THE INFLUENCE OF SMALL STATES ON SUPERPOWERS

THE INFLUENCE OF SMALL STATES ON SUPERPOWERS

Jamaica and U.S. Foreign Policy

RICHARD L. BERNAL

The University of the West Indies Press
Jamaica • Barbados • Trinidad and Tobago

The University of the West Indies Press
7A Gibraltar Hall Road, Mona
Kingston 7, Jamaica
www.uwipress.com

A catalogue record of this book is available from the National Library of Jamaica.

ISBN: 978-976-640-666-0 (print)
978-976-640-667-7 (Kindle)
978-976-640-668-4 (ePub)

Cover design by Robert Harris

Printed in the United States of America

Contents

Contents

Foreword

The Influence of Small States on Superpowers: Jamaica and U.S. Foreign Policy

Having come to Washington, D.C., from Arkansas, a small, rural state in the American South, I've often felt a particular kinship with the ambassadors of Caribbean nations. Serving as the face and voice of a smaller country in Washington can be both highly rewarding and deeply frustrating, sometimes simultaneously. Getting your issues onto policymakers' radar can be difficult, no matter how pressing those issues may seem to you and your government, because Washington tends to be preoccupied with global crises and its collective attention span for anything beyond urgent matters is strictly limited.

Nonetheless, for the creative, clever, and persistent ambassador, Washington is not impenetrable, nor is the U.S. government impossible to influence. With an understanding of how the city operates, a keen sense of timing, and an ability to put one's own priority issues within the context of the overall Washington agenda, a skilled envoy can help a small state to have outsized influence in the United States and beyond.

Richard Bernal was a master at the ambassador's craft. As Jamaica's top representative in Washington during the 1990s, he proved to be as effective an ambassador for his country—and indeed the entire Caribbean region—as any of the ambassadors from the Western Hemisphere during that time period. In my role first as Chief of Staff to President William J. Clinton and then as Counselor and Special Envoy for the Americas from 1993 to 1998, I carefully observed and closely interacted with each ambassador from the Western Hemisphere to the White House. There were many fine representatives during that time, but Ambassador Bernal was right at the top. A strong advocate for his views, he had a knack for making his case effectively and seemingly effortlessly, and by the end of his tenure, had achieved an impressive record of success.

The Influence of Small States on Superpowers: Jamaica and U.S. Foreign Policy is a record of Ambassador Bernal's time in Washington as Jamaica's senior envoy. But it is much more than that. This monumental study offers informative observations on how small nations can influence the foreign policy actions of much larger countries on specific issues of importance. Some will find in the book a "how to" guide for the ambitious ambassador in Washington. For myself, I found a pleasing reminder of the work that we were able to accomplish together along with other allies and friends during a particularly fruitful time in hemispheric affairs. I also found important lessons for regional interaction going forward.

Grounding his argument in international relations theory, Ambassador Bernal finds that traditional approaches are nonetheless inadequate to explain the daily reality that smaller nations face in the conduct of their foreign affairs. Virtually alone among many of his contemporaries, he recognizes and celebrates the many avenues of access in Washington that allow for nations the size of Jamaica to exercise targeted, meaningful influence, whether it be taking advantage of divided government (including bureaucratic cleavages), working through the think tank and business communities, or mobilizing a vocal diaspora. He also explicitly recognizes the importance of framing relevant issues within the context of U.S. policy priorities, in order to build momentum for progress and ultimate resolution.

On the one hand, Jamaica enjoys certain advantages, particularly of public awareness. Journalist James Reston once observed that "Americans will do anything for Latin America except read about it," yet many Americans are familiar with Jamaica—for its tourism, its music, and its exceptional athletes, all of which are truly world-class.

At the same time, as the Western Hemisphere emerged from its Cold War overhang and the Manley government came back into office, Jamaica had a problem. The island nation needed financial help but did not have the political support in Washington to get it done. In previous years the Manley government had been close to the Castro regime in Cuba, sparring frequently with the Reagan Administration. As Ambassador Bernal makes clear, there was no particular reservoir of goodwill for the new government; and, as the Cold War receded, U.S. assistance budgets were headed downward just at the time Jamaica faced growing debt pressures.

Similarly, during the 1990s, the flow of illegal drugs through the Caribbean increased and Jamaica was tagged with the perception that its cooperation with the United States in narcotics control efforts were insufficient. To complicate matters further, the North American Free Trade Agreement (NAFTA) went into action in 1994 and threatened to undermine trade preferences granted to Jamaica and other Caribbean nations under the Caribbean Basin Initiative.

While leaders in Washington may have perceived those issues as relatively minor at the time, each was of real political and economic significance to the respective governments in Kingston. That meant that, however pessimistic international relations theory might be about the likelihood of success, Jamaica needed to find a way to convince the United States that it was in its own interests to act. Ambassador Bernal's compelling narrative describes how concrete progress on each of these topics was achieved. His keen insights can also be applied to issues facing the Caribbean Basin today, not just the hardy perennials of trade and drugs, but also the need for cleaner, low cost energy and the impact on island nations of global climate change, among other shared priorities.

Still, when it comes to the conduct of international diplomacy, personal relationships and likeability cannot be overlooked. No matter how persuasive the case for one's views, progress is impossible if those views are never heard in corridors of influence. Paid advertisements in the Washington Post and on the walls of the Washington Metro are insufficient. In the words of the "Survivor" television series, small country ambassadors in Washington must outwit, outplay, and outlast their competition for policymakers' limited attention.

In practice, that means an ambassador has to be a presence, physically and substantively. Showing up is important, even when you are not specifically asking for anything. I well recall numerous meetings I had with Ambassador Bernal in my office in the West Wing of the White House, both alone and with other ambassadors and government officials he might have brought in for courtesy calls. Like many others in Washington, I developed a relationship of trust with Ambassador Bernal that we could both then rely upon in pursuit of our respective national interests.

During the 1990s, Jamaica did play an important role in helping to shape U.S. policy toward the Caribbean Basin, and Richard Bernal was a critical reason for that success. His book reminds us how much can be achieved when small states and superpowers find ways to work together. It is an important contribution to our understanding of regional politics, economics, history, and international relations, and a useful guide for the future.

—Thomas F. McLarty, III
White House Chief of Staff for President Bill Clinton

Acknowledgments

The research for and writing of this book started back in 1999. This project would not have been possible without the forbearance and support of my wife Margaret whose reading and writing allowed me to do the same. My work benefitted from the peace of mind and encouragement of a happy family life with my sons Brian and Darren. My determination to complete the years of reflection and research that have gone into this book was constantly energized by Nile and Elle. I was emboldened to write and publish a book by the example of my father Franklin who published three books.

The research process has benefitted from a small coterie of friends and mentors who have consistently encouraged me during the preparation of the manuscript. Librarians, typists, and proofreaders in Jamaica and the United States too numerous to mention have helped by responding to my numerous requests. The archival material was meticulously organized and preserved by Mrs. Dianne Smith-Brown and some additional material was loaned by Dennis Neill. Much of the typing of the early versions was done by Janice Rowe-Barnwell. Kia Penso helped with editing and structuring a keep chapter. Sha-Shana Crichton gave valuable legal advice on intellectual property rights and copyright matters. This book could not have been completed without the advice, organizing skills, diligence, and conviviality of Nicola Martin. Parts of the manuscript were read by George Dalley, Prof. Anthony Bogues, Steve Lamar, Dr. Diane Thorburn, Prof. Franklin Knight, Steve Lande, and Ann Wrobleski.

My awareness of matters beyond the national was aroused by the travels of my father while acting as an advisor to the federal government of the West Indies Federation and those I came in contact with such as Sir Fred Phillips. My interest in international affairs and foreign policy was excited by foreign travel in my early teenage years, during which I had the good fortune of exposure to Jamaican diplomats such as Ambassador Sir Edgerton Richardson at the United Nations, Alan Morais at the Jamaica High Commission in London, and Ashton Wright, Jamaica's High Commissioner to Trinidad and Tobago. They were civil service contemporaries of my father in the government of Jamaica. In my undergraduate studies I developed a strong interest in international economics and learning about this subject has been a lifelong passion. The initial interest was honed by imbibing political economy perspectives that located economics in the context of the world economy thanks to Norman Girvan in particular and to Donald Harris, George Beckford, and Clive Thomas. This approach deepened at the New School for Social Research with David Gordon, Anwar Shaikh, Gita Sen, and Robert Heilbroner. While doing graduate studies my interest in international representation increased by interactions with G. Arthur Brown of the United Nations Development Programme and Dudley "Jack" Clarke at the International Monetary Fund/World Bank. I gained considerable knowledge from working for Sir Alister McIntyre at the University of the West Indies and I have continued to learn from him.

My education in the practical dimension of international relations came through working with Ambassador Alfred Rattray and David Coore as supporting technical staff in the outreach of the People's National Party during the 1980s. What I know of diplomacy I learned by osmosis by working with the brilliant, charismatic, and remarkably persuasive Michael Manley on international economic issues, especially the deliberations and reports of the South Commission and the Economic Policy Committee of the Socialist International. In the course of participating in these exercises I benefitted from interaction with Manmohan Singh and Stuart Holland and being in the presence of and being able to observe at close quarters Julius Nyerere, Willi Brandt, Jimmy Carter, and Carlos Andre Perez. After my appointment as Jamaica's ambassador to the United States of America and Permanent Representative to the Organization of American States (OAS) I had the guidance Prime Minister P. J. Patterson, the consummate statesman, and the latitude granted to me to exercise my initiative by Ministers of Foreign Affairs, David Coore and Dr. Paul Robertson. Throughout the learning process Ambassador Don Mills was an inspirational mentor and exhilarating pedagogue.

The saga that I have related and the events and accomplishments in which I participated were aided by an outstanding staff at the Embassy of Jamaica in Washington, D.C., and the Jamaican Mission to the OAS. I do not single out anyone least I offend by omission. I am truly grateful for the work of these colleagues, all of whom have become ambassadors or taken up positions in international organizations. Mr. Keith Brooks worked with me throughout my entire tour of duty with excellence and unfailing good humor. The team of lobbyists, in particular George Dalley supported by Denis Neill, Ann Wrobleski, Steve Lamar, and Walter Jones provided indispensable guidance and support. I benefitted from access to some "wise men" whose advice was invaluable, most especially the "griot" of Caribbean affairs, Leo Edwards, the always insightful strategic thinking Richard Fletcher, and the indefatigable example of Randall Robinson, who was willing to pay the price for doing the right thing. Members of my "kitchen cabinet" shared their experience including Dr. Gladstone Bonnick of the World Bank and Sam Stevens Steve of the International Monetary System. Steve Lande was a true friend in the struggle for the CBI and CBERA. Jamaica had no better and more consistent friends than Congressman Charles Rangel and Ambassador Andrew Young. The Jamaican community was a constant inspiration and never failed to respond to any request to assist their beloved homeland. The wealthy and powerful Americans whose second home was in Jamaica were always willing to do for Jamaica.

I place on record my appreciation for the cooperation that was extended to me by four U.S. ambassadors to Jamaica: Glen Holden, Stanley McLelland, Gary Cooper, and Sue Cobb, and to Charge d'Affaires Lacy A. Wright Jr. Among the many Americans with whom I interacted Richard Feinberg, Senior Advisor, National Security Council, Thomas "Mack" McLarty, White House Chief of Staff and Special Envoy for the Americas, and Secretary of State Colin Powell were outstanding.

Being ambassador of Jamaica to the United States of America was not a job, it was a calling. It was a privilege to serve in the knowledge that service is its own reward.

During your ten years as Ambassador, you have earned respect and admiration throughout this country thanks to your effective representation of the interests of Jamaica and the Caribbean region. The United States has benefited from your cooperation on a wide range of issues of mutual interests.

— Excerpt from letter by Secretary of State General Colin Powell

Abbreviations

AAMA	American Apparel Manufacturers Association
ACP	African, Caribbean, and Pacific Group
AGOA	Africa Growth and Opportunity Act
AID	United States Agency for International Development
ATMI	American Textile Manufacturers Institute
BIT	Bilateral Investment Treaty
CACTAC	Central American and Caribbean Textiles and Apparel Council
CARIBCAN	Caribbean-Canada Trade Agreement
CARICOM	Caribbean Community
CBC	Congressional Black Caucus
CBERA	Caribbean Basin Economic Recovery Act
CBEREA	Caribbean Basin Economic Recovery Expansion Act
CBI	Caribbean Basin Initiative
CBTPA	Caribbean Basin Trade Partnership Act
CLAA	Caribbean/Latin American Action
EAI	Enterprise for the Americas Initiative
ECLAC	United Nations Economic Commission for of Latin America and the Caribbean
ESC	English Speaking Caribbean
EU	European Union
FDA	U.S. Food and Drug Administration
FEDEPRICAP	Federación de Entidades Privadas de Centroamérica, Panamá y República Dominicana
FTAA	Free Trade Area of the Americas
GDP	Gross Domestic Product
GOJ	Government of Jamaica
GNP	Gross National Product

G77	Group of 77
IADB	Inter-American Development Bank
IBA	International Bauxite Association
IMF	International Monetary Fund
INCSR	International Narcotics Control Strategy Report
INS	Immigration and Naturalization Service
IPR	Intellectual Property Rights
JCF	Jamaica Constabulary Force
JLP	Jamaica Labour Party
JPL	Jamaica Progressive League
MLAT	Mutual Legal Assistance Treaty
MNC	Multinational Corporation
NAACP	National Association for the Advancement of Colored People
NAFTA	North American Free Trade Agreement
NAJASO	National Association of Jamaican and Supportive Organizations
NCOCA	National Coalition on Caribbean Affairs
NIEO	New International Economic Order
NGOs	Non-Governmental Organizations
NSC	National Security Council
OAS	Organization of American States
OECS	Organization of Eastern Caribbean States
OMB	Office of Management and Budget
ONDCP	Office of National Drug Control Policy
OPEC	Organization of Petroleum Exporting Countries
PL 480	Food for Peace Program
PNP	People's National Party
SIDS	Small Island Developing States
UN	United Nations
USTR	Office of the U.S. Trade Representatives
WTO	World Trade Organization

ONE

Objective and Organization

Global powers and the United States more so than any other country are in danger of diplomatic overstretch as they attempt to cover international affairs across the world. Pragmatism dictates that they concentrate on countries whose actions they view as having the potential to impact their interests and this does not include small developing countries with the exception of a few that have strategic importance to the United States, e.g., Panama, Taiwan, Cuba. Therefore the foreign policy of the United States is predicated on the assumption that what small developing countries do can safely be disregarded. The conventional wisdom is that small developing countries exert limited if any influence on the foreign policy of large powerful global powers, in particular the United States of America.

This case study of Jamaica-U.S. relations demonstrates that even a small developing country can succeed in influencing the foreign policy of the United States. This is all the more noteworthy because Jamaica was not a country that assumed much significance or attention in U.S. foreign policy.[1] In other words, Jamaica had no special circumstances that it could leverage to influence U.S. foreign policy. The implication of Jamaica's success is that most countries might be able to do so and therefore the United States has to contend with a much larger number of countries. This book challenges the conventional wisdom based on the experience of the small developing country of Jamaica in its relations with the United States and raises the vitally important question: Should Washington worry and does the United States have to adjust how it executes its foreign policy? These questions are most pertinent at a time when both the White House and the Congress are inclined to reduce the amount of resources devoted to foreign policy. Mandelbaum argues that frugality will be the hallmark of U.S. global leadership in what he calls a cash-

1

strapped era. "Mounting domestic economic obligations will narrow the scope of America in the second decade of the twenty-first century and beyond. Because the United States will have to spend so much more than it has in the past on obligations at home . . . it will spend less than it has in the past on foreign policy. Because it will be able to spend less, it will be able to do less. Just what the United States will and will not do will be the most important issue in international relations in the years ahead."[2] The scaling down of U.S. global engagement was mooted during the late 1980s by historian Paul Kennedy in "The Rise and Fall of Great Powers"[3] and while his thesis has been criticized it did serve to point to the relationship between the economic health of a superpower and its ability to meet the costs of an expanding global role.

The narrative of this study is an examination and explanation of how a small, developing country can influence the foreign policy of a large, powerful developed country. The countries selected for study are Jamaica, a small developing country and the United States of America, a global superpower. Jamaica-United States relations are examined during the decade between mid-1991 and mid-2001. This period was selected for study because (a) the period encompasses several complete episodes of Jamaica's influence on U.S. foreign policy, (b) it provides a sufficiently long period to enable some conclusions to be drawn, and (c) the conventional academic research is enhanced by information derived from the personal experience of the author who was a lead participant in the events retold. The conclusion of the documentation and analysis is that Jamaica was successful in influencing U.S. policy.

CONTRIBUTION

The contribution of this book is three-fold. First, this study points to the need for a review of the standard conclusion provided by international relations theories, namely that a small developing country can and will have little or no influence on the foreign policy of large, powerful developed countries such as the United States. The foreign policy of small countries or small states is inevitably one of dependent foreign policy. However, during the years under review (1991–2001), Jamaica was able to influence U.S. foreign policy. To the extent that this was not an exception, then it indicates that other small countries, of which there are a large number, given propitious circumstances, could accomplish the same result. If small developing countries like Jamaica can influence the foreign policy of the United States, then this raises a serious concern for the United States. The experience of Jamaica needs to be examined carefully to glean the insights of how Jamaica accomplished influencing U.S. foreign policy. The lessons of the Jamaican experience will require a re-examination of existing international relations theory, with a view to remedying what must now be regarded as a lacuna.

Second, this study will fill a lacuna in the literature, as there are no in-depth scholarly studies on how a small developing country attempted to, and did, in fact, influence U.S. policy. There is literature on United States-Jamaica relations but it does not delve into the mechanics of operational-izing foreign policy. The available literature falls into two categories.

There are no book-length studies of U.S. policy towards Jamaica and therefore to discern an overall description of U.S. policy towards Jamaica requires the extraction and piecing together of Jamaica-specific U.S. poli-cies from the literature on U.S. policy towards part of the Caribbean or Latin America and the Caribbean. The literature from which to garner information on U.S. policy towards Jamaica suffers from the following weaknesses: (1) Several book-length studies and short articles[4] address U.S. policy towards the Caribbean as a whole and many treat the period before 1991–2000[5]; (2) There are several studies that are partial in scope dealing with particular issues, e.g., the Caribbean Basin Initiative[6] or a particular episode, e.g., U.S. intervention in Grenada.[7] This extensive lit-erature does not provide an outline of an overall policy; (3) The Carib-bean (inclusive of Jamaica) is subsumed under the wider rubric of U.S. policy towards Latin America,[8] and in many instances, the treatment of the Caribbean concentrates on Cuba;[9] (4) The issue of U.S. policy is ad-dressed in terms of the Caribbean Basin,[10] with the discussion primarily devoted to Central America.[11]

There are no book-length studies of Jamaica's foreign policy towards the United States during the period examined in this book. The extent to which the subject is treated in the existing literature is partial, i.e., as part of reviews of Jamaica's overall foreign policy and naturally policy to-wards the United States assumes prominence.[12] Surprisingly in some publications the discussion of policy towards the United States receives limited treatment.[13] An article that focused on the place of the English-speaking Caribbean (ESC) in U.S. foreign policy since the early 1960s concludes that the ESC was not important and received episodic atten-tion.[14] There are two informative book-length studies of Jamaica's foreign policy that are valuable but are focused on periods prior to 1991, for example by Persaud[15] for the period 1962–1980 and Henke[16] for the years 1972–1989. Foreign policy issues are discussed in Levi's biography of Michael Manley but its coverage ends before the period that is the subject of this book.[17] Some studies in which Jamaica is treated as part of the Caribbean predate the 1991 starting point of this study.[18] Some short articles treat aspects of Jamaica's foreign policy such as its role in the United Nations[19] and the Organization of American States.[20] Studies of United States-Caribbean relations are informative and useful, but do not examine in detail the question of how the Caribbean has attempted to influence U.S. policy towards the region.[21] The international relations literature on the ESC devotes virtually no attention to the mechanics of attaining the region's foreign policy objectives in the United States.[22]

There are memoirs of diplomats, but many are autobiographical, cover experiences in countries other than the United States[23] or focused on a specialized incident, and are of general interest only. For example, the reflections of Anatoly Dobrynin, who served 24 years as the Soviet Union's Ambassador to Washington, D.C., treat the unique relationship between the two superpowers,[24] a very different interaction than that between the lone superpower and a small, developing country. Some insights can be gained from the reminiscences of a Canadian Ambassador, though the book does not provide a formal analysis.[25] Again this book is of general interest because of the unique peaceful co-existence of these neighbors. Similarly the recollection of a recent British Ambassador has to be understood in the context of the so-called "special relationship."[26] Ambassador Bernardo Vega,[27] the Ambassador of the Dominican Republic to the United States, has published his diary of his tour of duty in the years 1995 to 1999. In addition to the diary of events that indicates what the life of an active ambassador is like he includes a number of his public statements that touch on some of issues covered by this study. More peripheral to the subject matter of this study are recollections of diplomats in countries other than the United States, for example, James Blanchard who served as U.S. ambassador to Canada[28] and Frank Ortiz who served in a variety of places including Barbados.[29]

These books do provide some first-hand information about how diplomats have operated; however, these accounts are part history and part biography in which the ambassador is the central figure in the drama. This weakness means these accounts do not constitute in-depth studies that explore in sufficient detail how countries try to influence U.S. foreign policy. In this regard the present study differs by treating the activities of the ambassador as integral but as part of the explanation involving other factors. This study does have the advantage of extensive conventional documentary sources being corroborated and enriched by the recollections of the Jamaican ambassador to the United States during the time period of the study. This balance differentiates this study from the few books written by individuals who were actually involved in the diplomatic process of influencing U.S. foreign policy. This study is therefore the first of its kind and most definitely the first study of Jamaica's attempts to influence U.S. foreign policy.

Third, beyond its contribution to the discipline of international relations, the book's archival, documentary, and analytic value can provide practical lessons, which can contribute to guidelines for the practice of diplomacy in the U.S. arena, for small states in particular and states in general. The intention is not to provide the diplomatic neophyte to Washington, D.C., with a manual,[30] but to allow readers to draw their own conclusions on how to utilize the information provided. The practical diplomatic techniques recommended by a former Guyanese High Commissioner to Canada is of some interest; however this is tangential given the differences between the Canadian and U.S. political systems.[31] Little else of direct relevance is available, because the tradition of senior public servants writing autobiographies is yet to emerge in Jamaica. The limited literature that exists either does not focus on foreign policy or is devoted to an interlude in the "foreign service" and not involving the United States.[32] The only memoir of a Jamaican diplomat, that by Donald Mills, is devoted primarily to issues and activities during his tenure as Jamaica's ambassador to the United Nations.[33]

ORGANIZATION

The study consists of eight chapters. Chapter 1 provides an overview of the topic and the objective of the study and outlines the organization of the analysis. The research on which the study is based (a) draws on books, articles, and newspapers, (b) is supplemented by papers, files, and recollections of the author's tenure as the Ambassador of Jamaica to the United States of America and Jamaica's Permanent Mission to the Organization of American States, and (c) uses interviews with persons involved in the events recounted.

The focus of this study is outside the ambit of the traditional subject matter of international relations, hence, there is limited applicability of existing theories of international relations. The study encompasses an examination of intra-state politics, specifically how activities in the domestic political environment and interest group politics[34] influence foreign policy in the United States, rather than inter-state relations. Therefore, the approach, which is most useful, is a pragmatic combination of international relations theory and models of domestic interest group politics. This point is elaborated in chapter 2, which provides a succinct review of the current theories of international relations and the literature on small states,[35] which emphasizes the limited ability of small states/countries to influence policy towards them by larger, more powerful countries. Given the limitations of the approaches reviewed it was necessary to examine the literature on interest group politics and to combine this with pertinent elements from the approaches reviewed to create an interest group model of foreign policy. The approach developed is a more appropriate conceptual and analytic framework in which to locate and inform the study of how a small developing country can exert sufficient influence on a large developed country to affect its foreign policy.

Chapter 3 presents two dimensions of the relationship between Jamaica and the United States. To place this relationship in the proper context, the chapter begins with a historical,[36] social, economic, and political overview of Jamaica and provides a comparison of Jamaica and the United

States, showing the substantial differences in size and level of development. The overview also reveals the extent to which the Jamaican economy is dependent on the United States against this background the two sides of United States-Jamaica relations are examined. First is an overview of U.S. foreign policy towards Jamaica and the ESC. Second, Jamaica's foreign policy towards the United States. is examined, with particular attention to those aspects that directly impinge on issues discussed in this study. Reference is made to the ESC[37] because the United States treats the region as a unit in its foreign policy[38] and because some of the objectives Jamaica pursued in the United States during the period of study were shared with the other states of the ESC and Central America, who collaborated in their pursuit. Against this background the main objectives of Jamaica's foreign policy towards the United States in the period 1991 to 2001 are outlined.

U.S. policy towards Jamaica has commonalities with the broad objectives and strategies of U.S. foreign policy[39] towards Latin America and the Caribbean. The ESC, including Jamaica, only became an arena for U.S. foreign policy during the 1960s, although there are antecedents between World War II and 1962 while Jamaica was still a British colony.[40] The time period of this study 1991–2001 means that attention is devoted to foreign policy during the administrations of George Bush[41] and Bill Clinton,[42] taking cognizance of events and developments in the Kennedy,[43] Johnson, Nixon, Carter,[44] and Reagan years. The period examined involves a transition from the Reagan administration's clearly defined and implemented foreign policy towards the Caribbean region,[45] centered around the Caribbean Basin Initiative, to the traditional, episodic, reactive mode during the terms of Presidents George Bush and Bill Clinton.

Chapter 4 discusses how foreign governments influence the process of the formulation and implementation of U.S. foreign policy. It is based on a well-established literature[46] on the process of the formulation of U.S. foreign policy. The reader who is knowledgeable about the U.S. political system and the formulation of foreign policy can omit reading this material. The policy formulation process involves the executive branch,[47] legislature,[48] state bureaucracy,[49] media,[50] lobbyists,[51] think-tank community,[52] and business sector,[53] and emerges from their interaction.[54] The conduct of U.S. foreign policy is the result of a complex, constantly shifting interaction among interest groups, institutions, and other actors, and reflects the trade-off between competing objectives and actors.[55] Based on a review of this literature, a simple model of the process of foreign policy formulation and the principal actors involved is posited. This is shown in figure 1.1.

The model of U.S. foreign policy formulation is extended to include the activities of foreign governments, businesses, and foreign residence communities. This enhanced model will be employed to describe and analyze how foreign governments attempt to and do influence the pro-

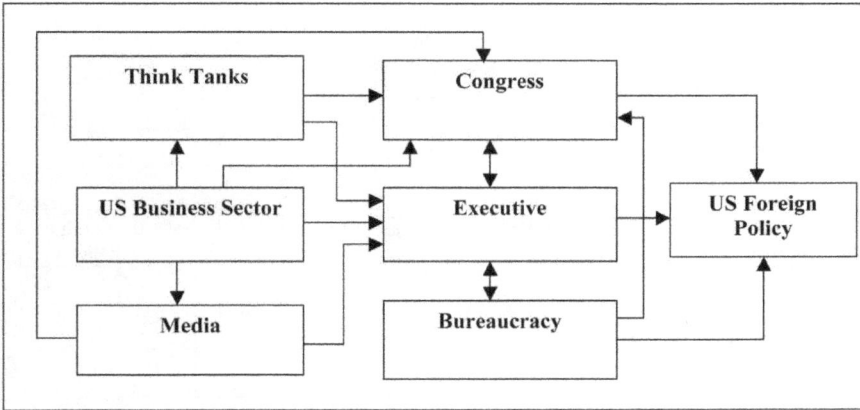

Figure 1.1. Formulation of U.S. Foreign Policy.

cess of foreign policy formulation. The model, as applied to attempts by foreign governments to influence U.S. foreign policy towards their country, is illustrated in Figure 1.2. This framework will be applied to analyze each case study.

The literature on attempts by foreign governments, businesses, and resident communities to influence U.S. foreign policy is reviewed. This exercise is essential background to the examination of attempts by Jamaica to influence U.S. foreign policy. The bulk of the research material documents the activism of Canada,[56] Mexico,[57] Japan,[58] and Israel.[59] Cognizance will be taken of differences in capacities for influence between powerful countries, e.g., Japan; strategic allies, e.g., Israel; or groups of countries, e.g., European Union; which have some leverage and small countries such as Jamaica, which are of marginal importance and have very limited human and financial resources. This task is made difficult by the fact that many of the studies of Jamaican foreign policy are comparative studies in which Jamaica is one of a group of countries.[60]

Against the background of Jamaica's foreign policy objectives in the United States, provided in chapter 3, the campaign to influence U.S. policy will be documented. In each case the key objectives and the strategies and campaigns pursued by Jamaica will be described and discussed. The criteria for selection of the case studies of Jamaica's attempts to influence U.S. policy were ability to document these campaigns and their importance to Jamaica. The documentation of these events is based on published sources, access to unpublished information, and the actual involvement in these campaigns by the author. The case studies selected were those of most concern to Jamaica during the period 1991–2001.

The following three chapters present the case studies of how Jamaica influenced U.S. policy on debt relief, foreign aid, narcotics cooperation,

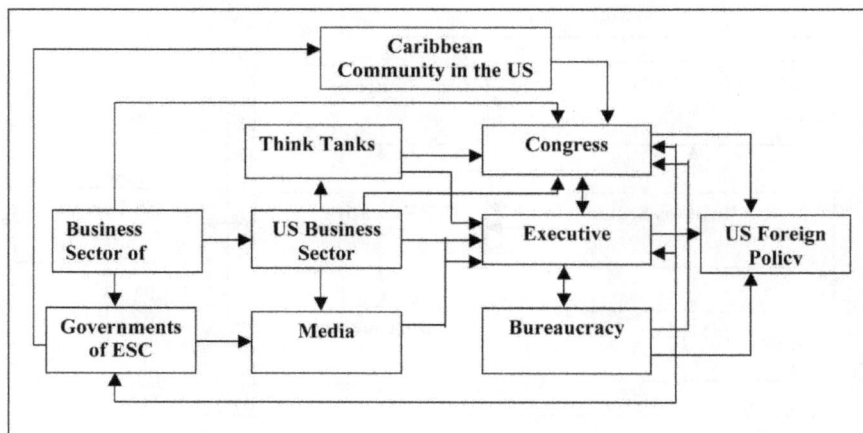

Figure 1.2. Attempts by Governments to Influence U.S. Foreign Policy.

and trade policy. The issues of debt relief and foreign aid are treated together because they were one campaign, since debt relief was regarded as a form of aid. Like securing certification of cooperation on drugs, these were instances where Jamaica acted alone. The campaign to shape U.S. trade policy by securing legislation to enhance the Caribbean Basin Initiative (CBI) was conducted in collaboration with Caribbean and Central American countries.

Chapter 5 reviews and analyzes the government of Jamaica's campaign to maintain foreign aid and secure debt relief. These were separate objectives, but the campaign in quest of both entailed substantial overlaps, both as regards the rationale, i.e., economic support and the U.S. institutions that were lobbied, e.g., Congress, State Department, and Treasury. This case study illustrates how a small country can influence U.S. foreign policy by mobilizing a domestic constituency and convincing, and then collaborating, with the Executive to get action from the bureaucracy and the Congress. There were opposition elements to be confronted and there was a lack of awareness in all sectors of the body politic. The campaigns for debt relief and aid are discussed separately but are included together in this chapter, because they were conducted simultaneously and were based on the same overall strategy.

The campaign to have Jamaica certified as fully cooperating with the United States on counter narcotics measures is examined in chapter 6. It documents a short intensive campaign to convince an inter-agency process involving several agencies and departments. There were no competing constituencies, as the process was almost entirely between the bureaucracy and executive on one side and the government of Jamaica on the other. The lesson from this campaign is the importance of building relations of trust with key officials and keeping a constant flow of information on what Jamaica was doing to control the production, export, and transshipment of narcotics.

A small country may seek to influence U.S. foreign policy by its own individual efforts, or by collaborating with other countries that have a common interest in a particular policy issue. Such was the case of the trade policy of the United States towards the Caribbean and Central America, originally expressed in the Caribbean Basin Economic Recovery Act (CBERA) of 1983 commonly known as the Caribbean Basin Initiative (CBI) and the Caribbean Basin Economic Recovery Expansion Act (CBER-EA) of 1990. The campaign to maintain and enhance the CBERA was an example of collaboration with other small states in a common endeavor. This complex campaign involving close and continuous cooperation between the countries of the Caribbean and Central America, sustained over a period of several years, is the subject matter of chapter 7. There was vigorous opposition from organized labor, a split in the U.S. business community between the textile and apparel interests, and a Congress not highly motivated to do trade legislation.

The case studies presented in the book have related episodes in which Jamaica was successful in influencing U.S. foreign policy, either by its own efforts, or in conjunction with other countries. In reality, every attempt to influence U.S. foreign policy did not come to fruition, e.g., trying to change U.S. policy on the European Union's preferential banana import regime. This type of experience can yield lessons, which are as important as those derived from the successes.

Chapters 5, 6, and 7 present case studies documenting how Jamaica, a small country, was able to influence the foreign policy of the superpower United States during the decade 1991 to 2001. Chapter 8 is devoted to explaining why Jamaica succeeded in influencing U.S. foreign policy and extracts and summarizes the principal lessons derived from the conduct of Jamaica. The lessons point to the type of actions and requirements for such actions that a small state must undertake if it is to influence the United States. The fact that the lessons derived from events that took place some time ago does not diminish their contemporary relevance and utility to the ongoing quest of small states/countries to influence U.S. foreign policy.

The circumstances at present remain essentially the same in terms of the institutions, culture, and decision making processes of the political system in the United States. This is not to say that nothing has changed but merely to point out that these changes have not fundamentally altered the gravamen of this book. Use of the Internet and information and communications technology (ICT) referred to as digital diplomacy or e-diplomacy (including the use of Twitter and Facebook) is arguably the most impactful recent developments.[61] By considerably reducing the cost of gathering and disseminating information modern ICT has increased exponentially the capacity to influence public opinion and the thinking of policy makers. This has been advantageous to small countries because it has furnished them with the means to reach an almost limitless audience and therefore considerably enhanced the capacity to mobilize support for a country's objectives. Instantaneous communication means that decisions have to be made in real time and consequently strategy and tactics have to be quickly redacted and this can pose a challenge for human and financial resources of small countries. Malone,[62] based on interviews with several diplomats of different nationalisties who served in different countries, concludes that modern information technology does not change the role of a diplomat because while there is more potential for outreach, decisions on what, how, and to whom have to be made by skilled, informed, and knowledgeable diplomats. Modern information and communication technologies have not fundamentally altered the contemporary U.S. key institutions, culture, and practices that constitute the American political system and therefore do not lessen the challenge confronting a small country attempting to influence U.S. foreign policy. There is no diminution in the value of the lessons learned from the Jamaica experience. These lessons remain vitally important. By allowing readers to garner the lessons emanating from the experience of Jamaica it is hoped that this can inform the conduct of those currently engaged in attempting to influence U.S. foreign policy, particularly by small developing countries.

NOTES

1. Richard L. Bernal, "The Unimportance of the English Speaking Caribbean in U.S. Foreign Policy as told by Presidents and Secretaries of State," Caribbean Journal of International Relations & Diplomacy, Vol. 1, No. 1 (February, 2013) pages 132–50.

2. Michael Mandelbaum, The Frugal Superpower. America's Global Leadership in a Cash-Strapped Era (New York: Public Affairs, 2010) pages 3–4.

3. Paul Kennedy, The Rise and Fall of Great Powers (New York: Vintage Books, 1987).

4. Ken I. Boohoo, "U.S.-Caribbean Relations in the Post-Cold War Era: Implications for Globalization and Development" in Ramesh Ramsaran (ed.), Caribbean Survival and the Global Challenge (Kingston: Ian Randle Publishers, 2002) pages 149–62.

5. John Bartlow Martin, U.S. Policy in the Caribbean (Boulder: Westview Press, 1978).

6. Richard Newfarmer (ed.), From Gunboats to Diplomacy. New U.S. Policies for Latin America (Baltimore, Johns Hopkins, 1984) Chapter 14, Anne Krueger, Economic Policies at Cross-Purposes. The United States and Developing Countries (Washington, D.C.: Brookings Institution, 1993) Chapter 7, and Abigail B. Bakan, David Cox, and Colin Leys (eds.), Imperial Power and Regional Trade. The Caribbean Basin Initiative (Waterloo: Wilfred Laurier University Press, 1993).

7. Thomas Carothers, In the Name of Democracy, U.S. Policy Toward Latin America in the Reagan Years (Berkeley: University of California Press, 1991) Chapter 3 and George P. Shultz, Turmoil and Triumph Diplomacy, Power and Victory of the American Ideal (New York: Charles Scribner and Sons, 1993) chapter 20.

8. Harold Molineu, U.S. Policy toward Latin America. From Regionalism to Globalism (Boulder: Westview Press, 1990) and Albert Fishlow and James Jones (eds.), The United States and the Americas. A Twenty-first Century View (New York: W.W. Norton, 1999).

9. Abraham F. Lowenthal and Gregory F. Treverton (eds.), Latin America in a New World (Boulder: Westview Press, 1994) and Abraham F. Lowenthal, Partners in Conflict. The United States and Latin America in the 1990s (Baltimore: Johns Hopkins University Press, rev. ed., 1990).

10. Jean Grugel, Politics and Development in the Caribbean Basin. Central America and the Caribbean in the New World Order (Bloomington: Indiana University Press, 1995) pages 125–58.

11. Margaret Daly Hayes, Latin America and the U.S. National Interest. A Basis for U.S. Foreign Policy (Boulder: Westview Press, 1984) Chapter 3 and John D. Martz (ed.), United States Policy in Latin America. A Quarter Century of Crisis and Challenge, 1961–1986 (University of Nebraska, 1988).

12. Vaughan Lewis. "Issues and Trends in Jamaican Foreign Policy 1972–1977" in Carl Stone and Aggrey Brown (eds.), Perspectives on Jamaica in the Seventies (Kingston: Publishing House, 1981), Vaughan A. Lewis, "The Small State Alone. Jamaican Foreign Policy, 1977–1980," Journal of Inter-American Studies and World Affairs, Vol. 25, No. 2 (May 1983) pages 139–70, and Paul Ashley, "Jamaican Foreign Policy in Transition: From Manley to Seaga" in Jorge Heine and Leslie F. Manigat (eds.), The Caribbean and World Politics: Cross Currents and Cleavages (New York: Holmes & Meier, 1988) pages 144–62.

13. Don Mills, "Jamaica's International Relations in Independence" in Rex Nettleford (ed.), Jamaica in Independence. Essays on the Early Years (Kingston: Heinemann Caribbean, 1989) pages 131–71 and Diana Thorburn and Dana Marie Morris, Jamaica's Foreign Policy. Making the Economic Development Link (Kingston: Caribbean Policy Research Institute, June, 2007).

14. Richard L. Bernal, "The Unimportance of the English Speaking Caribbean in U.S. Foreign Policy as told by Presidents and Secretaries of State," Caribbean Journal of International Relations & Diplomacy, Vol. 1, No. 1 (February, 2013) pages 132–50.

15. Randolph B. Persaud, Counter-Hegemony and Foreign Policy. The Dialectics of Marginalized and Global Forces in Jamaica (Albany: State University of New York Press, 2001).

16. Holger Henke, Self-Determination and Dependency. Jamaica's Foreign Policy 1972–1989 (Kingston: University of the West Indies Press, 2000) and for a short synopsis see Holger Henke, "Jamaica's International Relations. Between the West . . . and the Rest," Jamaica Journal, Vol. 34, nos. 1-2 (August, 2012) pages 32–37.

17. Darrell E. Levi, Michael Manley. The Making of a Leader (Kingston: Heinemann Publishers Caribbean, 1989).

18. Jacqueline Anne Braveboy-Wagner, The Caribbean in World Affairs: The Foreign Policies of the English-speaking States (Boulder: Westview Press, 1989).

19. H. S. Walker, "Jamaica and the United Nations," Jamaica Journal, Vol. 25, No. 3 (October, 1995) pages 2–9.

20. Richard L. Bernal and Vilma McNish, "Jamaica in the Organization of American States," Jamaica Journal, Vol. 26, No. 3 (March/April, 1997) pages 33–36.

21. Anthony Maingot, The United States and the Caribbean (London: Macmillan, 1994).

22. Vaughan A. Lewis (ed.), Size, Self-determination and International Relations: The Caribbean (Mona: Institute of Social and Economic Research, University of the West Indies, 1976), Basil A. Ince (ed.), Contemporary International Relations of the Caribbean (St. Augustine: Institute of International Relations, University of the West Indies, 1979), Richard Millet and W. Marvin Will (eds.), The Restless Caribbean. Changing Patterns of International Relations (New York: Praeger Publishers, 1979), and Anthony Bryan, J. Edward Greene, and Timothy Shaw (eds.), Peace, Development

and Security in the Caribbean. Perspectives to the year 2000 (London: Macmillan, 1990).

23. Eleni Kounalakis, Madam Ambassador: Three Years in Budapest (New York: New Press, 2015).

24. Anatoly Dobrynin, In Confidence: Moscow's Ambassador to America's Six Cold War Presidents 1962–1986 (New York: Times Books, 1995).

25. Allan Gotleib, I'll be with you in a minute Mr. Ambassador (Toronto: University of Toronto Press, 1991) and Allan Gotleib, Washington Diaries. 1981–1989 (McClelland and Stewart, 2006).

26. Christopher Meyer, DC Confidential. The Controversial Memoirs of Britain's Ambassador at the Time of 9/11 and the Iraq War (London: Weidenfeld & Nicolson, 2006). The accomplishments of the Ambassador reflect the extent to which Prime Minister Tony Blair worked assiduously to cultivate the relationship of being the closest ally to President George W. Bush. See James Naughtie, The Accidental American: Tony Blair and the Presidency (New York: Public Affairs, 2004).

27. Bernardo Vega, Diario de una Mision en Washington (Santo Domingo: Fundacion Cultural Dominicana, 2002).

28. James J. Blanchard, Behind the Embassy Door. Canada, Clinton, and Quebec (Chelsea: Sleeping Bear Press, 1998).

29. Frank V. Ortíz, Ambassador Ortiz: Lessons from a Life of Service (Albuquerque: University of New Mexico Press, 2005) pages 116–25.

30. John Shaw, The Ambassador: Inside the Life of a Working Diplomat (Capital Books, 2006).

31. Robert J. Moore, Third World Diplomats in Dialogue with the First World (London: Macmillan, 1985).

32. Ashton Wright, No Trophies Raised (Kingston: Ashton Wright, 1994).

33. Don Mills, Journeys and Missions at Home and Abroad (Kinston: Arawak Publishers, 2009).

34. Roger Hilsman, The Politics of Policymaking in Defense and Foreign Affairs. Conceptual Models and Bureaucratic Politics (New York: Prentice Hall, 3rd ed., 1993).

35. Christine Ingebritsen, Iver Neuman, Sieglinde Gstohl, and Jessica Beyer (eds.), Small States in International Relations (Seattle: University of Washington Press/Reykjavik: University of Iceland Press, 2006).

36. Franklin W. Knight and Colin A. Palmer (eds.), The Modern Caribbean (Chapel Hill: University of North Carolina, 1989), and Eric Williams, From Columbus to Castro. The History of the Caribbean 1492–1969 (London: Andre Deutsch, 1970).

37. For the purposes of this study the ESC consists of Antigua and Barbuda, Bahamas, Barbados, Belize, Dominica, Grenada, Guyana, Jamaica, Montserrat, St. Kitts and Nevis, St. Lucia, St. Vincent and the Grenadines, and Trinidad and Tobago. The ESC can be studied as a group because of (1) the commonality of history, characteristics, problems, and objectives among the countries; (2) the U.S. treats these countries as a homogenous entity for foreign policy and administrative simplicity. U.S. foreign policy towards the Caribbean distinguishes between the ESC and Cuba, Haiti, and the Dominican Republic, and (3) the ESC states are members of the Caribbean Community and with the exception of the Bahamas form the Caribbean Common Market (CARICOM) through which they coordinate their foreign policies.

38. The overview of U.S. foreign policy towards the Caribbean provides an important context in which to locate U.S. policy towards Jamaica but is not required reading for following the argument of the book; a knowledge of this would enhance the understanding of the reader.

39. Walter McDougall, Promised Land, Crusade State (New York: Houghton Mifflin, 1997), William Appleman Williams, The Tragedy of American Diplomacy (New York: W.W. Norton, revised edition, 1972), Stephen E. Ambrose and Douglas G. Brinkley, Rise to Globalism. America Foreign Policy since 1938 (Harmondsworth: Penguin, 8th revised edition, 1997), Walter La Feber, The American Age. United States Foreign

Policy at Home and Abroad Since 1750 (New York: W.W. Norton and Company, 1989).

40. Richard N. Gardner, Sterling Dollar Diplomacy in Current Perspective (New York: Columbia University Press, 1980), William Roger Louis, Imperialism at Bay. The United States and Decolonization of the British Empire (New York: Oxford University Press, 1978), and Stephen G. Rabe, Eisenhower and Latin America. The Foreign Policy of Anti-communism (Chapel Hill: University of North Carolina Press, 1988).

41. George Bush and Brent Scowcroft, A World Transformed (New York: Alfred A. Knopf, 1998).

42. Warren Christopher, In the Stream of History (Stanford: Stanford University Press, 1998) and Richard A. Melanson, American Foreign Policy since the Vietnam War (New York: M.E. Sharpe, 1996) chapters 5–6.

43. Dean Rusk, As I Saw It (Harmondsworth: Penguin, 1991).

44. Gaddis Smith, Morality, Reason and Power. American Diplomacy in the Carter Years (New York: Hill and Wang, 1986).

45. Thomas Carothers, In the Name of Democracy, U.S. Policy Toward Latin America in the Reagan Years (Berkeley: University of California Press, 1991).

46. Robert A. Pastor, Congress and the Politics of U.S. Foreign Economic Policy 1929-1976 (Berkley: University of California Press, 1980), Roger Hilsman, The Politics of Policy-making in Defense and Foreign Affairs. Conceptual Models and Bureaucratic Politics (New York: Prentice Hall 3rd. ed., 1993), and Stephen Cohen, Joel R. Paul, and Robert A Blecker, Fundamentals of U.S. Foreign Trade Policy (Boulder: Westview Press, 1996).

47. Stephen E. Ambrose, "The Presidency and Foreign Policy," Foreign Affairs, Vol. 70, No. 5 (Winter, 1991/92) pages 120–37, and Theodore C. Sorenson, "The President and the Secretary of State," Foreign Affairs, Vol. 66, No. 2 (Winter, 1987/88) pages 231–48.

48. Thomas Mann (ed.), The Question of Balance: The President, the Congress and Foreign Policy (Washington, D.C.: Brookings, 1990), James M. Lindsay, Congress and the Politics of the U.S. Foreign Policy (Baltimore: Johns Hopkins University Press, 1994), Barbara Hinckley, Less than Meets the Eye. Congress, the President and Foreign Policy (Chicago: University of Chicago, 1994).

49. Stephen D. Krasner, "Are Bureaucracies Important? (Or Allison in Wonderland)" Foreign Policy, No. 7 (Summer, 1972) pages 159–79.

50. Bernard C. Cohen, The Press and Foreign Policy (Princeton: Princeton University Press, 1963), James M. Fallows, Media Rules. How the American Press Undermines American Diplomacy (New York: Patheon, 1996), Charles Bray, "The Media and Foreign Policy," Foreign Policy, No. 6 (Fall, 1974) pages 109–25, W. Lance Bennett and David L. Paletz (eds.), Taken by Storm: The Media, Public Opinion and U.S. Foreign Policy in the Gulf War (Chicago: University of Chicago, 1994), and Daniel Hallin, The Uncensored War (Oxford: Oxford University Press, 1986).

51. Jeffrey H. Birmbaum, The Lobbyists (New York: Times Books, 1992) and Bruce C. Wolpe, Lobbying Congress. How the System Works (Washington, D.C. Congressional Quarterly Press, 2nd ed., 1996).

52. Thomas Medvetz, Think Tanks in America (Chicago: University of Chicago Press, 2012), James A. Smith, The Idea Brokers. Think Tanks and the Rise of the New Policy Elite (New York: Free Press, 1991), David Ricci, The Transformation of American Politics. The New Washington and the Rise of Think Tanks (New Haven: York University Press, 1993), Robert D. Schulzinger, The Wise Men of Foreign Affairs. The History of the Council of Foreign Relations (Oxford: Oxford University Press, 1984), and Peter Gross, Continuing the Inquiry. The Council of Foreign Relations from 1971 to 1996 (New York: Council on Foreign Relations, 1996).

53. Robert F. Smith, The United States and Cuba. Business Diplomacy 1917-1960 (New Haven: College and University Press, 1960), David Horowitz, Corporations and the Cold War (New York: Monthly Review Press, 1969), David Vogel, Fluctuating Fortunes. The Political Power of Business in America (New York: Basic Books, 1989),

Michael Parenti, Democracy for the Few (New York: St. Martins Press, 5th edition, 1988), William Greider, Who Will Tell the People? The Betrayal of American Democracy (New York: Simon and Schuster, 1992), and Steve Coll, Private Empire: ExxonMobil and American Power (New York: Penguin Press, 2012).

54. John Dumbrell, The Making of U.S. Foreign Policy (Manchester: Manchester University Press, 2nd ed., 1997) and Philip J. Briggs, Making American Foreign Policy, President-Congress Relations from the Second World War to the Post-Cold War Era (Lanham: Rowman and Littlefield Publishers, 2nd ed., 1994). For a discussion of the impact of this interaction on U.S. foreign policy towards Latin America and the Caribbean, see Robert Pastor, Whirlpool. U.S. Foreign Policy Toward Latin America and the Caribbean (Princeton: Princeton University Press, 1992).

55. Ralph G. Carter, Essentials of U.S. Foreign Policy Making (New York: Pearson, 2014), James M. McCormick (ed.), Essentials of U.S. Foreign Policy Making (Lanham: Rowman & Littlefield Publishers, 6th ed., 2012), and I. M. Destler, Making Foreign Economic Policy (Washington, D.C: Brookings Institution, 1980).

56. Charles F. Doran and Joel J. Sokolsky, Canada and Congress: Lobbying in Washington (Halifax: Centre for Foreign Policy Studies, 1986).

57. George W. Grayson, "Lobbying by Mexico and Canada" in Robert A. Pastor and Rafael Fernandez de Castro (eds.), The Controversial Pivot. The U.S. Congress and North America (Washington, D.C.: Brookings Institution Press, 1998) pages 70–94.

58. Pat Choate, Agents of Influence. How Japan's Lobbyists in the United States Manipulate America's Political and Economic System (New York: Alfred Knopf, 1990).

59. Edward Tivnan, The Lobby. Jewish Political Power and U.S. Foreign Policy (New York: Simon and Schuster, 1987) and John J. Mearsheimer and Stephen M. Walt, The Israel Lobby and U.S. Foreign Policy (New York: Farrar, Straus and Giroux, 2008).

60. George A. Fauriol, Foreign Policy Behavior of Caribbean States. Guyana, Haiti and Jamaica (Lanham: University Press of America, 1984) and J.A. Braveboy-Wagner, The Caribbean in World Affairs. The Foreign Policies of the English-Speaking Caribbean (Colorado: Westview, 1989).

61. Jovan Kurbalija, "The Impact of the Internet and ICT on Contemporary Diplomacy" in Pauline Kerr and Geoffrey Wiseman (ed.), Diplomacy in a Globalizing World (Oxford University Press, 2012) and Joshua Fouts, Social Media, Virtual Worlds and Public Diplomacy," World Politics Review, October 13, 2009. http://www.worldpoliticsreview.com/articles/4440/social-media-virtual-worlds-and-public-diplomacy. Accessed October 9, 2014.

62. David D. Malone, "The Modern Diplomatic Mission" in Andrew F. Cooper, Jorge Heine and Ramesh Thakur (eds.), The Oxford Handbook of Modern Diplomacy (Oxford: Oxford University Press, 2013) pages 124–41. See page 138.

TWO

Small States in International Relations

The United States of America and Jamaica differ vastly in size and level of development and hence their relations have been conducted in the context of significant asymmetries in power and influence. This was certainly the case during the period examined, 1991 to 2001, when the United States was acknowledged to be the single superpower. The enormous differences in size and the levels of development between the United States and Jamaica are documented in the first section, which presents data illustrating this reality.

The second section examines theories of international relations to arrive at a suitable methodology for analyzing the relationship between the United States and Jamaica. The review of the literature reveals two broad approaches based on how they treat differences in power among states/countries. Power is the capacity or ability to direct or influence the behavior of others or the course of events and the power of a country is a complex amalgam of different types of power.[1] Since power is not exercised in a vacuum, the extent to which a country/state has power depends on the power of other countries. All things being equal or as economists say, ceteris paribus, the smaller the country/state, the less power it will have and the more likely it will be subject to the power of larger, more developed countries/states. This is the logic common to both approaches. The traditional approach, which still exerts a dominant influence over the field of international relations, is based on a model of an atomistic world in which it is simply realistic to recognize differences in power among states/countries, and these asymmetries certainly exist among other things because of differences in size. The larger the difference in size between two countries/states is the larger the differences in power, capacity for independent policy, and sovereignty. The alternative approach understands and explains differences in power as being rooted in the structure of the world, both in the economic and political senses. In some versions power differentials are inherent in the structure and gives effect to the logic of capitalism on a global scale. Differences in economic power and concomitant political and military power are systemic. Smaller countries/states, bar exceptional circumstances, are the subject of the exercise of power with little option to resist unless they exit the system of global capitalism or transform their role in the international division of labor or world system.

The two paradigms suffer from an inadequacy of exploring the degrees of autonomy small states have for independent policy, foreign and internal. The inability of small states to influence the foreign policy of larger, more powerful counties is taken as axiomatic, ruled out by systemic structural asymmetries, a consequence of power differentials extant in the real world. These approaches do not admit the possibility that a small state can influence the foreign policy of a more powerful state, let alone a superpower like the United States. For example, Jean Grugel states that the "international relations of the state located in the Caribbean Basin are dominated above all by the presence and power of the U.S. . . . In all the states of the Caribbean Basin, therefore, decision-making internally, political and economic, is permeated with U.S. influence."[2] The underlying assumption is, other than in very rare and exceptional situations, autonomous action by small states to influence more powerful countries/states is simply unrealistic or foreclosed by the structure in which countries/states find themselves.

Like every other law of social sciences there are exceptions to the rule, hence both approaches can accommodate exceptions when small states exert self-determined influence over their own affairs. These situations arise from special circumstances and the opportunity to capitalize on them may be temporary and short-lived, depending on the conjuncture. Among the most notable and often cited examples is Iceland's declaration of the two hundred mile exclusive fishing zone and their defense of the maritime boundary. It was a rare exception made possible by very propitious circumstances, not ordinarily available to small countries/states. Less spectacular was Braveboy-Wagner's suggestion that Trinidad was able to leverage its energy resources to gain some influence in some arenas.[3] The success of Jamaica in exerting influence on U.S. foreign policy on several issues cannot be dismissed as an exception as will be demonstrated later in the text. While no government is completely devoid of the capacity to influence the external world, the Jamaica-U.S. experience challenges traditional notions that in circumstances of substantial asymmetries, the capacity of the smaller, less developed state to influence the larger, more powerful country is extremely limited. An explanation of this experience, which is clearly in the ambit of the discipline of international relations, will require modification, adjustment, or extension of the existing theories of international relations. Bishop's review of international relations literature leads him to the conclusion that there has been a "failure to adequately problematize small states" and explains, "the discipline was never really able to get beyond the thorny question of what is small? Dissatisfaction with this impasse further institutionalized the marginalization of the topic."[4]

How and why Jamaica was able to achieve influence over U.S. foreign policy has to be comprehended against the background of how foreign governments go about trying to influence U.S. foreign policy. This in turn requires an understanding of how foreign policy is formulated and implemented in the U.S. political system. An exercise of this type necessitates integration of two separate yet related social science disciplines, international relations and political science.

As the focus of the study is outside the ambit of the traditional subject matter of international relations, there is limited applicability of existing theories. This is especially true when examining the relations between a superpower, the United States, and a small developing country, Jamaica. The third section conducts a brief survey of the literature on small states to establish, by the definitions offered, that Jamaica is best described as a small developing country. The study encompasses an examination of both intra-state politics, specifically how activities in the domestic political environment and interest group politics[5] influence foreign policy in the United States, and inter-state relations. Samuel Huntington explains that "for an understanding of American foreign policy it is necessary to study not the interests of the American state in a world of competing states but rather the play of economic and ethnic interests in American domestic politics."[6] Therefore, the approach that is most useful for the purposes of this study is a pragmatic combination of the literature on international relations theories, small states, and models of domestic interest group politics. These approaches are reviewed in the following sections, but this review must be preceded by an establishment of the differences between the United States and Jamaica. This relationship is one in which Jamaica is highly dependent on the United States in economic terms as is evident in trade, investment, and tourism.

DIFFERENCES IN SIZE AND DEVELOPMENT

There are very significant differences in size and level of development between the United States and Jamaica. These differences can be measured and compared by using a variety of indices of size, in particular population, land area, and gross domestic product (GDP). The most frequently used indicator of size is population. Table 2.1 reveals that the United States had a population of 270 million in 1999 compared to Jamaica with a population of 2.57 million. A second commonly used indicator is the size of a country's land area because it is a proxy for the amount and diversity of natural resources. The size of land area of Jamaica is approximately 0.1 percent of that of the United States. A third, and perhaps the most useful indicator of economic size, is the level of GDP, which measures the aggregate wealth or output produced in an economy. The GDP also provides an indication of the magnitude of a country's domestic market, thereby offering some indications of the possible limitations to specialization of production and exploitation of economies of scale. The GDP figures shown in table 2.1 are expressed in 1990 U.S. dollars and show the enormous difference between the world's largest economy, the United States, and Jamaica. In 1999 the GDP of Jamaica was $7,446 million compared with $9,256,150 million in the United States. The GDP of the United States is approximately 1,243 times that of Jamaica, which means that every 7.5 hours, the United States produces the equivalent of Jamaica's GDP, i.e., the total goods and services produced in a year.

A fourth indicator of size is the disparity between corporate entities in the United States and Jamaica. These differences are enormous, as is shown in table 2.1. Firms in small economies, especially small developing economies, are all small in comparison with firms in large or developed countries and multinational corporations. The total sales of the largest U.S. firm, General Motors, was U.S. $164,068.9 million at the time that sales of the largest Jamaican firm, Grace Kennedy, were U.S. $312 million. Wal-Mart, the largest employer in the United States has a staff complement of 675,000 compared to Jamaica's top employer, Lascelles Demercado, which employs 6,800 people.[7] Export firms in small developing countries are minute by global standards, e.g., 74 percent of exporting firms in Jamaica have less than 100 employees.[8]

Differences in size, especially when these disparities are large, are usually taken, and reasonably so, as an indication of asymmetries in

Table 2.1. Comparison of United States and Jamaica

INDICATOR	UNITED STATES	JAMAICA
Area (thousands of sq. kilometers)	9,089	11
Population (millions 1995)	263.1	2.5
GDP (millions of constant 1990 $)	6,173,900	4,171
Largest Company (sales in $ millions)	General Motors 164,069	Grace Kennedy 312

Source: World Bank, World Development Report 1995 (Washington, D.C.: World Bank 1995), Business Week, March 24, 1997, The Caribbean's Top 100 Public Companies (Bridgetown: Caribbean Communications Inc., 1996), and The Fortune 500, http://archive.fortune.com/magazines/fortune/fortune500_archive/full/1997/101.html.

power and influence in the relationships between such states. However another important criterion is the difference in levels of development and in this regard, a widely used proxy is GNP per capita. As shown in table 2.1 the United States had a GNP per capita of $30,600 in 1999, which is far higher than Jamaica's $2,330. The United States is clearly a much more developed country than Jamaica judged by any and all of the development indicators used by the World Bank.[9] It is not necessary to adduce any data on differences in power such as size of armed forces, size of government budget, etc. Suffice it to simply state the obvious, which is, the superpower status of the United States allows the country to exercise power and influence in a manner which no other state was able to do in the period of analysis, 1991–2001. This fact alone overrides any issues about disparities of size and development.

Jamaica's Economic Dependence on the United States

Jamaica's economy is closely linked to that of the United States and the extent of dependence is evident in trade, capital flows, tourism, and remittances. (1) The United States is Jamaica's main trade partner, being both the main source of imports and the largest export market for Jamaican goods. (2) The United States has been the main source of foreign direct investment in Jamaica and the stock of U.S. investment is the largest of all foreign investors. (3) Jamaica is extremely dependent on the United States for tourism, with Americans accounting for 68 percent[10] of total tourist arrivals. (4) Remittances have been an important inflow of foreign exchange in Jamaica, with the United States being the largest source country.

SMALL STATES IN INTERNATIONAL RELATIONS THEORIES

The analysis of relations between the United States and Jamaica must adequately recognize the peculiarities of small states and take into account, in a way that is integral to the analysis, the asymmetries that exist between states and affects their relationships. In order to explore this type of asymmetric relationship, it is helpful to locate the discussion in the literature on small states and small economies. There is a well-developed literature on small states and what have been described as "ministates" and "microstates,"[11] as well as a parallel body of work on small economies.[12] Resort to this literature is necessary not only because of proximity to the subject matter of this study, but also because international relations theories offer little that is directly pertinent to foreign policy among asymmetric states. To establish this conclusion it is necessary to survey the main theories of international relations and explain why they are inadequate for the task of this study, before examining the literature on small states.

Surveys of theories of international relations have grouped these theories in a variety of ways, none of which is particularly useful for the purpose of this study. Little and Smith[13] classify the theories into three groups: the balance of power approach, the interdependence approach, and the dominance/dependence approach. Holsti suggests that the theoretical literature is characterized by three approaches: realism, dependency, and global society.[14] These typologies miss the fundamental basis for classifying theories of international relations, which is how they understand and treat the issue of asymmetries among countries/states. While not engaging in a detailed discussion of different theoretical approaches to the study of international relations, it is necessary to present a succinct overview of the current theories of international relations, grouped into two broad categories, based on how they view asymmetries among countries/states.

The approach, which I have entitled "atomistic asymmetries," with its focus on pluralism and interdependence, offers little insight when analyzing asymmetries. The "structural asymmetries" approach is not sufficiently enlightening because there is presumption of an immutable character to the asymmetries, which are inherent in global economic or international political systems. Neither broad approach suffices for the task at hand, which is to locate and inform the study of how a small country/state exerts influence over a far more powerful country/state, in the formulation of the foreign policy of the more powerful country/state. A more appropriate conceptual and analytic framework for the proposed task involves drawing on the literature on small states and domestic politics.

ATOMISTIC ASYMMETRIES

This approach to international relations is based on the recognition of asymmetries among states in an atomistic world. It acknowledges that these asymmetries give rise, in the real world, to differences in power and in these circumstances, the more powerful dominate the less powerful. These dynamics can change as states weaken or gain in power. In the real world small countries/states exert little influence over the more powerful. The weakness of the paradigm is its inability to explain how and why power differentials emerge and how they might be changed and has little predictive analytic value and even less use as a basis for prescriptive advice on policy. The evolution and mutation of this approach has given rise to different theories of international relations, which are reviewed below.

Realism

Realism is one of the longest prevailing approaches to the study of international relations and arguably the most influential paradigm, having dominated the discipline for nearly half of a century. Hans Morgenthau, E. H. Carr, and Kenneth Waltz are the most prominent proponents of realism. The dominance of this approach has been reduced by critiques and the emergence of other approaches, but nevertheless it remains a standard part of the repertoire. Realist theory assumes that the world is anarchic and the international system is one in which conflict is an ever present possibility. Nation-states are the fundamental actors and unit of analysis and are assumed to act rationally to safeguard and maximize their national political and economic power.[15] In this state-centric approach, the state is a territorially based, sovereign political unit with a central decision making unit, i.e., the government.

The early approaches to international relations have been aptly described as "liberal internationalist"[16] because they view relations among states as harmonious, i.e., with "idealism" or "utopianism."[17] The erosion of the plausibility of utopian thinking dates back to the work of Niebuhr[18] in the early 1930s and gathered pace with the imminence of World War II. In 1939, E. H. Carr, a Marxist historian, published *The Twenty Years Crisis, 1919–1939*, a book that became essential reading in the discipline for many years.[19] Carr pointed to the naiveté of concepts such as the harmony of interests (also an assumption of Classical economics of the nineteenth century) and the probability of collective security in a world divided been the "haves" and the "have-nots." Their different circumstances and aspirations made conflict inevitable, as the "well off" sought order to preserve the status quo and those who experienced deprivation could not accept this reality. Conflict was not an aberration born of misunderstanding, but inherent and systemic.

In 1948, Morgenthau published "Politics Among Nations,"[20] which became one of the standard texts for students of international relations, going into several editions and printings. The gravamen of his argument is simply that international relations is the study of states pursuing interests and this is best understood in terms of power. He took as axiomatic that the state is the key actor in the international arena and assumed that states have clearly defined interests, which he attributed to the power-seeking behavior rooted in human nature. It is taken for granted that a state, like a person, can have interests. The notion of the "national interest" subsumed a diversity of interests. The national interest centers on the pursuit of power, i.e., the ability to make others do your bidding, since it is by the exercise of power that national goals can be achieved. "International politics, like all politics, is a struggle for power."[21] The need for power is also systemically driven by the state of anarchy in international affairs, which exists because of the absence of a hegemonic power or an international organization, which can impose order. The methodology of realist scholarship is empiricism; in particular, comprehending the mode of decision-making of leaders, statesmen, diplomats, and policy makers. This requires deciphering the truth about reality, rationally and objectively, eschewing what is subjective and judgmental.[22] Despite the seminal status attained by "Politics Among Nations," there were obvious weaknesses, e.g., the distinction between power as an end in itself or as a means to an end. An integral concept was the balance of power, which was discussed in terms of a few large states, hence there is nothing said specifically about small states. However, the implication of Morgenthau's argument is that less powerful states (including small developing countries) will have little or no influence on the foreign policy of more powerful states.

Waltz achieved notoriety with a 1959 book titled *Man, The State and War*,[23] which was a historical review of the causes of war between states. He introduced the concept of levels of analysis, postulating three levels or "images," namely human nature; domestic, economic, and political systems of states; and the anarchy of the international environment in which states coexist. Waltz felt that the failure to distinguish these levels is a weakness in Morgenthau's works, e.g., whether the quest for power derives from the anarchical character of international politics or from human nature. He suggested that there were three levels of analysis: the international level, which has inter-state relations and the international system in its purview; the domestic level, which encompasses social, cultural, and political aspects of individual states; and the individual level, where the personal and psychological traits of leaders and statesmen are considered. Rosenau[24] subdivides the domestic level into state, society, and intermediating institutions and Jervis[25] expands the approach to four levels by adding the bureaucratic process.

Central to the critique of realism is its overarching preoccupation with a state-centric approach to international relations, its omission of domestic politics as a factor in the formulation and implementation of foreign policy, its reductionist notion of the overarching importance of the pursuit of national power, and its simplistic differentiation among states of "greater powers and lesser states."[26] At a methodological level the empiricism of the realists did not provide a theory with much explanatory power, indeed it was stylized facts in search of a theory. In fact, Halliday has argued that many in the discipline adopted the position that facts were enough.[27] This fundamental flaw was what the behaviorists sought to remedy, arguing that many of the fundamental concepts depended on unsubstantiated implicit assumptions about human behavior, resulting in theories that had little predictive value and limited explanatory power. They attempt to introduce a scientific empiricism by employing quantitative methods from other social science disciplines. The behaviorists also recognized that the realists did not have a theory of the state, which explained the interaction between domestic politics and foreign policy and sought to shed light on this lacuna by introducing decision-making models. The classic tract of this genre of literature is Allison's *Essence of Decision*,[28] which proposed three models (a) the rational actor model, which presumes that decisions are the result of the rational calculation of a single actor, (b) the organizational process model in which a multiplicity of organizations jointly make decisions, and (c) the bureaucratic politics model, which attempts to situate foreign policy decisions in a wider milieu of domestic politics in which decisions are affected by factors unrelated to foreign policy.

A further complication, which was introduced into the debate on decision-making, was the recognition that decision-makers could be swayed by their misperceptions and preconceptions. This cognitive dimension has received increasing attention as thinkers analyze the role of ideas and ideologies in the formulation of foreign policy, notably in the scholarship of Hunt,[29] Goldstein,[30] and Goldstein and Keohane.[31]

The recognition of theoretical weaknesses in realism and the much greater importance of economic issues in contemporary international relations gave rise to a variation of realism, which has come to be known as neo-realism.[32] This revision of realism did not abandon the core concepts of the state, power, conflict, and the balance of power. Bull, for example, views the world as an anarchical society on a global scale and is concerned to establish the conditions under which order will prevail in interstate relations. The possibility of order in the society of states depends on "institutions" such as the balance of power, war, international law, and diplomacy, which have functions or roles in maintaining international order.[33] Krasner attempted to demonstrate empirically the validity of the realist assumption of the state as a rational actor[34] and argued that the prospects for order in the world economy do not depend on international regimes because these are unlikely to regulate or attenuate the anarchy inherent among unequal states. In his study of Third World states in international economic relations he concludes that small, poor states in the South seek redress for their lack of power by supporting authoritarian regimes, which allocate resources rather than taking their chances in free markets. On the other hand the powerful, rich states of the North support market allocation because of their competitive advantages. The attempts of the Third World to create a New International Economic Order are properly understood as a challenge to global liberalism and an effort to change the rules of the game. This did not come to fruition and like any competition or conflict between the North and South will be resolved in favor of the more powerful states.[35] Waltz is just as pessimistic about the prospects for less powerful states in what he views as an anarchic world with states of different capacities. The big powers win out over small powers in a milieu where the balance of power is central and the nature of international relations is determined by the number and character of great powers.[36]

Interdependence

Keohane and Nye[37] describe the international system as characterized by what they call "complex interdependence" which is a situation not adequately conceptualized by realist theory. They do not repudiate realism's assumptions about the structure and processes of international politics but point out that the realist approach is only valid for events in some circumstances, at particular times. In their quest for a more nuanced reading of realism they promoted the examination of "transnational relations" among non-state actors such as multinational corporations, thus expanding international relations beyond the strictures of inter-state relations[38] to include an increasing array of actors,[39] in particular transnational, trans-governmental, and nongovernmental players. Complex interdependence like realism is an ideal type, which accurately portrays a condition prevailing in the international system only in specific circumstances.

According to Keohane and Nye,[40] complex interdependence is reflected in the increase in the number and variety of actors in international relations and differs from issue to issue. In the realist new international relations, there is a single dominant objective that the realists assume to be for national security. With interdependence theory, there is no overarching objective, which is immutable in all circumstances because any of a number of other goals or issues can take precedence in situations of complex interdependence. Interdependence among states makes the use of violence less likely or viable as an option because power is not confined to military power but different types of power exist and coexist. In their case studies, Keohane and Nye establish that realism does not have explanatory use in all situations and thereby undermine the simple conclusion that the more powerful state will be dominant in relations with less powerful states. This is an important notion, which takes into consideration the more complex perspective of interdependence among states with different levels of power, a differentiation that could derive from differences in size and level of development.

STRUCTURAL ASYMMETRIES

The theories that fall under the rubric of structural asymmetries are characterized by their identification of asymmetries as existing as a function and logic, inherent in global economic or political systems.

Dependency

The dependency approach or school[41] views the world and the international system as dominated by capitalism on a global scale. Inherent in this type of economic system is a "center–periphery" or "metropolis-satellite"[42] dichotomy, which coincides with development and underdevelopment. In this dualist concept, whose intellectual heritage derives from Prebisch[43] and the UN Economic Commission for Latin America (ECLA),[44] and structuralists such as Furtado[45] it is the center that exercises hegemony over the dependent periphery.[46] This periphery approach has the advantage of linking the domestic or national, and the foreign or international in an integrated and systemic way. It also treats asymmetries not merely as a historical context but as inherent in the structure of a global capitalist system. It characterizes relations of unequal power and disparities in levels of development as relations of dependency in which the center is dominant. They explain this dualism as historical in origin and inherent in the structure and functioning of capitalism, which has always been global. The center–periphery relationship is one of dominance and dependence but not one of outright conflict because the ruling class in the periphery benefits from, and indeed has, an integral and dependent role in accumulation on a world scale. The structure and functioning of capitalism on a world scale permits only what Frank has termed "the development of underdevelopment" in the periphery.[47] There is a process of polarization that produces development in the center and underdevelopment in the periphery or as Sunkel describes it, a single global process involving transnational integration and national disintegration.[48] Frank, Sunkel, and others stress that the polarization and center-periphery dichotomy is reproduced at the global level as well as within national economies. Critics have questioned the mechanism of exploitation or surplus extraction. However, the main propositions of dependency thinkers have been supported by empirical data.[49]

In addition to the structural factors that inhibit transformation of center-periphery relation, accomplices who perform a "sub-imperialist"[50] role and are a particular genre of bourgeoisie, variously described as "lumpenbourgeoisie"[51] and "comprador capitalists," reinforce dependence. The notion of a collaborating class was an integral aspect to the analysis of colonialism and neo-colonialism in the work of authors like Frantz Fanon.[52] Sunkel advanced the discussion beyond the simple dualist concept, by explaining that the part of the economy of the periphery that is closely integrated with the center has more in common with the center than with the rest of its national economy and the social counterpart of this is a section of all classes that are locked in with the center. He states "A complex of activities, social groups and regions in different countries which conform to the developed part of the global system and which are closely linked transnationally through many concrete interests as well as by similar life styles, ways and levels of living and cultural affinities."[53] These co-opted strata of classes use their influence and leverage to consolidate and defend, rather than change their country's dependent relations with the developed capitalist countries of the "center." They employ systemically reinforced positions to maintain political power and even opt for coercion rather than redistributive and social welfare policies. This has prompted many of the authors of this persuasion to suggest that the option for change is to exit from the existing structure of world capitalism in a transition to socialism. It has been argued that dependency is flawed because it incorrectly forecloses the possibility of development, e.g., industrialization.[54]

The dependency approach explicitly rejects the view of the world as a collection of atomistic nation-states acting rationally in pursuit of their clearly defined national interests. It employs a perspective that is holistic and structuralist, with the result that even bilateral relations among states have to be understood in structural and systemic terms. The prescriptions for an underdeveloped and dependent country are pessimistic, as both external and internal structures militate against having sufficient influence to change the character to external relations. The possibilities are even more constrained in the case of small states in the periphery, because of their greater dependence. This approach gives little credence to the possibility of the dependent country have sufficient influence to affect the policy towards it by the dominant country. This possibility is by definition stymied by structural aspects of dependency and the subjugated status of the ruling classes in the periphery. Dependency, like Marxism, does take international relations beyond the state-centric approach of realism and interdependence, to incorporate class analysis and the role of major non-state actors such as multinational corporations.

The extrapolation of a theory of international relations from dependency has given rise to "theories of dependent foreign policy," which make the fundamental point that the dependent country's foreign policy will be at least constrained and will exhibit compliance to the dominant country. Jeanne Hey warns that deterministic interpretations should be avoided both because this is a misinterpretation of the dependency approach and because Ecuador's experience in the 1980s displays some degrees of freedom. She explains that: "Dependence serves to constrain the options available to Ecuador's policy makers, to circumscribe their foreign policy ambitions, and at times to determine what behavior they follow." But the "dependent relationship proved critical to Ecuador's foreign policy process, but did not lead to a single set of foreign policy outcomes."[55]

Marxism

The Marxist approach[56] to society, politics, and the economy is holistic and based on historical materialism. It is a political economy framework integrating a superstructure with an economic substructure, which is determinant in the last instance. It starts from the premise that there is dialectic between opposites, and in capitalism this takes the form of conflict between the capitalists and the working class, and between development and underdevelopment.[57] Lenin[58] elaborated and extended the thoughts of Marx on capitalism as a global system and referred to capitalism on a global stage as imperialism in which monopolies, cartels, and finance capital become the driving forces. It must be noted that there is a considerable literature on imperialism, which is written from a non-Marxist perspective,[59] some of which pre-dates Lenin's famous pamphlet, notably Hobson,[60] and which shares several of the tenets and conclusions of the Marxist school,[61] particularly that imperialism is associated with or inherent in capitalism.[62] The less powerful and the underdeveloped countries are dominated by and exploited by the developed capitalist countries.

While this paradigm recognizes that policy, including foreign policy, emerges from a milieu of class conflict, it yields the lone conclusion that the most developed and powerful capitalist countries will have their way with little or no influence from the weaker and less developed states. The more recent expositions, e.g., "Western Marxism"[63] or neo-Marxism including Gramsci,[64] Lukacs,[65] Althusser, Mandel,[66] Magdoff,[67] Amin,[68] Emmanuel,[69] Poulantzas,[70] and Baran and Sweezy[71] rejected the reified, mechanical, and deterministic interpretations of Marx (including by Marxist-Leninists) and offer a more nuanced reading of the original texts of Marx and Engels. A number of scholars have suggested that a historical materialism approach can enrich the study of international relations.[72] If the more sophisticated contemporary interpretations of Marxism are employed, it can enhance the perspective[73] of imperialism as a structured relationship of dominance, rooted in global capitalism and involving an amalgam of economic, political, social, cultural, and military aspects. In this approach dialectic materialism is not interpreted in a deterministic manner and recognizes that even hegemonic dominance is tempered by degrees of resistance and less than absolute compliance by the subjugated country, even a small one.

World Systems

The work of Wallerstein[74] and those who have followed this holistic approach, e.g., Chase-Dunn[75] and Hopkins,[76] proceed from the fundamental assumption that based on history, the appropriate framework of analysis is the world as a system, and the best way to comprehend the world system is a historical approach. The methodology of historical analysis eschews what has been called "the cult of individualism"[77] and is Braudelian[78] in scope and sweep. Their intensive examination of the history of the modern era concentrates on the rise and consolidation of capitalism, which for them is the defining development of this era and which has its origin in "the long sixteenth century." The global expansion of capitalism occurred through the geographical spread of the market, an international division of labor, the rise of powerful states in Europe, the development of different forms of labor control, and various forms of political control. Wallerstein outlines a structure of the world as a system in which there are three functional components in the international division of labor—the core, the periphery, and in between, the "semi-periphery." The semi-periphery has a political function as well as an economic, namely it helps to stabilize the world system by acting as a buffer between the "core hegemons" (dominant powers) and the exploited periphery.

The world systems model shares with Marxism and the dependency approach, the tenet that the world is the appropriate unit of analysis, the primacy of the logic of capitalism at the world level over that of the nation-state, the dominance by the developed capitalist countries and the dependence of the less developed countries, and the development/underdevelopment polarization inherent in capitalism. The work of leading thinkers in the three perspectives influenced each other[79] and there were debates and exchanges.[80] Dependency and World Systems approaches have incorporated ideas from Marxist thinking, including the concept of surplus, ironically one of the points on which Marxists differentiate themselves, preferring the concept of surplus value.[81] Some well-known texts on international relations treat these three approaches together, e.g., Viotti and Kauppi group them under the rubric of globalism[82] and Little and Smith collect excerpts under dominance and dependence.[83]

World systems theory does elaborate on how the periphery can succeed in attempts to resist or influence the dominant core hegemons, whereas Marxism and dependency hold out revolution, exit from capitalism, and a transition to socialism.[84] Only C. Y. Thomas takes account of small size in his argument for the transformation from dependence to socialism as the only way to achieve genuine development.[85] The question of how size affects the character of center-periphery relations and the possibilities for influence and change is not addressed in the world systems, Marxist, and dependency approaches. This is the case even if different types of situations are distinguished in the periphery, e.g., periphery/semi-periphery, periphery/sub-imperialist, periphery/imperialism intermediary, and peripheral industrialized/non-industrial or non-competitive peripheral countries.[86]

Critical Theory

Cox[87] starts from the position that existing theories of international relations can explain how a particular world order is maintained and more importantly how it can be changed. Existing theoretical approaches are problem-solving theories and seek to improve the operations of existing institutions. These theories are ahistorical and time-bound because they take present institutions and social power relations as permanent, when in reality they are not fixed and hence, must be transcended by the development of critical theory. The objective of critical theory[88] is, following Marx, not just to understand the world but also to change it, in contrast to problem-solving theory, which serves some particular national, sectoral, or class interests.

International relations can best be understood by the analysis of structures that consists of three interrelated levels or spheres of activity (a) social forces engendered by the production process, (b) forms of state, and (c) world orders, i.e., the specific configuration of forces that define relations between states. He recognizes the rise and decline of three hegemonic world orders and acknowledges that a diffusion of power can occur when there is a "counter-hegemonic historic bloc" of social forces[89] of dominant and acquiescent groups. Through the internationalization of the state, states become part of a complex hierarchical political structure at the global level. Cox explains that the process results in different forms of state corresponding to the different positions of countries in the world economy. The reshaping of specific state structures in accordance with the overall international political structure is brought about by a combination of external pressures and realignments of internal power relations among domestic social groups. As internationalization proceeds, it provokes countertendencies of domestic social groups, which have been disadvantaged or excluded in the new alignment.[90]

World Society

The approach that has been labeled International or World Society, for want of a more precise term, is an eclectic attempt to formulate a holistic approach to international politics, which takes as its starting point a rejection of conventional international relations theory.[91] Burton proposes the concept of world society in which inter-state relations is only one type of relationship in a wide array of transnational linkages.[92] He contends that concepts like national power, balance of power, and national interest have been overtaken by contemporary reality. Burton uses systems theory to focus on conflict resolution and argues that conflict among states is often caused by dysfunctional internal decision-making. He draws a distinction between two kinds of conflict resolution, i.e., puzzle-solving and problem-solving. The former only addresses the symptoms while the latter seeks to transform the situation into a positive-sum scenario. Conflict can only be resolved when eight basic needs of the parties involved are satisfied. [93] The importance of this approach is its recognition of domestic (internal) factors in the decisions, which affect relations among states; however there is no discussion of difference in size.

INADEQUACY OF THEORIES OF INTERNATIONAL RELATIONS

The main approaches to the study of international relations give very limited attention to the formulation of foreign policy and how the involvement of other states in this domestic political process can have an impact. Or, the treatment is so "dirigiste" that it inadvertently excludes the possibility of a small state influencing the foreign policy of a large powerful country. The realism school focuses attention on the inter-state international policy arena and does not develop fully the aspect of domestic political processes that determine foreign policy. The early advocates of realism were preoccupied with differences in national power. Later, more nuisance approaches did incorporate the role of domestic politics in foreign policy formulation; however, these approaches essentially consist of elaborating on how foreign policy is formulated by delineating and identifying the principal domestic political actors. Within this paradigm there are a variety of approaches that seek to explain national decision making. Some of these approaches are quite elaborate analytic models but they give scant attention to the possibility of external actors in the formulation and execution of foreign policy.

The interdependence school introduces the dimension of transnational relations among a multiplicity of actors, including important non-state actors like the multinational corporations. The approach does not, however, adequately recognize the possibility of less powerful actors such as small states being able to influence the foreign policy of a far more powerful country such as the United States.

The dependence school makes a breakthrough by linking the domestic politics of interacting states by deploying the overarching framework of global capitalism; it establishes the structural links through the center-periphery dichotomy. The center and periphery are two aspects of the global operation of capitalism and domestic politics in nation-states and are catenated by the structure of a global economic system. The dependent character of the insertion of the periphery in the global capitalist system results in a characterization of the domestic politics in the periphery as subservient to a transnational capitalist class, based primarily in the center. The Marxist approach, particularly the thinking of "Western Marxism," is far more sophisticated in its elaboration of the dynamics of class structure and the dialectic of political processes in capitalist societies. However, the dominant influence is the economic power of the capitalist class and its transnational character. The world systems approach suffers from the same weaknesses as the Marxist and dependency schools, even while introducing variations such as the semi-periphery and its ill-defined role as a buffer between the core hegemony and the underlying periphery.

Critical theory does recognize the necessity to locate the analysis in particular settings where national and class interest may vary. However, its central focus is the configuration of forces, which define the character of relations between states, but relies on the use of dominance and power asymmetries. In this approach, the analysis of the intervention in the domestic politics of interacting states is not adequately developed. The world society approach is an eclectic approach to international politics, which is based on the recognition of interstate relations as part of an array of transnational linkages within world society. The importance of this approach is its recognition of domestic political factors; however, there is no discussion of the asymmetries that arise from differences in the size of the nation-state.

These approaches, while to some extent recognizing the importance of domestic political processes in influencing international relations, need to be strengthened. This can be accomplished by drawing on the literature on interest group politics and in particular, how interest groups affect foreign policy. This will obviate the weaknesses of oversimplified approaches to understanding the relationship between foreign policy and domestic political processes. The approach employed in this study relies on the integration of interest group politics with international relations theory.

This survey of international relations theory yields the conclusion that in a relationship between two states that differ vastly in power, size, and level of development, the smaller, less developed, and weaker state has virtually no influence on the foreign policy of the other. In a relationship between the United States of America and Jamaica, this literature on international relations would lead to the conclusion that Jamaica cannot and in fact does not exercise any discernable influence on the foreign policy of the United States towards Jamaica. The reality however, as documented in the study, is that the activities of the government of Jamaica did indeed have a noticeable effect on the foreign policy of the United States towards Jamaica. The case studies of the government of Jamaica's lobbying on debt, foreign aid, trade policy, and certification for narcotics cooperation, constitute a sufficient basis for generalization, especially since the disparities were so substantial. In other words, if such a small state can significantly influence the formulation and implementation of U.S. foreign policy, then it is certainly a possibility in situations where the disparities are not as significant. Therefore, the contribution of this study to international relations theory is to indicate the need to improve the explanatory power of the existing approaches by taking into account in-sights that can be derived from the literature on interest group politics.

The contribution to international relations of this study is beyond the analysis and documentation of United States-Jamaica relations, as it dem-onstrates that a small state can influence the foreign policy of even the most powerful country through involvement in the domestic politics of foreign policy formulation. The case studies indicate both the possibility and process of a small state influencing the foreign policy of a large, powerful country. There are however, limits to the capacity for influence even for the most well thought out and executed plan. In the U.S. political system, which affords greater possibilities for the intervention in domes-tic politics of foreign governments and other entities, a critical determi-nant of the outcome is financial resources. As illustrated by the failure to change U.S. banana policy, vast disparities in financial resources limit the capacity of small states to influence the domestic politics of U.S. foreign policy. The central point remains that international relations theories must give greater attention and more incisive analysis to the domestic politics of foreign policy formulation so that it can encompass the real world possibility of interstate influence in the context of considerable asymmetries of all kinds.

Theories of international relations, including those that recognize the importance of domestic politics as a determinant of foreign policy, con-clude that in a relationship between two countries that differ consider-ably in size, development, and power, the smaller state will have little or no influence on the foreign policy of the larger, more powerful state. While this generalization has overall validity, it is not a correct assess-ment or prediction in some situations. The contribution of this study is to demonstrate that in certain circumstances, a small, much less powerful country can influence the foreign policy pursued towards it by a much larger and far more powerful country. This proposition is based on the examination and analysis of relations between the United States and Ja-maica during the period 1991 to 2001. Given the vast differences in size, development, and power between the sole superpower, the United States, and Jamaica, the fact that a small, developing country actually influenced United States foreign policy towards it, raises important is-sues that need to be more adequately addressed by theories of interna-tional relations. If a small state such as Jamaica can influence foreign policy of the most powerful country in the world, then other more endowed states could do the same and perhaps more. Therefore, even though the experience of Jamaica was exceptional in general and even unique in some respects, it cannot simply be dismissed as an exception to the proverbial rule. The implication is that more attention should be de-voted to establishing the circumstances that are propitious for small state influence, and understanding what are the modalities and techniques of small states achieving influence in the context of substantial disparities in size, development, and power in relation with other states. These are questions that the discipline of international relations must adequately recognize and incorporate into new or modified theories of international relations. The importance of correcting this lacuna in international relations theory goes beyond the scholarly quest for better theory and a more complete discipline to its pertinence to the real world of international affairs. Asymmetries among states is reality with which states must contend in the daily conduct of foreign policy and this a particularly acute issue for the large number of small states, especially in their bilateral relations. In bilateral relations, the lack of leverage of small states cannot be offset by the equality of rights in multilateral institutions nor can group tactics necessarily obviate the power disparity that small states encounter in interactions with larger, more powerful countries.

The number of small countries and states in the world has increased significantly in recent decades; in particular, there has been a proliferation of small states and economies. At the end of World War I, there were 62 independent countries, by 1946 that number had risen to 74 and at present there are almost 200 countries. Most of these are small countries, indeed, there are 87 countries with populations of less than 5 million, 58 have fewer than 2.5 million people, and 35 have less than 500,000 people.[94] Given the large number of small countries, the issue of "smallness" must be addressed both as a political and economic phenomenon. The issue of small countries/states/economies must be examined and their participation ensured in all international organizations and agreements if a truly inclusive international community and global economy is to exist. This fact has been recognized in recent years, for example, the Summit of the Americas Declaration of Principles, in December, 1994 states that the formation of a free trade area among 34 countries would be a complex and unprecedented undertaking, "particularly in view of the wide differences in the levels of development and size of the economies existing in our hemisphere." The heads of state and government further committed the participating countries to "facilitate the integration of the smaller economies and increase their level of development." Subsequent Ministerial Declarations have noted the necessity of facilitating the integration and the importance of increasing the opportunities for the smaller economies to participate fully in the FTAA in a manner that promotes their growth.

The specific situation is that between the single superpower, the United States of America and Jamaica, a small developing country. In addition to the enormous disparity in size, level of development, and power, the unique "openness" of the U.S. political system and the separation of powers must be taken into account in any theoretical approach that is used to analyze how a foreign government can or has influenced U.S. foreign policy towards it. The most appropriate method of tackling this dilemma is to transcend the omissions and inadequacies of existing theories of international relations through a judicious incorporation of models of interest group politics. This introduces practical political considerations and modalities to a discipline characterized by theorizing at a highly abstract plane, which obscures the mechanics of foreign policy formulation and implementation that are critical to a small state trying to influence the policy of the United States

SMALL STATE: DEFINITION

The issue of small states in the field of international relations has prompted two directions in research. First is the effect of the proliferation of small states on the international system and even the need to limit this "undesirable" tendency.[95] Second, there is literature that focuses on how small size, i.e., limited resources, affects the power of these states and their capacity to influence external events and the behavior of other states.[96] The constraining effect of small size, i.e., limited resources on the capacity to execute foreign policy[97] is the premise underlying a voluminous and growing literature describing the foreign policies of small countries, including case studies of the foreign policy of individual or collaborating groups of countries including those of the English-speaking Caribbean.[98] These studies are historical and empirical and do not significantly advance the understanding of how small states can influence the foreign policy of larger, more developed, and more powerful countries, other than reiterating the obvious value of cooperation among groups of small states. Braveboy-Wagner argues that the small states of the English-speaking Caribbean, acting as CARICOM, exert some influence through alliance with a superpower or with larger groups of developing countries such as the African, Caribbean, and Pacific group.[99] Fauriol's comparative study of Guyana, Haiti, and Jamaica, while insightful on decision-making, doubts the efficacy of cooperation among small states and cautions that it "may provide little beyond an undeniably important psychological lift."[100]

Central to the discussion is to agree on a definition of a small state, small country, and/or a small economy and it is to this question that attention must now be directed. Small states/countries have been described by a variety of nomenclature and attempts to define this phenomenon have emerged in three streams of literature. First, there are terms dealing with the political phenomenon of the nation-state with the most frequently used term being "small states." The small state category is sometimes further subdivided to differentiate "micro-states" or "very small states."[101] When the development dimension is included, the result is the concept of "small developing states,"[102] in contrast with small states that are developed, e.g., Luxembourg, Monaco, and Liechtenstein. The term "ministate economies" has also been used.[103] Second, the terms

encompassing economies include "small economies,"[104] "smaller economies," "small developing economies,"[105] "small vulnerable developing
economies," and "small island economies."[106] Third, there are terms that
seek to capture environmental characteristics such as "islandness" and
locational remoteness that, when combined with developing status, have
given rise to a literature on "small island developing states." All three
concepts attempt to define size using a variety of measures. The literature
on each approach is reviewed below.

Small States

The definition of a small state is a debate that has not produced a
consensus. This is the conclusion of Sutton[107] based on a recent comprehensive review of the literature on small states. Some writers, e.g., Jainarain,[108] use the term small country instead of small state and the usage
inevitably suffers from the same problems as other more commonly used
nomenclature. There is considerable variation among the quantitative criteria proposed by various authors, e.g., Braveboy-Wagner recalls: "there
was a consensus of sorts in the 1960s that very small countries (ministate
or microstate) could be defined as having a population of less than 1
million inhabitants."[109] Taylor,[110] Harris,[111] Hein,[112] and Clarke and
Payne's[113] use of less than 1 million is consistent with this generalization
but Armstrong and Read[114] regard below 3 million as the appropriate
threshold. Bartson extends the range for being classified as a small state
to 10–15 million in population.[115]

Using 1 million or more in population resulted in a group of countries
within which there was considerable differences. Some are developed
and some are developing, leading Baldacchino to focus on "developing
microstates."[116] To capture the small end of the countries, De Smith[117]
speaks of a "very small state if it has a population of less than 150,000."
Other authors have differentiated small countries into three or more categories. Plischke employed population size range of fewer than 5 million
for small states, less than 300,000 for microstates, and those under 100,000
he designates as "submicrostates."[118] Ross classifies as small states, those
with populations between 1–5 million, "mini-states" are those with populations of 100,000 to 1 million, and those with populations below 100,000
are micro-states.[119] Applying 25 socioeconomic criteria, Liou and Ding
was able to identify nine distinct clusters of small states.[120]

Yet another approach to establishing what is a small economy or small
state, is to treat small as a relative concept that can be ascertained empirically by examining a distribution of economies or states based on a particular quantitative measure and identifying a cluster at the "small" end
of the spectrum. The result is a relative concept with those at the small
end being referred to as "smaller economies"[121] or "smaller powers."[122]
Bernal, in defining small developing economies, employs a combination

of land area, population, and per capita GDP and compared a range of countries concluding that the small developing economies were those that were small in a relative sense.[123]

The lack of a consensus on what is a small state is not surprising, since any definition of a small state, small economy, or small country in quantitative terms would invariably include a judgmental element because size is a relative concept. The result is that the term small state is used to describe some states that are not among the smallest but small relative to very large countries. Definitions of the term small state differ but most of the literature in international relations and foreign policy studies posit a small state as any state that is not a global power. The consequence of this loose relative size approach is to include under the rubric of a small state countries such as Denmark,[124] Slovenia,[125] Armenia, Georgia,[126] Yemen,[127] and the Baltic countries. These are to be sure, small relative to the great powers and this bifurcation leads Amersfoort and Klinkert to oversimplify the issue of definition of small states during the era 1900–1940, by stating that "it is obvious that whatever criterion, most states in the interwar world are to be considered small."[128]

Small Economies

Attempts to arrive at a definition in quantitative terms are the most advanced in the economic conceptualization of small economies or small developing economies. The question of how to define a small economy is not a new one, and definitions have historically varied widely. Definitions based on quantitative criteria vary considerably because they employ different criteria and exhibit a significant arbitrariness in the selection of boundary points. Size of population is the most frequently used criterion, with the cut-off point ranging widely among authors, e.g., Vital suggested below 20–30 million,[129] Adelman and Morris[130] and Maizels[131] pick less than 20 million, Kuznets,[132] Streeten,[133] and MacDonald and Novo[134] selected an upper limit of 10 million, while Chenery and Syrquin[135] used 5 million and Chenery and Taylor used a population of less than 15 million.[136] A less frequently used criterion is GDP or gross national product (GNP), e.g., an ECLAC (UN Economic Commission for Latin America and the Caribbean) study chose GNP of less than $15 billion.[137] The problem with GDP and GNP is that as time passes they are no longer useful guides to size because these aggregates have grown and/or increased by inflation. This being the case, when GDP or GNP is being employed it is often applied in conjunction with population and/or land area. Downes has sought to reduce the arbitrariness of choosing a combination by developing a single-valued index of country size, which combines demographic, economic, and geographic dimensions.[138]

In many instances two or more criteria were employed in combination of population, land area, or GDP. Demas opted for a population of 5 million or less and less than 20,000 square miles of usable land.[139] Jaina-rain[140] chose a population of 5 million, an area of 25 million hectares, or national product of U.S. $5 billion. Jalan decided on population below 5 million, GNP below U.S. $2 billion, and arable land of less than 25,000 square kilometers.[141] This type of approach has created as many problems as it has solved because economic data are time sensitive, e.g., what is a large GDP or GDP per capita income at present may very well appear small in ten years. Definitions of a small economy or small state may have to be revised over time if GNP or population is employed as the measure. For example, in 1985 the Commonwealth Secretariat used a population cut-off point of 1 million,[142] but by 1997 had revised the upper limit to 1.5 million.[143] Even with periodic upward revision of population, there will be cases of countries that fall outside the designated boundary but that share the characteristics of those within the boundary. In these instances the decision has been to include them despite being over the cutoff point. This was the agreed procedure when Jamaica fell outside the population stipulation of both the Commonwealth Secretariat and the World Bank.[144]

Small Island Developing States

Conrad opines: "On an island, you are disconnected, with water all around you. On an island you are alone, even if you share the place with others. The location is by definition eccentric, because it acknowledges that there is a centre elsewhere."[145] What Conrad says about the state of mind that occurs in islands is obviously about small islands, not Australia or Great Britain. The concept of small island developing states (SIDS) and the less frequently used "small island developing countries" incorporates size, development, and "island"[146] to emphasize environmental vulnerability. Although the usefulness of islands as a categorization has been questioned[147] the concept evolved in the United Nations system and was recognized as a category of country by the United Nations in 1994, by the Programme of Action for the Sustainable Development in SIDS (Barbados Programme of Action). The UN includes 51 countries in this category and many authors do not engage in the debate over definition but simply apply this definition.[148] The notions of island and nation have been combined by Srebrnik to describe some countries as "small island nations"[149] and with microstate to yield "island microstate."[150]

VULNERABILITY AND RELATIVE POWERLESSNESS

Small nations don't have a foreign policy. . . . They have merely a policy of existence.—C.S. Sulzberger, *New York Times*.[151]

After reviewing the three streams of the literature I conclude that the "differentia specifica" of small countries, small states, small nations, small economies, small developing economies, and small island developing states, is their vulnerability and relative powerlessness to respond to external events, including the policies of larger, more developed, more powerful countries, especially to a superpower such as the United States. Sutton speaks of this situation as the Caribbean being a "subordinated state system."[152] Vulnerability is evident in the impact of external events over which they have no control and limited resilience, or little or no capacity to respond or retaliate. These events can take one of three types namely, (1) economic, e.g., exogenous shocks such as a substantial spike in the price of oil. This is treated at length in the literature on small economies and small developing economies. (2) Political, i.e., arising from the deliberate action of another country or group of countries or an international institution. (3) Environmental, more specifically natural disasters, which when they affect a small country they have a catastrophic impact on the entire physical area of the country such as when Hurricane Ivan hit Grenada in 2004. This is in contrast to when Hurricane Katrina hit New Orleans but did not affect the entire United States of America.

Focusing on the political dimension, it is clear that vulnerability to bilateral political action by other states is indicative that small states suffer from a disparity in power compared to large developed countries and superpowers, in particular the United States of America. Vulnerability means having little or no influence to prevent or change the policy actions and direct interventions by larger, more powerful states.[153] It is this vulnerability that leads Rothstein to declare that a small state is "a state which recognizes that it cannot have security primarily by the use of its own capabilities, and must rely fundamentally on the aid of other states, institutions, processes or developments to do so."[154] A well-established school of thought argues that small states or countries are weak, i.e., do not have the economic and military resources to exercise power in international relations or even to defend themselves.[155] Weak states have to give compliance to the demands and policies of more powerful states. The Commonwealth Secretariat study on small states pointed to the vulnerability to external intervention by larger, more developed, and more powerful states.[156] This powerlessness is vividly illustrated by the decision of the United States in successfully having the World Trade Organization (WTO) declare the European Union's (EU) preferential banana regime to be incompatible with WTO rules. Consequently the EU had to disband the regime with the result that the banana industry collapsed in Grenada, Jamaica, St. Lucia, and St. Vincent.

Handel's review of the literature dates back to 1980 and reveals a conclusion that is still valid that not all weak states are synonymous with small states/countries, and all small states are weak states. Mini-states are at the extreme end of a continuum running from superpowers through great powers, middle powers, and weak states.[157] The logical converse of small states/countries being weak and having to give compliance is that they do not exercise any significant influence over more powerful states/ countries. This may be described as impotency in foreign policy. Naturally this compliance exists to the greatest extent when the dominant state is a superpower such as the United States. In special circumstances, small states/countries have managed to assert themselves and exert some influence on external events and the policies of other countries. Hence, the fatalistic reasoning that argues that small states/countries are vulnerable and therefore weak in relation to larger, more developed countries and therefore have little or no influence on the foreign policy of the dominant country as to be nuanced.

There are examples of small states asserting themselves and achieving some amount of influence over external events, for example, Iceland in keeping control of fish stocks in its coastal waters. Iceland was a small island state, which gained its political independence in 1944. The economy was almost entirely dependent on the fishing industry, with cod being by far the most important catch. Faced with a decline in the catch of cod after 1954, Iceland extended its territorial limit to 12 miles in 1958. Britain protested the action of an exclusive fishing zone and was supported by France, Germany, Spain, Belgium, Denmark, and the Netherlands. Thanks to the activity of the minuscule Iceland coast, guard Britain accepted the 12-mile limit in February, 1961. In September 1971, Iceland extended its limit to 50 miles and despite clashes with British vessels on the high seas, extended its jurisdiction to 200 miles on October 15, 1975. The small island state of Iceland changed the international rules governing ocean fishing in spite of attempted coercion by the British in what has become known as the "Cod Wars." By 1976, most countries had accepted and claimed their own 200–mile exclusive zones.[158]

The history of Iceland demonstrates the exception to the rule of small states having no influence on their external relations. Bishop reminds those tempted by euphoria that "such resilience can be fleetingly ephemeral"[159] and there can be pyric victories such as the WTO ruling in favor of Antigua in its case against the United States over international Internet gaming. Iceland's enduring vulnerability was revealed by its inability to prevent the implosion of its economy resulting from the devastating impact of the global financial crisis.[160] Some of the literature that makes the point of small states asserting or resisting is not considered pertinent here because they comprise episodes of countries that are definitely much larger than the ones being discussed in this study. Baker Fox's famous study of Finland, Norway, Spain, Sweden, and Turkey during World War II falls into this category.[161] Similarly Katzenstein's study of small states in world markets focuses on European countries.[162]

Jamaica: Small Developing Country

This survey, while not exhaustive, has covered enough literature to reveal that there is no single definition that enjoys anything like consensus. Nor is there a single concept or term for small country, state, economy, or nation; indeed there is a bewildering variety of nomenclature. To a large extent, what is a small state is in the eye of the beholder. Hey argues that "no strict definition is necessary either to employ smallness as an analytical device or to glean findings about foreign policy behavior from it."[163] The fundamental point is that small is best understood as a relative concept, i.e., a small country is a country that is small relative to other countries. If like Jamaica, the small country is also a developing one, then it is a small developing country. This approach is made easier in this study because although Jamaica is small by a variety of criteria and is classified as small by the Commonwealth Secretariat and the World Bank, it is also small by comparison with the United States. Similarly in contrast to the United States, Jamaica is clearly a developing country.

INTEREST GROUP POLITICS

There is a tendency to personify nation-states as the basic actors in the international system. Decision-making theory seeks to understand the behavior of the key decision-makers. Put simply, state action is the action taken by those acting in the name of the state.[164] Perception is central to the conceptual framework of decision-making theory, hence the worldview of decision-makers is a more important objective reality. This approach has led to a vast literature, which attempts to discern the underlying values and assumptions[165] and determine how these form a worldview, which informs the perceptions and decision-makers.[166] The development of this approach was accompanied by "psychological approaches to the study of foreign policy decision-making."[167] In reality, there is a plurality of decision-makers and institutions and policy emanates from the interplay of these several contending actors.

The "pluralist" models of the U.S. political system are based on the assumption that like free markets, the ideal outcome is the result of competition between individuals who are free to vote in elections, and interest groups, which influence politicians and political parties, and ultimately influence political decisions.[168] One of the early exponents of pluralist democracy spoke of "the balance of group pressure,"[169] a perspective that regards all interest groups as having a chance to shape political decisions and believes that this type of process can lead to a harmonious outcome. A major flaw in the model was the fact that interest groups differ considerably in their capacities, as they differ in resources, expertise, and organizing capacity. Numerous critics dismissed the naiveté of the model, pointing out that it was at variance with reality, and that in the real world power and influence was wielded by those with the most resources, specifically business and the wealthy, upper class elites, e.g., E. E. Schattschneider.[170] The Marxists, e.g., Paul Sweezy,[171] had all along maintained that the United States was a capitalist society and economy, and therefore was a class society in which economic and political power was controlled by the capitalist class. C. Wright Mills highlighted that political power was held and exercised by an integrated "power elite," consisting of the top levels of economic, military, and political institutions and they were drawn from the same social class.[172] The extreme and increasing concentration of wealth and income is the United States is extensively documented by G. William Domhoff[173] and others, to demonstrate the existence and cohesion of a small ruling class. These results are inevitable social manifestations of a systemic trend, inherent in what Baran and Sweezy have termed monopoly capital.[174] The retort to this well-documented critique was to suggest as Dahl did, that wealthy elites do not always take action with perfect clarity of purpose nor are their actions always consistent or rational in pursuit of their interests.[175] Some theorists made reference to the influence of business and the wealthy, which was offset by other interest groups such as organized labor, invoking Galbraith's concept of "countervailing power."[176]

INTEREST GROUP MODEL OF FOREIGN POLICY

The dominant paradigm in the analysis of foreign policy has been inter-state theory from a pragmatic position. The focus of this approach has been to assume the rationality of the internal political decision-making process, and therefore states are assumed to pursue their national interest in a rational manner. However, there are severe limitations to this approach and a new departure occurred with what is called the "realist" approach, which views the world as atomistic and focuses on inter-state relations. The world is anarchic, hence conflict is inherent and cooperation is the exception. Power[177] is the central concept with states seeking to rationally maximize and exercise their national power.[178] In this scenario, order is attained and maintained by balances of power between states.[179] The intellectual origin of this approach can be traced as far back as Thucydides, with other precursors including Machiavelli and Clausewitz.[180] The realist paradigm was modified by a discussion in which some argued that the balance of power was inherent and systemic,[181] while the protagonists posit its achievement by purposive action and diplomacy. The systemic hypothesis is of course too determinist to be very useful,[182] but Kissinger's argument that the balance of power is created by statesmen in the prosecution of national foreign policy,[183] is also inadequate. Allison sought to justify the "rational actor model," by positing that rationality could be ascribed when the state selects that alternative whose consequences rank highest in the decision-makers' "payoff function" (hierarchy of goals).[184]

The realist's model overlooks the complexity of foreign policy formulation and consequently, it oversimplifies the relationship between foreign policy and domestic policies. This glaring inadequacy prompted the famous "levels of analysis" debate in which some theorists advanced two levels,[185] the international and the domestic and others proposed three, four, or five by adding the individual,[186] the bureaucratic,[187] and sub-dividing the domestic level.[188] The underlying assumption of the realist approach is rationality, which abstracts from the pluralistic reality of foreign policy formulation. The "bureaucratic politics" approach was developed as a critique of the rational actor model, and attempts to incorporate the amalgam of forces and institutions, which influence foreign policy decisions. The leading proponents, Halperin[189] and Destler,[190] enriched foreign policy analysis by focusing on how competing factions in the state bureaucracy influence presidential decisions; however, they neglect the role of Congress and interest groups.[191] Reality is still more complex as Hilsman and colleagues point out because like-minded factions and alliances cut across the various departments of government.[192]

One interpretation of the bureaucratic politics model is that the President's ability to direct foreign policy is limited by the difficulty of overcoming inertia and competing self-serving interests of various agencies in the bureaucracy. Rivalries and conflicts between National Security Council (NSC) and the State Department characterized the Kennedy, Johnson, Nixon, and Carter Administrations.[193] However, Ambrose's review of the period 1941 to 1991 leads him to the conclusion that rather than being increasingly constrained by the bureaucracy and Congress "the Oval Office is where foreign policy for better or worse has been made."[194] Krasner argues that the problem with U.S. foreign policy is not management of bureaucratic politics but "confusion over values" and the need for "reformulation and clarification of objectives," which the President is best placed to undertake.[195] "The inside story of American foreign policy making since World War II is the story of Presidents, courtiers and barons and how they worked with and against one another." Courtiers are "the people and institutions tied to the President as person and politician" and a baron is "a senior official formally in charge of an important domain within the Presidential realm."[196] Presidents are politicians, and like every individual have biases, preferences, friendships, philosophy, allegiances, and idiosyncrasies, all of which influence their decisions. Destler, Gelb, and Lake conclude that the result of these internecine wars[197] is the "incapacity to conduct a steady and sensible foreign policy."[198]

Therefore the link between domestic politics and U.S. foreign policy formulation and implementation must take account of inter- and intragovernmental "politics," incorporate how domestic politics impacts and influences the institutions of government such as the President and Congress, and understand the attempts and influence of foreign entities such as governments, international institutions such as the United Nations/ Organization of American States (UN/OAS), and multinational corporations. These interactions are not adequately illuminated by international relations theory; however, by a combination of international relations theory and the theory of interest group politics, the analysis of foreign policy formulation and implementation can be enhanced, as is illustrated in figure 1.1. The combination enables the analysis to recognize the asymmetries of inter-state relations, which is tackled in all approaches to international relations and delineate the actors and interactions inherent in domestic political economy of foreign policy. The incorporation of the theory of interest group politics permits encompassing the recognition of class, wealth, and power, which is such an integral part of Marxist, dependency, and world systems approaches while sharpening the analysis by identifying trans-class interests and groups that coalesce around a particular issue. This type of analysis is particularly apt for the U.S. political system and especially revealing in understanding how foreign governments affect foreign policy by influencing the actors in domestic politics.

CONCLUSION

The theory of international relations has dealt with the issue of small states in two ways. First, is the effect of the proliferation of small states on the international system and the need to limit what is regarded as an undesirable tendency. It is undesirable from the perspective of diluting the influence and power of large developed countries in international affairs and multilateral institutions. Second, there is some literature on the difficulties that small states face because of their limited resources and capacity to execute foreign policy. These however do not establish a clearly identifiable theoretical approach and do advance the understanding of how small states influence international affairs, in particular the foreign policy of large and more powerful countries. The issue raised by this study, which earmarks an extension of the established literature in international relations, is how a small state can influence the policy of large and powerful states towards them.

The different theoretical approaches to international relations outlined in this chapter share a common assumption, namely that small states cannot have an influence on the behavior and foreign policy on large, powerful states. This arises from the simplistic and deterministic manner in which inter-state relations are treated. In the circumstances being examined by this case study it necessitates rethinking these paradigms. This study examines how a small state, Jamaica, can and did influence the foreign policy of the most powerful country, the United States.

The principal conclusion that a survey of international relations theory yields is that in a relationship between two states, which differ vastly in power, size, and level of development, the smaller, less developed, and weaker state has virtually no influence on the foreign policy of the larger, more developed, and more powerful. In a relationship between the United States of America, a superpower and Jamaica, a small, developing country, the literature on international relations would lead to the conclusion that Jamaica cannot and in fact does not exercise any discernable influence on the foreign policy of the United States towards Jamaica. However, the reality as documented in this study reveals that the activities of the government of Jamaica did indeed have an identifiable effect on the foreign policy of the United States towards Jamaica. The case studies of the government of Jamaica's lobbying on debt, foreign aid, trade policy, and certification for narcotics cooperation, constitute a sufficient basis for arguing that a small, developing state can influence the United States, a large, developed, and powerful state. This conclusion would not have been revealed by the application of extant international relations theory but was derived by supplementing international relations theories with the literature on interest group politics. Granting the uniqueness of the U.S. political system and how foreign policy is formulated and executed within that system may not permit a general proposition about relations between states of different sizes, levels of development. and power, but documenting one such occurrence means that there is "a case to be answered." Moreover there is every likelihood that there are several such instances because there are numerous small, developing states actively trying to influence the foreign policy of larger, more developed, and more powerful states, including the United States. There is therefore a demonstrated need for theories of international relations to be revised or revamped to take account of such situations. The contribution of this study to international relations theory is to indicate the need to improve the explanatory power of the existing approaches by taking into account insights that can be derived from the literature on interest group politics.

Moving from the applicability of the general proposition that a small state can influence the foreign policy of a large, much more powerful state, to the particular circumstances of a small state influencing U.S. foreign policy, it is necessary to point out that the U.S. political system provides more degrees of freedom than that of other large, powerful developed countries. While this is not the place to expand on this statement it is sufficient to briefly comment on the uniqueness of the U.S. political system.

Influencing the formulation and execution of the foreign policy of another country invariably requires involvement in the domestic political process. In attempting to influence foreign policy, the representatives of another country must be scrupulous not to breach the unwritten but established limits of open involvement in the domestic political process of another country. The acceptable limits vary from country to country but the political process in the United States is particularly open. In the case of the United States there are unique features that permit the legitimate action with the legislature to influence the formulation and execution of U.S. foreign policy, which is unlike any other country's political process. For example, it is permissible and has become accepted practice that foreign governments and foreign entities openly lobby individual members of the legislature. In other political systems this would not be acceptable conduct of representatives of a foreign government. While discreet or covert lobbying occurs in every political system, it is usually focused on the leadership of the executive and a few key members of the legislature and bureaucracy. This is in sharp contrast to the U.S. system where representatives of foreign governments and entities can openly campaign, including giving testimony before congressional and senatorial bodies with the stated objectives of influencing U.S. foreign policy. Therefore, an examination of how Jamaica tried to influence U.S. foreign policy must go beyond the traditional inter-state relations, which has been the focus of the discipline of international relations. It must devote considerable attention to the domestic politics of the formulation and execution of U.S. foreign policy. In doing this, it requires breaking new ground in international relations because the existing approaches/paradigms do not provide an adequate analytic framework to adequately explain the impact of a small state, Jamaica, on the foreign policy of the dominant superpower, the United States.

SUMMARY

The United States of America, a superpower and Jamaica, a small developing country differ vastly in size, economic development, and power; therefore, their relationship is one of very significant asymmetries. The period between 1991 and 2001 was when the United States was the single superpower. Theories of international relations conclude that where there are significant asymmetries the smaller countries can exert little or no appreciable influence on the foreign policy of the larger, more developed, more powerful country. The literature on small states/small countries confirms that this is the dilemma confronting small states/small countries and the few exceptions as is the case with every "law" arise from unique circumstances. This generalization of lack of ability to influence larger, more developed, more powerful countries applies to an even greater extent when the two countries involved are a superpower and a small developing country, as was the case with the United States and Jamaica.

The thesis advanced by this book is that a small country can influence a more powerful country including a superpower. The case studies use the experience of Jamaica and the United States during the decade 1991–2001 to demonstrate that this actually occurred.

The literature on international relations theories takes as axiomatic the inability of small states to influence the foreign policy of larger, more powerful counties, ruled out by power differentials based on systemic structural asymmetries extant in the real world. Given this limitation it is necessary to supplement and combine that literature with insights from interest group politics to create an appropriate methodological template for analyzing the relationship between the United States and Jamaica. This approach allows an understanding of the possibility that a small state can influence the foreign policy of a more powerful state, let alone a superpower like the United States because it permits the integration of domestic politics into the analysis of the relationship. The explanatory value of domestic politics in international relations is particularly pertinent in an examination of foreign policy formulation and implementation in the U.S. political system.

NOTES

1. This issue is explored in Joseph S. Nye, The Future of Power (New York: Public Affairs, 2011).

2. Jean Grugel, Politics and Development in the Caribbean Basin. Central America and the Caribbean in the New World Order (Bloomington: Indiana University Press, 1995) page 125.

3. Jacqueline Anne Braveboy-Wagner, "Opportunities and Limitations of the Exercise of Foreign Policy Power by a Very Small State: The Case of Trinidad and Tobago," Cambridge Review of International Affairs, Vol. 23, No. 3 (2010) pages 407–27.

4. Matthew Louis Bishop, "The political economy of small states: The enduring vulnerability?," Review of International Political Economy, Vol. 19, No. 5 (December, 2012) pages 942–60. See page 946.

5. Roger Hilsman, The Politics of Policy-Making in Defense and Foreign Affairs. Conceptual Models and Bureaucratic Politics (New York: Prentice -Hall, 3rd ed., 1993).

6. Samuel P. Huntington, "The Erosion of American National Interests," Foreign Affairs, vol. 76, No. 5 (1977) page 42.

7. Richard L. Bernal, The Integration of Small Economies into the Free Trade Area of the Americas, Policy Papers on the Americas, Vol. IX, No. 1 (Washington, D.C.: Center for Strategic and International Studies, February, 1998) pages 23–24.

8. Donald J. Harris, Jamaica's Export Economy. Towards a Strategy of Export-led Growth, Critical Issues in Caribbean Development No. 5 (Kingston: Ian Randle Publishers, 1977) Table B.01.

9. World Development Report 2000/2001 (Washington, D.C.: World Bank, 2001).

10. Master Plan for Sustainable Tourism Development–Jamaica (London: Commonwealth Secretariat, 2002) page 23.

11. Elmer Plischke, Microstates in World Affairs. Policy Problems and Options (Washington D.C.: American Enterprise Institute for Public Policy Research, 1977).

One definition of a microstate is less than 6 million see Steven L. Spiegel, Dominance and Diversity. The International Hierarchy (Boston: Little Brown, 1972) pages 112–13.

12. William G. Demas, The Economics of Development in Small Countries with Special Reference to the Caribbean (Montreal: McGill University Press, 1965).

13. Richard Little and Michael Smith (eds.), Perspectives on World Politics (London: Routledge, 1992).

14. K. J. Holsti, The Dividing Discipline. Hegemony and Diversity in International Theory (Boston: Allen and Unwin, 1985) pages 15–81.

15. For a discussion of different types of power and the use of power see Klaus Knorr, Power and Wealth (London: Basic Books, 1973) and Joseph S. Nye, The Future of Power (New York: Public Affairs, 2011).

16. Liberal internationalism in its pristine and contemporary forms is reviewed in Scott Burchill, "Liberal Internationalism" in Scott Burchill and Andrew Linklater (eds.), Theories of International Relations (London: Macmillan Press, 1996) pages 28–66.

17. James E. Dougherty and Robert L. Pfaltzgraff, Contending Theories of International Relations. A Comprehensive Survey (New York: Harper Collins, 3rd edition, 1990) pages 4–7.

18. Reinhold Niebuhr, Moral Man and Immoral Society (New York: Charles Scribner's Sons, 1932).

19. E. H. Carr, The Twenty Years Crisis, 1919–1939. An Introduction to the Study of International Relations (London: Macmillan, 1939; Harper and Row, 1964).

20. Hans Morgenthau, Politics Among Nations. The Struggle for Power and Peace (New York: Alfred A. Knopf, originally published in 1948, 5th ed., 1978).

21. Morgenthau, page 25.

22. Morgenthau, pages 4–5.

23. Kenneth Waltz, Man, The State and War (New York: Columbia University Press, 1959).

24. James Rosenau, "Pre-Theories and Theories of International Politics" in R. Barry Farrell (ed.), Approaches to Comparative and International Politics (Evanston: Northwestern University Press, 1966) page 43.

25. Robert Jervis, Perception and Misperception in International Politics (Princeton: Princeton University Press, 1976) page 15.

26. James E. Dougherty and Robert L. Pfaltzgraff, Jr., Contending Theories of International Relations. A Comprehensive Survey (New York: Harper Collins Publishers, 3rd ed., 1990) page 81.

27. Fred Halliday, Rethinking International Relations (London: Macmillan Press, 1994) page 24.

28. Graham T. Allison, The Essence of Decision. Explaining the Cuban Missile Crisis (Boston: Little, Brown and Company, 1971).

29. Michael H. Hunt, Ideology and United States Foreign Policy (New Haven: Yale University Press, 1987).

30. Judith Goldstein, Ideas, Interests and American Trade Policy (Ithaca: Cornell University Press, 1993).

31. Judith Goldstein and Robert O. Keohane (eds.), Ideas and Foreign Policy (Ithaca: Cornell University Press, 1993).

32. This explanation of the emergence of neo-realism is derived from Fred Halliday, Rethinking International Relations (London: Macmillan, 1994) page 31.

33. Headley Bull, The Anarchical Society. A Study of Order in World Politics (London: Macmillan, 1977) pages 71–73.

34. Stephen Krasner, Defending the National Interest. Raw Material Investments and United States Foreign Policy (Princeton: Princeton University Press, 1978).

35. Stephen Krasner, Structural Conflict. The Third World Against Global Liberalism (Berkeley: University of California Press, 1985).

36. Kenneth Waltz, Theory of International Politics (New York: Random House, 1979).

37. Robert O. Keohane and Joseph S. Nye, Power and Interdependence. World Politics in Transition (Boston: Little, Brown, 1977).

38. Robert O. Keohane and Joseph S. Nye (eds.), Transnational Relations and World Politics (Cambridge, Mass.: Harvard University Press, 1972).

39. Robert O. Keohane and Joseph S. Nye (eds.), Transnational Relations and World Politics (Cambridge, Mass.: Harvard University Press, 1972).

40. Robert O. Keohane and Joseph S. Nye, Power and Interdependence. World Politics in Transition (Boston: Little, Brown, 1977).

41. Surveys of these theories are presented in Cristobal Kay, Latin American Theories of Development and Underdevelopment (London: Routledge, 1989) pages 88–196 and Norman Girvan, "The Development of Dependency Economics in the Caribbean and Latin America: Review and Comparison," Social and Economic Studies, Vol. 22, No. 1 (March, 1973) pages 1–33.

42. Andre Gunder Frank, Capitalism and Underdevelopment in Latin America. Historical Studies of Chile and Brazil (New York: Monthly Review Press, 1967).

43. Raul Prebisch, "Commercial Policy in the Underdeveloped Countries," American Economic Review, Vol. 49, No. 2 (May, 1959) pages 251–73.

44. The Economic Development of Latin America and its Principal Problems (Santiago: United Nations Economic Commission for Latin America, 1950).

45. Celso Furtado, Development and Underdevelopment. A Structuralist View of the Problems of Developed and Underdeveloped Countries (Berkeley: University of California Press, 1964).

46. Theotonio Dos Santos, "The Structure of Dependence," American Economic Review, Vol. 60, No. 2 (June, 1970) pages 231–36, Theotonio Dos Santos, "The Crisis of Development Theory and the Problem of Dependence in Latin America" in H. Bernstein (ed.), Underdevelopment and Development. The Third World Today (Harmondsworth: Penguin, 1973), Fernando Henrique Cardoso, "Dependency and Development in Latin America," New Left Review, No. 74 (1972) pages and "Associated-dependent Development: Theoretical and Practical Implications" in A. Stepan (ed.), Authoritarian Brasil: Origins, Policies and Future (New Haven: Yale University Press, 1973), Fernando Henrique Cardoso and Enzo Faletto, Dependency and Development in Latin America (Berkeley: University of California Press, 1979), Andre Gunder Frank, Capitalism and Underdevelopment in Latin America (New York: Monthly Review Press, 1967), and Anibal Pinto and Jan Knakal, "The Centre-Periphery System Twenty Years Later," Social and Economic Studies, Vol.22, No.1 (March, 1973) pages 34–89.

47. Andre Gunder Frank, "The Development of Underdevelopment in Latin America" in Andre Gunder Frank (ed.), Latin America. Underdevelopment or Revolution (New York: Monthly Review Press, 1969).

48. Osvaldo Sunkel, "Transnational Capitalism and National Disintegration inn Latin America," Social and Economic Studies, Vol. 22, No. 1 (March, 1973) pages 132–76.

49. Vincent A. Mahler, Dependency Approaches to International Political Economy. A Cross-National Study (New York: Columbia University Press, 1980), Raymond Duvall et al., "A Formal Model of Dependencia Theory. Structure and Measurement" in Richard Merritt and Bruce Russett (eds.), From National Development to Global Community (London: George Allen and Unwin, 1981) pages 215–61 and David Sylvan and associates, "The Peripheral Economies. Penetration and Distortion," in William R. Thompson (ed.), Contending Approaches to World System Analysis (Beverly Hills: Sage Publications, 1983).

50. Cristobal Kay, Latin American Theories of Development and Underdevelopment (London: Routledge, 1989) pages 147–49 and 166–70.

51. Andre Gunder Frank, Lumpenbourgeoisie. Lumpendevelopment, Dependence, Class and Politics in Latin America (New York: Monthly Review Press, 1973).

52. Frantz Fanon, The Wretched of the Earth (New York: Grove Press, 1963).

53. Osvaldo Sunkel, "Transnational Capitalism and National Disintegration in Latin America," Social and Economic Studies, Vol. 22, No.1 (March, 1973) pages 132–76.

54. Bill Warren, "Imperialism and Capitalist Industrialization," New Left Review, No. 81 (1973) pages 3–45. For a rebuttal see Philip J. O'Brien, "Dependency Revisited" in C. Abel and C. M. Lewis (eds.), Latin America, Economic Imperialism and the State. The Political Economy of the External Connection from Independence to the Present (London: Athlone Press, 1985).

55. Jeanne A. K. Hey, Theories of Dependent Foreign Policy and the Cast of Ecuador in the 1980s (Athens: Ohio University Center for International Studies, 1995) page 270.

56. Fred Halliday, Rethinking International Relations (London: Macmillan, 1994) pages 47–73.

57. The possibility of an exception to the systemically related polar opposites of development and underdevelopment was espoused by Bill Warren, Imperialism. Pioneer of Capitalism (London: Verso, 1981).

58. V. I. Lenin, Imperialism. The Highest Stage of Capitalism (New York: International Publishers, 1939, originally published in 1917).

59. P.T. Moon, Imperialism and World Politics (London: Macmillan, 1926), Leonard Woolf, Economic Imperialism (London: Swarthmore Press, 1920), and E.M. Winslow, The Pattern of Imperialism (New York: Columbia University Press, 1948).

60. J. A. Hobson, Imperialism (Ann Arbor: University of Michigan Press, 1965, first published in 1902).

61. For a survey of Marxist theories of imperialism see Roger Owen and Bob Sutcliffe (eds.), Studies in the Theory of Imperialism (London: Longman Group, 1972) pages 13–70 and Anthony Brewer, Marxist Theories of Imperialism (London: Routledge and Kegan Paul, 1980).

62. Fieldhouse collects both Marxist and non-Marxist theories of imperialism under the rubric of capitalist imperialism; see D. K. Fieldhouse (ed.), The Theory of Capitalist Imperialism (London: Longmans, 1967). This distinguishes these theories from those that use the term imperialism for any relationship of dominance, e.g., William S. Ferguson, Greek Imperialism (New York: Biblo and Tanner, 1941).

63. For a review of this literature see Perry Anderson, Considerations of Western Marxism (London: New Left Books, 1976) and New Left Review and Perry Anderson (ed.), Western Marxism. A Critical Reader (London: Verso, 1978).

64. Stephen Gill, "Gramsci and Global Politics: Towards a Post-Hegemonic Research Agenda" in Stephen Gill (ed.), Gramsci, Historical Materialism and International Relations (Cambridge: Cambridge University Press, 1993) pages 1–18.

65. Georg Lukacs, History and Class Consciousness: Studies in Marxist Dialectics (Cambridge: MIT Press, 1972).

66. Ernest Mandel, Late Capitalism (London: New Left Books, 1975).

67. Harry Magdoff, The Age of Imperialism. The Economics of U.S. Foreign Policy (New York: Monthly Review Press, 1969).

68. Samir Amin, Accumulation on a World Scale (New York: Monthly Review Press, 1974) and Samir Amin, Unequal Development (New York: Monthly Review Press, 1976).

69. Arghiri Emmanuel, Unequal Exchange. A Study of the Imperialism of Trade (New York: Monthly Review Press, 1972). For an analysis of Emmanuel's theory see Richard L. Bernal, "Emmanuel's Unequal Exchange as a Theory of Underdevelopment," Social and Economic Studies, Vol. 29, No. 4 (December, 1980) pages 152–74.

70. Nicos Poulantzas, Political Power and Social Classes (London: Verso, 1978) and Nicos Poulantzas, Classes in Contemporary Capitalism (London: New Left Books, 1975).

71. Paul Baran and Paul Sweezy, Monopoly Capital (New York: Monthly Review Press, 1966).

72. Stephen Gill (ed.), Gramsci, Historical Materialism and International Relations (Cambridge: Cambridge University Press, 1993).

50 *Chapter 2*

73. Some non-Marxist scholars share the principal conclusions of Marxists, e.g., Johan Galtung, "A Structural Theory of Imperialism," Journal of Peace Research, Vol. 13, No. 2 (1971) pages 81–98.

74. Immanuel Wallerstein, The Modern World System I. Agriculture and the Origins of the European World-Economy in the Sixteenth Century (New York: Academic Press, 1974) and The Modern World System II. Mercantilism and the Consolidation of the European World Economy, 1600–1750 (New York: Academic Press, 1980).

75. Christopher Chase-Dunn, "Core-Periphery Relations: The Effects of Core Competition," in Barbara Hockey Kaplan (ed.), Social Change in the Capitalist World-Economy (Beverly Hills: Sage Publications, 1978) pages 159–77, "Interstate System and Capitalist World-Economy: One Logic or Two?" in W. Ladd Hollist and James N. Rosenau (eds.), World-System Structure. Continuity and Change (Beverly Hills: Sage Publications, 1981) pages 30–53, Global Formation. Structures of the World Economy (Cambridge: Basil Blackwell, 1989), and Christopher Chase-Dunn and Richard Rubinson, "Toward a Structural Perspective on the World-System," Politics and Society, Vol. 7, No. 4 (1977) pages 453–76.

76. Terrace K. Hopkins and Immanuel Wallerstein (eds.), Processes of the World System (Beverly Hills: Sage, 1981) and Terrace K. Hopkins and Immanuel Wallerstein (eds.), World-System Analysis. Theory and Methodology (Beverly Hills: Sage Publications, 1982).

77. E. H. Carr, What is History? (London: Macmillan, 1961) page 33.

78. Fernand Braudel, Civilization and Capitalism. 15th–18th Century (New York: Harper and Row, 1981–1984) Vols. 1–3.

79. Ronald H. Chilcote, "Issues in the Theory of Dependency and Marxism," Latin American Perspectives, Vol. VIII, Nos. 3 and 4 (Summer and Fall, 1981) pages 3–16 and C. Ramirez-Faria, The Origins of Inequality between Nations (London: Unwin Hyman, 1991).

80. Samir Amin, Giovanni Arrighi, Andre Gunder Frank, and Immanuel Wallerstein, Dynamics of Global Crisis (New York: Monthly Review Press, 1982).

81. Robert Brenner, "The Origins of Capitalist Development: A Critique of Neo-Smithian Marxism," New Left Review, No. 104 (July-August, 1977) pages 25–92.

82. Paul R. Viotti and Mark V. Kauppi, International Relations Theory. Realism, Pluralism, Globalism (New York (Macmillan, 2nd edition, 1993) pages 449–75.

83. Richard Little and Michael Smith (eds.), Perspectives on World Politics (London: Routledge, 2nd edition, 1991) Part III.

84. Samir Amin, Imperialism and Unequal Development (New York: Monthly Review Press, 1977).

85. Clive Y. Thomas, Dependence and Transformation. The Economics of the Transition to Socialism (New York: Monthly Review Press, 1974).

86. Samir Amin, Capitalism in the Age of Globalization (London: Zed Books, 1997).

87. Robert Cox, "Social Forces, States and World Orders: Beyond International Relations Theory," Millennium: Journal of International Studies, Vol. 10, No. 2 (1981) pages 126–55, Production, Power and World Order. Social Forces in the Making of History (New York: Columbia University Press, 1987) and Approaches to World Order (Cambridge: Cambridge University Press, 1996).

88. Richard Devetak, "Critical Theory" in Scott Burchill and Andrew Linklater (eds.), Theories of International Relations (London: Macmillan, 1996) pages 179–209.

89. Robert W. Cox, Production, Power, and World Order. Social Forces in the Making of History (New York: Columbia University Press, 1987) page 394.

90. Robert W. Cox, Production, Power, and World Order. Social Forces in the Making of History (New York: Columbia University Press, 1987) pages 253–54.

91. John Burton, International Relations. A General Theory (Cambridge: Cambridge University Press, 1965).

92. John Burton, World Society (Cambridge: Cambridge University Press, 1972) page 43.

93. John Burton, Frank Dukes, and George Mason, Conflict. Resolution and Prevention (London: Macmillan, 1990) and John Burton (ed.), Conflict. Human Needs Theory (London: Macmillan, 1990).

94. "Small but Perfectly Formed," The Economist, January 3, 1998, page 65.

95. Elmer Plischke, Microstates in World Affairs. Policy Problems and Options (Washington, D.C.: American Enterprise Institute, 1977).

96. Annette Baker Fox, The Power of Small States (Chicago: Chicago University Press, 1959), David Vital, Inequality of States. A Study of the Small Powers in International Relations (Oxford: Clarendon Press, 1967), and Robert L. Rothstein, Alliances and Small Powers (New York: Columbia University Press, 1968).

97. Annette Baker Fox, The Power of Small States (Chicago: University of Chicago Press, 1959), David Vital, The Inequality of States. A Study of Small Powers in International Relations (Oxford: Clarendon Press, 1967), Robert L. Rothstein, Alliances and Small Powers (New York: Columbia University Press, 1968), George L. Reid, The Impact of Very Small Size on the International Behaviour of Microstates (Beverly Hills: Sage Publications, 1974), Barry Buzan, "Peoples, States and Fear" in Edward E. Azar and Chung-In Moon (eds.), National Security in the Third World: The Management of Internal and External Conflicts (Cheltenham: Edward Elgar, 1988), and Sir Ronald Sanders, Crumbled Small. The Commonwealth Caribbean in World Politics (London: Hansib Publications, 2005).

98. Vaughn A. Lewis (ed.), Size, Self-Determination and International Relations. The Caribbean (Mona: Institute of Social and Economic Studies, University of the West Indies, 1976), Basil Ince (ed.), Contemporary International Relations in the Caribbean (St. Augustine: Institute of International Relations, University of the West Indies, 1979), Basil Ince, Anthony Bryan, Herb Addo, and Ramesh Ramsaran (eds.), Issues in Caribbean International Relations (Lanham: University Press of America, 1983), Jacqueline Anne Braveboy-Wagner, The Caribbean in World Affairs. The Foreign Policies of the English-Speaking Caribbean States (Boulder: Westview Press, 1989), and Anthony T. Bryan, J. Edward Greene, and Timothy Shaw (eds.), Peace, Development and Security in the Caribbean (London: Macmillan, 1990).

99. Jacqueline Braveboy-Wagner, "The English-Speaking Caribbean States: A Triad of Foreign Policies" in Jeanne A. K. Hey (ed.), Small States in World Politics (Boulder: Lynne Reinner Publishers, 2003) pages 31–51.

100. Georges A. Fauriol, Foreign Policy Behavior of Caribbean States. Guyana, Haiti, and Jamaica (Lanham: University Press of America, 1984) page 252.

101. Jacqueline Braveboy-Wagner, Small States in Global Affairs. The Foreign Policies of the Caribbean Community (CARICOM) (New York: Palgrave Macmillan, 2008) page 8.

102. Jacqueline Braveboy-Wagner, Small States in Global Affairs. The Foreign Policies of the Caribbean Community (CARICOM) (New York: Palgrave Macmillan, 2008) page 11.

103. Vincent Galbis, "Ministate Economies," Finance and Development, Vol. No. (June, 1984) pages 36–38 and T. N. Srinivasan, "The Costs and Benefits of Being, a Small, Remote, Island, Landlocked or Ministate Economy," World Bank Research Observer, Vol. 1, No. 2 (1986) pages 205–18.

104. Richard L. Bernal, The Integration of Small Economies in the Free Trade Area of the Americas, CSIS, Policy Paper on the Americas, Vol. IX, Study No. 1. (Washington D.C.: Center for Strategic and International Studies, February 2, 1998).

105. Richard L. Bernal, "Special and Differential Treatment for Small Developing Economies" in Roman Grynberg (ed.), WTO at the Margins. Small States and the Multilateral Trading System (Cambridge: Cambridge University Press, 2006) pages 309–55, Richard L. Bernal, "Globalization and Small Developing Countries: Challenges and Opportunities" in David Peretz, Rumman Faruqi, and Eliawony J. Kisanga (eds.), Small States in the Global Economy (London: Commonwealth Secretariat, 2001) pages 39–51 and Richard L. Bernal, "Globalization and Small Developing Countries: The

Imperative for Repositioning," in Denis Benn and Kenneth Hall (eds.), Globalization: A Calculus of Inequality (Kingston: Ian Randle Publishers, 2000) pages 88–128.

106. Benito Legarda, "Small Island Economies." Finance and Development, Vol. 21 (June, 1984) pages 42–43.

107. Paul Sutton, "The Concept of Small States in the International Political Economy," The Round Table: The Commonwealth Journal of International Affairs, Vol. 100, No. 413 (2011) pages 141–53.

108. Iserdeo Jainarain, Trade and Underdevelopment. A Study of the Small Caribbean Countries and Large Multinational Corporations (Georgetown: Institute of Development Studies, University of Guyana, 1976).

109. Jacqueline Braveboy-Wagner, Small States in Global Affairs. The Foreign Policies of the Caribbean Community (CARICOM) (New York: Palgrave Macmillan, 2008) page 11.

110. Charles L. Taylor, "Statistical Typology of Microstates and Territories: Towards a Definition of a Micro-state" in J. Rapaport, E. Muteba, and J. Therattil, Small States and Territories: Status and Problems, United Nations Institute for Training and Research Study (New York: Arno Press,1971) pages 183–202.

111. William S. Harris, "Microstates in the United Nations. A Broader Purpose," Columbia Journal of Transnational Law, Vol. No. 9 (Spring, 1970) page 23.

112. P. Hein, "The Study of Microstates" in Edward Dommen and Phillipe Hein (eds.), States, Microstates and Islands (London: Croom Helm, 1985).

113. Colin Clarke and Tony Payne (eds.), Politics, Security and Development in Small States (London: Allen and Unwin, 1987).

114. H. Armstrong and R. Read, "Determinants of Economic Growth and Resilience in Small States" in Lino Briguglio, Gordon Cordina, and E. Kisanga (eds.), Building the Economic Resilience of Small States (London and Malta: Commonwealth Secretariat and University of Malta, 2006).

115. R. P. Bartson, "The External Relations of Small States" in August Schou and Arne Olav Bruntland (eds.), Small States in International Relations (New York: John Wiley and Sons, 1971).

116. Godfrey Baldacchino, "Bursting the Bubble: The Pseudo-Development Strategies of Microstates," Development and Change, Vol. 24, no. 1 (1993) pages 29–51.

117. Stanley A. De Smith, Microstates and Micronesia: Problems of America's Pacific Islands and Other Minute Territories (New York: New York University Press, 1970) page vii.

118. Elmer Plischke, Microstates in World Affairs. Policy Problems and Options (Washington, D.C.: American Enterprise Institute, 1977) page 18.

119. Ken Ross, "The Commonwealth A Leader for the World's Small States," Round Table, Vol. 86, No. 343 (1997) 411–19.

120. F. M. Liou and C. G. Ding, "Subgrouping of Small States Based on Socioeconomic Characteristics," World Development, Vol. 30, No. 7 (July, 2002) pages 1289–306.

121. Richard L. Bernal, The Integration of Small Economies in the Free Trade Area of the Americas, CSIS, Policy Paper on the Americas, Vol. IX, Study No. 1 (Washington, D.C.: Center for Strategic and International Studies, February 2, 1998), Barbara Kotschwar, "Small Countries and the Free Trade Area of the Americas" in Miguel Rodriguez Mendoza, Patrick Low, and Barbara Kotschwar (eds.), Trade Rules in the Making. Challenges in Regional and Multilateral Negotiations (Washington, D.C.: Brookings Institution Press/ Organization of American States, 1999) pages 134–58, and Tom Crowards, "Defining the Category of Small States." Journal of International Development, Vol. 14, No. 2 (March 2002) pages 143–79.

122. Jean-Luc Vellut, "Smaller States and the Problem of War and Peace: Some Consequences of the Emergence of Smaller States in Africa," Journal of Peace Research, Vol. 4, No. 3 (1967) pages 252–69.

123. Richard L. Bernal, The Integration of Small Economies into the Free Trade Area of the Americas, CSIS Policy Papers on the Americas, Vol. IX, Study No.1 (Washington, D.C.: Center for Strategic and International Studies, February 2, 1998).

124. Henrik Larsen, Analysing the Foreign Policy of Small States in the EU: The Case of Denmark (London: Palgrave Macmillan, 2005) and Carsten Holbrand, Danish Neutrality: A Study in the Foreign Policy of a Small State (Oxford: Oxford University Press, 1991).

125. Zlatko Sabic and Charles Bukowski, Small States in the Post-Cold War World; Slovenia and NATO Enlargement (New York: Praeger Publishers, 2002) and Milan Jazbec, The Diplomacies of Small States: The Case of Slovenia with Some Comparisons from the Baltics (London; Ashcraft Publishing, 2001).

126. Asbed Kotchikian, The Dialectics of Small States: Foreign Policy Making in Armenia and Georgia (VDM Verlag, 2008).

127. Ahmed Norman Almadhagi, Yemen and the U.S.A: A Super-Power and a Small-State Relationship 1962–1994 (London: I.B. Tauris, 1996).

128. Herman Amersfoort and Wim. Klinkert (eds.), Small Powers in a World of Total War 1900–1940 (Leiden: BRILL, 2011) page 1.

129. David Vital, The Inequality of States. A Study of the Small Powers in International Relations (Oxford: Clarendon Press, 1967).

130. Irma Adelman and Joan Taft Morris, Economic Growth and Social Equity in Developing Countries (Stanford: Stanford University Press, 1973) page 106.

131. Alfred Maizels, Exports and Economic Growth in Developing Countries (Cambridge: Cambridge University Press, 1968) Chapter 1.

132. Simon Kuznets, "Economic Growth of Small Nations" in E. A. G. Robinson (ed.), Economic Consequences of the Size of Nations (London: Macmillan, 1960) page 5.

133. Paul Streeten, "The Special Problems of Small Countries," World Development, Vol. 21, No. 2 (1993) page 197.

134. Scott B. MacDonald and Andrew R. Novo, When Small Countries Crash (New Brunswick: Transaction Publishers, 2011) page 6.

135. Hollis B. Chenery and M. Syrquin, Patterns of Development, 1950–1970 (London: Oxford University Press, 1975).

136. H. B. Chenery and L. Taylor, Development Patterns: Among Countries Over Time," Review of Economics and Statistics, Vol. 50, No. 4 (1968) pages 391–416.

137. A Regional Integration Fund of the Free Trade Area of the Americas, ECLAC, LC/R 1738, July 10, 1997.

138. Andrew S. Downes, "On the Statistical Measurement of Smallness. A Principal Component Measure of Country Size," Social and Economic Studies, Vol. 37, No. 3 (September, 1988) pages 75–96.

139. William G. Demas, The Economics of Development in Small Countries with Special Reference to the Caribbean (Montreal: McGill University Press, 1965) page 2.

140. Iserdeo Jainarain, Trade and Development. A Study of the Small Caribbean Countries and Large Multinational Corporations (Georgetown: University of Guyana, 1976) page 47.

141. B. Jalan, "Classification of Economies by Size" in B. Jalan (ed.), Problems and Policies of Small States (London: Croom Helm, 1982) pages 17–38.

142. Vulnerability: Small States in the Global Society (London: Commonwealth Secretariat, 1985).

143. A Future for Small States: Overcoming Vulnerability (London: Commonwealth Secretariat, 1997) pages 8–9.

144. A Future for Small States. Overcoming Vulnerability (London: Commonwealth Secretariat, 1997) and Small States. Meeting the Challenges of the Global Economy (London and Washington, D.C.: Commonwealth Secretariat/ World Bank, 2000).

145. Peter Conrad, Islands. A Trip through Time and Space (London: Thames and Hudson, 2009) page 6.

146. A. J. Dolman, Islands in the Shade: The Performance and Prospects of Small Island Developing Countries (The Hague: Institute of Social Studies Advisory Service, 1984).

147. Percy Selwin, "Smallness and Islandness," World Development, Vol. 8, No. 12 (1980) pages 945–51.

148. Richard L. Bernal, "China and Small Island Developing States," Africa-East Asian Affairs, The China Monitor, Issue 1 (August 2012) pages 3–30.

149. Henry Srebrnik, "Small Island Nations and Democratic Values," World Development Vol. 32, No. 2 (2004) pages 329–41.

150. John Connell, Sovereignty and Survival: Island Microstates in the Third World (Sydney: University of Sydney, 1988).

151. Robert L. Rothstein, The Weak in the World of the Strong. The Third World in the International System (New York: Columbia University Press, 1980) page 52.

152. Paul K. Sutton, "The Caribbean as a Subordinate State System, 1945–1976," Hull Papers in Politics No. 16, Dept. of Politics, University of Hull, 1980).

153. This issue is discussed along with preventative measures that the international community should take to assist microstates in Sheila Harden, Small Is Dangerous. Micro States in a Macro World (London: Palgrave Macmillan, 1985).

154. Robert L. Rothstein, Alliances and Small Power (New York: Columbia University Press, 1968) page 29.

155. Alan K. Hendrickson, Diplomacy and Small States in Today's World, The Dr. Eric Williams Memorial Lecture, Twelfth Lecture, 22 May, 1998, page 5.

156. Commonwealth Secretariat, A Future for Small States: Overcoming Vulnerability (London: Commonwealth Secretariat, 1997).

157. Michael Handel, Weak States in the International System (London: Frank Cass and Co., 1990) pages 9–67.

158. For a succinct account of Iceland's extension of its exclusive economic zone see Mark Kurlansky, Cod: A Biography of the Fish That Changed the World (London: Penguin, 1998) pages 153–73.

159. Matthew Louis Bishop, "The Political Economy of Small States: The Enduring Vulnerability?," Review of International Political Economy," Vol. 19, No. 5 (December, 2012) pages 942–60. See page 953.

160. Asgeir Jonsson, Why Iceland? How One of the World's Smallest Countries Became the Meltdown's Biggest Casualty (New York: McGraw-Hill, 2009) and Roger Boyes, Meltdown Iceland: Lessons on the World Financial Crisis from a Small Bankrupt Island (New York: Bloomsbury, 2009).

161. Annette Baker Fox, The Power of Small States (Chicago: Chicago University Press, 1959).

162. Peter J. Katzenstein, Small States in World Markets: Industrial Policy in Europe (Ithaca: Cornell University Press, 1985).

163. Jeanne A. K. Hey, Small States in World Politics. Explaining Foreign Policy Behavior (Boulder: Lynne Reiner, 2003) page 2.

164. Richard C. Snyder, H. W. Bruck, and Burton Sapin, Foreign Policy Decision Making. An Approach to the Study of International Politics (New York: Free Press, 1962) page 65.

165. Cecil V. Crabb, Policy Makers and Critics. Conflicting Theories of American Foreign Policy (New York: Praeger Publishers, 1976).

166. Robert Jervis, Perception and Misperception in International Politics (Princeton: Princeton University Press, 1976).

167. Ole Holsti, "Cognitive Process Approach to Decision Making," American Behavioral Scientists, Vol. 20, No. 1 (September– October, 1976) pages 11–32 and D. Sylvan and S. Chan (eds.), Foreign Policy Decision-making: Perception, Cognitive and Artificial Intelligence (New York: Praeger Press, 1984).

168. Robert A. Dahl, Who Governs? (New Haven: Yale University Press, 1961).

169. Arthur Bentley, The Process of Government (Cambridge: Belnap Press of Harvard University, 1967).

170. E. E. Schattschneider, The Semi-sovereign People: A Realist's View of Democracy in America (New York: Rinehart and Winston, 1960).

171. Paul M. Sweezy, The Theory of Capitalist Development (New York: Monthly Review Press, 1942).

172. C. Wright Mills, The Power Elite (New York: Oxford University Press, 1956).

173. G. William Domhoff, Who Rules America? (Englewood Cliffs, NJ: Prentice-Hall, 1967), Who Rules America Now? (New York: Simon and Schuster,1983), and The Higher Circles. The Governing Class in America (New York: Vintage Books, 1971).

174. Paul Baran and Paul Sweezy, Monopoly Capital (New York: Monthly Review Press, 1968).

175. Robert A. Dahl, Who Governs? (New Haven: Yale University Press, 1961) page 272.

176. John Kenneth Galbraith, American Capitalism (Harmondsworth: Penguin, 1952) page 111.

177. For a discussion of the concept of power see Karl W. Deutsch, The Analysis of International Relations (Englewood Cliffs: Prentice Hall, 2nd ed., 1978) pages 23–52 and Klaus Knorr, Power and Wealth (New York: Basic Books, 1973).

178. Hans J. Morgenthau, Politics Among Nations. The Struggle for Power and Peace (New York: Knopf, 5th ed., 1978).

179. Kenneth N. Waltz, Theory of International Politics (Reading: Addison-Wesley, 1979).

180. Paul R. Viotti and Mark V. Kauppi, International Relations Theory. Realism, Pluralism and Globalism (New York: Macmillan, 2nd ed., 1993) pages 37–43.

181. Waltz, op. cit., and Kenneth N. Waltz, "Realist Thought and Neorealist Theory," in Charles W. Kegley (ed.), Controversies in International Relations Theory: Realism and the Neoliberal Challenge (New York: St. Martin's Press, 1995).

182. Ernst B. Haas, Beyond the Nation State (Stanford: Stanford University Press, 1964).

183. Henry A. Kissinger, A World Restored. The Politics of Conservatism in a Revolutionary Age (New York: Grosset and Dunlap, 1964).

184. Graham T. Allison, Essence of Decision. Explaining the Cuban Missile Crisis (Boston: Little, Brown and Company, 1971).

185. J. David Singer, "International Conflict. Three Levels of Analysis," World Politics, Vol. 12, No. 3 (April, 1960) pages 453–61, and Arnold Wolfers, Discord and Collaboration (Baltimore: Johns Hopkins University Press, 1962) pages 3–24.

186. Kenneth N. Waltz, Man, the State, and War: A Theoretical Analysis (New York: Columbia University Press, 1959).

187. Robert Jervis, Perception and Misperception in International Politics (Princeton: Princeton University Press, 1976).

188. James Rosenau, "Pre-Theories and Theories of International Politics" in R. Barry Farrell (ed.), Approaches to Comparative and International Politics (Evanston: Northwestern University Press, 1966) pages 27–92.

189. Morton H. Halperin, Bureaucratic Politics and Foreign Policy (Washington, D.C.: Brookings Institution, 1974).

190. I. M. Destler, Presidents, Bureaucratics, and Foreign Policy (Princeton: Princeton University Press, 1972).

191. John Dumbrell, The Making of U.S. Foreign Policy (Manchester: Manchester University Press, 2nd ed., 1997) page 20.

192. Roger Hilsman, Laura Gaughran, and Patricia A. Weitsman, The Politics of Policy Making in Defense and Foreign Affairs. Conceptual Models and Bureaucratic Politics (Englewood Cliffs, NJ: Prentice-Hall, 3rd ed., 1993) page 88.

193. Kenneth W. Thompson "The President, the Congress and Foreign Policy: The Policy Paper," in Edmund S. Muskie and Kenneth W. Thompson (eds.), The President, the Congress and Foreign Policy (New York: University Press of America, 1986) pages 3–34. See page 16.

194. Stephen E. Ambrose, "The Presidency and Foreign Policy," Foreign Affairs, Vol. 70, No. 5 (Winter, 1991/92) pages 120–37. See page 137.

195. Stephen D. Krasner, "Are Bureaucracies Important? (Or Allison in Wonderland)," Foreign Policy, No. 7 (Summer, 1972) pages 159–79.

196. I. M. Destler, Leslie I. Gelb, and Anthony Lake, Our Own Worst Enemy. The Unmaking of American Foreign Policy (New York: Simon and Schuster, 1984) page 167.

197. Destler et al., pages 166–237.

198. Destler et al., page 262.

THREE

Jamaica and Its Relations with the United States

The first part of this chapter provides an overview of Jamaica's history, society, economy, governance and politics, and national character and culture. It does not set out to provide a detailed description and analysis of all aspects of Jamaica's history, society, and economy. The section that is devoted to national character and culture is introduced by a general discussion of how national character and culture influence the foreign policy of countries. The second part reviews Jamaica's foreign policy towards the United States. Starting with a section on U.S. policy towards Jamaica and the English-Speaking Caribbean (ESC). What emerges is that Jamaica and the ESC is a low priority and has lacked visibility in overall U.S. foreign policy, and consequently focused engagement has been episodic. The following section consists of a history of Jamaica's foreign policy. This is a prerequisite of an examination of foreign policy towards the United States. The final section surveys the objectives and issues of Jamaica's foreign policy towards the United States and is deliberately weighted to place more emphasis on those aspects that are most pertinent to the subsequent analysis. For example, domestic politics, social change, and economic development undoubtedly affected foreign policy, but fascinating as these factors are, this is not the focus of this work and is clearly beyond its scope.[1] The influence of these on Jamaica's foreign policy are discussed only in so far as it has a direct bearing on how Jamaica sought to influence U.S. foreign policy towards it. The overview is essential background and is not intended to be comprehensive and therefore in many instances the narrative is of necessity rather terse.

PART I: OVERVIEW OF JAMAICA

Location and proximity of a country to the United States and/or to interests considered by the United States to be vital have been important determinants of U.S. foreign policy towards that country or that part of the world. Jamaica is situated in the Caribbean at latitude 18 degrees north and longitude 77 degrees west and is about 588 miles (946.3 kilometers) southwest of Miami, Florida. The island has land area of 4,411 square miles (11,420 square kilometers). It is 146 miles (235 kilometers) long and varies from 22 miles (35.4 kilometers) to 51 miles (82.1 kilometers) wide. Jamaica's location is close to Cuba and Puerto Rico, two countries about which the United States has "special" relationships. Shipping lanes for oil and important raw materials pass close by Jamaica and airline routes to South America pass directly over Jamaica. Indeed Jamaica is just over one hour's flying time by jet aircraft from Miami, a fact that has accounted for much of the expansion of the island's tourist industry. Indeed, the ability of providing continuous aircraft surveillance and protection for bauxite shipped from Jamaica to the Gulf Coast ports of the United States was a consideration stimulating U.S. investment in the export of bauxite from Jamaica.

The climate and topography of the island has been significant in its economic development as it has been the basis of agriculture and tourism, which together with bauxite have been the dominant sectors and exports of the economy. The varied terrain has allowed the cultivation of a wide range of crops from sugar and bananas on the plains to coffee in the hills. The highest point is the Blue Mountain Peak, which is 7,402 feet (2,256 meters) above sea level. The tropical climate with daytime temperatures averaging between 80–85ºF and nights that are about 10 degrees cooler, especially in the hilly areas, has been favorable to agriculture and tourism. There is no change of season although temperatures and humidity vary slightly between the middle of summer and the middle of winter. December to February is normally the coolest time of the year. The island experiences the heaviest rainfall during the months of May and October. July and August are usually the driest periods and the mean annual rainfall is about 78 inches (200 centimeters).[2] Hurricanes have on occasions inflicted serious damage on agriculture and tourism. The hurricane season is from June to October, but direct hits have been infrequent, e.g., Jamaica suffered direct hits in 1951 and in September 1988 causing extensive damage to property and production.

The capital and commercial center is Kingston, a city of approximately one million people that is situated on the southeastern coast of the island on a natural harbor, which is one of the largest in the world. Montego Bay, on the island's northwest coast, is the second largest city and the center of the tourism industry. Kingston and its environs are home to

over three-quarters of a million people and have steadily extended towards Spanish Town, another sizeable town.

History

Jamaica was inhabited by Taino Arawak[3] Indians when Christopher
Columbus first visited the island in 1494 on his second voyage to the so-
called "New World." A mountainous island with well-watered fertile
plains[4] but sparse wildlife and no significant deposits of precious metals
attracted little settlement and only intermittent colonialism. Although
Spain developed an enormous colonial empire[5] it was never firmly established in Jamaica where the preoccupation was the quest put eloquently
by C. L. R. James: "Christopher Columbus landed first in the New World
at the island of San Salvador, and after praising God enquired urgently
for gold."[6] In 1665 the English captured the island from the Spaniards
without encountering much resistance. After the English conquest, Jamaica became the stronghold of buccaneers[7] who transformed Port Royal, then the island's commercial center, into the infamous "richest and
wickedest city in the new world."[8] By the eighteenth century, Jamaica
had become a slave plantation economy and one of the world's most
important producers of sugar, then an extremely valuable commodity.
Sugar and its by-products, molasses and rum were produced from sugar
cane grown and milled on slave plantations. The production and export
of sugar in tropical colonies of European countries was an integral part of
the "triangular trade" involving sugar traded to Europe, and manufactured goods transported to Africa in exchange for slaves bound for the
colonies. The enormous profits derived from the mercantilist trade system of European colonial powers were critical to the emergence of capitalism. The profits from the slave trade[9] of the 17th and 18th centuries
provided capital, which helped to finance the Industrial Revolution in
England.[10]

After nearly two hundred years of slavery in the British Empire it was
abolished in 1834, a generation before it was outlawed in the United
States, by a combination of developments in capitalism in England, crisis
in the mode of political domination, the abolition movement, and by the
fierce and continuous resistance by slaves.[11] This resistance was particularly persistent and strong in Jamaica, prompting one author to speak of
"the slaves who abolished slavery."[12] Defiant and highly developed maroon society emerged early in Jamaica and achieved autonomy from the
colonial authorities, which was formally recognized by a treaty with the
Crown.[13] The traditions established in this era have imprinted in the
personality traits and national character of modern day Jamaicans, for
example, fearlessness about death and a willingness to resort to violence
in resolving disputes.[14] The tradition of resistance and struggle has contributed to the audacity of Jamaicans, a supreme confidence in their ca-

pacity to achieve whatever they want or need and adaptability[15] to their circumstances and to change those circumstances. Leaders, heroes, and those who elicit admiration and attaining status are those who have fought against injustice.[16] It is the quality and spirit exemplified in the goals and exploits of Marcus Garvey and in Michael Manley's belief and confidence when changing the tax regime governing the multinational corporations in the bauxite industry and in the quest for a new international economic order.

After nearly two hundred years, slavery had left an indelible mark on the structure of the economy, the society, and the people.[17] The abolition of slavery did not fundamentally change the structure and operation of the Jamaican economy, which continued as a plantation economy based on wage labor with the production and export of sugar under colonial preferential marketing arrangements as the dominant economic activity until well into the twentieth century. The lack of economic transformation was in large measure attributable the dominance of sugar and rum and to the colonial policy of discouraging industrialization as a strategy of diversification and economic development.[18] There was no diversification in the economic structure of the country until the emergence of the banana industry during the early part of the twentieth century. Exports remained concentrated on the British market but imports reflected the decline in dominance of Britain as a source of manufactured goods. Trade with Canada and the United States, which was important even in the eighteenth century[19] steadily increased in value as Jamaica sourced an expanding share of its imports from these countries.

Governance and Politics

During its three centuries as a British colony, Jamaica was variously administered by a governor and a planter-controlled legislature and by Crown Colony rule from London with a return to limited representative government in the late nineteenth and early twentieth centuries. In the late 1930s there was serious civil disorder whose antecedents have their origins in grievances dating back to the late nineteenth century[20] and the inter-war years[21] but more immediately stemmed from a prolonged period of unmitigated deprivation, poverty, and unemployment. At the forefront of protests were workers on the Kingston docks and sugar estate laborers organized by the embryonic trade union movement. This coincided with the rise of nationalism among elements of the middle class resulting in the birth of modern political parties. The People's National Party (PNP) was formed under the leadership of Norman Manley[22] in 1938 and the Jamaica Labour Party (JLP) was formed by Alexander Bustamante[23] in 1943 and these two parties have dominated Jamaican politics ever since. Both parties are closely linked to a major trade union, the JLP with the Bustamante Industrial Trade Union and the PNP with the

National Workers Union. The demand for political change[24] resulted in adult suffrage in 1944 and culminated in internal self-government in 1955.[25] The disturbances of the late 1930s coincided with growing nationalism both within the country and by nationals living overseas. A contemporary activist recalls that the "most articulate call for organizing the growing national spirit came from Jamaicans living overseas."[26] The events of the era set in motion a momentum that eventually led to political independence in 1962.

Universal adult suffrage was granted in 1944 in the wake of the disturbances of the late 1930s. Previous elections dating back to the seventeenth century had been conducted on a restricted franchise based on ownership of land. From 1957 to 1962, Jamaica was a member of the defunct West Indian Federation,[27] which incorporated ten of Britain's Caribbean colonies. On August 6, 1962 Jamaica became an independent country. Despite the collapse of the West Indies Federation,[28] Jamaica has participated in various regional institutions including the Caribbean Community (CARICOM).[29] Jamaica is an active member of the United Nations (including serving on the Security Council on two occasions), the Organization of American States,[30] the African, Caribbean, and Pacific (ACP) group of countries, the Commonwealth, the Caribbean Community (CARICOM), the International Monetary Fund (IMF), World Bank, the World Trade Organization (WTO), the Inter-American Development Bank, and the Association of Caribbean States.[31]

Jamaica has a democratic system of government organized on the Westminster model of parliamentary democracy based on the United Kingdom system.[32] The parliament consists of an appointed Senate of 21 members, 13 of whom are nominated by the party forming the government and 7 by the opposition. A House of Representatives consisting of 60 members is chosen in general elections held at intervals of five years. There are two major political parties, which evolved during the late 1930s and early 1940s, the People's National Party, which has been the majority party since October 1989 (during the entire period covered by this study) and the Jamaica Labor Party. The head of government is the Prime Minister, who is assisted by a cabinet minister and is responsible for the executive functions of the government. The Queen is formally the head of state, and she is represented by a Governor General, whose duties are purely formal and ceremonial. The Constitution (1962) is the basis for government. Local government is administered through the 13 parish councils (Kingston and St. Andrew are jointly administered) with councilors elected in separate local government elections, which are held for parish councils. These elections, like the general elections, are contested on party political lines.

Politics in Jamaica like other small societies is highly personal as key decisions are made by very few individuals and interpersonal relationships are particularly intense as respective roles are carried out by persons who know each other well and in many instances are relatives. Other aspects identified by Buddan and Reviere include greater central-ization, informal personal relations, limited number of constituents per elected representative, and more face-to-face contact between leaders and the public such that relatively minor issues can engage the attention of top officials and politicians.[33] In the case of Jamaica small society politics was taken to its apogee as the politics of modern Jamaica from the 1930s until the late 1960s was dominated by two cousins, Norman Manley and Alexander Bustamante. This special relation of respect and admiration[34] was acknowledged and transcended political differences. For almost all of the first 50 years the People's National Party was led by Norman Manley and his younger son Michael Manley. Elder brother Douglas served as a Member of Parliament and Minister of Government.

Mass media communication includes two daily national newspapers and several weekly or biweekly community-oriented newspapers, spe-cialist magazines, several radio stations, and two television stations. Sev-eral cable television companies are in operation providing subscribers with foreign programming for a fee; in addition many Jamaicans have satellite receivers. Access to media has been an integral part of the life of Jamaicans with daily morning and evening broadcasts of the BBC news being part of the standard routine of the average Jamaican. This exposure over many years has created a heightened awareness of international affairs and an understanding enhanced by the travel and migration of large numbers of Jamaicans. The public has been very engaged in inter-national issues such as relations with the IMF, the struggle against apart-heid, the U.S. invasion of Grenada, and U.S.-Cuba relations. The October, 1980 general election was called to decide whether or not Jamaica should continue to adhere to IMF stabilization programs. The 1983 general elec-tion called by the Seaga government resulted from a disagreement be-tween the government and the opposition PNP led by Michael Manley over whether Jamaica should support the U.S. invasion of Grenada. The PNP refused to contest the "snap" election and remained outside of Par-liament until the next general election in 1989. External events were also a factor in the 1962 general election when the JLP seized on the visit to Kingston a ship from the Soviet Union to claim that this was proof that the PNP intended to go Communist if they won the election. It is not clear whether the Communist bogey had any effect on the electoral results but the theme was resurrected in the 1980 election when the JLP pointed to the PNP's close relation with Cuba and what it portrayed as Castro's tutelage of Michael Manley.

Society

Jamaica's population at the end of 1996 was estimated at 2.52 million people, with the majority being young, e.g., about 32 percent being 14 years old and under. The overall sex ratio was 99.3 males per 100 females. Males are predominant in the under 20 year old age group, while females predominate in the 60 and over age group. The annual population growth during the 1990s has been about 1.1 percent.[35] Fertility rates have declined steadily reflecting improved education, contraceptive use, and female employment opportunities and morbidity rates have decreased as a result of better health care and economic development. Emigration has also been an important factor in restraining the growth of population and the emergence of a diaspora, which is an integral part of Jamaica's society and economy[36] as reflected in remittances. The overseas Jamaicans are mainly in the United States, in particular the greater New York area, the United Kingdom, and Canada, in particular Toronto.

The experience of migration has created a people with the facility and confidence for dealing with foreigners and a comfort level in foreign countries. This capacity has been reinforced by the high level of exposure to foreigners through the tourist industry, which has extensive linkages with other economic sectors and touches nearly every aspect of Jamaican life, especially in areas of the country where the industry is concentrated. The ability to mediate foreign cultures and coexist with people of different ethnic and cultural backgrounds dates back to the eighteenth century when Africans were introduced into the island as slaves. Ironically, Caribbean people are among the earliest "globalized" people both by their mode of existence, which has involved continual movement and their exposure to other cultures and the forced assimilation of foreign cultures and languages. Knight's description of the Caribbean is apt for Jamaica when he speaks of "an eclectic blend of almost all the peoples and cultures of the world."[37]

Emigration has been heavy since the late nineteenth century, mainly due to high unemployment and persistent poverty affecting both rural and urban areas. In the early decades of the twentieth century[38] Jamaicans went abroad in search of employment including to Panama to build the Canal,[39] to Costa Rica[40] and Cuba[41] to work in sugar and banana cultivation, and to the United States to reap apples, tobacco, and sugar cane[42] after World War II. In the 1950s Jamaicans started migrating to Britain[43] and soon after to Canada. Migration has alleviated overpopulation and unemployment[44] and provided an invaluable stream of remittances but may have deprived the society of some of its most enterprising citizens and dismembered families. This physical separation of family members has contributed to the prevalence of the matrifocal family structure[45] and juvenile delinquency.

The indigenous population of the island was decimated by ruthless exploitation,[46] slavery, and disease following the arrival of Columbus and Spanish colonization, a process driven by an obsession with the search for gold. There are no discernible remnants of the original inhabitants or the Spanish colonists. During English colonialism the English,

Irish, and Africans who were forcefully brought in as slaves to work primarily on sugar plantations were the people who populated the island. After the abolition of slavery in 1834 there was a major existential crisis in plantation economy and society[47] as the former slaves wherever possible abandoned the sugar plantations and the resulting shortage of labor prompted the British to bring in workers from India[48] and China.[49] The ethnic composition of Jamaicans[50] was principally African accounting for over 90 percent, followed by East Indian (3 percent), Chinese (2 percent), European (less than 1 percent), and other groups (4 percent). An estimated 30 percent of the population is of mixed ethnic origin reflecting the intermingling of different racial groups. This structure remained basically the same into the 1990s.

The mix of different ethnic groups and races is mirrored in the emergence of Creole culture resulting from the interrelation of European and African cultures with more recent but subsidiary infusion of Asian culture. Creole culture is characterized by a tension and a simultaneous blending of the two cultures in an ongoing process bearing the imprint of the experiences of slavery and colonialism. Indeed, for Lamming "the most authentic meaning of the word Caribbean is the organization of labour in the region by people particularly from Asia and Africa, and the responses of their labour to imperial rule, including the way in which they organized successful rebellions against this rule."[51] Colonialism dominated class structure, dictated social mobility, and controlled the character and extent of education until well into the twentieth century, indeed, the "immersion in European culture came to be directly related to the submerging of African ideas."[52] Indigenous expressions particularly of the peasant and working classes exhibit strong African retentions.[53] The creation of a Creole culture of necessity involved a conscious struggle against the imposed English culture, a process evident in the arts, for example in the works of poet and novelist Claude McKay, whose "If I Must Die"[54] is a clarion call to rebellion. Sherlock and Bennett see this as part of the second emancipation, the "emancipation of the spirit," and an essential sequel to the earlier emancipation from physical bondage.[55]

Jamaicans are a very religious people, but religion is not a divisive factor. Religious groups include Anglicans, Roman Catholics, Baptists, Methodists, Presbyterians, and fundamental groups. Jamaica also has one of the oldest synagogues and Jewish communities in the Western Hemisphere. Numerous indigenous derivatives of Christianity have emerged, mixing with African religious continuities[56] to form new religions, most notably Rastafarianism.[57] The Rastafarian movement has spread throughout the world and has a visibility out of proportion to the number of adherents because of its association with "ganja" as a religious sacrament and the prominence of Rastafarians in Reggae music, including global music icon Bob Marley.[58]

Branded across every social, economic, and psychological aspect of Jamaican life is the brutal experience of three hundred years of slavery.[59] The hurt and discomfort with such a cruel history is just "below the surface," indeed slavery "still casts its shadow" over the society.[60] Several contemporary behavior patterns and social institutions can only be adequately explained by reference to the period of slavery, for example, family forms.[61] Nobel winning St. Lucian poet Derek Walcott muses: "who in the New World does not have a horror of the past, whether his ancestor was torturer or victim? Who, in the depth of his conscience, is not silently screaming for pardon or for revenge?"[62] The psychologically dehumanizing and physically brutal experience of over 200 years of slavery is indelibly etched[63] in "collective unconscious"[64] of the Jamaican people and many aspects of contemporary behavior are attributed to this history. The well-known aggressiveness of Jamaicans has been attributed to the sources of African slaves brought to the island and the extreme brutality of slavery as practiced in Jamaica as compared to other venues.[65]

The class-color correlation, which was at the core of plantation society, continued with very little change after emancipation. The social structure of Jamaica was rigid, hierarchical, and coincided closely with color lines until as recently as the 1970s. In the era of slave plantation society, which existed until 1834, the social structure consisted of the ruling/owning class of white expatriates from Britain,[66] the slaves who were black Africans and their descendants, and a minute intermediated strata of poor whites and free colored people. Broadly speaking there were "two Jamaicas" well into the nineteenth century.[67] As the intermediate class slowly emerged during the nineteenth century and the first half of the twentieth century class structure took the shape of a pyramid in which class and color were closely correlated, consisting of a small White ruling/owning class at the apex, a very large Black working class and peasantry,[68] and in between a small Brown middle class.[69] The limited availability of public education[70] during the colonial era severely restricted social mobility and not until political independence did education became available to the working class. A more variegated social stratification evolved as the economic structure experienced diversification with the emergence of tourism, bauxite, and manufacturing. Cultural pluralism, which had reinforced the traditional class dichotomy, gave way over time to a dynamic interaction of European and African cultures to form "Creole culture."[71] For most of the last 300 years the dynamics of the intertwining has occurred during colonialism, which sought to enforce the dominance of the colonizer.[72]

The class structure has remained polarized in spite of a period of Democratic Socialism in the 1970s under the Michael Manley government during which there was an espousal of redistribution of income and means of production.[73] Despite this interlude the class structure has remained largely unchanged and reflects the traditional, highly uneven distribution of income and an extreme concentration of ownership. For example, in the late 1960s the pattern of land ownership was highly uneven with 293 owners of farms over 500 acres accounting for 43.2 percent of total farm land while 151,705 small farmers with less than 5 acres held 15.4 percent of total farm land.[74] Ownership and income are concentrated in a small capitalist class, the core of which consists of 21 families, who are close-knit by intermarriage and interlocking corporate directorates.[75] Associated with this pattern of ownership is a highly uneven distribution of income, i.e., the richest 4 percent of the households received 30 percent of total income, while at the other extreme 20 percent of the households received 19 percent of total income.[76] An influential part of the class structure has been foreign managerial personnel and expatriate owners consequent on the important role of direct foreign investment, predominantly United States in the Jamaican economy.[77]

Economy

Jamaica is a small, highly open developing economy with a land area of 4,411 square miles and a population of 2.5 million. Inherent in small size is a limited quantity and range of natural resources[78] and a small national market which deprives many lines of production from attaining economies of scale and scope. Jamaica's Gross Domestic Product in 1990 was USD$4,592,208,212 and per capita income was USD$1,921.

Functioning of the Economy[79]

An economy that has the structure described in the preceding section is a disarticulated economy. It is externally dependent, i.e., output responds to external demand, and output for both external and national markets has substantial import content. The import content of all forms of economic activity is high, e.g., in excess of 40 percent in tourism,[80] 20 percent in export agriculture, 34 percent in bauxite/alumina, 25 percent in construction,[81] and 57 percent in manufacturing.[82] The high import content is a problem compounded by the limited capacity to produce local substitutes. This means that there is limited internal dynamic growth, reinforced and exacerbated by the limited inter-sectoral linkages. Another critical aspect of dependence is that many of the decisions about resource allocation are made by multinational corporations with global profit maximization objectives, resulting in decisions not always in the best interest of the national economy. Foreign capital inflows traditionally finance the current account deficit and account for 30 percent of gross domestic investment.[83]

Economic growth is determined by an increase in productive capacity or an increase in utilization of productive capacity. An increase in both capacity and utilization necessitates an increase in the real volume of imports. The volume of imports is determined by the quantum of foreign exchange available to the economy and import prices. Foreign exchange earnings derive from two sources, (a) export earnings, and (b) capital inflows, both of which are essentially exogenously determined. Export earnings are determined by the exogenous factors of export prices and export demand, and by export supply, which depends partly on the availability of imported inputs. Capital inflows may take the form of aid, commercial loans, and foreign investment, all of which are exogenously determined while being sensitive to domestic economic performance, policy, and management. The dependence of the economy is made more acute by the fact that export earnings derive from a few exports, in particular bauxite and alumina, which account for over 65 percent of total exports.

Disarticulated economies have a limited dynamic for economic growth. Economic growth takes place only under special circumstances, i.e., a situation in which the particular dependent capitalist economy is able to supply one or some of the commodities required by the process of global accumulation at a price that compares favorably with alternative sources. These commodities may be labor, raw materials, or labor intensive manufactured consumer goods. A period of growth in the world economy is neither a necessary nor sufficient condition, but it can reinforce the expansionary development of a commodity. Economic growth takes place in response to global capital accumulation, the dynamic of which is concentrated in the developed capitalist section of the world economy. The endemic and systematic tendency of disarticulated economies is to crisis, i.e., stagnation of output and employment. Disarticulated economies are passive participants in the global accumulation of capital in the world capitalist economy. They are not integral to the process; they are periodically integrated or marginalized to varying degrees depending on their ability to provide goods and services needed by global accumulation. The fragility and volatility of economic growth in this type of economy derives from its disarticulated structure, which causes growth to be determined by, and vulnerable to exogenous factors. Capital accumulation is fragile and does not have a self-sustaining character because the exogenous determinants are continually changing. These are the changing needs of global accumulation and the changing ability of an individual country to supply those commodities.

The structural rigidities and distortions of disarticulated capitalist economies limit their capacity for adaptability. The small size of the economy further compounds vulnerability and constrains adaptability. Disarticulated economies experience underdevelopment, which may exhibit two tendencies. These are (a) economic growth through integration in the world economy under favorable circumstances, generating growth but not self-sustaining capital accumulation and development and (b) stagnation by marginalization from process of global accumulation, because of unfavorable external conditions.

Disarticulated economies have an externally dependent process of growth because structural distortions and rigidities deprive it of the capacity for internally dynamic growth. Foreign capital does not transform the process of growth from externally dependent into self-sustaining growth, but reinforces the dependent character of growth.[84] Self-sustaining growth is not possible unless there is a process of structural transformation, which reduces external dependence by linking demand and production, reducing import content, creating inter-sectoral linkages, and creating the capacity to produce a wider range of manufactured goods. This involves economic development, which is a process with a quantitative dimension, i.e., structural transformation. The capacity for self-sustaining economic growth is the end product of a process of economic development.

The small size of the market results in imperfections such as the existence of monopolies and oligopolies because the market is too small to support more than one or a few producers.[85] The lack of economies of scale and the absence of a competitive dynamic in the market lead to high production cost and prices, which are not internationally competitive for both exports and for domestic consumption. Firms are small by global standards and compared to those in the United States, e.g., the largest firm in the United States in 1996–97 was General Motors Corporation, which had annual sales of U.S. $164 billion compared to U.S. $312 million by Grace, Kennedy and Company, Jamaica's largest firm.[86]

Jamaica has a small, highly open economy. Major productive sectors are tourism, bauxite/alumina, informatics, agribusiness, agriculture, and manufacturing. Traditionally the economy has been dependent primarily on agricultural exports, in particular sugar and banana, until the emergence of bauxite and alumina production in the late 1950s. Despite a policy of import substitution industrialization in the 1960s manufacturing did not become the leading sector that it was anticipated to be; however, the production of apparel for export primarily to the U.S. market developed significantly after the passage of legislation giving effect to the Caribbean Basin Economic Recovery Act in 1983. By the early 1990s export agriculture had declined as a source of export earnings although it remained a critically important source of employment. Tourism increased steadily to become the largest earner of foreign exchange sector.[87] Tourism together with the bauxite/alumina sector were the twin drivers of economic growth.

Structure of the Economy

Jamaica was a "plantation economy"[88] dominated by sugar until bananas displaced it briefly during the 1930s[89] when the island was the

largest exporter in the world. The two crops remained the most important exports (accounting for 55.4 percent of total exports in 1950),[90] until
the emergence and development of bauxite exports in the 1960s when
Jamaica was the world's leading exporter. Exports of bauxite were the
largest merchandise export throughout the 1990s, while sugar and bananas have contracted considerably.

The mineral industry is dominated by bauxite and alumina, which
commenced in the 1950s. Jamaica has bauxite reserves of some 2 billion
tons, which are of high quality and easily accessible. The industry expanded rapidly from the late 1950s through the 1960s when Jamaica became the world's largest producer of bauxite. Following the substantial
decline in the bauxite/alumina industry in the 1980s, due to an international recession in the aluminum industry, there has been expansion in
production during the 1990s. Gypsum, marble, and high-purity lime-
stone are produced for local use and for export. Small marble-extracting
operations are taking place, and further expansion is expected in this
area. Crude oil, the main energy source, is all imported but is processed
locally for use by all entities except the bauxite companies that import
their own supplies of processed petroleum products.

Agriculture has been dominated by exports of sugar, rum, molasses,
bananas, coffee, tobacco, citrus, cocoa, and pimento. Production of food-
stuffs and livestock for the domestic market has been dwarfed by export
agriculture, which garnered most financial, infrastructure, and technical
support from the public sector and utilized the best land. Yet domestic
agriculture was the mainstay of the vast majority of farmers who were
small farmers.[91] The fishing industry expanded considerably in the
1980s, especially in the area of inland fishing. Forests, including state
plantations and privately owned stands as well as natural forests, cover
24 percent of Jamaica's total land area. Rising production costs and high
levels of illegal cutting have caused a decline in the sector's relative economic significance in recent years. Although its share of GDP declined
the sector remain an important source of employment. Those who could
not find employment in agriculture drifted into urban areas where they
formed a large and growing informal sector. This sector encompasses a
wide range of activities that coexists with the formal economy. The informal sector consists of entities that are outside the purview of the state
including illegal activities and has become a major sources of employment.[92]

A vigorous and sustained attempt was made at creating a manufacturing sector by a strategy of import substitution industrialization, which
was the accepted wisdom for developing countries in the 1960s. The initial developments occurred in food processing and later involved assembly of manufactured goods with the aid of high tariffs and import duties
and capitalizing on wages lower than in the industrialized countries. The
manufacturing sector contributes nearly 18 percent of the country's gross

domestic product and provides about 10.5 percent of total employment in the country. Most nontraditional manufacturing in Jamaica is dependent on imported raw materials. Plant size and scale of operations were geared mainly to the domestic and Caribbean Community (CARICOM) markets, although there is increased emphasis on production for international markets. This sector has declined marginally over the previous year due to high interest rates, the reduction in tariffs and import duty rates, and the several devaluations of the Jamaican dollar. The effects of these negative factors have almost been nullified by the growth in the textile and garment industry, especially with respect to exports to the United States. Approximately 75 percent of Jamaica's manufacturing exports during the 1990s were from this subsector, and incentives are available under the Export Industry Encouragement Act and the Jamaica Export Free Zone Act. Export manufacturing is carried out in export free zones located in Kingston and Montego Bay, where income tax incentives and duty-free status apply. Free zone manufacturing activities were expanded in the 1980s, responding to opportunities offered under the Caribbean Basin Economic Recovery Act (CBERA), particularly in the areas of garment assembly and ethanol production. A slump in the apparel market overseas and competition from Mexico created a setback, but the island's free zones are now expanding, improving their services and promoting garment/textile manufacturing and assembly, electronics, food processing, footwear, and furniture. Call centers and information processing firms providing services to the global market have grown both in the free zone and in Kingston. Tourism began to emerge with the advent of steam ships and has been encouraged as a means of diversifying the economy and reducing its dependence on the export of agricultural products. In recent years tourism has been the largest earner of foreign exchange and a principal source of employment. In 1990 foreign exchange earnings from tourism amounted to USD$740 million from 1.24 million visitors compared to USD$1.3 billion from 2.2 million visitors in 2000. The importance of the sector lies not only in being the largest earner of foreign exchange but derives from the extensive linkages with other sectors in the economy and its employment of a wide range of labor from the world class chef to unskilled workers, including a significant share of women. The expansion of the tourist sector has served to demonstrate that Jamaica and Jamaican owned, managed, and staffed enterprises can be competitive in a sensitive global industry.

The banking and insurance industries are primarily locally owned and controlled and are well diversified but the largest commercial banks were Canadian owned.[93] The largest bank was the Canadian Scotia Bank, which before the establishment of a central bank was the banker of the government. In the banking sector, private commercial banks and merchant banks account for most of the financial activity, though there was at least one private development bank. The state-owned National Development Bank and the Agricultural Credit Bank, both of which on-lend through approved financial institutions, play an important role in providing development financing. There has been a thriving stock exchange since the 1960s and money and capital markets are well developed.

Jamaica's traditional merchandise exports are dominated by bauxite and alumina, which together accounted for over one-half of total merchandise exports. Other significant contributors in this sector are sugar, bananas, coffee, and rum. Nontraditional exports including manufacturing have expanded significantly since the 1980s. Jamaica's principal trading partners in order of importance are the United States, the United Kingdom, Canada, and CARICOM. International trade with the United States accounts for over 50 percent of total trade, over 50 percent of exports are destined to the United States, and the dependence on the United States for imports constitutes an even higher share of total imports. There are also trade links with Russia, which buys pimento and bauxite, and with Japan, which provides a strong market for Jamaican Blue Mountain coffee, considered to be one of the finest coffees in the world. Jamaica is a member of the WTO and benefits from market access through specialized trade arrangements, including preferential agreements such as the CBI, Caribbean-Canadian Trade Agreement (CARIBCAN), the Lomé Convention, CARICOM-Venezuela Agreement, and CARICOM-Colombia Agreement.

National Character, Culture, and Tradition

The culture, character, traditions, history, and even myths of a country influence everything they do from the way they play football[94] to their foreign policy. Culture affects foreign policy in respect to the goals chosen and the manner in which foreign policy is executed. This is a well-established tenet of international relations and the literature is replete with supportive evidence. A pellucid example is the relationship between the myths of the Western frontier that are deeply embedded in the American psyche and U.S. foreign policy. This is given definitive treatment in Richard Slotkin's magisterial classic: "Gunfighter Nation."[95]

When President George W. Bush told Saddam Hussein to get out of Baghdad by midnight he was enacting and articulating the well-known role of the sheriff in western movies. The moniker "sheriff" is not repugnant to Americans, indeed, it is acceptable. Haass discusses the role of the United States in the aftermath of the Cold War by using the analogy of the "reluctant sheriff."[96] Bush warned Saddam that if he did not leave by the deadline the U.S. armed forces would rain down "Shock and Awe." This is analogous to a scene in the western movie "Tombstone" when Wyatt Earp warns the cowboys who had just carried out a terrorist killing of one of his brothers that he was coming for them and "hell is coming with me." There is a myth and tradition that the United States was by providence blessed with the role of global sheriff to vanquish the bad guys, variously the communists of the Cold War era and the terrorists of the contemporary period. The fact that Bush was proceeding without the mandate of the United Nations conforms to the western myth of the lone man standing up for what is right without the support of others of like mind but are not brave enough to stand with him. This is a recurring theme in the western movie genre, the most famous portrayal of which was Gary Cooper, the sheriff in "High Noon" facing a gang of outlaws abandoned even by his deputy and without the support of his wife.

The western movie was as Lenihan explains "a heroic myth eulogizing America's greatness"[97] and has been potent symbolism of the American ideal. The western iconography has been effectively used by a variety of politicians from Teddy Roosevelt[98] to Ronald Reagan to Bill Clinton to George W. Bush.[99] No one better personified the persona of the western cum American character and ideals than the mediocre actor named John Wayne.[100] The fact that the United States was proceeding alone was in conformity to the western movies' "idealization of socially responsible individualism."[101] A member of a posse in pursuit of outlaws in the 1943 movie "The Avenging Rider" declares "I have got all the authority I need right here in my holster."[102] The arrival of the cavalry in all western movies is greeted with gratitude by those rescued, hence the expectation of U.S. troops that Iraqis would welcome their arrival. The arriving character in "The Stranger from Texas" announces: "I'm not here to start trouble, I'm here to end it."[103]

Nothing including total annihilation is ruled out for those designated as the enemy that threatens civilization made synonymous with American society and American values. Slaughter of the Native American Indian was justified to protect civilization or the American way of life from savages, i.e., people of a different race.[104] This as a constant theme in western movies; for example an army captain in the movie "The Savage" declares: "There is only one solution: exterminate them: burn their villages. That's the only way to bring civilization to these parts."[105] When Bush said you are either "with us or against us" in his address to Congress on September 20, 2001, he was a Walter Mitty version of a character in the movie "The Alamo" who opines: "The enemy of my enemy is my friend."[106] Coyne explains the role of westerns in American identity: "the Western's overall thrust sanctified territorial expansion, justified dispossession of the Indians, fuelled nostalgia for a largely mythicized past, exalted self-reliance and posited violence as the main solution to personal and societal problems."[107]

Nations like individuals have personalities and these are often reinforced by a culture and a tradition of behavior. Jamaicans have a long history of being fearless fighters against injustice and a willingness to stand up for their rights regardless of the consequences. The aggressiveness of Jamaicans is compounded by a spirit of audacity, i.e., not only the willingness to try anything but the confidence that they will succeed. The entry of a Jamaican bobsled team in the winter Olympics is an example of the mindset and attitude. The origin of this pattern of behavior is in the slave revolts and the example of the Maroons[108] who achieve an autonomous state within the British colony recognized by a formal treaty. Slave revolts had such an impact on slavery in Jamaica that Richard Hart felt the most apposite description of the phenomenon was "the slaves who abolished slavery."[109]

The tradition of resistance and fighting for freedom lives on in what Carl Jung called the "collective unconscious"[110] of Jamaicans. Rex Nettleford observes that "the tradition of black assertion has never left Jamaican life. There was from the late eighteenth and early nineteenth century slave rebellions, Paul Bogle in 1865, 1968, and the young sufferers."[111] The audacity is exemplified by the exploits of a Jamaican woman, Mary Seacole[112] in the Crimean War. During the 1920s Marcus Garvey[113] established a global organization of people of African descent called the Universal Negro Improvement Association. He exercised global leadership in the struggle for the human rights and liberation of people of African descent and their liberation from discrimination and colonialism. His work and writings[114] had a profound impact and was the consciousness from which subsequent leaders emerged. There were other Jamaicans[115] and Caribbean people active in the Harlem Renaissance and in the struggle over these issues in the early twentieth century in the United States[116] but Garvey's impact was world-wide. His ideas are a direct antecedent of the Black Power movement[117] in the United States and in Rastafarians in Jamaica.[118] Malcom X attributes enormous significance to Garvey's influence when he said, "Every time you see another nation on the African continent become independent you know that Marcus Garvey is alive. Had it not been for Marcus Garvey and the foundations laid by him, you would find no independent nations in the Caribbean today. All of the freedom movement that is taking place right here in America today was initiated by the work and teachings of Marcus Garvey."[119]

Garvey's activities took place in the context of English-speaking Caribbean people constituting almost 25 percent of the population of Harlem[120] in 1920. They made important contributions to the development of a Black aesthetic through culture, politics, and the arts.[121] Jamaican poet and novelist Claude McKay "penned" the poem "If We Must Die," which became an anthem for struggle against racism and colonialism and was emblematic of his own political activism.[122] Resistance is a leitmotif in Jamaican cultural expressions. The attitude is evident in the lyrics of many of the songs of Bob Marley notably "Stand Up for Your Rights." Marley honed many of his themes from the study of the tenets of Rastafarianism,[123] an indigenous Jamaican religion that challenged many aspects of the status quo in Jamaican society and an approach that resonated internationally to other people deconstructing similar social, racial, and cultural issues. The Rastafarian movement continued in many respects ideas from earlier struggles and the thinking of Marcus Garvey.[124]

The Great Depression was a period of worldwide turmoil and no less so in Jamaica and the Caribbean. Unrest by the working class on the sugar estates and on the docks in Jamaica in the late 1930s was a transformative moment in the fight against British colonialism and initiated the final stage of decolonization.[125] The agitation received a flip with the return of Jamaican soldiers and airmen after World War II.

Jamaica's penchant for not being confined by convention was demonstrated when Jamaica entered a bobsled team in the Winter Olympics in Calgary, Canada in 1988 and in the 1994 Winter Olympics in Lillehammer, Norway. The four sled team finished 14th ahead of Austria, Canada, France, Russia, and the United States. The audacity to try the undone is an exemplar of a strong sense of self-confidence. The accretion of sporting feats builds over time a belief and a confidence. This is not engrained in a people only by political achievements and artistic accomplishments but has been repeatedly reinforced by world leading athletic feats. This began when Jamaicans won gold medals in track events in the 1948 Olympics. The fact of Jamaica, a tiny island with a population of a million and still a British colony, beating the rest of the world must certainly open anew psychological horizons. That athletic tradition has continued and today Jamaica has the fastest man, Usian Bolt, and fastest woman, Shelly-Ann Fraser-Pryce. Patrick Robinson acknowledges the talent and the tradition but highlights the highly organized system of identification of talent and its development through coaching and fierce competition.[126] This is an important point because it is not just exceptional talent that would flourish anywhere but the organized development of the talent. The achievement is no longer essentially individual but is national and systemic and therefore indicative of Jamaica's capacity to continue to excel.

Tradition is an important confidence booster. The early athletes that started the tradition in sprinting were aware that even before their successes the tiny island nation could lay claim to having produced in George Headley arguably the greatest batsman in Test Cricket. Jamaicans could draw on having been one of the world's most important sugar producers, the world's largest banana exporter in the 1930s, and then largest producer of bauxite in the world in the 1960s. Jamaica has been renowned for its world famous Blue mountain coffee, rum, ginger (Canada Dry Ginger Ale), and marijuana. Perhaps more than any other product has been reggae music, which has become a recognized global genre.[127] Bob Marley is known throughout the world and his classic "One Love" was named Song of the Century (twentieth century) by the British Broadcasting Corporation.

Raggae, a contemporary music from Jamaica, has become a genre for social protest and commentary. It was as Erna Brodber explains "black space" with origins in postcolonialist nationalist politics, Garvey, Rasta-fari, and Black Power. [128] The most prominent exponent of the genre, Bob Marley spoke out for the need to fight against "isms and schisms." As Carolyn Cooper explains raggae has been appropriated and adapted in a variety of cultural contexts across the world and thereby the revolution-ary ethos that is at the heart of Jamaican reggae music is translated into local languages that articulate the particular politics of new and different contexts. [129]

Tradition consolidated around the conviction that Jamaica as distinct from Jamaicans could influence international events, and this began to emerge in 1959 when Jamaica, not yet politically independent under the leadership of Premier Norman Manley, was the first country to place a trade embargo on South Africa ruled mercilessly by apartheid. At that time Jamaica did not have responsibility for its own foreign affairs. With this example it was no wonder that Michael Manley had the audacity to champion the cause of the world's poor in his call for a new international economic order. When he campaigned against apartheid he was continu-ing a tradition. It was at the instigation of Jamaica that the Common-wealth adopted the Gleneagles Agreement in 1977 to sever sporting ties with South Africa. His tireless role in the international diplomatic strug-gle to end apartheid in South Africa was recognized when he was awarded a gold medal for distinguished service in the struggle against apartheid. P. J. Patterson never felt he had to agree with the United States out of deference to their superpower status and refused to support the U.S. invasion of Iraq and spoke against this action in the United Nations.

Prime Minister Hugh Shearer of the small newly independent Jamaica in his speech to the United Nations General assembly of 1963 was bold enough to propose that the United Nations devote a year to human rights. [130] Indeed the year 1968 became the International Year of Human Rights. In June 1967, the UN General Assembly also accepted Jamaica's proposal for an international conference to review progress in the field of human rights. The committee established to organize the program of activities for the International Year of Human Rights was chaired by Jamaica's then Permanent Representative to the UN, the late Sir Egerton Richardson. Jamaica projected its image by the establishment of a Marcus Garvey award for a person that improved race relations and it was awarded to Dr. Martin Luther King. [131] Distinguished Jamaican diplomats have served in very influential positions in the UN process and in the UN system. In his time ambassador Donald Mills [132] was one of the most highly regarded ambassadors to the UN, chaired the Security Council for two years, and was a leading spokesman for the developing countries, chairing the Group of 77 and the Non-aligned Movement. Jamaica has had a seat on the Security Council for two terms. Ambassadors Lucille Mair and Patricia Durrant contributed to breaking the so-called "glass ceiling" for women in the UN system. The tradition lives on with the

announcement by the United Nations of the winning design that has
been selected for a monument called the Arc of Return to be erected to
commemorate the memory of the millions who died during the transatlantic slave trade. The proposal for the permanent memorial was made
by Jamaica at the United Nations in 2007.

Jamaica in the first decade of its political independence started to
verbalize that it was its intention not to slavishly align itself with the
United States. While this was not yet a declaration much less the practice
of a non-aligned foreign policy it does represent the embryonic recognition of such a course. Shearer stated as early as 1964 that: "we are no-
body's Government except the people of Jamaica. We happen to be next
door to the United States, but Jamaica does not take instructions from the
United States or any superpower. If it happens that our views coincide
with theirs, that's good for them. If it happens that our view and the view
of Russia coincides, that's good for them. But we do not take instructions.
We are guided by our own policy." [133] This was displayed when Jamaica
supported China's entry to the UN.

PART II: UNITED STATES, JAMAICA, AND THE CARIBBEAN

This section reviews United States-Jamaica relations against the background of relations between the United States and the ESC. The policies
of the United States towards the region will be treated extensively in
chapter 4 and the focus here is on the policy of Jamaica with some reference to issues common to the policy of the ESC as a whole towards the
United States. This is essential to explain the context in which to locate
the case studies of attempts to influence U.S. policy in the foreign policy
of the region. Against this background, the campaign to influence U.S.
policy towards Jamaica will be documented. Five key objectives and the
strategies and campaigns pursued by Jamaica will be described and discussed in subsequent chapters.

Invisible in U.S. Foreign Policy

One of the major obstacles to influencing U.S. foreign policy towards
the ESC is the limited importance the United States attaches to the region.
In the post-World War II era, U.S. foreign policy has been crisis driven,
i.e., attention has been devoted to countries or regions if they are viewed
as crises, which pose a direct threat to U.S. interests. The ESC has traditionally been regarded by the United States as a safe area, which only
rarely experienced low-intensity conflicts. Indeed, U.S. foreign policy toward the ESC has been episodic, and even then, the policy pursued has,
in most instances, been a subset of a wider regional policy, for example,
the isolation of Cuba. The periods in which the United States has focused

on the ESC have not been accompanied by policy specifically designed for the subregion. This is clearly demonstrated by the Caribbean Basin Initiative, which was motivated by elimination of armed, radical political movements in Central America against the overall backdrop of a global anticommunist strategy rather than the economic development of the ESC. However, the CBI served to bolster market-fundamentalist, pro-U.S. regimes such as the Seaga Government in Jamaica during 1980–1989. In the absence of a comprehensive consistently applied policy, the United States has resorted to short-term intervention. These episodes involve the interference in the Guyanese electoral process to ensure the ouster of Jagan's avowed Marxist Party, the destabilization of the Democratic Socialist government of Michael Manley in Jamaica; and the invasion of Grenada to complete the demise of the Bishop-led New Jewel Coalition. These episodes occurred in the early 1960s, late 1970s, and early 1980s, respectively, and the duration of each intervention was very short.

During the last 50 years, Jamaica and the ESC have not been a priority for U.S. foreign policy. Indeed, the ESC has been invisible in U.S. foreign policy. The lack of visibility of the ESC is evident in the paucity of studies and commentary on this issue in the literature on U.S. foreign policy in the post-World War II period. The validity of this contention is substantiated by a review of the memoirs of leading foreign policy actors, more specifically the published works of Presidents and Secretaries of State.

Dean Rusk, Secretary of State in the Kennedy and Johnson administrations, chronicled his tenure in 617 pages, including discussions on the Cuban missile crisis and Bay of Pigs and the intervention in the Dominican Republic, but there is no discussion of the ESC.[134] The significance of the political independence of Jamaica and Trinidad and Tobago in the early 1960s seems have escaped his attention. It is curious that this significant political transformation, which meant that Britain had relinquished control over security and foreign policy, did not elicit even passing comment.

In the rethink of U.S. foreign policy, which was stimulated by the end of the Cold War, the Caribbean received virtually no consideration. Typical of this tendency is former President Nixon who called on the United States to "seize the moment," mentioning Cuba but not the Caribbean, except in a fleeting remark on the need to abolish sugar quotas.[135] National Security Advisor, Zbigniew Brzezinski exhibited a similar myopia in his grand design, which seemed odd and preoccupied with traditional global issues.[136] Of the "flashpoints"[137] of the post-Cold War era, e.g., terrorism and migration, the Caribbean, in its widest geographic connotation, i.e., including Colombia, prompted concern because of the escalation of drug trafficking. Together with the emergence in the United States of "ethnic crime organizations" in the 1980s, the Jamaican drug "posses"[138] introduced a new security issue in U.S. foreign policy towards Jamaica.

Neither Jamaican or the ESC are mentioned in President Carter's memoirs, as the focus is on retelling the Camp David Accord, the Iranian hostage crisis, and the Panama Canal Treaty negotiations. He records, however, that the Bahamas' offer to allow the Shah of Iran to reside there was accepted but the Shah chose Mexico.[139] Cyrus Vance[140] recalls his stint as Secretary of State as dominated by the Camp David negotiations, the Israeli-Egypt peace agreement, the Panama Canal treaty, and Iranian hostage crisis. The recollections do not include the ESC.

The exception is Secretary of State George Schultz who in his memoirs discusses U.S. intervention in Central America and the invasion of Grenada.[141] However, despite the attention to the events of 1983 in Grenada, it is not clear that a coherent long-term policy, specifically developed and implemented for the ESC, was in place before or after this episode. The action of the Reagan Administration in Grenada really derives from and must be understood as part of a hemispheric-wide anti-communism policy, which dates back to the beginning of the Cold War. Initially, the ESC was exempt from military intervention because up until the 1960s, the states of the ESC were under British colonial rule and therefore, while physically in the United States' "backyard," they were in the British sphere of influence. Grenada also must be seen as a continuation of a policy of military intervention that the United States has employed since the early part of this century and whose motivations do not derive from an overarching, anti-communist strategy but reflect an arrogant use of overwhelming military superiority to ensure a government compliant with U.S. interests and policies. These two tenets of U.S. foreign policy in Latin America and the Caribbean were fused in a political conjuncture in which President Reagan wanted to send a decisive signal (at minimum cost) of his resolve to fight communism or the threat of communism. Indeed, Schultz describes the Grenada invasion as "a shot heard around the world."[142]

The foreign policy of the Carter Administration towards Latin America and the Caribbean was deeply divided between the traditional Cold War approach and an attempt to introduce a more enlightened approach. The latter approach sought to inculcate a Wilsonian moral leitmotif by introducing human rights concerns. Carter sought to permanently change U.S. policy from "paternalism or punishment or retribution when some of the South Americans don't yield to our persuasion."[143] This was exemplified by a less combative approach to Cuba and the response to the emergence of the Bishop regime in Grenada. However, Cold War considerations reasserted prominence in handling the Somoza—Sandinista imbroglio and in the resort to an attempted military rescue of hostages in Iran. The rise to prominence of the hardliners was helped by the Soviet invasion of Afghanistan in 1979 and the rhetoric of Ronald Reagan during the presidential election campaign. In this milieu, there was not a clear policy toward the ESC because of the divergence of foreign policy perspectives in the U.S. government, in which there were instances of old-style tactics, such as towards Jamaica and new approaches as exemplified by the renegotiation of the Panama Canal Treaty.[144]

From the late 1970s, the Central American region had been experiencing an extremely severe economic and political crisis. There was civil war in Nicaragua and El Salvador and violence and instability in Guatemala and Honduras.[145] The U.S. government was convinced that there were radical, anti-U.S. groups that were infiltrated and aided by communists.[146] The foreign policy of President Reagan was dominated by a virulent, "no holds barred" strain of anti-communism[147] involving covert CIA actions such as mining harbors and supplying arms to the Contras in Nicaragua, military involvement in El Salvador, and the military invasion of the tiny island of Grenada. The use of force as necessary in itself and as a way of maintaining the credibility of the U.S deterrent was a strongly held view of many influential senior foreign policy officials, e.g., Jeanne Kirkpatrick[148] and Henry Kissinger.[149]

Former President Bush and his national security advisor, Brent Scowcroft, in their book "A World Transformed,"[150] focus their attentions on the end of the Cold War but in the 566 pages make no reference to the English-speaking Caribbean. There are a few brief references to Nicaragua and Cuba in the context of the Cold War. While the book does not claim to be an all-encompassing overview of the foreign policy, that the Caribbean does not figure in the issues and events regarded as influencing the so-called transformation of the world is indicative of the region's low priority in U.S. foreign policy. Similarly, Secretary of State Warren Christopher in his 1998 book of his most important speeches has nothing to say about the ESC. In many instances, the Caribbean is simply subsumed in the phrase "Latin America and the Caribbean" while the discussion deals entirely with the large Latin American states as emerging markets for the United States Chairman of the Republican Party, Haley Barbour, while criticizing the Clinton Administration for treating Latin America and the Caribbean as a "secondary interest" in overall foreign policy, is guilty of the same oversight. In his discourse on country-specific policy priorities, he mentions Cuba and Haiti and Central America's need to be included in the North American Free Trade Agreement (NAFTA) to encourage and stabilize democracy.[151]

James Baker makes no mention of any of the countries of the ESC or the region as a whole in his memoirs of his tenure as Secretary of State during 1989 to 1993.[152] Warren Christopher, Secretary of State during the first Clinton Administration, included only two speeches on Latin America and the Caribbean in a volume dominated by the Middle East, Iraq, Bosnia, China, and Russia.[153] The tract on Latin America mentions Cuba but in the Caribbean, however, the restoration of democracy in Haiti is the theme of one address. This limited presence in the region, in the foreign policy agenda, is not surprising as the Clinton-Gore campaign

platform was dedicated almost entirely to domestic issues.[154] Christopher's biography[155] does not make mention of the Caribbean, not surprisingly since during his tenure he gave scant attention to the region.

Lowenthal is correct when he states that when "Latin American policy
considerations clash with other U.S. interests, as they often do, and
choices have to be made, improved relations with Latin America turn out
in practice to be a low-priority concern."[156] This assessment describes the
reality of the dilemma of the lack of sustained attention to the English-
speaking Caribbean by the United States. This lack of priority is so evident that it has come to characterize the thinking of non-government
entities interested in U.S. foreign policy. In offering proposals for U.S.
foreign policy for the twenty-first century, some leading think tanks over-
look the Caribbean and even neglect Latin America. The fixations continue to be Asia, in particular China, the former Soviet Union, in particular
Russia, the Middle East, and trade with Europe.[157] This mind set is illustrated by Sandy Berger of the National Security Council whose spirited
defense of Clinton's foreign policy and recommendations to the incoming
Bush Administration were that the "cornerstone" of national security
"remain" alliances with Europe, Asia, and "former great-power adversaries."[158]

PART III: JAMAICA'S FOREIGN POLICY

This section provides an introduction to Jamaica's foreign policy with the
motivations and capacity for foreign policy being dealt with in the first
section, which is followed by an overview of United States-Jamaica relations to set the stage for an examination of Jamaica's foreign policy towards the United States, which is outlined later in the chapter.

Motivation and Capacity for Foreign Policy

Jamaica has always been highly motivated to be very active in international affairs and hence has had an assertive, and at times aggressive
foreign policy. The motivation derives from the vulnerability of the economy both in terms of its acute dependence on imports of oil, raw materials, manufactured goods, and capital goods and its reliance on one or two
exports. The devastating impact of the increases in oil prices in the 1970s
illustrated the severe vulnerability of the economy. The economy is also
severely affected by inflation in prices in world markets particularly since
it is a price-taker because it is a small purchaser of goods and services.
There is a tendency for exports to be uncompetitive by global standards
because of (a) wage levels, which are high relative to other developing
country producers, e.g., bananas, sugar, (b) lack of economies of scale
due to small scale of production, e.g., manufacturing, sugar, (c) small

units of production experience lower levels of efficiency in all export sectors including tourism, (d) market structures that are monopolies, oligopolies, or imperfect do not generate the pressures that impel innovation and price sensitive production, and (e) the insulation from global competition until the 1980s by entrenched protectionism and import substitution industrialization policies.

Acute vulnerability certainly provided strong motivation to successive governments to pursue an active foreign policy even before the country attained its political independence. However what is more important to explaining the activism of leaders and governments is the self-confidence, even audacity, to confront and successfully challenge much more powerful governments, entities, institutions, and actors. This assertiveness emanates from the tradition of struggle against slavery and the colonial authorities, and the innate self-confidence, which is such an integral component of the Jamaican personality. The traditions, culture, and personality of Jamaicans are reflected in the attitude and conduct of its leaders and citizens in the goals and execution of the country's foreign policy. The proposition that culture, tradition, and personality of countries influence how they act in international affairs is neither new nor controversial. That the United States visualizes itself as the world's sheriff is not unrelated to its culture. Wills points tellingly to John Wayne being the number one movie star as late as 1995 as an indication of the adherence of Americans to the myths he portrayed in movies, particularly westerns.[159] The conviction that the United States has a "manifest destiny" that compels it to undertake a certain role in world affairs has been and still is pandemic in U.S. thinking in policy circles and in the wider society. Great Britain in an earlier era felt justified in its colonial policy because of the belief that it had been ordained to carry "civilization" to lesser mortals. Even the style and comportment of a nation is subject to the influence of culture, for example how West Indians play cricket[160] or how the Dutch way of playing soccer is related to the concept of space in their culture.[161]

The post of Minister of Foreign Affairs and Foreign Trade is one to which in general the most able and/or experienced persons were assigned; in fact the post is frequently combined with that of Deputy Prime Minister as was the case of Hugh Shearer in the Seaga government of 1980–1983. In some instances the Foreign Minister has been a former Prime Minister, e.g., Hugh Shearer, or later became Prime Minister, as was the case of P. J. Patterson. In David Coore, Prime Minister Michael Manley not only had an exceptional lawyer and economist but a life-long friend, confidante, and political colleague, and a former Deputy Prime Minister. They were supported in their work by a Foreign Service, which was regarded as an elite within the civil service because as a career it attracted the so-called "brightest and the best." Diplomatic representation benefited on many occasions from "political appointees" who were either accomplished outsiders, e.g., Dr. Lucille Mair,[162] pioneer in gender studies at the University of the West Indies and Dereck Heaven, a former member of parliament and minister of government, or distinguished civil servants, e.g., Sir Edgerton Richardson, former Financial Secretary and Don Mills, Head of the Central Planning Unit. Some of the political appointees were outstanding persons in their professions such as lawyers Douglas Fletcher and Alfred Rattray, both of whom served as ambassadors to the United States and OAS.

The example of those who have made an impact on international events is also an important ingredient in the attitude of Jamaican leaders and officials. The achievements of Marcus Garvey, his global reach and the international network of branches of the Universal Negro Improvement Association were a confidence booster and role model. Jamaicans (and other persons from the English-speaking Caribbean) were in the vanguard of movements for change in the United States and Europe from the early twentieth century.[163] No Black Nationalist or Black Power movement[164] is without debt to Garvey or any Third World Marxist untouched by Trinidadian C. L. R. James,[165] nor is St. Lucian W. Arthur Lewis' paternity of development economics in question.[166] Triumphs in sport, e.g., test cricket from the 1930s and track and field, starting with Herb McKinley's 1947 world record and continuing with gold medals in the 1948 Olympics inspired pride and confidence[167] and reinforced the "can do" attitude. The comparative ease with which Norman Manley negotiated changes to the royalty paid by the bauxite companies[168] and the granting of political independence from Great Britain were seen in Jamaica as a vindication of his skills rather than the desire of the British to relinquish their colonial role. An important aspect of the Jamaican assertiveness is the disposition to challenge authority, which is evident in so many facets of behavior that it must be regarded as a part of the Jamaican personality and culture.[169]

Nettleford points out that global developments require the top levels of political leadership to have the diplomatic and negotiating skills to deal with "outside powers" and this was a quality of Jamaican leaders from the era of Bustamante and Norman Manley. "Subsequent Prime Ministers and Ministers of External Affairs followed in their wake, bringing someone like Michael Manley in the Seventies to international prominence."[170]

The feeling that Jamaica could change the international circumstances that affect its economic development reached new heights of confidence with advent of Michael Manley. Manley could draw assurance from the fact that his father Norman had excelled at Oxford University and was awarded a medal for his service during World War I. He in turn had proven equal to the challenge at the London School of Economics and in the Royal Canadian Air Force. Manley was convinced that if Jamaica identified its best talent, which no doubt was world class, and planned and executed to the best of its ability and with the support of a fully briefed and mobilized country, it could achieve any objective. Jamaica at its best was a David for any Goliath cum IMF, multinational corporations, or U.S. government. No problem was incapable of solution: not managing developing country debt, not building a new international economic order, and not terminating apartheid. Furthermore he shared a conviction with his fellow Jamaicans that not only was everything in international politics and economics the concern of Jamaica but Jamaica must be involved and moreover could make a difference. Manley by his charisma and oratory unleashed a special sense of pride and self-assurance.[171]

A sober pragmatism and a depressed highly indebted economy tempered the orientation and style of the foreign policy of the "new" Manley government. An immediate priority was improving relations with the United States and the International Monetary Fund with which the Manley government of 1976–1980 had a troubled relationship. The need to rehabilitate relations with the IMF was even more urgent given the extent to which it had deteriorated during the Seaga regime. On a larger scale, relations with the United States were in disarray as the Republican administration of George Bush felt that Seaga had betrayed their trust and made off with a large sum of money lavished on him during the halcyon days of the first Reagan Administration. Cooperation with Congress had been poisoned by a land dispute between the Seaga government and John Rollins,[172] a wealthy and powerful Delaware-based businessman. Rollins, one of the largest donors to the Republican Party, nationally and in Delaware mobilized sympathetic support in both the House of Representatives and the Senate. Debt relief and foreign aid required Congressional approval but both would have been blocked pending resolution of the imbroglio with Rollins, who had substantial investments in hotel property dating back to the late 1960s. The task of creating a rapport with Bush was also made difficult by the fact that his return to the post of Prime Minister was "disturbing to many U.S. conservatives."[173]

There are two factors of critical importance to note in discussing Jamaica's foreign policy towards the United States. First, the fundamental reality of relations between the United States and Jamaica has been and still is the enormous asymmetry between them in size, economic development, and power. Second, Jamaica's foreign policy in several cases had similar goals to that of other states in the ESC and also was executed in collaboration with governments of the ESC acting as CARICOM.

The objectives of Jamaica's foreign policy towards the United States were to be left free to exercise its political independence, sovereignty, and right of self-determination in international affairs. More specifically it wished to be free of U.S. hegemony to the maximum extent possible and be able to pursue an independent foreign policy. This of course is an ideal with little chance of attainment but the degrees to which this was achieved were, and are, important. Whether free or constrained in foreign policy the most important goal for Jamaica was to promote economic development and the United States, as its main economic partner, in terms of a source of investment capital and imports and as an export market, must play a central part. Jamaica constantly sought improved access to the U.S. market, and increased private foreign investment, loans, aid, tourists, remittances, debt relief, and opportunities for migration and employment. Cooperation and assistance in economic development, the fight against drug trafficking, and in times of natural disasters were attributes Jamaica hoped for and sought in the foreign policy of the United States. While these motives and objectives remained the essential agenda over time, various administrations in Jamaica attempted to attain them in different ways.

The overriding concern of the United States has been the repercussion of events in the Caribbean for its national security variously defined as a changing amalgam of communism, migrants, drugs, and strategic raw materials. Economic interests were secondary as the economies of the ESC are small export markets and offer limited investment opportunities. Defined as its "backyard" the United States practiced unbridled hegemonic unilateralism despite the fact that for the most part governments in the region sought for partnership.

The primary interest of the ESC has been economic, acutely aware of their economic vulnerability. But the vulnerability of the small states of the ESC is more wide ranging. Prime Minister L. Erskine Sandiford of Barbados explains that "we are aware of the fragility and vulnerability of our microstates. Our vulnerability is manifold. Physically, we are subject to hurricanes and earthquakes; economically, to market decisions taken elsewhere; and now politically to the machinations of terrorists, mercenaries and criminals." [174] In an economic sense dependency was at an extreme in the smallest countries, e.g., in Dominica nearly all the economic activity is related to the export of a single primary product, bananas, to a single external market through a single multinational corporation. This is a situation aptly described by Prime Minister Kenny Anthony of St. Lucia as "the dependency of mono-cultural imperialism." [175]

The foreign policy of some small states is so obsessed with garnering foreign aid that they can best be described as "aid seeking economies." Patsy Lewis suggests that "Caribbean countries view their proximity to the United States as leverage in accessing financial resources. This meant adopting an anticommunist posture, particularly for Eastern Caribbean states" and "supporting the United States in international forums." [176] Unfortunately this has not yielded the amount of aid anticipated serving to prove that in dealing with the United States good behavior is not rewarded because it is expected. However, some spirit of self-determination has been exhibited by even the smallest and most needy states, e.g., although supporting the U.S. invasion of Grenada, the government of

Dominica's voting record in the UN in the same year differed from that of the United States.[177]

The political leaders of the region have been courageous in resisting insensitive policies and overbearing conduct by the United States, notably Michael Manley, Eric Williams, Forbes Burnham, and Maurice Bishop. The region has fearlessly pursued policy with which the United States disagrees and even attempted to discourage or reverse, e.g., relations with Cuba. The basis that has emboldened the ESC, is regional cooperation and solidarity. As early as 1947, Jamaica's Norman Manley called on the region to "create a large enough area, small although it will be in the face of the colossi who bestride the world today, but a large enough area to give us a voice and pull and power over those international affairs which in the long run determine the peace and prosperity" of the peoples of the region.[178]

There have been several instances of disagreement between the United States and the small states of the ESC dating back to the colonial period. One such was the renegotiation of the 1941 agreement for a military base in Chaguaramas in Trinidad.[179] In 1940, the United States exchanged "over-aged ships" with Britain for 99-year leases on naval or air bases in Antigua, the Bahamas, Guyana, Jamaica, St. Lucia, and Trinidad. Among the factors that contributed to the unnecessarily hostile disputes was the intransigent attitude of the United States claiming that the base was critical to defense of the Caribbean and indeed the South Atlantic[180] and insensitive to the fact that the area had been designated as the site for the capital of the West Indies Federation.

Security has been an issue in which the United States and the ESC have a long history of disagreement. The United States has always viewed the Caribbean Sea and the Panama Canal as an indispensable security zone. The United States has sought to secure this area by having bases in Cuba, Panama, Puerto Rico, Trinidad, and Jamaica and satellite and oceanographic facilities in these territories as well as Barbados and Antigua. The United States evinced no interest in having direct control over the British colonies in the Caribbean. In identifying and liquidating British assets to pay for armaments the United States made it clear that apart from bases in the Caribbean it wanted no territory. According to Secretary of the Treasury Morgenthau: "There is one thing I know that I can say Mr. Roosevelt (President Franklin D) that we don't want any of those islands . . . I know he doesn't want Jamaica, I know he doesn't want Trinidad and I know he doesn't want British Guiana."[181]

Bases in the Caribbean colonies were secured from Britain under the Destroyers—Bases Agreement of September 1940 and the Leased Bases Agreement of March 1941.[182] Under the "United States Defense Areas in the Federation of the West Indies," February 10, 1961, the United States agreed to return 80 percent of the land acquired in 1940 (900 acres in Antigua, 33,000 acres in Jamaica, and 21,000 in Trinidad). The expiration date of the original 99-year lease was changed from 2039 to 1977. This was only after a contentious and very unpleasant set of negotiations over Chaguaramas, which lasted from 1957 to 1961. Eric Williams described the conduct and positions of the U.S. government as colonialist and imperialist inimical to political independence and sovereignty.[183] In turn the United States at one time regarded Williams as "communist, racist and anti-American,"[184] but by the time of the Johnson Administration, Secretary of State Dean Rusk regarded him as merely "not always friendly."[185]

There have also been disagreements with Barbados, e.g., the St. Lucy oceanographic research facilities established in 1956 by the United States was returned to Barbados in March 1979 "after bitter words on both sides." There was a confrontation over CBI between the United States and Barbados because Barbados initially refused to furnish tax information on foreign investors but subsequently acceded to the CBI.[186] This type of resolute resistance to the United States is indicative of a self-confidence of countries whose leaders have always felt a capability in foreign affairs despite their small size. Prime Minister Errol Barrow of Barbados articulated this view as "Every state, however small, can play a useful part in international forums, a highly responsible role in the sub hemisphere to which it belongs and an important role in its immediate environment."[187]

There has been a long-standing suspicion, which has continued to the present, among many in the ESC region, about the "true" objectives of the U.S. policy. Dr. Eric Williams' study of history led him to the view that the United States had designs on the Caribbean from the early nineteenth century as part of its manifest destiny.[188] Prime Minister Eric Williams was always concerned about the imperialist[189] character of U.S. policy towards the ESC as he maintained that the United States had pursued "a policy to its so-called backyard, the Caribbean and Central America. As far back as 1898 the New York Times described the Caribbean Territories as 'the great American archipelago misnamed the West Indies.' Between 1893 and 1933 the United States intervened 30 times in Central America. One Senator saw the Caribbean population as part of the 'savage and senile peoples' whose control was America's manifest destiny. Letters to President Wilson in 1913 described Puerto Ricans as 'a race of mongrels of no use to anyone,' who should not be granted autonomy, and for whom 'a Governor from the South should be appointed."[190]

The National Security Council summed up the collective strategic interest of the United States and NATO in the West Indies in the following words: "The strategic location of the islands has caused the United States to establish on them certain military installations which contribute to the air and sea defenses of the Western Hemisphere. Some of the U.S. peacetime facilities on the islands are important as tracking stations for essential missile development work, while others are important to military training activities. In the event of war, certain of these installations will be important to the defense of the Panama Canal, the southern approaches to the United States, and the shipping routes between Latin and North America. Additionally, these facilities are important to the initial and continuing defenses of the continental United States."[191]

The attitude of the United States towards the ESC has not changed very much over the decades. Elliot Abrams, Assistant Secretary of State for Inter-American Affairs during the Reagan Administration, wrote as follows:

> American impressions of the Caribbean as a land of rum and beaches are belied by the region's past—and future—as an area of instability. While democracy is deeply rooted in a few countries, its hold is shaky at best in several others. Moreover, several island nations have economies so small and inefficient that they have little to export but their populations. The refusal of Bermudians to vote for independence last year may show that they, at least, have understood the point: In an increasingly troubled region, reliance on a foreign power for security and prosperity may be the most sensible form of nationalism. And the only available foreign power is the United States.[192]

Arrogance, paternalism, and racism have on many occasions resulted in poor U.S. diplomacy. Speaking of U.S. puppet Trujillo, Franklin D. Roosevelt quipped, "He may be a S.O.B. but he is our S.O.B."[193] Insensitivity and heavy-handedness have derailed many reasonable U.S. proposals, antagonized leaders, and undermined personal relations. In 1973, the normally deferential government of Jamaica declared the U.S. Ambassador, de Roulet, persona non grata, after he had intervened in domestic party politics in an attempt to influence the 1972 general elections. He was concerned about what Manley might do in regard to the U.S. multinational corporations in the bauxite industry. Levi recounts that de Roulet felt that then Prime Minister Shearer was "a well-dressed and courteous Negro" and "knew where his bread was buttered" and sought to boost his standing by arranging a meeting with President Nixon, "a highly unusual event in United States-Jamaican relations."[194] In the early 1980s, the Ambassador of the United States to the Eastern Caribbean, Frank Ortiz, told Prime Minister Bishop of Grenada that if Grenada developed close ties with Cuba it would "complicate" relations with the United States. He also alluded to the possible termination of U.S. aid,[195] a stance in keeping with thinking in Washington, which even considered imposing a blockade.[196] Bishop reciprocated with equal clumsiness in a public speech where he "warned" that "no one, no matter how mighty and powerful they are, will be permitted to dictate to the government and people of Grenada whom we can have friendly relations with and what kind of relations we must have with other countries. We are not in anybody's back yard."[197] This unsophisticated approach continues into the late 1990s. During the United States/Jamaica negotiations for a Ship

rider agreement, I had the temerity to point out to the chief U.S. negotiator that the agreement would have to be reciprocal, prompting, after an
incredulous silence, the unwitting reply: "no, it is not reciprocal."[198] He
was surprised by my declaration oblivious of the improbability of the air
wing of the Jamaica defense force pursuing.

Part of the explanation for the lack of sensitivity in the conduct of U.S.
foreign policy lies in the fact that the State Department allocates its best
staff to "trouble spots," and conversely the less able to areas like the ESC.
For example, a Carter Administration official described the staff of the
U.S. Embassy in Jamaica in the 1970s as "an assembly of misfits . . . if
someone was medically not in shape and needed to be close to home,
they would assign them to Jamaica."[199] On the other hand the ESC has
deployed its most able diplomats, many of whom were very influential
political appointees to serve in Washington, D.C. However relations with
the United States involve a multiplicity of interests, which are the responsibilities of different ministries especially in trade and financial matters.
In the case of Barbados the ministries of trade and finance have "dominated" foreign policy during the first 30 years of independence.[200] On the
whole effective execution of foreign policy is limited by the ability to
maintain only a few very small foreign missions.[201]

By 1950 the United States was very dependent on strategic raw materials and commodities such as rubber from colonies in Africa, Asia, and
the Caribbean.[202] This became an important consideration affecting U.S.
foreign policy in general[203] and policy on decolonization in particular,
and had implications for policy towards the Caribbean. Guyana and Suriname supplied 82 percent of United States imports of bauxite and alumina at the end of World War II[204] and Jamaica became a leading supplier
by the 1960s.[205] Secure access to critical raw materials has been an enduring factor in U.S. foreign policy not only because policymakers perceive it
to be in the national interest but also because of the political power
wielded by U.S. multinational corporations.[206]

The year 1959 was a "watershed" in United States-Caribbean relations
because of the Cuban revolution and the formation of the West Indies
Federation. The Cuban revolution placed the Caribbean firmly on the
Cold War agenda and hence the region received more attention and began to be viewed from the perspective of a vulnerable area close to the
border of the United States. This coincided with a major attempt by the
British Government to shed its colonies in the Caribbean region by forming a political federation of 10 small colonies.[207] Knight points out that
this policy was a "part of its decision to push modified self-government,
the British authorities revived the old idea of a regional confederation.
The idea had floated about the colonial office since the later part of the
nineteenth century."[208] However, as Gordon Lewis has pointed out "the
federation was the work, almost exclusively, of British officials and West
Indian politicians. There was little of a movement of enthusiastic popular

opinion behind it."[209] Despite the problems attendant on the federation, the United States welcomed the idea of a West Indies Federation as it was consistent with its stance on post-war decolonization. The United States supported a 10–15 year process of decolonization of the British Empire and this timetable was to be applied to the British West Indies.[210]

The federation was short-lived as even the negotiations on its forma-tion were protracted and acrimonious.[211] Divisive issues included the powers that the capital should exercise, the site of the Federal capital, and Jamaica's decision to build an oil refinery thus adversely affecting Trini-dad's exports to Jamaica. The internal political dynamics in Jamaica were a critical factor in the demise of the Federation,[212] as well as the lack of "a pervading consciousness of West Indian unity and nationhood" among the politicians or populace.[213] Eric Williams attributed the demise to the "centuries old inter–island jealousies, inept Federal leadership and the desire to pursue competitive rather than complementary strategies of economic development."[214]

The foreign policy of Jamaica and the ESC countries in the 1960s was dominated by the need to maintain preferential trade arrangements with Britain and the European Common Market, particularly for sugar and bananas. This preoccupation was central to the international relations of the region even in those countries whose economies were not dependent on these commodities as the most important sources of foreign exchange earnings, e.g., Jamaica, Guyana, and Trinidad and Tobago. Vaughan Lewis describes Jamaica's foreign policy as "relative passivity"[215] and Wiltshire-Brodber described this period of Trinidadian foreign policy as "conservative pragmatism" in which "the desire to conserve the econom-ic preferences from the colonial relationship was initially paramount. Even where Third World initiatives were made, they were used diplo-matically to bolster support for this relationship and remained largely symbolic."[216] The governments of the independent states of the ESC as-serted their opposition to apartheid in South Africa, banned all trade, and called for sanctions. Trinidad and Tobago voted with the majority of the international community to admit China to the United Nations although Barbados and Jamaica abstained. The region rallied solidly in support of Guyana and Belize against the spurious territorial claims of Venezuela[217] and Guatemala. None of these issues and developments had significant implications for relations with the United States.

The vulnerability of the small states of the ESC had long been recog-nized by the political leadership; hence shortly after the collapse of the political federation discussions began on economic integration arrange-ments. In May 1968, the twelve states formed the Caribbean Free Trade Association (CARIFTA) and subsequently deepened their integration by establishing the Caribbean Common Market and Community in 1972.[218] In addition to economic integration one of the fundamental objectives of the Treaty of Chaguaramas is "the coordination of the foreign policies of

Member States."[219] The Caribbean Development Bank was created in 1969.

In September 1961 at the height of the Cold War Jamaica began negotiating with Britain for independence. In this milieu Norman Manley, the leader of the Jamaican government delegation indicated that after independence Jamaica would be aligned with the West.[220] It is likely that this was motivated by the desire to forestall any resistance by the United States and Britain to independence. Shortly after Jamaica became independent in August 1962, the government through Prime Minister Alexander Bustamante declared, "I am for the West and the United States of America . . . I am for the West. I am against communism."[221] During the period 1960 to 1971, Jamaica's foreign policy was one of close alignment with the United States. *The Economist* magazine records that "Sir Alexander Bustamante has shown a characteristic lack of reserve in his gestures of friendship and trust towards the United States, inviting the establishment of a military base, among other things."[222] The United States had turned down the offer by Jamaica to have a military base, but in June 1963, the two countries signed a defense pact.[223] The position of the government represented the prevailing thinking in Jamaica at the time particularly among the leadership of the business community.[224] Based on a survey in the early 1960s, Bell reported that "the climate of opinion among Jamaican leaders was much more favorable in reaching a decision to align with the United States and Western powers than to reach a decision either to remain neutral or to align with the communist countries."[225]

Vaughan Lewis' description of Jamaica's foreign policy in the first decade of independence as "relative acquiescence and conformity to the American-dominated Western international arena"[226] is apt because there was some assertiveness. Within three months of attaining independence Jamaica came to attention in international affairs when Hugh Shearer, Minister of Foreign Affairs, in Jamaica's maiden address to the United Nations General Assembly suggested an international year for human rights.[227] The proposal was accepted and the UN designated 1968 as the International Year for Human Rights. Shortly after Jamaica voted against the United States in support of membership for China in the UN, Jamaica made vocal its positions on issues that did not abut frontally with the United States but that the United States would have viewed as a nuisance, e.g., support for UN membership for China, and the ending of apartheid in South Africa and colonialism in Africa. Jamaica was the first or among the first to impose a ban on the importation of goods from South Africa.

Jamaica's foreign policy changed dramatically between the 1960s and the 1970s and in a manner that the United States did not approve of. The 1970s were a period in which Jamaica experienced profound social change and a radicalization of politics emanating from both internal factors and international developments.[228] The milieu of the late 1960s was a confluence of insipient nationalism, nativistic black consciousness, and a resurgence of leftist political philosophies and a re-emergence of radical political activity. External influences imbricated and interpolated with national developments in a complex dialectic, for example, blending the ideas of Garvey, Black Power,[229] and Rastafarianism.[230] The legitimacy of the institutions and traditions of the Westminster model of democracy was being questioned or dismissed as the paraphernalia of "politricks" not politics.[231] The Michael Manley led People's National Party became the government of Jamaica in 1972 with convictions about social justice, restructuring the post-colonial economy into a self-reliant economy, and a non-aligned foreign policy.[232] There was a firm conviction that nationals or the government should partner foreign investors in the development process if Jamaica were to become a self-reliant economy. Jamaica's ambassador to the United States, Douglas Fletcher, speaking to U.S. businessmen in October 1972 explained: "the joint venture approach is the most appropriate mechanism for combining foreign capital and technology with Jamaican capital, human resources and materials" and "the joint venture approach is not related to a preconceived notion regarding the proportion of ownership which must be in local or foreign hands."[233]

A major issue in United States-Jamaica relations occurred over the renegotiation of tax agreements between the government of Jamaica and the U.S. multinational corporations in the bauxite industry. The Manley government was successful in increasing the tax take through the imposition of a production levy; however, the process was at times contentious. The 1974 annual report of the Embassy of Jamaica in Washington, D.C., recounts the episode as a difficult experience. The report[234] states that the relationship between the governments of Jamaica and the United States improved following the ouster in 1973 of the United States Ambassador de Roulet from Jamaica. On July 19, 1973, U.S. ambassador to Jamaica de Roulet in testimony to the Senate Committee on Foreign Relations claimed that he had made a "deal" with Manley that the United States would not intervene in the general elections in a way adverse to Manley and that if he became Prime Minister he would not nationalize the United States owned bauxite companies.[235] Manley denied categorically any such arrangement and demanded the recall of the U.S. ambassador. The negotiations conducted by the Bauxite Commission and the aluminum companies were the most important event and the Embassy was involved at various stages.

Prime Minister Manley visited Washington following his visit with Prime Minister Trudeau to meet with Secretary of State Kissinger. This meeting set the stage for the bauxite negotiations that followed shortly after. As a result of this meeting, the companies could not rely automatically on the U.S. government to pressure the government of Jamaica since the Prime Minister had received the assurances of Secretary Kissinger

that they would only take an interest in what was regarded as a "commercial negotiation." As the negotiations developed, faltered, and
reached an impasse, there were a series of exchanges between the two
governments; essentially, it was an exchange of information though, at
certain times, there was subtle pressure from the various parts of the
Administration. In an effort to counteract an unfavorable publicity campaign mounted by the companies, the government employed a public
relations consultant, A. F. Sabo Associates, who prepared in conjunction
with a firm of public relations consultants in Kingston, a kit on bauxite.
This was distributed to Congressmen, to Permanent Representatives at
the United Nations, Ambassadors to the White House and the OAS, journalists, and others. The Deputy Prime Minister spoke at a luncheon
hosted by the Ambassador to explain to a number of journalists the Jamaican position regarding the negotiations. Apart from the almost daily
contact with the Department of State, the Embassy met with select colum-
nists and Congressmen to explain Jamaica's position. This resulted in two
very positive columns in the *Washington Post* and the *Washington-Star
News*. One of the lead negotiators recalls that: "We knew some of the
companies approached them (the U.S. government) and tried to get them
to intervene and they refused" because of the "strategy by Manley. It
recognized the need to keep people informed and forestall any adverse
action."[236] The then Foreign Minister Senator Dudley Thompson recalls
that at every stage of the process the Jamaican government kept its U.S.
counterpart fully briefed and therefore differences between the two sides
did not lead to animosity.[237] Girvan in noting the lack of acrimony between the two sides pointed to the irony that the new arrangements did
not reduce dependency on the aluminum multinational corporations and
argues that this brought into being a new alliance between corporate
managers and "buro-political managers" of the government of Jamaica.[238] The willingness of Jamaica to take on the multinational corporations in the bauxite industry whatever the outcome certainly demonstrates what I regard as a prominent and distinctive feature of the Jamaican personality, namely audacity. The components of this behavior are
the confidence that anything can be achieved regardless of the obstacles,
unbridled aggression, and a willingness to suffer the consequences of the
actions taken. This quality when combined with ingenuity, information,
and education can produce surprising results.

Between 1972 and 1980 when Michael Manley was Prime Minister,
Jamaica's foreign policy became one of non-alignment[239] and the advocacy of the new international economic order (NIEO), neither of which
found favor with the United States. As early as 1970, Manley felt that
Jamaica needed to overcome its "insularity" in foreign affairs.[240] Manley's foreign policy is best described as one of concentric circles. (a) Economic and political cooperation begins most logically and naturally
amongst one's neighbors,[241] hence the first priority for alignments were

CARICOM[242] and Caribbean neighbors such as the Dominican Republic, Haiti, and Cuba. (b) Beyond the region natural areas of cooperation are the African, Caribbean, and Pacific countries with which Jamaica participated in various agreements such as the Lomé agreement.[243] (c) After the ACP group the next wider circle is the Group of 77 (G77) and the Non-Alignment Movement.[244] There was concern throughout the Caribbean about the advisability of pursuing a non-aligned foreign policy and concerns about whether this would jeopardize traditional allies such as the United States.[245] (d) The socialist block countries were potential allies in certain areas of our foreign policy objectives and they represented a critical element in the balance of forces and could help neutralize "the raw power of economic imperialism."[246] Manley believed very strongly that Third World countries faced a common development dilemma, which derived from differences in power, wealth, and economic development between themselves and the developed countries. He explained that "the rationale of the Third World is not a matter of ideology or politics but a matter of economic conditions . . . those who are of a similar economic condition and similarly disadvantaged must make common cause."[247]

Jamaica joined the Organization of American States in 1969 and attended the Third Conference of Heads of States and Governments of the Non-Aligned Movement in 1970 as a full member, but was represented by a low level delegation.[248] Manley felt that Jamaica should "seek to avoid being sucked into the East/West polarization and play our part in the building of a third, non-aligned political force."[249] In October 1973, in the context of the Arab/Israeli War, members of the Organization of Petroleum Exporting Countries (OPEC) raised the price of oil and imposed an oil embargo on certain Western countries that were particularly supportive of Israel. Ambassador Mills explains that this "demonstration of the potency of the 'oil weapon' set the stage for the issuing of the challenge by Third World countries by way of the demand for the New International Economic Order (NIEO), these countries believing that they had now developed the necessary solidarity and leverage."[250]

The relationship between Jamaica and the United States improved with the assumption to office of the Carter Administration. In 1977, the Carter Administration took a number of steps to give Manley its blessing and reverse the acrimony of the recent past. Rosalynn Carter, the U.S. ambassador to the United Nations, the assistant secretary of state for inter-American affairs, and a host of lesser officials visited Kingston. The practice of using Caribbean ambassadorships as payoffs for campaign contributions was ended and a career foreign service officer, Loren Lawrence, was named to Jamaica. Manley signed a loan agreement with the International Monetary Fund (IMF) and began the painful process of deflating his economy. Carter responded with a promise of increased aid, to be channeled through a collective effort of donor-countries to help the Caribbean as a whole and Jamaica in particular. At the end of 1977, Manley was warmly received at the White House.[251] The Carter Administration "exerted pressure on the IMF. . . . Andrew Young went directly to Carter on this and let the IMF know informally that the United States wanted a favorable agreement for Jamaica."[252] Andrew Young visited Jamaica and the Manley government received development aid from the United States in June 1978. Stephens and Stephens observed that "by mid-1979 a growing concern in the Carter Administration and in Congress about developments in the region (that is, Nicaragua, El Salvador, Grenada), along with the ascendancy of the Brzezinski wing and its 'get tough on Communism' line, also affected the relations with Jamaica."[253] Manley's visit to Moscow in 1979 appeared to provide credence to the so-called leftward drift of his party and government.

Manley's leadership and Jamaica's activism in the Non-Alignment Movement,[254] G77, the International Bauxite Association (IBA),[255] and the debate over the NIEO incurred the wrath of the United States. The IBA was viewed by some as a "new OPEC in bauxite."[256] Indeed, it was a speech at the Non-Aligned Movement conference in Cuba in 1979 that was the "last straw" for the United States. During the Havana speech of 1979, Manley had indicated support for the pro-independence movement in Puerto Rico. Ambassador Alfred Rattray, Jamaica's Ambassador to the United States, recalls that this created "difficulties."[257] Manley himself recalled that the United States was "very upset by this speech,"[258] perhaps "consternation"[259] might be a more apt description. Manley's daughter and biographer records "my father always felt that it was his refusal to oblige Washington and remain neutral on this issue (Cuba's involvement in the war in Angola) which earned him the enmity of senior American policy makers, not only jeopardizing any hope of aid, but triggering the CIA's destabilization tactics on the island."[260] This came against a background of growing concern and displeasure by the United States at Jamaica's relations with Cuba.

In 1973, Jamaica established full diplomatic relations with Cuba. Cubana airline began weekly air service to Jamaica in 1974, Manley visited Cuba in 1975, and Castro visited Jamaica in 1977. Relations with Cuba were as part of a program of expanded economic relations with socialist countries.[261] The U.S. government repeatedly expressed concern about Jamaica's relations with Cuba and while not asking specifically to downgrade relations with Cuba they expressed their displeasure.[262] Perhaps the incident that soured U.S. relations with Jamaica was Jamaica's public support for Cuban troops sent to Angola in 1975. Manley recalls that: "Jamaica took the position that the Cuban troops invited by the Angolan government were legitimate. This obviously incensed elements in the U.S. administration. From that moment relations with the United States became increasingly strained."[263] In late 1975, U.S. Secretary of State Henry Kissinger visited Jamaica ostensibly for a vacation and held unofficial talks with Manley during which he warned Manley not to go ahead with recognition of the MPLA in Angola and support for Cuba's assistance to the MPLA. Manley was affronted and refused.

Payne has suggested that the "gains attained were massively outweighed by the consequential loss of support from traditional sources. Nowhere was this truer than in the case of Cuba. Whatever tangible benefits to Jamaica resulted from Cuban aid, there can be no doubt about the negative net effect of the close ties that were established. In U.S. government circles Cuba's relationship with Jamaica was perceived as part of a conscious Cuban design to spread the influence of communism with the Caribbean. Alternative explanations, couched in the language of an honorable solidarity between under-developed countries, were regarded as naïve at best and a deliberate deception at the worst reckoning." [264] The U.S. unwillingness to listen to and try to understand views like those enunciated by the Manley government has been described as "self-inflicted deafness." [265]

Jamaica's Ambassador to the United Nations, Don Mills became Chairman of the Group of 77 for 1977–1978; however, this reflected the esteem in which he was held rather than a strategy planned by Jamaica. Nevertheless it provided visibility and influence to Jamaica. Jamaica's leadership role was highlighted further by P. J. Patterson, Minister of Industry and Tourism who was the leading negotiator for the African, Caribbean, and Pacific (ACP) countries with the European Economic Community for the Lomé Convention. Dudley Thompson, the Foreign Minister, spearheaded the establishment of the Law of the Sea Conference and Jamaica was elected to the Security Council of the United Nations.

Jamaica's relations with the United States were aggravated by a vicious campaign of misinformation in the local and U.S. news media. One of the most vulgar articles of this genre appeared in *Newsweek* in February 1977. "I recently talked to senior intelligence men in Britain, France and Venezuela, to non-CIA sources in the United States and — in Jamaica itself — to former Special Branch intelligence officials recently fired by Manley. These sources claim that Fidel Castro's grand design calls for a Marxist axis running across the Caribbean from Guyana to Jamaica to Havana. Along with the talk of re-rapprochements with the United States, Castro's agents are steadily building their influence in Kingston. Cuba has the biggest embassy in town, and two-thirds of its staff are said to be DGI agents. Cuban airliners shuttle in and out at all hours, loading and unloading crates and people with no questions asked and no records kept." . . . "Ever since Manley returned starry-eyed from a 1975 visit to Cuba, he has relied heavily on Castro's aid and advice. Under Cuban guidance he has moved to reduce the role of private enterprise." Whether Manley intends it or not, Jamaica could become the next country to go to Marxist. [266]

It was widely believed that the Central Intelligence Agency (CIA) was involved in trying to prevent Manley from being re-elected in 1976 or to remove him from office,[267] especially after former CIA agent Philip Agee[268] publicly claimed that there were 9 CIA agents operating in Jamaica as officers of the U.S. embassy. Manley attributed the involvement of the CIA to "punishment for our support of Cuba's defense of Angola against South Africa."[269]

Tension between the United States and Jamaica had its origin both in the displeasure over the foreign policy of the Manley government and domestic policy following the PNP's declaration in late 1974 that it was committed to democratic socialism. Although it was basically a form of Fabian socialism it was accompanied by ambiguous and at times inflammatory rhetoric, e.g., the PNP's Principles and Objectives stated that "Sovereignty over the national economy is a fundamental pre-condition for complete national independence. To achieve this, our natural resources, the banking and financial system and foreign trade must be brought under the national control."[270] What national control meant was open to widely differing interpretations from private ownership by Jamaicans to state ownership. The same publication spoke of "Social ownership and/or control of the means of production, distribution and exchange"[271] and explained "Social ownership though fundamental, is not the only basis for the exercise of social control. Control can be exercised directly by the people through co-operative and other participatory institutions and indirectly by the State acting on behalf of the working people or by worker participation in private enterprise."[272]

The economic strategy that accompanied the PNP's democratic socialism and the aspirations for a non-aligned foreign policy, encountered difficulties because Jamaica was compelled to avail itself of borrowing from the International Monetary Fund (IMF). In 1977 Jamaica entered into an IMF stabilization program and when this collapsed it agreed to an Extended Fund Facility (EFF) in 1978. The EFF, which is a three-year agreement, was interrupted in late 1979 when Jamaica did not meet the conditionality.[273] The rationale and policy measures of the IMF programs were in many respects in conflict with economic objectives and policies of the Manley administration[274] and foreclosed the option to pursue a certain type of development strategy.[275] After much debate the PNP government in March 1980 decided not to renegotiate the stabilization program with the IMF, but pursued its own stabilization policy without funding from the IMF. Manley decided to call a general election in October 1980 to allow the country to decide on a return to IMF policies or to pursue what became known as a "Non-IMF Path." The draconian austerity resulting from the IMF programs contributed significantly to the erosion of support for the Manley government.[276] The PNP suffered a massive defeat in the general election resulting in Seaga and the JLP becoming the government. Of those voting for the JLP, 31 percent indicated that their main reason was economic hardship and 26 percent cited fear of communism.[277]

Newly elected Prime Minister Edward Seaga immediately declared his fidelity to the United States: "The Jamaican electorate in an historic decision on October 30, 1980 by the widest margin of votes in our political history, laid to rest the body of democratic socialism in Jamaica as the deceased client of the Cuban state, as a proxy for Marxist ambitions and intentions in the area."[278] Seaga lost no time in returning "Jamaica's foreign policy to the unalterable pro-West position of earlier JLP government" remarked a former diplomat.[279] The pro U.S. policy was in large measure motivated by raw opportunism as Payne explains that the "Seaga government's rabidly anti-Cuban politics cannot be properly understood without grasping the broader thinking, which did underlay the crudity of some of the gestures. This was to demonstrate to the U.S. government the sincerity and extent of its commitment to the fight against communism in the Caribbean. The quid pro quo was to be the provision of sufficient U.S. economic assistance to prevent the re-emergence of socialist politics in Jamaica or any other part of the region."[280] Seaga lost no time in suggesting a large injection of U.S. aid, indeed in November 1980, he called for a Mini-Marshall Plan for the Caribbean. The concept was discussed in July 1981 at a conference in the Bahamas, involving the U.S. Secretary of State and the foreign ministers of Canada, Mexico, and Venezuela. The meeting broke up in disarray because of differences over whether assistance should take the form of trade or aid, how aid could be provided, and whether Cuba, Nicaragua, and Grenada should be excluded.[281] The attempt by the United States to include Canada, Colombia, Mexico, Venezuela, and even Trinidad[282] as donors was unsuccessful. A modified concept became the Caribbean Basin Initiative, the centerpiece of Reagan's policy towards the Caribbean and Central America. It generated considerable enthusiasm among those salivating at the prospect of foreign aid and expectations of increased exports to the U.S. market. Others were skeptical and even cynical; for example, Manley saw it as a manifestation of a U.S. policy of global bilateralism, which "explicitly discriminates between the members of the region in accordance with current perceptions of political conformity."[283]

In foreign policy circles in Washington, D.C., the widely held view of the role of Cuba in the Caribbean was expressed by a 1980 report of the Council for Inter-American Security, which saw the Caribbean as "the soft underbelly" of the United States: "there remains the glaring problem of the Soviet Union's growing military and intelligence presence in Cuba . . . Cuba at some point must be held liable for working with the Soviets on a successful policy of subversion and destabilization in the hemisphere. At the same time, we must shore up our remaining friends in the area and carry out, for once, some preventive measures."[284] The Reagan Administration provided over $.5 billion in aid to Jamaica, indeed during 1981 and 1982 Jamaica received more U.S. aid than during the years 1946 to 1980.[285] Reagan also sought to boost private foreign investment in Jamaica by asking David Rockefeller, the chairman of Chase Manhattan Bank to lead a committee of senior business executives to promote investment in Jamaica. The much-heralded committee commenced work in March 1981 but investment remained tardy. The paucity of investment was compounded by the tapering off of U.S. aid as skepticism increased in Washington, D.C., over Seaga's unwillingness to stick to IMF prescribed stabilization programs. In late 1986 the U.S. import quota for Jamaican sugar was reduced.[286]

The differences between Seaga and the IMF were a direct consequence of the deflationary impact of the IMF policy measures including devaluation, tight monetary policy, cuts in fiscal expenditure, increased taxation, and lay-offs in the public sector during the early 1980s. Between 1983 and 1985 real wages fell by 17 percent and the share of wages and salaries in national income plummeted from 62 percent to 54 percent.[287] By the mid-1980s the Reagan Administration had become disillusioned with the Seaga government, which it had hoped would become a model of private sector–led growth in juxtaposition to the Cuban model. Assistant Secretary of State for International Affairs, Elliott Abrams is reported to have warned Seaga to "straighten up and fly right."[288] Jamaica's economic malaise continued and by 1988 the United States no longer regarded Jamaica its "most committed client state"[289] as a viable model; this disenchantment was compounded by the fact that "the Caribbean was no longer a U.S. foreign policy priority."[290]

A major rift, which was not repaired for many years, developed between the countries of the English-speaking Caribbean that were members of CARICOM over whether to request and/or support U.S. military intervention in Grenada in 1983.[291] The episode was precipitated by a military coup against the government of Maurice Bishop during which Bishop and some members of his government were brutally murdered. A self-proclaimed Marxist faction within the New Jewel Movement seized state power, an unprecedented event in the history of a region renowned as peaceful and with an unbroken record of electoral democracy. The Governor General of Grenada requested help from the CARICOM states, Britain, and the United States to restore order and democracy. The Organization of Eastern Caribbean States (OECS), which consisted of the eight smallest states, invited the United States to invade Grenada. The CARICOM governments were split over what action to take. With Eugenia Charles in the lead, Dominica, Barbados, and Jamaica decided to take part in a military intervention and sent troops to do peacekeeping duties following the U.S. military invasion. Guyana, Trinidad and Tobago, Belize, and the Bahamas abstained and it was later revealed that the supporting governments had knowledge of and had agreed to the U.S. invasion.[292] Manley and the PNP publicly denounced the U.S. invasion as

Manley saw it as unnecessary, cynically motivated, unprincipled, and compromising[293] to Caribbean sovereignty.[294] The United States had long been dismayed by the construction of an international airport by Cuba, relations with North Korea, Libya, and Iraq, economic aid from the Soviet Bloc,[295] and the rhetoric and policies of the Bishop regime.[296] The foreign policy of the PRG was intended to support the pursuit of a "non-capitalist path" of development, an ill-defined concept even in theory, and would have been extremely difficult in the most favorable international political circumstances, which the early 1980s certainly was not.[297]

Ironically, the longest standing radical regime in the ESC, the government of Forbes Burnham was tolerated because the opposition party was led by an avowed and unrepentant Marxist-Leninist, Cheddi Jagan. The United States had engineered the removal of Jagan from political office, and while not comfortable with Burnham, overlooked his policies including foreign policy that was "frequently in conflict"[298] with those of the United States, e.g., non-alignment, state control of the economy and relations with close Cuba, China, Libya, and the Soviet Union. The Burnham regime supported Castro in Cuba, the Sandinistas in Nicaragua, Bishop in Grenada, and the Palestinian Liberation Organization and denounced Israel.[299]

While Grugel is correct in recognizing that in the states of the Caribbean Basin "decision-making internally, political and economic, is permeated with U.S. influence,"[300] the ESC has asserted its independence. The ESC have been friendly towards the United States and in many instances have been allies; however, the United States has frequently expressed its disappointment with the lack of fidelity to U.S. policy objectives, e.g., in voting with the United States. Taking 1983 as an illustration, the voting convergence was 40 percent for Barbados and Trinidad and Tobago, 50–60 percent for the other countries, and 70–90 percent for St. Lucia.[301] The U.S. government officials found it hard to contain their annoyance at the unwillingness of ESC governments to adhere to U.S. positions on international issues, but it was effrontery beyond the limits of tolerance when leaders in the region criticized the United States. For example, when the U.S. ambassador issued a "dire warning" to Bishop's Peoples Revolutionary Government about relations with Cuba, the microstate of Grenada publicly rebuked the United States. "We do not recognize the right of the United States of America to instruct us on whom we may develop relations with . . . rudeness and meddling in our affairs and no one, no matter how mighty and powerful they are, will be permitted to dictate to the government and people of Grenada."[302]

A new security issue in U.S.-ESC relations emerged during the late 1980s, an issue that would assume increasing importance; that issue was drug trafficking. As drug use and abuse increased in the United States, politicians and government officials were forced by public opinion to devote more attention to both the demand and supply sides of the drug

scourge. Naturally, the United States focused more resources on preventing narcotics from entering the United States and part of that stepped-up
campaign was preventing or at least reducing marijuana and cocaine
being transshipped from South America through the Caribbean Basin.
Efforts were also directed at the elimination or reduction of marijuana
grown in several countries of the ESC. Symbolic of this focus on drug use
and drug trafficking was the establishment of the annual drug cooperation program in 1986. The United States found cause for concern in fact
that the ESC was an area that produced marijuana, through which cocaine was smuggled, and where some governments were struggling to
cope. This was compounded by suspicions that some governments and/
or some government officials were compromised or actively involved in
or deliberately tolerating the drug trade. Several Ministers of Government in the ESC were suspected by the United States of aiding and abet-
ting drug dealers, e.g., Lynden Pindling, Prime Minister of the Bahamas,
a country that was estimated to be the source of 40 percent of the cocaine
reaching Florida from South American sources.[303] The view that there
were corrupt government officials in the ESC was reinforced when in
September 1985 the Chief Minister and two other Ministers were convicted in Florida and a former Minister of Belize were convicted in North
Carolina.[304] The globalization of drug trafficking inevitably encompassed
the small states of the ESC with a resulting internationalization of corruption and violence.[305] In this milieu, Miami not Havana was the source of
subversion and security threats in the Caribbean.

By the end of the 1980s Jamaica like the rest of the ESC was confronting a new and rapidly changing international situation in which traditional relations with large powers such as the United States and Britain
had evolved beyond the original rationale. These relations were about to
be restructured unilaterally and the governments of the ESC urgently
needed to rethink old assumptions and develop new economic strategies
and fresh modes of mediating the encounter with the new economic and
geo-political trends. Relations with the former colonial power had certainly witnessed a marginalization from lingering post-colonial guilt.
Gonzales speaks of relations that developed as having reached "a pla-
teau"[306] and Pastor and Fletcher call for "the United States and the Caribbean to contemplate new forms of economic and political association."[307]
Greene warns of the necessity "to objectively evaluate the role and future
of regional integration as a mechanism for peace and security."[308] This
recognition of the need for change in international relations was occur-
ring when the integration movement in the ESC was at a low ebb because
of wide differences in economic development strategies and foreign policies.

Michael Manley became prime minister for the third time when the
PNP won the 1989 general election. His goals and convictions remained
the same but he put himself and the PNP through an intensive and com-

prehensive re-think of the means to achieve their objectives. As he put succinctly: "The world has changed. Jamaica has changed. And I think I have changed."[309] The advent of George Bush to the presidency in the United States ushered in a more sophisticated and nuanced approach to foreign policy, which provided an atmosphere in which Manley and Jamaica could reposition themselves. The rapprochement that was achieved might not have occurred during the "anti-communist monotheism" of the Reagan era.

During the course of the 1990s U.S. policy in the Americas was one of undulation and interaction between unilateralism and multilateralism, and might best be described as "multi-bilateralism."[310] Dominguez, however, argues that "the relative balance" between unilateral and multilateral actions in the Americas had shifted during the Bush and Clinton Administrations towards multilateralism. A measure of the decline of U.S. hegemony in global affairs and the tampering influence of incipient multilateralism in the Inter-American system was the invasion of Haiti in 1994 because the United States sought the approval of the United Nations before taking military in Haiti. This was the first time that this has happened. Dominquez points out that they have been shifted by the United States towards "hemispheric multilateralism" in the 1990s, which he attributes to this strategy being more cost-effective,[311] i.e., reduced bilateral foreign aid and greater reliance on multilateral and hemispheric financial institutions such as the World Bank and the Inter-American Development Bank. Nye has argued that the increasing resort to multilateralism in U.S. foreign policy was inevitable given the relative decline in all forms of power other than military; indeed on a growing number of issues such as international financial instability, climate change, and drug smuggling the United States cannot go it alone.

The global economy and the international political framework, which have existed since World War II, are in an advanced stage of metamorphosis. The speed and the profundity of the changes involved in globalization[312] have been so dramatic that most people have not realized that the world is not changing; it has changed. This transformation ushers in a new era, and those countries that are slow to adjust and adapt to the new economic environment will be progressively marginalized from the mainstream of global economic activity.[313] The global changes are not simply a change in the weather; they constitute a change in climate.

The nature and conduct of international relations has also been altered profoundly during the last two decades. The post-World War II political architecture collapsed with the end of the Cold War, leaving the United States as the single superpower. The implosion of the Soviet Union, the fragmentation of Eastern Europe, the rise of the newly industrialized economies in Asia and Latin America, and intensifying tri-polar economic rivalry with the United States, Japan, and the EU, have combined to change the dynamics of international affairs. In the immediate future, international relations will be more complex because of diversity and proliferation of political actors, the evolution of governance in response to the erosion of the sovereignty of the nation-state, and the need for new forms of management of the global economy.

The strategic importance of the ESC including Jamaica to the United States and Europe has declined in recent years.[314] This is a reflection of the end of the Cold War, and the fact that the region's principal exports of agricultural products and critical raw materials, e.g., sugar, bananas, and bauxite, are no longer as important to the United States and the EU. These products are readily available from other regions and in some cases at lower prices. The security concerns of the United States have changed dramatically in the post-Cold War era; current priorities include the Middle East, China, Iraq, and North Korea, as well as the rehabilitation of the Soviet Union and Eastern Europe. Unlike those countries, the ESC is characterized by well-entrenched and stable democracies, so that despite its proximity, it has received less attention from the United States.

U.S. policy towards the ESC in the Clinton era was based on the template of the Miami Summit of the Americas objectives and processes, which reflect a new hemispheric multilateralism. The Summit was proposed in December 1993 by the United States and the hemisphere was mobilized between January and June 1994. The two previous summits were held in 1956 and 1967 but had little lasting impact. The Miami Summit contained 23 initiatives and plan of action, and set in motion the Free Trade Area of the Americas.[315] This process was reviewed and commitments renewed at the Second Summit of the Americas in Santiago, Chile in 1998. The Summit represents not a new departure in U.S. policy towards Latin America and the Caribbean but an approach based more on multilateralism than on the traditional hegemonic unilateralism. The objectives of U.S. policy remained basically those of the past, namely security and economic, updated to take account of the end of the Cold War, resurrection of electoral democracy, and transnational crime[316] centered on drug trafficking. However, the Summit was a triumph for those in the Clinton Administration who pushed to place the region on the U.S. foreign policy agenda. This was a not inconsiderable achievement because as Feinberg points out "lacking in strong bureaucratic constituencies, free of major conflict, and facing the ever-present anti-hemispheric forces, Latin America was not a strong candidate for presidential attention." Alas, more so for the Caribbean except for the so-called "hot potatoes" of Cuba and Haiti.[317] The United States-CARICOM Summit in 1996 was a belated response to pressure from disgruntled governments in the Caribbean and Central America (similar summits was held at about the same time). The United States-CARICOM meeting of 1996 sought to balance the security interests of the United States with the economic concerns of the ESC leaving both parties less than satisfied.[318]

JAMAICA'S FOREIGN POLICY TOWARDS THE
UNITED STATES IN THE 1990S

The Following Issues Dominated U.S.-Jamaica Relations During the 1990s

Enhancement of the CBERA

The United States is the largest trading partner and source of capital flows of the CARICOM. CBI nations are a significant market for U.S. exports: in 1999, U.S. exports to CBI countries totaled $19.8 billion, 333 percent more than in 1995 and represents about 3 percent of total U.S. exports. It is estimated that about 50 cents of each dollar spent in the Caribbean Basin is spent back in the United States compared with only 10 cents of each dollar spent in Asia. In 1995 Jamaica purchased 75 percent of its imports from the United States. The Caribbean Basin is in aggregate now the tenth largest export market for the United States, surpassing other U.S. trading partners such as France. Presently, the United States/ Caribbean relationship supports more than 400,000 jobs in the United States and many more throughout the Caribbean.

The Caribbean Basin Initiative came into effect in 1983 by the enactment of the Caribbean Basin Economic Recovery Act (CBERA). Subsequently, in 1990 the Caribbean Basin Economic Recovery Expansion Act (CBEREA) added several improvements and made the CBERA into a permanent program. In May 2000 the U.S. House of Representatives and the Senate passed the United States-Caribbean Basin Trade Partnership ACT (CBTPA) as part of the Trade and Development Act of 2000 and President Clinton signed it into law on May 18, 2000. The bill, which became effective on October 1, 2000, represents an enhancement of access to the U.S. market, in particular, the textile provisions and those for other products excluded under the CBERA. The duration of these provisions will be for eight years ending in September 2008.

The NAFTA undermined the benefits of the CBERA because Mexico enjoyed more favorable access to the U.S. market. This placed the small, undiversified economies of CBI countries at a competitive disadvantage in terms of access for apparel exports to the United States. The preferential access to the U.S. market provided to Mexico under the NAFTA compounded the advantages that Mexico already enjoyed, i.e., inexpensive labor, cheap energy, lower transportation costs, and economies of scale. The progressive lowering of tariffs and removal of quotas for Mexico has caused a reduction in some of the Caribbean Basin's most valuable exports, because quotas and tariffs limited CBI apparel exports. Mexico's share of total U.S. apparel imports increased from 4.2 percent in 1993 to 11.0 percent in 1997, while U.S. imports from Jamaica, by far the largest CARICOM supplier, declined from $531 million in 1995 to $422 million in 1998. Some existing productive capacity was lost in the region as many factories have closed and relocated to Mexico. Imports from other CARI-COM countries stagnated or declined or ceased altogether, compared to the pre-NAFTA period when imports from CARICOM countries were increasing.

The new legislation was a significant step towards parity of market access between Mexico and the CBI countries, particularly as it related to apparel. This includes the immediate elimination of duties and quotas on apparel and textile luggage products made from fabrics wholly formed and cut in the United States of U.S. yarns (807A), or from fabrics wholly formed in the United States of U.S. yarns, cut in countries covered by the CBI 809. HR 434 also provided tariff treatment under rules of origin identical to NAFTA for goods previously excluded, i.e., footwear, tuna, petroleum products, and watches and watch parts.

In July 2000, the USTR announced that CBI countries would have to meet certain eligibility criteria in order to be considered for trade benefits and report on such activity by October 2, 2000. The eligibility criteria covered a range of issues including: (a) The country's demonstrated commitment to WTO Uruguay Round Agreements; (b) The status of government policy towards workers and workers' rights; (c) The country's commitment to participate in negotiations toward the completion of FTAA negotiations; (d) The extent to which the country had taken steps to become a party to and implement the Inter-American Convention Against Corruption; and (e) contribute to efforts in international to develop and implement international rules in transparency in government procurement.

Having to meet eligibility criteria was worrying to most CBI governments because it appeared to be an attempt by the United States to push a parallel political agenda. All CBI countries were named as beneficiaries on October 2, 2000. However discussions continued between the CBI states and the U.S. government on implementation issues.

In April 1999, prior to the Financial Stability Forum (FSF) and Financial Action Task Force (FATF) reports, financial advisories were issued by the United States and the United Kingdom against Antigua and Barbuda. The U.S. Treasury also issued an advisory against the Bahamas in July citing deficiencies in their legal, supervisory and regulatory systems. These countries were deemed to be tax havens with harmful fiscal regimes and serious deficiencies in counter money laundering systems. These actions led to a barrage of adverse media coverage. Ironically, money laundering is not confined to offshore financial centers, as all banking systems are vulnerable to this scourge. The concerns, which centered on money laundering, have since been addressed by strengthening investigative and regulatory authorities. Subsequently the UK advisory was modified but the United States has not announced any alterations to its advisory.

The government of Jamaica was committed to fighting transnational crime and has implemented far-reaching legislation to counteract money laundering. The United States has played and must continue to cooperate in building the capacity to meet this challenge. Jamaica in spite of limited resources has implemented several administrative and legislative measures in its endeavor to ensure that its financial system is insulated as far as possible from criminal elements but will require technical assistance from the United States and the OECD countries.

Maintaining the Level of U.S. Aid

Since the 1960s, the United States has supported the process of structural adjustment, economic reform, trade liberalization, and economic growth in the ESC countries. U.S. foreign aid has played an important role in the expansion of physical infrastructure, the improvement of institutional capacity, and the training of human resources in the Caribbean. During the 1980s, U.S. development assistance to the region averaged $200 million per annum. Since then there has been a sharp reduction. For evidence of this one has only to look at U.S. foreign assistance to Jamaica, which declined from $165.6 million in 1985 to approximately $15 million per annum since 1995. The ESC governments view this trend as unfortunate and unwise since development assistance has and continues to contribute to supporting private sector-led growth and investment. The United States has been a vital source of funding for the following programs: facilitating economic liberalization; promoting institution-building and public sector efficiency; supporting debt reduction; providing assistance to the social sectors to cushion the effects of economic adjustment on the poor; improving natural resource management; assisting in efforts to combat the international narcotics trade; funding environmental protection; disaster relief; and investment promotion. Declining U.S. assistance may negatively affect Jamaica's capacity to carry out these programs at a continued high level.

Debt Relief

The servicing of a large external debt can cripple the economic growth of developing countries because it uses scarce foreign exchange, constrains fiscal expenditure, and reduces import capacity. Jamaica experienced debt problems during the late 1970s and 1980s and received debt relief from various debt restructuring exercises, e.g., the Paris Club and via new instruments, e.g., debt swaps. Following the 1990 economic summit in Houston longer maturities and more generous grace periods were extended to debtor countries,[319] but this like the debt relief initiatives in the Enterprise for the Americas Initiative (EAI) focused on official bilateral debt. Jamaica was pleased to benefit from relief on bilateral debt but wanted its principal problem of debt to multilateral financial institutions such as the World Bank, addressed by rescheduling. What at the time seemed like a preposterous idea, eventually was partially realized when some of the ESC countries have benefited from debt relief under the Heavily Indebted Poor Countries (HIPC) Initiative, formally launched by the IMF and the World Bank in 1996. In 1999, Guyana benefited from debt relief under the program, receiving approximately USD$440 million. In November 2000, Guyana received approval from the IMF and World Bank for an additional USD$590 million in debt relief through December 2001 under the Enhanced HIPC Initiative.

Cooperation Against Drug Trafficking

Cooperation on security matters is one of the most important and there have been both problematic and successful aspects of the Caribbean/U.S. collaboration. Jamaica along with the other ESC states have been fully committed partners in the fight against narcotic drugs and other aspects of transnational crime. The governments of the ESC region have consistently emphasized the link between economic opportunity and social stability, which are the best antidotes to the drug trade and transnational crime. Unfortunately this link has never been fully appreciated or acknowledged by the United States; rather there has been a thinly disguised suspicion that this was just another ploy by the aid-seeking Caribbean governments to induce more U.S. aid.

The fact that small island states in the Caribbean are located close to major production points of drugs and are also major markets for drugs, encourages drug smuggling and the multi-national drug trafficking groups to begin to locate increasingly in small island states. Efforts to combat drug smuggling have proven to be an expensive exercise, diverting substantial resources from social investment such as education and health. In addition, resources available to the police and military forces in small island states are limited, particularly equipment such as motor vehicles, ships, airplanes, and surveillance equipment, and this makes it difficult, despite the strong commitment of governments in this area, to fight the scourge of illicit drug and firearms trafficking.

At various times some ESC countries have been included in the Department of State's list of major transit countries, according to the most recent International Narcotics Control Strategy Report (INCSR). In each case, the Report noted that the country or territory lies on the cocaine trafficking route from South to North America. In addition, six countries have been listed as major money-laundering countries, which are defined as those countries whose financial institutions engage in currency transactions involving significant amounts of proceeds from international narcotics trafficking. During the period examined in this study ESC governments have received full certification from the United States, which signifies that these countries were taking steps individually or in conjunction with the United States to fulfill the obligations as parties to the UN 1988 Convention Against Illicit Traffic in Narcotic Drugs and Psychotropic Substances.

The small states simply do not have the institutional capacity or human and financial resources to tackle the major drug cartels. General McCaffrey is correct when he speaks of the hemispheric narcotics control effort not as a war but as a long-term engagement. The crimes derived from drug trafficking have high impact on small nations and small populations. Money laundering, drug use, political corruption, intimidation, and violent crime have all increased in the region over the last two decades as a result of its strategic location. Each nation faces the challenge of ensuring that it does not become a weak link in the fight against transnational organized crime. The geographic location of Jamaica literally in the middle of the Caribbean sea and the hemisphere between the main sources of supply and the insatiable appetite of the enormous United States has placed a significant burden on Jamaica to continue to undertake aggressive interdiction efforts to curtail the movement of drugs through the region. As the United States commits itself to more robust anti-narcotic efforts in source nations, due attention must be paid to ensuring that a compatible strategy with adequate resource support is developed with respect to transit countries. Jamaica warrants greater U.S. support because it is both a transit country and a source country.

The governments in the region continue to undertake significant eradication programs for marijuana crops as a corollary to their far-reaching efforts to interdict the flow of hard drugs to the United States. The support given by the U.S. government to regional security forces by way of donated aircraft and vessels has improved the capacity to challenge the well-funded and well-organized criminal organizations involved in narcotics trafficking. Many ESC states have entered into maritime cooperation agreements, which has facilitated cooperation and helped to more effectively challenge the drug traffickers and other players in organized crime. It is critical that the United States strengthen its support for the anti-narcotics programs through enhanced training, technical assistance, and resource allocation commensurate with the magnitude of the threat posed by the cartels.

Preserve the EU Banana Regime

The export of bananas is vital to the economic, social, and political fabric of many states some of whom depend on the industry for more than 50 percent of their export revenue. The banana exporting countries fought a gallant rearguard action to prevent the United States and its cohort of Central American and Latin American banana producing countries from dismantling the EU banana regime. The United States position on bananas was instigated by and driven by the large campaign contributions of a single giant multinational corporation, namely Chiquita. In mid-2001 the European Union member states (at a European Ministers Meeting) gave their backing to the European Commission's proposals for the adoption of a first-come, first-served method. The United States, Latin American producers, and the Caribbean all agree that the Europeans' decision to rally behind a first-come, first-served method of allocating quotas and licenses (this would be transitional to a tariff-only system), is not in the best interest of all parties with a substantial interest in the trade.

Preserve Market Arrangements for Sugar and Rum

Sugar producers of the CBI region repeatedly voiced their concern about the efforts by Mexico to accelerate the expansion of its sugar quota to the U.S. market at a faster rate than agreed in the side letter signed at the time of the NAFTA Agreement. Under this agreement, Mexico's quota will increase to 250,000 metric tons by 2001. The United States is permitted to allocate a global quota of 1,117,195 metric tons per annum as notified to the WTO; within that quota, the portions assigned to Caribbean countries have declined sharply over the years. The individual country quotas are now at levels that barely make shipping economical. Any measure that results in further loss in preferential access to the U.S. market could have significant economic and social consequences in the region, particularly given the low world market prices. The Caribbean countries urged the U.S. government not to entertain Mexico's request for an expansion of its sugar quota, unless that quota could be accommodated without a reduction in the quotas currently allocated to the Caribbean countries. On September 22, 2000, the USTR announced the country-by-country quota allocations for raw cane sugar, refined sugar, and sugar-containing products for fiscal year 2001. Out of the total pool of a tariff rate quota of 1,117,195 metric tons, which the United States has offered, Jamaica has been allocated 11,584 metric tons.

The lobbying efforts were effective, particularly given the pressure exerted by Mexico to have their demands accommodated. Meetings were held with Congressional officials and Government officials to present the CBI region's peculiar concerns and the potential disadvantage that reduced quotas would occasion for their local producers and exporters. Those efforts were successful and the tariff rate quotas were calculated based on each country's historical trade to the United States.

The expansion of the "zero for zero" agreement between the United States and the European Union would be inimical to Caribbean interests. This would further jeopardize the access of rum exports from the Caribbean to the EU and the U.S. markets. On a positive note, under the Trade and Development Act of 2000, rum imported from the region into Canada, then blended and bottled for re-export to the United States has been granted duty-free access. The Act provides that liqueurs and "spirituous beverages" produced in Canada from CBI rum be given duty-free access where this rum accounts for at least 90 percent by volume of the alcoholic content of these liqueurs and spirituous beverages. The region's rum industry stands to benefit substantially from the increased market access.

Illegal Guns

The battle to stem the flow of illicit guns has been a major area of concern for Jamaica where the murder rate and other violent crimes have reached astonishing levels. In its dialogue with the United States. The traffic in illegal weapons emanating mainly from the United States has played a significant role in increased violence and criminal activity in the region. The ESC states including Jamaica have joined the United States in signing the Inter-American Convention against the Illicit Manufacturing of and Trafficking in Firearms, Ammunition, Explosives and Other Related Materials and are committed to efforts to stem the flow of guns to the region. In this area we need the continued support of the United States. The United States continues to provide support to the region in its effort to trace guns used in criminal activity and the assistance provided by the BATF in this regard is important. However, Jamaica viewed the illicit trafficking of firearms as dangerous and urged the United States to strengthen measures to curtail the outflow of illegal guns to Jamaica, not unlike Jamaica's commitment to stemming the trafficking of drugs to the United States. Due to the seriousness of the problem, at great expense Jamaica implemented sophisticated security measures at ports of entry to try to address the inflow of illegal guns.

Migrations and Deportation

The migration both legally and illegally from economically depressed areas to countries where jobs and higher wages are available is likely to be more pronounced in the next decade or two, as Latin American and Caribbean population growth rates persist at high levels and as some countries of the hemisphere experience limited economic growth and development. Migration has always been a major political issue in the United States, although the growth of the economy will require workers from abroad, given the aging of its population.[320] Migration to the United States has been a critical factor relieving unemployment in Jamaica and a significant number of working age people migrate to the United States from the region. Immigrants to the United States between 1988 and 1998 as a percentage of population in ESC countries is high-ranging from 39.9 percent in Guyana to 3.5 percent in the Bahamas, with 8 percent in the case of Jamaica.[321]

One area of grave concern for Jamaica has been the problem of deportation of criminals. This problem, exacerbated by U.S. legislation adopted in 1996, has had a serious impact on the social fabric of Jamaican society particularly given the paucity of resources to deal with the impact of criminal returnees many of whom have little ties to the communities to which they are returned. The destabilization caused by the deportation of criminals was a problem of major proportion for all the small countries of the Caribbean and Central America. The incidents of deportation from the United States to Caribbean countries increased steadily despite the pleas from these governments for the United States to be sensitive to the capacities of their law enforcement agencies to deal with the influx of criminal "deportees." Recidivism among these deportees contributes to an escalation of crime because of the access to sophisticated weapons and links to transnational crime groups.

Under the Anti-terrorism and Effective Death Penalty Act and the Illegal Immigration Reform and Immigration Responsibility Act of 1996, the term "deportation" was changed to "removal" and the definition of a felony broadened. These Acts further limited the discretion of the Immi-gration and Naturalization Service and mandated the deportation of im-migrants for acts classified as misdemeanors under state law but defined as "aggravated felonies" for the purposes of immigration law. The new definition applies to offenses that occurred before, on, or after the date of enactment of the legislation. These changes have resulted in many hard-ship cases including the detention and removal of long-stay permanent residents including elderly persons, for minor offenses some of which were committed long ago. The deportations of persons who have lived in the United States since childhood is an area of particular concern, as in many cases these persons have no viable ties in the region. This exacer-bates problems within the receiving states because these persons have no established means of support upon their return and are prone to become involved in criminal activities. In the period 1995–1999, the number of deportations to the CARICOM countries doubled.[322] Similarly the num-ber of deportees from the United States to Jamaica almost doubled from 834 in 1998 to 1,620 in 2000.[323] The World Bank points out that Jamaica is the country in the Caribbean with the largest flow of deportees relative to its population.[324]

Jamaica would benefit from the enactment of legislation to restore some discretion to the Immigration and Naturalization Service (INS) and reverse some of the unintended consequences of the 1996 legislative measures. In drafting new legislation the responsible agencies should consider such factors as the ties of the individual to the United States and their length of stay in the country, the impact of deportation on U.S.-based families, the nature of the offenses, their lack of connection to the states to which they are returned, and the adverse impact that deporta-tion has on Jamaica and similarly small developing countries.

Special Treatment for Small Developing Economies in the FTAA and WTO

There has been a trend during the decade of the 19990s towards reduction or elimination of preferential trading arrangements poses a major challenge. The dismantling of preferential trade arrangements such as the WTO ruling on bananas, indicates that fundamental changes have profoundly affected Jamaica and the ESC. Measures should be designed to address the concerns and interests of small, developing economies and these should not be limited to measures that avoid putting small economies at a disadvantage, but should be proactive in promoting the growth and development of smaller economies.

First, Jamaica and other small developing economies should be allowed to undertake commitments to the extent consistent with their adjustment capacity, development, financial and trade needs, and their administrative and institutional capabilities for implementation. Given the small size of firms in smaller economies and the small scale of production and the limited size of the market, export sectors will require a longer period of adjustment than larger firms and larger, more developed economies. Hence, there must be asymmetrically phased implementation of rules and disciplines, permitting a longer adjustment period for smaller economies.

Second, the small, developing countries such as Jamaica will have to improve their capacity to mediate the encounter with the global marketplace. Technical assistance for capacity building should aim to (a) contribute to efforts by small economies to undertake the structural, institutional, and legislative adjustment, (b) promote the development of adequate institutional capacity including training to improve their handling of negotiations and implementation of the international trade agreements, and (c) assist small economies in fulfilling their obligations under the various international agreements, in particular, commitments under the WTO.

CONCLUSION

This chapter provided a social, economic, political, and historical overview of Jamaica as a background to the review of Jamaica's foreign policy towards the United States and makes reference to the commonalities with the English-speaking Caribbean. The dominant feature of U.S.–Jamaica relations is the disparities in power, size, and economic development between the United States and Jamaica. Nevertheless, Jamaica has a tradition of resistance to hegemony, which has its origins in the long history of fighting against oppression in the forms of slavery and colonialism. This has given rise to an audacity that is uniquely Jamaican and that imbues the behavior of individuals, organizations, and the society as a whole. Assertiveness and feistiness are expected of the government by the Jamaican public in handling international relations, especially in standing up to larger more powerful states that appear to be taking advantage of Jamaica. Indeed, Persaud[325] makes the very perceptive observation of an "exceptionalism," which characterized the foreign policy of very different governments in Jamaica.

Foreign policy was sometimes aimed at ingratiating with the United States, as was the case when the Bustamante/Shearer government of the 1960s sought to differentiate itself from other developing countries by virtue of being a "middle income country," democratic, politically stable, and racially harmonious.[326] The straightforward mendicancy of the Seaga regime of the 1980s was predicated less on the conviction that Jamaica was inherently "special," but more on the need to convince the United States that Jamaica had a special role in the geo-politics of the Caribbean in the 1980s. Seaga capitalized on Reagan's simplistic anti-communism and for a couple of years was a special project of the Reagan Administration. The United States abandoned Seaga after his unwillingness to adhere faithfully to the orthodox macroeconomic stabilization policy designed by the IMF. The unique treatment of Jamaica by the United States ended when it discerned Seaga's opportunism and lack of genuine ideological credentials

This tradition of special pleading and assertiveness became bravado in the 1970s when the daring Michael Manley and his government successfully challenged the aluminum multinational corporations and the IMF (with less success) as part of a deeply felt belief in the necessity to change the status quo in the world. Manley and his foreign policy team had the audacity, skills, and the belief in the morality and justice of their cause to play a role in global affairs, far larger than warranted by Jamaica's size, in the attempt to create a new international economic order (NIEO). Manley believed that a NIEO was possible "only through united action that the Third World can hope to reduce its dependence, create economic viability and give meaning to its independence. If the commitment to independence is serious, there can be no compromise in the struggle for the new international economic order and the task of building Third World unity."[327] The Manley administrations attained a leadership role on behalf of the Third World, as contributing to uniting these states in "a kind of world trade union of the poor."[328] The adroit diplomacy of Manley came very close to establishing the Common Fund[329] when he convened a meeting in Runaway Bay, Jamaica with participation from Schmidt of West Germany, Trudeau of Canada, Fraser of Australia, Obasanjo of Nigeria, and Perez of Venezuela.[330] Jamaica achieved a special status in international affairs; for example it was Jamaica that sponsored the resolution calling for the United Nations International Year of Human Rights.[331]

This study does not examine every issue in U.S.-Jamaica relations but concentrates on those issues that ended in a resolution and that furnish the best illustrations of how Jamaica attempted to influence U.S. foreign policy towards Jamaica. Those issues are automatically ruled out of consideration because they are unresolved at the time of writing, e.g., treatment of small developing economies in the FTAA and in the WTO, migration and deportation, off-shore financial services, and taxation policy. Some issues have been the subject of considerable cooperation, e.g., money laundering and illegal firearms, and therefore do not provide instances of attempts to influence U.S. policy to the extent that warrant a detailed case study. In some situations the process of influence was relatively simple as in the case of maintaining sugar quotas and hence this is mentioned to illustrate a particular point rather than be subjected to extensive expositions. The issues that have been subjected to detailed analyses are the enhancement of the CBI, the struggle to maintain the EU banana regime, securing debt relief, preventing a reduction of foreign aid from the United States, and ensuring certification of cooperation with the United States on counter drug trafficking, which was a critical aspect of overall cooperation with the United States on narcotics.

NOTES

1. Randolph B. Persaud, Counter-Hegemony and Foreign Policy. The Dialectics of Marginalized and Global Forces in Jamaica (Albany: State University of New York Press, 2001).

2. R. M. Bent and Enid L. Bent-Golding, A Complete Geography of Jamaica (London: Collins, 1966).

3. The term Taino Arawak is used following Franklin W. Knight, The Caribbean. The Genesis of a Fragmented Nationalism (New York: Oxford University Press, 2nd edition, 1990) page 7. In the historiography different authors have used both Arawak and Taino. For descriptions of the Arawaks in Jamaica see Frank Cundall, Historic Jamaica (Kingston: Institute of Jamaica, 1915) pages 1–6 and Clinton V. Black, History of Jamaica (London: Collins, 1958) pages 9–22.

4. The name Jamaica is derived from the Arawak "Xayamaca," which means "Land of Wood and Water."

5. C. H. Haring, The Spanish Empire in America (New York: Harcourt, Brace and World, 1947) and J. H. Parry, The Spanish Seaborne Empire (London: Hutchinson and Co., 1966).

6. C. L. R. James, The Black Jacobins.Toussaint L'Ouverture and the San Domingo Revolution (New York: Random house, 1963) page 3.

7. Franklin W. Knight, The Caribbean. The Genesis of a Fragmented Nationalism (New York: Oxford University Press, 1990) pages 97–105 and Clinton V. Black, History of Jamaica (London: Collins, 1958) pages 47–71.

8. Robert F. Marx, Pirate Port. The Story of the Sunken City of Port Royal (London: Pelham Books, 1968).

9. Philip D. Curtin, The Atlantic Slave Trade (Madison: University of Wisconsin Press, 1969) and Robin Blackburn, The Making of New World Slavery. From the Baroque to the Modern 1492–1800 (London: Verso, 1997).

10. Eric Williams, Capitalism and Slavery (London: Andre Deutsch, 1964). See also Ralph Davis, The Rise of the Atlantic Economies (London: Weidenfeld and Nicolson, 1973).

11. Robin Blackburn, The Overthrow of Colonial Slavery 1776–1848 (London: Verso, 1988).

12. Richard Hart, The Slaves Who Abolished Slavery (Mona: University of the West Indies Press, 1985).

13. Carey Robinson, The Fighting Maroons of Jamaica (Kingston: Collins and Sangsters-Jamaica, 1969), Mavis C. Campbell, The Maroons of Jamaica 1655–1796. A History of Resistance, Collaboration and Betrayal (Trenton, N.J.: Africa World Press, 1990), Beverley Carey, The Maroon Story. The Authentic and Original History of the Maroons in the History of Jamaica (Gorton town, Jamaica: Agouti Press, 1997), and Richard Price (ed.), Maroon Societies. Rebel Slave Communities in the Americas (Baltimore: Johns Hopkins University Press, 1979) pages 227–92.

14. Laurie Gunst, Born Fe Dead (New York: Henry Holt, 1995).

15. Michael Manley noted this quality of West Indians in the way they played cricket and how this affected the game. See Michael Manley, A History of Cricket (London: Andre Deutsch, 1988) page 379.

16. Higman's study of Caribbean history leads him to conclude that the "central heroes of Caribbean history, official and unofficial, attained their status by fighting against injustice." See Barry W. Higman, Writing West Indian Histories (London: Macmillan, 1999) page 203.

17. A variety of aspects of slavery are captured in Hilary Beckles and Verene Shepherd (eds.), Caribbean Slave Society and Economy: A Student Reader (New York: New Press, 1993).

18. Richard l. Bernal, "The Great Depression, Colonial Policy and Industrialization in Jamaica," Social and Economic Studies, Vol. 37, Nos. 1 and 2 (March-June, 1988) pages 33–64.

19. Selwyn Carrington, The West Indies During the American Revolution. A Study in Colonial Economy and Politics (Leiden: 1987), Selwyn Carrington "The United States and Canada: The Struggle for the British West Indian Trade," Social and Economic Studies, Vol. 37, Nos. 1 and 2 (March–June, 1988) pages 69–106, and Peter K. Newman, "Canada's Role in West Indian Trade Before 1912," Inter-American Economic Affairs, Vol. XIV, No. 1 (March, 1960) pages 25–49.

20. Thomas C. Holt, The Problem of Freedom: Race, Labor, and Politics in Jamaica and Britain, 1832–1938 (Baltimore: Johns Hopkins Press, 1991) and Patrick Bryan, The Jamaican People: 1880–1902 : Race, Class and Social Control (Kingston: University of the West Indies Press, 2002).

21. James Carnegie, Some Aspects of Jamaica's Politics 1918–1938 (Kingston: Institute of Jamaica, 1973).

22. Rex Nettleford (ed.), Manley and the New Jamaica. Selected Speeches and Writings 1938–1968 (London: Longmans Caribbean, 1970), Rex Nettleford, "Manley and the Politics of Jamaica," Social and Economic Studies, Vol. 20, No. 3 (September, 1971) Supplement, and Victor Stafford Reid, The Horses of the Morning. About The Rt. Excellent N. W. Manley, Q. C., M. M. National Hero of Jamaica. An Understanding (Kingston: Caribbean Authors Publishing, 1985).

23. George Eaton, Alexander Bustamante and the Modern Jamaica (Kingston: Kingston Publishers, 1975).

24. The events and implications of this period are treated in detail in Colin A. Palmer, Freedom's Children. The 1938 Labor Rebellion and the Birth of Modern Jamaica (Chapel Hill: University of North Carolina Press, 2014), Richard Hart, Rise and Organize. The Birth of the Workers and National Movements in Jamaica 1936–1939 (London: Karia Press, 1989), Richard Hart, Towards Decolonization. Political, Labour and Economic Development in Jamaica 1938–1945 (Kingston: Canoe Press, University of the West Indies, 1999), Ken Post, Arise Ye Starvelings. The Jamaican Labour Rebellion of 1938 and Its Aftermath (The Hague: Martinus Nijhoff, 1978), and Ken Post,

Strike the Iron. A Colony at War: Jamaica 1939–1945 (Atlantic Highlands, N.J.: Humanities Press, 1981).

25. For a study of politics during the years 1944 to 1962 see Trevor Munroe, The Politics of Constitution Decolonization. Jamaica, 1944–1962 (Mona: Institute of Social and Economic Research, University of the West Indies, 1972).

26. Lady Bustamante, The Memoirs of Lady Bustamante (Kingston: Kingston Publishers Ltd., 1997) page 48.

27. David Lowenthal, The West Indies Federation. Perspectives on a New Nation (New York: Columbia University Press, 1961).

28. Hugh W. Springer, Reflections on the Failure of the West Indies Federation (Cambridge, Mass.: Center for International Affairs, Harvard University Press, July, 1962).

29. The official source book on CARICOM is CARICOM Secretariat, CARICOM. Our Caribbean Community (Kingston: Ian Randle Publishers, 2005). For Jamaica's policy in the Caribbean after the break-up of the West Indies Federation see R.B. Manderson-Jones, Jamaican Foreign Policy in the Caribbean 1962–1988 (Kingston: CARICOM Publishers, 1990). For an overall history see Anthony J. Payne, The Political History of CARICOM (Kingston: Ian Randle Publishers, 2008). For a recent review of the state of CARICOM see Terri-Ann Gilbert-Roberts, The Politics of Integration. Caribbean Sovereignty Revisited (Kingston and Miami: Ian Randle Publishers, 2013).

30. Richard L. Bernal and Vilma McNeish, "The Caribbean in the OAS," Jamaica Journal, No. 26-3 (December, 1998) pages 33–36.

31. Norman Girvan, Cooperation in the Greater Caribbean: The Role of the Association of Caribbean States (Kingston: Ian Randle Publishers, 2006) and Cedric Grant, "The Association of Caribbean States and United States-Caribbean Relations" in Ransford W. Palmer (ed.), The Repositioning of United States-Caribbean relations in the New World Order (Westport: Praeger, 1997) pages 27–50.

32. Gladstone E. Mills, Westminster Style Democracy: The Jamaican Experience (Kingston: Grace Kennedy Foundation, 1997).

33. Robert Buddan, The Foundations of Caribbean Politics (Kingston: Arawak Publications, 2001) pages 15–18 and Bill Reviere, State Systems in the Caribbean (Mona: Institute of Social and Economic Studies, University of the West Indies, 1990) pages 59–92.

34. Busta's admiration for N.W. Manley as a lawyer was unbounded. He never failed to refer to him as "my cousin Norman, the greatest lawyer in the West Indies." See Ashton Wright, No Trophies Raise (Kingston: Ashton G. Wright, 994) page 51. Edna Manley's diaries speak of her husband's "fondness" and "affection" for Bustamante. See Rachel Manley (ed.), Edna Manley. The Diaries (Kingston: Heinemann, 1989) passim.

35. Economic and Social Survey. Jamaica (Kingston: Planning Institute of Jamaica, various years).

36. Delano Franklyn (ed.), The Jamaican Diaspora. Building an Operational Framework (Kingston: Wilson Franklyn Barnes, 2010). In 1995 an estimated 31.2 percent of households received remittances, see Namsuk Kim, The Impact of Remittances on Labor Supply: The Case of Jamaica, World Bank Policy Research Working Paper 4120 (Washington, D.C.: World Bank, February, 2007) page 8.

37. Franklin Knight, The Caribbean. The Genesis of a Fragmented Nationalism (New York: Oxford University Press, 1990) page 308.

38. For a report of the quality of life in those years see Erna Brodber, The Second Generation of Freemen in Jamaica, 1907–1944 (Gainesville: University Press of Florida, 2004).

39. Olive Senior, Dying to Better Themselves. West Indians and the Building of the Panama Canal (Kingston: University of the West Indies Press, 2014) and Velma Newton, The Silver Men: West Indian Labour Migration to Panama, 1850–1914 (Kingston: Ian Randle Publishers, 2004).

40. Aviva Chomsky, West Indian Workers and the United Fruit Company in Costa Rica, 1870–1940 (Baton Rouge: Louisiana State University Press, 1996) and Ronald N. Harpelle, The West Indians of Costa Rica. Race, Class and the Integration of an Ethnic Minority (Kingston: Ian Randle, 2001).

41. Tracey E. Graham, Jamaican Migration to Cuba, 1912–1940, Doctoral Dissertation, Department of History, University of Chicago, March 2013.

42. Alec Wilkinson, Big Sugar. Seasons in the Cane Fields of Florida (New York: Alfred A. Knopf, 1989).

43. R. B. Davison, Black British. Immigrants to England (London: Oxford University Press, 1966), Nancy Foner, Jamaica Farewell. Jamaican Migrants (London: Routledge and Kegan Paul, 1979), and Vivienne Francis, With Hope in Their Eyes (London: Nia, 1998).

44. Gene Tidrick, "Some Aspects of Jamaican Migration to the United Kingdom 1953–1962," Social and Economic Studies, Vol. 15, No.1 (March, 1966) pages 22–39.

45. Edith Clarke, My Mother Who Fathered Me. A Study of the Family in Three Selected Communities in Jamaica (London: Allen and Unwin, 1957).

46. The ruthlessness of Columbus and the early Spanish conquistadors is documented in Hans Koning, Columbus. His Enterprise (New York: Monthly Review Press, 1976) and Kirkpatrick Sale, The Conquest of Paradise (New York: Alfred A. Knopf, 1990).

47. Douglas Hall, Free Jamaica 1838–1865. An Economic History (Kingston: Caribbean Universities Press, 1969) and William A. Green, British Slave Emancipation. The Sugar Colonies and the Great Experiment 1830–1865 (Oxford: Oxford University Press, 1976).

48. Verene Shepherd, Transients to Settlers: East Indians in Jamaica in the Late 19th and Early 20th Century (London: Peepal Tree Press, 1991).

49. Walton Look Lai, Indentured Labor, Caribbean Sugar: Chinese and Indian Migrants to the British West Indies, 1838–1918 (Baltimore: Johns Hopkins University Press, 2004).

50. Mary Manning Carley, Jamaica. The Old and the New (London: George Allen and Unwin, 1963) pages 106–125.

51. George Lamming, "Concepts of the Caribbean" in Frank Birbalsingh (ed.), Frontiers in Caribbean Literature in English (London: Macmillan, 1996) pages 1–14. See page 3.

52. Erna Brodber, "Socio-cultural Change in Jamaica" in Rex Nettleford (ed.), Jamaica in Independence. Essays on the Early Years (Kingston: Heinemann, 1989) pages 55–74. See page 61.

53. For a discussion of aspects of African retentions see Margaret E. Crahan and Franklin W. Knight (eds.), Africa and the Caribbean. The Legacies of a Link (Baltimore: Johns Hopkins University Press, 1979) and Mervyn C. Alleyne, Roots of Jamaican Culture (London: Pluto Press, 1988).

54. Wayne Cooper (ed.), The Passion of Claude McKay. Selected Prose and Poetry 1912–1948 (New York: Schocken Books, 1973) page 124.

55. Philip Sherlock and Hazel Bennett, The Story of the Jamaican People (Kingston: Ian Randle, 1998) page 344.

56. On African religions see Mervyn Alleyne, Roots of Jamaican Culture (London: Pluto Press, 1988) pages 76–105.

57. Leonard Barrett, The Rastafarians. Sounds of Cultural Dissonance (Boston: Beacon Press, 1977), Joseph Owens, Dread. The Rastafarians of Jamaica (Kingston: Sangsters Bookstores, 1976), and A. Barrington Chevannes, Rastafari: Roots and Ideology (Syracuse: Syracuse University Press, 1995).

58. For the influence and expression of Rastafarianism in the life and songs of Bob Marley see Stephen Davis, Bob Marley (London; Arthur Barker, 1983), Timothy White, Catch a Fire. The Life Bob Marley (Holt, Rinehart and Winston, 1983), and Cedella Booker with Anthony Winkler, Bob Marley. An Intimate Portrait by His Mother (London: Viking, 1996).

59. Orlando Paterson, The Sociology of Slavery. An Analysis of the Origins, Development and Structure of Negro Slave Society in Jamaica (London: Granada Publishing, 1967) and Edward Brathwaithe, The Development of Creole Society in Jamaica, 1770–1820 (Oxford: Clarendon Press, 1971). See also relevant sections of Orlando Patterson, Slavery and Social Death. A Comparative Study (Cambridge, Mass.: Harvard University Press, 1982).

60. Brian Meeks, Radical Caribbean. From Black Power to Abu Bakar (Kingston: University of the West Indies Press, 1996) page 3.

61. Fernando Henriques, Family and Colour in Jamaica (London: Eyre and Spottiswoode, 1953).

62. Derek Walcott, "The Muse of History" in Derek Walcott, What the Twilight Says. Essays (New York: Farrar, Straus and Giroux, 1998) pages 36–64. See page 39.

63. As post-slavery traumatic stress syndrome, see Joy Angela Degruy, Post Traumatic Slave Syndrome (Joy Degruy Publications Inc., 2005) and Omar G. Reid, Post Traumatic Slavery Disorder: Definition, Diagnosis, and Treatment (Conquering Books, 2005).

64. Frieda Fordham, An Introduction to Jung's Psychology (Harmondsworth, England: Penguin, 1953) pages 22–23.

65. For a discussion of this proposition see Robert Buddan, The Foundations of Caribbean Politics (Kingston: Arawak Publications, 2001) page 45.

66. Richard S. Dunn, Sugar and Slaves. The Rise of the Planter Class in the English West Indies, 1624–1713 (New York: W. W. Norton, 1972) pages 149–87 and L. F. Ragatz, The Fall of the Planter Class in the British Caribbean, 1763–1833. A Study in Social and Economic History (New York: American Historical Association, 1928).

67. Philip D. Curtin, Two Jamaicas. The Role of Ideas in a Tropical Colony 1830–1865 (Cambridge, Mass.: Harvard University Press, 1955).

68. On the emergence of the peasantry see Sidney W. Mintz, From Plantation to Peasantries in the Caribbean (Washington, D.C.: Woodrow Wilson International Center for Scholars, 1984).

69. M. G. Smith, Plural Society in the West Indies (Berkeley: University of California Press, 1965), Fernando Henriques, Family and Colour in Jamaica (London: Eyre and Spottiswoode, 1953) pages 33–63, and Madeline Kerr, Personality and Conflict in Jamaica (London: Collins, 1963) pages 93–104.

70. Errol Miller, "Educational development in independent Jamaica" in Rex Nettleford (ed.), Jamaica in Independence. Essays on the Early Years (Kingston: Heinemann Caribbean, 1989) pages 205–28.

71. Edward Braithwaite, The Development of Creole Society in Jamaica, 1770–1820 (Oxford: Clarendon Press, 1971), R. T. Smith, "Social Stratification, Cultural Pluralism and Integration in West Indian Societies" in S. Lewis and T. Matthews (eds.), Caribbean Integration (Rio Praedas: University of Puerto Rico, 1967) pages 233–50, and Lloyd Brathwaite, "Social Stratification and Cultural Pluralism," Annals of the New York Academy of Sciences, Vol. 83 (1960) pages 816–36.

72. Rex Nettleford, Caribbean Cultural Identity. The case of Jamaica. An Essay in Cultural Dynamics (Kingston: Institute of Jamaica, 1978) pages 1–46.

73. For an outline of the philosophy of the PNP and the Manley led government of 1974 to 1980, see Richard L. Bernal, "IMF and Class Struggle in Jamaica, 1977–1980," Latin American Perspectives, Vol. 11, No. 3 (Summer, 1984) pages 53–82 and Richard L. Bernal, "Jamaica: Democratic Socialism Meets the IMF," in Jill Torrie (eds.), Banking on Poverty: The Global Impact of the IMF and World Bank (Toronto: Between the Lines, 1983) pages 217–40.

74. Census of Agriculture 1968–1969. Jamaica Final Report, Vol. 3, Part A (Kingston: Department of Statistics, 1974) page 14.

75. Stanley Reid, "An Introductory Approach to the Concentration of Power in the Jamaican Corporate Economy and Notes on its Origins," in Carl Stone and Aggrey Brown (eds.), Essays in Power and Change in Jamaica (Kingston: Jamaica Publishing House, 1977) pages 15–45.

76. The statistics are for 1958 but estimates for 1972 reveal no change. See E. Ahiram, "Income Distribution in Jamaica, 1958," Social and Economic Studies, UWI, Vol. 13, No. 3 (September 1964), pages 36–69, Jamaica Socio-Economic Report (Washington, D.C.: Inter-American Bank, July 1979), Vol. 1, page 49, and Derick Boyd, Economic Management, Income Distribution, and Poverty in Jamaica (Westport: Praeger Publishers, 1988).

77. Norman Girvan, Foreign Capital and Economic Underdevelopment in Jamaica (Kingston: Institute of Social and Economic Research, University of the West Indies, 1971), Norman Girvan, Corporate Imperialism. Conflict and Expropriation (New York: Monthly Review Press, 1979), and Richard L. Bernal, "Foreign Investment and Development in Jamaica," Inter-American Economic Affairs, Vol. 38, No. 2 (Autumn, 1984) pages 3–21.

78. Allison A. Fenton, Trevor A. Jackson, and Dennis A. Minott, Natural Resources, Assessment and Development: A Regional Study in CARICOM Territories. Report prepared for the CARICOM Secretariat (July, 1984) pages 1–46.

79. This section draws on Samir Amin, "Accumulation and Development: A Theoretical Model," Review of African Political Economy, No. 1 (August –November, 1974) pages 9–26, Theotonio Dos Santos, "The Structure of Dependence," American Economic Review, Vol. LX, No. 2 (May, 1970) pages 231–36, and Osvaldo Sunkel, "Transnational Capitalism and National Disintegration in Latin America," Social and Economic Studies, Vol. 22, No. 1 (March, 1973) pages 132–76.

80. Owen Jefferson, The Post War Economic Development of Jamaica (Mona: Institute of Social and Economic Research, University of the West Indies, 1972) pages 178–79.

81. S. Daniel, A. A. Francis, D. Nelson, B. Nembhard, and D. H. Ramjeesingh, "A Structural Analysis of the Jamaican Economy, 1974. An Application of the Input-Output Technique," Social and Economic Studies, Vol. 34, No. 3 (September, 1985) pages 1–69.

82. Structural Adjustment of the Jamaican Economy, 1982–1987 (Kingston: National Planning Agency, 1982) page 9.

83. Richard L. Bernal, The Political Economy of IMF Programs in Jamaica 1977–1984 (Doctoral Dissertation, New School for Social Research, May 1988) pages 79–80.

84. Norman Girvan, Foreign Capital and Economic Development in Jamaica (Mona: Institute of Social and Economic Studies, University of the West Indies, 1971) Chapter 8, discusses the Jamaican experience in the 1950s and 1960s.

85. Mahmood Ali Ayub, Made in Jamaica. The Development of the Manufacturing Sector, World Bank, Staff Occasional Paper, No. 31 (Washington, D.C.: World Bank, 1981) pages 62–63.

86. Richard L. Bernal, The Integration of Small Economies in the Free Trade Area of the Americas, Center for Strategic and International Studies, Policy Papers on the Americas, February 2, 1998, page 24 and Richard L. Bernal, "Nano-firms, Integration and International Competitiveness: The Experience and Dilemma of the CSME" in Kenneth Hall (ed.), CARICOM. Perspectives on its Pertinence in the Twenty-First Century (Mandeville: Northern Caribbean University Press, 2012) pages 198–224.

87. D. Ramjee Singh, A. Birch, and Hilton McDavid, "Impact of the Hospitality-Tourism Sector on the Jamaican Economy, 1974–1993," Social and Economic Studies, Vol. 55, No. 3 (September, 2006) pages 183–207.

88. Lloyd Best, "A Model of Pure Plantation Economy," Social and Economic Studies, Vol. 17, No. 3 (September, 1969) pages 283–326 and George L. Beckford, Persistent Poverty. Underdevelopment in Plantation Economies of the Third World (New York: Oxford University Press, 1972).

89. Gisela Eisner, Jamaica 1830–1930. A Study of Economic Growth (Manchester: Manchester University Press, 1961).

90. Owen Jefferson, The Post-War Economic Development of Jamaica (Mona: Institute of Social and Economic Studies, University of the West Indies, 1972).

91. For a detailed study of small farming see David Edwards, An Economic Study of Small Farming in Jamaica (Mona: Institute of Social and Economic Studies, University College of the West Indies, 1961).

92. Michael Witter, "The Informal Economy of Jamaica" in Dennis Pantin (ed.), The Caribbean Economy. A Reader (Kingston: Ian Randle Publishers, 2005) pages 434–63.

93. Daniel Jay Baum, The Banks of Canada in the Commonwealth Caribbean (New York: Praeger, 1974).

94. David Winner, Brilliant Orange. The Neurotic Genius of Dutch Football (London: Bloomsbury Publishing, 2000).

95. Richard Slotkin, Gunfighter Nation. Myth of the Frontier in Twentieth-Century America (Norman: University of Oklahoma Press, 1998).

96. Richard N. Haass, The Reluctant Sheriff: The United States After the Cold War (New York: Council on Foreign Relations Press, 1997).

97. John H. Lenihan, Showdown. Confronting Modern America in the Western Film (Chicago: University of Illinois Press, 1980) page 10.

98. Teddy Roosevelt went to great lengths to create an image of himself which matched the hero in western movies. See Evan Thomas, The War Lovers. Roosevelt, Lodge, Hearst and the Rush to Empire, 1898 (New York: Little, Brown and Company, 2010).

99. Michael Coyne, The Crowded Prairie. American National identity in the Hollywood Western (London and New York: I. B. Taurus Publishers, 1997) pages 1–2.

100. Gary Wills, John Wayne's America: The Politics of Celebrity (New York: Simon and Schuster, 1997).

101. John H. Lenihan, Showdown. Confronting Modern America in the Western Film (Chicago: University of Illinois Press, 1980) page 15.

102. Jim Kane, Western Movie Wit and Wisdom (Houston: Bright Sky Press, 2007) page 107.

103. Jim Kane, Western Movie Wit and Wisdom (Houston: Bright Sky Press, 2007) page 235.

104. John H. Lenihan, Showdown. Confronting Modern America in the Western Film (Chicago: University of Illinois Press, 1980) pages 55–89.

105. Jim Kane, Western Movie Wit and Wisdom (Houston: Bright Sky Press, 2007) page 44.

106. Jim Kane, Western Movie Wit and Wisdom (Houston: Bright Sky Press, 2007) page 97.

107. Michael Coyne, The Crowded Prairie. American National Identity in the Hollywood Western (London and New York: I. B. Taurus Publishers, 1997).

108. Bev Carey, The Maroon Story: The Authentic and Original History of the Maroons in the History of Jamaica, 1490–1880 (Kingston: Agouti Press, 1997), Carey Robinson, The Fighting Maroons of Jamaica (Kingston: William Collins and Sangster (1971), Carey Robinson, The Iron Torn: The Defeat of the British by the Jamaican Maroons (Kingston: LMH Publishing Company, 2007), and Mavis Campbell, The Maroons of Jamaica 1655–1796 (Africa World Press, 1988).

109. Richard Hart, Slaves Who Abolished Slavery: Blacks in Rebellion (Mona: University of the West Indies Press, 2002).

110. Jung states: "in addition to our immediate consciousness, which is of a thoroughly personal nature and which we believe to be the only empirical psyche . . . there exists a second psychic system of a collective, universal, and impersonal nature which is identical in all individuals. This collective unconscious does not develop individually but is inherited. It consists of pre-existent forms, the archetypes which can only become conscious secondarily and which give definite form to certain psychic contents." C. G. Jung, The Archetypes and the Collective Unconscious (London: 1996) page 43.

111. Rex Nettleford, Mirror Mirror. Identity, Race and Protest in Jamaica (London and Kingston: William Collins and Sangsters Jamaica, 1970) page 120.

112. Mary Seacole, Wonderful Adventures of Mrs. Seacole in Many Lands (London: Penguin, 2005) and Jane Robinson, Mary Seacole: The Most Famous Black Woman of the Victorian Age (New York: Basic Books, 2004).

113. A. Jacques Garvey, Garvey and Garveyism (Kingston: A. Jacques Garvey, 1963), Edmund David Cronon, Black Moses. The Story of Marcus Garvey and the Universal Negro Improvement Association (Madison: University of Wisconsin Press, 1968), Tony Martin, Race First. The Ideological and Organizational Struggles of Marcus Garvey and the Universal Negro Improvement Association (Westport: Greenwood Press, 1976), Rupert Lewis, Marcus Garvey. Anti-Colonial Champion (London: Karia Press, 1987), Rupert Lewis and Patrick Bryan (eds.), Garvey. His Work and Impact (Mona: ISER, UWI, 1988), and Colin Grant, Negro with a Hat. The Rise and Fall of Marcus Garvey (Oxford: Oxford University Press, 2008).

114. A. Jacques Garvey, The Philosophy and Opinions of Marcus Garvey (New York: Augustus M. Kelly, 1967) and A. Jacques Garvey and E. U. Essien-Udom (London: Frank Cass, 1977).

115. Joyce Moore Turner, Caribbean Crusaders and the Harlem Renaissance (Urbana and Chicago: University of Illinois Press, 2005).

116. Winston James, Holding Aloft the Banner of Ethiopia. Caribbean Radicalism in Early Twentieth Century America (London: Verso, 1998).

117. Theordore Vincent, Black Power and the Garvey Movement (Forestville: Ramparts Press, 1972).

118. Four of the founders of Rastafarianism were influenced by the thinking of Garvey. See Leonard Barrett, Rastafarians: Sounds of Cultural Dissonance (Boston: Beacon Press, 1977).

119. A. Jacques Garvey, Garvey and Garveyism (Kingston: A. Jacques Garvey, 1963).

120. Winston James, Holding Aloft the Banner of Ethiopia. Caribbean Radicalism in Early Twentieth Century America (London: Verso, 1998) page 12.

121. Louis J. Parascandola (ed.), "Look for Me All Around You": Anglophone Caribbean Immigrants in the Harlem Renaissance (Cleveland: Wayne State University Press, 2005) and Joyce Moore Turner, Caribbean Crusaders and the Harlem Renaissance (Chicago: University of Illinois Press, 2005).

122. Wayne F. Cooper, Claude McKay: Rebel Sojourner in the Harlem Renaissance: A Biography (Baton Rouge: Louisiana State University Press, 1987).

123. Barry Chevannes, Rastafari: Roots and Ideology (Syracuse University Press, 1994).

124. Horace Campbell, Rasta and Resistance: From Marcus Garvey to Walter Rodney (Africa World Press, 1987).

125. Ken Post, Arise Ye Starvelings: The Jamaican Labour Rebellion of 1938 and its Aftermath (The Hague: Martinus Nijhoff, 1978) and Richard Hart, Towards Decolonisation. Political, labour and economic conditions in Jamaica 1938–1945 (Mona: Canoe Press, University of the West Indies, 1999).

126. Patrick Robinson, Jamaican Athletics: A Model for 2012 and the World (Arcadia Books, 2009).

127. Carolyn Cooper (ed.), Global Raggae (Mona: University of the West Indies Press, 2012).

128. Erna Brodber, "Raggae as Black Space" in Carolyn Cooper (ed.), Global Raggae (Mona: University of the West Indies, 2012) pages 21–36.

129. Carolyn Cooper, "Jamaican Popular Music A Yard and Abroad" in Carolyn Cooper (ed.), Global Raggae (Mona: University of the West Indies, 2012) pages 1–19.

130. Hartley Neita, Hugh Shearer. A Voice for the People (Kingston: Ian Randle Publishers, 2005) page 193.

131. "The Government in 1966, decided that one of the ways in which Jamaica would mark the International Year was by the award of a Prize for Human Rights. The Prize would be named after one of Jamaica's national heroes—Marcus Garvey—would carry a cash award of £5,000, and would be awarded for outstanding contribution in the field of race relations. The Government through the Mission circulated the govern-

ments of Member States and Observer Missions as well as the Specialized Agencies and the Non-Governmental Organizations, details of the Code of Procedure agreed upon, and requested their nominations. Following announcement of the award of the Prize to the late Dr. Martin Luther King the Mission notified all the Governments and Organizations of the award." Jamaica at the UN, 1968. Government of Jamaica Ministry Paper No. 57, May 30, 1969.

132. Don Mills, Journeys and Missions: At Home and Abroad (Kingston: Arawak Publishers, 2009).

133. Hartley Neita, Hugh Shearer. A Voice for the People (Kingston: Ian Randle Publishers, 2005) page 207.

134. Dean Rusk, As I Saw It (Harmondsworth: Penguin, 1991).

135. Richard Nixon, Seize the Moment. America's Challenge in a One-Superpower World (New York: Simon and Schuster, 1992) page 264.

136. Zbigniew Brzezinski, Out of Control. Global Turmoil on the Eve of the 21st Century (New York: Charles Scribner and Sons, 1993).

137. Robin Wright and Doyle McManus, Flashpoints. Promise and Peril in a New World (New York: Alfred A. Knopf, 1991).

138. Laurie Gunst, Born Fi' Dead. A Journey Through The Jamaican Posse Underworld (Henry Holt Co., 1995).

139. Jimmy Carter, Keeping Faith: Memory of a President (New York: Bantam Books, 1982) pages 452 and 469.

140. Cyrus Vance, Hard Choices, Critical Years in America's Foreign Policy (New York: Simon and Schuster, 1983).

141. George P. Schultz, Turmoil and Triumph. Diplomacy, Power, and the Victory of the American Ideal (New York: Charles Scribner and Sons, 1993) pages 323–45.

142. George P. Schultz, Turmoil and Triumph. Diplomacy, Power, and the Victory of the American Ideal (New York: Charles Scribner and Sons, 1993) page 323.

143. Gaddis Smith, Morality, Reason and Power. American Diplomacy in the Carter Years (New York: Hill and Wang, 1986) page 109.

144. Smith, Morality, Reason and Power. American Diplomacy in the Carter Years. (New York: Hill and Wang, 1986) Chapter 5.

145. Central America in Crisis. A Programme for Action (Washington, D.C.: Washington Institute for Values in Public Policy, 1983).

146. Communist Interference in El Salvador (Washington, D.C.: U.S. Department of State, Special Report No. 80, February 23, 1981) pages 1–8.

147. "For Reagan, anticommunism was an article for faith." Indeed, "there was not doubt that he (Reagan) came to office holding sincere and strong convictions about the dangers of communism—and of the use of force to combat it." See Haynes Johnson, Sleepwalking Through History, America in the Reagan Years (New York: W. W. Norton and Company, 1997) page 254.

148. Alan Gerson, The Kirkpatrick Mission. Diplomacy Without Apology. America at the United Nations 1981–1985 (New York: Free Press, 1991).

149. David Landau, Kissinger. The Uses of Power (Boston: Houghton Mifflin, 1972).

150. George Bush and Brent Scowcroft, A World Transformed (New York: Alfred A. Knopf, 1998).

151. Haley Barbour, Agenda for America. A Republican Direction for the Future (Washington, D.C.: Regency Publishing, 1996) pages 263–68.

152. James Baker, The Politics of Diplomacy: Revolution, War and Peace 1989–1992 (New York: Putnam Publishers, 1995)

153. Warren Christopher, In the Stream of History. (Stanford: Stanford University Press, 1998).

154. Governor Bill Clinton and Senator Al Gore, Putting People First (New York: Times Books, 1992) page 109.

155. Warren Christopher, Chances of a Lifetime (New York: Simon and Schuster, 2001).

156. Abraham F. Lowenthal, "Latin America and the Caribbean: Toward a New U.S. Policy" in John P. Lewis and Valeriana Kallab (eds.), U.S. Foreign Policy and the Third World (New York: Praeger, 1983) page 51.

157. Foreign Policy in the 21st Century. The U.S. Leadership Challenge (Washington, D.C.: Center for Strategic and International Studies, September, 1996) and Kim R. Holmes and James G. Moore, Restoring American Leadership: A U.S. Foreign and Defense Policy Blueprint (Washington, D.C.: Heritage Foundation, 1996).

158. Samuel R. Berger, "A Foreign Policy for the Global Age," Foreign Affairs, Vol. 79, No. 6 (November/December, 2000) pages 22–39.

159. Garry Wills, John Wayne's America. The Politics of Celebrity (New York: Simon and Schuster, 1997).

160. C. L. R. James, Beyond a Boundary (London: Hutchinson and Co., 1963).

161. David Winner, Brilliant Orange. The Neurotic Genius of Dutch Football (London: Bloomsbury, 2000).

162. Lucille Mair, Rebel Women (Kingston: Institute of Jamaica, 1975).

163. Winston James, Holding Aloft the Banner of Ethiopia. Caribbean Radicalism in Early Twentieth-Century America (London: Verso, 1998).

164. "All Black Power advocates understandably turn to Garvey for ideological strength and sustenance." See Rex Nettleford, Mirror Mirror. Identity, Race and Protest in Jamaica (London and Kingston: William Collins and Sangsters Jamaica, 1970) page 128.

165. On the Marxism of James see Anthony Bogues, Caliban's Freedom. The Early Political Thought of C. L. R. James (London: Pluto Press, 1997).

166. Robert L. Tignor, W. Arthur Lewis and the Birth of Development Economics (Princeton: Princeton University Press, 2005).

167. James Carnegie, Great Jamaican Olympians (Kingston: Kingston Publishers, 1996).

168. Carlton E. Davis, Jamaica in the World Aluminium Industry 1938–1973 (Kingston: Jamaica Bauxite Institute, 1989) pages 151–251.

169. It is evident in popular music, see Carolyn Cooper, Sound Clash: Jamaican Dancehall at Large (New York: Palgrave Macmillan, 2004).

170. Rex Nettleford, Political Leadership in the Commonwealth Caribbean. Responsibilities, Options and Challenges at End of Century (Mona: School of Continuing Studies, University of the West Indies, 1994) pages 6–7.

171. "Everybody seemed a few inches taller, backs straighter, heads held higher." See Peter Abrahams, The Coyaba Chronicles. Reflections on the Black Experience in the 20th Century (Kingston: Ian Randle, 2000) page 267.

172. Drury Pifer, Hanging the Moon. The Rollins Rise to Riches (Newark: University of Delaware Press, 2001) pages 175–87.

173. H. Michael Erisman, "The Caricom States and U.S. Foreign Policy: The Danger of Central Americanization," Journal of Interamerican Studies and World Affairs, Vol. 31, No. 3 (Fall, 1989) pages 141–82. See page 176.

174. Kenneth O. Hall (ed.), Integrate or Perish. Perspectives of Leaders of the Integration Movement 1963–1999 (Mona: University of the West Indies Press, 2000) page 220.

175. Didacus Jules and Tennyson S. D. Joseph (eds.), At the Rainbow's Edge. Selected Speeches of Kenny D. Anthony 1996–2002 (Kingston: Ian Randle Publishers, 2004) page 157.

176. Patsy Lewis, Surviving Small Size. Regional Integration in Caribbean Ministates (Kingston: Ian Randle Publishers, 2002) page 63.

177. Irving W. Andre and Gabriel J. Christian, In Search of Eden. The Travails of a Caribbean Mini State (Upper Marlboro: Pond Case Press, 1992) pages 204–7.

178. Rex Nettleford (ed.) Manley and the New Jamaica (London: Longman, 1971) page 166.

179. Paul K Sutton (ed.) Forged From the Love of Liberty. Speeches of Dr. Eric Williams (Port of Spain: Longman Caribbean, 1981) pages 301–15.

180. The struggle is recounted in Colin A. Palmer, Eric Williams and the Making of the Modern Caribbean (Kingston: Ian Randle Publishers, 2006) Chapter 3.

181. Benn Steil, The Battle of Bretton Woods. John Maynard Keynes, Harry Dexter White and the Making of the New World Order (Princeton: Princeton University Press, 2013) page 102.

182. Fitzroy Baptiste, War, Cooperation and Conflict: The European Possessions in the Caribbean, 1939–1945 (New York: Greenwood Press, 1988).

183. Eric Williams, Forged From the Love of Liberty—Selected Speeches of Dr. Eric Williams. Compiled by Dr. Paul K. Sutton (Longman Caribbean, 1981) pages 301–15.

184. Eric Williams. From Columbus to Castro. The History of the Caribbean 1492–1968 (London: Andre Deutsch, 1970) page 207.

185. Sahadeo Basedeo and Graeme Mount, The Foreign Relations of Trinidad and Tobago, 1962–2000. The Case of a Small State in the Global Arena (Port of Spain: Lexicon Trinidad, 2001) page 9.

186. Neville C. Duncan, "Domestic Policy and International Relations" in Trevor A. Carmichael (ed.), Barbados. Thirty Years of Independence (Kingston: Ian Randle Publishers, 1996) page 60.

187. Diplomacy and Development: A Review of the Foreign Policy of Barbados (Bridgetown, Barbados: Ministry of Foreign Affairs, 1987) page 4.

188. Eric Williams, From Columbus to Castro. The History of the Caribbean 1492–1968 (London: Andre Deutsch, 1970) pages 409–28.

189. Eric Williams, From Columbus to Castro. The History of the Caribbean 1492–1968 (London: Andre Deutsch, 1970) pages 407–27.

190. Eric Williams, Forged From the Love of Liberty—Selected Speeches of Dr. Eric Williams. Compiled by Dr. Paul K. Sutton (Longman Caribbean, 1981) page 423.

191. Fitzroy Baptiste, "The Federal Process in the West Indies as Seen by the United States, 1947–1962," Social and Economic Studies, Vol. 48, No. 4 (December, 1999) pages 209–10.

192. Elliot Abrams, "The Shiprider Solution Policing the Caribbean," The National Interest, Vol. 43 (Spring, 1996) pages 86–92. See page 86.

193. Eric Williams, From Columbus to Castro. The History of the Caribbean 1492–1968 (London: Andre Deutsch, 1970) page 465.

194. Darrell E. Levi, Michael Manley, The Making of a Leader, (Kingston: Heinemann Publishers (Caribbean) Ltd., 1989) page 139.

195. Gaddis Smith, op-cit., page 126.

196. Michael Massing, "Grenada Before and After," The Atlantic Monthly, February 1984, page 81 (pages 75–87).

197. Gaddis Smith, page 126.

198. Confidential notes of Ambassador Richard Bernal.

199. Evelyn Huber Stephens and John D. Stephens, Democratic Socialism in Jamaica (Princeton: Princeton University Press, 1986) page 126.

200. Neville C. Duncan, "Domestic Policy and International Relations" in Trevor Carmichael (ed.), Barbados. Thirty Years of Independence (Kingston: Ian Randle, 1996) pages 52–66. See page 64.

201. Jacqueline Braveboy–Wagner, "Caribbean Foreign Policy," Caribbean Studies, Vol. 1, No. 3 (Third Quarter, 1988) pages 77–89. See page 87.

202. Philip W. Bell, "Colonialism as a Problem in American Foreign Policy," World Politics, Vol. 5 (1952) pages 86–109.

203. Edward S. Mason, "American Security and Access to Raw Materials," World Politics, Vol. 1 (1949) pages 149–1962 give an indication of the thinking at the time.

204. Eric Williams, From Columbus to Castro. A Caribbean History 1492–1968 (London: Andre Deutsch, 1970) page 201.

205. Norman Girvan, Foreign Capital and Economic Development in Jamaica (Mona: Institute of Social and Economic Research, University of the West Indies, 1971).

206. Stephen D. Krasner, Defending the National Interest. Raw Materials. Investments and U.S. Foreign Policy (Princeton: Princeton University Press, 1978).

207. For an account of the genesis and evolution of the West Indies Federation, see Lloyd Braithwaite, "Progress Toward Federation, 1938–1956," Social and Economic Studies, Vol. 6, No. 3 (June 1957) pages 133–84.

208. Franklin W. Knight, The Caribbean, the Genesis of a Fragmented Nationalism (New York: Oxford University Press, 2nd ed., 1990) page 300.

209. Gordon Lewis, The Growth of the Modern West Indies (New York: Monthly Review Press, 1968) page 352.

210. Fitzroy Baptiste, "The Federal Process in the West Indies as Seen by the United States, 1947–1962," Social and Economic Studies, Vol. 48, No. 4 (December, 1999) pages 185–210. See pages 186 and 201.

211. Overand R. Padmore, "Federation: The Demise of an Idea," Social and Economic Studies, Vol. 48, No. 4 (December, 1999) pages 21–65.

212. David Coore, "The Role of the Internal Dynamics of Jamaican Politics on the Collapse of the Federation," Social and Economic Studies, Vol. 48, No. 4 (December, 1999) pages 65–82.

213. Sir Fred Philips. Caribbean Life and Culture. A Citizen Reflects (Kingston: Heinemann, 1991) page 54.

214. Eric Williams, From Columbus to Castro, page 508.

215. Vaughan Lewis, "Issues and Trends in Jamaican Foreign Policy 1972–1977" in Carl Stone and Aggrey Brown (eds.), Perspectives on Jamaica in the Seventies (Kingston: Publishing house, 1981) page 44.

216. Rosina Wiltshire-Brodber, "Trinidad and Tobago Foreign Policy 1962–1987: An Evaluation," in Selwyn Ryan (ed.), Trinidad and Tobago. The Independence Experience 1962–1987 (St. Agustine: Institute of Social and Economic Studies, University of the West Indies, 1988) pages 281–302. Page 282.

217. Jacqueline A. Braveboy-Wagner. The Venezuelan-Guyana Border Dispute. Britain's Colonial Legacy in Latin America (Boulder: Westview Press, 1984).

218. Carifta and the New Caribbean (Georgetown: Commonwealth Caribbean Regional Secretariat, 1971), The Caribbean Community in the 1980s, Report by a Group of Experts (Georgetown: CARICOM Secretariat, 1981), R. B. Manderson-Jones, Jamaican Foreign Policy in the Caribbean 1962–1988 (Kingston: Caricom Publishers, 1990), and Christoph Mullerleile, CARICOM Integration, Progress and Hurdles. A European View (Kingston: Kingston Publishers, 1996).

219. Treaty Establishing the Caribbean Community, Chaguaramas, 4th July 1973 (Georgetown: Caribbean Community Secretariat, June, 1987) page 4.

220. Richard Hart, The End of Empire. Transition to Independence in Jamaica and Other Caribbean Region Colonies (Kingston: Arawak Publications, 2006) pages 298–99.

221. George Eaton, Alexander Bustamante and Modern Jamaica (Kingston: Kingston Publishers, 1975) page 202.

222. "Jamaica, Free to Go Where?," The Economist, August 11, 1962, page 519.

223. Michael Kaufman, Jamaica Under Manley. Dilemmas of Socialism and Democracy (London: Zed Books, 1985) page 86.

224. Wendell Bell and J. William Gibson Jr., " Independent Jamaican Faces the Outside World," International Studies Quarterly, Vol. 22, No. 1 (March, 1978) pages 5–48.

225. Wendell Bell, Jamaican Leaders. Political Attitudes in a New Nation (Berkeley: University of California Press, 1964) page 168.

226. Vaughan Lewis, "Issues and Trends in Jamaican Foreign Policy, 1972–1977" in Carl Stone and Aggrey Brown (eds.), Perspectives on Jamaica in the 70s (Kingston: Kingston Publishers, 1981) page 43.

227. Hartley Neita, Hugh Shearer. A Voice for the People (Kingston: Ian Randle Publishers, 2005) pages 191–93.

228. Larry Lacey, Violence and Politics in Jamaica, 1960–1970 (London: Manchester University Press, 1972), Carl Stone, Class, Race and Political Behavior in Urban Jamaica (Mona: Institute of Social and Economic Research, University of the West Indies,

1973), and Obika Gray, Radicalism and Social Change in Jamaica, 1960–1972 (Knoxville: University of Tennessee Press, 1991).

229. Garvey is a forerunner of the Black Power movement of the 1960s in the United States; see Theodore G. Vincent, Black Power and the Garvey Movement (New York: Ramparts Press, 1970). This is the case even when this intellectual debt is not acknowledged; see Stokely Carmichael and Charles V. Hamilton, Black Power. The Politics of Liberation (New York: Vintage Books, 1967).

230. For examples of the intermingling of these three ideational systems see I. Jabulani Tafari, A Rastafari View of Marcus Mosiah Garvey. Patriarch, Prophet, Philosopher (Kingston: Great Company Ja. Ltd., 1996) and Burning Spear, see 100th Anniversary (Island Records, 1976), Social Living (Island Records, 1980), and Hail H.I.M. (Heartbeat, 1994).

231. Trevor Munroe, For a New Beginning. Selected Speeches. 1990–1993 (Kingston: Caricom Publishers, 1994) page 104.

232. Michael Manley, The Politics of Change (London: Andre Deutsch, 1974).

233. Speech by Ambassador Fletcher at Business Luncheon in New York, October 25, 1972.

234. Embassy of Jamaica Annual Report 1974 (Washington, D.C.: Embassy of Jamaica, 1974) page 1.

235. Hearings before the United States Senate, Subcommittee on Multinational Corporations of the Committee on Foreign Relations (Washington, D.C.: Government Printing Office, 1973) pages 109–34.

236. Patrick H. O. Rousseau, Negotiating Change. Pat Rousseau and the Bauxite Negotiations 1974–1977 (Kingston: Heinemann Educational Books (Caribbean) Ltd., 1987) page 67.

237. Interview with Senator Dudley Thompson, October 18, 2000.

238. Norman Girvan, Corporate Imperialism (New York: Monthly Review Press, 1979) page 115.

239. For a brief account of the Non-Alignment Movement up to the time that Manley demitted office in 1980 see Gwyneth Williams, Third World Political Organizations (London: Macmillian, 1981) pages 46–65.

240. Michael Manley, "Overcoming Insularity in Jamaica" Foreign Affairs, Vol. 49, No. 1 (October, 1970) pages 100–110.

241. Michael Manley, Jamaica. Struggle in the Periphery (London: Third World Media Ltd./Writers and Readers Publishing Corporative Society, 1982) page 66.

242. For a review of Jamaica's policy towards CARICOM see R. B. Manderson-Jones, Jamaican Foreign Policy in the Caribbean, 1962–1988 (Kingston: CARICOM Publishers, 1990).

243. Michael Manley, Jamaica. Struggle in the Periphery (London: Third World Media Ltd./Writers and Readers Publishing Cooperative Society, 1982) page 66.

244. Michael Manley, Jamaica. Struggle in the Periphery (London: Third World Media Ltd./Writers and Readers Publishing Cooperative Society, 1982) page 67.

245. Vaughan A. Lewis, "The Commonwealth Caribbean Policy of Non-Alignment" in Basil A. Ince (ed.), Contemporary International Relations of the Caribbean (Port of Spain: Institute of International Relations, 1979) pages 1–11.

246. Michael Manley, Jamaica. Struggle in the Periphery (London: Third World Media Ltd./Writers and Readers Publishing Cooperative Society, 1982) page 67.

247. Speech by Honorable Michael Manley Prime Minister of Jamaica at Howard University, 10th August 1972, page 22.

248. Locksley Edmondson and Peter Phillips, "The Commonwealth Caribbean and Africa: Aspects of Third World Racial Interactions, Linkages and Challenges," in Basin A. Ince (ed.), Contemporary International Relations in the Caribbean (St. Augustine: Institute for International Relations, University of the West Indies, 1979) pages 33–55. See page 46.

249. Michael Manley, Jamaica. Struggle in the Periphery (London: Third World Media/Writers and Readers Publishing Cooperative Society, 1982) page 66.

250. Don Mills, "Jamaica's International Relations in Independence" in Rex Nettleford (ed.), Jamaica in Independence: Essays on the Early Years, (Kingston: Heinemann Publishers (Caribbean) Ltd. 1989) page 143.

251. J. Daniel O'Flaherty, "Finding Jamaica's Way," Foreign Policy (Summer, 1978) page 138.

252. Evelyne Huber Stephens and John D. Stephens, Democratic Socialism in Jamaica (Princeton: Princeton University Press, 1986) page 175.

253. Evelyne Huber Stephens and John D. Stephens, Democratic Socialism in Jamaica (Princeton: Princeton University Press, 1986) page 205.

254. Michael Manley, Up the Down Escalator: Development and the International Economy, A Jamaican Case Study (London: Ándré Deutsch Ltd. 1987) pages 96–114 and 227–38.

255. Norman Girvan, Corporate Imperialism. Conflict and Expropriation (White Plains, N.Y.: M.E.Sharpe, 1976) pages 143–51.

256. C. Fred Bergsten, "A New OPEC in Bauxite," Challenge May 31, 1977, pages 12–20.

257. Holger Henke, Between Self-Determination and Dependency: Jamaica's Foreign Relations, 1972–1989 (Mona: University of the West Indies Press, 2000) page 48.

258. Michael Manley, Up the Down Escalator: Development and the International Economy, A Jamaican Case Study (London: Ándré Deutsch Ltd, 1982) page 175.

259. Holger Henke, Between Self-Determination and Dependency: Jamaica's Foreign Relations, 1972–1989 (Mona: University of the West Indies Press, 2000) page 48.

260. Rachel Manley, Slipstream. A Daughter Remembers (Kingston: Ian Randle Publishers, 2000) page 201.

261. Richard L. Bernal, "Restructuring Jamaica's Economic Relations with Socialist Countries, 1974–1980," Development and Change, Vol. 17, No. 4 (October, 1986) pages 607–34.

262. Michael Manley, Jamaica. Struggle in the Periphery (London: Writers and Readers Publishing Cooperative Society, 1982) pages 175–79.

263. Michael Manley, The Poverty of Nations. Reflections on Underdevelopment and the World Economy (London: Pluto Press, 1991) page 85.

264. Anthony Payne, Politics in Jamaica (Kingston: Ian Randle Publishing, Revised Edition, 1994) page 159.

265. Ali A. Mazrui, "Uncle Sam's Hearing Aid," in Sanford J. Unger (ed.), Estrangement. America and the World (Oxford: Oxford University Press, 1985) pages 179–92. See page 189.

266. Arnaud De Borchgrave, "Cuba's Role in Jamaica ," Newsweek, February, 1977.

267. Ellen Ray, "CIA and Local Gunmen Plan Jamaican Coup," Counterspy, Vol. 3, No. 2 (December, 1976).

268. Philip Agee, Inside the Company. A C.I.A. Diary (New York: Stonehill, 1975).

269. "The Manley/Levitt Exchange," Small Axe, No.1 (1997) page 82.

270. Principles and Objectives. People's National Party (Kingston: People's National Party, 1970) page 6.

271. Principles and Objectives. People's National Party (Kingston: People's National Party, 1970) page 23.

272. Principles and Objectives. People's National Party (Kingston: People's National Party, 1970) page 26.

273. Norman Girvan, Richard L. Bernal, and Wesley Hughes, "The IMF and the Third World: The Case of Jamaica, 1974–1980," Development Dialogue, No. 2 (1980) pages 113–15.

274. Richard L. Bernal, "IMF and Class Struggle in Jamaica, 1977–1980," Latin American Perspectives, Vol. 11, No. 3 (Summer, 1984) pages 53–82.

275. Norman Girvan and Richard L. Bernal, "The IMF and the Foreclosure of Development Options: The Case of Jamaica," Monthly Review, Vol. 38, No. 9 (February, 1982) pages 48–68.

276. Richard L. Bernal, "The IMF and Class Struggle in Jamaica, 1977–1980," Latin American Perspectives, Vol. 42, No. 3 (Summer, 1984) pages 53–82.

277. Carl Stone, The Political Opinions of the Jamaican People 1976–1981 (Kingston: Blackett Publishers, 1982).

278. Edward Seaga, Speech to the Annual Meeting of the Council of the Americas, New York, December 5, 1980.

279. R. B. Manderson-Jones, Jamaican Foreign Policy in the Caribbean 1962–1988. Kingston: CARICOM Publishers, 1990) page 144.

280. Anthony J. Payne, Politics in Jamaica (Kingston: Ian Randle Publishers, Revised Edition, 1994) pages 160–61.

281. Fitzroy Ambursley, "Jamaica from Michael Manley to Edward Seaga," in Fitzroy Ambursley and Robin Cohen (eds.), Crisis in the Caribbean (London: Heinemann, 1983) pages 72–104. See page 94.

282. Sahadeo Basedeo and Graeme Mount, The Foreign Relations of Trinidad and Tobago, 1962–2000. The Case of a Small State in the Global Arena (Port of Spain: Lexicon Trinidad, 2001) p. 55.

283. Michael Manley, The Integration Movement, the CBI and the Crisis of the Mini-State," Caribbean Affairs, Vol. 1, No. 1 (January-March, 1988) pages 6–15. See page 10.

284. A New Inter-American Policy for the Eighties (Washington, D.C.: Council for Inter-American Security, 1980) page 46.

285. Tom Berry, Beth Wood, and Deb Preusch, The Other Side of Paradise. Foreign Control in the Caribbean (New York: Grove Press, 1984) page 162.

286. Anthony Payne, Politics in Jamaica (Kingston: Ian Randle, 1994) page 111.

287. Kari Polanyi Levitt, The Origins and Consequences of Jamaica's Debt Crisis 1970–1990 (Mona: Consortium School of Graduate Studies Social Science, University of the West Indies, 1991) page 17.

288. Timothy Ashby, Missed Opportunities: The Rise and Fall of Jamaica's Edward Seaga (Indianapolis: Hudson Institute, 1989).

289. Anthony Payne and Paul Sutton, Charting Caribbean Development (London: Macmillan, 2001) page 107.

290. Kathy McAfee, Storm Signals. Structural Adjustment and Development Alternatives in the Caribbean (London: Zed Books, 1991) page 128.

291. For a history of origins, conduct, and demise of the government of Maurice Bishop see Grenada. Whose Freedom? (London: Latin America Bureau, 1984) and Hugh O'Shaughnessy, Grenada. Revolution, Invasion and Aftermath (London: Sphere Books, 1984).

292. Anthony Payne, Paul Sutton, and Tony Thorndike, Grenada: Revolution and Invasion (New York: St. Martin's Press 1984) pages 151–53.

293. Cheddi Jagan, The West on Trial. The Fight for Guyana's Freedom (Berlin: Seven Seas Books, 1972).

294. Darrel E. Levi, Michael Manley. The Making of a Leader (Kingston: Heinemann, 1989) pages 237–38.

295. Frederic L. Pryor, "Socialism via Foreign Aid: The PRG's Economic Policies with the Soviet Bloc," in Jorge Heine (ed.), A Revolution Aborted. The Lessons of Grenada (Pittsburgh Press, 1990) pages 153–80.

296. Maurice Bishop, Forward Ever! Three Years of the Grenadian Revolution (Sidney: Pathfinder Press, 1982) and Chris Searle, Grenada. The Struggle Against Destabilization (London: Writers and Readers Publishing Cooperative, 1983).

297. Anthony Paine, "The Foreign Policy of the People's Revolutionary Government," in Jorge Heine (ed.), A Revolution Aborted. The Lessons of Grenada (Pittsburgh: University of Pittsburgh Press, 1990) pages 123–51.

298. Harold Alexander Lutchman, From Colonialism to Co-operative Republic. Aspects of Political Development in Guyana (Rio Piedras: Institute of Caribbean Studies, 1974) page 248.

299. Festus Brotherson Jr., "The Foreign of Guyana, 1970–1985: Forbes Burnham's Search for Legitimacy," Journal of Interamerican Studies and World Studies, Vol. 31, No. 3 (Fall, 1989) pages 9–36.

300. Jean Grugel, Politics and Development in the Caribbean Basin. Central America and the Caribbean in the New World Order (Bloomington: Indiana University Press, 1995) page 125.

301. Carl Stone, "Buying Power," Weekly Gleaner, April 28, 1987, page 18.

302. W. Richard Jacobs and Ian Jacobs, Grenada. The Route to Revolution (Habana: Casa de las Americas, 1980) page 136.

303. Christoph Mullerleile, Caricom Integration. Progress and Hurdles. A European View (Kingston: Kingston Publishers, 1996) page 181.

304. Christoph Mullerleile, op. cit., page 181.

305. Anthony P. Maingot, The United States and the Caribbean (London: Macmillan, 1994) Chapter 7.

306. Anthony P. Gonzales, "Recent Trends in International Economic Relations of the CARICOM States," Journal of Interamerican Studies and World Affairs, Vol. 31, No. 3 (Fall, 1989) pages 63–95.

307. Robert A. Pastor and Richard D. Fletcher, "Twenty-first Century Challenges for the Caribbean and the United States: Toward a New Horizon" in Jorge I. Dominguez, Robert A. Pastor, and R. DeLisle Worrell (eds.), Democracy in the Caribbean. Political, Economic and Social Perspectives (Baltimore: Johns Hopkins University Press, 1993) pages 255–76.

308. J. Edward Greene, "External Influences and Stability in the Caribbean" in Anthony T. Bryan, J. Edward Greene, and Timothy M. Shaw (eds.), Peace, Development and Security in the Caribbean. Perspectives to the Year 2000 (London: Macmillan, 1990) page 222.

309. Robert Borosage, "Lonely Manley," Mother Jones, March-April, 1991, pages 26–29. See page 26.

310. Don Mills, The New Europe, the New Order and the Caribbean (Kingston: Grace, Kennedy Foundation, 1991) page 71.

311. Jorge I. Dominguez, "The Future of Inter-American Relations: States, Challenges and Likely Responses" in Jorge I. Dominguez (ed.), The Future of Inter-American Relations (New York: Routledge, 2000) pages 3–34. See pages 26 and 32.

312. For an analysis of the implications of globalization for Jamaica and the English-speaking Caribbean see Don D. Marshall, Caribbean Political Economy at the Crossroads, NAFTA and Regional Development (London: Macmillan, 1998) Chapters 3 and 4, Richard L. Bernal, "Globalization and Small Developing Countries: The Imperative for Repositioning," in Denis Benn and Kenneth Hall (eds.), Globalization: A Calculus of Inequality (Kingston: Ian Randle, 2000) pages 88–128, and Richard L. Bernal, "The Caribbean in the International System: Outlook for the First 20 years of the 21st Century" in Kenneth Hall and Denis Benn (eds.), Contending with Destiny. The Caribbean in the 21st Century (Kingston: Ian Randle, 2000) pages 295–325.

313. Hilbourne A. Watson, "Global Restructuring and the Prospects for Caribbean Competitiveness: With a Case Study of Jamaica," in Hilbourne A. Watson (ed.), The Caribbean in the Global Political Economy (Boulder: Lynne Rienner/Kingston: Ian Randle, 1994) pages 67–90 and Richard L. Bernal, Strategic Global Restructuring and the Future Economic Development of Jamaica, North South Agenda Paper No. 18 (Miami: North-South Center, University of Miami, May, 1999).

314. Anthony P. Gonzales, "World Restructuring and Caribbean Economic Diplomacy" in Lloyd Searwar (ed.), Diplomacy for Survival: CARICOM States in a World of Change (Kingston: Frederick Ebert Stiftung, 1991) pages 1–18.

315. Richard Feinberg, who initiated the idea while responsible for Latin America and the Caribbean within the National Security Council, wrote the definitive work on this subject. See Richard Feinberg, Summitry in the Americas. A Progress Report (Washington, D.C.: Institute of International Economies, 1997).

316. Tom Farer (ed.), Transnational Crime in the Americas (New York and London: Routledge, 1999), Ivelaw Griffith, "Transnational Crime in the Americas: A Reality Check," and Monica Serrano, "Transnational in the Western Hemisphere" in Jorge I. Domiquez (ed.), The Future of Inter-American Relations (New York and London: Routledge, 2000) pages 63–86 and 87–110, and Anthony Bryan, Transnational Crime (Miami: North-South Centre, University of Miami, 2000).

317. Feinberg, op. cit, page 4 and pages 55–62.

318. The CARICOM negotiating team was jointly led by Ambassador Richard Bernal (economic aspects) and the Attorney General of Barbados, David Simmons (security aspects).

319. World Bank, Annual Report 1991 (Washington, D.C.: World Bank, 1992) page 65.

320. Peter G. Peterson, Gray Dawn: How the Coming Age Wave Will Transform America and the World (New York: Times Book, Random House, 1999).

321. Max J. Castro, Immigration and Integration in the Americas (Miami: North South Centre, University of Miami, Agenda Paper No. 46, May, 2001) page 7.

322. Richard L. Bernal, "U.S. Caribbean Relations at the Dawn of the Twenty-First Century" in Richard L. Bernal, Anthony T. Bryan, and Georges A. Fauriol, The United States and Caribbean Strategies. Three Assessments, Policy Papers on the Americas, Vol. XII, Study 4 (Washington, D.C.: Center for Strategic and International Studies, 2002) pages 3–25. See Table V.

323. Bernard Headley with Michael D. Gordon and Andrew MacIntosh, Deported (Jamaica: Bernard Headley, 2005) page 64.

324. Crime, Violence and Deportees: Trends, Costs and Policy Options in the Caribbean, World Bank Report No. 37820 (Washington, D.C.: World Bank, May, 2007).

325. Randolph B. Persaud, Counter-Hegemony and Foreign Policy. The Dialectics of Marginalized and Global Forces in Jamaica (Albany: State University of New York Press, 2001).

326. Randolph B. Persaud, Counter- Hegemony and Foreign Policy. The Dialectics of Marginalized and Global Forces in Jamaica (Albany: State University of New York Press, 2001) pages 120–23.

327. Michael Manley, Jamaica. Struggle in the Periphery (London: Writers and Readers Publishing Cooperative Society/ Third World Media Ltd., 1982) page 106.

328. Michael Manley, "Address to Parliament," May, 1974.

329. The Common Fund is explained in Michael Manley, Up the Down Escalator. Development and the International Economy- A Jamaican Case Study (London: Andre Deutsch, 1987) chapter 7.

330. Michael Manley, The Poverty of Nations. Reflections on Underdevelopment and the World Economy (London: Pluto Press, 1991) page 94.

331. Randolph B. Persuad, Counter-Hegemony and Foreign Policy. The dialectics of Marginalized and Global Forces in Jamaica (Albany: State University of New York Press, 2001) page 127.

FOUR

How Foreign Governments Attempt to Influence U.S. Foreign Policy

The model of the U.S. foreign policy formulation presented in chapter 1 concentrated on domestic factors and must be extended to include the activities of foreign governments, businesses, and foreign residence communities. This chapter will employ the enhanced model described in chapter 1 to analyze how foreign governments attempt to influence the process of foreign policy formulation in the United States. The model, which is illustrated in figure 4.1, is the framework that will be applied to analyze each case study. The discussion draws on the literature on attempts by foreign governments, businesses, and resident communities to influence U.S. foreign policy. This exercise is essential background to the examination of attempts by the government of Jamaica to influence U.S. foreign policy. The bulk of the research material documents the activism of Canada,[1] Mexico,[2] Japan,[3] and Israel.[4] In reviewing the literature it is necessary to be cognizant of differences in capacities for influence between powerful countries, e.g., Japan; strategic allies, e.g., Israel; or groups of countries, e.g., EU, which have some leverage, and small countries such as Jamaica that are of marginal importance and have very limited human and financial resources.

Foreign governments attempt to influence U.S. policy by (1) direct contact with the various branches, departments, and agencies of the U.S. government, (2) contact with the media and think tanks that can influence U.S. government, (3) alliance with its business associations and firms, and (4) where possible by mobilizing their migrant communities in the United States. Foreign governments often employ professional lobbyists and public relations firms to advise, guide, assist, and support in "furthering" their views and attaining their objectives. In some situations foreign governments may find that they can cooperate with and act in

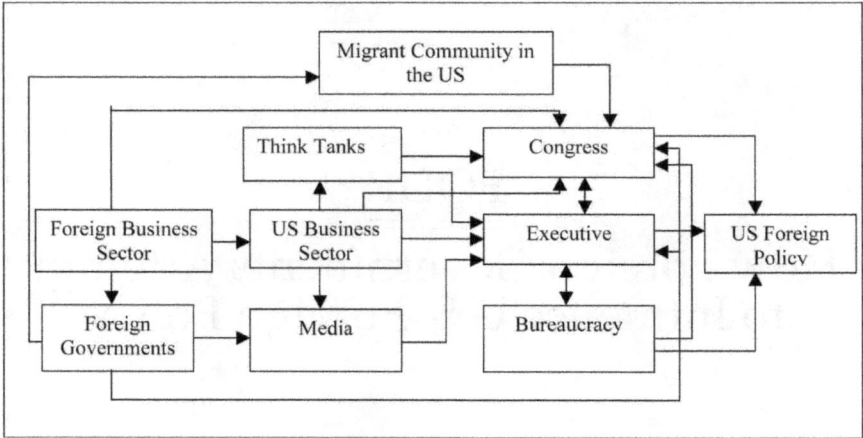

Figure 4.1.   Attempts by Foreign Governments to Influence U.S. Foreign Policy

concert with domestic U.S. interests. These interests and alliances vary between issues, political situation, and continually shifting circumstances. In some cases, the foreign government representatives in Washington may join with the executive to lobby Congress in support of, or in opposition to, or to modify a specific piece of legislation or draft legislation. For example, the government and business sectors of Canada and Mexico lobbied shoulder to shoulder with the Clinton Administration to secure Congressional approval of the NAFTA. The only constant in the highly fluid Washington politics is that there are no fixed alliances and with very few exceptions, there are no friends, only contacts whose interests coincide on a particular issue at a given moment in time in a particular political conjuncture. A friend and supporter on one issue may at the same time be a virulent and impeccable opponent on another issue. These realities epitomize the Mafia dictum "it is not personal, it is just business." Continuous change is the only constant. It is the mode of existence and the nature of the context of operations.

The chapter is divided into two parts. The first is devoted to a general discussion of how foreign governments have attempted to influence U.S. foreign policy towards their respective countries. The second part provides an overview of the means and channels that Jamaica has sought to employ in its attempt to influence U.S. foreign policy, particularly during the 1990s.

PART I

The Executive

Most foreign governments are aware of the balance of power between the President, the Congress, and the Judiciary in the U.S. political system, but focus much of their efforts on influencing U.S. policy on the White House. Meetings between heads of government are of course the highest level of inter-government interaction, and are seen as pivotal in having a foreign government's perspective taken into account in the formulation and implementation of U.S. foreign policy. The issue areas in which the President has full and direct control are not as numerous as foreign governments perceive; nevertheless the White House can exert enormous pressure on Congress and the bureaucracy to ensure that the President's wishes are translated into policy. Foreign governments, particularly those where the same political party controls both the Executive and the legislature, are often frustrated when the President is not able to immediately command that decisions be implemented.

The principal problem of this level of diplomacy is that meetings between the head of a foreign government and the President are the exception and not the rule. Indeed, only those representing countries that the United States regards as powerful and important have repeated access to the President. For most countries, opportunities to meet with the President are few and brief, even in exceptional circumstances. It is not uncommon for a President's four-year term to run its course without meeting for extended conversation, all but a small coterie of "world leaders." Contact for most heads of government is confined to a few fleeting moments of greeting and exchange of pleasantries at international meetings. Usually, heads of state are confined to meeting the Secretary of State or Vice President, if he is an integral part in foreign policy. Ministers of Foreign Affairs often find they have to meet with senior officials other than the Secretary of State, or will have to wait until the Secretary of State's calendar can accommodate their request for a meeting. Ambassadors to Washington, D.C., may have virtually no contact of a substantive nature with the Secretary of State during their tenure and only have a chance to have a meaningful exchange with the President during the presentation of their credentials. In some instances, credentials are presented to the Secretary of State in order to facilitate early and expeditious accreditation. In the case of small states of limited strategic value to the United States, access to the highest political levels is extremely restricted and may be confined to "crisis situations." One of the most effective means of influencing U.S. policy is a meeting between a country's head of government and the President. For example, the meeting between President Clinton and five Prime Ministers of Jamaica, the Bahamas, Barbados, Guyana, and Trinidad and Tobago in August 1993 was instrumental in leading to a renewed focus by the United States on its policy towards the region. The meeting caused the Administration to pause, reflect, and update their policy towards the English-speaking Caribbean (ESC). The meeting also permitted the Prime Ministers and their Foreign Ministers to meet and interact with Vice-President Al Gore, Secretary of State Warren Christopher, Secretary of Commerce Ron Brown, Ambassador Alec Watson of the State Department, Anthony Lake and Richard Feinberg of the National Security Council, and Mickey Kantor, U.S. Trade Representative.[5]

Congress

The U.S. political system is unique among democracies because it allows anyone or any institution, domestic or foreign, to openly lobby its legislature. In most political systems intervention by foreign government representatives is confined to interacting with the Executive or Bureaucracy. The formulation of U.S. foreign policy includes attempts at influencing foreign business and foreign government officials and entities, as shown in figure 4.1.

Foreign governments endeavor to influence U.S. foreign policy and trade policy by interacting with domestic partners with whom they share common objectives. They make representations to the Executive and the Bureaucracy and lobby Congress. The willingness to openly lobby members of Congress has increased in the last 10–15 years. Prior to this, some ambassadors felt that such direct contact with Senators and Congressmen was an "impropriety." Ambassador Heeney of Canada, commenting on his tenure in Washington in the 1950s, advised that "For an ambassador to intervene directly with a member of either House of Congress is a delicate, risky undertaking which may easily backfire: the legislative branch is traditionally resentful of anything approaching foreign interference or attempted pressure . . . direct recourse to congressional friends should be reserved for the most critical situations in which no practical alternative was available."[6] In recent years ambassadors have had no such reservations, on the contrary, some ambassadors have been very active in lobbying Congress.[7]

The lobbying of Congress by foreign governments can be made more effective by operating with the advice and contacts of a lobbying firm. No matter how good an ambassador and his staff are they are not able, even in a long tenure, to develop the range and number of contacts that a firm in the lobbying business for ten or more years can develop. In addition, there are types of information that Americans, especially former colleagues, will share with each other, which they will hesitate to provide to a diplomatic representative of a foreign government. Jamaica's employment of Neil and Company was instrumental in assisting Ambassador Bernal to quickly develop contacts in Congress among both members and staff. Neil and Company recorded in their 1994 annual report to the government of Jamaica that "we have succeeded in reinforcing Ambassador Bernal's well-established positions as the leading Caribbean diplomat in Washington, which reinforces Jamaica's pre-eminence in the policy-making community and serves to educate policy makers on Jamaica's perspectives on important foreign aid, financing and trade issues. Ambassador Bernal is often the diplomat-of-choice for consultation on Caribbean affairs." The report continued by stating that, "Ambassador Bernal was able to testify before the House Ways and Means Committee only after we had secured a special waiver of the Committee's standing rules preventing foreign government witnesses from testifying at hearings. As a result of the positive reception of that appearance, however, we were able to arrange for Ambassador Bernal to be invited to testify before the Committee two additional times this year, surpassing the precedent he himself set a year ago."[8]

Lobbyists

Many foreign governments employ lobbyists, and these activities are governed by the Foreign Agents Registration Act of 1938, which required those who lobby on behalf of foreign governments or political parties to register with the Justice Department. In 1995 the law was amended, and broadened the definition of foreign lobbyists to include individuals who lobby on behalf of foreign-owned commercial enterprises. It required them to register with the clerk of the House and the secretary of the Senate. At the end of the 1990s there were an estimated 10,000 to 20,000 lobbyists operating in Washington, D.C.[9] About 600 lobbyists have registered with the Justice Department as "agents" representing foreign governments or parties,[10] an increase of 50 percent since the late 1970s.[11] However, the Justice Department has estimated, for instance, that the number of unregistered foreign agents ranges from 30 percent to 60 percent of all those registered.[12] Many of these lobbyists are former Members of Congress or former high-ranking officials in the Federal government. The Center for Public Integrity has documented that 47 percent of the former senior officials of the U.S. Trade Representative registered as agents representing foreign clients.[13]

Under the current regulations, all persons must be registered as foreign agents with the Department of Justice if they act as agents, representatives, employees, or servants and engage directly or through any other person in any of the following activities:[14] (a) political activity in the United States on behalf of the foreign principal, (b) public relations counsel, publicity agent, information-service employee, or political consultant for the principal, (c) soliciting, collecting, disbursing, or dispensing contributions, loans, money, or other items of value for the foreign

principal, and (d) representing the interests of the foreign principal before any agency or official of the government of the United States.[15]

The ability to influence events depends on the amount of support that
can be mobilized and consolidated among entities and groups with similar interests. Joining forces creates a larger critical political mass in addition to what has been termed "a synergy that can exceed the effectiveness
of its components."[16] The efficacy of lobbying can be enhanced if the
lobbying firm, sometimes with the Embassy, can mobilize the U.S. resident community of that country's nationals to support policies in the
interest of their homeland. Experience has demonstrated that the activities of foreign lobbyists or agents who lack strong indigenous support
achieve only limited or transient influence on American foreign policy.[17]
Examples of successful lobbying based on domestic, grassroots support
are the American Israel Public Affairs Committee (AIPAC), and the
Greek and Irish lobbies.[18] Where the community is not well organized, or
lacks the tradition of voting in their countries of origin, or has not been
sufficiently galvanized by any issue, there is usually an absence of involvement. The Hispanic community is an example of a primarily politically dormant community, which has only recently attracted attention.[19]
Historically they have had little political presence and exercised clout in
only a limited number of Congressional jurisdictions. Immigration has
been the only issue around which they have coalesced and it has allowed
the Hispanic community to coalesce on a national level.

In the late 1980s, Japanese corporations were spending an estimated
$100 million a year on political lobbying in the United States and another
$300 million building a nationwide grassroots political network to influ-
ence public opinion. Together, the Japanese government and Japanese
companies employed ninety-two Washington law, public relations, and
lobbying firms on their behalf, compared with 55 for Canada, 42 for
Britain, and 7 for the Netherlands.[20] Choate's comment that Japan's lobbying was "an ongoing political campaign as though it were a third major political party"[21] is an exaggeration, but the Japanese lobbying presence has been considerable.

In the 1990s the Mexican government found the services of various
lobbying firms indispensable in their campaign to secure Congressional
approval of the NAFTA. One of their lead negotiators explained: "we
found the assistance of lobbyists extremely important. They helped us
understand the intricacies of the U.S. legislative process where we were
bound . . . to be involved. There was no way we could have acquainted
ourselves with the system without the intelligent help of our lobbying
team."[22] In 1996 foreign governments, corporations, and individuals reported that they spent $64 million specifically on lobbying governmental
entities. These figures probably understate the full range of foreign lobbying activities and expenditures. Covert campaign contributions by

foreign governments and foreign nationals to American elections are a problem that congressional committees have investigated.[23]

A good lobbying firm can be very helpful in ensuring exposure, making contacts, and networking for a country's ambassador. One foreign diplomat described the role of their lobbyists as forming "the scaffold that gives structure to the whole and in their subtle way makes the system work."[24] A lobbyist can be very important in introducing a new ambassador, especially if a new campaign is to be launched or an unpleasant issue has arisen. However, lobbyists cannot substitute for a good ambassador and a hard-working professional embassy staff, as there are tasks that can only be done by the ambassador, and meetings and events in a sovereign country that can only be represented by its ambassador. The ideal situation is when both lobbyists and ambassador are highly motivated, energetic, and operating in close coordination. Neil and Company in their 1991 report[25] to the government of Jamaica stated: "the Ambassador came to Washington with a desire to establish contacts with key players on Capitol Hill and the intention of solidifying congressional support for Jamaica. The lobbyists were able to facilitate this effort by arranging numerous congressional visits for the Ambassador targeting friends of Jamaica and the committees and Members of Congress with influence over policy directly affecting Jamaica. In this way the lobbyists helps the ambassador to become an active, visible Ambassador who is widely recognized as a leader of the Caribbean diplomatic corps."

Gaining access to key Members on Capitol Hill often requires being recognized as an expert on an important issue. Part of our strategy for 1991 was to promote Ambassador Bernal as an expert on regional, particularly Caribbean, economic matters. Included within this rubric is the debt issue. We have disseminated newspaper articles written by the Ambassador to Members of Congress who work in the area of trade and economic policy. We have arranged for the Ambassador to appear on panels both in Washington and elsewhere and through an effective letter writing campaign, we have ensured that Ambassador Bernal's viewpoint and thus, that of the government of Jamaica, is known to the members and staff prior to their deciding on issues or voting on legislation that directly impacts Jamaica.

In addition to cultivating a close personal and working relationship between Ambassador Bernal and Members of Congress who may serve on committees dealing with foreign affairs or economic policy, we have also helped to establish close ties with its members of Congressional Black Caucus (CBC). As it grows in number and as certain of its members become increasingly senior, the Congressional Black Caucus, as an organization, becomes more influential and powerful. Fortunately, Black Caucus Members have traditionally supported Jamaica in Congress. This support has often been crucial in the appropriations and authorization processes. Realizing that this support cannot be taken for granted, however, we arranged for the Ambassador to meet regularly with members of this group and to become acquainted personally with them. These efforts have led to continued strong and consistent support from the Black Caucus."[26]

The services of a lobbyist can be especially useful if a foreign government has to confront a distasteful issue, as these go-betweens can filter out the country's counterargument or alternative view or explanation. No matter how immoral the government, or how disreputable their conduct or unpalatable the cause, for the right price, it is always possible to engage a lobbyist. The firm of O'Connor and Hannon succeeded in preventing the cut-off of aid to a government in El Salvador, which was implicated in death squad killings and the murder of six Jesuit priests by the military.[27]

Mexico's Campaign for NAFTA [28]

In order to secure NAFTA, Mexico spent an estimated total of $45 million, with as much as $15 million spent in 1993. This involved a revolution in the diplomacy of Mexico in Washington, D.C., from the "unobtrusiveness in the pre-NAFTA period." The old style reflected not wanting to intrude in U.S. internal affairs, fatalism about what could be achieved, limited resources, "cautious envoys," the ambassador's lack of outreach (1983–1988), and "the embassy's inertia." Mexican expenditure on lobbying increased from $412,419 in 1988 to $9,518,971 in 1992 exceeding what more affluent countries were spending, e.g., Canada (also involved in NAFTA) spent $4,967,145.

Two very important aspects of the Mexican campaign were, first, the hiring of numerous influential former U.S. government officials. In addition to former government officials and former Senate and House members, Mexico hired top lobbying firms with connections to both Republicans and Democrats, e.g., the Brock Group; law firms, e.g., Sharman and Sterling,; public relations firms, e.g., Burson-Marsteller; and trade specialists, e.g., Manchester Trade. Second, a very able and highly influential political appointee was made Ambassador to the United States. He was allowed to increase the staff in the Mexican Embassy in Washington, D.C., from 65 to 85, including expertise from outside the foreign ministry so that "the Embassy's personnel (were) more specialized, but they were better prepared, as evidenced by their holding more advanced degrees than their predecessors." A considerable asset was the fact that the Ambassador was able to exert more influence both in the United States and Mexico, because he was able to speak and act with the authority of the President. In the United States, the standing and influence of a country's ambassador is to a considerable extent determined by his or her proximity and access to the highest levels of political power in the government, which he or she represents. In some situations, the ambassador is far more influential than the country's Minister of Foreign Affairs and in some instances, passed up a ministerial post to serve as ambassador to the United States for personal reasons or because the government regarded relations with the United States as its foreign policy priority.

Media

The foreign policy decision-making process in the United States is influenced by public opinion because the President and more so the members of Congress who have to seek reelection every two years are sensitive to what is carried in the media. With the exponential growth of media, the role of public opinion is increasingly apparent and pervasive in the policy process. However, the relationship between media and foreign policy is one of interdependence with influence being exerted in both directions.[29] The nexus is extremely complex with many instances in which public opinion determines the direction of policy; however, the administration is often in a position to sway public opinion. Even in cases where the White House goes against public opinion, e.g., aid to the Contras by the Reagan Administration, public opinion did at least constrain the implementation and duration of the policy.[30] All governments seek to manipulate or even influence the content, perspective, and timing of new broadcasts and print reporting. Opinions vary from those that argue that the press is trusting of and even deferential to the foreign policy establishment.[31] Others such as Entman[32] regard the media as being effectively manipulated by the U.S. government and ends up in the famous words of Edward Herman and Noam Chomsky, "manufacturing consent."[33]

One of the most effective techniques of influencing the White House and the Congress, both of which are acutely sensitive to public opinion, is to arrange to have a government's view widely, frequently, and favorably presented in the media. This can take many different forms depending on the audience, the objective, and the issue. A particular perspective may be aired or articulated by a well-known personality or acknowledged expert or prominent person, either by persuading them or inducing them by payment or favors. This is best accomplished by utilizing the expertise and connections of a public relations firm or media consultant. In circumstances where financial limitations do not permit resorting to professional services, a government might try to place an opinion editorial in leading nationally circulated newspapers such as the *Washington Post*, the *Wall Street Journal*, and the *New York Times*. Some ambassadors have been able to break the unwritten rule of not publishing articles written by currently serving ambassadors by having opinion editorials published in various newspapers, most notably in the *Post* and the *Journal*.

Cohen has suggested that in each major power, one newspaper stands out as an organ of elite opinion.[34] In the United States in economic matters it is the *Wall Street Journal* and in Washington, D.C., the bible of politics is the *Washington Post*; on all issues including international affairs the *New York Times* is highly regarded. All three papers influence public opinion and the information supplements what U.S. government policymakers get from official sources. Certain network newscasts are influential because they often provide live coverage of events and reach a larger audience than print media. Sometimes a paper is not a national voice but is useful because of its willingness to cover a certain issue or region of the world. For example, the *Miami Herald* was important because of its willingness to cover Latin America and the Caribbean.

If a government can afford to spend the required amount of money, it can purchase advertisements in newspapers or even special supplements, the cost of which might be offset by private sector advertisements. In some circumstances a foreign government can arrange to have its case pleaded in public by surrogates, either genuine or concocted for the purpose, by advertisements in the press or spots on television. A good example of this type of well-funded, media campaign is the one Mexico launched to secure acceptance and passage of NAFTA when it realized that the American public was split 46 percent in favor and 44 percent against. This costly media blitz involved targeting 31 major media markets with the aim of influencing key undecided members of Congress. All Mexican government agencies and several U.S. government departments were involved in the campaign, designed and managed by the giant public relations firm of Burson-Marsteller. The intensity of the campaign can be gauged by the fact that in one four week period, at least 45 major news stories and more than 30 positive editorials were published.[35] Spending and manpower on such an enormous scale is obviously an option available only to the largest and wealthiest countries.

Whatever the perspective, it is beyond dispute that the media can have an influence on U.S. foreign policy. This is important for small states that are trying to get visibility for their issue and to shape the debate on issues of concern to them. The problem is that being of little importance and not being a newsworthy crisis such as a military coup and starving children it is very difficult to get the attention of major news media. In addition, if the small country is competing against a domestic interest that is willing to spend then it can nullify or even overwhelm the efforts of the small country. A clear example of this was Chiquita's dominance of the print media on the United States-European Union dispute over the EU's preferential banana import arrangements.

Under the direction of Ambassador Bernal the information officer assigned to the Embassy of Jamaica compiled and kept up to date a media list. This list identified persons of Jamaican and Caribbean origin in all major media and in cities where there were large communities of Caribbean persons. Each major city throughout the United States had a Caribbean music and news program on weekends and they would accommodate all requests for interviews and briefings. This was an inexpensive way for the Jamaican ambassador to reach the Caribbean community because it was only a long distance call and not air travel. The media list was vital to get coverage and indeed to prevent or counteract negative reportage. For example, an advanced warning from Jamaican Joy Elliott in Reuters prevented the news service from carrying a harmful erroneous item that purported that Ambassador Bernal attended a certain Congressional Black Caucus, which he had not. An exchange of late night calls prevented the incorrect information from being carried.

Migrant Communities in the United States

The United States is a multicultural, multi-ethnic society in which migrant communities have always exerted some influence on U.S. foreign policy. The history of that influence in the twentieth century according to Smith[36] can be divided into three periods. In the first stage, from the 1910s to the 1930s, the most active groups were the Irish, Germans, Scandinavians, and Italians, who acted as a restraint on U.S. involvement in international affairs. By contrast, in the second stage during the Cold War, virtually all the ethnic groups strongly supported an assertive anti-communist policy. A third phase, beginning with the end of the Cold War, has witnessed the disintegration of the consensus and the emergence of a wide variety of ethnic and national loyalties coexisting with patriotism, creating a situation of divided loyalties. In recent years, migrant communities and second generation ethnic groups have become more influential in U.S. society and its international relations[37] as their numbers and share of total population have increased. Perhaps the most successful ethnic community lobbying on foreign policy is the Jewish community.[38] Refugee groups have also gained attention; as Shain explains, "while 'white Anglo-Saxon' domination over foreign policy may have been powerful enough to exclude 'nonwhite' ethnic voices from the policy process, the policy elite's preoccupation with communism allowed American doors to open to Third World refugees and, eventually, to the views they expressed."[39] This group has definitely exerted a powerful influence on U.S. foreign policy towards supporting Israel. The success is evident in the fact that economic and military aid to Israel has exceeded that provided to any other country.[40] One of the most powerful lobbying organizations is the American Israel Public Affairs Committee (AIPAC), which has 55,000 members, a staff of 150 people, and a budget exceeding U.S.$15 million. It wields significant influence in Congress because it has often been decisive in the Jewish vote in local and national elections.[41]

U.S. policy towards Cuba has been to tighten or at least maintain the embargo, despite the inclination of Bush and Clinton towards constructive engagement. The rigidity in policy, which has persisted despite a steady escalation of calls for the relaxation or abolition of the embargo,[42] is testimony to the pressure generated by Cuban-Americans. This relatively small community (7 percent of the voting population in Florida)[43] concentrated in Miami and southern Florida has wielded a disproportionate influence through consistent voting behavior, well-organized public campaigns, and financial contributions.[44] It is a remarkable feat that despite their small number, they have held U.S. foreign policy hostage even beyond the end of the Cold War. The Cuban American National Foundation (CANF) and the Free Cuba Public Affairs Committee were able to buy influence in Congress by making huge financial contribution to both parties. These Cuban-American organizations were by far the largest contributors to the 17 Hispanic members of Congress during the 1991/1992 elections. They gave $694,896 during 1981 to 1992, compared to $75,050 by the eight other Hispanic PACs.[45] High on the list of recipients were the following powerful politicians: Senator Jesse Helms, Representative Dan Burton (co-sponsors of the Helms Burton Act), Congressman Bill Richardson (later Secretary for Energy), Congressman and later Senator Robert Torricelli, and Congressman and later Senator John McCain (unsuccessful candidate for the Republican Party Presidential nomination).[46] Others accepting contributions were Senator Lloyd Bentsen (later Secretary of the Treasury), Senator Dan Quayle (later Vice President), George Bush (Vice President and later President)[47] and Joseph Lieberman (Vice Presidential candidate).[48] The CANF, formerly led by flamboyant Bay of Pigs survivor and millionaire businessman Jorge Mas Canosa, had an annual budget of over $3.5 million.[49] The CANF uses every avenue of influence from speaking engagements at the prestigious Council on Foreign Relations, to disseminating a constant stream of printed propaganda,[50] to organizing conferences and testimony to Congressional hearings.

The Greek-American community in the United States was successful in pressing the Congress to impose an arms embargo on Turkey in 1975, despite opposition in Congress and the Ford Administration and in spite of the importance of Turkey as an ally to the United States and its strategic geographical position in the U.S. defense cordon around the Soviet Union during the then raging Cold War.[51] Although there were misgivings in Congress and concern in the Ford Administration, the campaign had strong public support. The objective of the embargo was to end the Turkish military presence in northern Cyprus and pressure Turkey to negotiate a settlement of dispute with Greece over Cyprus. The embargo was phased out in stages until 1978, when the old arrangements were restored and did not achieve its objective. However, the campaign demonstrated what a relatively small ethnic minority community could accomplish when there is a well-organized campaign of mobilization. Americans of Greek ancestry with a strong attachment to the homeland of their forebearers rallied to the defense of their land of origin, against what they regarded as the aggression and wrongful occupation of territory that Greece and Greeks had traditionally thought of as theirs. It is instructive as the campaign demonstrates that small ethnic communities with deep-rooted "ancient affections," to use Woodrow Wilson's term, can change U.S. foreign policy in a direction contrary to established perceptions of national interest.

Alliances among Migrant Communities

In their attempts to advance their interests, migrant communities often seek alliances with other such groups in order to increase their critical mass in political terms and increase their leverage. Such alliances are easier to forge if these communities have a common interest, e.g., opposition to U.S. immigration policy. The bases for the creation of inter-communal alliances vary from issue to issue since they are often ethnic, e.g., Arabs opposed to U.S. support for Israel or people of African descent pressing for aid for Africa to assist in the fight against AIDS. Religion can be a powerful force in uniting different nationalities, e.g., the case of Muslims in respect to U.S. foreign policy towards the Balkans or the Middle East. These coalitions are often difficult to mobilize and maintain over the course of an extended campaign, as there are centrifugal forces that overwhelm or fragment the sometimes-tenuous centripetal impulses. Even when a campaign can galvanize widespread sentiment, it is problematic to translate this into political pressure because of constraints such as money, the illegal status of sections of the migrant community, and the lower voter turnout in migrant groups. Some issues divide migrant communities along class, ethnic, linguistic, and/or ideological lines, e.g., the Sandinista-Contra civil war.

Well-established communities are in a better position to press their demands than newly arrived migrant communities, because they are viewed as having the legitimacy of being born Americans and are not disparaged as being "aliens" who should not be complaining, and least of all criticizing, U.S. foreign policy. Migrants publicly complaining about U.S. policy are often admonished that they should not be in the United States if they disagree with U.S. foreign policy and are advised to go back to their "own country." Cultural and historical differences can pose subtle and complex problems for establishing and operating political alliances. This dilemma is illustrated by the assumption of a close affinity between African-Americans and Africans both in the United States and in their native lands. Similarly migrants from Central America and Latin America assume a "natural brotherhood" with Hispanic Americans only to find that class, color, race, and nationality override all but family ties.

The migrant community from the ESC has always experienced an affinity with African-Americans, since the earliest period of contact, a trend that became more pronounced over time. As Basch points out, "West Indians were assigned by the dominant groups—i.e. whites—to the same sociopolitical space as Black Americans. This meant that West Indian relations with the wider society were largely mediated by Black American institutions, a situation destined to produce ambivalent feelings between the two groups, largely mediated by West Indian relations with the wider society.[52] Several important leaders of black political activism in the United States on both domestic and foreign policy issues were of Caribbean origin or were descendants of migrants from the ESC. The best known of these leaders was Marcus Garvey[53] from Jamaica. Other influences from the ESC include activist George Padmore from Trinidad, Marxist intellectual C. L. R. James[54] from Trinidad, poet Claude McKay from Jamaica, and musician Bob Marley from Jamaica. Winston James has observed that, "Caribbean migrants were indeed present in socialist and black nationalist organizations in numbers well out of proportion to their weight within the American population. Moreover, many held leadership positions within such movements."[55] The relationship is a complex one. It is not without differences, which cannot be assumed away because both groups share a racial profile and common cultural heritage that is supposed to be an automatic and intuitive bond.

The patriotism of citizens who identify themselves, or can be differentiated as, "hyphenated Americans" is frequently brought into question if such groups disagree with U.S. foreign policy towards their ancestral homeland. In fact their patriotism, loyalty, and even trustworthiness is questioned even if they indicate tacit support or express their compliance with U.S. foreign policy. The supposition of "divided loyalties" or what some prefer to describe as "conflicted loyalties"[56] remains widespread, as it avoids impugning the patriotism of those who have a strong sense of ethnic identity. The most graphic and notorious episodes involved the disgraceful treatment of Japanese-Americans during World War II, for which there has been no apology or restitution. While these pogroms are not likely to be repeated in this day and age, there is still a residue of nativism and pervasive racism.

Business

The influence of the business sector, particularly large corporations, on U.S. foreign policy, especially economic policy, is well documented.[57] Wiarda, while dismissing the Marxist notion of the control of big business over government policy in capitalism, states, "business influence over foreign policy extends far beyond traditional lobbying efforts. It now includes business largely running or controlling large areas of U.S. foreign economic policy."[58] Foreign governments, in collaboration with their business associations and large corporations, attempt to network with U.S. business associations, such as the American Chamber of Commerce, to influence Congress, the President, and the bureaucracy, both directly and indirectly, through the media. On matters of common interest, foreign governments and their business communities see U.S. companies that operate in their country as natural allies. This business-to-business relationship can enhance the attention given to the objectives and issues of a foreign government, because the White House and Congress are particularly "responsive" to the views expressed by U.S. corporations.

It is often the case that there is not unanimity throughout all sectors of the U.S. business community on any given policy issue. This makes it even more imperative to have strategic business alliances with U.S. firms, which can advocate a position that is in the interest of both themselves and the foreign government, but that they articulate as their issue of concern and their proposals for U.S. policy. For example, this type of business-to-business collaboration is the alliance between the United States and Caribbean sugar producers, to preserve the U.S. bilateral sugar quota system and to cap Mexican exports of sugar to the United States, permitted by a side letter of NAFTA.

Another leading example is the Caribbean/Latin American Action (CLAA), an association of business leaders from major U.S. and Caribbean corporations. It is a non-profit corporation incorporated in 1980 and funded primarily by contributions from companies in the region or concerned about the region. The CLAA, from its headquarters in Washington, D.C., has lobbied in favor of U.S. aid to the region, the 936 funds program, and the Caribbean Basin Initiative (CBI). The CLAA had its origins in the late 1970s when the committee for the Caribbean was founded to encourage the U.S. government and private sector to address issues of concern to Caribbean countries. In 1980, it was renamed the Caribbean/Latin American Action and in 1990 its mandate was expanded to include South America.[59] At the beginning of December each year, CLAA hosts a major conference in Miami, which brings together political leaders from the region, high-level U.S. officials, and U.S. and Caribbean business leaders. In addition to the annual conference, CLAA has arranged several private/public sector fora on offshore finance, tourism, telecommunications, and the Free Trade Area of the Americas (FTAA).[60] The CLAA played an important role in pushing for enhancement of the CBI by presenting a business perspective to the Administration and Congress supporting new legislation on the CBI.

Bureaucracy

The ambassador to the United States, supported by the Embassy in Washington and the associated consulates, represents the apogee of a foreign government's diplomatic apparatus in the United States. The ambassador and embassy, while targeting the bureaucracy, in particular the

State Department, seek to develop contacts among all the entities that play a role in the formulation of U.S. foreign policy. In recent years, foreign diplomats have begun to interact with a wide range of specialized sections and agencies in the U.S. bureaucracy. This has been made necessary by the decentralized nature of the structure of U.S. government bureaucracy and the extensive use of the inter-agency process as a mechanism for the formulation of U.S. policies that either constitute foreign policy or impact on U.S. relations with foreign governments. The process of certifying foreign governments as cooperating with the United States on counter-narcotics campaigns illustrates the diverse multiplicity of government entities that have a role in this process. The numerous layers of bureaucracy include the agencies that collect information and monitor anti-drug trafficking programs of foreign governments, the inter-agency process that evaluates the data and makes a recommendation to the President who in turn, after perusing the report of the inter-agency process, announces the outcome and informs Congress by way of a mandated report.

Several of the most important departments and agencies of the U.S. government have offices in foreign countries, for example USAID, the Central Intelligence Agency (CIA), and the Drug Enforcement agency (DEA). The most important external office is the embassy that reports to the State Department. The embassy usually has a wide range of skills covering all aspects of relations with the host country. The Washington-based bureaucracy depends on information from the "field" and takes account of the views from their staff in the particular country. A government wishing to influence U.S. foreign policy must seek to shape the feedback going to Washington, D.C. It was not infrequent that U.S. officials based in Jamaica developed strong empathy with Jamaica and at times were viewed in Washington as having "gone native." Many officials sought a second and even a third posting in Jamaica and most of those whose final posting was Kingston have participated in U.S. organizations supporting Jamaica such as the "Friends of Jamaica." Others have retained direct links with particular projects or organizations.

An important but often neglected dimension of the foreign policy bureaucracy is the U.S. embassy and U.S. ambassador in the foreign country, trying to influence U.S. policy. The State Department puts significant reliance on reports, information, views, and perspectives from its diplomatic representative in forming impressions of a particular foreign country and in formulating policy towards that country. The U.S. ambassador can exert considerable influence on the bureaucracy, the Congress, and the White House, if that person is a political appointee with access to the President. The ambassador of a country to the United States must develop a close working relationship with the U.S. ambassador to his or her country. The U.S. ambassador can also play an important role in lobbying Congress in support of foreign aid allocations and legislation affecting the country to which the ambassador is accredited.[61]

Jamaica's ambassador to the United States during 1991–2001, Richard Bernal had a very close working relationship with the four U.S. ambassadors who served in Jamaica during those years. The U.S. ambassadors to Jamaica in this period were Ambassador Glenn Holden, during the Administration of President George Bush, Ambassador Gary Cooper, during the first Administration of President Bill Clinton, Ambassador Stanley McLenand, during the second Clinton Administration, and briefly with Ambassador Sue Cobb, in the Administration of George W. Bush. Bernal met, or spoke by telephone, with his counterpart on nearly all of his frequent trips to Jamaica. Similar contact was made when the U.S. ambassador visited Washington, D.C., and other cities or conferences in which both ambassadors were present. Regular telephone calls were exchanged between the ambassadors in Washington, D.C., and Kingston, and correspondence was shared to ensure that both ambassadors were working in tandem and towards the same goals.

On August 9, 1972, ackees were officially banned from entering the United States because the United Bureau of Foods (UBF) was concerned that the product contained hypoglycin-A, a toxicant that could result in illness and even death. The decision was based on literature available to the bureau that provides evidence that ackee contains toxic substances. The Bureau had no evidence to assure itself that toxic material was eliminated during the processing stage. The Bureau suggested that manufacturers provide evidence that toxic substances are eliminated in processing and requested assurances that processing makes the product safe for consumption.[62]

The issue was how to measure the level of toxin with sufficient accuracy to establish that if canned under the proper conditions, the level of toxin would be below the safety threshold set by the U.S. government. The product was not certified for exportation to the U.S. market until July 2000. During the ensuing period, the government of Jamaica with the support of its private sector, made numerous attempts to have the ban rescinded. The Jamaican community in the United States, primarily the Jamaica Progressive League and the business community that imported the product, lobbied the U.S. government to permit the importation of canned ackees. The campaign continued on and off throughout the 1970s and 1980s. Ambassador Alfred Rattray met with the USDA in October 1978 in an attempt to resolve the matter, stating that ackee was safely consumed in Jamaica and elsewhere in the world. The Ambassador also suggested that there could be a warning label on the cans. However, he was informed that it would be necessary to submit a petition convincing U.S. authorities that the consumption of ackee was safe. If the petition were successful, it would result in an agreement between the two governments, stipulating appropriate production processes. The Jamaican officials were also informed that a petition might take up to two years to be resolved.[63] The struggle continued throughout the 1980s with Ambassador Keith Johnson writing several letters to Congressman Charles B. Rangel, asking him to intervene with the FDA. On March 12, 1987, Rangel wrote to the United States Trade Representative (USTR) and received a reply on June 3, 1987, which reiterated an unchanged position by the USFDA.

Commencing in the early 1990s a decision was made to revive the lobbying effort and to revisit the issue in view of new scientific techniques for treating toxicity. The campaign involved mobilizing support in Congress and presenting new scientific evidence to the U.S. authorities. On August 11, 1993, a government of Jamaica team led by Ambassador Richard Bernal and involving Mr. James Kerr, Jamaica Bureau of Standards and scientific experts, Dr. George F. Wilson, Director, Jamaica Agricultural Research Programme, Jamaica Agricultural Development Foundation, and Dr. Juliette Newell, met with Mrs. Ellen McCloskey and a team from the U.S. Department of Agriculture in Washington, D.C. The basis for re-opening the discussions was the presentation of new scientific techniques on the measurement of the level of toxin in tree opened canned ackees, developed by researchers at the University of Florida and the Jamaica Bureau of Standards. It demonstrated that the level was so low as to be almost undetectable. On the following day the Ambassador sent a letter[64] to the U.S. Food and Drug Administration (USFDA) requesting the lifting of the "alert" on ackee.

On April 20, 1999, a Jamaican delegation including Ambassador Richard Bernal, Dr. André Gordon, Technical Advisor, Technological Solutions Ltd., Mr. John Mahfood, Grace Kennedy and Company, Mr. James Kerr, Chemist, Jamaica Bureau of Standards, and Mr. Norman McDonald, President, CANCO, met with a 15-person team from the USDA and new techniques for measuring toxins in processed ackee were presented. The U.S. response was favorable and a commitment was made to visit the canning factories in Jamaica and in conjunction with the Jamaica Bureau of Standards, certify those that met U.S. standards. A five-member delegation from the USDA and the FDA visited Jamaica in September 7, 1999 and in July 2000, the United States lifted the ban on the importation of ackees canned in Jamaica and certified two factories[65] as meeting U.S. standards.

The resolution of this long-standing dispute was primarily due to the intervention of the U.S. ambassador to Jamaica, Stanley McClelland, who used his political contact with the President to ensure prompt action by the U.S. authorities. This intervention came against the background of presentation of scientific evidence on the safety of canned ackees. The actual negotiations involved the private sector, the Jamaican Exporters Association, the Embassy of Jamaica, the government of Jamaica, representatives of the United States Embassy in Jamaica, and the United States

Food and Drug Administration. It was also a personal triumph for the U.S. ambassador, Stanley McLelland, who made a personal campaign of getting the ban lifted during his three-year tour of duty to Jamaica.

Think Tanks

Think tanks play an important role in the identification of foreign policy objectives, the analysis of issues, and the recommendation of policy measures. Most of these institutions are independent, although some have a distinctive philosophical orientation and are generally autonomous elements in the U.S. foreign policy process. Their influence derives from their espousal of views to all entities in the foreign policy process and their influence on policy makers, international organizations, and public opinion. Their status and impact derives in many instances from the fact that they provide a platform for senior officials, formally in decision-making positions in the Executive and bureaucracy, who in most instances are waiting to resume a position in the bureaucracy. This gives certain credence to their views and warrants attention since they may occupy foreign policy decision-making roles in the future. Foreign governments have generally resorted to trying to influence their policy research agenda by funding research on relations between the United States and their own country or region, or a particular international issue of significance to their national interests. In some instances, the business sector of a foreign country will act as surrogate for a foreign government by funding research, the exchange of views through conferences, and in some instances will establish, in collaboration with U.S. business interests, partnerships to facilitate dialogue and the propagation of shared views. These partnerships are usually institutionalized in the form of business organizations, which put out policy documents or host policy discussions and strictly speaking are not think tanks in the conventional connotation.

The European Institute[66] in Washington, D.C., is an example of this type of organization. The Institute is a Washington, D.C., based public-policy organization devoted to European-U.S. affairs. It brings together Americans and Europeans in an independent and non-partisan forum. Its goal is to maintain and renew the transatlantic relationship while European integration proceeds and the Atlantic Alliance evolves. Participants include representatives of governments, corporations, universities, experts, journalists, NGOs, and contributing individuals. The Institute supports its mission among 24 countries and 80 U.S. and European corporations by organizing and facilitating a range of activities: (a) working groups that meet on a regular basis to address specific issues, (b) briefings by government and business leaders, (c) off-the-record roundtable discussions with senior officials, (d) publication of *European Affairs*, a quarterly policy journal, and ad hoc reports. The guiding principle for all activities is to maintain a balance of representation between Europeans and Americans in the public and private sectors.

PART II

Employment of Lobbyists by the ESC

The governments of the ESC countries have in general employed professional lobbyists only during periods of crisis,[67] largely because of the prohibitive costs. Antigua, the Bahamas, and Trinidad and Tobago have only employed lobbyists for short periods, as the governments of the ESC countries have typically used lawyers to address specific issues or concerns. Jamaica is the exception, having retained a lobbying firm, A. F. Sabo and Associates, during 1981–1989. In 1989, when Michael Manley replaced Edward Seaga as Prime Minister, the lobbying arrangements were changed. The Manley government hired a lobbying firm, Neil and Company, in 1989 and later in the 1990s the contract was shared between two firms. The banana export countries retained the services of a lobbyist, Ross-Robinson and Company and briefly utilized lawyers and a public relations firm during that period. The sugar exporting countries of the ESC retained the services of Ed Greaves in Washington, D.C. None of the other governments of the ESC retained lobbyists during the 1980s. They did however spend money on tourism and investment promotion.[68]

As issues such as debt relief, investment, and trade became more important than foreign assistance in the bilateral relationship between the United States and the Caribbean, the Caribbean had to widen its alliances and recruit new allies to encourage policies to foster strong commercial links between the United States and the Caribbean.

Use of Lobbyists by Jamaica

The earliest resort to government relations support by the government of Jamaica took place during the negotiations with U.S. multinational corporations producing bauxite and alumina in Jamaica. These negotiations were at times tense and Jamaica retained the services of A.F. Sabo and Associates. In 1980, Edward Seaga, leader of the opposition, thought it advisable to have professional advice on public relations in the United States. Sir Edgeton Richardson, Jamaica's Ambassador to the United Nations, introduced Ann Sabo to Seaga. After winning the election in October 1980, Mr. Seaga hired A. F. Sabo and Associates, which commenced paid services in early 1981 and continued with the central government until 1984, when they were retained by the Jamaica National Investment Promotions Ltd. until 1990. Prime Minister Seaga became the first head of government to visit the newly elected President Ronald Reagan. Sabo and Associates helped to design and manage an intensive campaign for Jamaica to play a lead role in the early development of the CBI. Through their Washington office, they arranged meetings and numerous telephone calls between Seaga and members of Congress. In those days, meetings between diplomats of foreign governments and members of Congress were infrequent. Sabo organized visits of teams including spokespersons from the Jamaican business sector, executives of U.S. companies that were members of the Jamaica American Chamber of Commerce. These teams were supported by briefings and talking points from members of staff of Sabo's Washington, D.C., office. The campaign targeted Congressmen whose districts imported Jamaican bauxite and alumina or exported to Jamaica.[69]

Before Michael Manley was elected in 1989 he was aware that he carried "baggage" that might prove detrimental to him in establishing a positive relationship with the government of the United States. He knew that in the election of 1980, Edward Seaga, with the help of conservatives in the United States had succeeded in painting him as a communist sympathizer and having the election in Jamaica seen by some ideologues in the United States as a battle between democracy and communism. Manley, who had become quite sophisticated about the U.S. political process during the 1980s when he visited the United States regularly on the lecture circuit, was aware of the complexity of appealing to different constituencies in Washington. In addition, he wanted to have government relations counsel in Washington who could assist him in assuring the government of the United States that he was returning to power with different economic plans and policies, and that he was no longer going to govern as a democratic socialist, emphasizing the New International Economic Order and champion third world relationships such as that with Cuba.

After interviewing several firms, Michael Manley decided to retain the services of Neil and Company, who had been introduced to him by Richard Fletcher[70] through Harry Smith, who as a businessman involved in the shipment of PL 480 surplus food had done business in Jamaica. Neil and Company won out over several lobbying firms, including Ron Brown, then at Patton Bogg.

Richard Bernal (later Ambassador to the United States), General Manager of the Workers Savings and Loan Bank, was a member of the panel who interviewed firms bidding for the contract with the Manley government. Bernal pointed out that Neil and Company knew "absolutely nothing about Jamaica." After an embarrassing pause, a red-faced Neill replied that that was true but "we know Washington." Bernal went on to forcefully insist that if they were going to service the government of Jamaica they needed to employ staff that knew something about Jamaica, preferably someone with a Jamaican background. This point was not lost on either Neill or Manley. At the time Neil and Company commenced working for Jamaica, Dalley, an American of Jamaican parentage was ready to leave the post of Chief of Staff to Congressman Charlie Rangel to join the private sector. During his first visit to Washington as Prime Minster in 1989, Dalley asked Manley, who he had come to know well during his visits to Washington to lecture in the 1980s, whether he would be willing to become a client. He responded that he would love to have Dalley work for him in Washington, but before knowing of Dalley's intention to leave Rangel's employment, he had decided to hire Neil and Company as his government relations counselors. What Manley did, however, was to introduce George Dalley to Denis Neill and it make it clear to Denis that his hiring Dalley to be a part of the team to service Jamaica would be a good idea and would contribute to the immediate establishment of a positive working relationship. Neil took the hint and Dalley began working for Neil and Company on June 1, 1989, on the Jamaica account.

Neil and Company assisted in smoothing Manley's relationship with the government of the United States, thanks to Manley's convincing arguments that he had spent his time out of power in the 1980's in a serious rethink and was convinced that the way for economic development to be achieved in Jamaica was through the development of a vibrant private sector, operating in an enabling free market environment. In addition, the lobbyists helped the Manley government project itself as a staunch and effective ally of the United States in the war against drugs, which in 1989–1990 was a major concern of U.S. policymakers. Prime Minister Manley came to the United States, and in one-on-one meetings with members of Congress and Senators, and in Congressional testimony, spoke of his commitment to join the United States in the fight against the menace of trafficking in dangerous narcotics in the region and proposed an innovative regional approach to the problem to be led and funded by the United Nations.

The lobbyists worked with friends of Jamaica in the Congress, especially with members of the Congressional Black Caucus, but also with Delaware Senators Biden and Roth, thanks to the help of multimillionaire John Rollins, who appreciated that Manley had been willing to solve a land dispute Rollins had with the government of Eddie Seaga. In addition to opening the doors to Republican Party leaders to whom John Rollins was a major contributor, Manley's willingness to settle the Rollins land dispute established his credentials as a leader who was ready to work with the U.S. investors and the private sector. The lobbyists obtained increased U.S. assistance to Jamaica, working particularly with Bill Gray on the House Appropriations Committee and Bob Kasten on the Senate Appropriations Committee, to increase U.S. government anti-narcotics assistance to Jamaica and to maintain current levels of foreign assistance for the social programs such as the alleviation of poverty in Jamaica.

In 1993, Dalley moved to the law firm of Holland and Knight and the contract for the provision of advice and counsel to the government of Jamaica was shared between Neil and Company and Dalley, with the division of labor to be determined by the Ambassador and by mutual agreement. Simultaneously Neil and Company encountered financial problems and went out of business, its assets being acquired by a lobbying organization named the Jefferson Group. The Government of Jamaica has continued its relationship with the Jefferson Group and its successor, Jefferson Waterman International, and with Dalley at Holland and Knight. In mid-2000, Dalley established his own government relations practice.

During the latter half of the 1990s the lobbying team for Jamaica consisted of George Dalley of Holland and Knight and Ann Wrobleski and Steve Lamar of Jefferson Waterman International. See appendix B. Jamaica also benefitted from the services of Hazel Ross-Robinson of Ross-Robinson Associates who was retained by the banana exporting countries of the English-speaking Caribbean. See appendix C.

The tasks of the lobbyists on behalf of Jamaica have shifted over the years towards a greater emphasis upon the securing of beneficial trade legislation, and away from the obtaining of higher levels of foreign and anti-narcotics assistance, although both of these assistance programs continue to be funded by the U.S. government in Jamaica. The major lobbying effort since the passage of legislation by the United States to create the North American Free Trade Agreement in 1994 has been to achieve legislation to restore parity of access to the U.S. market for the nations of the Caribbean Basin, who lost the superior access they had previously had under the Caribbean Basin Initiative. As a result of Mexico gaining preferential access to the U.S. market through the NAFTA, Jamaica experienced diversion of investment, particularly in the apparel assembly industry to Mexico, and loss of jobs. After five years of effort, the campaign finally succeeded in 2000 in securing the passage of legislation to provide CBI parity, now called CBI enhancement, to that provided by the U.S. market to Mexico under the NAFTA.

Use of a Public Relations Firm by Jamaica

To complement the work of the lobbyists, Neil and Company, the government of Jamaica hired Fenton Communications to handle public relations in North America, effective June 1, 1989. The firm, which was headed by David Fenton, with Leila McDowell as account executive, had assisted Michael Manley while he was leader of the opposition. The immediate and most important task was to reintroduce Manley to the U.S. government, media and the public and overcome the image of that of a socialist and close friend of Fidel Castro. Typical of this image is a report by the Associated Press on May 11, 1989, which stated "Florida business leaders were impressed — although some are still cautious — after meeting the 'new' Michael Manley, leading Jamaica again a decade after his socialist government fell."[71] One of the early positives for the campaign in the United States was Manley's resolute determination to fight drug trafficking at a time when Jamaica was seen as struggling with a serious drug problem. In May, the *Wall Street Journal* carried an article on the front page, which portrayed Jamaica as fighting a losing battle against drug smuggling in the port of Kingston.[72] On May 23, 1989, the conservative *Washington Times* in an editorial called on the Bush Administration to support Manley in his fight against drugs.[73] On June 9, 1989, at the 12th annual TransAfrica dinner, Manley announced his new initiative for a multinational strike force against drugs, operating under the auspices of the United Nations. Manley's idea was acclaimed in the influential *Washington Post*,[74] Reuters, Associated Press, Interpress, Knight Ridder newspapers, *Miami Herald*,[75] and the MacNeil-Lehrer NewsHour. Without the work of Fenton Communications, the Manley drug initiative would not have received the amount of attention that it did and the re-imaging of Michael Manley might not have occurred as quickly and as effectively. The lobbyists and the public relations firm combined to ensure that members of Congress were aware of Manley's innovative proposal. It was not accidental that in July "the Senate unanimously passed an amendment to the State Department Authorization Bill approving Mr. Manley's proposal. Sponsored by Senators Arlen Specter (R-Pa) and John Kerry (D-Ma), they applauded Manley's anti-drug plan as worthy of praise and strong support. The House passed a similar resolution in June."[76]

Use of Lobbyists by Trinidad and Tobago

In late 1991 when Patrick Manning was elected as Prime Minister of Trinidad and Tobago, he and his primary advisors, Lenny Saith who became Minister of Planning and Wendell Mottley, who became Minister of Finance in the new government, decided it would be in the interest of the new government to raise its profile in Washington as a means of becoming engaged in the policy dialogues affecting the Caribbean and to develop a constituency of support for the nation in the Congress. Trinidad and Tobago had not previously felt the need for an enhanced presence in Washington because it did not have particular need for assistance from the United States or from the multilateral development institutions.

Trinidad and Tobago's oil and gas production produced sufficient revenue to create a relationship with the United States of a different nature than that of the rest of the nations of the Caribbean and to obviate the need for aid. The new government, however, felt the need to diversify the economic base and to attract investment from the United States for this purpose. Government Relations counsel (lobbyist) was hired to assist the government of Trinidad and Tobago become better known as a positive investment destination and to introduce the newly enhanced private sector oriented economic policies and investment climate as well as the existence of specific opportunities in Trinidad and Tobago to potential investors. Neil and Company, in the person of George Dalley aided by Vicki Asceveda, assisted the government by advising on the establishment of an investment promotion agency that would provide information on opportunities for investment in Trinidad and Tobago and facilitate the interest of potential investors. The Jamaica Promotion Agency (JAMPRO) was cited as a model and used as such in the formation of the Trinidad and Tobago Development Corporation (TIDCO).

George Dalley encouraged the visit to Washington of the Prime Minister and his senior Ministers and introduced them to the Clinton Administration policymakers, who were in a position to inform inquiring potential U.S. investors of the strength of the economy of Trinidad and Tobago and the pro-investment economic policies of the new government. The U.S. federal government agencies who are responsible for interfacing with U.S. investors abroad such as the Department of Commerce, the Overseas Private Investment Corporation (OPIC), the Export-Import Bank (EXIM), and the Office of the U.S. Trade Representatives (USTR), are influential with such investors and thus it is essential that the personnel in these agencies become cognizant of and impressed with the foreign government's willingness to attract and support new investment from the United States.

Trinidad and Tobago were helped in managing their case with these agencies, and with other policy makers in the U.S. government, by the U.S. energy companies who had been historically engaged in oil and gas production in Trinidad and Tobago. These companies, led by AMOCO, were willing to assert their own positive experience and lend their voices and resources to our efforts to introduce the new government and its intention to attract new investment to diversify and grow the economy. It is significantly beneficial in promoting the interests of a Caribbean government in Washington if there is a community of U.S. businesses that have had a positive experience in the nation and a good relationship with the U.S. government. The role of the government relations advisors was to motivate the U.S. business community to assist the government in its efforts to raise and enhance its recognition, to develop a program to maximize their effectiveness with federal government officials, and in making the case for the economic significance of the trade and commercial relationship between the United States and Trinidad and Tobago, to them and to influential members of Congress.

The Congressional Black Caucus

The Congressional Black Caucus (CBC) was formed in 1970 and originally had nine members. Its first prominent action was a boycott of President Nixon's State of the Union address in 1973 because he had refused to meet the CBC to discuss police brutality and the 1969 killing of Black Panthers Fred Hampton and Mark Clark. The meeting took place after the boycott.[77] Over the years, the CBC has shown strong interest in developments in Africa and the Caribbean and has been consistent advocates seeking to influence U.S. foreign policy towards these regions. In the mid-1980s, membership had grown to 20 and the principal foci were civil rights issues and sanctions against South Africa. The CBC was very active in the campaign to dismantle apartheid in South Africa. The 1992 elections, which followed the reconfiguration of congressional districts, led to an increase to 39 members, 38 Democrats and one Republican. Carol Moseley Braun became the first African-American woman to be elected to the Senate. The CBC, led by its chairman, Ronald V. Dellums, initiated and passed legislation in 1990 that denied military aid to the Mobutu regime in Zaire and required that economic aid be channeled through private voluntary organizations.[78] Another notable campaign was the effort to change U.S. policy towards deposed Haitian president Aristide. Demonstrations outside the White House led to the arrest of several CBC members, including Kweisi Mfume, Ron Dellums, and Alice Hastings.[79]

African-Americans have assumed a powerful role in the Democratic Party, e.g., Ron Brown was Chairman of the party until he became Secretary of Commerce in the Clinton Administration. African-Americans have also held the posts of Secretaries of Agriculture, Transport, and Energy. In addition, African-Americans accounted for almost 20 percent of the delegates at the 1992 Democratic National Convention.[80] The increased influence of the CBC can be judged by press coverage; the *Washington Post* in 1982 describes the experience of the Caucus as one of "frustration."[81] By 1985 *Congressional Quarterly* reported that the CBC was "striving for influence,"[82] in 1989 the *Washington Times* reported that President Bush met with the Caucus to develop "co-operation,"[83] but by 1993 *Congressional Quarterly* reported that the Caucus was "flexing its muscle" on the budget.[84]

Under the astute and articulate leadership of Ambassador Douglas Fletcher, rapport was established between the Embassy and the Congressional Black Caucus, especially with its Chairman, Charles Rangel. Senator Dudley Thompson attended the Black Caucus dinner on September 28, 1974. This was an important breakthrough as, previous to this, the Caucus's main interest in foreign affairs was Africa. In 1981 the Caucus initiated the 1st Annual Caribbean Seminar, which over the years included knowledgeable Caribbean speakers such as Professor Franklin Knight of Johns Hopkins University, and had participation by political representatives of both principal parties in Jamaica. Michael Manley addressed the seminar twice, first on November 21, 1981, and then on September 27, 1985. During the 1980s, representatives of the Seaga government kept in touch with the Caucus and sought to strengthen its connection with the Caribbean. The contact with the CBC was widened and deepened after Manley returned to the prime ministership. Manley would personally meet with members of Congress in their offices on "the Hill." It was always flattering for them to receive a visit from a prime minister.

American Friends of Jamaica

Many wealthy Americans own vacation homes in Jamaica, notably in Round Hill and Tryall on the outskirts of Montego Bay. They develop a bond of friendship with the people and the country. They contribute to many Jamaican charities and were promoters of the country. In the 1990s they included wealthy and powerful corporate executives such as Ralph Lauren, Bob Pittman (founder of MTV, COO of AOL Time-Warner), William "Bill" Rhodes (senior vice-chairman of Citigroup and Citibank) who was head of Citibank in Jamaica in 1969, John Rollins (a top contributor to the Republican Party), and Mandy Ourisman (Ourisman Automotive Enterprises) whose wife Mary became U.S. ambassador to Barbados and the Eastern Caribbean countries during 2006–2008. They can be mobilized to exert their influence, which derives from their corporate standing, business connections, political contributions, and their social and political contracts. They were always willing to help Jamaica and happy to have the ambassador at their social functions. Ambassador Bernal and more so his wife with the help and encouragement of Frank Pringle a wealthy Jamaican who was Minister of Tourism and a Senator got to know many of this group. Engagements with this group of wealthy Americans were useful on several occasions such as the influence of John Rollins on the Congressional delegation of Delaware. Invitations from this group could end up with meeting Johnny Cash or being seated between U.S. Supreme Court Justice Sandra Day O'Connor and Rev. Leo J. O'Donovan, S. J., president of Georgetown University at a Christmas lunch. In addition some American investors were consistent boosters of Jamaica. None were more consistently active than Braxton and Debbie Moncure, operators of luxury villas in Bluefield on the south coast of Jamaica.

Summary

How and why Jamaica was able to achieve influence over U.S. foreign policy has to be comprehended against the background of how foreign governments go about trying to influence U.S. foreign policy. This in turn requires an understanding of how foreign policy is formulated and implemented in the U.S. political system. Influencing foreign policy in the United States involves working with the executive, legislature, and the various departments of the bureaucracy. It also involves engaging the domestic actors that influence the White House and the Congress. This includes think tanks, the business sector, and the Caribbean Diaspora community. Foreign governments seek to transmit their views by utilizing the mediums of influence such as lobbyists and the media. The degrees of freedom available to foreign governments to use various avenues of influence are unique in the American political system.

Caribbean Community in the United States[85]

The 1990 Census recorded 688,730 people who claimed that their primary ancestry was West Indian. The largest group was Jamaicans, who numbered 435,024, almost 64 percent of the total. The next largest nationalities were from Guyana (81,665), Trinidad and Tobago (76,270), Barbados (35,455), Belize (22,922), and the Bahamas (21,081), and the rest (16,000) from other countries. Some 386,256 people, or 56 percent of West Indians in the United States, live in the New York City metropolitan area (including Connecticut and New Jersey), with the vast majority in New York itself. The next largest concentration was in Florida (117,549) and there was a significant presence in California, Massachusetts, and the Washington, D.C.–Maryland–Virginia area. The U.S. Census Current Population Survey (March 1997) indicated that in 1996, there were 506,000 people who had been born in Jamaica, but this is an underestimate because children born in the United States to Jamaican immigrants were not included. It is estimated that the West Indian population in the United States may be over one million.

The West Indian migrant community was very small until the mid-1960s, when it grew rapidly. The earliest community organizations were burial societies, church-related groups, and credit unions, and were not involved in domestic political matters. Those organizations that were explicitly political devoted their attention to issues in the Caribbean, particularly universal adult suffrage, internal self-government, and independence, e.g., the Jamaica Progressive League. The Jamaica Progressive League (JPL) was formed in 1936, and became the registered U.S. representative and fundraiser for the People's National Party in Jamaica. During the 1940s and 1950s, the "dues paying membership ran into thousands"[86] and gave psychological support and advice to newly arrived migrants. The focus of West Indian community organization shifted from primarily supporting its members to greater involvement in political matters from the mid-1960s. The JPL, which has its headquarters in New York, has been active in lobbying on immigration. The membership is minute, especially in the branches, e.g., in Washington, D.C., its membership has dwindled to a handful because of problems amongst the leadership.

Although Caribbean migrant families keep in close touch across the continental United States,[87] a nationwide Caribbean community or umbrella organization of significant size has not emerged or existed on a sustained basis. The earliest attempts to form a nationwide, pan-West Indian organization were made in the 1950s with the formation of Caribbean American Inter-cultural Organization (CAIO). It was limited to "educating" congressional and government officials because its tax-exempt, non-profit status prevented lobbying. The National Association of Jamaican and Supportive Organizations (NAJASO) was formed in the July 4, 1977, at the instigation of Alfred Rattray, then Jamaica's ambassador to the United States and with the assistance of the Embassy of Jamaica, which represented the coming to fruition of an idea that had been discussed for many years. This non-profit, tax-exempt, umbrella organization had a membership of 50–70 Jamaican community organizations throughout the United States. The Caribbean Action Lobby (CAL), was founded in 1980 by Trinidad-born, Los Angeles Congressman Mervyn Dymally, and New York-based activists of various nationalities. The CAL lobbied in Washington on immigration issues and U.S. policy toward the Caribbean,[88] but unfortunately, it collapsed because of internal disputes in the early 1990s.

The Brooklyn-based Caribbean American Chamber of Commerce and Industry (CACCI), founded in the mid-1980s by Grenadian-born Roy A. Hastick, has focused primarily on promoting small business and trade between CARICOM and the United States. It has generated some support from companies doing business in the West Indian community. Hastick, Dr. Marco Mason of the Caribbean Women's Health Association, and other groups secured public funding in 1985 to establish the Caribbean Research Center at Medgar Evers College in Brooklyn. *Carib News*, a New York-based weekly newspaper founded by Karl B. Rodney, a Jamaican, covers Caribbean affairs and issues affecting the West Indian community in the United States. The paper provides a forum for West Indians throughout the United States and the Caribbean. The circulation of *Carib News* is about 60,000, with 25 percent of its readers outside the New York metropolitan area.

According to the 1990 Census, only 36.7 percent of the West Indians in the United States were naturalized, one of the lowest rates of all immigrant groups and only 25 percent of West Indians interviewed in New York City said they were U.S. citizens. Shirley Chisholm, for example, born in Brooklyn of Barbadian parents, reached the U.S. Congress, the first person of West Indian descent to have achieved this status "by identifying herself with African-American rather than with West Indian interests." Jamaican born Una Clarke ran as an openly West Indian candidate and was elected to represent Brooklyn in the New York City Council in 1991.[89] Congresswoman Sheila Jackson-Lee, of Houston, Texas, who was born in the United States of Jamaican parents, was elected in the early 1990s. Since then she has established an outstanding reputation as a highly intelligent, savvy, informed, and articulate individual and has been a powerful advocate for Caribbean issues such as CBI enhancement and bananas.

West Indian migrants first inserted themselves into the U.S. political process by organizing support groups for African American candidates, e.g., "Caribbeans for Percy Sutton" and "Caribbeans for Koch," organized in New York by Grenadian dentist Dr. Lamuel Stanislaus.[90] In recent years the number of elected Caribbean officials at city and state levels has increased and this may augur well for the future. However, the Caribbean migrant community in the United States has not been able to unite behind Caribbean-born candidates at the level of Congressional elections. A recent example is the attempt by Jamaican-born Una Clarke, Councilwoman for Brooklyn, to unseat incumbent Democratic Congressman Major Owens whose support for Caribbean issues has justifiably been criticized. The Clarke campaign was weakened by opposition from some factions of Jamaicans, including Councilman Perry, who actively campaigned for Owens.

Lobbying by the Caribbean Community

Perhaps the single most effective way to advance the Caribbean agenda is to establish ways in which it can be aligned with domestic U.S. policy concerns. In this way, it will be possible to build trans-border coalitions of the interests, spanning the United States and the Caribbean, that converge on a policy position. In this regard, the most effective lobbying is done through advancing arguments that address the self-interests of Americans. An alliance for the lobbying of Caribbean interests in Washington, which therefore includes the constituency comprised of those U.S. citizens who benefit from a strong Caribbean relationship, will be effective because it represents beneficiaries of the policy who can frame the issues in terms of domestic constituency politics.

There is particular benefit in mobilizing support for addressing foreign policy issues, for which there is generally an insufficient interest and a negligible constituency. The lobbying for foreign assistance that has been most effective is that undertaken by Caribbean Americans in support of assistance to their country of origin. It is therefore a priority goal for those concerned about the Caribbean to mobilize support for the Caribbean within the Caribbean-American community. Caribbean Americans who are citizens are traditionally interested and active in politics, but they have not turned their attention and activism toward advocacy for the Caribbean. As the Caribbean community is presently strategically located in jurisdictions represented by key decision-makers affecting trade policy and foreign assistance (notably in Connecticut, represented by a member of the Trade Subcommittee of the Committee on Ways and Means and the Chair of the Western Hemisphere Committee of the Senate Foreign Relations Committee and in New York, represented by the Chairman of the Senate Finance Committee) there is potential for effective lobbying for increased assistance to the Caribbean through activating Caribbean Americans and Caribbean American organizations.

Sometimes by adroit maneuvering and astute power politics, the complex and usually convoluted process of foreign policy decision-making can be abbreviated or bypassed. Normally, major decisions involve about 20 agencies and as many as 100 officials in a long process of meetings that can take several months. Such decisions, in the absence of a major crisis, are achieved by what is known as bureaucratic end runs.[91] One such end run was the decision on the Summit of the Americas, which Feinberg, Senior Director for Inter-American Affairs in the NSC, says was made in 36 hours in a decision chain that went from NSC to vice president to president.[92]

In July 1997, veteran community leaders such as Leo Edwards and Dr. Alston Meade formed the National Coalition on Caribbean Affairs (NCOCA) as a 501 (c)(3). The objective of NCOCA is to "address" issues that impact on Caribbean communities within the United States and the Caribbean region. From its inception, it has been active in lobbying on banana, immigration, and CBI issues through correspondence and meetings with the State Department, National Security Council, and members of the Congressional Black Caucus.[93]

The Association of Caribbean American Leaders, which was organized in 1999 by City Council member Una Clarke of Brooklyn, New York City, is an association of elected officials. It now has members from New York, Texas, and Georgia. The membership includes city councilors, state delegates, majors, judges, and a member of Congress.[94] The Association has been active on issues affecting the Caribbean and has served to demonstrate that Caribbean people resident in the United States retain a strong interest in, and are concerned about, U.S. policy towards the Caribbean. The Association has lobbied and was helpful to the campaign to secure passage of the CBI Enhancement legislation.[95] Clarke was instrumental in inserting the words "the Caribbean" in the Democratic Party platform for the 1996 Presidential elections. The tireless Delegate Shirley Nathan Pulliam is a respected regular in Washington, D.C., and Maryland political circles.

One of the most important mechanisms for the Caribbean community to influence U.S. policy on issues of concern to the Caribbean was the annual conference organized by Jamaican Karl Rodney and his newspaper, *Carib News*. Starting in 1995 and hosted in a different Caribbean venue each year it brought together members of the Congressional black Caucus and the political leadership of the Caribbean countries.

Networking Prominent Jamaicans in the United States

Jamaicans as a whole have done well in the United States and several individuals have achieved prominence. These prominent Jamaicans who are U.S. citizens can exercise influence in their professions, in local politics, and in national affairs. Ambassador Bernal and his wife assiduously and enthusiastically initiated and engaged prominent Jamaicans. Some were nationally and internationally known such as General Colin Powell (later Secretary of State) and Harry Belafonte, and others were top executives such as Walt Braithwaite, a vice president at Boeing in Seattle and Smith of Kaiser in Baton Rouge or CEOs of their own companies such as Bert Mitchell, founder of the largest firm of CPAs. Others were leading doctors, e.g., Dr. Prendergast of the Mayo clinic, prominent lawyers, and distinguished professors. Very important were those Jamaicans in political positions. The two most active were Councilwoman Una Clarke of New York and Shirley Nathan-Pulliam of Baltimore. It was Una Clarke that ensured that the word "Caribbean" appear in the Democratic Party platform. Una Clarke's daughter Yvette Clarke became a Democratic member of the U.S. House of Representatives from New York. She joined Sheila Jackson-Lee, U.S. Representative for Texas's 18th congressional district (Houston) since 1995 who has Jamaican parents. There were several Congressional staffers with Jamaican connections; the most high-ranking was Gloria Simmonds-Wright, who was a senior staffer with Newt Gingrich who as Speaker of the House of Representatives would never have the time for Jamaica or the Caribbean. George Dally was chief of staff for Congressman Charlie Rangel and later a lobbyist for Jamaica, and Hazel Ross-Robinson worked in Congressman Bill Gray's office.

Jamaicans in all positions were always willing to help their country when asked and were effective even when they were not in executive jobs, for example, a Jamaican woman who was secretary to the Vice-President of CNN. After networking Jamaicans next was identifying persons of Caribbean origin, e.g., Mervyn Dymally, Democrat of Trinidadian heritage who represented a district in California in the U.S. House of Representatives during 1981–1993 or persons who represented districts with large Caribbean populations most importantly Charles Rangel, Democrat, representing New York's 13th congressional district continuously since 1971 and Donna Christian-Christensen was the non-voting Delegate from the United States Virgin Islands to the House since 1997. At the direction of ambassador compiled a list of Congressional "staffers" and this proved most useful in garnering and disseminating information on the "Hill."

Alliances with U.S. Domestic Interests

In the struggle between Mexico and the Caribbean and Central America to influence U.S. foreign policy, it was reasonable to assume that Mexico would prevail. Mexico, after all, has more resources and is a country that the United States regards as critically important. What tipped the balance was the fact that the interests of the U.S. business community coincide with those of the sugar exporters and governments of the Caribbean and Central America. In the course of obtaining a favorable outcome, Jamaica, along with other Caribbean and Central American countries, sought to influence the decision-making process by interacting with the White House, Congress, and USTR. The principal actors in the process of making a ruling on U.S. sugar import policy are shown in figure 4.2.

As Mexican sugar production increased, the Mexican government and private sector launched a campaign to increase the amount of Mexican sugar allowed into the United States. This required a countervailing campaign by U.S. sugar producers and the states of the ESC and Central America to limit the size of the quota for sugar imported into the United States from Mexico under the NAFTA. The necessity to limit Mexican exports to the United States arose because the only way Mexican sugar

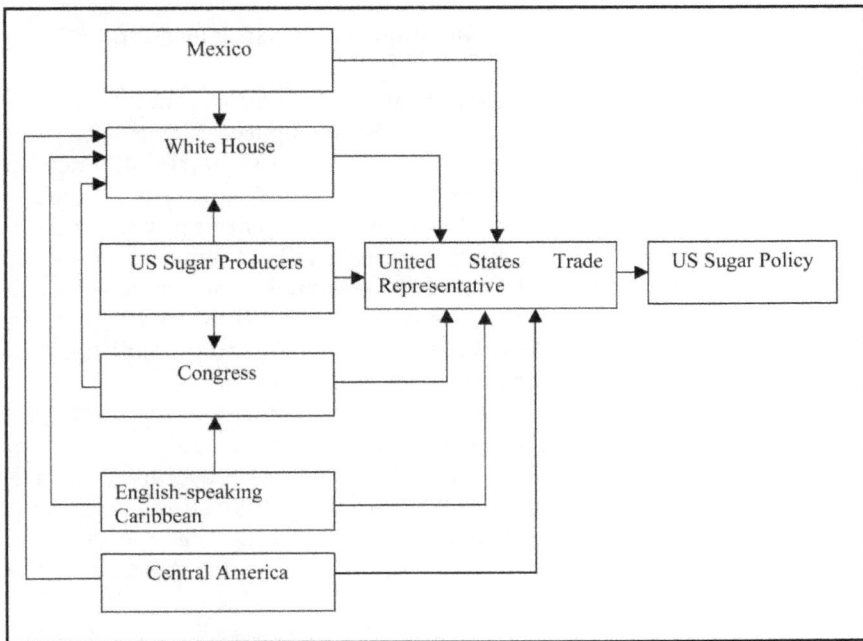

Figure 4.2.   Influencing U.S. Sugar Policy.

could be absorbed by the U.S. market would be by reducing the amount of sugar allowed in under the system of bilateral sugar quotas. The sugar exports of the ESC to the United States are determined annually as part of the quota system. An increase for Mexico could have resulted in an across the board reduction for all beneficiary countries of the bilateral quota system. To achieve a cap on Mexican sugar, the sugar exporting countries of the ESC (Barbados, Belize, Guyana, Jamaica, and Trinidad and Tobago) worked in unison with the beneficiary countries of Central America. Both collaborated with U.S. producers of sugar, whose interests coincided, as they too wanted to exclude or limit the volume of sugar permitted into the U.S. market from Mexico. Eventually Mexico was limited to 250,000 tons by a side letter (agreement) to the NAFTA.

The White House was approached by all the interested parties but demurred to lead on an issue, which became increasingly sensitive. Public opinion and organized labor were convinced that NAFTA was causing job losses and was debilitating to the U.S. economy. The administration could not afford to appear to be further opening access to the U.S. market in this milieu, as this would have been extremely unpopular. Increased imports of sugar would be opposed vigorously by U.S. sugar producers, possibly with the support of the wider agricultural lobby. The White House intimated to the U.S. Trade Representative's Office (USTR), the agency responsible for handling the decision on whether to maintain the cap on Mexican sugar imports, that more Mexican sugar was in the words of one insider, "not on at this time" and that they should "find a way to shut it down."

The USTR received missives and visits by all the concerned parties. In addition, the ESC made their case to the State Department with the hope that it would be a friend in court and exercise a salutary influence on USTR. The National Security Council was also made aware of the implications for drugs and migration of reduced export earnings and employment in the sugar industry in the region, especially in Jamaica, where the industry's viability was tenuous. Congressional representatives who were "friends" of the Caribbean or of U.S. agriculture or involved in foreign affairs issues were alerted to the importance and possible harmful repercussions of increased access for Mexican sugar.

The private sector sugar interests of the 15 countries in the Caribbean and Central America that participate in the U.S. tariff rate sugar program, known as the CBI Sugar Group, retained the services of a lobbyist specializing in sugar matters. Ed Graves,[96] a knowledgeable, experienced, and ever watchful lobbyist was instrumental in ensuring that the views of those opposed to increased Mexican sugar imports were heard in the "right places at the right time."

Media in the Caribbean

Media in Jamaica and the Caribbean can have an impact on U.S. foreign policy because the U.S. embassy picks up reports and opinion editorials in the local media and transmits them to the State Department and National Security Council. This can be useful because the media is uncensored and can purvey information that the government cannot. In addition, coverage and opinions in local media can influence both public opinion indirectly and directly affect decisions by the political directorate. In the 1990s Jamaican media had grown beyond two daily newspapers and two radio stations, which in addition to carrying news hosted widely listened to daily talk shows.

In addition, there is Caribbean media in the United States, most notably *Carib News*, a weekly newspaper operating in New York. The paper is owned by Carl and Faye Rodney, a Jamaican family. It began operation in 1982 and by the late 1990s it was printing 50,000 copies and had an estimated readership of 250,000. Particularly influential were the columns written by Tony Best, a respected Barbadian journalist. Best was in a position to make observations and comments that Caribbean diplomats and regional officials preferred not to say publicly. The newspaper gave voice to Ambassador Bernal through opinion editorials[97] and interviews[98] on a wide range of issues that would not have made it into U.S. media. The influence of *Carib News* was enhanced by the frequent citations in the *Congressional Record*.

CONCLUSION

The U.S. political system more, than any other, is open to foreign governments openly seeking to influence the Executive, legislature, and bureaucracy using all legitimate means ranging from the services of lobbyists to dispensing views favorable to their cause through the media. On any given issue, a foreign government will simultaneously pursue its objectives using several different channels. An important aspect of influencing U.S. policy is building alliances with U.S. domestic interest groups, particularly big business. Where the country involved can mobilize migrant communities in the United States, it can significantly influence decisions by members of Congress. This chapter has served to illustrate the channels available, the alliances created, and the experiences of some foreign governments who have influenced or seek to influence U.S. foreign policy.

NOTES

1. Charles F. Doran and Joel J. Sokolsky, Canada and Congress: Lobbying in Washington (Halifax: Centre for Foreign Policy Studies, 1986).
2. George W. Grayson, "Lobbying by Mexico and Canada" in Robert A. Pastor and Rafael Fernandez de Castro (eds.) The Controversial Pivot. The U.S. Congress and North America (Washington, D.C.: Brookings Institution's Press, 1998) pages 70–94.
3. Pat Choate, Agents of Influence. How Japan's Lobbyists in the United States Manipulate America's Political and Economic System (New York: Alfred Knopf, 1990).
4. Edward Tivnan, The Lobby. Jewish Political Power and U.S. Foreign Policy (New York: Simon and Schuster, 1987).
5. Briefing Book, Visit of the Hon. Prime Minister of Jamaica to Washington, D.C., August 26–31, 1993 (Embassy of Jamaica, Washington, D.C., August 25, 1993).
6. Arnold Heeney, The Things That Are Caeser's. Memoirs of a Canadian Public Servant (Toronto: University of Toronto Press, 1972) page 127.
7. Allan Gotlieb, I'll Be with You in a Minute, Mr. Ambassador. The Education of a Canadian Diplomat in Washington (Toronto: University of Toronto Press, 1991).
8. Summary of Accomplishments of Neil and Company on behalf of Jamaica, 1st Session, 103rd Congress, 1994, page 13.
9. Patricia D. Woods, The Dynamics of Congress. The Guide to the People and the Process of Lawmaking (Washington, D.C.: The Woods Institute, 1999) page 114.
10. Roger H. Davidson and Walter J. Oleszek, Congress and Its Members (Washington, D.C.: Congressional Quarterly Press, 7th ed. 2000), page 352.
11. Kevin Phillips, Arrogant Capital (New York: Little, Brown and Company, 1994) page 90
12. Deborah M. Levy, "Advice for Sale," Foreign Policy, No. 67 (Summer, 1987) pages 64–86.
13. William Greider, Who Will Tell the People. The Betrayal of American Democracy (New York: Simon and Schuster, 1992) page 398.
14. U.S. Department of Justice, Criminal Division. The Foreign Agents Registration Act of 1938 as Amended and the Rules and Regulations Prescribed by the Attorney General (Washington, D.C.: Department of Justice, n.d.).
15. "Latin American and Caribbean Lobbying for International Trade in Washington, D.C." United Nations Commission on Latin America and the Caribbean (ECLAC) LC/G.1632. LC/WAS/L.9, June 29, 1990.
16. Charles S. Mack, Lobbying and Government Relations (Connecticut: Quorum Books, 1989) pages 107.
17. Charles McC. Mathias, Jr. "Ethnic Groups and Foreign Policy," Foreign Affairs, Vol. 59, No. 4 (Spring, 1981) pages 978–79.
18. A good description of the AIPAC can be found in Smith, op. cit, pages 215–29.
19. Betty Liu, "Presidential Rivals Feel the Power of Hispanic Voters," Financial Times, October 4, 2000.
20. David C. Korten, When Corporations Rule the World (West Hartford: Kumarian Press, 1995) page 147.
21. Pat Choate, "Can a Keiretsu Work," Harvard Business Review (September, 1990) pages 187–97.
22. Hermann von Bertrab, Negotiating NAFTA. A Mexican Envoy's Account (Westport: Praeger, 1997) page 15.
23. Roger H. Davidson and Walter J. Oleszek, Congress and its Members (Washington, D.C.: Congressional Quarterly Press, 7th ed. 2000), page 352.
24. Hermann von Bertrab, Negotiating NAFTA. A Mexican Envoy's Account (Westport: Praeger, 1997) page 16.
25. Neil and Company, Jamaica's Annual Report 1991 (Washington, D.C.: 1992).
26. Annual Report for 1991 (Washington, D.C.: Neil and Company, 1992).
27. William Greider, Who Will Tell the People. The Betrayal of American Democracy (New York: Simon and Schuster, 1992) page 256–57.

28. Based on Hermann von Bertrab, Negotiating NAFTA. A Mexican Envoy's Account (Westport: Praeger, 1997).

29. Patrick O'Heffernan, Mass Media and American Foreign Policy: Insider Perspectives on Global Journalism and the Foreign Policy Process (Norwood, NJ: Ablex Publishing Co., 1991).

30. Richard Sobel, Public Opinion in U.S. Foreign Policy. The Controversy over Contra Aid (Lanham: Rowman and Littlefield Publishers, 1993).

31. William A. Dorman and Mansour Farhing, The U.S. Press and Iran: Foreign Policy and the Journalism of Deference (Berkeley: University of California Press, 1987).

32. Robert M. Entman, Projections of Power: Framing News, Public Opinion, and U.S. Foreign Policy (Chicago: University of Chicago Press, 2003).

33. Edward S. Herman and Noam Chomsky, Manufacturing Consent (New York: Pantheon, 1988).

34. Bernard C. Cohen, The Press and Foreign Policy (Princeton, NJ: Princeton University Press, 1963) page 136.

35. Hermann von Bertrab, Negotiating NAFTA. A Mexican Envoy's Account (Westport: Praeger, 1997) page 25.

36. Tony Smith, Foreign Attachments. The Power of Ethnic Groups in the Making of American Foreign Policy (Cambridge: Harvard University Press, 2000) pages 47–84.

37. Louis L. Gerson, The Hyphenate and Recent American Politics and Diplomacy (Lawrence: University of Kansas Press, 1964), Lawrence H. Fuchs, The American Kaleidoscope: Race, Ethnicity and the Civic Culture (Hanover, N.H.: University Press of New England, 1990), and Alexander DeConde, Ethnicity, Race and American Foreign Policy: A History (Boston: Northeastern University Press, 1992).

38. Bernard Reich, The United States and Israel: Influence in the Special Relationship (New York: Praeger Publishers, 1994), David H. Goldberg, Foreign Policy and Ethnic Interest Groups: American and Canadian Jews Lobby for Israel (Westport: Greenwood Press, 1990), and Bernard Gwertzman, The Lobby: Jewish Political Power and American Foreign Policy (New York: Simon and Schuster, 1988).

39. Yossi Shain, Marketing the American Creed Abroad: Diasporas in the U.S. and Their Homelands (New York: Cambridge University Press, 1999).

40. Mohammed Rabie, The Politics of Foreign Aid: U.S. Foreign Assistance and Aid to Israel (New York: Praeger, 1988)

41. Cecil V. Crabb, Jr., Glenn J. Antizzo, and Leila E. Sarieddine, Congress and the Foreign Policy Process, Modes of Legislative Behavior (Louisiana: Louisiana State University Press, 2000) pages 145–46.

42. Dave Juday, "Lift the Embargo," Editorial, Wall Street Journal, August 26, 1994, Peter Hakim and Moses Naim, "The Case for Trading with Cuba," Journal of Commerce, December 30, 1994, Wayne Smith, "Don't Isolate Cuba–Open It to New Ideas," Christian Science Monitor, August 25, 1994, Andrew Zimbalist, "The Great U.S.–Cuba Embargo Debate (Cont'd). Ease Tensions," Miami Herald, March 23, 1994, Jeremy Morgan, "Give Castro A Carrot," New York Times, February 17, 1994, "End the Cold War Against Cuba," Journal of Commerce, February 9, 1993, and Steven Greenhouse, "New Calls to Lift Embargo on Cuba," New York Times, February 20, 1993.

43. William M. Leogrande, "Enemies Evermore: U.S. Policy Towards Cuba After Helms-Burton," Journal of Latin American Studies, Vol. 29 (1997) pages 211–21.

44. Carla Anne Robbins, "Dateline Washington: Cuban-American Clout," Foreign Policy, No. 88 (Fall, 1992) pages 162–82.

45. Rick Mendora and Sarah Acosta, "The D.C. Cash Flow," Hispanic Business, October 1993, pages 20–26. See page 25.

46. Rick Mendora and Sarah Acosta, "The D.C. Cash Flow," Hispanic Business, October 1993, page 26.

47. John Spicer Nichols, "The Power of the Anti-Fidel Lobby," The Nation, October 24, 1988, pages 389–91. See page 390.

48. Peter H. Stone, "Cuban Clout," National Journal, February 20, 1993, pages 449–53. See page 451.

49. Peter H. Stone, "Cuban Clout," National Journal, February 20, 1993, page 450.

50. Adolfo Leyva De Varona, Propaganda and Reality: A Look at the U.S. Embargo Against Castro's Cuba (Miami: Cuban American National Foundation, July 1994).

51. Laurence Halley, Ancient Affections, Ethnic Groups and Foreign Policy (New York: Praeger, 1979).

52. Linda G. Basch, "The Politics of Caribbeanization: Vincetians and Grenadians in New York," in Constance R. Sutton and Elsa M. Chaney, Caribbean Life in New York: Sociocultural Dimensions (New York: Center for Migration Studies of New York, 1987) pages 160–81. See page 169.

53. Edmund David Cronon, Black Moses. The Story of Marcus Garvey and the Universal Negro Improvement Association (Madison: University of Wisconsin Press, 1968), Richard L. Bernal, "The Significance of Garvey," New World Quarterly, Vol. 5, No. 4 (1972) pages 69–72, Tony Martin, Race First. The Ideological and Organizational Struggles of Marcus Garvey and the Universal Negro Improvement Association (Westport: Greenwood Press, 1976), Rupert Lewis and Maureen Warner-Lewis (eds.), Garvey. Africa, Europe, the Americas (Kingston: Institute of Social and Economic Research, 1986), and Rupert Lewis and Patrick Bryan (eds.), Garvey. His Work and Impact (Kingston: University of the West Indies, 1988).

54. Anthony Bogues, Caliban's Freedom. The Early Political Thought of C.L.R. James (London: Pluto Press, 1997).

55. Winston James, Holding Aloft the Banner of Ethiopia. Caribbean Radicalism in Early Twentieth-Century America (London: Verso Press, 1998) page 122.

56. Tony Smith, Foreign Attachments. The Power of Ethnic Groups in the Making of American Foreign Policy (Cambridge: Harvard University Press, 2000) page 24.

57. An exception to this is Mark Smith who sees the influence of business as benign and even munificent. See Mark A. Smith, American Business and Political Power. Public Opinion, Elections and Democracy (Chicago: University of Chicago, 2000).

58. Howard J. Wiarda, American Foreign Policy: Actors and Processes (New York: Harper Collins College Publishers, 1995) page 99.

59. 1997 Caribbean Basin Profile, (Washington, D.C.: Caribbean Latin American Action/Caribbean Publishing Co., 1996) page 6.

60. Caribbean/Latin American Action, Annual Report 1999–2000 (Washington, D.C.: Caribbean/Latin American Action, 2000) page 7.

61. David D. Newsom, Diplomacy and the American Democracy (Bloomington: Indiana University Press, 1988) page 51.

62. Embassy of Jamaica Telegram No. 141, August 9, 1972.

63. Ackee File, Part I, July 1972–November 1974, Embassy of Jamaica.

64. Letter to Janice Oliver, Acting Deputy Director for Systems and Support, U.S. Food and Drug Administration from Richard Bernal, Ambassador of Jamaica to the United States, August 13, 1993.

65. Ackee File Part II, April 1999, Embassy of Jamaica.

66. European Institute, Washington, D.C., April, 2001.

67. Jacqueline Braveboy-Wagner, Caribbean Diplomacy. Focus on Washington, Cuba and the Past Cold War Era (New York: Caribbean Diaspora Press, 1995) pages 39–40.

68. "Latin American and Caribbean Lobbying for International Trade in Washington, D.C." United Nations Commission on Latin America and the Caribbean (ECLAC) LC/G.1632. LC/WAS/L.9, June 29, 1990, page 10.

69. Interview with Anne Sabo, October 12, 2000.

70. Former Senator and Minister of State in the Ministry of Finance and Planning in the PNP government of 1976–1980. Then a senior official at the Inter-American Development Bank.

71. "Florida Business Leaders Still Wary With New Manley," Miami Times, May 11, 1989.

72. Daniel Machalaba, "Even Legitimate Ships are Falling Victim to Drug Smugglers," Wall Street Journal, May 24, 1989, page A1.

73. "The 'New' Jamaica," Editorial, Washington Times, May 23, 1989.

74. Michael Isikoff, "Jamaican Urges Anti-Drug Force," Washington Post, June 11, 1989.

75. R. A. Zaldivar, "Jamaican Leader Urges Global Anti-Drug Squad," Miami Herald, June 10, 1989.

76. Jamaican Prime Minister Proposing International Anti-Drug Strike Force, Media Advisory for August 18, 1989, Fenton Communications, Washington, D.C.

77. Kweisi Mfume with Ron Stodghill II, No Free Ride. From the Mean Streets to the Mainstream (New York: Ballantine Books, 1996) page 319.

78. Winsome J. Leslie, Zaire. Continuity and Political Change in an Oppressive State (Boulder: Westview Press, 1993) page 147.

79. Kweisi Mfume with Ron Stodghill II, No Free Ride. From the Mean Streets to the Mainstream (New York: Ballantine Books, 1996) page 339.

80. David Bositis, Blacks and the 1992 Democratic National Convention (Washington, D.C.: Joint Center for Political and Economic Studies, 1992) page 22.

81. Elizabeth Bumiller, "The Caucus and the Cause," Washington Post, September 20, 1982.

82. Nadine Cohodas, "Black House Members Striving for Influence," Congressional Quarterly, April 13, 1985 pages 675–81.

83. Jeremiah O'Leary, "Bush, Black Caucus meet, open way for co-operation," Washington Times, May 24, 1989.

84. Kitty Cunningham, "Black Caucus Flexes Muscle On Budget – and More," Congressional Quarterly, July 3, 1993, pages 1711–15.

85. Douglas W. Payne, Emerging Voices. The West Indian, Dominican and Haitian Diasporas in the United States, Policy Papers on the Americas, Vol. IX, Study 11 (Washington, D.C.: Center for Strategic and International Studies, October 22, 1987).

86. Philip Kasinitz, Caribbean New York. Black Immigrants and the Politics of Race (Ithaca: Cornell University Press, 1992) page 114.

87. Christine Ho, Salt-Water Trinnies (New York: AMS Press, 1991) page 108.

88. Philip Kasinitz, Caribbean New York. Black Immigrants and the Politics of Race (Ithaca: Cornell University Press, 1992) pages 224–25.

89. Douglas W. Payne, Emerging Voices: The West Indian, Dominican and Haitian Diasporas in the United States, CSIS Americas Program Policy Papers on the Americas, Vol. IX, Study 11, Washington, D.C.: Centre for Strategic and International Studies, October 22, 1998) pages 5–6.

90. Philip Kasinitz, Caribbean New York. Black Immigrants and the Politics of Race (Ithaca: Cornell University Press, 1920) pages 166–76.

91. Richard E. Feinberg, Summitry in the Americas. A Progress Report (Washington, D.C.: Institute of International Economics, 1997) page 60–61.

92. Morton Halperin, Bureaucratic Politics and Foreign Policy (Washington, D.C.: Brookings Institution, 1974) pages 189–218 and William Taylor Amos, Jr., and Lawrence Kort, American National Security: Policy and Process (Baltimore: Johns Hopkins Press, 4th ed., 1993) page 225 and passim.

93. NCOCA. National Coalition on Caribbean Affairs, Creating New Strategies to Meet New Challenges (Washington, D.C.: NCOCA, 1997).

94. Members of the Association of Caribbean Leaders are: Councilwoman Una Clarke, Brooklyn, New York, Chair; Delegate Shirley Nathan Pulliam, Baltimore, Maryland; Councilman Noel Spencer, Chester, New York; Mayor Allan Thompson, Spring Valley, New York; Council member Veronica Airey-Wilson, Hartford, Connecticut; Assemblyman Roger Corbin. Nassau County, New York; Representative Henrietta Turnquist, Decatur, Georgia; Assemblywoman Pauline Rhodd-Cummings, Far Rockaway, New York; District Attorney Robert Johnson, Bronx, New York; Judge Sam D. Walker, Mount Vernon, New York; Congresswoman Sheila Jackson Lee, Houston, Texas; Commissioner Hazel Rogers, Fort Lauderdale, Florida; Assemblyman Patrick Williams, Mineola, New York; Councilman William McKoy, Paterson, New Jersey;

Mayor Sam Brown, Miami Lakes; and Senator John Sampson, State Senator, 19th District, New York.

95. Michael D. Roberts, "Lobbying Washington on Caribbean Issues: Historic First" Carib News, July 6, 1999 and Michael D. Roberts, "Caribbean-American Lobbying Group Meets with Clinton's Special Envoy at White House" Carib News, July 6, 1999.

96. Ed Graves, of Ed Graves and Associates, is a veteran of 12 years as a chief of staff for a U.S. senator and has been a lobbyist for 17 years. It was his responsibility to monitor the U.S. sugar program and make sure that the client countries maintain their share of the U.S. sugar quota.

97. Richard L. Bernal, "U.S. Attitude to Jamaica and Its Caribbean Neighbors. A Jamaican Perspective," Carib News, Week Ending August 8, 2000.

98. Tony Best, "U.S.-European Banana Settlement Faces New Hurdle," Carib News, week ending May 1, 2001.

FIVE

Foreign Aid and Debt Relief

Jamaica's economic circumstances by the end of the 1980s were such that the government of Michael Manley, who assumed office on the February 10, 1989, felt it was urgent and imperative to seek debt relief and financial support. The United States because of its global economic preeminence, its dominance in decision-making in the Bretton Woods institutions, and as the major economic partner of Jamaica was the primary target of Jamaica's quest for debt relief and development assistance. The objectives of Jamaica's campaign in the United States were, first, to secure debt relief directly from the United States and indirectly from other sources based on the political influence of the United States and second, to forestall a reduction in U.S. aid and if possible to increase the amount of U.S. aid. The accomplishment of Jamaica's twin goals would require the creation of a favorable disposition towards Jamaica in the White House, Treasury, State Department, and Congress. The political atmosphere in Washington, D.C., both in the administration and in Congress was not propitious for the attainment of either goal. An additional complication was the lingering but outdated perception particularly among conservatives[1] that a Manley led government was still democratic socialist in its philosophical orientation. This entailed a carefully planned campaign to first, re-image Michael Manley and the PNP government in Jamaica and second, make the case that Jamaica was a country that both needed and deserved U.S. support in the forms of aid and debt relief.

This campaign was designed primarily by the lobbying firm of Neil and Company and the public relations firm of David Fenton in close conjunction with Prime Minister Michael Manley and after May 1991 with Ambassador Richard Bernal.[2] These efforts began before Manley became Prime Minister but moved into high gear when Manley assumed power in February 1989. Before regaining the post of Prime Minister

Manley was frequently in the United States for speaking engagements and lectures as a means of earning a living. During these trips he maintained contacts with a wide range of people and institutions. During these years he engaged a variety of officials in different branches of the U.S. government. Richard Fletcher, a former Minister of State in the Ministry of Finance in the late 1970s at the Inter-American Development Bank, was instrumental in selecting and arranging these appointments. The campaign moved into a more strategically organized operation with the hiring of a lobbyist.

The gravamen of the campaign that was emphasized was explaining that Manley and the PNP had abandoned democratic socialism and were genuinely and actively committed to private sector led, market driven economic policies. This was no easy task because there was a lingering skepticism about Manley because of his policies and actions in the 1970s. Manley earned the ire of the United States because of the expulsion of the U.S. ambassador who had tried prevent his election and who made untrue public allegations about a deal not to increase taxation of U.S. multinational corporations in the bauxite industry.[3] His friendship with Fidel Castro, increased taxation on multinational corporations in the bauxite industry, and his exposition of democratic socialism put a stain on relations with the Nixon and Ford administrations.[4] Ronald Reagan in his diaries had characterized Manley as "a Cuban backed pro-communist."[5] The United States was explicit in its displeasure over Manley's support for Cuban troops in the liberation struggles in Angola and Southern Africa when Henry Kissinger met with Manley.[6] Increased taxation of bauxite production in Jamaica was greeted by the *Washington Post* as "the biggest increase in any raw material price since . . . the Organization of Petroleum Exporting Countries quadrupled the price of oil."[7]

While his social and economic goals remained unchanged, the Michael Manley that took office in 1989 was much changed in his thinking about how to achieve the goals. An important aspect of his approach to economic development was a greater recognition of the market and the role of the private sector. The changed perspective on economic policy was the end product of a careful rethinking of the experience of his 1971–1980 period in office, a profound understanding that the geopolitics of the 1990s was very different from the 1970s, and domestic political changes.[8] While in opposition in the years 1980 to 1989 Manley engaged the private sector in a sustained dialogue at two levels, first personally with the top business leaders and second, a technical team representing the PNP (Dr. Richard L. Bernal, Dr. Omar Davies, and Dr. Peter D. Phillips) met regularly with a team from the Private Sector Organization of Jamaica. In an interview with *Newsweek* magazine he explained that: "The world has evolved, I have evolved."[9]

The Jamaican electorate accepted his much modified economic platform as was evident in his overwhelming electoral victory. The problem he faced was how to convince foreign governments including that of the United States and international financial organizations of both the modified thinking and of his commitment to the policies he was espousing. In order to accomplish this he and the PNP would have to overcome lingering impressions and some very strongly held views about policies of his government during the 1972–1980 period when the PNP professed a commitment to Democratic Socialism.

The process of exposure to the new thinking started in the late 1980s and was facilitated by Manley's frequent speaking engagements and lectures at universities in the United States, Canada, England, and Europe. In the course of his overseas travels he was available to the media (print, television, and radio) for interviews. During the years in opposition he kept in touch with Congressman Charlie Rangel, the Congressional Black Caucus, Randall Robinson of Trans-Africa, the Liberal wing of the U.S. think tank community such as Saul Landau[10] of the Institute for Policy Studies, the British Labour Party, in particular Stuart Holland MP, and the European parties that were members of the Socialist International. Manley sought to raise international awareness of the debt crisis of developing countries when he chaired the Economic Committee of Socialist International, which produced the report "Global Challenge. From Crisis to Cooperation: Breaking the North-South Stalemate."[11] He was a member of the South Commission chaired by Julius Nyerere and spoke of the international debt with illustration from the Jamaica experience in his books.[12] Prior to becoming ambassador Richard Bernal, while teaching development and international economics at the University of the West Indies, worked as an economic advisor to Manley and attended both the Socialist International Committee on Economic Policy and the South Commission and was fully aware of Manley's views on debt and debt relief. Manley's 1987 book *Up the Down Escalator* located the debt crisis of the Third World as rooted in the structure and functioning of the world economy. He stated that "the debt burden being carried by the Third world nations individually and collectively is simultaneously the result and the measure of all the factors in the world economy."[13]

DEBT RELIEF

By 1989 when Michael Manley became Prime Minister, Jamaica and several Caribbean countries had become heavily indebted[14] with the largest debtor being Jamaica. Jamaica's external debt (government and publicly guaranteed) stood at USD$3.93 billion in 1990.[15] The debt was large in relation to their total output and productive capacity with the debt/GDP ratio being almost 100 percent in 1990. This meant that the debt was the equivalent of one year's worth of the total goods and services produced by Jamaica, or put another way, it would require one year's total output of all economic activity to repay the debt. The servicing of the external debt had become the single most important constraint to adjustment, stabilization, and sustained economic growth. The debt service ratio, i.e., the share of foreign exchange earnings from the export of goods and services required for debt repayment, was high. In 1990 it was 210 percent,[16] which meant that just under half of all foreign exchange was not available to the economy to purchase essential imports such as oil, food, spare parts, capital goods, and medicine.

The high debt servicing ratios were made more onerous by the fact that the highly indebted countries were simultaneously encountering a negative net transfer of resources, i.e., inflows from new loans was exceeded by the outflows for repayment of principal and interest. In Jamaica in 1988, the net transfer on debt was negative, i.e., repayment exceeded new loans by U.S. $128 million. This was extremely debilitating to these developing countries, which on the contrary, should aim to receive a net inflow of resources to reinforce the process of economic growth and facilitate structural transformation. In many countries debt repayment was the major factor that prevented the reduction of fiscal deficits and reduced the capacity of the government to provide infrastructure, health, education, and security. Debt indicators are provided in table 5.1.

Jamaica's debt had more than doubled, from approximately U.S. $1.87 billion in 1980 to over U.S. $4.15 billion in 1990. The debt/GDP ratio moved from 82.2 percent in 1980 to 110.9 percent in 1991. The worsening debt situation was evident in the increase in debt repayments and the increase in negative net transfers. Debt repayment for the region increased by 259 percent. During 1986 to 1991, Jamaica transferred overseas more than it received in each year totaling U.S. $1 billion for the six-year period.

Special Case of Jamaican Debt

The crisis of Jamaican debt was a distinct situation and was therefore a special genre of debt problem, namely, small middle-income developing countries whose outstanding debt was owed largely to official debtors. This type of debt situation had not received sufficient attention as debt relief had focused primarily on the commercial bank debt of low-

Table 5.1.   Debt Indicators for Jamaica 1980–1990 (U.S. $ Million)

Year	Total Debt	Debt/GDP	Debt Service	Debt Service/Exports (%)	Net Transfer
1980	1,866.8	82.2	574.0	12	24.0
1990	4,152.8	97.8	663.54	28	-144.84

Source: World Bank, World Debt Tables 1992–93, Bank of Jamaica.

income countries, in particular those in Africa. Bilateral or inter-government debt had been the subject of numerous and repeated rounds of rescheduling through the Paris Club. However, the issue of debt owed to multilateral institutions such as the International Monetary Fund, the World Bank, and the Inter-American Development Bank (IADB) had not been tackled because these institutions did not reschedule debt.

Debt owed to "official creditors," i.e., multilateral institutions and bilateral development assistance agencies, by Jamaica was extremely high. The share of official debt in public and publicly guaranteed long-term debt was 85.9 percent and debt due to multilateral institutions was 39.9 percent. In Jamaica, bilateral debt was a particularly large share of total external debt accounting for 46.4. For further data see table 5.2.

The dominant share of official debt in the long-term debt of Jamaica indicates that the debt was accumulated in the quest for economic development through projects and infrastructure and/or stabilization cum adjustment. Repayment escalated because of adverse external developments, natural disasters, policy imperfections, and inadequate management. One of the dilemmas of the debt crisis was that there seemed to be no reward for good behavior, i.e., countries that made strenuous efforts to achieve stabilization and adjustment and pursued sound economic management and who were reliable in their debt repayment, did not receive more favorable treatment in terms of debt rescheduling from commercial banks, governments of creditor countries, and multilateral institutions, in particular, the IMF. The inconsistencies in the secondary market also seemed to reward those debtors who did not honor their obligations, instead of rewarding countries that abided by their repayment schedules and conducted their fiduciary affairs responsibly. This is illustrated by the fact that countries that were reliable in their debt servicing found that their debt was sold in the secondary market at a higher price than the debt of countries that were in arrears or that were refusing to accept terms offered by creditors.

Table 5.2. Composition of Public and Publicly Guaranteed Long-Term Debt of Jamaica by Type of Creditor (1980–2000). (U.S. $ Millions)

Year	Multilateral	Bilateral	Commercial	Other, incl. bonds
1980	29.1	25.0	21.9	24.0
1991	34.7	50.5	9.0	5.7
2000	33.0	36.1	3.9	26.9

Source: Bank of Jamaica.

The Debt Policy Process

The process of influencing U.S. policy on international debt involved having an impact on the decisions taken by the Treasury within the overall policy framework set out by the Executive. Truman of the Federal Reserve emphasizes that "U.S. policy on international debt is a responsibility that is shared within the U.S. government; the Treasury Department, the State Department, the White House, the Congress and the Federal Reserve are all involved in various aspects of that policy, and its implementation includes an even longer list of institutions."[17] When policy involves monies foregone, e.g., for debt relief or to be spent lobbying, Congress becomes very important. The National Security council is also a "player" because it briefs the President each morning. The views of the White House, the Treasury, and the Congress are influenced by media coverage of the debt crisis of developing countries and by the technical policy studies produced by experts and think tanks. In its campaign to influence debt policy the government of Jamaica with the assistance and advice of its lobbyists and public relations firm concentrated on the Executive, the Treasury, and Congress. The campaign also involved sharing ideas with think tanks and bringing to the public's attention through the media the urgency for debt relief for countries like Jamaica. This process is outlined in figure 5.1.

Strategy

Jamaica responded to its situation of heavy external indebtedness by rescheduling debt owed to transnational commercial banks and rescheduling bilateral debts owed to governments of developed countries through a mechanism known as the "Paris Club." However, by the late 1980s Jamaica owed a large share of its external debt to multinational

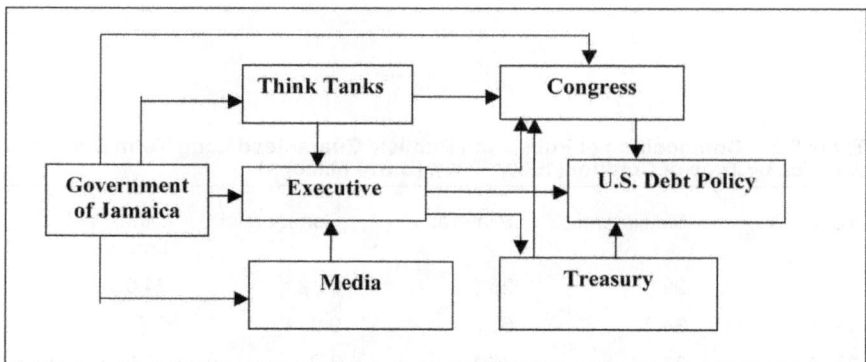

Figure 5.1.   Influencing U.S. Debt Policy.

financial institutions, in particular the World Bank and the International Monetary Fund. These institutions did not reschedule debts owed to them because they argued that would undermine their financial viability. The IMF pointed to the fact that it operated as a revolving fund and any disruption in the stream of repayment would eventually lead to the exhaustion of the fund to the ultimate detriment of the member countries that needed to borrow. While there is an apparent validity to this claim, the IMF like any prudently managed financial institution can permit a certain amount of rescheduling while maintaining solvency. The World Bank argued that an important part of its resources were raised on private capital and rescheduling would jeopardize this capacity by lowering the Bank's triple A rating. This is a most specious argument because the World Bank's credit rating depends not on the balance sheet but derives from the fact that its principal shareholders were the richest and most developed countries and therefore their virtually unlimited capital stood behind the institution. The Manley-led government of Jamaica increased its efforts to (1) continue to reschedule commercial bank debt and bilateral debt, (2) convince the IMF and the World Bank and the developed countries, in particular the United States, to permit rescheduling, and (3) encourage developed countries to cancel all or at least some of the debts owed to them by developing countries, especially the most vulnerable, both the poorest and the smallest economies. The deserving developing country debtors were those whose governments were making an effort to "put their house in order" but who needed the financial breathing space that reduced debt payments could provide.

The United States was the dominant power in international economic affairs as it was the largest source of lending to developing countries both in terms of foreign aid, lending by U.S. owned commercial banks, and as the largest contributor to the IMF, World Bank, and Inter-American Development Bank. As the country with the largest share of votes in the IMF, World Bank, and the IADB the United States' "word was law" in these institutions. The policy also set the tone and parameters of the bilateral aid and debt policies of other developed countries. The Netherlands and the Scandinavians were the first to exhibit flexibility and empathy in dealing with Third World debt, an example of enlightened humanitarianism, which percolated by slow osmosis to the United States. In this conjuncture influencing U.S. policy was the critical determinant of whether and to what extent any aspect of Jamaica's quest for debt relief would come to fruition. This dictated that the focus of Jamaica's campaign was the United States with the goal of changing U.S. policy on how the debt problem of developing countries would be handled.

By 1989, Michael Manley and the PNP were elected, and Jamaica's external burden had become a serious constraint on economic growth. External indebtedness escalated rapidly after the oil price shock of the mid 1970s because of borrowing from transnational commercial banks by the government of Jamaica.[18] A second wave of borrowing by the Seaga administration, this time from bilateral donors and multilateral financial institutions, in particular the IMF and World Bank, compounded the debt problem. Indeed, by the mid–1980s Jamaica was locked into "a vicious circle of foreign indebtedness,"[19] a situation in which it was necessary to borrow to ensure repayment. Also by the late 1980s the debt crisis of developing countries was at a stage where traditional and conventional techniques of debt restructuring were not sufficiently generous and flexible to provide meaningful debt relief. The debt crisis of developing countries erupted when Mexico declared in August 1982 that it could not pay its debts. By 1985 an attempt was made to address the problem of the 15 most indebted developing countries. This effort was led by James Baker, U.S. Treasury Secretary and became known as the Baker Plan, a combination of debt rescheduling and new money. The effect of the Baker Plan was to extend the repayment schedule but the stock of debt was not reduced. By the late 1980s the problem of debtor countries was not lack of liquidity but insolvency forcing the recognition that a reduction of the stock of debt could not be avoided. In March 1989 the task could not be postponed and Treasury Secretary Nicholas Brady launched the Brady Plan, which allowed the commercial banks to exchange their claims on developing countries for tradable instruments with less risk to principal and interest, allowing them to get the debt off their balance sheets, and in exchange the banks agreed to debt relief linked to a commitment to stabilization and economic reform.[20]

The new demarche in U.S. foreign policy towards Latin America, which was represented by the Enterprise of the Americas Initiative in 1990, recognized that substantial debt relief was necessary to stimulate economic recovery in Latin America and the Caribbean.[21] The decade of the 1980s in Latin America has come to be known as the lost decade because most countries experienced low growth or contraction of economic activity. Of course the problem that received the most attention was the commercial bank debt of a few Latin American countries, specifically Argentina, Brazil, and above all Mexico. The size of the debt owed by these countries threatened the viability of the most exposed transnational commercial banks, including some of the largest U.S. banks. Commercial bank debt of developing countries had been the subject of creative thinking, which resulted in some innovative mechanisms for debt relief.[22] Bilateral debt relief, however, was confined to less than generous debt rescheduling arrangements. Therefore, for developing countries whose debt was largely owed to bilateral agencies and multilateral financial institutions, the prospects for substantial relief were very limited. The dilemma is typified by the situation of Jamaica by the late 1980s.

The debt of developing countries emerged as a major problem in the late 1970s and persisted and worsened during the 1980s. Jamaica's debt problem escalated during this period and had reached dangerous proportions by the time that the Michael Manley led People's National Party (PNP) government assumed office in 1989. An important aspect of this problem was debt to official creditors because at the end of 1990, 84 percent of Jamaica's external debt was owed to official creditors, of which 48 percent was due to bilateral donors.[23] The difficulty faced by countries like Jamaica was that multilateral financial institutions (MFIs) like the World Bank did not permit rescheduling. In addition, bilateral donors have been slow to provide the magnitude of debt relief that would have been meaningful. In an effort to influence the political and policy making environment in the direction of more generous debt relief than had been provided through Paris Club rescheduling exercises and to induce MFIs to commence rescheduling, the Manley government launched an intellectual offensive. This was led by Mr. Manley who used every opportunity to speak and write about the debt problem, proposing new mechanisms of debt relief. He argued that the burden of debt payments was a major cause of the poverty of developing countries.[24] Manley started to push the idea of debt relief even before he was in office. For example, he chaired the Committee on Economic Policy of the Socialist International in 1985 and produced a report titled "Global Challenge" that stated that an international solution to the debt crisis was imperative and if not "unilateral declarations of default by more countries are not only a real threat but virtually inevitable."[25] In the United States he drove the issue at the Carter Center's consultation[26] with leaders from Latin America and the Caribbean on a "New Hemispheric Agenda"[27] in March 2014.

In an article on developing country needs in the 20th anniversary issue of the influential U.S. journal, *Foreign Policy*, Manley argued that the "debt crisis threatens not only individual countries, but the functioning of the world economy as well. It constrains world trade, inhibits capital inflows, hampers growth and per capita income, and generates tremors of increasing severity in the international banking system. . . . A way must be found to halt the debt-deflation spiral that saps the world economy of much of its vitality. Sufficient debt relief to developing countries would restore the import capacity of debtor countries and free resources to resuscitate world trade. Such an expansion in world trade would alleviate the trade deficits of debtor countries. Moreover, debt relief would prompt a resumption of capital flows to developing countries that would stimulate economic growth. . . . The Brady Plan represents a conceptual breakthrough because for the first time debt reduction has been contemplated by the United States as part of an overall strategy to cope with Third World debt; however, it does not do enough. The extent of its relief for foreign exchange payments is relatively small, and it evolves considerable new lending, which tends to perpetuate the cycle of debt. . . . A solution must proceed from the recognition that governments in developed countries, transnational commercial banks, multilateral lending institutions, and governments of Third World countries are all partly responsible for the debt crisis."[28]

Ambassador Bernal took his cue from Prime Minister Manley and set about trying to influence the intellectual and policy making environment in Washington institutions by speaking at think tanks, having meetings with members of Congress, presenting testimony to Congress,[29] and having publications in the media and scholarly journals. In an opinion editorial in the *Washington Post*, the Ambassador argued, "the United States cannot be an oasis of well-being in a sea of poverty. The debt crisis of Caribbean countries has adverse implications for both the United States and the Caribbean. Given the relatively small size of the debt and given that debt reduction for reconstruction and development is not unprecedented, the United States could afford bilateral debt relief as proposed by the Enterprise for the Americas Initiative."[30] The ambassador also advocated multilateral debt relief in an article in the widely read popular publication, the *International Economy*. Bernal stated that "the multilateral institutions cannot simultaneously urge reduction measures on other creditors while eschewing any form of rescheduling. The argument that the viability and credit rating of these institutions would be jeopardized is not credible since their soundness derives not from their operations but from the backing of the developed countries. If supplementary resources or charter changes are required to enable these institutions to undertake debt restructuring then this must be done quickly."[31]

Mr. Manley was a rare exception among heads of government because he was willing to meet in person or speak by telephone with members of Congress and Senators. During his visit to Washington in May 1991 he held meetings with Congressmen Charlie Rangel and Bill Gray. In addition, he pursued the debt relief topic in his meeting with President Bush. The Prime Minister, who was accompanied by Dr. Peter Philips, Minister of State and Richard Bernal, Ambassador to the United States, also raised the issue of debt relief with Vice President Dan Quayle. However, this turned out to be futile because the team was not able to explain to Vice President Quayle what debt relief meant. The Ambassador followed up on this initiative by attending a Redskins game at which he was sure to have five minutes with the Vice President during halftime. He took the opportunity to raise debt relief with Vice President Quayle but with little success, as the concept still seemed to elude the Vice President. Manley and the Jamaican team forged an understanding on the debt issue with David Mulford, Under Secretary for International Affairs for the Department of the Treasury. He was the key official in the leadership of the Bush administration's international debt strategy, and the formulation and implementation of the Baker and Brady Plans.

Think Tanks

The debt burden in developing countries and its adverse implications for economic growth became an issue in academic and policy-making circles during the late 1970s. At that time the substantial increase in the price of oil placed severe strains on the import capacity of the developing countries, many of whom either borrowed excessively from transnational commercial banks or deflated their already struggling economies. The result was a severe crunch between rapidly escalating debt servicing and limited foreign exchange earnings. In this regard Jamaica was typical, having borrowed on the assumption that the surge in oil prices was temporary and it soon found itself locked in a "vicious circle of foreign indebtedness."[32] During the 1980s when commercial banks reduced their lending to developing countries or experienced difficulty in securing payment on schedule despite several debt restructuring agreements, developing countries including middle income countries began to borrow from multilateral financial institutions. This development coupled with the increasing debt of the poorest countries to bilateral agencies led to a second dimension of the debt crisis, namely debt to multilateral and bilateral institutions. This proved to be a difficult new development because multilateral financial institutions, in particular the IMF and the World Bank, were not permitted to reschedule debt servicing.

A voluminous literature developed analyzing the cause and consequences of the debt situation of developing countries, whether this was a crisis for the international monetary system and making suggestions on how the problem could be managed and/or solved.[33] Despite many innovative and practical proposals for debt relief, governments in developed countries, commercial banks, and the IMF and the World Bank continued stout resistance to the adoption of measures that could be regarded as debt forgiveness/cancellation, and even the terms and conditions of rescheduling arrangements were far from generous. The Washington based think tanks were very active in this debate particularly given their proximity to the IMF and the World Bank and the dominant position of the U.S. Treasury in international financial matters. Among the influential institutions were the Institute for International Economics and the Overseas Development Council. Despite different perspectives there was a recognition by the end of the 1980s that developing country debt required a "much more effective response."[34]

TransAfrica Forum, an organization headed by Randall Robinson, lobbied very actively in support of debt relief for highly indebted countries in Africa and the Caribbean including Jamaica. Robinson and Manley, who was guest speaker on two occasions at the annual TransAfrica dinner, had a warm friendship and an intellectual rapport and shared ideas on debt relief. Robinson's proposed bill called for the total write-off of bilateral debt owed by CARICOM countries as of January 1, 1991. It also requested the President to actively encourage multilateral creditors to provide debt relief to these countries. The objectives of the bill appeared overly ambitious; however, TransAfrica realized that the bill would inevitably be weakened during the legislative process and hence it was necessary to begin from a strong negotiating position.[35] There were a number of environmental non-governmental organizations (NGOs) that advocated debt-for-nature swaps, most notably Thomas Lovejoy,[36] the originator of the concept of debt for nature swaps, Randall Curtis of the Nature Conservancy, Barbara Hofkinson of the World Wildlife Fund, and Peter Seligmann of Conservation International. This approach to debt relief gained visibility from the increased awareness about environmental issues among the American public and because as Chairman of the Federal Reserve Alan Greenspan put it: "None of us had forgotten the Latin America debt crisis of 1982."[37] Bill McGibben's title "The End of Nature"[38] is emblematic of the heightened consciousness about the environment.

Congress

Any cancellation or reduction of debt owed to the U.S. Federal government and to institutions in which the United States is a major contributor such as the IMF and the World Bank required congressional action. The rationale for this is that any non-repayment requires additional fiscal resources to be found. Therefore, initiatives proposing debt cancellation or reduction had to be authorized under some existing legislation or required new legislation to be passed, hence debt reduction had to be authorized by Congress as part of the Enterprise for the Americas Initiative.[39] This requirement limited the changes of getting authorization for debt relief since parochial attitudes in the House regarded this as a "handout" to the profligate and a diversion of resources, which could be applied to projects in the districts or states, which members represented. They felt that it was not a policy that their electorates would be sympathetic to or would support, therefore many members who saw the merits of debt relief for developing countries were in trepidation of openly expressing their support and those that did felt constrained to endorse very small sums.

The Embassy and the lobbyists mounted a comprehensive daily campaign to secure debt relief arguing that this was in the economic self-interest of the United States as debt relief would free resources that would be used for investment and the purchase of imports from the United States. For example, correspondence to Senator Bob Graham on July 9, 1992, states that "the short-term relief provided by this bill would greatly improve regional economies which, in turn, would provide expanded export opportunities for U.S. goods and services. The United States is already the Caribbean and Latin America's largest trading partner and the overall volume of trade could increase dramatically due to Enterprise for the Americas Initiative debt modification."[40] Similar arguments were used in letters sent to Senators Hatfield, Kasten, D'Amato, Harkin, Johnston, DeConcini, Lautenberg, Leahy, Inouye, Specter, and Rudman.[41] Efforts to lobby Congress were supported by the Jamaican community organizations who were asked by the Embassy to focus on congressmen and senators in areas where there was a concentration of Caribbean citizens, e.g., in New York, Hartford, and Florida. The West Indian Commission on its visit to Washington for hearings with the Caribbean community also lobbied Congress for debt relief.[42] The Administration and debtor countries operated in tandem, for example, Secretaries Brady and Baker in their letter to Thomas S. Foley, Speaker, U.S. House of Representatives in July 1992 relied on economic self-interest as the justification for debt relief. The Secretaries stated that "we also need to proceed with full implementation of the debt reduction proposals advanced under the EAI. By reducing countries' bilateral debt to the United States, we can provide critical incentives to sustain important economic reforms while helping Latin American and Caribbean countries escape the shadow of debt that discourages investors. Particularly for the smaller countries in the region such as Costa Rica, El Salvador, and Jamaica, debt reduction under the EAI would substantially reduce their overall external debt burdens and provide important support for market-oriented economic reforms."[43]

Representative Kika de la Garza, Democrat, Texas used his position as chair of the Committee on Agriculture of the House of Representatives to push through legislation to permit debt for environment swaps under the Enterprise for the Americas Initiative. The House Agriculture Committee approved H.R. 4059 on June 30, 1992, permitting countries to repurchase up to 40 percent of their outstanding and rescheduled debt owed to the U.S. Department of Agriculture's Commodity Credit Corporation on the condition that the country commits to spend the funds released to carry out certain environmental activities.[44]

There were many members of Congress who were politically uncomfortable with using resources to provide debt relief to foreign governments when there were alternative uses in their districts. They were concerned not to appear to be coddling profligate countries at the expense of domestic issues. One of the most obstinate opponents was David Obey, Chairman of the House Foreign Operations House Sub-Committee but he was eventually overwhelmed by the vociferous support of the majority of members[45] and by the carefully arranged pressure from key members of the Congressional Black Caucus.[46]

Executive

The political acumen of the leadership in the Bush Administration led to an understanding of the implications of the excessive debt burden particularly after Mexico defaulted, shaking the foundations of many of the largest U.S. commercial banks. The spectre of social conflict and political instability loomed over many Latin American countries important to the United States such as Brazil, Argentina, and Venezuela, as well as the prospect of renewed civil war and guerilla movements in Peru, Nicaragua, Guatemala, and El Salvador. However, their inclinations were constrained by the ultra-conservative disposition of the U.S. Treasury, which consistently failed to grasp the wider social, political, and economic consequences of a deepening of the debt crisis. Eventually, action to keep the Mexican economy from collapsing inspired innovative measures including the Brady Bonds. The debt for nature swaps and debt write-downs became part of a wider multi-pronged approach to the promotion of economic growth and political stability in Latin America and the Caribbean.

The government of Jamaica and its lobbyists understood that the keys to debt relief were, first, the political acceptance of necessity of debt relief by President Bush and second, that Jamaica be seen as worthy of debt relief. Manley set out to persuade Bush on the importance and urgency of debt relief as a means of assisting economic growth in developing countries struggling to emerge from the malaise of the so-called "lost decade" of the 1980s. Vice President Dan Quayle visited Jamaica in January 1990 as part of a three day swing through Latin America and the Caribbean following the U.S. invasion of Panama. While Manley expressed disagreement with the U.S. action in Panama he convinced Quayle that "Potentially any reduction in foreign assistance makes it more difficult for us to pursue the war on drugs, because that war costs money."[47] Quayle that occasion announced an additional $10 million in P.L. 480 assistance to Jamaica. With debt relief and increased aid as priorities Prime Minister Michael Manley met with President George Bush in Washington, D.C., on May 3, 1990, at which time the debt issue was discussed in depth. Meetings were also held with Secretary of the Treasury Nicholas Brady, Acting Secretary of State Lawrence Eagleburger, the House Foreign Affairs Committee, and the Senate Foreign Relations Committee.[48]

The issues raised and the proposals advanced in 1990 were revisited and reemphasized during a similar meeting in May 1991. These discussions served to acquaint the U.S. government at the highest levels with the unique situation of debtor countries like Jamaica, which were highly indebted to both commercial banks and official lenders. Successive Paris Club negotiations had reduced Jamaica's burden of debt repayment to commercial institutions by rescheduling repayments. This left a substantial share of external debt owed to multilateral financial institutions, in particular the IMF and the World Bank, and bilateral donor agencies such as USID. The ideas that Manley advanced dealt with the cancellation of bilateral debt and the unprecedented idea of rescheduling debts owed to the IMF and the World Bank.

The dialogue on debt relief was helped considerably by the comfort and respect that developed between Michael Manley and George Bush. The relationship was so good that when Manley demitted office because of ill health the President hosted him at a small dinner[49] in the private quarters of the White House and extended to him the hospitality of Blair House. This type of cordiality had not existed since Manley met with President Jimmy Carter on December 16, 1977, at the White House. On that occasion Manley and Carter met for one hour and 15 minutes and then had lunch for another hour and a half.[50]

Media

There was a bifurcation of views on the issue of debt relief for developing countries expressed in the media as the conservative financial press such as the *Wall Street Journal* and *Business Week* continued to purvey the conventional wisdom, which had so clearly been overtaken by reality by the late 1980s and early 1990s. The far less influential, liberal press argued the case for debt relief on humanitarian grounds and was joined by some neo-conservative spokespersons concerned about the nexus between debt, poverty, and communism.

In addition to the issue of whether the United States should facilitate or even condone debt relief there was the question of which countries needed and more importantly which governments should be granted this "benefit." Jamaica was by the late 1980s undoubtedly a country needing debt relief. Should a government led by Seaga be assisted, having doubled the country's external debt in its first couple years in office, or could a Manley government tied to democratic socialism but with a weak economic management record including two aborted IMF programs be trusted to make use of debt relief? Manley had to live down the image of a socialist, pro-Cuba radical, which was the standard fare in the print media in the 1970s and 1980s. This was no easy task given the virulence of the branding. For example, Arnaud de Borchgrave of *Newsweek* magazine described Manley's electoral victory in 1977 as "made possible, in part, by direct support by Cuba's secret service" and "the Soviet Union is expected to open an embassy in Kingston. The Cubans are already well entrenched. . . . Whether Manley intends it or not Jamaica could become the next country to go Marxist."[51] Arnaud de Borchgrave was found to be guilty of plagiarism and exposed in May 2012.[52]

Fenton Communications was instrumental in increasing Manley's presence in U.S. media. This was not a difficult task given that Manley was mediagenic and an articulate and persuasive advocate. He was much

sought after because of his worldwide reputation as a leader of the so-
called Third World. Media contact was not left to the initiative of the
media but was sought in a proactive media engagement policy. Meetings
were arranged with key journalists and influential media, e.g., the editorial board of the *Washington Post* in May 1990 and highly visible media
events, e.g., the Morning Newsmaker at the National Press Club in Washington, D.C., in May 1990.

Bureaucracy

The views prevailing in the bureaucracy were predominantly of the
conventional type even where as in the case of the State Department there
was an appreciation of the link between debt and instability. The dominant approach was that provided by the Treasury, which eschewed non-
economic considerations while admonishing debtors to stay the course
even if this required the most severe fiscal contraction. The Treasury
maintained "ownership" of the issue both on the grounds of jurisdiction
and technical expertise and only exhibited a modicum of flexibility when
the banks themselves took the lead in rescheduling and pressuring the
U.S. government to ensure the safety of their loans by participating in
financing packages for large debtor countries such as Mexico. By 1990
some of the large U.S. banks including Citibank were in sufficient difficulty to warrant the intervention of the Treasury and the Federal Reserve.[53] It was "widely accepted"[54] that Latin America's massive debt-
service burden had become unsustainable and substantial debt relief was
urgently needed to avoid economic, social, and political fallout.

Manley's rehabilitation with various branches of the U.S. government
in the year to 18 months before he regained the post of prime minister
was guided by and facilitated by a highly respected Jamaican in Washington, D.C. Richard Fletcher, a senior official at the Inter-American Development Bank and former Minister of State in the Ministry of Finance
in the Manley government of 1971–1980, advised on strategy, arranged
meetings, and accompanied Manley to appointments. He was helped to
rebuild Jamaica's relations with the International Monetary fund, the
World Bank, and the Inter-American Development Bank through his contacts with colleagues in these institutions. He was instrumental in the
decision to employ a lobbyist.

Government of Jamaica

The struggle to get debt relief to be accepted as prudent policy by the
U.S. government was a difficult one as foreign governments were unable
to generate widespread public support and support in Congress for debt
relief for developing countries. The balance of forces shifted when the
U.S. banks began to pressure the Executive and bureaucracy, i.e., Treas-

ury and Federal Reserve to participate in bailing them out where their portfolios contained a significant share of uncollectable loans. Liberal elements coincided with conservative views when arguing that the U.S. government should play a role in resolving the debt crisis even if this involved committing U.S. government funds. Jamaica and Guyana were the countries from the region most affected and it was in this milieu that Jamaica exerted leadership on this issue with Michael Manley being a most persuasive advocate and lobbyist. All ministers of government of Jamaica were mandated to raise the issue of debt relief in all of their meetings with U.S. officials and their itineraries in Washington, D.C., always included appointments designed to further the issue.

Jamaica was well served by an outstanding Minister of Foreign Affairs during these years in which debt relief was a priority for Jamaica. David Coore was a brilliant student and head boy of Jamaica College where his life-long friendship with Michael Manley began. In 1942 he was awarded the 1942 Jamaica Scholarship. He studied economics at McGill University in Canada and read law at Oxford University in the United Kingdom; he was called to the Bar at the Middle Temple. On returning to Jamaica he worked in the chambers of Norman Manley, regarded as Jamaica's foremost attorney. This is no doubt how he became involved in the People's National Party. He was the Member of Parliament for St Andrew West Central from 1967 to 1976, and St Andrew West from 1976 to 1978. He served in many capacities in the PNP including vice-president and Chairman. He was Deputy Prime Minister and Minister of Finance from 1972 to 1978 and then held senior positions in the Inter-American Development Bank. He was a member of the Joint Select Committee who helped draft the Jamaica Constitution in 1962, "when his legal expertise proved invaluable."[55] He was Minister of Foreign Affairs and Foreign Trade from 1989 to 1993. He brought to this task a breadth of knowledge of world affairs,[56] his brilliance, unflappable calm, political experience, legal erudition, and great sense of humor. Having lived and worked in Washington, D.C., he understood the U.S. system of government and was close to Michael Manley politically and personally.

Subsequently the post was filled by Dr. Paul Robertson, a bright former university lecturer had worked very closely with Mr. Manley and held several senior positions in the PNP including General Secretary. He held a PhD in political science from the University of Michigan and was a lecturer at Howard University and the University of the West Indies, Mona, Jamaica.

Lobbyist

The services of the lobbying firm contributed to spreading the recognition that Jamaica was serious about economic reform in a private sector-led growth process but was constrained by a heavy burden of debt.

The lobbyist in tandem with the Embassy of Jamaica disseminated this message to Congress, the State Department, the Treasury, and the Executive through meetings, speaking engagements, and letters. The interest of the government of Jamaica in debt relief coincided with attempts by the Bush Administration led by Deputy Secretary of the Treasury Robert Mulford, in providing debt relief as part of the Enterprise for Americas Initiative (EAI). Jamaica's campaign was so successful that it became the first country to receive debt relief under the EAI. The *Wall Street Journal* reported that Jamaica would be the chief beneficiary of debt reduction funding because it "aggressively lobbied behind the Washington firm Neil and Company and had help from senior Democrats, including Texas Congressman Charles Wilson, Congressman Charles Rangel and Majority Leader Whip William Gray."[57]

The Campaign

The principal actors involved in shaping the outcome of the campaign for debt relief in Jamaica were the Executive, Congress, the Bureaucracy in particular the Treasury, the media, think tanks, and the ESC governments. The Treasury was the main determinant of U.S. policy on relief on heavily indebted developing countries. The Treasury took cognizance of the political directives from the White House and in turn advised the President on the technical aspects and financial limitations of various methods of debt relief. The Treasury was notoriously conservative in its philosophy and policies and new ideas were reluctantly received, usually in the face of imminent disasters such as a default by Mexico. The Congress was in a constitutionally mandated position to approve or veto policies with financial implications.

The campaign by Jamaica took place in a context in which developing country debt had become a major problem for the global community. No major international meeting was complete without a discussion of the "debt crisis," whether at the United Nations or at the International Monetary Fund. The governments of developed countries were inured to the supplicants from the so-called "Third World" because these were regarded as profligate and inept in the conduct of their economic and fiscal affairs. Mismanagement was to be corrected by deflationary stabilization programs under the tutelage of the IMF. Rescheduling of debt was prohibited in the case of multilateral financial institutions, e.g., the World Bank, and severely discouraged for debt owed to private creditors, including transnational commercial banks.[58] These hard line attitudes were ameliorated during the late 1970s and the decade of the 1980s because commercial banks were forced to reschedule debts, which to a considerable extent were the result of careless overlending that was associated with the recycling of Petro-dollars. Flushed with Petro-dollars, the banks lent without undertaking adequate sovereign risk analysis. The banks relied on the IMF to minimize the interruptions in debt servicing and prevent any losses.

The governments in the developed countries whose transnational commercial banks were involved in lending to developing countries were pressured and persuaded to "enforce" debt servicing by debtor countries. In the early years of the debt crisis, the governments of the United States and Western European countries performed this role from conviction but later were impelled by an exaggerated fear that their banks would be jeopardized by non-payment. The U.S. banking sector became active in shaping U.S. policy by lobbying the Treasury and Congress, both directly and by supporting research in think tanks. The output of the think tanks and financial periodicals were for a time regurgitated by the popular media. Over time, however, rising current of opinion questioned the orthodox explanations and policy prescriptions. The alternative view emerged from academics, the developing countries, humanitarian NGOs, notably Oxfam, and radical political organizations. These views expanded from leftist journals, e.g., *Monthly Review*, a Marxist publication to permeate liberal groups and eventually became part of mainstream discussions to the point where the morality of bailing out the banks was questioned across the spectrum of political thinking. The think tanks became central to the debate over what the United States should do about the burgeoning debt of developing countries[59] because all participants employed technical studies to support their perspectives and recommendations. Economists of various perspectives provided a wide menu of debt relief options.[60]

FOREIGN AID

The foreign aid policy of the United States emanates from a process involving the Congress and the bureaucracy in the form of the U.S. Agency for International Development of the State Department being the primary determinants with input from the White House, the National Security Council, and the Department of State. USAID was established in 1961 by President John F. Kennedy to implement international development assistance programs in forms authorized annually by the Congress acting under the Foreign Assistance Act. At times it has been an independent federal agency, and sometimes as a part of the State Department. The media, think tanks, and the U.S.-based Jamaican community have some influence on the decisions made by Congress and the Executive because they influence the political environment in which decisions about foreign aid and its allocation are made. A foreign government seeking to influence this process needs to interact with all of these entities and political actors. The process by which the government of Jamaica influenced USAID policy is shown in figure 5.2.

The Foreign Aid Process

The formulation of the U.S. foreign aid package for Jamaica is a lengthy process, taking one and one-half years before the aid is actually provided to Jamaica. The design begins in Kingston, is studied again and reviewed by the various Executive agencies in Washington, is studied again by the Congress, and concludes with the Congressional vote and passage into law. The initial "request" for aid for Jamaica is generated by the U.S. Embassy in Kingston, as is the case for all countries that receive U.S. bilateral aid, after the Administration has sent to each Embassy its general budgetary guidelines. The U.S. Embassy in Kingston plays a central role in helping Jamaica define the extent of its participation in U.S. security and economic assistance programs. It also helps define the relationships between aid levels and U.S. national interests and policy objectives in Jamaica. The Embassy submits four detailed reports to Washington on the assistance programs. Planning documents are prepared for both security and economic assistance, providing the general outlines of the planning for each program. In addition, separate programming documents are also compiled, which discuss the details of how the requested aid will be spent. The two security assistance program reports, like the two economic assistance reports, are the result of coordinated efforts among senior officers in all departments and agencies within the U.S. embassy in Kingston, including a personal review by the Ambassador. These documents express the Embassy's view of what should be provided in assistance for Jamaica. They include Jamaica's perceptions of its needs, but reflect more strongly the biases of the Embassy. As a conse-

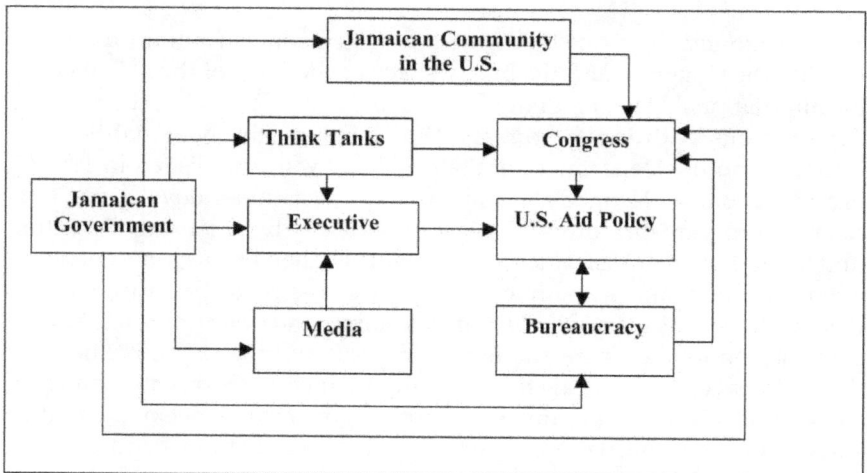

Figure 5.2.   Influencing U.S. Aid Policy

quence, AID's submission for economic assistance may be at odds in some respects with the desires of the government of Jamaica. To change the mix of aid submitted by the Embassy in Kingston, Jamaica must influence the proposal inside the administration in Washington.

The Embassy reports described above are next sent to the inter-agency process involving the Department of State, the Department of Defense, USAID, the National Security Council (NSC), the Office of Management and Budget (OMB), and the Department of the Treasury. These agencies begin their reviews of the reports from a regional perspective, before dealing with individual countries. They evaluate Jamaica's economic and military program levels according to Jamaica's defense capability, U.S. foreign policy objectives, and U.S. national security interests. The USAID reviews the documents and establishes the basic levels, terms, and conditions that it deems appropriate for aid to Jamaica. At the same time, the Defense Security Assistance Agency (DSAA) conducts a similar review of the military programs. Representatives from the Department of State, the National Security Council, the Department of the Treasury, and OMB participate in both reviews. A few months after the submission of the reports and the completion of an initial "staffing," or evaluation, within the Department of State, Defense, and USAID, an interagency program review is conducted. The Politico-Military Affairs Bureau (PM) of the State Department, which chairs the interagency review group, drafts a timetable for completing the budget submission. It also establishes the framework to be used by the State Department Regional Bureaus in presenting their proposals of program funding levels for each country within their respective regions.

At the same time, USAID conducts similar meetings to review economic assistance. These meetings are first country specific, then regional, and finally deal with the worldwide program. The participants in these meetings are drawn principally from within AID, but include representatives of the State Department's Economic Bureau, the NSC, OMB, and the Treasury Department. After the "worldwide wrap-up" within USID, the Administrator makes his final decisions on country levels, terms, and conditions. His decisions with respect to Jamaica are based principally on advice from USID's Bureau for Program and Policy Coordination. These decisions then become the official USAID position for the next steps of the process.

The final review within the bureaucracy takes place in the office of the Deputy Secretary of State. The Deputy Secretary's review of the interagency recommendations are supposed to resolve any outstanding issues, such as the inclusion of additional recipient countries, or changes to military assistance or economic assistance programs. Sometimes, all issues are resolved at the interagency level, and this review checks off or "clears" these decisions as recommendations to the Secretary of State. The annual program funding levels recommended by the Deputy Secretary are then forwarded to the Secretary of State for his approval. Generally the Secretary of State will approve these proposals unchanged.

The proposals for aid are then sent to the Office of Management and Budget (OMB) for final evaluations and adjustments to the funding levels. This final review is made in the context of the entire U.S. budget, and often the levels proposed by the interagency group will be reduced by OMB and sent back to the State Department. The final decision on these levels can then only be made by the President following Cabinet-level discussions.

In accordance with the U.S. Constitution, once the Administration has determined its foreign aid program, it must submit the program to the Congress for review and approval. The Congress approves the program in three separate steps: first, it approves the total foreign aid budget within the U.S. budget; second, it authorizes the Administration to spend the foreign aid funding; and third, it approves (appropriates) the actual funds to be spent. The first Congressional review in this process is exactly the same for all U.S. programs, both foreign and domestic. This review is designed to ensure that U.S. government spending is approved within the context of the entire budget; only later will the proposal be reviewed in the context of a foreign policy. The first review is very brief insofar as it pertains to Jamaica: Jamaica's programs are included in a worldwide budget where they are dwarfed by big budget items such as U.S. defense and health programs. Jamaica is unlikely to be mentioned during the review. The second and third Congressional reviews of foreign aid programs are very detailed and redundant. It is during these reviews that any Congressional statements for and against Jamaica's programs would be made. The formal proposal for Jamaica's aid comes to the Congress as a part of the Executive Branch's draft Foreign Assistance Authorization Bill, the legislation authorizing the President to spend money to conduct foreign policy. This is the first detailed Congressional review of Jamaica's programs.

The House Foreign Affairs Committee and Senate Foreign Relations Committee and their respective subcommittees review the proposals for foreign aid and conduct hearings to examine the authorization request. In the House Foreign Affairs Committee, there is usually a hearing by the Western Hemisphere Affairs Subcommittee (under whose jurisdiction Jamaica's programs fall) dedicated specifically to a review of the Administration's policy. In the Senate Foreign Relations Committee, Jamaica's program is usually addressed in a hearing by the Western Hemisphere and Peace Corps Affairs Subcommittee. During these hearings, Congress will generally request that testimony be provided by senior officials of the Executive Branch, the Secretary of State, and the Secretary of Defense.

Following these hearings, the subcommittees and committees will proceed to amend (or "mark up") the President's proposed draft legislation to incorporate each committee's views. The revised proposal (in the form of a legislative "bill") is then voted upon within the committees and submitted to the House and Senate, respectively, for a Floor vote. On the Floor, the bill faces the same amendment process as in committee, and any decision made by the committees can be modified on the Floor of the House or Senate. Each committee and each chamber of Congress act independently of the others. While both generally base their actions on the President's proposals, they each do what they wish. A proposal only becomes law after both chambers have approved it and the President signs the "bill." Thus, most actions by one committee or one chamber of Congress are considered preliminary, and may be changed at some later point.

Since the bills prepared in each chamber almost always differ, a joint House-Senate Conference Committee must reconcile the differences. When this is completed, the Joint Conference Committee "reports out" an agreed-upon bill, which is then resubmitted to each chamber for final consideration. Since the bills considered in each chamber at this stage are identical, an affirmative vote in both chambers will result in a final authorization enactment, which needs only the signature of the President to become law.

The Congressional review and approval of the appropriations bill is the same as that for the authorization bill. The bill must be separately debated and amended by the Appropriations Committees and sent to the Floor of each chamber for passage. Following that, a joint House-Senate Conference Committee must again approve the legislation, which, after final approval by the two chambers,[61] is seen by the President for his signature.

In the event that a new appropriations bill is not passed in a given fiscal year (which ends on September 30 of each calendar year), the fiscal year may enact a "Continuing Resolution" which essentially permits foreign assistance funding for the new fiscal year to continue at the same level as the preceding year, or at an adjusted level as determined by Congress. After legislative enactment of the authorization and appropriations bills or a substitute "Continuing Resolution," the annual security assistance budget development process is almost complete. All that remains is for the Administration to allocate the funds to individual country programs. Within 30 days after enactment of an appropriations bill, the Executive Branch must make a final allocation of the amounts appropriated. The State Department then presents to Congress an Operating Year Budget (OYB), under which it will operate foreign aid programs for that year. Generally, the allocations reflect the country levels proposed and justified in the initial budget submissions to the Congress. However, they also include changes made by Congress (earmarks of assistance levels or prohibitions on assistance, for example) and they accommodate any cuts made in the overall levels of specific accounts by allocating reductions in proposed country programs. At this point the foreign aid cycle is complete. By the time the final legislation is approved, and the Operating Year Budget finalized, the next year's security assistance program development cycle has begun, and the 10-month long, detailed planning and programming process is once again fully underway. In this sense, the U.S. government is constantly working on two separate foreign aid planning cycles: the one for next year, as well as that for the following year.

Importance of U.S. Aid

Foreign aid from the United States has played an important role in supporting public sector development projects and social programs in the ESC. The United States began providing foreign aid to the ESC in the mid-1950s. The crisis in British Guiana in 1953 prompted the United States to conclude Technical Assistance Agreements with British Guiana and Jamaica in 1954–1955. The specific objectives were to counter the communist threat and promote increased output of strategic raw materials.[62] During the 1960s foreign aid was regarded as an important instrument for promoting development in the newly independent countries of the Caribbean. As one of the leading Caribbean thinkers explained, "The fact is that small independent nations such as Trinidad or Jamaica need help for a period of time in order that their economies may become self-sustaining. As independent countries they are seeking aid for economic and social development, and they turn in particular to the United States. They have based their claim not on poverty but on their record in development."[63] The 1980s was the period in which the largest flows to the region took place with Jamaica being one of the largest beneficiaries. Jamaica received almost $1 billion of foreign aid from the United States during the 1980s (see table 5.3). However, by the late 1980s there was a very sharp reduction in aid to the region representing a shift in U.S. priorities and less apprehension about the security of the Central American region. This shift in policy was partly due to the post-Vietnam syndrome and the fact that following the end of the Cold War, anticommunism had not been replaced by another rationale, which gave coherence to U.S. foreign aid. The American public was no longer seized with the importance of foreign policy and perceived on impelling need for foreign aid. A crisis of disinterest emerged, which required new ways of engaging the public in U.S. foreign policy.[64] Indeed, sensing this mood, Clinton in his 1992 campaign pledged to spend less on international affairs and foreign aid.[65]

The Political Atmosphere

The political atmosphere in Washington shifted in the latter part of the 1980s because the threat of communism was not regarded as palpable in

Table 5.3. USAID Economic Assistance to Jamaica 1980-1999 (US$ Mil)

YEAR	*ESF	**DA	PL480	TOTAL
1980	00.0	2.68	10.02	12.70
1981	41.00	12.92	17.11	71.03
1982	90.46	28.95	17.51	136.92
1983	59.35	22.18	20.11	101.64
1984	55.00	32.64	20.57	108.21
1985	81.00	34.26	40.34	155.61
1986	58.57	26.07	37.58	122.22
1987	25.93	18.09	39.94	83.96
1988	0.50	39.24	35.75	75.49
1989	12.90	51.82	47.06	111.78
1990	13.73	14.44	41.60	69.77
1991	10.00	16.82	45.12	71.94
1992	22.25	15.31	36.07	73.63
1993	3.00	40.38	34.28	77.66
1994	0.00	9.14	20.00	29.14
1995	0.00	11.44	10.00	21.44
1996	0.00	8.31	21.20	29.51
1997	0.00	11.03	10.00	21.03
1998	0.00	11.04	5.00	16.04
1999	0.00	6.12	10.00	16.12

Source: USAID Overseas Loans and Grants; USAID LAC Data Book 1999: Planning Institute of Jamaica, PL480 data
* Economic Support Funds; ** Development Assistance

Central America and the Caribbean. The second Reagan Administration reduced the level of foreign aid.[66] It was also a time when there was a major re-evaluation of the efficacy of foreign aid as an instrument of foreign policy, a renewed questioning of the contribution of aid to economic growth in developing countries, and pressure for a shift in the focus of foreign aid away from the traditional role in economic development to humanitarian concerns, sustainable development, and strengthening of democracy. In this milieu, the traditional opponents of aid renewed their criticisms of aid. For example, The Heritage Foundation claimed that much of U.S. foreign aid "goes to support avowed adversaries of the United States and hostile, non-aligned nations," citing the fact that, "$1 billion, or 13.6 percent of last year's (1997) bilateral assistance, went to countries that voted against the United States at least half of the time in the United Nations." They also disparaged the focus on basic human needs as, "turning aid that had been seen as a temporary crutch into what has become a permanent dole."[67] Public opinion had shifted in the late 1980s to regarding spending on domestic issues as being more important than foreign aid.[68] At that time Peter Tarnoff, president of the Council on Foreign Relations described the mood as "many Americans tired of paying for an activist foreign policy and strong national defense are demanding that their President pay more attention to, and spend more money on, domestic matters."[69]

Political events in the Caribbean viewed through the Cold War prism accounted for a gigantic increase in U.S. aid to the region according to USAID officials. The political happenings that caught the attention of U.S. policy makers were "Jamaica's transition from defiant, independent socialism to free markets, Guyana's non-aligned socialism shifted towards democratic capitalism, and the rise and fall of a Marxist government in Grenada." However, the "most fundamental change that reconfigured aid's policies in the Caribbean was the increased emphasis on private sector development."[70] The Reagan Administration also set out to "re-establish uncontested U.S. political and economic hegemony in our backyard"[71] namely Central America and the Caribbean. Jamaica became a showcase[72] for the Reagan Administration as a capitalist success to counter the Cuban model. USAID was concerned that the "failure of the aid program in Jamaica would confirm the view of those in the Caribbean and elsewhere in the third world that cooperation with the IMF and stimulation of the private sector is a hopeless endeavor."[73] McAfee notes that the "Reagan Administration pulled out all the stops to assist Seaga and keep its new Caribbean free enterprise showboat afloat."[74] During the 1980s, Jamaica was by far the largest recipient of U.S. foreign aid in the Caribbean. Indeed, in 1981 and 1982, Jamaica received more assistance than in the entire post-war period. During the halcyon period of 1981 to 1985, Jamaica ranked as the second or third highest per capita recipient of aid funding worldwide and tenth in absolute terms. This was in sharp contrast to the 1960s and 1970s when U.S. aid was modest.

Aid from the United States dropped precipitously after the mid-1980s reflecting the reduced concern about leftist regimes in Central America (Sandinistas in Nicaragua) and the Caribbean (democratic socialism in Jamaica, cooperative socialism in Guyana, and Bishop in Grenada), less angst about Cuban influence, and disenchantment with the failure of the Seaga regime to be a successful private enterprise model to counter the interest in the Cuban model. It was also a time when there was criticism and reevaluation of U.S. aid policy and activities it supported from both the "conservative"[75] and the "radical" ends of the political spectrum. These views continued a debate over the efficacy of foreign aid in promoting economic growth in developing countries that dates back to the 1950s and remains an unresolved debate in development economics. Notable critics include Milton Friedman[76] and P. T. Bauer who was still firing salvos in the mid-1980s[77] although there were studies that demonstrated the positive returns from aid.[78] In the 1990s there was another blossoming in the United States of the perennial debate about aid effectiveness. Public opinion regarded domestic issues as more important than development issues and relations with less developed countries.[79] It was in this political atmosphere[80] that the second Reagan Administration shifted towards lower levels of foreign assistance.[81] Jamaica and the Caribbean were targeted for serious reductions in aid from the beginning of the 1990s and this continued throughout the decade as Congress sought to garner additional resources for Eastern Europe after the implosion of the Soviet Union. By the early 1990s, "aid fatigue" had emerged in the United States as political support for foreign aid weakened and even for supporters of aid the purpose of aid was being reviewed.[82] Congressman Obey and academic Lancaster summarize the situation facing the Bush Administration as the need for a design "that can win support at home, and that the United States can afford [and] that must be done in the much broader context of cutting the federal budget deficit."[83]

At the same time there was strong sentiment in favor of domestic issues instead of foreign aid and international engagement. In addition there were influential voices calling for a new demarche in U.S. foreign policy towards Latin America and the Caribbean. For example, Pastor and Fletcher suggested that "the time has come to consider a new stage in the region's development and its relationship with the United States" and that "the United States should offer a bold economic initiative."[84]

Justifying Aid for Jamaica

The government of Jamaica was not a foreign policy priority for the United States as it was neither a crisis nor a country of strategic value. Jamaica had one advantage, namely, it was regarded in U.S. political and policymaking circles as the "leader of the Caribbean" and "the country whose example was followed sooner or later by other Caribbean countries."[85] In addition, the activism of successive governments in international affairs and the prominent worldwide profile of Manley and Seaga's closeness to the Reagan Administration had created a recognition factor for Jamaica. By 1991 members of Congress and policymakers were aware of Manley, Seaga, and Jamaica. There was however a perception that the Manley Administration of 1972–1980 had been socialist and was on friendly terms with Fidel Castro and Cuba. There were many Americans of all "walks of life" who even believed, vaguely recollected, or had read or heard that Jamaica under Manley's rule had been in danger of going communist and some persons had the impression that Manley was a communist and close ally of Castro. The fact that the Peoples National Party (PNP) under the leadership of Michael Manley had declared itself democratic socialist in 1974 was widely misunderstood both in Jamaica and abroad, especially in the United States, to mean a prelude to communism or having the potential to mutate in that direction. This "Red Scare" was deliberately propagated by political opponents inside and outside of Jamaica, in particular, through a virulent propaganda campaign by the Seaga and the Jamaica Labour Party[86] and malicious misrepresentations in local and international media. In reality the inflammatory rhetoric and reckless statements by the "Leftists" in the PNP provided an abundance of material for opponents and caused considerable confusion and consternation even among supporters of the PNP. Manley conceded that "I certainly wouldn't do the deeds any differently but I would certainly moderate the language."[87]

Michael Manley and the PNP during the eight years in opposition rethought their philosophy and, while not changing the goals, decided to change the means of attaining them, prompting one commentator to describe the new policy as "market-led socialism."[88] Specifically it reverted to an economic strategy of private sector, market driven economic growth. On regaining power Prime Minister Manley spoke of "a radical change of direction" in which there would be the "free play of market forces in the determination of prices" as this was the "only way that we begin to ensure, in the long run, efficient use of our resources."[89] The new economic policy had to be explained to overseas institutions and foreign government so as to minimize any possibility of a wait and see attitude as this could delay the allocation and disbursement of urgently needed resources. Perhaps the most important arena in which it was necessary to convince decision makers was in Washington, D.C., where some of the key persons and institutions exhibited an initial skepticism. The image of Michael Manley was of a brilliant and articulate leader of international stature who was a passionate crusader to change the world in a way that would ensure the betterment of the peoples of the so-called Third World. This was a noble cause that no well thinking person could disagree with but the methods Manley advocated, e.g., the new international economic order,[90] the Common Fund,[91] and non-alignment[92] aroused concerns among those who were well off in the status quo. His active leadership role and advocacy of these ideas through the Socialist International, e.g., the Brandt/Manley Report,[93] which called for changes in the structure and management of the world economy, did not endear him to Republican administrations of 1980–1988.

In order to reimage Manley and reposition Jamaica, Manley decided to enlist the services of a lobbyist and a public relations consultant and to appoint a new ambassador to the United States who was an economist intimately involved with economic policies of the PNP party and the government. With this team in place in Washington a wide ranging campaign was undertaken, led by Manley himself, and supported by Foreign Minister Coore and G. Arthur Brown, the highly regarded Govenor of the central bank. An integral component of the strategy to persuade and convince Washington was lobbying the Congress for aid and debt relief. Another very serious problem that had to be overcome was the reputation gained during the Seaga regime when Jamaica became known for unkept promises about economic policy, mismanagement, resisting IMF policy advice, excessive borrowing, and fiscal profligacy. A former Department of Commerce official vividly expressed the United States view as: "Despite $1 billion in U.S. development assistance and the close friendship of the Reagan administration, Edward Seaga failed to transform Jamaica's economy during more than eight years in office, becoming a disappointment, as well as a political embarrassment." [94]

The gravamen of Jamaica's presentations to U.S. government officials and members of Congress in support of aid was that Jamaica was committed to free market economics, economic reform, and structural adjustment but urgently required financial support in the form of loans, debt relief, and aid. For example, the Ambassador stated this in several testimonies to various Committees of Congress. [95] Over the years, the United States and the Caribbean Basin nations have developed an important economic partnership, partly as a result of U.S. assistance and trade programs. For Jamaica, the United States was a very important economic partner and supporter of its development program. Indeed, over the past decade, Jamaica has been a major recipient of U.S. foreign aid to the Caribbean region. The United States has been a vital source of funding because these resources were used to:

1. Facilitate economic liberalization and private sector-led growth;
2. Promote institution building and public sector efficiency;
3. Support debt reduction;
4. Assist the social sectors to cushion the effects of economic adjustment on the poor;
5. Improve natural resource management;
6. Combat the international narcotics trade;
7. Fund environmental protection; and
8. Provide disaster relief

Ultimately, Jamaica was seeking to reduce its traditional reliance on official assistance and to finance development through a combination of domestic and foreign private capital flows. However, this long-term goal could only be achieved with continued U.S. support for Jamaica's comprehensive economic reform and development programs. Jamaica was acutely aware of the budgetary constraints in the United States. Furthermore, given the end of the Cold War and pressing domestic concerns, Congress and American public opinion favored a reduction in foreign assistance programs. The government of Jamaica welcomed the refocusing of the U.S. aid program towards sustainable development, with an emphasis on entrepreneurial development, assistance to the social sectors, and popular participation in the development process. Nevertheless, while the rationale for this new approach was clearly understood, a reduction in development assistance should be a phased process, which must be sensitive to Jamaica's development needs. Sudden and drastic foreign aid cuts would adversely affect Jamaica's structural transformation efforts.

The United States had supported the process of economic reform and trade liberalization in Jamaica. The Jamaican Government was implementing a "comprehensive and uncompromising economic reform program" that had brought positive results and that had "created private sector-led, market-driven economic growth." U.S. assistance principally in the form of Economic Support Funds, which now have been totally phased out, had helped Jamaicans make that adjustment by providing the government with budgetary allotments to facilitate economic reform. It was pointed out that as the economy has expanded, so too has the capacity to import from the United States, its largest trading partner from which Jamaica imported 70 percent of its goods and services. Imports from the United States had experienced annual growth of 13.6 percent since 1985.

Development assistance (DA) from the United States had also played an important role in sustaining Jamaica's economic growth and reform programs by helping Jamaica undertake critical social programs in areas such as education and public health, and created employment through the promotion of micro-enterprise development. Jamaica's collaboration with USID had improved the management of health services and helped to establish better and more widely understood family planning practices, and the prevention of the transmission of AIDS and other deadly diseases. U.S. funding also contributed to the construction of low-cost housing, the provision of low-income families with access to potable water, and the alleviation of youth unemployment. Food aid to Jamaica through the PL480 program has been a tremendous success, benefiting vulnerable and disadvantaged groups. Since the 1970s, Jamaica has graduated from the Title II grant program to receiving a combination of Title I (the soft loan program) and GSM, the credit guarantee program administered by the USDA and guaranteed by the Commodity Credit Corporation.

The United States has been an important supporter of private sector development but the government of Jamaica is looking to private sector sources and foreign direct investment to generate additional capital to finance Jamaica's development needs. U.S. government support has been instrumental in facilitating private investment in Jamaica, strengthening a complementary partnership that ultimately generates U.S. jobs and exports. The Overseas Private Investment Corporation has supported dozens of projects in Jamaica, to the amount approaching $1 billion since it began in 1963. The administration and Congress should give consideration to the strengthening of a mutually beneficial trading partnership. In the long-term, as foreign aid is phased out, it can only be replaced by a sound and commercially viable trade and investment relationship. Jamaica has long recognized the importance of such a relationship with the United States. Bilateral trade flows have expanded by more than 10 percent a year since the mid-1980s; moreover, U.S. investors are playing an active role in Jamaica's growing private sector.

The Caribbean Basin Initiative (CBI) has formed an important basis for the United States/Jamaican and United States/Caribbean partnership to flourish. The Administration is developing a proposal to strengthen this CBI framework to help CBI countries cope with trade and investment diversion from Mexico under the NAFTA and prepare a road map for their full participation in the FTAA. In this regard, Jamaica is ready and committed to further cementing that partnership by undertaking the obligations of a free trade agreement with the United States. Indeed, in the past two years alone, Jamaica and the United States have taken steps in that direction by signing a Bilateral Investment Treaty (BIT) and an Intellectual Property Rights (IPR) agreement. Jamaica has also led the Caribbean in negotiating tough textile anti-circumvention language with the United States.

Jamaica continues to face heavy debt service obligations, owed primarily to bilateral donors such as the United States. Recently, the United States has made valuable concessions that have provided important debt relief to support reform efforts. This debt relief frees scarce foreign exchange resources for crucial imports and reduced debt servicing helps to lower fiscal expenditure, thereby contributing to Jamaica's growth. Debt relief has also channeled local currency debt repayments into environmental management funds, building a sustainable environmental framework for development. Ultimately, because of debt relief, Jamaica has been one of the few countries to reduce its stock of external debt and debt servicing. Nevertheless, debt service obligations remain high and currently absorb approximately one-half of the government's annual budget. By comparison, in the United States, where public debate has highlighted the burden of the U.S. government budget deficit, debt service is less than 20 percent. As Jamaica allocates such a high percentage of the public sector budget for debt servicing, it is unable to pursue other ongoing development priorities. In this regard, Jamaica welcomes the enactment of new mechanisms to effect debt reduction through buybacks and swaps.

The Jamaican government is irrevocably committed to maintaining a comprehensive anti-drug campaign based upon a two-pronged approach, focusing both on supply and demand reduction. To curtail the supply of drugs, the government is engaged in a campaign to eradicate marijuana growing in the remote mountainous regions of the country and to strengthen capabilities to interdict and punish drug offenders.

Already Jamaica has succeeded in reducing marijuana production and has passed legislation on asset forfeiture and money laundering, and implemented a Mutual Legal Assistance Treaty (MLAT) with the United States. The United States has made an important contribution through the support of economic and security assistance, training, and other material and assets, and Jamaica is actively working with U.S. government agencies to strengthen cooperation across a range of activities. Jamaica is keenly aware that without a demand for illegal drugs, there would be no (drug) industry. Therefore, there must be an effort to stem demand for drugs in Jamaica. Critically acclaimed programs are being funded that focus on rehabilitating former drug addicts and on providing drug eradication to vulnerable groups. These supply and demand-related programs place considerable pressure on the Jamaican government's budget, particularly at a time when there is considerable effort to fund other social programs while curtailing the growth of fiscal expenditure. With continued U.S. assistance, Jamaica can maintain its aggressive efforts, both to stop the harmful flow of drugs into the United States and to provide viable alternatives for Jamaicans to induce them out of illegal narcotics activities. Any reduction in U.S. funding of counter narcotics programs would put additional financial burdens on the Jamaican government at a time when it is undertaking critical economic reforms. U.S. assistance sustains an important partnership in the effort to combat international narcotics trafficking.

The U.S. foreign assistance program in Jamaica should be viewed as an investment in the economic well-being of the United States, not as outflows of money. The mutual benefits of foreign assistance are well documented and need to be clearly recognized in order to forestall any further cuts in aid programs. If aid must be reduced, it must be done in a phased and orderly manner. One way to ensure this is through the creation of a Development Fund for Latin America and the Caribbean, which can offset aid cuts while providing a comprehensive policy vehicle for new types of assistance in the future. Strengthening our common economic relationship will provide an additional framework through which aid flows can be replaced by advantageous commercial linkages.

Operationalizing the Campaign

The amount of foreign aid allocated to a country and in what form is a decision that emerges from a long process starting with the recommendations of the U.S. Embassy and AID mission in that country and meandering through the bureaucracy in Washington, D.C. Once the Administration submits its proposals to Congress, the real battle begins because Congress has the final say and has the power to modify the proposals received from the Administration. Given the unique openness of the U.S. political system foreign governments and their lobbyists can actively intervene in the decision-making process. In lobbying the Congress, a foreign government can enlist the support of the community of its nationals who are resident in the United States as well as think tanks and the media. This complex political process is shown in figure 5.2.

The strategy to garner foreign aid from the United States involves two phases: first, to create a favorable impression of the country and establish the need for U.S. foreign aid, and second, to show that the country is deserving of aid, more specifically, that the country is friendly or even better, an ally and best of all, compliant with U.S. demands. This case can also be strengthened, where it can be demonstrated that there is a credible internal threat such as leftist guerilla movements, e.g., Colombia, or externally, communist subversion, e.g., El Salvador, and of course, if a link can be demonstrated between sources of internal instability and forces of external instigation or material and/or financial support, e.g., Nicaragua. The United States is most receptive to supplication where the country has strategic value because of its geographic location, e.g., Turkey. These themes are easily understood by members of Congress when approached with plausible evidence by the executive and the bureaucracy. Spokespersons from the countries needing or wanting aid can reinforce and compliment the proposals from the bureaucracy and the Executive. Officials in all branches of the U.S. government are steeped in the philosophy that aid can promote prosperity, which is regarded as the most lasting defense against communism and other radical ideologies. "For our own security and well-being, and as responsible free men we must seek to share our capacity for growth, and the promise of a better life, with our fellow men around the world. This is what aid is all about." as explained by President Johnson.[96] There is also a ready response to the use of foreign aid as an instrument of foreign policy, as expressed in the dictum "Aid is designed to win friends and influence people."[97]

Where the case for foreign aid rests only on economic need and where the request for an allocation of foreign aid does not originate with the bureaucracy or Executive, the country wanting aid has to initiate the request with the Executive and bureaucracy who in turn sometimes, in collaboration with the originating country, make proposals to Congress. In these circumstances, the country wanting U.S. aid must meet the criteria of friend, ally, or servile follower or be of strategic importance. If the country doesn't fall into any of these categories, it must establish that it is not hostile and is well disposed towards the United States or friendly. In addition to this, the requesting country must establish that development assistance will be a critical input in its economic strategy, which must be that of a private enterprise market economy. It is also important to demonstrate that the resources provided by the United States will be used in a manner that the United States regards as appropriate. What is regarded as an appropriate use for U.S. development assistance includes some perennials such as physical infrastructure, education, and a variety of other uses depending on what is in vogue in economic policy, e.g., privatization was regarded as a must in the 1980s and social safety nets and poverty alleviation programs were fashionable in the 1990s.

Jamaica was a country that during the 1980s was regarded as a lackey and was for a time promoted by the United States as a private enterprise model to counter any lingering attraction that the Cuban model had for countries such as Nicaragua, Peru, Guyana, and Grenada. The return of Michael Manley to the Prime Ministership of Jamaica in 1989 came at a time when the Seaga regime had been written off in U.S. government circles as corrupt and incompetent and being guilty of wasting an enormous amount of U.S. foreign aid. Manley's return to power was greeted in the United States in the bureaucracy and private sector with skepticism about his conversion to free market economics from democratic socialism which he and his party, the PNP, professed during the period 1974–1980. In Congress and the press, opinions were divided between those who recognized Manley's leadership and genuine humanitarianism in the 1970s, and who were convinced that this was the core of his being, whether he pursued a state-led or a market-led economic strategy, and those for whom Manley was a sheep in wolf's clothing, who had not relinquished socialist inclinations and was still a close friend of Fidel Castro. In this context, the first phase of Jamaica's quest for U.S. foreign aid and debt relief was to dispel suspicion and doubt about Manley and to explain his economic policy. Having laid this groundwork, the second phase of the campaign was to explain exactly how and for what aid and debt relief would be used.

In order to rehabilitate Manley and the PNP government, the services of a lobbyist and a public relations firm were retained. Part of the strategy was to help the Executive and bureaucracy to lobby the Congress for aid and debt relief under the rubric of the Enterprise for the Americas Initiative. This was made easier by the fact that Manley and his government helped to shape the EAI and genuinely believed in and were committed to the tenets of the EAI. There was also self-interest in that the EAI had to come into existence before debt relief under its rubric could be administered. The statement by press secretary Fitzwater on President Bush's meeting with Prime Minister Michael Manley on May 15,1991, stated that the "President thanked the Prime Minister for his strong endorsement of the free-trade agreement with Mexico and the Enterprise for the Americas Initiative (EAI)" and that the "President noted that Jamaica has played a constructive role in encouraging the participation of CARICOM members in the process of trade and investment liberalization through the EAI."[98] Consistent with this stance Ambassador Bernal was elected chairman of the Organization of American States Working Group on the Enterprise for the Americas Initiative.[99]

Lobbyists

The use of lobbying services from a well-established firm proved to be invaluable to the efforts of the government of Jamaica to maintain and increase the level of foreign aid from the United States. Neil and Company had on their staff roster several former senior government officials as well as former congressional staffers. Therefore, the firm was well placed to lobby Congress on behalf of Jamaica as it had done successfully for other countries. Alertness and attention to detail allowed Neil and Company and the Embassy of Jamaica to have part of the ESF funds originally destined for Pakistan but blocked because of political problems between Washington and Islamabad, reallocated to Jamaica in 1991.

The lobbyists had as their first task to prevent reductions to the amount of aid granted to Jamaica, particularly given the huge reduction in aid since the heyday of the Reagan era (see table 5.3). The second task was to retain and if possible increase aid allotted to Jamaica and the third was to oppose restrictive terms and conditions on aid programs to Jamaica. [100] In the early 1990s when the aid campaign was at the core of Jamaica's goals, the Chairman of the House Foreign Affairs Committee (HFAC) was Dante Fascell, a Democrat from Florida and long time supporter of Caribbean issues. The lobbyists and the embassy concentrated their efforts on friends in the Western Hemisphere Subcommittee and the HFAC, knowing that in the debate on the floor of the House on the Foreign Assistance Authorization Bill, the aid allocated to Jamaica would not attract much attention. There was the ever-present specter of archconservative, Senator Jesse Helms, the doyen of parliamentary obstructionism who strongly opposed foreign aid. In lobbying the Senate and House, Prime Minister Manley was willing to interact directly with members; for example, on his visit to Washington, D.C., in May, 1991, he met with Congressmen Charles Rangel and Major Owens and spoke by telephone with Senators Biden, Dodd, and Kerry.

Congress

Unfortunately "foreign economic aid tends to be viewed as a set of international welfare payments, to be traded off against domestic welfare programs." [101] Members of Congress had to be convinced that aid was necessary and that Jamaica should be a beneficiary although it was well off by comparison with Africa. In addition, members had to be encouraged to support aid allocations especially when there were pressing needs in their districts, such as health and education services and infrastructure. Michael Manley's international reputation as a crusader against apartheid and for the world's poor ensured that members were always eager to meet with him and his charisma invariably persuaded them to support Jamaica's cause or at least neutralized potential reservations. Face to face meetings were reserved for the most important members such as Congressman Charles Rangel, while the ambassador knocked on as many doors and the lobbyist gave attention to the most conservative elements.

One of the important functions of the lobbyist was to ensure the visibility of Jamaica and the issues of concern to the Jamaican government in the various fora and discussions in Congress. For example, the lobbyist would ensure that all foreign assistance authorization bills included language commendatory of Jamaica and calling for U.S. development assistance for Jamaica. Typical of these efforts were the insertion of language in Congressional documents in the fiscal year 1994.

a. The Report accompanying the Foreign Assistance Authorization Bill of 1994 includes the following: "Jamaica in the past year has continued to implement its bold and far-reaching program of economic reform. . . . Continued U.S. assistance to Jamaica serves as important encouragement for Jamaica to continue along this economic path. . . . With U.S. assistance, Jamaica has continued over the past year to implement development programs, provide feeding programs for the poorest of the poor, reform the administration of health care, and effectively combat the illegal trade in narcotics. In the committee's view, Jamaica deserves continued U.S. assistance in its efforts to provide its people with an enhanced quality of life."

b. The Report accompanying the Foreign Aid Appropriations Bill of 1994 includes the following: "The Committee notes with concern that bilateral assistance levels, particularly Economic Support Funds and Development Assistance, declined sharply during the past year for a number of Caribbean countries. For example, from fiscal year 1992 to fiscal year 1993, Jamaica saw its Development Assistance Funds and Economic Support Funds reduced. United States bilateral assistance has been critical in helping Caribbean countries sustain the momentum of their economic reforms while encouraging them to remain active partners with the United States to accomplish other development and anti-narcotics objectives. The Committee urges the Administration to allocate sufficient resources to Caribbean countries to promote economic development and regional stability."

c. The Report accompanying the Foreign Assistance Authorization Bill includes the following: "Over the past decade, our foreign aid and trade programs have focused on encouraging the development of market-oriented economies, supporting anti-narcotics efforts, and stimulating United States/Caribbean commercial links. . . . These efforts have succeeded in generating economic growth, which has advanced Caribbean living standards and creat-

ed a market for U.S. goods and services . . . .We should not, however, take these successes for granted. . . . Jamaica is still undertaking
difficult privatization programs and trade liberalization measures
that need our support. Continued U.S. assistance is still vital to
sustain these reforms."

Executive

A very important intervention in the foreign aid allocation process by
the White House was at the critical juncture when Manley had just returned to office and there was still some residual skepticism about Manley's sincerity about a free market economic strategy and before there
was time to prove this commitment. It came from an unexpected source,
namely Vice President Dan Quayle who met Manley during the 1990 visit
to Washington, D.C., in the course of which Manley invited Quayle to
visit Jamaica. The Vice President spent one day in Jamaica en route to or
from Latin America and it is reported that "they hit it off." On his return
to Washington, D.C., the Vice President took up the cause of Jamaica and
pushed within the Bush policy circle for increased aid for the Manley
government. It was Quayle who told the leadership in Congress that he,
the Vice President must have a substantial increase in foreign aid for
Jamaica[102] and that this was a priority for the Bush Administration. Although not highly regarded[103] Quayle's personal intervention was a
turning point because the "Hill" responded to the demand of the Vice
President because he still had "good connections" from his recent tenure
in the U.S. Senate from 1980 to 1988 and his two terms in the U.S. House
of Representatives.

Government of Jamaica

The government of Jamaica had limited exposure to systematic full
time lobbying before 1990. The government had used the services of the
government relations firm A. Sabo Associates during the bauxite levy
issue in the mid-1970s. However, the tenure of the lobbying firm was
brief and focused specifically on the bauxite issue. The interaction was
concentrated between the Executive and bureaucratic branches of the two
governments. There had been contact with Congress but not on the scale
and intensity that the activities in support of the CBI legislation entailed
in the early and mid-980s. Lobbying services were provided under the
direction of Anne Sabo and these continued until the early days of the
Manley Administration elected in 1989. The campaign for the CBI involved considerable work on the "Hill" by representatives of the public
and private sectors of the potential beneficiary countries in Central
America and the Caribbean. In this case, foreign governments were col-

laborating with the Reagan Administration to mobilize support in Congress for the CBI legislation.

In 1990, the government of Jamaica at the initiative and behest of Michael Manley took the decision to undertake a complete overhaul and upgrading of its representational capacity in the United States. This involved, first, contracting the services of a lobbying firm and a public relations firm, and second placing specially appointed community relations officer in New York to improve relations with the Jamaican community in the United States. The third component of the program was the upgrading of the Embassy of Jamaica starting with the appointment of a new ambassador. This revamping of representation was similar to that undertaken by the Mexican government to complete the negotiations for NAFTA and secure congressional passage of this agreement. Beginning in 1991, Prime Minister Manley and the Minister of Foreign Affairs and Foreign Trade began a process of modernization of its Embassy in Washington, D.C. The newly appointed Ambassador was a political appointee with close links to the political leadership of the PNP and the Cabinet. Ambassador Bernal took the initiative to upgrade the skills of the staff of the Embassy and reorganized the Embassy along functional lines. This was accomplished with the support of Minister Coore and his successor, Dr. Paul Robertson, against the strenuous opposition and persistent resistance of the career staff at all levels in the Ministry of Foreign Affairs and Foreign Trade.

Media and Think Tanks

The media played little or no direct role in the process of influencing the U.S. foreign aid process; however, the media over time began to delete remarks about Manley's policies in the 1970s and shifted to portraying Manley as committed to the market economy and economic reform and structural adjustment. The think tanks provided an important platform for the articulate Manley to explain his current policy direction to the American policy community. Manley gave addresses at several think tanks including the Heritage Foundation and the Overseas Development Council and universities such as Columbia University and Howard University. Ambassador Bernal, a former university academic, was very active in the think tank community. Indeed, on many occaisions he was the only ambassador present and almost at every event was the only developing country diplomat. Some of the contacts reinforced or made in the think tanks later became members of the U.S. government, for example, Richard Feinberg, formerly of the Overseas Development Council later to be in charge of Latin America and the Caribbean in the National Security Council. Several persons on the staff of think tanks were former U.S. government officials and gave valuable insights into the workings of the U.S. government system. They usual retained contacts and influence in their former departments and could be very helpful.

Business Sector

The campaign to reposition Jamaica in the minds of U.S policymakers, media, and Congress involved U.S. business interests "going to bat" for Jamaican issues as U.S. citizens or companies have more credence with U.S. audiences because they are independent of government. The Jamaican-American Chamber of Commerce in Kingston, especially its president in the early 1990s, Will Maloney, met with officials in Washington, D.C., to validate Jamaica's economic reform policies. Manley's official delegations for overseas missions almost always included representatives of the Jamaica's business sector and on some occasions, leaders from the trade union movement, e.g., the May 1990 visit to Washington, D.C., of Meyer Matalon, who was a close friend and advisor of Manley and leading entrepreneur and was frequently a member of official delegations. Matalon was assigned to represent the Prime Minister in some meetings, e.g., during Manley's visit to Washington, D.C., in May 1991, Matalon and Ambassador Bernal constituted the delegation that met with Deputy Secretary of State Lawrence Eagleburger.

The single most important and consistent U.S. businessman to support Jamaica's objectives in the United States was the wealthy Delaware based John Rollins who was a major donor to the Republican Party at both the national and state levels. Rollins, whose investments in Jamaica date back to the 1960s, deployed his lobbyist in Washington, Jim Mahoney to reinforce Jamaica's lobbying efforts. This support from Rollins was achieved when early in his term, Manley personally resolved a bitter, protracted dispute between Rollins and the government of Jamaica that arose from actions taken by the Seaga regime of the 1980s. Rollins claimed that land, which he had purchased during the 1960s, had been expropriated by Seaga who in turn asserted that a clause in the purchase agreement committing Rollins to certain developments on specified dates was in breach. Rollins complained to Congress and was able to block aid to Jamaica. By resolving this dispute Manley not only removed the block on foreign aid to Jamaica but also demonstrated that he was a man who kept his word and was genuinely committed to private sector development and the promotion and sanctity of private direct foreign investment. Rollins was no longer a critic of the Jamaican government but was a staunch advocate of the Manley government and was consistently helpful on issues of concern to Jamaica.

Jamaican Communities in the United States

The Jamaican community in response to a request for help from Ambassador Bernal was instrumental in garnering the support of Congresswoman Barbara Kennelly of Hartford, Connecticut for aid, debt relief, and the CBI. The Caribbean migrant community was also a motivating factor in the support of Albert Wynn of Prince George's County in Maryland, Alcee Hastings in Florida, and Major Owens of Brooklyn, New York. A connection with Jamaica was sometimes an important entrée and link, leading to interest in and support for issues of concern to Jamaica, e.g., Congresswoman Carolyn Maloney of New York whose father retired and lives in Jamaica. Another channel of access was through Jamaican Congressional staff members, e.g., it was only possible to get word to Newt Gingrich when he was Speaker of the House through his staff member, Mrs. Gloria Wright-Simmonds and Adrian Wright of Congressman DeFazio's office.

Jamaica's Accomplishments

Jamaica was successful in accomplishing its goals relating to foreign aid and debt relief.

1. Jamaica was successful in halting the decline in foreign aid from the United States. U.S. aid dropped by more than 50 percent from $155.6 million in 1985 to $75.5 million in 1988. Moreover Jamaica was able to raise aid to $111.8 million in 1989 and maintain the level of aid at about $70 million per year during the period 1990 to 1993. This was a remarkable achievement in a political environment not well disposed to aid and the lingering skepticism about Manley and the PNP government.

2. The government of Jamaica was successful in convincing the United States to grant debt relief. On August 23, 1991, Jamaica represented Senator the Hon. David Coore of Jamaica by signing an agreement with Deputy Secretary of the U.S. Treasury Department, John Robson, to reduce PL480 debt under the EAI. The Agreement provided for the reduction of Jamaica's stock of debt owed under the PL480 program by 80 percent from $270,909,240 to $54,181,805. To accomplish this Jamaica established its need and that it deserved this type of support from the U.S. government. In accomplishing this objective Jamaica had contributed to raising the awareness of the debt problem of developing countries and the importance of debt relief as a means of promoting economic recovery in heavily indebted countries.

3. Jamaica was one of the first countries to benefit from a debt for nature swap under the Enterprise for the Americas Initiative. In October 1991 Jamaica benefitted from a debt for nature swap.[104]

The value of the debt involved was $437,956, the purchase price was $300,000 and the conservation funds amounted to $437,956. It established an endowment fund for the Jamaica National Parks Trust (JNPT), a conservation trust fund dedicated to the conservation of biological diversity through support of Jamaica's national parks system, specifically the Montego Bay Marine Park and Blue and John Crow Mountains National Park. The main sources of funding were provided by USID ($190,000), Puerto Rico Conservation Trust ($100,000), and the Nature Conservancy ($10,000). Private sector financial institutions provide assistance, including American Express Bank, Pan Caribbean Bank, and several Jamaican stockbrokers.

CONCLUSION

Jamaica's campaign for debt relief was a multifaceted campaign aided by the advice of lobbyists, Neil and Company and a public relations firm, Fenton Communications. Prime Minister Manley gave personal leadership to this issue, which galvanized support in the Bush Administration, which was grappling with the escalation of Third World debt particularly in Latin America where default by Mexico or Brazil could have seriously undermined the U.S. banking system. The Embassy of Jamaica working closely with the lobbyist and the Prime Minister's office were able to gain recognition for the particular circumstances of Jamaica, more specifically that the majority of the external debts were owed to bilateral agencies and multilateral financial institutions. Jamaica was able to mobilize support in the think tank community, business sector in the United States and Jamaica, and in Congress to support economic reform in Jamaica. The argument was made that at this juncture an injection of foreign aid was needed and this should be complemented by debt relief, which would free foreign exchange for the development drive. The campaign was particularly successful in enhancing the understanding of Jamaica's dilemma and urgent needs. In Congress the empathy for Jamaica was reinforced by appeals to U.S. self-interests, namely that debt relief would promote U.S. exports and investment. These arguments were successful in garnering support from members who would normally have ignored the appeal; for example, Senator Bob Kasten of Wisconsin stated that he supported debt relief for the Caribbean because of the increased trade between Wisconsin and the Caribbean.[105] Many of the arguments advanced by spokespersons for the government of Jamaica in support of debt relief were also used to justify foreign aid to Jamaica. Both campaigns shared personnel and relied on the same strategy, which concentrated on effectively intervening in the political infighting on foreign aid in the Congress. Both campaigns benefitted from the personal involvement of the Prime Minister of Jamaica, Michael Manley and his charisma and persuasiveness. Lacy Wright, the Deputy Chief of Mission in the U.S. embassy in Kingston, described Manley as "the most brilliant extemporaneous English speaker I've ever heard."[106]

NOTES

1. Manley's election in 1989 was "disturbing to many U.S. conservatives." H. Michael Erismann, "The CARICOM States and U.S. Foreign Policy: The Danger of Central Americanization," Journal of Interamerican Studies and World Affairs, Vol. 31, No. 3 (Fall, 1989) pages 141–82. See page 176.

2. The then ambassador Keith Johnson and the Embassy in Washington, D.C., had virtually no involvement in the design of the campaign. The Ambassador was a political appointee of the previous government led by Edward Seaga and had been appointed because he had served at the United Nations when George Bush was U.S. Ambassador. It was said that "would get through the backdoor of the White House."

3. Darrel E. Levi, Michael Manley. The Making of a Leader (Kingston: Heinemann Publishers Caribbean, 1989) page 139.

4. Larry Rohter, "Michael Manley, Ex-Premier of Jamaica, Is Dead at 72," New York Times, March 8, 1997.

5. Roland Reagan, The Reagan Diaries, edited by Douglas Brinkley (New York: Harper Perennial, 2007) page 133.

6. Michael Manley, Jamaica. Struggle in the Periphery (London: Third World Media/ Writers and Readers Publishing Cooperative Society, 1982) pages 115–16.

7. "After Oil, Bauxite" Washington Post, June 3, 1974, cited in Carlton E. Davis, Jamaica in the World Aluminum Industry, Vol. II 1974–1988. Bauxite Levy Negotiations (Kingston: Jamaica Bauxite Institute, 1995) page 207.

8. For analysis of the change in the thinking of Manley and the PNP see David Panton, Jamaica's Michael Manley: The Great Transformation 1972–92 (Kingston: Kingston Publishers, 1993) pages 101–52.

9. Erik Calonius, "A comeback in Jamaica," Newsweek, Vol. 113, Issue 8, 20 February, 1989, page 29.

10. Saul Landau, The Dangerous Doctrine - National Security and U. S. Foreign Policy (Boulder: Westview Press, 1988).

11. Global Challenge. From Crisis to Cooperation: Breaking the North-South Stalemate (London: Pan Books, 1985) pages 95–99.

12. Michael Manley, Up the Down Escalator. Development and the International Economy. A Jamaican Case Study (London: Andre Deutsch, 1987).

13. Michael Manley, Up the Down Escalator. Development and the International Economy. A Jamaican Case Study (London: Andre Deutsch, 1987) page 10.

14. Richard L. Bernal, "Caribbean Debt Relief," Caribbean Studies, Vol. 4, No. 2, (June 1991) pages 45–58.

15. Data from World Development Indicators database.

16. Jamaica: 2003 Article IV Consultation—Staff Report; Staff Statement; Public Information Notice on the Executive Broad Discussion; and Statement by the Executive Director for Jamaica. IMF Country Report No. 04/76 International Monetary Fund March 2004.

17. Edwin M. Truman, U.S. Policy on the Problem of International Debt, International Finance Discussion Papers, Board of Governors of the Federal Reserve System, No. 357, July 1989, pages 1–2.

18. Richard L. Bernal, "Economic Growth and External Debt in Jamaica," in Antonio Jorge, Rene F. Higonnet, and Jorge Salazar-Carrillo (eds.), External Debt and Economic Growth in Latin America (New York: Pergamon Publishers, 1982) pages 89–108.

19. Richard L. Bernal, "The Vicious Circle of Foreign Indebtedness: The Case of Jamaica," in Antonio Jorge, Jorge Salazar-Carrillo, and Frank Diaz-Pou (eds.), External Debt and Development Strategy in Latin America (New York: Pergamon, 1985) pages 111–28.

20. The Brady Plan, http://www.emta.org/template.aspx?id=35 Accessed 2 September 2014.

21. Robert Devlin, "Economic restructuring in Latin America in the face of the foreign debt and the external transfer problem," CEPAL Review, No. 32 (August, 1987) pages 75–101.

22. Richard L. Bernal, "Resolving the Global Debt Crisis," Economia Internazionale, Vol. XL, Nos. 2–3 (Maggio-Agosto, 1987) pages 1–9 and Richard L. Bernal, "Resolving the International Debt Crisis," in Omar Davies (ed.), The Debt Problem in Jamaica: Situations and Solutions, Monograph No. 1, Department of Economics, University of the West Indies, Mona (September 1986) pages 82–114.

23. Percival James Patterson, "None But Ourselves," Budget Presentation 1991/92, May 9, 1991, page 8.

24. Michael Manley, The Poverty of Nations. Reflections on Underdevelopment and the World Economy (London: Pluto Press, 1991) pages 1–2, 88–89, and 113.

25. Global Challenge. From Crisis to Co-Operation: Breaking the North-South Stalemate (London: Pan Books, 1985) page 98.

26. Michael Manley was accompanied by David Coore and Richard Bernal.

27. "Latin American Leaders Meet to Examine Hemispheric Agenda," The Carter Center News, Spring, 1989, pages 1, 4–5.

28. Michael Manley, "Southern Needs," Foreign Policy, No. 80 (Fall, 1900) pages 40–51.

29. Richard L. Bernal, "Debt Relief for Caribbean Countries" in Hearings before the Subcommittees on Human Rights and International Organizations, Western Hemisphere Affairs and International Economic Policy and Trade of the Committee on Foreign Affairs, House of Representatives, One Hundredth First Congress, Second Session, June 28th, July 11, 18, 31 and September, 1990 (Washington, D.C., U.S. Government Printing Office, 1991) pages 225–38.

30. Richard L. Bernal, "A Way Out of the Caribbean Debt Trap," Washington Post, November 5, 1991.

31. Richard L. Bernal, "Next Stop, Caribbean Debt Relief," International Economy, Vol. 5, No. 4 (July/August 1991) pages 71–74.

32. Richard L. Bernal, "The Vicious Circle of Foreign Indebtedness: The Case of Jamaica," in Antonio Jorge, Jorge Salazar-Carrillo, and Frank Diaz-Pou (eds.), External Debt and Development Strategy in Latin America (New York: Pergamon, 1985) pages 111–28 and "Economic Growth and External Debt in Jamaica," in Antonio Jorge, Rene F. Higonnet, and Jorge Salazar-Carillo (eds.), External Debt and Economic Growth in Latin America (New York, Pergamon Publishers, 1982) pages 89–108.

33. These proposals are reviewed in Richard L. Bernal, "Resolving the International Debt Crisis," in Omar Davies (ed.), The Debt Problem in Jamaica: Situations and Solutions, Monograph No. 1, Department of Economics, University of the West Indies, Mona (September 1986) pages 82–114 and Richard L. Bernal, "Resolving the Global Debt Crisis," Economia Internazionale, Vol. XL, Nos. 2–3 (Maggio-Agosto, 1987) pages 1–19.

34. C. Fred Bergsten, America in the World Economy. A Strategy for the 1990s (Washington, D.C.: Institute for International Economics, 1988) pages 157–88.

35. Embassy of Jamaica Files, Third World Debt, May 1988.

36. Thomas E. Lovejoy, "Aid Debtor Nations' Ecology," The New York Times. New York, 4 October, 1984.

37. Alan Greenspan, The Age of Turbulence (New York: Penguin Press, 2007) page 157.

38. Bill McGibben, The End of Nature (New York: Random House, 1987).

39. Richard L. Bernal, "Enterprise for the Americas Initiative Act 1991" (H.R. 4059) in hearing before the Committee on Agriculture, House of Representatives, One Hundred Second Congress, Second Session, June 17, 1992 (Washington, D.C., U.S. Government Printing Office, 1992) pages 73–82.

40. Letter from Ambassador Richard Bernal to Hon. Robert Graham, United States Senate, July 9, 1992.

41. Embassy of Jamaica files, Jamaica's Debt Reduction Under the EAI, August 1991.

42. Letter from Ambassador Richard Bernal to Hon. Edolphus Towns, U.S. House of Representatives, July 20, 1992.

43. Letter from Nicholas Brady and James Baker III to Thomas Foley, Speaker, U.S. House of Representatives, July 1992.

44. Committee Approves Debt-for-Environment Swaps, News Release, Committee on Agriculture, U.S. House of Representatives, July 1, 1992.

45. Embassy of Jamaica files, Memorandum from George Dalley to Hugh Small, Minister of Finance, June 24, 1992.

46. Interview with Denis Neill, August 12, 2001.

47. Robert Pear, "Jamaican Criticizes Panama Invasion," New York Times, January 30, 1990.

48. The Official Working Visit to Washington, D.C., of the Right Honorable Michael Manley, Prime Minister of Jamaica, May 2 to May 4, 1990. Files of Neil and Company.

49. Apart from Bush and Manley, the guests were Speaker of the House, General Colin Powell and Ambassador Bernal and his wife.

50. Meeting with Prime Minister Michael Manley of Jamaica, White House Statement Issued Following the Meeting, December 16, 1977. http://www.presidency.ucsb.edu/ws/?pid=7024

51. Annaud De Borchgrave, "Cuba's Role in Jamaica," Newsweek, February 28, 1977, pages 37–38.

52. Erik Wemple, "Washington Times Columnist: Originality deficit?" Washington Post. 2012. Retrieved July 21, 2014.

53. Bob Woodward, The Maestro: Greenspan's Fed and the American Boom (New York: Simon and Schuster, 2000) pages 72–73.

54. Abraham F. Lowenthal, "Rediscovering Latin America," Foreign Affairs, Vol. 69, No. 4 (Fall, 1990) pages 27–41.

55. Delano Franklin, Letter to the Editor, Jamaica Observer, November 16, 2011, page 10.

56. Interview with Senator David Coore, Minister of Foreign Affairs and Foreign Trade, The Courier N 138 March–April 1993. www.nzdl.org/gsdlmod? Accessed 9 August, 2014.

57. David Rogers, "House Approves $21.5 Billion Bill on Energy and Water," Wall Street Journal, May 30, 1991.

58. Richard L. Bernal, "Transnational Banks, the International Monetary Fund, and External Debt of Developing Countries," Social and Economic Studies, Vol. 31, No. 4, December, 1982, pages 71–101.

59. William R. Cline, International Debt: Systematic Risk and Policy Response (Washington, D.C.: Institute of International Economics, 1984) and Thomas O. Enders and Richard P. Mattione, Latin America: The Crisis of Debt and Growth (Washington, D.C.: The Brookings Institution, 1984).

60. Proposals for debt relief are surveyed and analyzed in Richard L. Bernal, "Resolving the International Debt Crisis" in Omar Davies (ed.), The Debt Problem in Jamaica. Situations and Solutions, Monograph No. 1 (Mona: Economics Department, University of the West Indies, 1986) pages 82–114.

61. No specific limit is set for most countries.

62. Fitzroy Baptiste, "The Federal Process in the West Indies as Seen by the United States, 1947–1962," Social and Economic Studies, Vol. 48, No. 4 (December, 1999) page 208.

63. Philip Sherlock, "Prospects in the Caribbean," Foreign Affairs Vol. 41, No. 4 (July, 1963) pages 744–50. See page 750.

64. Daniel Yankelovich and I. M. Destler (eds.), Beyond the Beltway. Engaging the Public in U.S. Foreign Policy (New York: W. W. Norton, 1994).

65. Bill Clinton and Al Gore, Putting People First: How We Can All Change America (New York: Times Books, 1992) page 30.

66. Vernon W. Ruttan, United States Development Assistance Policy. The Domestic Politics of Foreign Economic Aid (Baltimore: Johns Hopkins University Press, 1996) page 131.

67. Doug Bandow, "Rethinking U.S. Foreign Aid," Heritage Foundation Backgrounder No. 653 (Washington, D.C.: the Heritage Foundation, June 1, 1998) pages 1–12, see pages 1–2.

68. Vernon W. Ruttan, United States Development Assistance Policy. The Domestic Politics of Foreign Economic Aid (Baltimore: Johns Hopkins University Press, 1996) page 141.

69. PeterTarnoff, "An End to Foreign Policy. The Need to Reconcile Foreign and Domestic Strategies," Harvard International Review, Vol. XIV, No. 4 (Summer, 1992) pages 4–6, see page 4.

70. Carole Henderson Tyson and Daniel J. Seyler, "U.S. Foreign Aid to the Caribbean in the 1980's" in Mark Sullivan (ed.), The Caribbean Basin: Economic and Security Issues, Study Papers submitted to the Joint Economic Committee, Congress of the United States, (Washington, D.C.: U.S. Government Printing Office, January 1993) pages 42–64, see page 43.

71. Tom Barry and Deb Preusch, Soft War (New York: Grove Press, 1988) page 17.

72. Scott D. Tollefson, "Jamaica. The Limits of a Showcase Policy," SAIS Review, Vol. 5, No. 2 (Summer–Fall, 1985) pages 189–204.

73. Kathy McAfee, Storm Signals, Structural Adjustment and Development Alternatives in the Caribbean (London: Zed Books, 1991) page 126.

74. McAfee, op. cit, page 126.

75. Doug Bandow (ed.), U.S. Aid to the Developing World: A Free Market Agenda (Washington, D.C: The Heritage Foundation, 1985).

76. Milton Friedman, "Foreign Economic Aid: Means and Objectives," The Yale Review, Vol. 47, No. 4 (Summer, 1958).

77. P. T. Bauer, "Foreign Aid: Issues and Implications" in P.T. Bauer, Reality and Rhetoric: Studies in the Economics of Development (Cambridge: Harvard University Press, 1984) pages 38–62.

78. Robert Cassen and Associates, Does Aid Work? (Oxford: Clarendon Press, 1986).

79. Vernon W. Ruttan, United States Development Assistance Policy. The Domestic Politics of Foreign Economic Aid (Baltimore: Johns Hopkins University Press, 1996) page 141.

80. For a review of U.S. aid trends at the end of the 1980s see Elliott Berg, "Recent Trends and Issues in Development Strategies and Development Assistance" and Ernest H. Preeg, "An Anatomy of the U.S. Foreign Assistance Program" in Richard E. Feinberg and Ratchick M. Avakov (New Brunswick: Transaction Publishers, 1991) pages 67–89 and 123–44.

81. Ruttan, op. cit., page 126.

82. Anne O. Krueger, Economic Policies at Cross Purposes. The United States and Developing Countries (Washington, D.C.: The Brookings Institution, 1993) page 36.

83. Comments made to Ambassador Bernal by several State Department officials on many occasions.

84. David R. Obey and Carol Lancaster, "Funding Foreign Aid," Foreign Policy, No. 71 (Summer, 1988) pages 141–55. See page 141.

85. Robert Pastor and Richard Fletcher, "The Caribbean in the 21st Century," Foreign Affairs, Vol. 70, No. 3 (Summer, 1991) pages 98–114. See page 99.

86. Holger Henke, passim.

87. Michael Kaufman, Jamaica under Manley. Dilemmas of Socialism and Democracy (London: Zed Books, 1985) page 206.

88. David Panton, Jamaica's Michael Manley: The Great Transformation 1972–92 (Kingston: Kingston Publishers, 1993) pages 151–52.

89. Michael Manley, Jamaica's New Economic Direction (Kingston: Jamaica Information Service, September 16, 1990).

90. Michael Manley, The Poverty of Nations. Reflections on Underdevelopment and the World Economy (London: Pluto Press, 1991) pages 88–109.

91. Michael Manley, Up the Down Escalator. Development and the International Economy. A Jamaican Case Study (London: Andre Deutsch, 1987) pages 115–40.

92. Carlton Davis, "Michael Manley's Foreign Policy of Non-alignment," Jamaica Journal, Vol. 34, Nos. 1–2 (August, 2012) pages 38–47. See page 40.

93. Global Challenge. From Crisis to Co-operation: Breaking the North-South Stalemate (London: Pan Books, 1985).

94. Timothy Ashby, Missed Opportunities: The Rise and Fall of Jamaica's Seaga (Indianapolis: Hudson Institute, 1989) page 10.

95. This section is based on testimonies to Congress by Ambassador Bernal, see Richard L. Bernal, "U.S. Foreign Assistance and Economic Reform," in Hearings before a Subcommittee of the Committee on Appropriations, House of Representatives, One Hundred Third Congress, Second Session, April, 1994 (Washington, D.C.: U.S. Government Printing Office, 1994) pages 768–76, "Foreign Aid to Jamaica," in Senate Hearings before the Committee on Appropriations. Foreign Operations, Export Financing, and Related Programs Appropriations. Foreign Operations Appropriations, 1995 (H.R. 4426) (Washington, D.C.: U.S. Government Printing Office, 1994) pages 768–76, "U.S. Foreign Assistance and Sustainable Growth in Jamaica" in Hearings before the Committee on Appropriations, Subcommittee on Foreign Operations, Export Financing, and Related Agencies, United States House of Representatives, One Hundred Fourth Congress, Second Session, April 25, 1996 (Washington, D.C.: U.S. Government Printing Office, 1996) pages 369–78, "U.S. Foreign Assistance and Sustainable Growth in Jamaica" in Hearings before the House Committee on Appropriations Subcommittee on Foreign Operations, Export Financing, and Related Agencies. April 24, 1997 (Washington, D.C.: U.S. Government Printing Office, 1997), pages 682–93, and "U.S. Foreign Assistance and Sustainable Growth in Jamaica" in Hearings before a Subcommittee of the Committee on Appropriations, U.S. Senate One Hundred Fifth Congress, First Session, May 22, 1997 (Washington, D.C.: U.S. Government Printing Office, 1998), pages 351–56.

96. Raymond F. Mikesell, The Economics of Foreign Aid (London: Weidenfield and Nicolson, 1968) page 6.

97. Charles P. Kindleberger, Power and Money (New York, McMillan, 1970) page 133.

98. Statement by Press Secretary Fitzwater on the President's Meeting with Prime Minister Michael Manley of Jamaica 1991-05-15. From the website of the George Bush Presidential Library and Museum.

99. Richard L. Bernal, "A Caribbean Perspective of the Enterprise for the Americas Initiative," Organization of American States Working Group on the Enterprise for the Americas Initiative, June, 1992.

100. Congressional/Administration Action Matrix (Washington, D.C.: Neil and Company, April 1, 1991) Chapter 6, page 8.

101. John P. Lewis, "Can We Escape the Path of Mutual Injury?" in John P. Lewis and Valeria Kallab (eds.), U.S. Foreign Policy and the Third World Agenda 1983 (New York: Praeger Publishers, 1983) pages 7–48. See page 20.

102. Interview with Denis Neill, August 12, 2001.

103. Garry Wills, "Late Bloomer," Time Magazine, April 23, 1990, pages 28–34.

104. Commercial Debt for Nature Swaps, World Wildlife Fund Center for Conservation Finance, December 9, 2003, page 1. Commercial Debt-for-Nature Swaps Full Table, https://www.cbd.int/.../wwf-commerci. Accessed 26 September 2014.

105. Work Plan for the Government of Jamaica 1993, Neil and Company, page 3.
106. Lacy Wright, Deputy Chief of Mission, U.S. Embassy, Kingston (1991–1995), Jamaica Country Readers, adst.org/wp-content/uploads/2012/09/. Accessed 30 August 2014.

SIX

Counter Narcotics Cooperation

The United States—with only 5 percent of the world's population—consumes 30 to 50 percent of the world's cocaine supply.[1] The international trafficking cartels rely upon an ever-changing network of suppliers and routes to move their product to the main consumer markets in the United States and Europe. Jonathan Winer, U.S. Deputy Assistant Secretary of State for Law Enforcement and Crime, sums up the problem: "The Caribbean is a significant drug transit zone because there are lots of harbors, lots of airstrips and governments without a lot of money."[2] Seven of the 32 countries that the United States identifies as "major drug-producing or drug-transit countries" are in the Caribbean Basin.[3] U.S. officials believe that roughly 20 percent of the 760 tons of cocaine annually produced in South America are transshipped to the United States through the Caribbean Basin.[4] Drug trafficking in the Caribbean has escalated since the mid-1980s due to increased production of marijuana in the region[5] and the expansion of the transshipment of cocaine originating primarily in Colombia. It has even been suggested that at one time in the 1980s marijuana was the largest cash crop in Belize and Jamaica.[6] The Eastern Caribbean "vector," i.e., Antigua and Barbuda, Barbados, Dominica, Grenada, St. Kitts and Nevis, St. Lucia, and St. Vincent and the Grenadines was said to be the "second largest" channel of cocaine entering the United States.[7] The growth of the drug traffic in the Caribbean is related to poverty, unemployment, and the lucrative earnings from drugs, and constrained capacity of governments in the region to counteract the vast resources and technology of transnational drug traffickers. This difficult situation has been compounded by the decline in banana production and export, precipitated by the United States led challenge to the EU banana regime and the heavy external indebtedness of some countries.[8]

The Caribbean was a serious concern for the United States because of its production of marijuana known locally as "ganja" and its central location on routes used to transport cocaine from Colombia. By the mid-1980s the United States estimated that Jamaica was responsible for 13–15 percent of the marijuana entering the United States. Haughton explains that, "So profound was the effect of globalization's effect on Jamaica's marijuana production and traffic in the 1980s that Jamaica surpassed Mexico and Colombia to become the number one producing and trafficking country in Latin America and the Caribbean and held on tightly to that status even in the 1990s and 2000s."[9]

By the 1990s narcotics use and trafficking was a vast, growing transnational criminal activity that affected all countries and may be having an adverse economic impact on important sectors such as tourism.[10] Drug trafficking is at the heart of transnational organized crime in the Americas because of the growth of drug use in the United States, the production of marijuana, cocaine, and more recently opium in Colombia and Mexico, and its transshipment through the Caribbean, managed by a new hybrid of businessmen, namely "narco-businessmen."[11] The drug traffic has become one of the more important causes of crime and violence in the Caribbean and "narco-criminality"[12] has an impact on most aspects of social, economic, and political activity. What Griffith has described as "geo-narcotics" has become a central theme of U.S. foreign policy towards the English-speaking Caribbean. The term seeks to capture the dynamics of drugs, geography, power, and politics that emanate from the multidimensional problem of drug production, consumption, trafficking, and laundering of the illicit gains and that caused security conflicts among states and non-state actors.[13]

CERTIFICATION OF COOPERATION ON NARCOTICS

The U.S. policy of reducing the supply of drugs entering the United States involves an annual evaluation by the bureaucracy of the extent to which foreign governments are cooperating with the United States. Since 1987, the U.S. government has annually evaluated narcotics control efforts around the world. The report, the International Narcotics Control Strategy Report (INCSR), was mandated by Congress and examines both supply and trafficking problems and efforts to curb such problems. Information for the report is solicited from U.S. embassies around the world and supplemented by data collected by the law enforcement and intelligence communities. While the State Department chairs the interagency group that compiles the report, the Departments of Justice, Treasury, Transportation, the National Security Council, and the Office of National Drug Control Policy (ONDCP) at the White House play active roles.

Separate from the report but better known and far more controversial, is the so-called "certification process" by which the U.S. government judges a country's narcotics control efforts. Only countries deemed to be major contributors to the U.S. drug problem are graded—countries that supply other countries or regions, are not judged although their efforts are examined in the INCSR. On certification questions, according to law the Secretary of State recommends to the President whether a country should receive a determination of full certification, decertification, or de-certification with a national security waiver. The President then sends the determinations to Congress, which has 60 days to overturn the Presidential decision. There is no requirement for the Congress to approve the Presidential determinations. Both the report and the certification decisions are made public on March 1, again according to U.S. law.

Aside from the publicity generated by the decision to decertify a country, that country may also not receive foreign assistance from the United States or be eligible for loans or insurance from the U.S. export credit agencies. In addition, the United States must vote against loans to that country in the international financial institutions. When the decision is made to decertify a country but also grant a national security waiver, it is generally so that assistance may continue to flow while also allowing the United States to express its dissatisfaction with narcotics control cooperation.

The objective of Congress when it established the certification process was to ensure the U.S. government's efforts to compel cooperation and to make the President accountable for vigorously prosecuting an international drug policy. Since 1986 when the decertification policy was established the objectives have widened because drug trafficking is seen as the core of a variety of organized transnational crime.[14] During the administrations of President Reagan and Bush, the certification process was predictable and benign. Decertification was reserved for rogue states, e.g., Iran and Syria, or countries that had limited cooperation with the United States, e.g., Burma and Afghanistan. In 1988 and 1989 Panama was placed on the decertification list just prior to the U.S. invasion to remove President Manuel Noriega for involvement in drug trafficking. Under President Clinton certification became far more rigorous. In 1994, Nigeria was decertified and in 1996 and again in 1997 Colombia was decertified; however, Mexico which was just as culpable and was given a national interest waiver.[15] It was widely felt that the decertification exercise harmed relations with Mexico and Colombia without producing any tangible results. The certification process has been controversial with critics arguing that the process provokes conflict rather than promoting cooperation because of the inaccuracy of its assessments and the short-term nature of its focus.[16] Supporters claim that the certification process works because since 1986 it has served to focus attention on the drug issue, raise awareness, and pressure governments to give more attention to this issue.[17] The very notion that the United States would exercise arbitrary judgment has always been objectionable to most countries.

Cooperation between the United States and the English-speaking Caribbean (ESC) on reducing drug trafficking has been good but there have been differences on where the emphasis should be placed. The United States concentrates on supply interdiction rather than demand reduction and the ESC has been sensitive to policies that impinge on their already limited sovereignty and have consistently requested more resources from the United States.[18] No country from the ESC has ever been decertified; however, some countries have been listed in the conditional category, e.g., Belize in 1997. On one occasion, Jamaica experienced some difficulties in ensuring certification. In anticipation of this difficulty and based on information both from United States and Jamaican government officials, Ambassador Bernal took the initiative to plan and lead the execution of a comprehensive and carefully calibrated campaign to ensure certification. The process began six months before the crucial decision-making meeting in late February in the conviction that Meg Greenfield was right when she said, "A lot of things needed to be fixed, but everything is fixable. Everything would be fixed with the proper political exertion."[19]

The policy of Congressional certification of countries designated by the President as cooperating fully with the United States on fighting the drug trade involves the Congress, bureaucracy, and the White House. The process of certification is shown in figure 6.1.

Bureaucracy

The sections of the State Department that handle counter narcotics collect data on countries deemed to be involved in drug trafficking, in

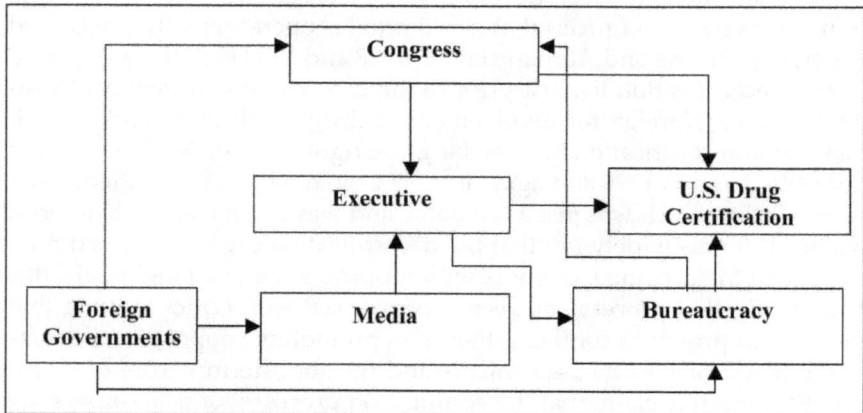

Figure 6.1. Influencing Certification of Cooperation on Narcotics.

particular if they are viewed as a source of drugs entering the United States. As noted the data gathering is conducted in close cooperation with the Drug Enforcement Agency, the Customs Service, and U.S. Coast Guard and other law enforcement and intelligence agencies. Depending on the level of cooperation with the foreign government, the estimates of drug production, trafficking, and transshipment are determined after dialogue with local law enforcement agencies. In the case of Jamaica, U.S. officials, both those based in Jamaica and those stationed in Miami (who oversee the Caribbean region) and in Washington, D.C., had regular meetings with the police and the Military Intelligence Unit of the Jamaica Defense Force. Meetings and dialogue with local authorities do not always produce an agreement on figures and the assessment of the effort being made by the government, even where the United States has a high regard for the effectiveness of local counter narcotics units and a very good working relationship with local officials. Differences can and do arise between the United States and local law enforcement bodies but can be resolved amicably if there is mutual respect and a history of close collaboration, as was the case between the United States and Jamaica. Misinformation can filter through or be misinterpreted, e.g., in one of the periodic meetings between the State Department and the Embassy of Jamaica in Washington, D.C., a U.S. official politely upbraided Jamaica for not using U.S. supplied helicopters and inquired why there was this falling off in effort. On return to the Embassy, Ambassador Bernal immediately telephoned Admiral Peter Brady, Chief of Staff of the Jamaica Defense Force, who informed the ambassador that the helicopters in question had not been in use because they were maintained by the United States who had grounded them because they were in need of spare parts that had not yet been provided by the U.S. government. A few minutes later the ambassador was able to clear up this misinformation to a very embarrassed and apologetic State Department official. The spare parts arrived in Jamaica shortly after this exchange.

During the 1990s the United States was in the habit of "raising the bar" each year for Jamaica to retain certification by the United States. Many of the elements or criteria that were introduced each succeeding year were not quantifiable tests and were open to a considerable amount of subjectivity by U.S. officials. While the United States has a list of criteria for certification, there is always the issue of "political will," which is almost impossible to quantify. A government may cooperate fully and not meet quantifiable targets, for example, because of unexpected setbacks. There was also the overall impression of a government that could be affected by statements by the head of state of the country, press reports of drug busts, the demeanor of the government in international fora in regard to U.S. policies and objectives, the severity of jail sentences for persons convicted of drug crimes, and the timely arrest of a prominent drug "don."

The governments of Jamaica and the United States maintained regular contacts on narcotics through the exchange of visits and meetings both in Washington, D.C., and Kingston. Officials from various agencies, Departments, and Congress on visits to Jamaica would meet with the head of the police force and the army as well as the Ministry of National Security and Justice. Each year the Minister of National Security and Justice, K. D. Knight visited Washington, D.C., and met with the highest levels of the Department of State, the Attorney General, the Federal Bureau of Investigation, and the Drug Enforcement Agency. For example, Minister K. D. Knight visited Washington, D.C., during April 12–14, 1995, and accompanied by senior officials from the Ministry of National Security and Justice and the Embassy of Jamaica in Washington, D.C., had meetings on April 12, 1995, with Mr. Charles Thompson, Department of Treasury, Ms. Anne Patterson, Department of State, and Mr. Mark Richards, Department of Justice. On April 13, 1995, he met with Ambassador Ms. Joan Higgins, Immigration and Naturalization Service (INS). On April 14, 1995, Minister Knight met with the Drug Enforcement Administration. On May 8, Ambassadors Richard Bernal and Gary Cooper (U.S. ambassador to Jamaica) met in Washington, D.C., to follow up on the meetings held by Minister Knight.

Executive

The President is required to submit to Congress not later than September 15 of the preceding fiscal year a report identifying each country determined to be a major drug transit or drug producing country as defined in section 481(e) of the Foreign Assistance Act of 1961. In the report the President must designate each country that has "failed demonstrably" to meet its counter narcotics obligations. Designated countries would be ineligible for foreign assistance unless the President determined that that assistance was vital to the U.S. national interest or that the country had made "substantial efforts" to improve its counter narcotics performance. The White House plays a limited role in the process tabulating the information for such decisions but it convenes the final decision-making meeting of the agencies involved. The White House is critical because of its role of sign off on the final certification decisions that will be submitted to the Congress. The finalizing of the decisions is really a political exercise that examines the report and the decisions, which flow from it in the context of U.S. foreign policy and the "state of mind" of the Congress. For example, the Clinton Administration was in a conundrum on several occasions as to whether it should decertify Colombia for the escalation of drug production, trafficking, and money laundering and risk destabilization of a regime beset by drug cartels and leftist guerrilla movements. The report had balanced criticism with commendation and set targets, which the Congress would be asked to support by approving additional funds. In the case of Mexico the Clinton Administration actually resorted to decertification to both pressure the Mexican government to improve its efforts to reduce the flow of drugs into the United States and demonstrate to Congress and the American public that it was tough on drugs.

The White House is instrumental in the certification process because the President and senior advisers participate in the ultimate meeting in the decision-making process. Therefore it is of critical importance to develop relations with senior White House officials and to keep them fully apprised of the efforts of a government in cooperating with the United States on counter narcotics programs. It is also pertinent for them to be aware of the efforts being made, the severe resource constraints, and the inadequacy of U.S. aid in view of the enormous task faced by small, poor developing countries. These officials should also be kept abreast of achievements of a government in its efforts to reduce drug trafficking and related criminal activities. In Jamaica's difficult episode of certification in 1996 and 1997, the friendship and mutual respect between Jamaica's Ambassador Richard Bernal and Mack McClarty, President Clinton's confidant and Special Envoy to the Americas, was of incalculable value.

When President Clinton and Prime Minister P. J. Patterson met in September 1995 they discussed a counter narcotics cooperation (among other issues) and the President signaled the intention to provide more assistance to bolster Jamaica's eradication and interdiction efforts. In December of 1995 Jamaica acceded the 1988 United Nations Convention Against Illicit Traffic in Narcotic Drugs and Psycho-tropic Substances.

Congress

The Congress has a largely passive role in the process because the major decisions are taken by the President but figures prominently in setting the tone of the report by indicating during its deliberations a view or mood. The disposition of members of Congress reflects currents in public opinion and the media towards the drug problem and expressed perceptions of whether the administration is or has done enough to reduce drug smuggling and drug use. Each year, for instance, at least one Senator and one member of the House can be expected to file legislation overturning the President's decisions regarding Colombia and Mexico. This act is the opening round in the public debate over certification and sets the tone for the next 60 days of coverage by the media.

The certification process is essentially an inter-agency process involving the State Department, the Drug Enforcement Agency, etc. It begins with an evaluation of the current year's estimates of drug production, transshipment, and money laundering and reviews the efforts of governments to reduce or control these by interdiction, legislation, and punishment. The agencies involved rely on direct assessments through visits and on receiving information from the agencies directly involved in counter narcotics activities as well as the views of the U.S. embassy in the particular country. The United States evaluates most countries based on their progress towards goals established yearly in consultation with the United States in bilateral agreements, which in turn, are backed by the 1988 United Nations Convention Against Illicit Drug Trafficking. The evaluation is an assessment of whether countries cooperated with the United States or took adequate steps on their own to meet the criteria spelled out in the 1988 Convention. Jamaica, a signatory to the 1988 Convention, also enjoyed a close working relationship with U.S. law enforcement and intelligence agencies.

One of the principal weaknesses of the process is that it is largely subjective and even where quantitative targets are involved, these are at best, guesstimates. This weakness is illustrated by the dilemma of the acreage of "ganja" production. If this year's total is the same as last year's, does it mean that this year's effort is a failure because it has not reduced production or is it a success because production has not increased? The State Department's International Narcotics Control Strategy Report of April, 1994 notes that "We cannot accurately estimate the total amount of drugs transiting Jamaica, the increase in seizure frequency in 1993, from 1992 levels—cocaine up 127 percent, marijuana up 16 percent—indicates cocaine and marijuana trafficking is on the rise." [20] The increased frequency of seizures is not interpreted as representing an improved effort by Jamaica, but on the contrary, that drug trafficking had increased. Another subjective aspect of the evaluation is the fact that the quantities of drug production and trafficking are at best, guesstimates arrived at jointly between the United States and Jamaican government agencies, sometimes only after long and contentious discussions. By their own admission, the U.S. government "can quantify the drug seizures reported by GOJ (Government of Jamaica), but cannot accurately estimate the total amount of drugs produced in or transiting Jamaica," [21] yet the same report states that "The increasing size of seizures of cocaine and marijuana along with occasional heroin seizures, gives evidence of Jamaica's dual roles as a major producer of 'ganja' (marijuana) and as an increasingly important drug trans shipment site." [22]

UNITED STATES-JAMAICA COOPERATION

While Jamaica consistently disagreed with the United States on certain policy issues, such as the U.S. policy towards the embargo, Jamaica and the United States had a good relationship. Cooperation on counter narcotics was therefore embedded in an overall relationship of cooperation. For example, during late 1994 Jamaica acceded to the request of the United States to dock a ship in the harbor of Kingston to process Haitians fleeing that country in pursuit of entry to the United States. This permission by the government of Jamaica assisted Haitian refugees to get immediate healthcare and accelerated processing and helped the United States to handle a politically inconvenient and controversial issue. In so doing "Jamaica really earned the gratitude of the United States."[23] This in turn boded well for another aspect of the relationship, namely the appointment of a new U.S. ambassador to Jamaica. Just days before the United States made their request Jamaica Prime Minister Patterson had instructed Ambassador Bernal to inform the State Department that the long absence of a U.S. ambassador in Kingston was "no longer an embarrassment but was now an affront." The hiatus was created when former Congresswoman Shirley Chisholm, who initially accepted the appointment, decided to decline because of problems with her eyesight. In preparation for the mission of Strobe Talbot, State Department and Congressman Bill Grey, Ambassador Bernal communicated the displeasure of the government of Jamaica and emphasized that the likelihood of an affirmative answer would be considerably enhanced if the mission provided the name of the new U.S. ambassador. When Talbot arrived in Kingston a few days later he announced to the government that the new U.S. ambassador would be Gary Cooper, business executive and decorated veteran with a distinguished service record in the Marine Corp. On assuming his post later that year he became the first African-American to serve as ambassador to Jamaica.

JAMAICA'S ANTI-DRUG POLICY

Jamaica produces marijuana, which is widely used by the local populace, and there is export of the drug to the United States as the principal market. This reflects both the demand for the drug and physical proximity to Jamaica. Use of marijuana and trafficking in the drug in the island and exporting the drug are illegal in Jamaica. Police investigations of narcotics trafficking increased from 3,117 during 1966–68 to 13,350 in the period 1982–84[24] and remained a serious problem in the 1990s. Jamaican criminals developed links with criminal networks overseas through their involvement in the narcotics trade and starting in the 1970s there was a steady increase in the number of Jamaican drug criminals migrating illegally to the United States and Great Britain. This movement of Jamaican drug criminals led to the formation of Jamaican drug gangs, notorious for their fearlessness and gun violence, known as "posses"[25] in the United States and "yardies" in Great Britain.

According to the International Narcotics Control Strategy Report between 1987 and 2000, Jamaica is regarded as a major producer and exporter of marijuana and is regarded as a significant transit country for cocaine originating in South America and more particularly Colombia. Heroine is virtually non-existent, nor is there production or movement of essential and precursor chemicals. Money laundering associated with drug trafficking is only alluded to as an emerging problem beginning in the late 1990s. These reports also state that Jamaica's climate, soil, and rainfall are ideal for the cultivation of cannabis or "ganja." The most commonly cultivated variety is sinsemilla, which is produced in two half-yearly crops. Four to six crops of other varieties can be grown each year. The island is regarded as an ideal transshipment point because its "long coastline and thinly stretched security forces provide favorable conditions for drug traffickers. Air traffickers take advantage of Jamaica's proximity to the United States; the island's unsecured airstrips are used to move cocaine and locally produced marijuana to the United States. The island's many ports, harbors and beaches provide loading sites for marijuana."[26]

In Jamaica the Ministry of National Security has overall responsibility for Buccaneer operations with the Jamaica Defense Force (JDF) and the Jamaica Constabulary Force (JCF)[27] providing operational leadership and daily direction of all eradication and interdiction forces. The JDF, in conjunction with the JCF, conducts year-round eradication and interdiction operations involving police and elements of JDF air, land, and sea forces. Resources, human and financial, to devote to campaigns against drug production and smuggling are a major problem for the government of Jamaica because of the tight fiscal situation in which the government has had to operate during the 1990s. Debt and structural adjustment programs have curtailed the capacity of Caribbean countries to put resources into the fight against drug trafficking.[28] The U.S. government supports the efforts of the Jamaican authorities by providing equipment including helicopters and training. The United States collaborates by providing information and participates in some missions. Securing U.S. assistance for its counter narcotics campaign requires a subtle balance of showing the persistent nature of the narcotics problem while demonstrating a sustained or increasing effort by local law enforcement agencies.

U.S. ASSESSMENT OF COOPERATION WITH JAMAICA

The assessment by the United States of Jamaica's efforts to combat drug production and smuggling includes an assessment of the strengthening of institutional capacity, passing of new or improved legislation, and of adherence to bilateral, hemispheric, and multilateral treaties. In this regard, Jamaica has an exemplary record, which has been lauded on numerous occasions by a variety of U.S. government agencies and departments. For a list of principal treaties signed and new legislation passed see table 6.1.

The fact that Jamaica had not passed the enabling act for the Mutual Legal Assistance Treaty (MLAT) had become a recurring irritant in the

Table 6.1. CHRONOLOGY OF COUNTER NARCOTICS LEGISLATION AND TREATIES

DATE	LEGISLATION/TREATY
1988	United States-Jamaica Bilateral Narcotics Agreement signed
1989	GOJ signs the 1988 UN Convention Against Illicit Traffic in Narcotic Drugs and Psychotropic Substances
October, 1989	Government of Jamaica (GOJ) hosted the Caribbean Ministerial Narcotics Law Enforcement Conference with participation of 150 officials from 20 countries and ten anti-narcotics organizations
March, 1990	GOJ's joint Information and Coordination Center became operational
1990	GOJ creates special port security corps to undertake security at the country's two international airports
1991	GOJ signed a "Supercarrier" Agreement obligating Air Jamaica to institute security measures against drug smuggling aboard its aircraft
July, 1991	The United States-Jamaica Extradition Treaty entered into force
1994	GOJ pass Asset Forfeiture Act
1995	GOJ passed the Mutual Legal Assistance Treaty (MLAT) enabling act and ratified the 1989 United States-Jamaica MLAT
1995	The National Council on Drug Abuse published a five year National Drug Strategy
December, 1995	GOJ acceded to the 1988 UN Convention
December, 1996	Money Laundering Bill enacted
May, 1997	United States-Jamaica Maritime Counter-narcotics cooperation agreement signed
November, 1997	GOJ amended the 1996 anti-money laundering act
February, 1998	United States-Jamaica Maritime Counter-narcotics cooperation agreement came into force by passage of legislation
1999	Legislation passed allowing GOJ to enter into agreements with other governments to share assets confiscated from drug traffickers
March, 1999	1996 Money Laundering Act amended
Late 1999	Legislation to create drug court passed

Source: Narcotics Files, Embassy of Jamaica, Washington, D.C.

cooperation on narcotics. The MLAT between the United States and Jamaica had been signed on July 7, 1989, and sent to Congress in October 1991. In his Letter of Transmittal to the Senate President George Bush described the importance of MLAT as "an effective tool to help to assist in the prosecution of a wide variety of modern criminals, including members of drug cartels, 'white-collar criminals,' and terrorists." The United States was particularly interested in Article 17 because it required that the "Requested State . . . make best efforts to locate a person believed to be in its territory and to communicate the results to the Requesting State."

When this issue was raised with Ambassador Bernal as a possible problem for certification, Ambassador Bernal told Ambassador Gelbard, a well-known hard liner in charge of narcotics in the State Department, "As Ambassador, I should give you a plausible explanation of why it hasn't been done and that we are making every possible effort to have this done as soon as possible. But I agree with you that it has been outstanding for far too long and I will do everything in my power to have this done expeditiously."[29] The Ambassador then brought this directly to the attention of the Prime Minister and the Minister of National Security and Justice, warning that this could be a factor in certification and strongly urging them to ensure early passage of this legislation. The heightened recognition and sense of urgency galvanized Minister Knight who effectively moved the legislation through the House of Representatives.

U.S. government agencies and officials take careful account of actions and pronouncements by the Prime Minister (or President) and Ministers of drug producing or transshipment countries as an indication of the seriousness of a government's commitment to combating the narcotics trade. For example, the State Department's 1989 mid-year update reported that, "since its election on February 9, 1989, the People's National Party (PNP) government has not wavered in its commitment to a vigorous anti narcotics program . . . one of Manley's first acts as Prime Minister was to appoint . . . a special Cabinet sub-committee responsible for mobilizing and coordinating all aspects of the national fight against drugs and drug trafficking."[30] In April 1996 the Prime Minister sent a team of senior officials led by Dr. K. D. Knight, Minister of National Security and Justice, to the United States for discussions on counter narcotics cooperation. The report records that the Prime Minister stated that "he wanted Jamaica to play a pivotal role in regional anti-narcotics efforts and agreed to host a Caribbean inter-Ministerial narcotics conference in Kingston . . . he also said he was willing to take the lead in establishing a regional anti-narcotics training center in Kingston."[31]

Media

The U.S. government views the ESC as a region that produces and exports drugs, i.e., marijuana, and is an area that is increasingly used for the transshipment of cocaine from Colombia to the United States. There is a widespread perception throughout the U.S. government, the public, and the media that the ECS is a major source of narcotics entering the

United States. This impression is maintained by a steady flow of articles in the print media, denigrating the efforts of governments in the region to reduce drug trafficking and portraying these societies as extremely corrupt and lacking in law enforcement. For example, *Time* magazine[32] in February 1996 in reference to Antigua said "Bird's son, Vere Jr. has been tied to a 1990 ploy to establish a school that would train mercenaries to fight for the Medellin cartel. He was also involved, they say, in covert gun shipments to the cartel through Antigua." It continued, "Prime Minister Bird denies that Antigua cossets drug lords or money launderers, but the island is increasingly dependent on drug money for its livelihood." It describes Trinidad as "another island that seems to have been lost to the drug cartels." In a similar manner, the *Washington Post*[33] carried a lead story purporting that Russia mobsters and drug cartels had combined forces to escalate money laundering, drug trafficking, and arms sales through the Caribbean. It was alleged that there were "meetings between Russian organized crime figures and representatives of the Cali cocaine cartel on the islands of Aruba, St. Vincent and Antigua." The weeks immediately preceding the decision on certification is a period when the media focus on stories about drug trafficking in foreign countries. Two weeks before the culmination of the certification process in 1998 was when the *Washington Post* chose to carry on its front page[34] and on another page and a half articles on drug trafficking and corruption in the Caribbean.[35] Not to be outdone the rival Washington, D.C., newspaper the *Washington Times* reported that Secretary of State Madeleine Albright called on the Caribbean governments to bolster their lax laws and law enforcement to fight drug trafficking, money laundering, and arms trafficking.[36] This was an inaccurate report since Ambassador Bernal attended the meeting referred to and no such statement was made. *The Economist*, known for its conservative language, declared in June 2000 that the Caribbean was being overwhelmed by "a tidal wave of drugs."[37] Even the normally banal *GQ* men's fashion magazine had carried a multipage exposé of a drug trafficker's activity in St. Kitts and Jamaica.[38]

Using the media is critical in forming a favorable image or impression of a foreign government's efforts to combat drug trafficking, or counteract harmful media coverage. Access to the media is particularly important for small countries with limited capacity to pay for professional public relations services. Counteracting bad publicity requires daily monitoring and quick response. For example, the *New York Times* carried a damaging article on October 24, 1996, which required a response. The response took the form of a letter to the editor on January 7, 1997, which appears as appendix D.[39]

The monitoring of the print media included influential foreign newspapers, which were widely read in the United States such as the *Financial Times* of London. For example, the *Financial Times* headlined a report on October 25, 1996: "Drugs Tide Rises around the Caribbean."[40] On February 6, 1997, just three weeks before the culmination of the certification process, the *New York Times* carried a damaging piece on Jamaica. The letter in appendix E was written to President Clinton on February 12, 1997 to correct the erroneous statements in the article.[41]

THE CAMPAIGN FOR CERTIFICATION

Certification became a problem for Jamaica during 1996/1997 because the data on Jamaica's counter narcotics effort in 1996 showed a sharp decline in a range of indices compared to 1995. The number of hectares of cannabis eradicated dropped by 32 percent from 695 in 1995 to 473 in 1996. Seizure of cocaine in 1996 (236 kilograms) was less than half of those in 1995 (751 kilograms). Arrest for drug offenses declined from 3,705 in 1995 to 3,263 in 1996. Table 6.2 provides narcotics data for Jamaica for the years 1987 to 1999. The 1997 State Department Report notes that "U.S. provided helicopters used to assist eradication efforts were grounded for safety reason for part of the year" and that harvestable cultivation had risen significantly in 1996 compared to 1995.[42] The report highlights the decline in arrests, cocaine seizures, and cannabis eradication, but makes passing reference to the 42.5 percent increase in the amount of cannabis seized during 1996.

The 1996 report[43] expressed dissatisfaction with the effort of the government of Jamaica. It stated that (a) the GOJ "did not take adequate steps to achieve several of the goals and objectives of the 1988 UN Convention," (b) "drug arrests, cocaine seizures, and cannabis eradication did not meet the goals and objectives of our bilateral letter of agreement" and admitted that the targets for drug arrests and cocaine seizures had been significantly increased, (c) Jamaica's money laundering act passed in December 1996 was too limited in scope and the recommendations of the "Kingston Declaration" (which includes the 40 recommendations of the Financial Action Task Force and the 19 recommendations of the Caribbean Financial Action Task Force), (d) "Action on drafting a precursor chemical bill was deferred in 1997," and (e) Negotiations between the United States and Jamaica for a maritime counter narcotics cooperation agreement that commenced in 1996, were stalled by Jamaica's declaration of exclusive law enforcement authority in its exclusive economic zone. Negotiations resumed in February 1997, in part due to the urging of Ambassador Bernal in discussions with Prime Minister Patterson and Minister of National Security, K. D. Knight.

During mid-1996, at a time when the efficacy of U.S. drug policy was being questioned,[44] officials in the State Department's Bureau for International Narcotics informed Ambassador Bernal of their grave concerns about Jamaica's counter narcotics efforts, and cooperation with the United States. An unspoken part of the problem was that the objectives and targets in the bilateral letter of agreement were simply unattainable. They had been increased unrealistically in 1995 over the protest and advice of the Jamaican national security officials. There were protracted negotiations over the 1996 goals, with Jamaica being unhappy with the final results. The critical area of dispute was over calculating the qualitative estimates and targets, which were unreasonable in view of the fluctuation in eradication, seizures, and arrests since 1987 (see table 6.2). Whether the push was from rogue elements in Washington, D.C., or from the U.S. ambassador, Gary Cooper, or there was common thinking in both capitals, is not clear.

Ambassador Bernal sensed the impending danger, alerted the Prime Minister and Minister of National Security and Justice, and initiated a campaign in September 1996. The campaign had two components. The first was to ensure that the government of Jamaica attained certain objectives before the completion of the U.S. evaluation process on which certification is based. The second was to communicate Jamaica's strenuous efforts, achievements, and "politically correct" pronouncements on narcotics. Jamaica's lobbyists were well placed to assist the Ambassador in this campaign. Ann Wrobleski was Assistant Secretary of State for Nar-

Table 6.2. NARCOTICS ERADICATION, SEIZURES, AND ARRESTS IN JAMAICA 1987–1999

YEARS	ERADICATION CANNABIS (hectares)	SEIZURES COCAINE (kilograms)	CANNABIS (metric tons)	TOTAL ARRESTS
1999	894	2.46	56.2	6,718
1998	705	1.161	35.9	7,352
1997	743	0.41	24.0	3,364
1996	695	0.24	53.0	3,263
1995	473	0.57	37.2	3,705
1994	695	0.18	46.0	886
1993	692	0.16	75.0	1,416
1992	456	0.49	35.0	1,149
1991	811	0.06	43.0	5,027
1990	833	0.76	29.0	5,432
1989	1,030	0.13	38.0	3,594
1988	1,510	0.01	0.53	3,725
1987	650	8.60	215.0	3,967

Source: International Narcotics Control Strategy Reports (Washington, D.C.: United States Department of State, 1987–2000).

cotics and Law Enforcement during the second Reagan Administration and negotiated the certification process on behalf of the Administration with the Congress. She then defended certification decisions made by both the Reagan and Bush Administrations before the Congress and in the media. George Dalley also served in the State Department earlier in his career and had also served as Chief of Staff to the leading anti-drugs House Democrat, Representative Charles Rangel (D-NY). On the instructions of Ambassador Bernal, the government of Jamaica's lobbyist prepared a list of the 100 most influenced persons in the evaluation process and certification decisions. This list covered the key agencies in the interagency progress, the White House, Congress (both Representatives and staff), and the press. One of the principal obstacles was the uncooperative disposition of Ambassador Cooper and the U.S. embassy in Jamaica. Ambassador Bernal and lobbyist George Dalley spent considerable time meeting with senior U.S. officials during the Caribbean and Latin American Action (CLAA) Miami Conference, December 8–11, 1996, countering misinformation about Jamaica's drug situation. Much of the misleading impressions of Jamaica's fight against drug trafficking appeared to emanate from the U.S. ambassador to Jamaica, Gary Cooper.

The certification process for Jamaica went "down to the wire" causing untold anxiety in both Washington and Kingston. The year began with a meeting between Ambassador Bernal and Assistant Secretary Robert Gelbard of the State Department on January 5, 1997—the second working day of the year. This exchange of views was followed by a meeting between the Jamaican Ambassador and Peter Romero and John Hamilton of the State Department on January 17, 1995.[45] The remarks made by Ambassador Bernal in both meetings are recorded below.[46]

> The government of Jamaica remained committed at the highest levels in combating illicit narcotics trafficking and in exercising leadership to promote regional cooperation in this front. In September, 1996 at the opening of the Caribbean Regional Drug Training Centre, Prime Minister Patterson delivered a speech strongly reaffirming this commitment.
>
> Jamaica has proposed a Hemispheric Conference on Illicit Trafficking of Drugs to be held in April in Kingston. Minister Knight asked me to convey again his invitation for you to visit Jamaica at your earliest convenience.
>
> Ship-rider Agreement—Jamaica has removed its exception to the 1988 Convention, eliminating obstacles to speedy negotiation of a Maritime Cooperation Agreement. We look forward to the United States accepting our invitation to complete negotiations in early 1997.
>
> Money Laundering—Legislation criminalizing money-laundering activities was enacted in late 1996. It institutes stiff penalties for those who engage in money laundering activities as well as those who aid in such activities.
>
> Extradition - Jamaica recently extradited three individuals to the United States and is preparing further extradition actions in the coming

weeks. Jamaica has pledged to arrest any individuals wanted by U.S. law enforcement agencies upon being advised of their locations.

Asset Seizure—Jamaica has assisted the United States, Canada, and the United Kingdom in 20 asset seizure cases under the MLAT. Jamaica hopes to move on 2 asset seizure cases under the terms of its asset seizure law in early 1997.

Conviction Rate—Jamaica's conviction rate exceeds 50 percent, contrary to reporting by the U.S. embassy, which incorrectly analyzed criminal statistics. The Minister of National Security is prepared to put a special anti-narcotics unit in the Department of Public Prosecutions (DPP) with the assistance of the U.S. government.

Eradication—In 1996, Jamaica eradicated 450 hectares of marijuana.

On December 3, 1996, K. D. Knight, Minister of National Security and Justice and Ambassador Richard Bernal met with Under Secretary of State for Global Affairs Timothy Wirth for about 30 minutes in Washington, D.C. Wirth was in charge of the International Narcotics and Law Enforcement Bureau, which is directed by Assistant Secretary Robert Gelbard, and therefore has oversight responsibility for the narcotics certification process. Gelbard had primary responsibility for formulating recommendations concerning certification; these recommendations required consensus with others in the State Department including Wirth and in other agencies. This meeting was held to try to ensure that when the final certification decisions are made in late February, Wirth would review the minutes of this discussion in his determination of whether to accept the recommendations advanced by Gelbard. With this in mind, the purpose of the meeting was to provide Wirth with enough information to raise his "comfort level" on the status of Jamaica's commitment to cooperating with the United States on counter narcotics activities.

During the six months prior to the meeting with Wirth and in some cases for longer periods, Beverly Eighmy, Bureau of International Narcotics and Law Enforcement and others in the State Department had raised a series of issues. While the United States was fixated on the Maritime Cooperation Agreement, it had constantly pointed to the need for progress in several areas to generate "critical mass" to show Jamaica's continued cooperation. Several sources at the State Department acknowledged that, while Jamaica's level of cooperation in the past had been superior, the rest of the region had been "moving ahead" on narcotics issues while Jamaica has lagged. Without further actions in the primary areas, administration officials told the Jamaican Embassy and the lobbyists that Jamaica faced a real threat of decertification. Although this eventuality was judged to be unlikely, Jamaica decided not to treat casually any possibility that the Administration would decertify or certify Jamaica with a "national interest waiver." At the end of 1996 the issues to be resolved were: (1) the lack of a Maritime Cooperation Agreement, and the continued exemption to the 1988 UN Convention; (2) the allegation that there was a "low rate" of conviction of drug offenders; (3) the lack of implementation of the asset seizure act; (4) lack of progress on speeding up the extradition of persons wanted by the United States; (5) lack of final passage of "meaningful" money laundering legislation.

The factors in Jamaica's favor were the excellent cooperation between the various law enforcement organizations and the increases in seizure rates and eradication efforts. However, there was a "what have you done for me lately" approach of U.S. policy makers, and the position that cooperative law enforcement efforts could not be substituted for performance in the five problem areas noted. While responding to U.S. concerns Jamaica chose to maintain the initiative in setting its own agenda for counter narcotics activities and made abundantly clear that its actions were motivated by a strong self interest in fighting the narcotics threat and did not derive from U.S. pressure or initiative. Because the meeting could not afford a detailed examination of the five problem areas, it was decided that the government of Jamaica would demonstrate progress on issues raised by the United States. Indeed, the United States in several instances did not adequately recognize the extent of Jamaica's achievements. For example, the U.S. complaint of a low rate of conviction of drug offenders was due to their view that only those who received a prison sentence were counted as a conviction. This was obviously erroneous as some convictions resulted in fines. Another example was the fact that there were asset seizure cases and extradition cases in the judicial process but not yet concluded, which the United States regarded as not pursuing asset forfeiture or extradition. An aspect of the Jamaican system of government, which was not fully appreciated by the United States, was the nature of the Jamaican judicial process. Similarly the United States showed a contemptuous attitude towards the legislative process in Jamaica, which is no less time consuming than that of the United States. Hence the U.S. demand for a quick fix of what it said were shortcomings in Jamaica's money laundering legislation.

There were intangibles that affected the perception of a country and impact on the judgmental aspect of the certification process. One of these qualitative factors is pronouncement on drugs and the fight against drug trafficking. Early in 1996, State Department officials complained of the apparent lack of high-level commitment to counter narcotics. In the last quarter of that year, the Prime Minister delivered a strong statement reaffirming Jamaica's commitment while Minister Knight has made at least two such statements. Jamaica pointed out that no senior U.S. narcotics officials had visited Jamaica during the Clinton Administration, and extended an invitation to Wirth to come for the signing of the Maritime Cooperation Agreement.

In September 1996 at the opening of the Caribbean Regional Drug Training Centre in Kingston, Prime Minister P. J. Patterson pointed out that the idea for such a center originated with the Government of Jamaica in 1989. The commitment to fighting drug traffic was reiterated in unequivocal terms stating, "I want to leave no one in any doubt of our political will and to pledge my on-going leadership to prevent drug use and to halt narcotics production."[47] He went on to enumerate Jamaica's numerous policy measures, improvements, and achievements in its counter narcotics program. The Prime Minister also stated, "Jamaica does not intend to permit any of its territorial space—whether in the air, on land or sea—to be abused by narcotics traffickers."[48] In the same vein he declared, "Drug cultivation on Jamaica soil will not be tolerated. Drug trafficking in and through Jamaican territory will meet with full and speedy resistance. Both will incur severe punishment."[49]

As late as February 21, 1997, less than 10 days before the completion of the certification process, Jamaica's lobbyists warned in a confidential memo to Ambassador Bernal that, "At this point, there remains a lack of consensus within the Administration on how Jamaica should be considered in this process. We understand from Administration sources that some offices and agencies, such as the State Department's Narcotics Bureau, are recommending a decertification with a national interest waiver while others, such as the Department of Justice, are pushing for full certification. We further understand that Jamaica is one of 2 or 3 countries for which no final consensus has been reached. Congressional sources have also confirmed that the Administration has been unable to reach a final decision on Jamaica."[50]

REPEATING A CONSISTENT MESSAGE

The Ambassador working with Jamaica's lobbyist Ann Wrobleski and George Dalley developed a script[51] (February 3, 1997), which was used as the speaking notes for verbal presentations and the basis for written communications.[52] The script is reproduced below:

1. Through a recent amendment to the Dangerous Drugs Act, Jamaica significantly strengthened penalties for drug-related convictions.
2. Throughout 1996 Jamaica has continued its commitment to halt drug trafficking and eradicate narcotics cultivation. In September 1996, the Prime Minister delivered a strong statement reaffirming Jamaica's commitment to fight narcotics trafficking and cooperate with the United States on bilateral and regional efforts to do the same. The Government of Jamaica has taken steps to implement the provisions of the 1994 Asset Forfeiture and Seizure Act, and is now working to coordinate 28 foreign requests for asset forfeiture. In two cases, using provisions of the recently MLAT, assets have been restrained pending forfeiture orders. In December 1996, the Government enacted domestic money laundering legislation to

augment and strengthen existing money laundering regulations. Through a recent amendment to the Dangerous Drug Act, Jamaica significantly strengthened penalties for drug-related convictions. In December 1996, Jamaica removed its exemption regarding ship-riders from the 1988 UN Convention, clearing the way for negotiation of a Maritime Cooperation Agreement. In September 1996, Jamaica opened a U.S.-sponsored regional drug training center at the Jamaica Police Academy. Three months later, 25 individuals, representing 10 countries in the region, were graduated. In 1996, Jamaica eradicated 472.5 hectares of marijuana and destroyed 2.78 million seedlings.

3. Jamaica is looking toward continued cooperation in 1997; although there is no evidence of illegal diversion of precursor chemicals in Jamaica, the Government expects to place precursor legislation before the Parliament in 1997. Jamaican negotiators and U S are now working to conclude a maritime cooperation agreement. Jamaica is eagerly awaiting the arrival of UH1H Helicopter spare parts, which were committed by President Clinton in 1995 and notified to the Congress at the end of FY 1996. The Government is now requesting a "security audit" of Jamaica's ports to improve surveillance against drug smuggling in Jamaican exports. The Government is expecting to increase the current 55-man complement of the JCF Narcotics Division. The Government is hoping to obtain assistance to set up and establish the Assets Forfeiture/Money Laundering Investigative Unit.

The script was used as the basis for letters to Congress, the bureaucracy, and to other influential actors in the certification process. In addition to letters, Jamaica's case was presented by a short "background note," and copies of favorable media reports and speeches of the Prime Minister and Minister of National Security. For example, the *Daily Gleaner*, the daily newspaper with the largest circulation in Jamaica, reported a major drug bust in the port in Kingston in its edition of December 4, 1997.[53] This article was either faxed or sent by mail with an accompanying cover letter. A typical letter read as follows: "As the process of preparation of the President's report on the cooperation between the United States and Jamaica and other nations in the region goes forward this month, I take the opportunity to share with you the record of the United States/Jamaican counter-narcotics relationship. During the past 10 years, we have enjoyed a strong and mutually beneficial relationship in our common cause against the trafficking in dangerous narcotics that pose a threat to both our societies. In fact, in each of those years, Jamaica's cooperation with the United States has been fully certified by the President during the annual narcotics partnership review process."[54]

THE LIST

The list used in the 1996/1997 campaign consisted of selected members of Congress, senior Congressional staff, senior officials in the inter-agency process, and influential friends. The members of Congress who were included in the list are shown in table 6.3.

The list also included friends and supporters such as: Dr. Robert A. Pastor, Director, Latin American and Caribbean Program, the Carter Center, Inc; former President Jimmy Carter, the Carter Center Inc; the Hon. Vernon Jordan of the law firm, Akin, Gump, Strauss, Hauer, and Feld; and the Hon. Andrew Young, former U.S. ambassador to the United Nations and former mayor of Atlanta. Certain key Congressional staff members were also on the list and these included: Roger Noriega, House International Relations Committee, and John Mackey, House International Relations Committee.

IMPORTANCE OF TIGHT COORDINATION

The U.S. government raised the issue of the need for a Jamaica/U.S. Maritime Counter Narcotics Agreement ("ship-rider agreement") and presented a draft agreement in February 1996. The draft was a model agreement presented to all countries that the United States wanted to sign such an agreement. During late 1996 and early 1997, one of the criteria, which the United States was using to judge Jamaica's cooperation, was if it had signed a ship-rider agreement or was making progress in negotiating a "ship-rider agreement." Jamaica declined to sign the draft agreement and insisted on negotiations. The negotiations began in late 1996 and were proceeding more slowly than the United States had wanted. The United States was surprised and frustrated that Jamaica did not immediately sign the draft agreement and pointed out that Trinidad and Tobago had signed the model agreement almost immediately when it was presented. The government of Jamaica recognized the contribution that such an agreement could make to Jamaica's fight against drug use and drug trafficking and was not deliberately stalling but insisted on engaging in negotiations, which were patiently and astutely led by Solicitor General Dr. Kenneth Rattray. The main problem for Jamaica was the wide ranging ambit of the draft agreement and the implications that it could portend. The issues in the negotiations were of two types, the substantive and the practical. The substantive issue was reciprocity in rights to enter the out party's territory although Jamaica at the time did not possess capacity to pursue drug traffickers into U.S. air space or coastal waters. The principal practical issue was working out a practical and effective protocol for request to pursue into Jamaican airspace and maritime borders. The key issue was how the request would be made and ensuring a

Table 6.3.   MEMBERS OF HOUSE AND SENATE WHO WERE SENT INFORMATION REGULARLY: 1996–1997

Bob Barr, U.S. House of Representatives	Jose Serra, U.S. House of Representatives
Sonny Callahan, U.S. House of Representatives	Robert Menendez, U.S. House of Representatives
Julian Dixon, U.S. House of Representatives	Carlos Romero-Barcelo, U.S. House of Representatives
Lee Hamilton, U.S. House of Representatives	Bill McCollum, U.S. House of Representatives
Alcee Hastings, U.S. House of Representatives	John Porter, U.S. House of Representatives
Dan Burton, U.S. House of Representatives	Steven Schiff, U.S. House of Representatives
Phil Crane, U.S. House of Representatives	Christopher Smith, U.S. House of Representatives
Porter Goss, U.S. House of Representatives	Maxine Waters, U.S. House of Representatives
Amo Houghton, U.S. House of Representatives	Cynthia McKinney, U.S. House of Representatives
Zoe Lofgren, U.S. House of Representatives	Ileana Ros-Lehtinen, U.S. House of Representatives
Dennis Hastert, U.S. House of Representatives	Charles Schumer, U.S. House of Representatives
Charles Rangel, U.S. House of Representatives	Esteban Torres, U.S. House of Representatives
Louis Stokes, U.S. House of Representatives	Melvin Watt, U.S. House of Representatives
Solomon Ortiz, U.S. House of Representatives	John Mica, U.S. House of Representatives
Carrie Meek, U.S. House of Representatives	Bob Livingston, U.S. House of Representatives
Michael Oxley, U.S. House of Representatives	Joe Biden, Jr. , U.S. House of Representatives
Elijah Cummings, U.S. House of Representatives	Christopher Dodd, U.S. House of Representatives
Edward Markey, U.S. House of Representatives	Charles Grassley, U.S. House of Representatives
Joseph Kennedy, U.S. House of Representatives	Nancy Pelosi, U.S. House of Representatives
Benjamin Gilman, U.S. House of Representatives	Dave Obey, U.S. House of Representatives

Clay Shaw, U.S. House of Representatives

Nita Lowey, U.S. House of Representatives

Edolphus Towns, U.S. House of Representatives

Sheila Jackson-Lee, U.S. House of Representatives

L. McIntosh Slaughter, U.S. House of Representatives

Michael McNulty, U.S. House of Representatives

Gene Green, U.S. House of Representatives

Earl Hillard, U.S. House of Representatives

Chaka Fattah, U.S. House of Representatives

Jessie Jackson, Jr. , U.S. House of Representatives

Elton Gallegly, U.S. House of Representatives

Ken Calvert, U.S. House of Representatives

Jon Fox, U.S. House of Representatives

William Jefferson, U.S. House of Representatives

Bobby Scott, U.S. House of Representatives

Major Owens, U.S. House of Representatives

Jim Ramstad, U.S. House of Representatives

Donald Payne, U.S. House of Representatives

Paul Coverdell, U.S. House of Representatives

Bob Graham, U.S. House of Representatives

Orrin Hatch, U.S. House of Representatives

Jesse Helms, U.S. House of Representatives

Patrick Leahy, U.S. House of Representatives

Connie Mack, U.S. Senate

Daniel Moynihan, U.S. Senate

William Roth, Jr. , U.S. Senate

John Kerry, U.S. Senate

Richard Lugar, U.S. Senate

Barbara Milkulski, U.S. Senate

Chuck Robb, U.S. Senate

Arlen Specter, U.S. Senate

Frank Murkowski, U.S. Senate

Robert Torricelli, U.S. Senate

Alfanso D'Amato, U.S. Senate

Mitch McConnell, U.S. Senate

---

rapid approval. Article 14 stipulates that permission must be sought from the local authorities for each mission. Requests can be submitted orally and a response should be made in three hours; in the absence of a response permission is deemed to be granted.

The principle of reciprocity was vital for Jamaica as recognition of Jamaica's sovereignty and to ensure that in the future if Jamaica had the capacity it could carry on pursuit into U.S. territory. Jamaica insisted and

held out for reciprocal rights and treatment until there was some movement from the U.S. team. I well recall that some U.S. officials were incredulous Jamaica had the temerity to assume that the agreement would be
reciprocal in rights. The attitude of many officials at the time was made
explicit by Elliott Abrams, former Assistant Secretary for Inter-American
Affairs in the Reagan Administration who extolled the practicality of the
ship-rider agreement for CARICOM by pronouncing that "in an increasingly troubled region, reliance on a foreign power (United States) for
security and prosperity maybe the most sensible form of nationalism."[55]
This caused offense throughout the Caribbean.

At one stage the United States threatened to call off or postpone further negotiations; however, Ambassador Bernal persuaded them to re-
institute the schedule of negotiations. Gelbard had decided to terminate
the negotiations and called Ambassador Bernal to inform him of the
decision. On the assurances of Ambassador Bernal that he was unaware
of such a letter and that the contents as read to him on the telephone by
Gelbard were totally incorrect, the negotiations were reinstituted. This
incident demonstrates the paramount importance of a foreign
government presenting a single position on a consistent basis to all
points of contact with the U.S. government both in the home country and
in the United States.

On May 6, 1997, the governments of Jamaica and the United States
completed the negotiations of a "ship-rider agreement," which was
signed in Bridgetown, Barbados in May 1997 on the occasion of the meeting between the Prime Ministers and Presidents of the Caribbean and
President Clinton. Legislation giving effect to the Agreement was passed
in early 1998. While this did not meet the pace the United States would
have liked they were reassured in the interim that Jamaica was fully
committed to bring the agreement into law. Continuous communication
with the U.S. government prevented any misunderstanding. For example, K. D. Knight, Minister of National Security, in a letter of November
20, 1997, to U.S. ambassador J. Gary Cooper, wrote, "In recent months
we both have been discussing various aspects of Jamaica/U.S. Bilateral
Co-operation on Narcotics Control and I find it necessary at this time to
bring you up to date with the progress made in relation to some of the
talking points."[56]

FOLLOW-UP

An important aspect of lobbying is to maintain contact on a continuous
basis and to avoid only resorting to networking when there is an urgent

need for help. This is often referred to as the "know 'em before you need 'em" strategy. In this regard, the campaign started six months before the certification date and involved communication on a regular basis involving written communication approximately every two weeks interspersed with face-to-face meetings. Having achieved a favorable outcome in the certification process, it was important to express appreciation to those who were supportive and even those who abstained from opposing or being critical. Hence, thank you letters were sent to the entire "list" both as an expression of appreciation and to ensure that the relationship was maintained intact for the future. The thank you letter on completion of the certification process in March 1997 is reproduced in appendix F.

Throughout 1996, Jamaica continued its commitment to halt drug trafficking and eradicate narcotics cultivation. In September 1996, the Prime Minister delivered a strong statement reaffirming Jamaica's commitment to fight narcotics trafficking and cooperate with the United States on bilateral and regional efforts to do the same.

The government of Jamaica has taken steps to implement the provisions of the 1994 Asset Forfeiture and Seizure Act, and is now working to coordinate 28 foreign requests for asset forfeiture. In two cases, using provisions of the recent MLAT, assets have been restrained pending forfeiture orders.

In December 1996, the government enacted domestic money laundering legislation to augment and strengthen existing money laundering regulations.

Through a recent amendment to the Dangerous Drugs Act, Jamaica significantly strengthened penalties for drug-related convictions.

In December 1996, Jamaica removed its exemption regarding shipriders from the 1988 UN Convention, clearing the way for negotiation of a Maritime Cooperation Agreement.

In September 1996, Jamaica opened a UNDCP-sponsored regional drug-training center at the Jamaica Policy Academy. Three months later, 25 individuals, representing 10 countries in the region, were graduated.

In 1996, Jamaica eradicated 472.5 hectares of marijuana and destroyed 2.78 million seedlings.

THE FINAL EPISODE

Jamaica was certified as cooperating fully with the United States in March 1997. But even on the day of the meeting in the White House to decide on certification there was considerable tension. On the fateful day the U.S. ambassador to Jamaica Gary Cooper informed the Ministry of Foreign Affairs that Jamaica had been decertified, setting off alarm bells throughout the highest levels of the government. Prime Minister Patterson telephoned Ambassador Bernal and sought confirmation. Bernal informed the Prime Minister that this was not possible since the White House meeting had not yet been convened and reaffirmed his earlier advice that all indications were that Jamaica would be fully certified. The Ambassador telephoned Mack McLarty to reconfirm previous indications. Ambassador Bernal also telephoned Ambassador Cooper who stated that this was his impression after talking with John Hamilton of the State Department. A call was immediately placed to Hamilton who denied making such a definitive statement or even a prediction but did confide that he was concerned about the outcome. Bernal called and reiterated to the Prime Minister and Minister of Foreign Affairs and Foreign Trade that Jamaica would be certified. At about mid-day Bernal was informed that Jamaica was certified and was asked to make no public comment until after the Secretary of State had publicly announced the certification decisions in the afternoon. Corroborating information came from Wrobleski who was attending a swearing-in ceremony at the State Department for Ambassador John Maisto when word spread through the group that only Belize had been decertified with a national interest waiver. Ambassador Bernal informed Prime Minister P. J. Patterson by telephone.

CONCLUSION

The campaign to secure certification for Jamaica during the nine months from mid-1996 to the end of February 1997 demonstrates that an astutely planned and executed strategy, coordinating all components in the United States and in Jamaica, monitoring and reacting to adverse events on a daily basis, and a proactive delivery of information and a consistent message to the Congress, bureaucracy, and the media can be successful. A very important part of attaining the desired outcome was supporting the campaign with the appropriate action, policies, and pronouncements by the government of Jamaica. In this regard Prime Minister P. J. Patterson and K. D. Knight, Minister of National Security played a vital role in ensuring full cooperation with the United States at the operational level. In addition, their speeches and the timing of policy actions were alert to the confirmation process. No matter how good the strategy and the message, the extensive contacts and good personal relationships of the team of lobbyists and the Ambassador made a significant difference to the final outcome.

NOTES

1. "Rethinking International Drug Control: New Directions for U.S. Policy," A Task Force Report by the Council on Foreign Relations (New York, NY: Council on Foreign Relations, February, 1997) page 49 and Ivelaw Lloyd Griffith, Drugs and

Security in the Caribbean. Sovereignity Under Siege (University Park, PA: Pennsylvania State University Press, 1997) page 55.

2. Douglas Farah, "Caribbean Key to U.S. Drug Trade," Washington Post, 23 September 1996.

3. Text of a letter from the President to the Chairman and Ranking Members of the House Committee on Appropriations and International Relations and the Senate Committees on Appropriations and Foreign Relations (Washington, D.C.: The White House, Office of the Press Secretary, 3 December 1996).

4. International Narcotics Control Strategy Report, March 1997 (Washington, D.C.: United States Department of State, Bureau of International Narcotics Matters, August 1997) pages 11 and 22.

5. Ivelaw Lloyd Griffith, Drugs and Security in the Caribbean. Sovereignty under Siege (University Park: Pennsylvania State University Press, 1997) pages 32–40 and 53–92.

6. Scott B. McDonald, Dancing on a Volcano: The Latin American Drug Trade (New York: Praeger, 1992) page 89.

7. International Narcotics Control Strategy Report, March 1997 (Washington, D.C.: United States Department of State, Bureau of International Narcotics Matters, August, 1997) pages 35.

8. Richard L. Bernal, "Debt, Drugs and Development in the Caribbean," Transafrica Forum, Vol. 9, No. 2 (Summer, 1992) pages 83–92 and Richard L. Bernal, Winsome J. Leslie, and Stephen E. Lamar, "Debt, Drugs and Structural Adjustment in the Caribbean," in Ivelaw L. Griffith (ed.), The Political Economy of Drugs in the Caribbean (London: Macmillan, 2000) pages 58–80.

9. Suzette A. Haughton, Drugged Out. Globalisation and Jamaica's Resilience to Drug Trafficking (Lanham: University of the Americas Press, 2011) page 63.

10. Gary Lee, "Crime in the Caribbean: A Reality Check," Washington Post, April 8, 2001.

11. Jorge G. Castaneda, The Mexican Shock. It's Meaning for the U.S. (New York: Free Press, 1995) page 165.

12. Gary Brana-Shute, "Narco-criminality and Political Economy in the Caribbean," in Ivelaw L. Griffith (ed.), The Political Economy of Drugs in the Caribbean (London: Macmillan, 2000) pages 97–112.

13. Ivelaw L. Griffith, Caribbean Security on the Eve of the 21st Century, McNair Paper 54 (Washington, D.C.: Institute for National Strategic Studies, National Defense University, 1996) page 33.

14. Anthony Bryan, Transnational Organized Crime: The Caribbean Context, Working Paper Series, Working Paper No. 1 (Miami: Dante B. Fascell North-South Center, University of Miami, October, 2000), Anthony Maingot, "The Decentralization Imperative and Caribbean Criminal Enterprises" in Tom Farer (ed.), Transnational Crime in the Americas (New York: Routledge, 1999) pages 42–170, and Ivelaw Griffith, "Transnational Crime in the Americas: A Reality Check" in Jorge I. Dominguez (ed.), The Future of Inter- American Relations (New York: Routledge, 2000) pages 63–86.

15. Mathea Falco, "America's Drug Problem and Its Policy of Denial," Current History, Vol. 97, No. 618 (April, 1998) pages 145–49.

16. Peter Hakim, "U.S. Drug Certification Process Is in Serious Need of Reform," Christian Science Monitor, March 27, 1997.

17. For a discussion from different perspectives see, Drug Certification and U.S. Policy in Latin America (Washington, D.C.: The Woodrow Wilson International Center, The Latin American Program, April 1988).

18. Trevor Munroe, "Cooperation and Conflict in the U.S.-Caribbean Drug Connection," in Ivelaw L. Griffith, The Political Economy of Drugs in the Caribbean (London: Macmillan, 2000) pages 183–200.

19. Meg Greenfield, Washington (New York: Public Affairs, 2001) page 19.

20. International Narcotics Control Strategy Report, April 1994 (Washington, D.C., United States Department of State, Bureau of International Narcotics Matters, April 1, 1994) page 197.

21. International Narcotics Control Strategy Report, March 1995 (Washington, D.C., United States Department of State, Bureau of International Narcotics Matters, March 1995) page 182.

22. International Narcotics Control Strategy Report, March 1995 (Washington, D.C., United States Department of State, Bureau of International Narcotics Matters, March 1995) page 180.

23. Lacy A. Wright, Jr.,Deputy Chief of Mission, U.S. Embassy, Jamaica, 1991–1995. The Association for Diplomatic Studies and Training Foreign Affairs Oral History Project, pages 1–113. www. adst. org/wp-content/uploads/2012/09/Caribbean-Islands.pdf.

24. Bernard Headley, The Jamaican Crime Scene. A Perspective (Mandeville: Eureka Press, 1994) pages 68–75

25. Laurie Gunst, Born Fi' Dead. A Journey Through the Jamaican Posse Underworld (New York: Henry Holt and Company, 1995) and Faye V. Harrison, "Drug Trafficking in World Capitalism: A Perspective on Jamaican Posses in the U.S." Social Justice. Vol. 16, No.4 (1989) pages 115–31.

26. International Narcotics Control Strategy Report, April 1993 (Washington, D.C., United States Department of State, Bureau of International Narcotics Matters, April 1, 1993) page 195.

27. Anthony Harriott, Police and Crime Control in Jamaica. Problems of Reforming Ex-Colonial Constabularies (Kingston: University of the West Indies Press, 2000).

28. International Narcotics Control Strategy Report, Mid-Year Update, August, 1989 (Washington, D.C., United States Department of State, Bureau of International Narcotics Matters, August, 1989) page 56.

29. Personal notes of Ambassador Bernal.

30. International Narcotics Control Strategy Report, March, 1997 (Washington, D.C., United States Department of State, Bureau of International Narcotics Matters, August, 1997) page 189.

31. International Narcotics Control Strategy Report, March 1997 (Washington, D.C., United States Department of State, Bureau of International Narcotics Matters, March, 1997) page 190.

32. Cathy Boothe and Tammerlin Drummond, "Caribbean Blizzard," Time Magazine, February 26, 1996.

33. Douglas Farah, "Russian Mob, Drug Cartels Joining Forces," Washington Post, September 29, 1997.

34. Serge F. Kovaleski and Douglas Farah, "Organized Crime Exercises Clout In Island Nations," Washington Post, February 17, 1998, page A1 and A10.

35. Douglas Farah, "Drug Corruption Over the Top," Washington Post, February 17, 1998 and Douglas Farah, "Double Identity," Washington Post, February 17, 1998.

36. Michelle Faul, "Albright Advises Islands to Hit Drugs," Washington Times, April 7, 1998.

37. "A Tidal Wave of Drugs," The Economist, June 24, 2000.

38. Jeff Stein, "The Caribbean Connection," GQ magazine, August, 1999, pages 164–71 and 209–11.

39. Files of the Embassy of Jamaica.

40. Canute James, "Drugs Tide Rises around the Caribbean," Financial Times, October 25, 1996.

41. Files of the Embassy of Jamaica.

42. International Narcotics Control Strategy Report, Mid-Year Update, March, 1996 (Washington, D.C., United States Department of State, Bureau of International Narcotics Matters, March, 1996) page 189.

43. International Narcotics Control Strategy Report, Mid-Year Update, March, 1996 (Washington, D.C., United States Department of State, Bureau of International Narcotics Matters, March, 1996).

44. Mathea Falco, "U.S. Drug Policy: Addicted to Failure," Foreign Policy, No.102 (Spring, 1996) pages 120–33.

45. Appointments Diary of Ambassador Dr. Richard L. Bernal, 1997.

46. Notes of Ambassador Bernal, January, 1997.

47. Delano Franklin (ed.), A Voice in Caribbean and World Politics. P.J.Patterson. Selected Speeches 1992–2000 (Kingston: Ian Randle Publishers, 2002) page 215.

48. Delano Franklin, op. cit., page 218.

49. Delano Franklin, op. cit., page 220.

50. Confidential Memorandum, Update on Narcotics from Ann Wrobleski, George Dalley, and Steve Lamar to Ambassador Richard L. Bernal, February 21, 1997.

51. Files from Jefferson Waterman, Inc.

52. Background on Jamaican Counter-Narcotics Efforts, Embassy of Jamaica and Jefferson Waterman International, February 3, 1997.

53. Glenroy Sinclair, "Drug Busts on the Ports," Daily Gleaner, December 4, 1997, page 1.

54. Files of Ambassador Bernal.

55. Abrams, Elliott. 1996. "The Shiprider Solution: Policing the Caribbean." National Interest, Vol. 43, No. 1 (Spring, 1996) pages 86–92

56. Letter from K. D. Knight, Minister of National Security of Jamaica to U.S. ambassador J. Gary Cooper, 20th November, 1997.

SEVEN

Trade Enhancement

The United States is and has been since World War II the main trading partner of the Central America and the Caribbean. In the case of Jamaica over 50 percent of imports are sourced from the United States and it is the destination for over one half of total exports. The trading relationship is reinforced by the fact that the United States is also the principal source of private foreign investment, involving many U.S. multinational corporations.[1] The value of U.S.-CBI trade has tripled in the last 15 years, moving from $12.6 billion in 1985 to $39.4 billion in 1999. Trade statistics for 1985–1999 are shown in table 7.1. U.S. exports to the region have generated a significant increase in employment as jobs dependent on exports to the CBI have increased from 118,840 in 1985 to 402,360 in 1998, a net increase of 283,520 jobs in 14 years (see Table 7.2). The growth in trade was given a substantial boost by the CBI, which came into effect in 1983 and the trade has been beneficial to both the United States and the countries of the CBI region although the United States has consistently maintained a favorable trade balance since the inception of the CBI (see table 7.1).

The Caribbean Basin Initiative came into effect in 1983 by the enactment of the Caribbean Basin Economic Recovery Act (CBI I). The CERA granted unilateral preferential trade benefits to countries in the Caribbean and Central America that met the specified eligibility criteria. The CERA provided duty free or reduced duties for a designated list of products until September 30, 1995. The CBI I did not provide duty free treatment for textiles, apparel, footwear, handbags, luggage, work gloves, flat goods, leather wearing not eligible under the generalized system of preferences (GSP), canned tuna, petroleum products, watches, and watch parts. Unfortunately, the products excluded from duty free treatment

Table 7.1.   United States/CBI Trade 1985-1999 (Millions of Dollars)

Year	U.S. Imports	U.S. Exports	Balance
1985	6,687	5,942	-745
1986	6,065	5,362	297
1987	6,039	6,906	867
1988	6,061	7,690	1,629
1989	6,942	9,023	2,081
1990	7,525	9,569	2,044
1991	8,372	10,013	1,641
1992	9,627	11,263	1,636
1993	10,378	12,428	2,050
1994	11,495	13,441	1,946
1995	12,673	15,306	2,633
1996	14,700	15,903	1,203
1997	16,877	18,432	1,555
1998	17,250	20,118	2,868
1999	19,607	19,816	209

Source: Calculated from Department of Commerce data.

happened to be products in which the CBI countries had a comparative advantage and therefore the most export potential.

In 1990 the Caribbean Basin Economic Recovery Expansion Act (CBI II) expanded the list of eligible products and made the CBI into a permanent program. However there were still types of apparel that were omitted from the duty free dispensation.

In May 2000 the U.S. House of Representatives and the Senate passed the United States-Caribbean Basin Trade Partnership (CBI III) as part of the Trade and Development Act of 2000 and President Clinton signed it into law on May 18, 2000. The bill, which became effective on 1 October 2000 represents an enhancement of access to the U.S. market, in particular, the textile provisions and those for other products excluded under the CBI I. The duration of these provisions will be for 8 years ending in September 2008.

The original conception of the CBI by the Reagan Administration anticipated a closely linked program of development financing in the form of U.S. foreign aid. However, this essential component was not included in the CBI legislation[2] nor were there any provisions for debt relief for those countries, which were highly indebted. The thinking in U.S. government circles was that the legislation by liberalizing access to the

Table 7.2. U.S. Jobs Dependent on Trade with the Caribbean Basin Nations

Year	Jobs Dependent on CBI	New Jobs Created Per Year
1985	118,840	
1986	127,240	8,400
1987	138,120	10,880
1988	153,800	15,680
1989	165,800	12,000
1990	191,380	25,580
1991	200,260	8,880
1992	225,262	25,002
1993	248,552	23,290
1994	268,814	20,292
1995	306,120	37,306
1996	318,060	11,940
1997	368,640	50,580
1998	402,360	33,720

Based on U.S. Department of Commerce formula of $1 billion in exports = 20,000 jobs.

U.S. market would stimulate private investment from both foreign and domestic sources. This prediction was not realized because the new trade provisions created export incentives but this did not generate the anticipated capital formation, which was critical to the establishment and expansion of export enterprises.[3] In 1984, U.S. assistance and export credits to the 24 CBI beneficiary countries amounted to $1.26 billion. By 1994 the level of assistance had dropped by more than $700 million to $544 million.[4]

Another concern in the CBI region about the original legislation was the limited duration set at 12 years making it difficult to attract long-term investment.[5] In 1986 as part of a major overhaul of the U.S. tax code, the U.S. Congress made a valuable source of private sector financing available for CBI projects. This pool of investment capital was generated through the investment of profits of U.S. companies operating in Puerto Rico under a tax credit contained in Section 936 of the U.S. tax code. The term "Section 936" refers either to a provision in the U.S. tax code or the credit contained in that provision. The Caribbean loan program is the mechanism through which 936 loans were made available to eligible CBI countries. These funds were made available to entrepreneurs and investors, who used the funds to finance investment and capitalize projects throughout the Caribbean. As a result, although Section 936 has been seen primarily as a tool to promote growth and employment in Puerto Rico, it emerged as a key financing source for investment and economic development throughout the Caribbean.[6] To a large degree, the Section 936 Caribbean loan program was developed to compensate for the lack of an investment component in the CBI. The Section 936 funds, which first became available to the Caribbean in 1988, filled a needed gap by providing a large pool of resources for financing private sector medium and long-term investments. These funds were also eligible for use in financing investment in industries outside of the purview of the CBI such as petroleum.[7] The Section 936 program was terminated in 1996 despite a strenuous lobbying effort by Puerto Rico, Central America, and the ESC[8] and generated pressure for the enhancement of the CBI.

THE CAMPAIGN

The original CBI did not provide complete free access to the U.S. market for all products from the CBI beneficiary countries as it excluded certain types of apparel, tuna, leather goods, and footwear. These were products in CBI designated countries that had a comparative advantage and therefore were the products that had the most potential for export. The governments and private sectors of the CBI countries began to lobby the U.S. administration and Congress to extend the product coverage to include all the excluded or restricted products. The persistent requests and agitation by the CBI states prompted the Subcommittee on International Economic Policy and Trade of the Western Hemisphere of the committee on Foreign Affairs to hold hearings in Bridgetown, Barbados in September 1987. The hearings involved members of Congress and senior government and business leaders from the ESC.

The campaign to secure enhancement of the CBI lasted from the late 1980s until 2000 with an interim upgrade of the CBI being passed in 1990 (see chronology of events in appendix G). The campaign involved efforts to convince the Bush and Clinton administrations to make the political decision to include CBI enhancement as part of the legislative program submitted to Congress to give effect to the objects of U.S. trade policy. Both administrations agreed that some modification of the CBI was necessary; however, the views of the White House were not necessarily in tandem with the expressed wishes of the CBI countries or the Congress. Much attention was devoted to having the "right bill" initiated in Congress and to garner sufficient support to have this enacted as legislation. This was an arduous and complex task because Congress exhibited no consensus on any aspect of U.S. trade policy as is evident in the enormous political effort that was required by the Clinton Administration to pass the NAFTA and the Uruguay Round agreements of the WTO. There was widespread apprehension about further opening of the U.S. market to exports from countries with sub-U.S. wages, fostered to a large extent by organized labor whose protestations bordered on the hysterical. In addition, there was a sort of "CBI fatigue" in Congress as many members felt that they had already "fixed" the CBI "problem." It was therefore hard to mobilize enthusiasm or willingness to devote the time necessary to drafting legislation and building sufficient supporting coalition. Indeed, this fatigue prompted the advocates of CBI improvement to call their desired legislation "NAFTA parity" to minimize the association with the expansion of CBI access and invoke the spectre of NAFTA damage to CBI in the same way in which NAFTA was perceived to be adversely affecting employment and investment in the United States. This was particularly the case with the improvement in market access for goods from the CBI region because the main issue was access for apparel made in the CBI countries from fabric made in the United States (807A goods), which was seen by some as creating jobs overseas at the expense of the United States. For example, in March 1995 the Committee on the Implementation of Textile Agreements (CITA) made a determination that imports from the Dominican Republic, Costa Rica, Honduras, El Salvador, Colombia, Turkey, and Thailand were causing serious damage to the domestic cotton and man-made fiber underwear industry.[9]

A major problem in garnering support for new legislation to enhance the CBI was the fact that the administration, bureaucracy, and Congress at no time heard a single message from U.S. business interests. On the contrary there a major split between the textile and apparel interests. The apparel interests strongly supported further liberalization of the U.S. market for apparel manufactured in the CBI countries but were vigorously opposed by the textile interests who wanted to restrict production of apparel to manufacturing using U.S. made fabric. The result was two widely differing messages being transmitted to Congress often in complex industry jargon, which confused would-be supporters and split the ranks of Congress.

THE ARGUMENTS PUT FORWARD BY THE ESC[10]

In 1983 the Committee on Ways and Means proposed legislation that led to the passage of the Caribbean Basin Initiative (CBI). This legislation recognized the considerable benefit to be derived by both the United States and the Caribbean from the liberalization of the trading relationship. It was motivated by security concerns and designed to stimulate investment, lock-in economic reform, and promote trade-led economic growth. The CBI witnessed an expansion of U.S.-CBI trade but the advent of the North American Free Trade Agreement (NAFTA) threatened to divert trade and investment from the CBI countries. This very real possibility prompted the CBI states to petition the Bush administration to ensure that this did not become an eventuality.[11] In 1994 the pro-CBI enhancement members of Congress drafted a bill to achieve this objective. This was H.R. 1403 The Caribbean Free Trade Act, which was vigorously supported by the CBI countries. The arguments put forward by the CBI countries in support of this bill are set out in detail in the rest of this section. This exposition in the pristine language serves to record the argumentation justifying the enhancement of the CBI, gives the authentic flavor of the period, and was the fundamental template on which later refinements and necessary political modifications were constructed.

The CBI has been responsible for unparalleled growth in trade between the United States and the Caribbean, acting as a catalyst for exports, investment, and employment creation in the economies of the United States and the Caribbean nations, such as Jamaica. In the first 10 years of the CBI, U.S. exports to the region surged by 100 percent and Caribbean exports to the United States climbed by close to 50 percent. In 1992, the United States posted yet another trade surplus with the Caribbean Basin—for the seventh year in a row. The Caribbean Basin now comprises the tenth largest market of the United States; for the Caribbean, the United States is by far the largest market. Combined trade (accounting for both imports and exports) between the United States and the Caribbean exceeded $20 billion in 1992, supporting 220,000 jobs in the United States and countless jobs throughout the Caribbean region.

As the growth process in CBI economies has been strengthened by increased U.S. investment and market access, import capacities have increased, resulting in increased purchases of U.S. goods and services. Each dollar spent by the Caribbean generates 60 cents worth of U.S. exports, while that same dollar in Asia would only generate 10 cents per dollar of U.S. exports. Jamaica for example, now purchases three quarters of its imports from the United States, as increased overall demand has inevitably led to the creation of exports, and more importantly, export-related jobs, in the United States.

In addition, the jobs created in Jamaica have often been in industries such as apparel manufacture, where U.S. employers can no longer offer globally competitive products if all stages are carried out in the United States. The CBI has given these U.S. firms the ability to rely for part of their production on the internationally competitive wage rates in the Caribbean, rather than losing their entire operations to low wage competitors in Asia. As a result, U.S. apparel manufacturers have been able to improve their costs of production and retain the global competitiveness of U.S. manufactured apparel exported throughout the world marketplace.

Finally, the access to the U.S. market provided by the CBI has encouraged economic reform and liberalization of economic policies in the region, particularly in Jamaica. Just as the promise of NAFTA has stimulated economic reform in Canada, Mexico, and throughout the region, we in Jamaica have had the incentive of the market access provided by the CBI to embrace the policies of privatization and economic deregulation that promote export driven, private sector-led development and growth.

"Jamaica believes that the CBI has served as a first, and vital, step in the path leading to expanded trade, investment and growth with the United States. The CBI supported economic reform to create genuine market economies and has laid the groundwork for mutual prosperity through sustained growth and stronger commercial links. If economic expansion is to continue, especially as the NAFTA negotiations are brought to a close, it is necessary that a mechanism be established, which will enable United States and Caribbean firms to enhance their current trade partnership. We believe that H.R. 1403—the Caribbean Basin Free Trade Agreement—will provide such a trade mechanism."

EFFECTS OF NAFTA ON THE CBI/UNITED STATES TRADE

The structure of trade in the region ensures that the impact of NAFTA will be substantial. Fifty to seventy percent of exports of CBI countries go to the three NAFTA countries. With such a significant proportion of the region's trade taking place with the United States, and given the importance of trade to economic growth, there is concern that NAFTA could result in trade diversion and not in trade creation.

The NAFTA could convert the CBI into a depreciated asset. It would erode CBI provisions and thereby place the small, undiversified economies of CBI countries at a competitive disadvantage in terms of access to the U.S. markets as it provides Mexico with removal of tariffs and quotas over specified adjustment periods. This would inadvertently create a situation in which Mexico, which already has inexpensive labor, cheap energy, lower transportation cost, and economies of scale, would now have a further advantage over the CBI countries. Although Mexico does not compete with the CBI region in all of its exports, a relaxation of import barriers for Mexico could cause a reduction in many of the Caribbean's most valuable exports.

Again, one of the best examples of this potential for displacement is in the area of textiles. Under NAFTA, Mexican textiles and apparel will benefit from a progressive tariff reduction over a ten-year period. This would introduce a new dimension of competition, creating a situation whereby CBI-produced garments made from U.S. textiles would have to compete at a price disadvantage against Mexican apparel made from Mexican textiles. This would displace both CBI apparel producers and U.S. textile manufacturers as importers sought the cheaper Mexican garments.

In the four years before NAFTA became effective on January 1, 1994, U.S. apparel imports increased at 23 percent per annum and those from Mexico rose at 24 percent a year. In 1994 apparel imports from the CBI region grew by 13 percent while imports from Mexico expanded by 33 percent. In 1995 there was a21 percent rise in imports from the CBI countries but imports from Mexico leapt by an incredible 52 percent.[12] These results are a direct result of the disparities in tariffs and duties between NAFTA and CBI. For every $10 f.o.b. value of a typical garment made in the CBI countries and entering the United States under heading 9802.00.80 contains $6.40 in duty-free U.S. components and $3.60 in dutiable foreign value-added. Applying the 1995 trade-weighted tariff for apparel of 16.1 percent to the foreign value-added yields a duty of $0.58 or an ad valorem equivalent of 5.8 percent.[13]

On a regional economic level, there could be an erosion of the economic gains of the past decade because NAFTA could cause the following:

Trade Diversion

The elimination of quota and phase-out of tariffs on Mexican products could remove or at least reduce the advantage enjoyed by CBI exports to the United States. This could cause a diversion of U.S. demand from suppliers in CBI countries to firms in Mexico, thus reducing CBI exports. This would aggravate the balance of payments difficulties of Caribbean economies.

Investment Diversion

As trade prospects and advantages in the Caribbean diminish, investors will begin to redirect their funds to Mexico. This diversion of investment is already evident from investment patterns throughout the region.

Relocation of Production Capacity

Existing productive enterprises, which had originally located in the Caribbean to take advantage of the access to the U.S. market, could transfer or close operations in preference for Mexican locations, which have the advantage of better access to the U.S. market access. NAFTA discriminates in favor of Mexico against the CBI region.

Contraction of Economic Activity

The loss of trade and investment opportunities would precipitate a decline in business confidence and economic activity, undermining development prospects throughout the Caribbean. Caribbean governments would inevitably find it more difficult to sustain their own economic reform and structural adjustment programs, becoming more reliant upon bilateral aid programs.

United States Jobs Losses

Ultimately, a large number of American jobs that depend on healthy Caribbean trade flows would be lost as commercial opportunities contracted in the Caribbean.

Trade Deficit Aggravated

The loss of U.S. export opportunities would reduce the stable trade surplus that the United States maintains with the Caribbean.

The CBI has served as a catalyst for the creation of jobs and economic development between the CBI countries and the United States, therefore the de facto elimination of CBI trade provisions could cause a long-term reversal in that economic relationship. This effect has already been documented as investors evaluate the provisions and likely implementation of NAFTA. The United States International Trade Commission (ITC), in a report entitled, "Potential Effects of a North American Free Trade Agreement on Apparel Investments in CBERA Countries," has concluded that "NAFTA will introduce incentives that will tend to favor apparel investment shifts away from the CBERA countries to Mexico."

LEGISLATION: H.R. 1403 BILL

The key elements of the bill were:

A. Creation of a Level Playing Field

H.R. 1403 recognizes the importance of trading relationships to the Caribbean by explicitly ensuring that a level playing field exists between Mexican and Caribbean exporters with regard to the U.S. market. This would involve upgrading CBI to cover those products that are exempted from duty free treatment under CBI, and those goods and services placed at a disadvantage vis-à-vis Mexico by the provisions of NAFTA. In a word, it would provide non-discriminatory access for Caribbean products in the U.S. market. For example, the textile and apparel sector is a key CBI export industry and is currently subject to many restrictions.

H.R. 1403 would create no special benefits for the CBI that wouldn't already exist for Mexico. Nor would it legislate special treatment for CBI producers in excess of that granted Mexico. Nor would it go into effect in the absence of an agreement on NAFTA. It would merely extend to the Caribbean, those provisions that would apply to Mexico under NAFTA. In this sense, H.R. 1403 embodies the spirit of a "free trade agreement" by guaranteeing that trade responds to free market forces, rather than artificial government barriers.

B. Parity as a Transitional Arrangement

H.R. 1403 establishes simultaneous and equivalent treatment for CBI countries and Mexico in terms of tariffs, rules of origin, and quota elimination. Any delay in the establishment of this parity principle could result in uncertainty, leading to trade and investment diversion from the Caribbean Basin. Even the uncertainty that would be engendered by a one-year delay could do serious damage to the trade-reliant economies of the Caribbean.

At the same time, H.R. 1403 establishes parity as a transitional arrangement to enable the economies of the CBI region to complete their process of economic reform, liberalization, and structural adjustment, which will put them in a position to move towards full reciprocity. Economic reform and market access must be simultaneous. A premature attempt by the CBI countries to provide full reciprocity could be detrimental to the process of adjustment, since export-led growth is only possible with stable market access.

C. The Three-Year Negotiation Period

Currently, the bill establishes parity for a three-year period, during which the Administration can begin and conclude negotiations for free trade agreements with CBI countries or CBI countries can accede to NAFTA. The three-year period should incorporate some flexibility, which would allow each nation to accommodate its own economic realities. A major concern is that the three-year period may represent an artificial deadline, cutting off on-going negotiations. One solution would include a provision allowing the Administration, after appropriate consultation with the Congress, to extend the three-year deadline in cases where negotiations are in progress and reasonably expected to result in a concluded agreement.

D. Long Term Reciprocal Arrangements

H.R. 1403 lays out the process through which negotiations for long-term free trade agreements can be executed with the United States. This title acts as further stimulant to the Caribbean economies to continue to implement trade liberalization and economic reforms in order to accede to full free trade negotiations with the United States.

It also puts the CBI countries on notice that preferential trade arrangements—such as the CBI or the LOME Convention—will not exist indefinitely. The region must adapt to the gradual erosion or elimination of preferential trade regimes in favor of reciprocal trading systems. In order to cope with this profound change, these economies must continue the process of adjustment and reform, to ensure that in the not too distant future they will be able to compete effectively in quality and price in the global marketplace.

E. Phased Reciprocity over an Appropriate Adjustment Period

Having utilized a transitional period based on similar market access to that provided to Mexico under NAFTA, CBI countries will be in a position to begin to phase-in reciprocity over a suitable period. A suitable adjustment period should take account of the small size and undiversified structure of Caribbean economies. Although H.R. 1403 does not expressly discuss these time frames, it implicitly endorses this mechanism. The form, specifics, and pace of reciprocity should be worked out between the United States and individual countries, possibly through the institutional mechanism of the Trade and Investment Framework Agreements, which were operationalized under the auspices of the Enterprise for the Americas Initiative.

F. Implementation of Side Agreements

H.R. 1403 would require that the negotiations of free trade agreements with Caribbean Basin countries include provisions pertaining to environmental, labor, and import issues that would be comparable to those in NAFTA. We support and fully endorse this concept and believe it is consistent with the principle of establishing a level playing field. In securing equal access to the U.S. market, we are prepared to maintain adequate environmental protection, universal safeguards for workers' rights, and mechanisms to protect the domestic economy from import surges.

Congress

Congress had been convinced by the Reagan Administration to pass the CBI in 1983 in the context of what was perceived to be a communist threat in Central America and the Caribbean. The evidence adduced was leftist guerilla movements in El Salvador and Guatemala, the Sandinista government in Nicaragua, and the Bishop government in Grenada. The Reagan government also had concerns about Jamaica where the Seaga government was been held up as a model of private sector-led development to counter the attraction of the Cuban model in countries like Guyana. By the late 1980s it was widely perceived in Congress that this threat had passed and the region was now stabilized having received preferen-

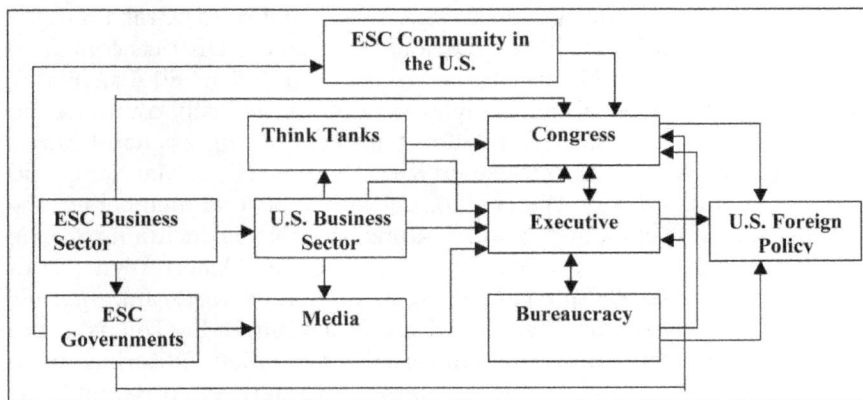

Attempts by ESC Governments to Influence U.S. Trade (CBI) Policy.

tial market access to the United States and a large injection of foreign aid during the 1980s. The original CBI legislation, however, still embodied quotas and tariffs on apparel, leather goods, and other items in which the CBI countries had a comparative advantage. In an attempt to expand market access for the these items so as to stimulate growth, employment, and investment an initiative was taken to enhance the CBI. This unfortunately commenced at a time when the awareness of the CBI region had declined, U.S. foreign policies had shifted, domestic economic issues had come to the fore, and there was "CBI fatigue."

The principal obstacles to the passage of new CBI legislation centered around building a sufficient critical mass of support for an issue that was not regarded as a priority since there was no vocal domestic community or leadership from the Executive demanding new legislation. In addition, the U.S. business community were apathetic except for the textile and apparel industries who were irrevocably split on what the new legislation should contain. This was occuring in a context where NAFTA was widely believed to be having an adverse impact on the rate of growth of apparel exports from the CBI region. Senator Bob Graham of Florida, a stalwart supporter of the CBI, advised Congress that "Caribbean trade is cheaper than Caribbean aid" and warned that "If we do nothing, I am concerned that NAFTA will divert trade from the Caribbean Basin, potentially making necessary to increase foreign aid to the region in order to bolster faltering economies."[14] Several menbers of the Congressional Black Caucus, prominent among whom was Representative Charles Rangel, were empathetic and pressed the issue in Congress and with the Administration, e.g., Representative Carrie Meek had "spoken personally with Ambassador Kantor."[15]

The leadership in Congress on the CBI issue consisted of those members committed to free trade, e.g., Congressman Crane (R), those whose constituencies benefitted substantially from exporting to the CBI countries, e.g., the Florida delegation, in particular Senator Bob Graham (D),[16] and Congressman Sam Gibbons (D), and those whose Districts contained large numbers of Caribbean citizens, e.g., Congressman Ed Towns (D), New York. There were also those who were philosophically committed to strengthening Caribbean-U.S. relations especially Congressman Charles Rangel (D), New York, Congressman Kwasi Mfume (D) of Maryland, and Congresswoman Maxine Waters (D), California. Several members of the Congressional Black Caucus were strong supporters including Carrie Meek (D) and Alcee Hastings (D) of Florida, and Albert Wyn (D) of Maryland. The Black Caucus haelped in numerous ways, for example Ambassador Bernal was interviewed on Congressman Ed Towns' radio and television programs, the ambassador's opinion editorials were placed in the official record of the House by Congressman Rangel, and each year at the conference that is part of the annual Black Causus Week there was a panel on Caribbean issues involving Congressional Representatives and Caribbean Ambassadors.

The opposition in Congress was fueled by a general apprehension about expanding market access for countries with lower wages than the United States because of a perception that jobs were being transferred overseas. In a 1998 poll, 58 percent of Americans agreed with the statement that foreign trade was "bad for the U.S. economy because cheap imports hurt wages." Only 32 percent agreed with the statement that trade was "good for the U.S. economy; it creates foreign demand, economic growth and jobs."[17] There were some prominent Congressional representatives such as Richard Gephardt who were opposed to free trade whether in the form of a trade agreement with Chile[18] or enhancing the CBI.

Some representatives in Congress were caught in the dilemna of wanting to support the enhancement of CBI, but disagreeing with other components in the legislative package, e.g., NAFTA and the Africa Trade Bill; others were worried about a backlash from organized labor who might accuse them of causing jobs to be lost in their district. The Caribbean felt very let down by some members of the Black Caucus who pledged their support for CBI Enhancement but voted against the Caribbean Partnership Act. The most glaring example was Congressman Major Owens who represented more Caribbean Americans than any other elected official. He was brought to "heel" after being harshly criticized by Caribbean radio programs in the New York area, and the *Carib News*, a New York based newspaper owned and operated by Jamaicans, Karl and Fay Rodney.[19] His support solidified when challenged for the Democratic Party nomination by Jamaican Councilwoman Una Clarke, during 2000.

A lobbyist can assist a government in disseminating its message by arranging for its visibility in publications that are read by policy-makers and congressional representatives. Jamaica's lobbyist, Neill and Company records that it "worked to reinforce Ambassador Bernal as a leading voice in support of Caribbean parity with NAFTA. As part of that strategy, we worked with Ambassador Bernal to develop positions and statements that he could advance, which would then be embraced by policy-makers and disseminated by the media. We then worked to circulate those statements for maximum effect." The following excerpts are examples of Ambassador Bernal's contributions on NAFTA parity for the Caribbean, which were communicated throughout Washington. These include: (a) "If NAFTA takes effect next January, United States/Caribbean commerce could erode by next spring," in *United States/Latin Trade*, May 1993. (b) "If NAFTA takes effect next January, United States/Caribbean commerce could erode by next Spring," in "The North American Free Trade Agreement Position Paper," Congressional Black Caucus News Release, June 24, 1993. (c) "If NAFTA takes effect next January, United

States/Caribbean commerce could erode by next spring, the caucus said,"
in the Bureau of National Affairs report on CBC NAFTA position, June
28, 1993. (d) "If NAFTA takes effect next January, United States/Carib-
bean commerce could erode by next Spring." – Congresswoman Barbara
Collins, reading from the CBC position paper during the House debate
on NAFTA, November 17, 1993.[20]

A critical role in the legislative process is played by the staff of the
Committee responsible for drafting the bill and mobilizing co-sponsors
and general support for the bill. The importance of committee staff is well
known to seasoned lobbyists but is often overloked by ambassadors and
representatives of foreign governemnts. A balance has to be struck between interacting with staff while forgoing face to face meetings with
Congressional Representatives and Senators. Meetings should always be
requested with the Representatives who will have their key staff official
present in the meeting but if a meeting cannot be arranged because of
sceduling or in the interest of time the alternative of an exchange with
senior staff members must not be refused. Such a meeting scores with the
staff member because it follows them and elevates their status among
their peers and in any case they are the persons who will be briefing the
members of Congress and writing the language in the bill. In the case of
the CBI there were two key staff members in the Ways and Means Committee, Mary Jane Wignott, staff director for the Democrats and Meredith
Broadbent, staff director for the Republicans. They were extremely hard
working and very knowledgeble and were of indispensible help on the
mechanics of the legislative process and in sharing their "readings" of the
politics of the process.

The Executive

The Clinton Administration throughout its eight years reiterated its
commitment to enhancing market access for the CBI countries by supporting new legislation. The President in particular repeatedly stated his
commitment to this objective; however, his directives to the bureaucracy
were not met with total compliance as the United States Trade Representative's (USTR) Office always had reservations. President Clinton that the
CBI should be upgraded because of the negative impact of NAFTA explaining that "one of the unintended consequences of our trade agreement with Canada and Mexico is that Mexico seems to get a comparative
benefit over the Caribbean countries, which we never intended to happen."[21] President Clinton's Special Envoy to Latin America and the Ce-
ribbean, Mack McLarty, a life long friend of the President and a sucessful
business executive with considerable diplomatic skills was a tireless and
effective advocate for CBI enhancement. When he chose to demit from
office it was a loss to the CBI cause before approprite legislation was

passed. His replacement Buddy McKay was never as influential as he did not have the "ear" of President Clinton as did Mack McLarty.

The CBI legislation was never a political priority for the Administration and therefore did not receive the kind of attention necessary for success, e.g., an organized campaign of persuasion in Congress. The CBI received the attention and conviction of the President's closest and most influential advisor, Thomas "Mack" McLarty, when he was special envoy to Latin America and the Caribbean. But even this effort was nothing compared to the campaign to secure the passage of the North American Free Trade Agreement, which was led by the President himself and involved most of the menbers of the Cabinet. Indeed, the CBI was not only of secondary importance but was even seen as complicating the Congressional approval of more important trade legislation such as the passage of NAFTA and the WTO. The statements of President Clinton[22] and U.S. Trade Representative Kantor were preoccupied with NAFTA, the Uruguay Round and APEC without any mention of the CBI.[23]

McLarty's advocacy was impeded repeatedly by organized labor working through other well placed officials such as Leon Panetta, then Chief of Staff of the White House. Some representatives of organized labor, especially in the textile and apparel industries resented grossly exaggerated figures of job losses, which without definitive proof were attributed to NAFTA and predicting more of the same if an enhanced CBI was to be approved by Congress. They argued that the jobs lost was Ross Perot's "great sucking sound." This ploy resonated with the American public who were never fully convinced of the benefits of free trade as was evident by the 76 percent who in the early 1990s believed that international trade agreements caused job losses.[24] They resorted to an even more pernicious gambit of pointing to cases of human rights abuses and lack of trade union representation in parts of Central America as both an unfair advantage and an abhorent breach of basic human rights. On at least one occasion the White House deferred pressing for the CBI during the finalization of the budget. The CARICOM countries were never cited by organized labor spokespersons for worker rights as they have world class standards. In the case of Jamaica, the country was always cited favorably in the annual report of the State Department to Congress on economic policy and trade practices.[25] Ambassador Bernal made it a central point to emphasize this as a "plus" for the countries of the ESC and an indication of their willingness to participate in fair trade.

The efforts of the Caribbean and Central American countries were ceaseless and consistent at every level of their governments and the business community. On every occasion when any of the Prime Ministers of the ESC states met either individually or collectively with President Clinton, the need to pass legislation upgrading the views to the U.S. market provided by the CBI was always emphasized. This was one of the priority issues when Prime Minister P. J. Patterson met with Clinton in Washington in 1995 and was a focal point of the United States-CARICOM Summit in Bridgetown, Barbados in May 1997. The Central American countries on several occasions sent joint Presidential and Ministerial delegations to Washington to make the rounds of the State Department, Congress, business associations, and the press. Ministers and Prime Ministers from the CARICOM states made lobbying for the CBI a core part of their missions to Washington but only on one occaision did a CARICOM Prime Minister (Prime Minister Panday of Trinidad and Tobago) go to Washington, D.C., specifically to press the case for CBI, and even then it was as part of a Central America-Caribbean team.

The political directorate used major fora and meetings in the United States to try to influence the legislative process, for example, the annual Miami Conference organized by the Caribbean-Latin American Action. Prime Minister P. J. Patterson of Jamaica in his keynote address to the conference of December 2000 stressed that the "CARICOM has campaigned long and hard for CBI enhancement. Ever since the passage of the NAFTA six years ago, CARICOM states have sought for a leveling of the playing field regarding access to the United States market so as to enable CARICOM and other CBI beneficiary nations to compete for new investments in the region on a more secure footing" and to emphasize that the CBI is "a larger market for the United States goods, than France, Brazil or even China." [26]

The visits of delegations of Presidents and Prime Ministers from the CBI countries served to highlight the importance of the enhancement of the CBI to the future of the region. It also ensured that there were meetings with the very highest levels of U.S. government, something that which diplomatic representatives find difficult to achieve. [27] For example, in September 1999, such a delegation from the region was able to meet with Senators Trent Lott (Majority Leader), Senator William Roth (Chairman of the Fanance Committee) and Senators Moynihan, Grassley, Graham, Nickles, and Coverdell. Similarly in the House, they had a single meeting with all the key members, namely Bill Archer, Chairman of the Ways and Means Committee, ranking Democrat Charles Rangel, Phil Crane, Chairman of the Trade Subcommittee, and ranking Democrat Sander Levin.

The security implications of trade and investment diversion from the CBI region because of NAFTA was a theme that was frequently stressed to the White House by the leadership on the region. The spectre of political instability was alluded to, increased drug trafficking was hinted at, and the possibility of increased illegal migrants was elicited in many presentations. The CBI enhancemant was also suggested as the appropriate transition to hemispheric free trade and a consolidation of economic reforms and the entrenchment of the market economy. At one stage the support of the governors throughout the United States was solicited as a way of pressuring the Clinton Administration to see the CBI as a partial solution to the vexed U.S.-EU banana dispute.[28]

Bureaucracy

The USTR was never convinced of the merits of preferential trade arrangements such as those in the extant CBI and was even more skeptical of the validity of further extending non-reciprocal trade arrangments to the region. Ambassador Barshefsky and her senior advisors were committed to free trade for all countries regardless of size and level of development. This objective was pursued at the multilateral, hemispheric, and bilateral levels and the priorities were on large markets such as the EU, Japan, and China. Considerable time and resources were absorbed in the negotiations for NAFTA and the subsequent difficult task of securing congressional passage but little effort by comparison was devoted to CBI enhancement. Barshefsky made this position explicit in testimony to the powerful Ways and Means Committee of the House of Representatives in February 1995 when she stated reservations on H.R. 553 The Caribbean Basin Trade Security Act rather than expressing the administration's full support when the Clinton Administration was publicly committed to upgrading the CBI. She put on the record that "the single most important objection that the administration has to the bill as currently drafted is that the bill provides benefits without corresponding obligations on the part of the Caribbean"adding the admonishment that the "CBI nations must begin now to do more to get ready for free trade than they have done thus far."[29]

The USTR did concede the need for CBI parity with NAFTA because Mexico benefitted from duty free treatment of apparel whereas apparel from the CBI countries were still subject to duties.[30] This was a point that Richard Feinberg in the National Security Council tried to emphasize within the Clinton Administration and assured the region that there would be "measures intended to allay their concerns over the impact of NAFTA on their economies."[31] The Assistant Secretary for Inter-American Affairs predicted in March 1994 that "we will announce momentarily measures thar will address the concerns of CBI countries about the impact of NAFTA on their trade with the United States."[32] Menbers of the Congressional Black Caucus sought to highlight the concerns of the CBI countries in the House and in their representations to the Administration. The State Department was consistently supportive of the CBI enhancement campaign because it saw this as a way of stablizing democracy in Central America and the Caribbean with minimum impact on the Federal budget. The Commerce Department was committed to the legislation as it believed that this could generate exports and employment. The views of the State Department and supportive members of Congress were treated askance and often downplayed on the basis that these sympathetic elements did not fully appreciate the procreative power of free trade and the rationale of U.S. trade policy.

The U.S. legislative system is the most open and transparent in the world as it permits all interested parties whether national or foreign to participate. The separation of powers is such that if the executive wants an act passed in the Congress it has to arrange for a bill to be introduced in the House and companion legislation in the Senate. In the process members of either chamber of Congress may modify the bill including in ways that the Administration disagrees with and may prompt the administration to lobby against that provision. If the provision is sufficiently abhorrent to the President he can try to have it expunged by announcing his intention to veto the bill when it is sent to him for signature. This is sometimes enough to kill off an obnoxious bill or provision in a bill but there are ways for Congress to override the President's veto; however, differences are usually settled or compromises negotiated before this eventuality. When foreign interests are involved situations have occurred where the Administration and a foreign government join forces to lobby against a bill introduced in Congress or the Administration opposes a bill that was tabled in Congress with concurrence and support of a foreign government or governments.

Situations in which foreign governments are involved in the legislative process are usually bills concerning foreign aid or trade. For example in the early 1980s the U.S. trade negotiations with Japan ended up with the U.S. and Japanese governments collaborating to forestall proposed legislation in Congress that would not be helpful to either side and complicate the negotiations. Prestowitz recalls that "top officials were testifying in Washington against the proposed legislation. The President had said he would veto it. To persuade the Japanese to make concessions, we had to frighten them by suggesting that, despite our best efforts, we might not be able to restrain Congress. Implicitly we were linking ourselves in common cause with the Japanese" and "the U.S. trade team became an advisor to the government of Japan on how to handle the U.S. Congress."[33]

In case of CBI enhancement the USTR was not able to agree with the pro-CBI group in the House led by Sam Gibbons, Phil Crane, and Charles Rangel and Bob Graham in the Senate. The USTR differed with the pro-CBI group on whether the CBI was a U.S. trade priority, on when if ever there was a propitious time to introduce CBI enhancement legislation, and what provisions the bill should incorporate. The USTR whether acting on its own contrary to public pronouncements by the President or acting with the knowledge of the White House consistently stalled the process of enacting legislation to upgrade the CBI. The USTR insisted that the Administration would "draft its own bill, which would build on prior proposals in an effort to obtain both industry and Congressional support"[34] when collaboration with the leadership in Congress was the most efficacious way to ensure congressional support.

First, the introduction of CBI related legislation would complicate and even jeopardize the passage of legislation to allow the GATT and NAFTA to come into operation and lowering tariffs had fiscal implications that would be difficult to justify in the contentious and protracted budget process and therefore the administration sought the inclusion of provisions on the GATT bill. The program was estimated to cost $200 million a year for five years. Later the same administration decided to pull the proposal ostensibly for the fiscal fallout but in reality the spectre of displaced unionized apparel workers would have cost the administration an undetermined number of votes for the overall GATT legislative package.

Second, the USTR was not in agreement with any version of the CBI bill that did not emanate from their chambers, even bills that were introduced in Congress that were acceptable to the pro-CBI members of Congress, the domestic industry, and the Central American and Caribbean countries. Indeed, the USTR always introduced their own bill with significant differences with those already tabled in Congress. Examples of different coexisting bills are show in appendices H and I. This complicated the process considerably because it caused fractions among the members who were willing to support CBI enhancement because it put them in the embarassing dilemma that if they supported the pro-CBI bill they would be out of sync with the Administration, which claimed to be in favor of CBI enhancement, and if they supported the Administration's bill they would have to part company with the pro-CBI coalition.

U.S. Business Sector

In the normal process of legislation, the members of the House and Senate pay very close attention to the needs and desires of the business community, not only because of their financial contributions, but because of their commitment to promoting business and commerce, although business never speaks with one voice and there are differing views. In this case there was a split between the textile sector and the apparel industry that was never fully resolved as they were deprived the legislation of full blown support from the U.S. business communty. The textile interests led by the American Textile Manufacturers Institute (ATMI) fought doggedly to prevent or severely limit the use of non-U.S. fabric in the production of apparel qualified for CBI treatment. This of course was an attempt to preserve export markets and to maintain production and employment in the manufacturing of textiles in the United States, a sector uncompetitive by global standards in most lines of production.

The apparel manufacturers were represented by the American Apparel Manufacturers Association (AAMA), which represents 23,515 manufacturers[35]; three-fourths have sales of under $20 million, 70 percent of

U.S. preduction, and 700,000 manufacturing jobs.[36] The AAMA was interested in the lowest cost of production for U.S. firms regardless of where the fabric was sourced and therefore did not support limiting fabric to U.S. made textiles. Spokespersons like Larry Martin, President of the AAMA were opposed to fabric limitations because their members wanted to source production from the CBI region at the lowest possible cost. Having already benefitted from lower than U.S. wages in the CBI countries, they sought to further lower cost of production by using non-U.S. fabric, whether regional in origin or imported from outside the United States-CBI ambit. The AAMA made the argument that upgrading the CBI to parity with NAFTA was essential because "the United staes cannot afford the advantage it created in its own backyard through the CBI. To remain competitive in the global market and to preserve a high valued-added U.S. employment base, our companies must be allowed to make full use of a partnership with the Caribbean Basin."[37]

Both the apparel and the textile sectors maintained well-financed and professionally staffed lobbying campaigns aimed at the White House, USTR, the Congress, and the media. Their different messages, especially when couched in the technical jargon of the textile-apparel industry, served to confuse all but the trade cognoscenti resulting in many members of Congress and their staff giving up in frustration, gaining no understanding of the issue. The protagonists waged an unrelenting campaign resulting in the legislation in different forms failing to pass the House on several occasions.

The U.S. business sector other than the textile and apparel companies showed little or no interest in the CBI, largely because many of these sectors or industries did not stand to gain directly from improved access to the U.S. market by CBI countries. Although most of the largest companies in the United States operate in the CBI, many of them were either engaged in the export of goods and services or their imports from the region were already given duty free, quota free entry. In the case of U.S. businesses in Jamaica, the list included numerous powerful multinational corporations such as Alcoa, Kaiser, Citibank, American Airlines, KPMG Peat Marwick, Johnson and Johnson, International Business Machines (IBM), Colgate Palmolive, Sherwin Williams, Xerox, 3-M, Esso Standard Oil, Shell, Texaco, Gillette, Goodyear, Hanes, McDonalds, Burger King, Holiday Inn, and Wyndham.[38] Despite repeated letters, meetings, and telephone calls with senior executives and their lobbyists and Washington representatives, there were virtually no tangible expressions of support for enhanced CBI legislation. In 1991, Ambassador Bernal went as far as meeting with David Rockefeller, founder of Chase Manhattan Bank in New York and Chairman of the U.S. Business Committee on Jamaica in the mid 1980s in the hope of capitalizing on his prominence. The meeting did reawaken his interest in Jamaica and he was persuaded to reconvene the committee to update members who were all executives of Fortune 500 companies on investment opportunities in Jamaica. He also was asked to support legislation to enhance the CBI, however, it was hard to identify his influence. A few U.S. companies did make representations to the bureaucracy and the Congress, i.e., Amoco Trinidad Oil Company[39] as well as Caribbean/Latin American Action.[40]

The American Textile Manufacturers Institute (ATMI) is the national trade association for the domestic textile industry. Member companies operate in more than 30 states and process approximately 80 percent of all textile fibers consumed by plants in the United States. The industry employs approximately 600,000 people. The Washington, D.C.-based ATMI is the U.S. textile industry's primary advocate with the legislative and administrative branches of the federal government as well as the news media. The ATMI's activities encompass lobbying, international trade, product and administrative services, communications, and economic information. Carlos Moore, executive vice president took the lead in the association's lobbying for new legislation to adjust the CBI. The ATMI represents the manufacturers primarily in the textile mill products industry and is "one the strongest and most influential"[41] industry associations that lobby Congress, the USTR, and the White House. The organization has a record of influence, for example, its role during the passage of NAFTA.

The Caribbean/Latin American Action (CLAA), an association of firms and business executives from the United States, Latin America, Central America, and the Caribbean lobbied vigorously for CBI enhancement, under the energetic leadership of its long serving executive director Peter Johnson and later on Tito Colorado. It certainly made an impact on American elected officials when Johnson could say before Congress that the CBI was in the interest of the United States and upgrading it was desired by the 120 U.S. corporations that were members of CLAA. The CLAA devoted a member of staff, Bennett Marsh, to following the CBI and regularly held briefings for ambassadors and officials from the embassies of CBI countries.

These meetings were a useful opportunity for CBI diplomats to exchange views with executives of CLAA and U.S. businessmen to plan strategy. The organization also annually hosted a week-end long retreat in Annapolis, Maryland, that brought together officials from embassies, U.S. government, and the business communities of the Caribbean and the United States. For example, the retreat on February 25–28, 1994, was attended by 60 persons included representatives from Caribbean embassies, the State Department, USTR, U.S. Agency for International Development, Department of Commerce, Department of Agriculture, Caribbean Association of Industry and Commerce, FEDEPRICAP, Caribbean Council for Europe, the House Subcommittee on Trade, AAMA, Greenberg Traurig, Holland and Knight, and Manchester Trade. Company executives included U.S. firms with investments in the CBI region, e.g., RJR

Nabisco, U.S. citizens managing subsidiaries in the Caribbean such as William Maloney of Tropicana Holdings in Jamaica, and major Caribbean firms, e.g., Goddard Enterprises of Barbados. In a rare appearance some of the most important businessmen from the ESC were in attendance, such as Sidney Knox of Neal and Massey of Trinidad and Tobago and Yesu Persaud of Demerara Distillers in Guyana.[42] The resulting Congresional testimonies and communiques of the CLAA consistently advocated the enhancement of the CBI and NAFTA parity on the basis that it was good for both the CBI countries and the United States.[43] The CLAA also produced the annual Miami Conference, the biggest gathering of U.S. and Caribbean private and public sector leadership, which over the last 20 years has been a platform to air Caribbean issues such as the CBI.[44]

Lobbyists

Trade legislation such as that required to effect an enhancement of the CBI attracts the attention of lobbysts, both those on contract to foreign governments, individual corporate clients, industry associations, and even the federal government and those who are soliciting business. Some large lobbying firms with a capability to service the full spectrum of issues before Congress and departmaents and agencies of the federal government keep a watching brief to provide information to its client list and to be prepared if approached on the issues by an existing or potential client. A big lobbying outfit must have an awareness of as many issues as is practical so that an existing client will not seek the services of other firm; in other words a large lobbying firm must be a one-stop lobbying "supermarket." A lobbying firm that is monitoring an issue for one client can recycle some and sometimes all of the information it has garnered to other existing or potential clients to arouse their need to be aware of the issue; hence the "leg-work" and expenses can be spread over several clients and generate a bigger return. Greenberg and Truig were prominent on behalf of a variety of domestic and overseas clients.

Many large corporations and industry associations such as the ATMA and the AAMA have an in-house lobbyst or lobbying section as well as a public relations officer or public relations firm. Some firms have former high level officials such as a former Secretary of the Treasury or Commerce or Agriculture on their board of directors or as a consultant with a view to deploying their influence and contacts in Congress or the White House or bureaucracy. Yet another model is to have on call a general lobbyist who would identify and arrange for the services of specialists when the situation warrants such highly specialized capability.

Lobbyists lubricate the legislative process by shuttling between the Congress and interested corporations and governments. They are particularly useful to foreign governments that do not have the contacts or the expertise to outline their concerns and goals to the key members of Congress. Several lobbying firms were involved on behalf of a variety of interested parties, both domestic and foreign. For example, former Congressman Bob Walker, President of the Wexler Group, was the convenor of the meeting between majority leader Senator Trent Lott (R-Mississippi) and Presidents and Prime Ministers of Central America and the Caribbean in September 1999. George Dalley of Holland and Knight was the central link in a similar meeting with Congressman Charles Rangel, ranking Democrat on the House Committee on Ways and Means.[45]

The specialist trade consultant is yet another species of operative providing advisory services to corporations, foreign governments, and business associations. They are lobbyists but are very small operations sometime an individual, but usually a former government official with knowledge of or experience in a particular area of trade. This might be a particular industry, e.g., apparel or a commodity, e.g., sugar or a specific trade pact, e.g., NAFTA or institution, e.g., the World Trade Organization, or a region of the world, e.g., Latin America. These consultants/lobbyists by assisting participants and injecting their knowledge and ideas in the legislative process, add "grease" to the wheels. Steve Lande of Manchester Trade, a former USTR official, was a knowledgeable "bee" dispensing pollen to the process of CBI enhancement on behalf of clients (Costa Rica, El Salvador, Honduras, and Guatemala) and in his own right. Lobbyists working for clients with the same or similar objectives often collaborate rather than compete on issues that involve many interested paties and require a majority in the House and Senate to ensure the desired outcome. This is in contrast to situations in which a member can single-handedly attach an amendment to a bill that may have absolutely nothing to do with the subject of the amendment. Collaboration facilitates a sharing of the workload, avoids duplication of effort, which can cause confusion, and allows each lobbyist to concentrate on their specialization. In the case of the CBI an informal coordinating committee was formed consisting of lobbyists, business organizations, and diplomatic representatives of CBI governments.

Think Tanks

The think tanks did not devote much attention to the issue of CBI enhancement as the Caribbean was either not part of their research agenda or represented a subset of concerns with U.S. foreign policy towards Latin America. For example, the Cato Institute in its review of the foreign policy of the two Clinton administrations only mentioned Cuba and even then listed it among the "second-tier problems."[46] Few major publications were devoted to this subject with the exception of the Centre for Strategic International Studies (CSIS)[47] and the North-South Center of the University of Miami. The CBI was mentioned in several publications dealing with wider issues such as Latin America, and U.S. foreign and

trade policy, e.g., by the North-South Center on NAFTA.[48] Expert witnesses from think tanks gave testimony to Congress, e.g., Professor Anthony Bryan of the North-South Center[49] and Georges A. Fauriol of CSIS.
Think tanks used the print media to help mobilize public opinion in
support of CBI enhancement.[50]

The limited engagement of the majority of think tanks was not for lack
of efforts to secure their active involvement in the issue. For example, a
determined attempt was made to garner the support of the Heritage
Foundation, the influencial conservative think tank that was regularly
opining on trade issues. The CBI was a preferential trade arrangement
and therefore ran counter to the free trade philosophy that it was prose-
lytizing. Some prominent scholars in think tanks developed an appreciation for the CBI issues, e.g., John Sewell, Overseas Development Council,
Peter Hakim, Inter-American Dialogue, and Joseph Tulchin, the Woodrow Wilson Center, but this did not extend to the institution sectors.

The work of some think tanks focused on trade issues other than the
CBI inadvertently made the passage of legislation to enhance the CBI a
more difficult task. Those think tanks that expressed concerns about the
harmful impact of NAFTA on employment in the United States helped to
create an atmosphere in which the majority of Americans believed that all
trade agreements resulted in increased unemployment and increased imports. Such claims were reaching and influencing an American public
where 61 percent admitted that they were "not knowledgeable about
trade."[51] A series of reports from the Economic Policy Institute (EPI)
proclaimed in graphic and shrill language the doom of "job destruction,"
"disappearing jobs," and "employment casualties" resulting from NAF-
TA.[52] This type of protectionist diatribe resonated with the public more
than the advocates of free trade and trade liberalization[53] from the highly
respected institutions like the Institute for International Economics,[54]
Center for Strategic and International Studies,[55] Organization for Economic Co-operation and Development,[56] and the Brookings Institution.[57]

The EOI made the fantastic claim that "Since 1994, 340,000 jobs have
been lost in the textile and apparel industries, primarily because of a
flood on imports from Mexico and the Caribbean."[58] This kind of apparently well researched missive served to intimidate Congressional Representatives whose inclination was to support trade liberalization and trade
bills like the CBI enhancement. Some members of Congress who had
been persuaded to support the passage of NAFTA were so worried about
the views of voters in their districts that they were afraid to support
legislation for CBI enhancement. This was a torturous dilemma for many
Democrats especially members of the Congressional Black Caucus who
depended heavily on the support of organized labor. The vast majority of
the CBC did stand up for their convictions and voted for the Africa
Growth and Opportunity Act (AGOA), which included provisions to enhance the CBI.

Media

The small countries of Central America and the Caribbean are limited in the amount of money they can afford to spend on the employment of professional lobbyists and therefore see the print media as a way of galvanizing public support for their causes. Opinion editorials appeared in the *Wall Street Journal*, the *Washington Post*, the *Journal of Commerce*, and the *Washington Times* written by Presidents of Central American countries, e.g., Costa Rican President Angal Rodriguez[59] and by the Ambassador of Jamaica to the United States.[60] The Executive through Thomas "Mack" McLarty[61] wrote opinion editorials in support of expanding trade with the Americas[62] and executives and spokespersons for the competing business interests frequently expressed their views in the media. Ambassader Bernal's opinion editorial in the *Wall Street Journal* gained considerate attention.[63]

There were two aspects of engaging the press on the CBI issue: first, to interest the major media houses in following the developments on the CBI, and second, to get the Caribbean perspective inserted in whatever coverage was given to the issue. Unfortunately, the CBI was not an issue that was regarded as a foreign policy priority by the mainstream media and could not compete with issues that were more exciting, e.g., the restoration of democracy in Haiti in the midst of stemming the tide of refugees or perennial controversies that appealed to a vocal constituency, e.g., the Arab-Israeli conflict. To get the issue on the agenda of influential media was not easy and the Caribbean had to resort to tactics such as a meeting between the editorial staff of the *Washington Post* and the ambassadors of the CARICOM countries, e.g., in 1992 with Mike Getler, managing editor for foreign affairs, or the occasional breakfast briefing by Ambassador Bernal at the National Press Club or speech at a think tank, e.g., the CSIS. These press opportunities had to capitalize on the visit of a Prime Minister/Minister[64] or some event or occurrence that was newsworthy from a U.S. point of view but could then be used to air a wide range of issues and proposals and to provide important background information. For example, Ambassador Bernal's media luncheon at the National Press Club was arranged because there was interest in Jamaica's positions on the EAI, Haiti, and drugs but the occasion was also used to present the case for NAFTA parity and to highlight Jamaica's economic reforms.[65]

Another technique was to attend a highly visible press conference and ask a question or make a comment on the CBI. The Caribbean and Central American spokespersons had to overcome the tendency of U.S. journalists to use only Americans as sources on foreign policy or trade matters. This had to be addressed by establishing representatives from the region as credible sources on the CBI issue. Regular testimonies to Congress, speeches to think tanks, and opinion editorials were used to spread the word and to establish Ambassador Bernal as a spokesperson or source on the CBI and other Caribbean issues. Once this had been done the Embassy did not have to initiate media contacts but also responded to requests for background information, comments, and interviews, e.g., the *Miami Herald* and the *Washington Post*. This type of relationship was also developed with the specialized trade press where very few Embassy officials felt sufficiently comfortable on technical issues, e.g., with the very influential *Inside U.S. Trade*.

In addition to the econmoic arguments justifying the modification of the CBI, the importance of its contribution to political stability and security were alluded to particulatly in regard to Central America. For example, President Callejas of Honduras warned even before the NAFTA negotiations were completed that it would "put the CBI countries at a comparative disadvantage with Mexico in attracting trade and investment."[66] In making the point of the adverse impact that NAFTA was likely to have on U.S.-CBI trade, care had to be exercised not to offend the proponents of current U.S. trade policy. For example when the Central Americans met Ambassador Carla Hills of USTR in August 1991 they raised their concerns only after expressing support for NAFTA and the Enterprise for the Americas.[67]

Another tactic employed to gain a sufficient number of votes to pass the enhanced CBI was to capitalize on the devasting impact of Hurricane Mitch in Central America by arguing that this made the CBI enhancement even more needed and urgent.[68] Thousands were made homeless, productive capacity was destroyed or damaged, and workers and farmers became temporarily unemployed. It was estimated that it would take years for the affected countries to restore the agricultural production and apparel manufacturing. The Minister of Foreign Trade of Costa Rica publicly implored the United States to provide "aid plus trade" to the region.[69] The campaign mainly by three Central American governments to capitalize on the misfortune caused by hurricanes elicited some empathy in Congress[70] and this allowed Congressman Phil Crane (D-Illinois), Chairman of the House Ways and Means Committee to introduce HR 984, the Caribbean and Central American Relief and Economic Stabilization Act. This Act was intended to improve trade benefits of the CBI and provide assistance to countries affected by Hurricanes Mitch and Georges. Empathetic voices such as Mack McLarty and Congressman Jim Kolbe (R) of Arizona took up the battle cry in support of CBI enhancement.[71] They were complemented by some think tanks and the U.S. apparel sector, e.g., the President of the American Uniform Company who wrote to Congressman Ben Gilman to express his "unqualified support for congressional efforts to include a CBI provision in the Hurricane Relief legislation currently being drafted."[72]

A concerted campaign was undertaken by the Embassy of Jamaica under the direction of the Ambassador using a list of Caribbean professionals in U.S. media, especially the print media to ensure that the CBI issue was featured and the Jamaican and Caribbean perspective was mentioned. This took the form of briefings either in person or more often by phone and making available information by fax to be passed to strategically placed journalists covering trade and/or foreign policy and/or the Caribbean. Such contacts can also be useful in situations requiring damage control, e.g., a Jamaican in Reuters calls the home of her ambassador at 1 am to alert him of a report stating that he had made damaging statements at a meeting of the Black Caucus. The ambassador, who had not attended any such meeting, was able to correct the erroneous report before it was disseminated.[73] Relations with the Caribbean community newspapers and local radio broadcasts were instrumental in keeping the Caribbean community across the United States informed and mobilized, e.g., *Carib News* in New York. Tony Best of the *Carib News* followed the CBI issue very closely and was the doyen of the purveyors of information and opinion to the ESC community.

Business Sector of the CBI Countries

The business sector of the CBI has a long history of lobbying in support of CBI legislation dating back to the original legislative process in 1983 and continuing on a reduced scale into the 1990s. The most involved were those associated with the manufacturing sector, in particular, those exporting apparel to the United States. The apparel sector is of particular importance to Jamaica and consequently the Jamaican private sector was active in letter writing and joining government officials in meeting with members of Congress, the State Department, USTR, and with their counterparts from Central America. The strategic alliance between the business sectors of the ESC and Central America was important in providing a consistent and unified position from the region. The Central American and Caribbean Textiles and Apparel Council (CACTAC) is an interest group that represents the textile and apparel industry members from all CBI countries. Among the leading spokespersons for the region was Peter King of Jamaica who was an active participant in CACTAC and other regional business organizations. The CACTAC has been the most organized and effective business sector organization participating in the lobbying effort. They made numerous visits at appropriate times and met with a wide cross-section of congressional leaders, government officials, and representatives of the U.S. textile and apparel industry. They were able to make common cause with the apparel manufacturers and apparel importers in the United States and were therefore able to reinforce the message from these interests and to present the U.S.-CBI business position.

The Federacion de Entidades Privados de Centro America y Panama, in San Jose, Costa Rica, was able to speak with one voice for the business sector of Central America. The organization was active in lobbying the U.S. government under the leadership of Jose Manuel Salazar, its Executive Director. At critical junctures business associations in the ESC and Central America were mobilized to write to or call on members of Congress and officials in the bureaucracy. These included at one time or another, the American Chamber of Commerce of the Dominican Republic, American Chamber of Commerce of Trinidad and Tobago, Costa Rican-American Chamber of Commerce, Guatemala's Non-Traditional Products Exporters Association, and the Haitian–American Chamber of Commerce and Industry.[74]

ESC Community in the United States

The Embassies of the ESC in parallel action with those of the Central American countries made the attainment of new CBI legislation a well understood and strongly supported objective of their respective communities in the United States. Jamaican community organizations wrote letters to Congress and lobbied local, state, and city officials in support of an enhanced CBI. Elected representatives of Caribbean origin were particularly effective in communicating their views to members of Congress and the Senate, e.g., Delegate Shirley Natham-Pulliam always ensured that members of Congress from Baltimore were fully briefed on the importance of the CBI to the Caribbean community. New York City Councilwoman Una Clarke was tireless in keeping the Congressional Representatives of New York State fully informed on the Caribbean perspective and led more than one delegation of elected Caribbean representatives and organizations to Washington, D.C., for meetings on "the Hill."[75] On one occasion the Jamaican community organizations in Hartford were instrumental in ensuring that their member of Congress attended an important hearing at which the Jamaican Ambassador was testifying. Congresswoman Barbara Kennelly had not indicated support for enhancing CBI despite letters from Ambassador Bernal. Her presence at a hearing on the CBI by the House Ways and Means Committee on Trade in 1993 was regarded as important. Ambassador Bernal mobilized the Jamaican community organizations in Hartford, Connecticut, to pressure her to attend. She attended the hearing and supported the CBI legislation

THE PROCESS

To come back to ask for even more preferential trade "benefits" and so soon after was ungrateful and greedy. This political atmosphere was one chacterized by a certain "fatigue" with the CBI issue and the CBI was no longer a security problem as it was perceived in the early 1980s when the CBI was first broached. Given the political context it was necessary to find some new and urgent rationale for addressing the CBI issue once again. The answer was obvious and genuine, namely the threat of NAFTA's harmful effect on U.S.-CBI trade, with apparel being a graphic example.[76] This would resonate with Congress where the apprehension about NAFTA's impact on the U.S. economy was palpable. This together with the need to exude a posture of not asking for "more" and to soft-peddle the term CBI required a repackaging of the issue. It was in this milieu that the new nomenclature, "NAFTA parity" was developed[77] to signal that there was a real problem that had to be dealt with and as quickly as possible to prevent the erosion of an important foreign policy and trade policy initiative which stood to the credit of Congress. The use of the term NAFTA parity was also intended to communicate that the CBI countries were not making a request for additional benefits but were merely asking for fair play by seeking a "level playing field" in hemispheric trade.

The prevailing wisdom among the Administration, Congress (Representaives and staff), and the lobbying cognoscenti was that another stand-alone CBI upgrade bill would not generate the necessary political traction especially as there were other more engaging or unavoidable bills on the legislative agenda. The rationale for the Administration's proposal of the Caribbean Basin Interim Trade Program/Initiative is instructive because it reveals the thinking on CBI policy. Treasury Secretary Lloyd Bentsen said that the proposal was made "because we believed it would be a good way to work towards our long-term goal of an expanded free trade area in the hemisphere by establishing some mutually beneficial measures to be taken by the United States and the CBI countries as building blocks."[78] It was decided with the concurrence of the anxious supplicants from the CBI region that the best possibility was to attach the CBI bill or provisions to a bill that had to be voted on and ideally one that could not be postponed.

First, it was thought that it could be attached or be part of a package with the legislation to ratify and bring into force the Uruguay Round Agreement. Unfortunately this bill encountered unanticipated and virulent debate about where it when too far by impinging on U.S. sovereignty and where it did not go far enough to protect vital U.S. interests such as intellectual property rights. The administration in tandem with the bureaucracy decided it was too risky and that it might complicate the passage of the far more important Uruguay Round legislation.

Second, having been unceremoniously dropped from the immediate legislative agenda of the administration the pro-CBI forces regrouped and look out for the next legislative vehicle. The opportunity seized on was to attach the CBI to the implementing legislation for NAFTA; however, this was fraught with even more difficulties and again the administration decided not to proceed, a decision that was disappointing to the CBI region but was a politically astute decision as the NAFTA vote was extremely close and bitterly debated. The NAFTA was eventually approved by a very narrow margin and only after a massive campaign in the administration with the personal involvement of President Clinton had "pulled out all the stops."

Third, after two failed attempts to attach the CBI bill or provisions to other pieces of legislation the strategy that emerged was to include it in a package of legislation that had to be approved by Congress. The one legislative function that Congress must execute annually is to pass the Federal budget. In 1995, Bill Archer, Chairman of the Committee on Ways and Means proposed the inclusion of "H.R. 553, The Caribbean Basin Trade Security Act, in the budget reconciliation bill" and further signaled that he intended to "consider it as a separate matter later this year."[79] The budget seemed to be the best "engine" to which to couple the CBI "car," so this was done, only to find that in succeeding years the CBI made it to the final reconciliation conference only to be omitted or passed over in "trading."

Fourth, a number of CBI bills were attempted in an atmosphere where all parties including the reluctant USTR felt that this was a long overdue commitment that needed to be fulfilled. The bills were beset by opposition from the textile industry and organized labor and would-be supporters were in trepidation of losing voters during their re-elections or financial contributions. The fact that the USTR always tabled its own bill at variance with those proposed in the House and Senate and with the optimistic urging of the CBI countries only made passage more difficult. Bills originating in Congress were passed in Committee on several occasions but never made it to a full House vote.

Finally, a long neglected issue, the persistent poverty and in places the increasing impoverishment of Africa and the decimation inflicted by the AIDS epidemic, aroused the compassion of the American public. It became an issue that no "right thinking" person could ignore and in response to a growing public sentiment and the forceful advocacy of the Congressional Black Caucus forcing the administration and Congress craft trade legislation for Africa. Although there were strongly expressed differences including among the Black Caucus on the appropriate bill, the Africa Growth and Opportunity Act together with the CBI bill was passed in May 2000, by 309–110 votes in the House and by 77–19 in the Senate.

CONCLUSION

Jamaica played a central role in the drafting and passage of the CBERA legislation in a political environment that was not particularly receptive. The outcome and the experience demonstrate that a small country by mobilizing strategic international alliances and building common interest with coalitions of domestic interests in the United States can influence U.S. foreign policy.

NOTES

1. Richard L. Bernal, "Foreign Investment and Development in Jamaica," Inter-American Economic Affairs, Vol. 38, No. 2 (Autumn, 1984) pages 3–21.
2. Vladimir N. Pregelj, "U.S. Foreign Trade and Investment Policy in the Caribbean Basin Region," in The Caribbean Basin Economic and Security Issues. Joint Economic Committee Print (S. Print. 102–10) (Washington, D.C.: Government Printing Office, 1993) page 332.
3. The U.S. International Trade Commission pointed out that, "Overall, levels of new investment in beneficiary countries (CBI) region remain disappointingly low." See annual report on the impact of the Caribbean Basin Economic Recovery Act on U.S. Industries and Consumers No. 2225 (Washington, D.C.: U.S. International Trade Commission, 1992).
4. Richard L. Bernal and Steve Lamar, Caribbean Basin Economic Development and the Section 936 Tax Credit. North-South Agenda Paper, No. 22 (Miami: North-South Center, University of Miami, December 1996).
5. Stephen A. Quick, "The International Economy and the Caribbean: The 1990s and Beyond," The Caribbean Basin: Economic and Security Issues Joint Economic Committee Print (S. Print 102–10) (Washington, D.C.: Government Printing Office, January 1993).
6. Bernal and Lamar (1996).
7. Bernal and Lamar (page 8).
8. Bernal and Lamar (1996), Richard L. Bernal, "936 Funds: Contributing to Jamaica's Development," (H.R. 5270) in hearing before the United States House of Representatives Committee on Ways and Means One Hundred and Second Congress, Second Session, July 21–22, 1992 (Washington, D.C.: U.S. Government Printing Office, 1992) pages 1075–78, Richard L. Bernal, "The Role of 936 Funds in Economic Development of Caribbean Countries," in Hearings before the Committee on Ways and Means, House of Representatives, One Hundred and Third Congress, First Session, March 23, 31 and April 1, 1993 (Washington, D.C.: U.S. Government Printing Office, 1993) pages 1305–10, and Richard L. Bernal, "A U.S.-Caribbean Tax Lifeline" The Journal of Commerce, April 16, 1993.
9. Brenda A. Jacobs, "U.S. Moves to Control 807 Trade," Bobbin, June, 1995, pages 12–17.
10. "The Caribbean Basin Initiative," in Hearings before the Subcommittee on International Economic Policy and Trade on Western Hemisphere Affairs of the Committee on Foreign Affairs, House of Representatives, One Hundredth Congress First Session, September 18 and 19, 1987 (Washington, D.C., U.S. Government Printing Office, 1987) pages 48–56; "NAFTA at Three: The Case for NAFTA Parity," Statement submitted to the House on Ways and Means Trade Subcommittee, House of Representatives, One Hundred Fifth Congress, First Session, September 11, 1997 (Washington, D.C.: Government Printing Office, 1998) pages 261–63; "The Caribbean Basin Free Trade Agreement Act" (H.R. 1403) in Hearing before the Subcommittee on Trade and the Subcommittee on Oversight of the Committee on Ways and Means, House of Representatives, One Hundred Third Congress, First Session, June 24, 1993 (Washington, D.C.: U.S. Government Printing Office, 1993) pages 68–75; Testimony on the Caribbean Basin Initiative to the Hearings before the Sub-Committee on 1987 International Economic Policy and Trade and on Western Hemispheric Affairs of the Committee on Foreign Affairs, House of Representatives, One Hundredth Congress, First Session (Washington, D.C.: Government Printing Office, 1988) pages 45–56.

11. Shelley Emling, "Hills to Hear Central Americans' Trade Pact Fears," Journal of Commerce, August 9, 1991.

12. Production Sharing: Use of U.S. components and Materials in Foreign Assembly Operations, 1991–95 (Washington, D.C.: United States International Trade Commission, USITC Publication No. 2966, May 1996) pages 5–1 to 5–3 and Second Report to Congress on the Operation of The Caribbean Basin Recovery Act (Washington, D.C.: United States Trade Representative, October 16, 1996) page 16–18.

13. Second Report to Congress on the Operation of The Caribbean Basin Economic Recovery Act (Washington, D.C.: United States Trade Representative, October 10, 1996) page 24.

14. Statement of the Hon. Bob Graham, Senator from the state of Florida, Hearing before the Subcommittee on Trade and the Subcommittee on Oversight of the Committee on Ways and Means, House of Representatives, One Hundred Third Congress, June 24, 1993 (Washington, D.C.: U.S. Government Printing Office, 1995) page 52.

15. Letter to Ambassador Dr. Richard L. Bernal from Representative Carrie Meek, Member of Congress, September 27, 1994.

16. Statement of Senator Bob Graham of Florida in Hearing before the Subcommittee on Trade of the Committee on Ways and Means, House of Representatives, One Hundred Fourth Congress, First Session, February 10, 1995 (Washington, D.C.: Government Printing Office, 1995) pages 8–10.

17. Robert B. Reich, "Trading Insecurities," Financial Times, May 20, 1999.

18. David S. Broder, "Gephardt Warns Against Trade Pact With Chile," Washington Post, March 14, 1995, page D2.

19. "NAFTA Vote Exposes False Friends," editorial, Carib News, November 18, 1997, and Tony Best, "U.S. Congress Rejects NAFTA Parity," Carib News, November 18, 1997.

20. Files of Neill and Company and various reports to the Government of Jamaica from Neill and Company.

21. Remarks by the President to the Wall Street Project Conference, The White House, Office of the Press Secretary, January 15, 1998.

22. President William J. Clinton, Remarks on the Global Economy at American University, February 26, 1993, Weekly Compilation of Presidential Documents, Vol. 29, No. 8, Monday, March 1, 1993, pages 229–330.

23. Michael Kantor, "Trade Central to America's Future in the World," U.S. Department of State Dispatch, Vol. 4, No. 20 (May 17, 1993) pages 352–53.

24. Susan Ariel Aaronson, Trade and the American Dream. A Social History of Postwar Trade Policy (Lexington: The University Press of Kentucky, 1996) page 134.

25. See for example, Report submitted to the Committee on International Relations, Committee on Ways and Means of the U.S. House of Representatives and the Committee on Foreign Relations, Committee on Finance of the U.S. Senate by the Department of State, February 1995 (Washington, D.C.: Government Printing Office, 1995) pages 387–92.

26. Delano Franklin (ed.), A Jamaican Voice in Caribbean and World Politics. P. J. Patterson. Selected Speeches 1992–2000 (Kingston: Ian Randle Publishers, 2002) pages 331–33.

27. Senators are Presidents or Cabinet members in waiting and less vulnerable to small migrant communities and it is notoriously difficult to have even a short meeting with them as they opt to relegate ambassadors to meeting with staff members. The most used technique is to agree to an appointment but be unavoidably tied up at the time and substituting staff members. To ensure that he and his foreign minister had access to Senator Sam Nunn, Ambassador Bernal traveled from Washington, D.C., to Montego Bay, Jamaica and along with Minister of Foreign Affairs and Foreign Trade David Coore attended the opening dinner of the Aspen Institute conference on Russia, Ukraine and the U.S. Response. As guests of honor the Jamaican tandem enjoyed an hour of cocktails with twenty members of the House and Senate. A valuable hour and

a half was spent at dinner with Senator Nunn who ended the evening knowing about Jamaica, its debt problem, and the need for CBI enhancement.

28. Letter to the Governors of all states from Ambassador Richard L. Bernal, February 22, 1999.

29. Statement of Hon. Charlene Barshefsky, Deputy United States Representative, Hearing before the Subcommittee on Ways and Means, House of Representatives, One Hundred Fourth Congress, February 10, 1995 (Washington, D.C.: U.S. Government Printing Office, 1995) page 19.

30. Second Report to Congress on the Operation of The Caribbean Basin Recovery Act of 1990 (Washington, D.C.: United States Trade Representative, October, 1996) pages 16–18.

31. Richard E. Feinberg, "Substantive Symmetry in Hemispheric Relations," U.S. Department of State Dispatch, Vol. 5, No. 11 (March 14, 1994).

32. Alexander F. Watson, "U.S.-Latin America Relations in the 1990's: Toward a Mature Partnership," U.S. State Department Dispatch, Vol. 5, No. 11 (March 14, 1994).

33. Clyde V. Prestowitz, Jr., Trading Places. How We Allowed Japan to Take the Lead (New York: Basic Books, 1988) page 281.

34. Letter to Ambassador Richard l. Bernal from Peter Allgeier, Associate U.S. Trade Representative for the Western Hemisphere, February 7, 1996.

35. Kitty G. Dickerson, Textiles and Apparel in the Global Economy (Englewood Cliffs, NJ: Prentice Hall, 2nd edition, 1995) page 394.

36. Testimony of Larry Martin, American Apparel Manufacturers Association, in Hearings before the Subcommittee on Trade of the Committee on Ways and Means, House of Representatives, One Hundred Fourth Congress, First Session, February 10, 1995 (Washington, D.C.: U.S. Government Printing Office, 1995) pages 93–96.

37. Letter to the Honorable President William J. Clinton from Larry Martin, President of AAMA, April 16, 1996. See "AAMA Letter on NAFTA Parity for CBI," Inside NAFTA, Vol. 3, No. 9, May 1, 1996, page 5.

38. Members Guide 1997 (Kingston: The American Chamber of Commerce of Jamaica, 1997).

39. All of these organizations submitted statements to Congressional Hearings, see Hearing before the Subcommittee on Trade of the Committee on Ways and Means, House of Representatives, One Hundred Fourth Congress, First Session, February 10, 1995 (Washington, D.C.: Government Printing Office, 1995) page 203.

40. Statement of Peter Johnson, Caribbean/Latin American Action in Hearings before the Subcommittee on Trade of the Committee on Ways and Means, House of Representatives, One Hundred Fourth Congress, First Session, February 10, 1995 (Washington, D.C.: U.S. Government Printing Office, 1995) pages 154–62.

41. Kitty G. Dickerson, Textiles and Apparel in the Global Economy (Englewood Cliffs, NJ: Prentice Hall, 2nd edition, 1995) page 394.

42. 1994 CLAA Retreat. List of Participants (Washington, D.C.: Caribbean Latin American Action, 1994).

43. Communiqué, Miami Conference on the Caribbean (Washington, D.C.: Caribbean Latin American Action, 1993).

44. Richard l. Bernal, Impact of NAFTA on the Apparel Industry in the Caribbean, Address to the Miami Conference, December 2, 1992.

45. CBI files, Embassy of Jamaica.

46. Jonathan G. Clarke, A Foreign Policy Report Card on the Clinton-Gore Administration, Policy Analysis No. 382 (Washington, D.C.: Cato Institute, October 3, 2000) pages 10–11.

47. Steve Lande and Nellis Crigler, "CBI and NAFTA Provisions Compared" in Georges A. Fauriol and G. Philip Hughes, U.S.-Caribbean Relations into the 21st Century (Washington, D.C.: Center for Strategic and International Studies, 1995) pages 29–42.

48. Bennett Marsh, "CBI in the Shadow of NAFTA" in Recommendations for a North American Free Trade Agreement and for Future Hemispheric Trade, Miami Report III (Miami: North-South Centre, 1992) pages 43–52.

49. Testimony of Anthony T. Bryan, Hearing before the Subcommittee on Trade of the Committee on Ways and Means, House of Representatives, One Hundred Fourth Congress, First Session, February 10, 1995 (Washington, D.C.: Government Printing Office, 1995) pages 170–72.

50. Stephen Lande and Ambler Moss, "Give Central America a Trade Break," Journal of Commerce, February 24, 1999.

51. Third Annual Survey of Public Opinion on International Trade (Washington, D.C.: The Association of Women in International Trade, 1999).

52. Robert E. Scott, North American Trade After NAFTA. Rising Deficits, Disappearing Jobs (Washington, D.C.: Economic Policy Institute, 1996), Jesse Rothstein and Robert E. Scott, NAFTA's Casualties. Employment Effects on Men, Women and Minorities (Washington, D.C.: Economic Policy Institute, 1997), Jesse Rothstein and Robert E. Scott, NAFTA and the States. Job Destruction is Widespread (Washington, D.C.: Economic Policy Institute, 1997), and Robert E. Scott, NAFTA's Hidden Costs. Trade Agreement Results in Job Losses, Growing Inequality and Wage Suppression for the United States (Washington, D.C.: Economic Policy Institute, 2001).

53. The debate over free trade and protectionism has gone on in the United States for most of the 20th century and the 1990s was no exception. For views for opposing perspectives see Jagdish Bhagwati, The World Trading System at Risk (Princeton: Princeton University Press, 1991) and Ralph Nader et al., The Case Against Free Trade. GATT, NAFTA and the Globalization of Corporate Power (San Francisco: Earth Island Books and Berkeley; North Atlantic Books, 1993) and Douglas A. Irwin, Free Trade Under Fire (Princeton: Princeton University Press, 2002). For a history of the debate see Susan Ariel Aaronson, Trade and the American Dream. A Social History of Postwar Trade Policy (Lexington: University Press of Kentucky, 1996).

54. Jeffrey Schott, The Uruguay Round. An Assessment (Washington, D.C.: Institute for International Economics, 1994) and Gary Clyde Hufbauer and Jeffrey J. Schott, NAFTA. An Assessment (Washington, D.C.: Institute for International Economics, 1993).

55. Robert A. Rogowsky, Linda A. Linkins, and Karl S. Tsuji, Trade Liberalization. Fears and Facts, Center for Strategic and International Studies, Washington Papers, No. 179 (Westport: Praeger, 1997).

56. Open Markets Matter. The Benefits of Trade Liberalization (Paris: Organization for Economic Cooperation and Development, 1998).

57. Gary Burtless, Robert Z. Lawrence, Robert E. Litan, and Robert J. Shapiro, Globaphobia. Confronting Fears About Open Trade (Washington, D.C.: Brookings Institution, Progressive Policy Institute and Twentieth Century Fund, 1998) and I. M. Destler, "Trade Policy at a Crossroad. An Approach for 1999 and Beyond," Brookings Review, Vol. 17, No. 1 (Winter, 1999) pages 27–30.

58. Robert E. Scott, Rebuilding the Caribbean. A Better Foundation for Sustainable Growth (Washington, D.C.: Economic Policy Institute, 2000) page 10.

59. Angel Miguel Rodriguez, "After Hurricane Mitch," Washington Post, November 24, 1998.

60. Richard L. Bernal, "Why Caribbean Nations Need Parity with NAFTA," The Miami Herald, February 4, 1993 "NAFTA Parity," Latin Trade, May 1993, "Caribbean Nations Need NAFTA, too," The Washington Times, October 1, 1993, "A Jamaican's Case for Trade Parity with NAFTA," The Wall Street Journal, March 22, 1996 and "Parity for the Caribbean," Journal of Commerce, July 2, 1997. September 18 and 19, 1987.

61. Judith Evans, "Big Mack Attack," LatinFinance, September 1997, pages 59–62.

62. Thomas F. McLarty III, "Trade Means Good Jobs for Americans," Washington Post, September 15, 1997.

63. Richard L. Bernal, "A Jamaican's Case for Trade Parity with NAFTA," *Wall Street Journal*, March 22, 1996.

64. For example, the visit of Deputy Prime Minister P. J. Patterson in December 1991 was the occasion for a press conference because he was having meetings with the IMF, World Bank, IADB, and Secretaries Lawrence Eagleburger and David Mulford.

65. Speaking Notes. Ambassador Bernal at Media Luncheon, the National Press Club, June 12, 1992 at 12:30 p.m. Files of the Embassy of Jamaica, Washington, D.C.

66. Rafael Leonardo Callejas, "Prosperity for the Americas," Journal of Commerce, February 3, 1991.

67. Further Suggestions for August 12th Central American meeting with Ambassador Hills, Manchester Trade, August 7, 1991.

68. Larry Martin, "A Humanitarian Trade Bill," Journal of Commerce, May 2, 1999.

69. Samuel Guzowski, "Aid Plus Trade Equals Relief," Journal of Commerce, April 2, 1999.

70. William Roberts, "Bipartisan Group of Senators Press for Caribbean Economic Package," Journal of Commerce, February 4, 1999.

71. Mack McLarty and Jim Kolbe, "Central America Needs Help, Not Handouts," Journal of Commerce, March 16, 1999.

72. Letter to Congressman Ben Gilman from Gary K. Smith, President of the American Uniform Company, February 2, 1999.

73. Diary of Ambassador Bernal.

74. All of these organizations submitted statements to Congressional Hearings, see Hearing before the Subcommittee on Trade of the Committee on Ways and Means, House of Representatives, One Hundred Fourth Congress, First Session, February 10, 1995 (Washington, D.C.: Government Printing Office, 1995).

75. George A. Dalley, "C'bean Leaders Contribute to Passage of CBI," *Carib News*, May 23, 2000.

76. This was a point made repeatedly by Prime Minister P. J. Patterson of Jamaica, see Delano Franklin (ed.), a Jamaican Voice in Caribbean and World Politics. P. J. Patterson. Selected Speeches 1992–2002 (Kingston: Ian Randle Publishers, 2002) page 133.

77. The term NAFTA parity was developed by Richard Bernal in discussion with Steve Lande. Several suggestions were aired and rejected including the Act for Caribbean Transformation but this was discarded because of the risk of being confused with ACT, a gay rights organization.

78. Letter to Ambassador Richard L. Bernal from Lloyd Bentsen, Secretary of the Treasury, October 5, 1994.

79. Letter to Ambassador Richard L. Bernal from Congressman Bill Archer, October 17, 1995.

EIGHT

Conclusions and Lessons

This final chapter consists of three parts covering what was accomplished, how it was accomplished, and why Jamaica was able to accomplish what it did. Part I very briefly states the achievements recounted in the case studies. The gravamen of these case studies is that they demonstrate that Jamaica, a small, developing country of little if any strategic importance to the United States was able to influence U.S. foreign policy during the decade covered by this study. Part II is devoted to explaining why Jamaica was successful in influencing U.S. foreign policy. Part III discusses the lessons to be derived from Jamaica's influence on U.S. foreign policy and points out why these are relevant and important. Extracting and adumbrating the lessons of the Jamaican experience can yield insights that can assist governments trying to influence the foreign policy of the United States. These lessons are of immediate contemporary relevance particularly to those who on behalf of their small countries are currently engaged in trying to influence U.S. foreign policy.

PART I: WHAT WAS ACCOMPLISHED

Jamaica, a small developing country of no particular strategic importance was able to influence the foreign policy of the United States of America, undoubtedly the sole superpower during the years 1991–2001. Specifically Jamaica was able to achieve the goals of:

1. Preventing the reduction of foreign aid and maintaining aid at a high level.
2. Securing significant debt relief.
3. Being certified as fully cooperating with the United States on counter narcotics.

4. Securing the passage of the Caribbean Basin Economic Recovery
    Act (CBERA) in collaboration with countries from the Caribbean
    and Central America.

PART II: WHY JAMAICA WAS SUCCESSFUL

The most important factors explaining the success of Jamaica in influencing U.S. foreign policy were:

The U.S. System of Government and Political Culture

The U.S. political system and political culture are unique in the degree
of openness to representatives of foreign governments. More than any
other country the U.S. system allows diplomats and foreigners, resident
and non-resident to lobby all departments of the U.S. government and
this is not regarded as interfering in the internal affairs of the United
States. Indeed, the representatives of foreign governments can call on
elected representatives to persuade them to pass legislation that could
affect U.S. foreign policy toward their countries. In many instances
foreign governments are competing with U.S. domestic interests for policy measures and financial resources.

The legislative process in both the House of Representatives and the
Senate is based on committees in which a single member of the House or
Senate can block a bill or add an amendment to a bill. This is particularly
the case if the person is chair of the committee or has seniority. What this
means is that lobbying can be intensive rather than extensive in emphasis. It is very expensive and time-consuming to directly engage all or the
majority of members of Congress on any issue and more so for issues
related to foreign policy or regions of the world that are not regarded as a
clear and present danger to national security. A further concentration of
the legislative process is that the drafting of the language in a bill is
assumed by the staff of the primary sponsor or by the staff of a few co-
sponsoring members of Congress. Lobbying is conducted in concentric
circles, starting with a core of committed supporters, then moving to
those that are most likely to be engaged (sometimes in opposition) or
whose interest can be aroused. A variety of motives may figure in engaging a member's interest. For example, Carolyn B. Maloney, Democrat of
the 12th district of New York was interested in Jamaica because her
mother had retired to live in Jamaica. The members of Congress from
Florida were in general supportive, e.g., Alcee Hastings because of the
importance of trade between that state and the Caribbean. Where there
were Caribbean voters, such as some districts of New York, New Jersey,
Maryland, Florida, and Connecticut the Congressional representatives

were supportive of Caribbean issues. Occasionally a Congressman would be empathetic to foreign policy or international trade issues.

In the early 1990s the State Department used to issue what were then called Travel Advisories warning Americans to think very carefully about traveling to a particular destination. A travel advisory was issued for Jamaica[1] based on an incident of violence in one of the poorest inner-city neighborhoods in Kingston. This was potentially damaging to the vitally important tourist industry. Ambassador Bernal met with the State Department to point out the likely damage and to protest that the incident in Kingston posed no threat to American tourists because the main vacation areas were more than two hours' drive away and 70–100 miles from Kingston. This was conceded but travel advisories were issued for entire countries. The country-wide warning was too blunt an instrument and hence on the advice of Bill Kirk, former staffer of Congressman Conyers, Ambassador Bernal met with the very senior and influential Congressman John Conyers Jr., Democrat from the 13th congressional district of Michigan, which is in Detroit. Conyers was at the time Chairman of the Legislation and National Security Subcommittee of the House of Representatives Committee on Government.

Jamaica's complaint joined those of travelers, travel agents, and tour operators who were confused by the travel advisories. Conyers had recognized that the system was "inconsistent and inadequate" and had requested that the General Accounting Office do a report on the issue. The report[2] confirmed the deficiencies and recommended changes. Thanks to the actions taken by Conyers, who was first elected in 1965, a report was prepared to have the system changed.[3] The Bureau of Consular Affairs of the State Department subsequently refined its warning to specify areas within countries. The validity of a more focused warning or alert is immediately obvious in the case of large countries such as Brazil or India but is vitally important in small countries such as Jamaica.

Jamaican National Character and Culture

The culture, character, traditions, history, and even myths of a country influence everything they do from how they play football[4] to their foreign policy. Hadfield-Amkhan explains: "These national characteristics are no mere menu of attributes, they portray the character of a given people, one in which their history, traditions, values and state institutions fuse into a form of collective self-reference."[5] Specifically culture affects foreign policy in respect to the goals chosen to pursue and the manner in which foreign policy is executed.

The history of China illustrates the importance of national character and culture in foreign policy. The Chinese are well known for their cultural predilection to take the long view both in drawing on the lessons of history and in the patience exercised in their diplomatic practice. Kissing-

er in his book *On China*[6] relates how Mao Zedong in formulating international strategy drew on Chinese wisdom and classic literature from as far
back as 221 B.C. These cultural aspects of the Chinese national character
were the leitmotif of the prolix diplomacy of the U.S.-China rapprochement initiated by President Nixon. U.S. frustration with the slowness and
subtlety of Chinese diplomacy[7] recalls British consternation when trying
to establish diplomatic relations in the 50 years before the start of the First
Opium War in 1839.[8]

Jamaican Exceptionalism

Every society, country, and nation exhibits a national character that
emanates from and is a reflection of its national culture. Every country
has a national character and while each national character is unique, the
national character of some countries are distinctive in that they all have
some influence on the foreign policy of their countries. National character
and the culture of which it is a reflection affect the goals, means, modalities, and style of foreign policy, e.g., in the United States. The influence
of national character and culture is evident even when there are contending aspects.[9] National character emanates from the enduring shared culture and personality characteristics that transcend economic, political,
and social differences within societies and countries and that give rise to
behavioral commonalities of a people, society, or country.[10] National cultures are unique and are all in a sense exceptional; however, the use of
the term "exceptionalism" is employed here to connote not only uniqueness but that apart from being different there is some quality that is
unusual and special and that characterizes few others.[11] In the United
States, where the concept emerged and is frequently used, the attribution
of exceptionalism to the United States is widely accepted. Few have
raised doubt about the United States as a case of exceptionalism.[12] The
United States is cited as exceptional because of a combination of history,
size, military power, economic development, superior political institutions, culture, diplomatic leadership, and religion. Jamaica, which without many of these strengths, has over many years demonstrated an exceptionalism in its foreign policy and in international affairs.

Without digressing it is worth spending a few extra lines on the concept of exceptionalism. "Exceptionalism" need not be based on factual
evidence and can be derived from myth because what is important is the
perception or belief by a person, social group, institution, society, or
country that it is exceptional in some way. This quality allows a country,
society, or culture even as small as Jamaica to project itself internationally
because it does not accept that it has to conform to prevailing rules or
accepted or conventional norms of behavior. Many countries have distinctive national personalities and in some cases the country is conscious
of or perceives that its distinctiveness makes it unique or at least different

from other countries, i.e., exceptional. Exceptionalism often becomes the rationale for foreign policy, i.e., policy towards the rest of the world whether in the form of withdrawal from international relations or engagement in some instances for domination and subjugation of other societies. The best known is China's policy of isolation from those it designated as "barbarians." A well-known example of outreach is the European view of having a civilizing mission to non-European societies based on the assiduously cultivated myth of the inherent superiority of the culture, religion, and race. In the United States, exceptionalism [13] manifested itself as the widespread conviction that America is a country uniquely blessed by providence with a "manifest destiny," a mandate to propagate across the globe the American brand of capitalism and democracy.

At the center of Jamaica's culture and national character is a tradition of resistance and struggle, and this is reflected in Jamaica's approach to foreign policy and relations with other countries and even more powerful countries. The former Governor General (head of state) of Jamaica, the Most Hon. Prof. Kenneth Hall characterizes the character of Jamaica's foreign policy as "the prominence of its interventions on global and international issues and earning from the international community the confidence to be selected to head many significant groups or to be the lead spokesperson on many of the determining north-south, south-south and global relations." [14] Persaud describes this as Jamaica's "international exceptionalism," [15] which owes much to internal factors and in particular its emergence can be traced to the need of the governments of the period to respond to social pressures. This pressure coincided with Jamaica's attempt to differentiate itself from poor and developing countries.

Jamaica as a society has always had exceptionalism in its approach to the world based on the proposition that "we little but we talawah." "Talawah" for Jamaicans mean they are strong and can do anything they set their mind to. This audacious attitude is built upon the view that we freed ourselves from slavery and colonialism and the tremendous accomplishments of outstanding individuals such as Nanny, Mary Seacole, Marcus Garvey, George Headley, Bob Marley, and Usain Bolt. It was Jamaican audacity that emboldened Garvey to coin the hortatory, clarion call to people of African descent: "Up, up you mighty race! You can accomplish what you will." The confidence to handle the external world emerged even while Jamaica was still a colony of Britain. The traits of the Jamaican personality include fearlessness, [16] determination, persistence, and unlimited confidence that anything can be achieved. Jimmy Cliff's "You can get it if you really want it" is emblematic of this spirit. Poet and novelist Kwame Dawes explains that Jamaicans take this attitude towards any task in any circumstances by the "suspension of a sense of scale." [17] Doreen Miller explains that: "The historical experience of Jamaicans predispose them to a belief that they can and will do what they think they can. Generally, they do not accept –no– as the final answer because they truly believe there is another way to achieve their goal . . . . Once a goal is set, the urge to achieve will not allow anyone to interfere or create obstacles . . . They take pride in making their own decisions and controlling their own destiny."[18] There are some data on the characteristics of the Jamaican character that reveal that Jamaicans are always willing to challenge the existing order and rules that give expression to that order. Geert Hofstede[19] developed a six-variable measure of cultures that when applied to Jamaicans yielded the follow descriptors: "conflicts are resolved by fighting them out . . . people believe there should be no more rules than are necessary and if they are ambiguous or do not work they should be abandoned or changed."[20]

Tradition of Assertiveness

The character of Jamaica's international relations is one of assertiveness and this evolved through a progression of three phases. The first was resistance to conforming to a subordinate position in dealing with other countries. This was evident even before political independence from British colonialism when Jamaica was the first country in the world to place a ban on goods from apartheid South Africa. Similarly, Norman Manley was afforded a meeting with President John F. Kennedy at the White House while Jamaica was still a British colony. The second phase was moving from resistance, which is a reactive mode of interaction, to the self-confidence to initiate policy on international issues. Hugh Shearer was the person who suggested the UN's International Year of Human Rights. Third, in the full flowering of assertiveness Jamaica sought to shape not only policy but to shape the international agenda and attempt to assume some leadership of groups of countries such as the Commonwealth, the ACP, the Non-Aligned Movement, and Socialist International. This audacity was emblematic of the leadership of Manley and Patterson who when necessary disagreed with the United States, the superpower. For example, Michael Manley, along with Barbados, Guyana, and Trinidad and Tobago breached the U.S. diplomatic embargo of Cuba when they established diplomatic ties with Cuba in 1973. Seaga in a very different sense was bold in the way he achieved some influence in the U.S. administration by ingratiating himself with Ronald Reagan and having Jamaica adopted as a model of dependent capitalism to counter the Cuban socialist model. Seaga was the first head of government to be received by President Reagan. Patterson was decisive in the rescue and provision of sanctuary in Jamaica for ousted Jean-Bertrand Aristide at a time when the United States did not want him to be anywhere near Haiti.

Resistance

The politics of Jamaica was dominated from the late 1930s by two "giants," Alexander Bustamante and Norman Manley. Bustamante regarded subservience to the UK and United States in foreign relations as the one feasible course. This was his pragmatism because he was a feisty trade union leader who had been imprisoned by the British colonial authorities during World War II. Norman Manley was a declared socialist who was Premier of Jamaica during the 1950s and who looked poised to be the first prime minister of an independent Jamaica. He was not known to be reliably pro-U.S. Despite being awarded a medal for military service in the British army in World War I he was regarded with suspicion by the U.S. government. Manley, then King's Counsel and member of the House of Representatives, was detained at Ellis Island when passing through the United States on his way from Britain to Jamaica. Vic Reid recalls that when he arrived at Idlewild Airport in February 1951 he was "grabbed by immigration authorities, interrogated and hustled off to Ellis Island."[21] He was released nine hours following a "massive intervention" by the British government, the NAACP, the Jamaica Progressive League, and American leaders.[22] He resumed his lecture tour to New York, Detroit, and Washington, D.C. The incident revived memories of earlier incidents incolving Jamaicans resisting racist treatment in the United States.[23]

Norman Manley led the People's National Party, which had a radical left wing. In the 1950s the four acknowledged leaders of the left were branded "communists" and expelled from the Party in April 1952.[24] It was alleged that they had been "forming a Communist cell within the Party." The PNP action was in response to "Pressure from within the party, and the charges of Communism levelled against the party from without by its critics."[25] There was also concern in the United States that "the Jamaican communists were being welded into a single strike force by aggressive and competent leadership,"[26] which may have played a role. The PNP mounted a program of internal political education and public relations to distinguish its democratic socialism from communism. Bogues reminds us that: "Michael Manley's intervention into party politics and trade unionism was against the Marxist-Leninist left. When, at the behest of the party leadership he conducted a massive speaking program amongst party members, it was to conduct a political education program on the differences between democratic socialism and communism. It is ironic that twenty-eight years later, both the U.S. political elite and the local conservative opposition would ferociously attack his regime as being communist."[27]

In 1959 under the leadership of Premier Norman Manley Jamaica was the first country to place a trade embargo on South Africa because of apartheid. At that time Jamaica was not yet politically independent and therefore did not have responsibility for its own foreign affairs. Norman Manley, Premier of Jamaica, a British colony, met with President John F. Kennedy on April 19, 1961 at the White House. This is a remarkable event given the fact that Jamaica was still a colony of Britain. The United States engaged because Manley was seen by the United States as "the outstanding West Indian statesman and is likely to be the first Prime Minister of the federation after its independence in 1962."[28] Manley spoke of matters of concern to both the West Indies and Jamaica. Secretary of State Dean Rusk's briefing memorandum to President Kennedy advised that, "We believe the principal objective of your meeting should be to convey to Mr. Manley a sense of the importance we attach to the successful establishment of an independent West Indian Federation. Recent reports from London, Kingston, and Port of Spain indicate that sentiment against the Federation of the West Indies is growing in the area. Mr. Manley may himself be having misgivings about Jamaica's adherence and some thoughts about the island seeking independence by itself alone."[29] The issues discussed were sugar (both quota and non-quota purchases[30]), bauxite, air agreements, and aid. Norman Manley stated that: "We want a much larger quota than has been allotted. Sugar is a matter of life and death to the West Indies."[31] In recommending that President Kennedy accede to the request for a meeting with Manley, Secretary Rusk pointed out that "Manley had publicly declared his opposition to neutralism and his devotion to principles of democracy."[32]

Self-Confidence

Once Jamaica became politically independent it began to view the United States as a benefactor and to make a pitch for aid. Writing in 1963 Sir Philip Sherlock explained that the "small independent nations such as Trinidad and Jamaica need help for a period of time in order that their economies may become self-sustaining. As independent countries they are seeking aid for economic and social development, and they turn in particular to the United States. They have based their claim not on poverty but on their record of development."[33] Prime Minister Bustamante immediately declared a desire for a defense pact with the United States. The United States advised that Jamaica's defense could best be accomplished by joining the Organization of American States (OAS). McGeorge Bundy's memorandum to President Kennedy in preparation for meeting Bustamante on June 27, 1962, stated: "We see membership in the OAS and accession to the Rio Pact as the best means of guaranteeing Jamaica's defense in the post-independence period."[34] Thanks to the resolute stance and diplomatic skill of Jamaica's then ambassador to the United States Sir Edgerton Richardson[35] Jamaica was persuaded to assert a more independent approach to Jamaica's accession to membership in the OAS in 1969. Jamaica did the unprecedented when it joined the OAS without breaking off diplomatic relations with Cuba or participating in sanctions or the embargo against Cuba despite pressure from the United States including the possible loss of aid from USAID.[36] Jamaica supported entry of the People's Republic of China to the UN in 1973. The government of Jamaica, Ministry Paper No. 60 of 1969 dealing with Jamaica's membership in the OAS stated: "As for being involved in crusades against ideologies through interference in domestic affairs, we are confident of our ability to avoid this in keeping with our policy of interfering, and of being determined to prevent others from interfering in our own domestic affairs."[37]

Jamaica sought to portray itself as a country that was democratic, politically stable, free of racial discrimination, and somewhat more economically advanced than the majority of other developing countries. An inflated national pride was an element of this but there was a deliberate strategy that was based on the view that separating Jamaica from the "pack" would yield advantages. The advantages anticipated were that Jamaica if perceived as a middle income country would be viewed as a more desirable investment location. Persaud described the policy as: "The challenge for Jamaica as the JLP saw it, was essential one of maneuvering within the established regimes of global liberalism. The American version of multilateralism which emerged after World War II, and codified in the Bretton Woods institutions was entirely consistent with the world view of the JLP. With the government's acceptance of American-inspired ideas and institutions, the quest for economic resources was to be prosecuted without causing any major rupture, vis-a-vis multinational corporations, international financial institutions, or bilateral relations with northern developed countries."[38]

Michael Manley's foreign policy breaks with the policy of the previous administration that always aligned with the West in the Cold War. Jamaica began to exhibit some independence on non-Cold War issues from the 1960s. Michael Manley dismissed the policy of the JLP as keeping Jamaica in a servile relationship with imperialism[39] and took this exceptionalism to new heights with non-alignment, the new international economic order, and support for Cuban troops in southern Africa. Jamaica's exceptionalism continued when Seaga despite his obeisance to the United States accomplished the feat of being the first head of government to meet with President Ronald Reagan. P. J. Patterson criticized the U.S. invasion of Iraq and provided sanctuary for the exiled former president of Haiti. The memorial to those who died in the slave trade at the United Nations in New York was proposed by Jamaica.

Audacity

Bravado is one attribute but it only becomes confidence when it is accompanied and reinforced by tangible accomplishments and so it was in the case of Jamaica. Michael Manley, faced with a serious economic crisis after the first oil crisis of 1973, realized that the best prospect for earning more foreign exchange and tax revenue was to extract it from the bauxite/alumina industry. The industry was controlled since its inception in the late 1950s by American and Canadian multinational corporations. Manley made the very daring decision to take on the multinational corporations by setting in motion a process of negotiation conducted by a team comprised entirely of Jamaicans and supported by an international diplomatic campaign masterminded and led by himself.[40] Jamaica was successful in the conduct of the negotiations but did not reach agreement on taxation and eventually imposed new taxation.[41] In the process Jamaica achieved what most people regarded impossible and this was a cathartic and transformative moment that gave the Jamaican nation an unprecedented confidence. The lead negotiator, Pat Rousseau, recalls "our establishing conclusively as a people that we were equal to all in basic skills and if we were willing to work hard and prepare extensively, we could even be superior to our opponents from the developed world" and by the end of the negotiation "we had dispelled their original view of us being mendicants with a tin cup asking for a handout . . . .had changed their views of us, seeing us then as well prepared formidable opponents."[42] Manley commented: "the Jamaican people at the moment when I announced the Production Levy in the sovereign Parliament of our country knew what it was to be citizens of a sovereign, independent nation."[43]

Expulsion of the U.S. Ambassador

On July 20, 1973, the government of Jamaica led by Prime Minister Manley declared that the U.S. ambassador to Jamaica, Vincent de Roulet, was "no longer persona grata"[44] for interfering in Jamaica's internal affairs. This designation refers to a foreign person whose entering or remaining in a particular country is prohibited by that country's government. It is the most serious form of censure that a government can apply to foreign diplomats. The ambassador was in the United States at the time and never returned to Jamaica. This type of action is permitted under the Vienna Convention[45] but it was a bold measure for a small state to take against the ambassador of the United States. He owed his appointment to contributions to the Republican Party by himself and his mother-in-law who was the owner of the New York Mets baseball team at the time.[46] He was appointed by President Nixon and assumed the post in October 1969. De Roulet was an unfortunate choice because he had no previous diplomatic experience and he showed himself to be inept and insensitive. He was described in *Harper's* magazine as an "unreliable amateur."[47] His conduct was so clumsy that it was said that he "outuglied the original Ugly American" while keeping a high profile with his luxury yacht.[48] Levi[49] relates that de Roulet thought Michael

Manley was a socialist and inimical to U.S. interests and tried to ensure that he would not be elected. "De Roulet devised a deal to keep Manley from being elected: boosting then-Prime Minister Shearer by arranging an appointment with President Nixon."[50] He felt comfortable in describing Shearer as "a well-dressed and courteous Negro" who "knew where his bread was buttered."[51] USAID provide $20 million to the Shearer-led government shortly before the election.[52] De Roulet's downfall was precipitated by testimony he gave to the Senate in which he claimed that both Shearer and Manley had assured him that they would not raise the issue of nationalization of bauxite, an allegation denied by both.[53] The action by the Manley government did no discernable damage to Jamaica-U.S. relations given the outrageous and inept conduct of de Roulet. However, it was a courageous action by a small developing country to have taken against a U.S. ambassador not knowing how the United States might react.

Michael Manley's Foreign Policy

The foreign policy of Michael Manley when he assumed the post of prime minister in 1972 was both a break from the policy of the JLP government that preceded him in office and a continuation of his father's thinking on foreign policy. Even before Jamaica attained political independence Norman Manley imposed an import embargo on products from South Africa. As pointed out by Carlton Davis the elder Manley did not have the legal or political authority to take such an action.[54] Norman Manley advocated the position that Jamaica should not be aligned with any bloc.[55] His life's work was extricating Jamaica from colonialism and the gaining of political independence. This was the mission of his generation, to which he said "mission accomplished." The mission of Michael Manley's generation was "reconstructing the social and economic society and life of Jamaica."[56]

To understand the foreign policy of Michael Manley it is necessary to know his political philosophy, e.g., economic development for all, self-determination; his personal ideals, e.g., justice, equal opportunity, fair play; and his political methodology, e.g., collective bargaining, skill versus power, socialism, the eventual triumph of reason, and his pragmatic analysis of the circumstances in which he was acting. Central to his political philosophy is the concept of social justice through equality of opportunity[57] both within Jamaica and in the international context. As Bogues puts it: "equality had a foundational aspect" for Manley, indeed was the "central political value" of his political practice.[58] His belief involved changing the rules that govern access to opportunities for all. In the international arena small countries in order to achieve economic development, have to help change the global rules, e.g., the new international economic order as an essential complement to a national strategy of self-reliant economic development. Manley was not an idealist as he demonstrated his political pragmatism in the changes in how he pursued his goals. Many observers and commentators misunderstood Manley's adjustments in tactics and strategy as changes in values and goals and even as opportunism. His goals, ideals, and values were consistent and unchanged but he adjusted his strategies to the local and international circumstances and the particular global conjuncture. Nettleford confirms that even as he embraced the neo-liberalism of the 1980s when he returned to power 1989, the goals of participatory democracy, of people empowerment, of social justice of 'transformation without hopelessly dividing the people', never left his vision." [59]

Manley's concept of a foreign policy was based on concentric circles of country (Jamaica), region (Caribbean), developing countries, the Non-Aligned Movement, and multilateral. Carlton Davis illustrates the link between Manley's personal ideals, political philosophy, and his foreign policy by explaining the ontology: "the individual, the family, the community, small or large, the country, the region and the developing world." [60]

This is Manley's concentric circles of foreign policy in his own words: "Economic and political co-operation begins most logically and naturally amongst one's neighbours. Distances are short and the likelihood of common understanding of issues and sharing of objectives most likely to occur. . . . As a natural extension of our commitment to the English-speaking brothers and sisters in the Caribbean, we were determined to bridge the gap which separated the English-speaking Caribbean from the rest." [61] Speaking of the role of regionalism he stated, "regionalism can provide the framework in which internal markets are increased, external bargaining power enhanced and international recognition maximized." [62] Manley's next circle: "Looking beyond the region . . . the African, Caribbean and Pacific countries. . . . From the ACP Group we move into the wider circle which formed the Group of 77 and the Non-Aligned Movement itself." [63] His impeccable logic was: "The Non-Aligned Movement represented our best political hope for the development of a third force in world politics." [64] This was a natural alliance because "the developing world is part of a common problem in its dealing with the metropolitan world (developed countries)." [65] Manley asserted that the "conflict of interest between these two groups is sharp, it is all-pervading" [66] and "the primacy of an identity of interests which are common to the Caribbean, Africa, Central America, India, South-East Asia and so on." [67]

As a former successful trade unionist Michael Manley's experience predisposed him to the conviction that it is possible to negotiate a mutually satisfactory agreement between parties of asymmetrical power and different interests. He was convinced that "in its dealings with the industrialized nations, the third world desperately needs the strength that can come from regional economic groupings; and, more general the development of a common economic diplomacy."[68] Similarly he spoke of "the necessity for the developing world as a whole to evolve a common strategy with regard to its economic dealings with the metropolitan nations."[69]

For Michael Manley economic transformation in a small dependent developing country of necessity involved reform of the external circumstances that restricted the degrees of freedom for such countries. His foreign policy was an indispensable extension of the internal economic development strategy. He sought to create a mixed economy by pursuing what he termed "a non-capitalist path of development to distinguish experiments like ours from the neo-colonialist model of capitalism of the Puerto Rican type and the Marxist-Leninist model of the Cuban type."[70] Non-alignment and the call for a new international economic order[71] were logical extensions and complements to the internal economic re-structuring.

Beyond the concentric circles he believed that he could leverage the third force of a united bloc of developing countries to exert an influence in multilateral fora as exemplified by his arranging a summit of six world leaders in Jamaica in 1978. The fact that he was able to assemble the heads of government of Canada, Germany, Australia, Nigeria, Norway, and Venezuela was a considerable and unprecedented accomplishment for the leader of a small insignificant developing country and was a measure of his stature in world affairs.

"The fundamental problem of the world today is not so much a question of conflicting ideologies as of the economic relationship between the developed economies of the metropolitan world and the less developed economies of the third world."[72] He saw the economic inequity as an economic and moral affront: "The very presence of such economic power in foreign hands represents a threat to the sense of independence of a country and a serious obstacle to its freedom of action in economic planning."[73] His solution was: "The key therefore must lie in joint ownership. It is only when control and ownership are shared reasonably between those who supply the initial capital and know-how on one hand, and those who supply the raw material and the labor on the other, that mutuality of interest can exist."[74] The international economic inequity was for Manley the fundamental feature of global capitalism and economic development required struggling against how this "imperialist" system operated. He developed and reiterated this point at the Non-Aligned Conference in Havana in 1979 when he stated that "We may call ourselves communists, socialists or humanists or simply progressive, but all [are] anti-imperialists."[75]

Prof. Anthony Bogues observes that Manley was born in a world dominated by colonial empires and his life experience was one of struggling for de-colonization and Manley's thinking evolved in an anti-colonial perspective.[76] Bogues, who worked closely with Manley both in the party and the government makes the insightful comment that Manley's vision in the 1970s was one of transformation, but by the mid-1980s it had become one of reform. Bogues attributes this ideological shift to Manley being "acutely aware of changes in the balance of forces in the world." He explains that at that juncture "Manley is thinking here that reform means improvement while transformation means change which carries with it improvement but changes in the power relationships in a society."[77] My own view based on working close with Michael Manley is that his change of approach from transformation to reform was not opportunism but a careful and deep rethinking of the internal and external circumstances. Eight years of Ronald Reagan and Margaret Thatcher in power made a profound change in world affairs that could not be ignored. Dr. Peter Phillips, who was minister of state in the prime minister's office in the Manley Administration of 1989–1993 explains that the tensions between the United States and Jamaica "were to be significantly amplified on account of the particular resonance that the socialist label would have had in Washington preoccupied with Cold-War competition between the so-called Eastern and Western blocs."[78]

Manley was devoted to freedom and that means a democracy in which the individual has the right and opportunity to influence decisions that affect their current and future conditions of life.[79] In my view this belief was extended to international relations in which Manley was committed to the democratic right of nations/countries to participate in the decisions that affect their current and future sovereignty, self-determination, and economic development. His commitment to freedom gave him a strong revulsion to all its impediments and impelled him to fight against the racism of the apartheid regime in South Africa and colonialism in Southern Africa. The tenet of freedom was also at the foundation of his commitment to the right of self-determination of all nations and countries.

Manley understood that to accomplish the type of economic transformation that would provide economic development that would uplift the majority of people in Jamaica it would be necessary to tackle both internal and international obstacles. He regarded the prevailing structure of the global economic order as a barrier to economic transformation and hence his push for a new international economic order.[80] Dudley Thompson,[81] Jamaica's Minister of Foreign Affairs, explains what Manley did to further the process of change. "He gave us a place and to do that he had to become a leader of the Third World. To become that he had to approach our position not as mendicants to the United States powers that opposed us but as proud leaders, and as such he led the Third World as a spokesperson by introducing the new international economic order and drawing on people like Nyerere to foster the Third World movement."[82] By a new international economic order he meant: "the techniques of political management of world trade and world finance that will lead to the progressive elimination of those wide disparities in wealth now existing between different sections of mankind and which are too great to be tolerated."[83]

Manley believed that it was in Jamaica's interest to diversify its international relations beyond maintaining the traditional friendships with Canada, Britain, and the United States. Hence he argued that "the perpetuation of dependence upon these three relationships is inimical to Jamaica's long term interests."[84] He sought to widen Jamaica's diplomatic relations with other developing countries and found natural allies in leaders who shared his political philosophy such as Carlos Andres Perez of Venezuela and Julius Nyerere of Tanzania. Part of diversifying Jamaica's economic relations was the development of relations with socialist countries.[85] The most important initiative was the export of bauxite to the Soviet Union and provision by Cuba of doctors to bolster public healthcare.

Manley had a sophisticated understanding of the need to find likeminded leaders in the developed countries and did this in fora such as the South Commission and Socialist International (SI) where he chaired the Committee on Economic Policy during the presidency of Willy Brandt. As a result of Manley's initiative SI produced in 1985 a report entitled "Global Challenge. From Crisis to Co-Operation: Breaking the North-South Stalemate."[86] The gravamen of the report set out in an introduction by Manley and Brandt was that the world was caught in a crisis, which in many ways is unprecedented and worse than that of the 1930s and called for planned collective reflation among like-minded governments. Reflation of the global economy had to be accompanied by redistribution and that required changes in the structure of the world economy. The developing countries would benefit from a combination of reflation in the North, redistribution in the North and South and restructuring of the world economy and North-South relations.[87] The four fundamental areas of reform in the world economy were (1) the terms of trade with the Common Fund as a partial solution; (2) the international division of labor with the need to restructure the concentration of industry in the North; (3) the international monetary system with the need to change stabilization policies of the International Monetary Fund as a central issue; and (4) multinational corporations with the call for a code of conduct.[88] These recommendations are paralleled in the report of the South Commission[89] of which Manley was a member.

He was very concerned about the role of multinational corporations (MNCs), viewing them as strangling economic growth in developing countries by depriving them of the full value of their exports and by retaining all of the profits from commodity exports. This was very much the thinking of the leading Caribbean economists at that time. The operations of MNCs were seen as antithetical to economic development. Beckford identified the MNC as maintaining persistent poverty in plantation economies[90] and Girvan pinpointed the MNC as central to the dependent

underdevelopment of mineral-export economies.[91] Girvan had been expressing this view from the late 1960s[92] and by the early 1970s it was
widely accepted that the MNCs in the bauxite industry in Jamaica needed
to contribute more to economic development.

U.S. Reaction to Manley's Foreign Policy

The United States was not disturbed by Manley's assumption of the
post of prime minister of Jamaica in 1972, but became increasingly concerned during the 1970s. This shift in perspective about Manley resulted
from a combination of several factors. First, Jamaica had reiterated several times since it became independent that it was with the West, hence
Manley's shift to non-alignment represented a new policy. This could
have been accommodated but second, Manley developed relations with
Cuba and a personal friendship with Fidel Castro. This was a pin prick
on a super-sensitive and irrational nerve in the American psyche. The
rhetoric of the PNP left after the general election of 1977 caught the attention of elements of the foreign policy community in Washington, D.C.
Third, Manley's advocacy for a new international economic order was
not getting the type of traction that would threaten U.S. global economic
interests but his new approach to the terms and conditions of operation
for bauxite producing multinational corporations was a worry not in
itself but if a small unimportant country could do it then other developing countries might be emboldened to try. The International Bauxite Association (IBA), which was an initiative of Manley, was interpreted by
some as portending a cartel to be used against the developed countries
that imported bauxite in the manner in which Organization of Petroleum
Exporting Countries (OPEC) had escalated oil prices. No less a person
than Fred Bergsten called it a new OPEC in bauxite.[93] Fourth, Manley's
strongly expressed support for the liberation struggles in Southern Africa
invoked a hostile reaction from the United States especially because it
entailed support for Cuban troops in Angola. Henry Kissinger in a face to
face meeting with Manley made pellucid the displeasure of the United
States.[94]

A certain amount of displeasure was spawned in the United States by
calls for a new international economic order (NIEO). This is to be understood by recalling the animosity ignited in the United States by OPEC's
increases in the price of oil. The call for a NIEO had achieved the status of
a United Nations Declaration. UN General Assembly resolution 3201 (S-
VI) May 1, 1974, states a commitment "to work urgently for the establishment of a new international economic order based on equity, sovereign
equality, common interest and cooperation among all states, irrespective
of their economic and social systems, which shall correct inequalities and
redress existing injustices, make it possible to reduce the widening gap
between the developed and the developing countries and secure steadily

accelerating economic and social development." The conservative attitude has been summarized as: "Concessions to ill-conceived demands inspired by the South would run the risk of arousing expectations that would be insatiable and unrealizable."[95] Today, the demand for a NIEO does not seem even very radical, but at the time the United States and Europe were not of a mind to accommodate any meaningful change. Mazower explains: "The terrifying worry to Washington was that differing European and American responses to this demand might break up the politico-economic alliance that upon which the post-war revival of capitalism and the emergence of the United States as a global power had been based. In retrospect such a fear seems almost preposterously overblown."[96] What cannot be discounted is the unwillingness of the dominant countries to yield gracefully and democratically to changes in the existing international economic order of which they were the main beneficiaries. This is what Diaz-Alejandro describes as "the historical tolerance of the dominant powers toward the exercise of selectivity by peripheral countries in their international linkages."[97]

The NIEO was a reformist project because it sought to change the rules in a way that would allow for a more equitable sharing of the gains from international trade and investment. It is not the apocalyptic vision of the Marxist paradigm in which capitalism is doomed to inevitable crisis born of the inherent contractions in the process of accumulation on a global scale. This perspective gave rise to terms like "late capitalism," e.g., Mandel[98] and the "transition to socialism," e.g., C. Y. Thomas[99] as the appropriate development strategy. The NIEO was about rebalancing of the gains from international economic relations such as that which originated with the concern over the terms of trade between commodities and manufactured goods and the countries that specialized in these two types of goods within a rigid international division of labor. Prebisch[100] and Singer[101] were concerned about the distribution of gains from international trade. Manley was seized of the validity of the adverse and long-term deterioration of the terms of trade between commodities and manufactured goods. He invested considerable political and intellectual energy to getting the Common Fund established.[102]

The issue of the inequity of international trade and depriving commodity exports, whether in colonial mercantilist trade arrangements of global free market situations, was a permanent facet of Caribbean thinking. The loss of the economic surplus through international trade was raised by Eric Williams in *Capitalism and Slavery*[103] and developed by the Plantation School[104] with parallel intellectual evolution in the Dependency School. The struggle by Jamaica to change the terms of integration into the global economy goes back to the colonial era and therefore there was a natural synchronicity between this thinking and the ideas of the NIEO. The diversification of international economic relations was simply a pragmatic action as part of a perfectly valid and legitimate attempt to reduce dependence on the developed capitalist countries and to create increased self-reliance by cultivating trading relations with other developing countries and socialist countries. This was not a radical action because at the time there were those who strongly advocated what at that time was called "de-linking." The de-linking was a logical outgrowth of the dependency school of development economics and neo-Marxist thinking, which was in vogue at the time as a counter to the orthodoxy of economic development thinking then prevalent. However, there were two versions: the more extreme version interpreted de-linking as minimizing economic contact with the capitalist world economy and a more pragmatic interpretation was as a strategy for a less dependent, more self-reliant development path. This was the difference between Gunder Frank's "development of underdevelopment"[105] and Cardoso and Faletto's "associated dependent development."[106] Similarly the calls for self-reliance at the time should not be confused with autarky.[107] Manley was no reckless radical as he demonstrated by opting for negotiation[108] with the multinational corporations in the bauxite/alumina industry rather than "nationalization," which was being advocated by some.[109]

The establishment of the International Bauxite Association and the successful negotiations with multinational corporations in the bauxite/ alumina was interpreted in some quarters in the United States as ominous developments. While press coverage in the United States was empathic to Jamaica's desperate economic situation, editorials in the influential *Washington Post* and the *New York Times* raised the specter of Jamaica's actions as echoing OPEC and portending cartelization of vital mineral commodities. An excerpt from the *Washington Post* is illustrative of this perspective. Jamaica's actions represented "the biggest increase in any raw material price since the Arabs clamped their oil embargo on the West during the war in the Middle East last fall and the Organization of Petroleum Exporting Countries quadrupled the price of oil"; the article went on to speculate as to whether Jamaica would be an example that would incite other commodity producers.[110]

Manley recalled that shortly after Jamaica announced its support for Cuban troops in Angola there was a "turning point" in U.S.-Jamaica relations that was evident in adverse articles in the U.S. press, a contraction of aid, and an increase in the staff of the U.S. embassy.[111] Manley made reference to an article by James Reston in the *New York Times* in March 1977 in which Reston alleged the expansion of Cuban influence in Jamaica.[112] Manley said that because of its friendship with Cuba in the course of exercising its "rights of sovereignty and non-alignment, Jamaica was marked for punishment."[113]

Manley's second term in office was viewed by some in the United States as socialist, pro-Cuban, and anti-American. For example, the Heritage Foundation had this to say: "reforms under the banner of democratic socialism measures ostensibly designed to decrease the island's still pervasive poverty, but which, coupled with Manley's pro-Cuban rhetoric began to take the appearance of creeping communism . . . Since 1974, Manley pushed his country closer and closer into the Soviet orbit, and developed particularly good ties to the Cuban government of Fidel Castro. Manley became a staunch supporter of Cuban interventionism in Africa and defended the placement of Soviet combat troops in Cuban bases. At the same time, he condemned the U.S. military presence in the area as imperialism."[114] This characterization of Manley was not helped by statements like the following, made in 1985 in the midst of the Reagan era. "Certainly, it is the wildest illusions to believe that the Soviet Union has an active blueprint for the subversion of Latin America lurking in some basement in the Kremlin."[115]

The deterioration of the U.S.-Jamaica relationship has been discussed in detail by Kaufman,[116] Stephens and Stephens,[117] Persaud,[118] and Henke.[119] The purpose of this section is to establish that when Manley returned to political office in 1989 he had to explain his changed thinking and rehabilitate himself and the PNP government in the U.S. foreign policy circles. This was a prerequisite to restarting U.S. aid, securing debt relief, and ensuring U.S. support from the IMF, World Bank, and the Inter-American Development Bank (IADB). The accomplishment of influencing U.S. policy towards Jamaica was made even more complex and difficult by the necessity to reposition Michael Manley in the eyes of the U.S. government. In this regard the greatest asset was Michael Manley himself, his charisma, his acuity of mind, and his persuasive articulation of policy issues.

Seaga's Foreign Policy

The Manley era 1972–1980 was a rupture from the apparently comatose posture of Bustamante who assured the United States that Jamaica would "be a firm ally of the United States and has no desire to play the neutral of seeking aid from East and West."[120] The foreign policy of the Seaga led government was a reversion to an extreme version of the JLP policy of the 1960s, put bluntly, we are with the West. It was also a reflection of Seaga's economic policy, which also dated back to the 1960s. He outlined this policy explained at the Commonwealth Finance Ministers meeting in 1969 as: "The first essential is that developing countries should ensure that a favourable climate exists for foreign investment" and "the second essential is for the establishment of the necessary institutional framework to facilitate foreign investment."[121] Financial aid from the United States was to be an essential private foreign investment and therefore the Seaga foreign policy was an aid seeking policy. This is a far cry from the declaration of Jamaica's first ambassador, Neville Ashenheim, in presenting his credentials to the president in 1962: "even in these material days, the kind of friendship we offer is an affair of the spirit and carries no price tag." [122]

Seaga's foreign policy was blatant political opportunism based on projecting Jamaica to the Reagan Administration as a model that the United States could contrast with the socialist inspired models in Nicaragua, Guyana, Grenada, and Cuba. At that time the United States was prone to seeing Soviet and Cuban influence everywhere in the Caribbean; hence there was an opportunity to do what Maingot calls "playing the Cuban card" [123] and what Stephens and Stephens call the "American Card." [124] The ideological disposition of the Reagan team was responsive to a political leader who claimed to be fighting to save democracy and capitalism from Cuban-supported socialism, which is how Seaga portrayed the Manley government of 1972–1980. A sense of the flavor of Seaga's characterization is: "The Cuban government became deeply involved with the PNP government newly elected in 1972. Cuba, it was obvious now saw Jamaica not just as a proven friend but as an ideological fellow-traveler in the socialist movement. . . . Jamaicans had felt uneasy with Castro in Cuba after the success of the revolution in 1959. . . . That disquiet . . . intensifies when Cuban missiles pointed threatening at the United States. The uneasiness about Cuban-type socialist contamination of the body politic in Jamaica grew further when Prime Minister Michael Manley was invited to ride with Fidel Castro in his Ilyushin jet to Algiers for his first meeting of the Non-Aligned Movement in September, 1973." [125] Manley visited Cuba and in turn Fidel Castro visited Jamaica. Historian Patrick Bryan explains that "warm relations with communist Cuba fanned the flames of anti-communist hysteria in Jamaica. It gave Edward Seaga the opportunity to capitalize on those sentiments, an opportunity Seaga grasped with both hands." [126]

Reagan had taken note of developments in Jamaica when Michael Manley was prime minister, as can be gleaned from a brief note he wrote on July 6, 1977. [127] Jamaica and Seaga receive several notations in the diaries, starting with the fourth recording of events on January 28, 1981, when he recorded that Prime Minister Seaga of Jamaica was the guest for his first state luncheon. Reagan, who had selected Jamaica as a showpiece [128] wrote: "He (Seaga) won a terrific election victory over a Cuban-backed pro-communist. I think we can help him & gradually take back the Caribbean which was becoming a Red lake." [129] Reagan maintained his interest in Jamaica throughout his eight years in office and visited Jamaica (and Barbados) in April 1982. He kept faith with Seaga and had regular contact with him and there were face-to-face meetings in February 1983 and October 1988. [130]

Seaga, thanks to the influence of John Rollins, a wealthy American businessman and Republican donor with investments in Jamaica, was the first head of government to be received at the White House by the newly elected Ronald Reagan. This was a considerable feat given the relative unimportance of Jamaica. In addition Seaga was sufficiently influential to get Reagan to visit Jamaica. Reagan's visit to Jamaica and Barbados in April 1982 was the first by a U.S. president since December 5–13, 1940, when President Franklin D. Roosevelt from the safety of his ship inspected British bases in Antigua, the Bahamas, St. Lucia, and Jamaica for possible American use. Reagan assured the region that "Our ties to the Caribbean are many and strong, and we mustn't let them be weakened by neglect . . . after all the Caribbean is our third border."[131]

Kenneth Hall observes that: "By aligning himself with the Reagan Administration in particular, he (Seaga) was able to create significant opportunities for leadership, less as an independent actor, but as an important agent of American policy in this hemisphere."[132] Seaga was also instrumental in the U.S. invasion of Grenada. In his autobiography[133] and diaries President Reagan made several comments on the invasion of Grenada.[134] He recorded on October 21, 1983: "I've OK'd an outright invasion in response to a request by 6 Caribbean countries including Jamaica & Barbados. They will all supply some troops so that it will be a multinational invasion."[135] He felt vindicated in this action because: "We have captured 700 Cubans, most of the Grenada military have faded back into the population"[136] and "They (the Cubans) were really going to move in & take over."[137] The connection as he saw it between events in Lebanon and Grenada is presented among a selected group of speeches published as a book.[138]

Manley February 1989–March 1992

The Michael Manley who took office in 1989 was much changed in his thinking about how to achieve the goals to which he was committed throughout his political life. An important aspect of his thinking was a greater recognition of the market and the role of the private sector. The changed perspective on economic policy was the end product of a complex rethinking of the experience of his 1972–1980 period in office and a profound understanding that the geopolitics of the 1990s were very different from those of the 1970s. The Jamaican electorate accepted the modified political platform and gave him and the PNP the largest majority of seats in the House of Representatives. However, the problem he faced was how to convince foreign governments including that of the United States and international financial organizations of both the modified thinking and of his commitment to the policies being espoused. In order to accomplish this he and the PNP would have to overcome impressions and some very strongly held views about the policies of the 1972–1980 period.

The process of exposure to the new thinking started in the late 1980s and was facilitated by Manley's frequent speaking engagements and lectures at universities in the United States, Canada, England, and Europe.

During the years of his opposition he kept in touch with members of the Congressional Black Caucus, the liberal wing of the United States think tank community, the British Labour Party, and the European parties that were members of the Socialist International. Among Manley's qualities were his intellect, confidence, and command of language, which gave him a willingness to engage anyone including hostile journalists, critics of all persuasions, and renowned scholars, as for example in the exchange of letters with Professor Kari Levitt.[139] By 1990, Manley had succeeded in convincing the outside world that he was seriously committed to his new approach. In January 1990 the *New York Times* reported that: "An American official said Mr. Manley had gone through a very impressive evolution as a political leader. For example, the official said, Mr. Manley has moved to sell state-owned industries, hotels and cement plants to private investors. In addition, the official said, Mr. Manley has been very tough on drug trafficking in Jamaica and has eradicated large amounts of marijuana being grown here (Jamaica). Our cooperation in the war on drugs could not be better, the American official said."[140] In March 1991 Manley is quoted as saying: "The world has changed. Jamaica has changed. And I think I have changed."[141]

Foreign Policy of P. J. Patterson

The conceptual template on which P. J. Patterson executed his foreign policy was the concentric circles framework of which he was one of the lead architects. He was Jamaica's Minister of Foreign Affairs during the years 1972 to 1975. During his tenure as Foreign Minister he was an exponent of developing country cooperation and coordination in their engagements and negotiations with developed countries. He served as President of the ACP/EU Ministerial Council and astutely led negotiations with the European Community on behalf of the ACP group of developing countries. In his capacity as Chairman of the ACP/EEC Ministerial Conference, he was instrumental in crafting the agreement for the first Lome Convention, which was signed in 1975. This agreement was the template for subsequent Lome conventions. His negotiating and diplomatic skills were acknowledged when he was asked to serve on several occasions as President and Spokesman of the ACP Ministerial Council.

He was an ardent regionalist and explained that this irrecoverable commitment did "not spring from any theoretical or sentimental motivations, but are rooted in the pragmatic appreciation that our own self-interest and the imperatives of being able to cope with the developments in the world around us, leave no other position."[142] For well over a decade he was in the role of senior statesman in CARICOM always able to get divergent views to coalesce into a pragmatic consensus. He envisioned CARICOM as an institutional arrangement for these small states to respond to global change. "The Community must be seen as a collective instrument available to the people of CARICOM to help construct resilience to adjust and adjust to these transformations in the global and regional environment."[143] CARICOM was essential in external relations to prevent the marginalization of the region and to reduce its vulnerability to political pressure, economic shocks, and environmental susceptibility. He declared that "The Caribbean Community can also be seen as an instrument for collective mitigation of the individual political and economic vulnerability of its members."[144] With no sentimentality he acknowledged that the migration may be limited: "Although the potential aggregate political and economic strength embodied by the Community is very modest by world standards and therefore is itself vulnerable as an entity, nevertheless a CARICOM that fulfils its potential can provide some degree of amelioration of the vulnerability stemming from the small size of individual members."[145]

He was never afraid to differ from the United States notably when he declined to allow the United States to send Haitian boat people to Jamaica instead of back to Haiti and provided safe haven for the exiled Haitian President Jean Bertram Aristide when he was returned from exile in Africa. He not only did not support the U.S. invasion of Iraq but was critical of this action in his address to the UN General Assembly. Patterson was a leading member of the PNP government, which developed a tradition of voting independently of the United States in the UN. On issues where the United States and the USSR voted differently in 1975 and 1979 Jamaica voted similarly to the United States 15.1 percent and 19.8 percent in those years.[146] Patterson publicly criticized the Helms-Burton Act because he said it "flies in the face of a basic premise of international law."[147] He was keenly aware of the implications for Jamaica's international trade and foreign policy of the formation of trade blocs such as the EU and NAFTA.[148] Navigating this context required a foreign policy in which Jamaica played an active role in the G-77, Non-Aligned Movement, G-15,[149] the ACP, and the Socialist International. Jamaica hosts several meetings of these organizations, for example, the Socialist International Committee for Latin America and the Caribbean met in Kingston, Jamaica, on September 1–2, 2000, hosted by the People's National Party. The Ninth Summit of the G-15 was held in Montego Bay, February 10–12, 1999.

Patterson had a very clear understanding of global affairs when he became Prime Minister of Jamaica in the early 1990s. He knew that the end of the Cold War ushered in a new global environment with the implication that "we are released from the inhibitive mindset of more than four decades of the Cold War, all nations are forced to redefine their role in the New World Order."[150] One of the prominent new features that he highlighted was the formation of economic/trading blocs such as the EU and NAFTA because "the rise of these powerful economic blocks have exerted tremendous pressures on Third World countries."[151] Concomitantly the break-up of the Soviet Union and its satellites in Eastern

Europe released several countries that became competitors with developing countries for aid, trade, and foreign investment. The implications of this development were, first, "the Latin American and the Caribbean Region is challenged to deepen and widen intra-regional relationships if we are to respond to the economic challenges which will be unleashed by the creation of NAFTA."[152] Second, "the prospect of a Single European Market obliges the countries of the Commonwealth Caribbean working together with the other countries in Africa and the Pacific, to preserve the preferences under Lome IV."[153] Patterson reaffirmed Third World solidarity when he reiterated: "the centrifugal forces unleashed by liberalized block based economy threaten the cohesiveness of the Third World and a unified response is most needed."[154] At the same time he chastised the developed countries at the G-15 in Cairo when he said, "The North must not use globalisation and the wider acceptance of the market system as an excuse for resiling from its responsibility to engage in the war to end poverty."[155]

There were issues on which Patterson was critical of U.S. policy toward the Caribbean region; in particular, he voiced concerns about the encroachment of the United States on the sovereignty of the Caribbean governments. He criticized, on several occasions, U.S. embargo against Cuba and specifically cited the Cuban Liberty and Democratic Solidarity Act (known in common parlance as the Helms-Burton Act) because among other things it "flies in the face of a basic premise of international law" namely territoriality.[156] He condemned aspects of U.S. counter narcotics policy describing this as a "flashpoint issue." "Some proposals made in order to eradicate the (drug) problem would see national sovereignty diluted, diminished or diluted all together through an uncritical application of the ship-rider principle and pressure to disregard our legal and constitutional provisions. . . . The permissive, uncritical and not clearly defined ship-rider type of arrangement now being touted as a necessity is really a latter day version of that generic type of intervention."[157] He had no hesitation in identifying transnational corporations as the drivers of the U.S. policy of dismantling the EU preferential banana regime, which was vital for the survival of the banana industry particularly in the smallest Caribbean states.[158]

Prime Minister Patterson was the senior statesman in CARICOM and was instrumental in ensuring that to the greatest extent possible CARICOM took common positions on foreign policy including on issues with the United States. Like Jamaica countries such as Barbados and Trinidad were trying to navigate the 1990s while constrained by varying degrees of external vulnerability.[159] Patterson was always willing to stand up for what he believed to be the right position; for example. he opposed the U.S. sanctions on Cuba and he did not support the U.S. invasion of Iraq.

Astute Political Leadership

During the period of this study 1991–2001 the government of Jamaica was led by two outstanding statesmen: Prime Ministers Michael Manley (until March 30, 1992) and Percival J. Patterson for the rest of the period. The issues of restoring U.S. aid and engineering debt relief took place under the leadership of Manley and the issues of cooperation on counter narcotics and the passage of the CBERA were handled under the stewardship of Patterson. Their personalities were different but they shared a view of the world and a willingness to fearlessly stand up for what they believed to be right and the diplomatic skills to attain and play a leadership role in world affairs.

Michael Manley was so engaging that just before he retired from the post of Prime Minister President George Bush held a dinner for him in his private quarters in the White House on March 24, 1992. Accommodation was provided for Manley at Blair House. The dinner was at a single table of President George Bush, Michael Manley, Glyn Ewart (later Mrs. Glyn Manley), Secretary of State James Baker, Treasury Secretary Brady, Deputy Treasury Secretary David Mulford, General Colin Powel, Speaker of the House of Representatives Tom Foley, Ambassador Glen Holden (U.S. Ambassador to Jamaica), and Mrs. Holden, myself, and my wife, Margaret. So persuasive was Michael Manley that Sir Shridath Ramphal recounts an anecdote: "Jimmy Carter's private meeting with Michael Manley on the Common Fund during the signing of the Panama Canal treaties led to a review of U.S. policy. It did not change American Policy; but an edict went out at official level never again to allow Michael Manley to be alone with the President." [160]

P. J. Patterson, a lawyer by profession, was an astute statesman who thought carefully about strategy and tactics and had less dependence on charismatic personality. He was very experienced in international diplomacy having served as Jamaica's minister of foreign affairs. Added to his gravitas was the fact he was the undoubted leader of the CARICOM and therefore the United States was always aware that in dealing with him he had the support of CARICOM and that he was the key to getting CARICOM to take policy positions. He was not willing to go along with U.S. positions if he disagreed and was prepared to incur the displeasure of the United States. In 2004, after President Jean Bertrand Aristides was ousted and transported from Haiti, Prime Minister P. J. Patterson dispatched a Member of Parliament, Sharon Hay-Webster, to the Central African Republic. She along with Randal Robinson and Congresswoman Maxine Waters persuaded the leadership of that country to release Aristide and his family so that they could go to Jamaica. The former Haitian leader and his family resided in the island for several months until the Jamaican government gained acceptance by the Republic of South Africa for them

to relocate there. This was a courageous decision because Aristide publicly claimed that he was ousted by a U.S. instigated coup.[161]

Matching the Ambassador to the Mission

It was important that the government selected a person to serve as
ambassador in the United States whose skills matched the agenda to be
pursued in Washington, D.C. Gail Scott, wife of a Washington-based ambassador and television anchorwoman points out that the posting in the
United States has changed over the years. Writing in 1999 she observed:
"In this most prestigious and pressurized post, ambassadors in Washington work hard and play less and less. Today's top diplomats are truly on
24-hour duty for political and commercial negotiating" and "Many ambassadors who are neither economists nor successful business executives
privately told me that they find commercial diplomacy, an aspect of their
job for which they aren't necessarily prepared. With the exception of a
few-such as . . . Jamaica's ambassador Bernal who is an economist and
banker."[162] Professor Anthony Payne states that Bernal: "as an economist, he was well-equipped to handle discussions with the IMF and the
World Bank and particularly well placed tin the Caribbean and Latin
American diplomatic corps in Washington to take advantage of the opening offered by President Bush's Enterprise for the Americas Initiative
(EAI) in 1990. As a result Jamaica was able to position itself at the forefront of the debate about how the Caribbean should react to the EAI and
all that it set in train."[163]

In the early 1990s the type of person appointed as ambassador to the
United States was changing from the traditional career diplomat to a
more technical person. Writing in mid-1990 David Brock captured this
change by saying: "Indeed, ambassadors posted to Washington today are
less statesmen-diplomats than lobbyists-intelligence agent" and called it
shirt-sleeve diplomacy. The new style ambassador is more likely to be a
well-connected politico or businessman than a stuffy, striped-pants graduate of a school of protocol. The Embassy Circuit, which ranked ambassadors by their social prowess, is dead; the new breed give working dinners
for serious people, rather than the type of glitzy affairs."[164]

Canadian ambassador Alan Gottlieb, when asked what he had
learned about how to be a good diplomat in Washington, D.C., responded: "Forget everything you ever learned about diplomacy."[165] The
Ambassador from a small, strategically unimportant, developing country
must be very creative and even unorthodox to get the message of their
country heard in Washington, D.C., where literally all interests, national
and foreign, are competing for the attention of Congress, the departments
of the Federal government, and the White House. The Ambassador has to
be innovative and unorthodox in his operations to first gain entry to
events and institutions that would not normally think of including the

diplomatic representative of an unimportant country. For example, when I wanted to lobby Vice President Dan Quayle I was not certain I could get an appointment with him so I accepted an invitation from an American friend to attend a Redskins game with tickets from his law firm. I was told that Quayle was attending and would be in the executive lounge during the half-time break. My host had access and I was able to speak with the vice president for a few minutes. Long enough to make my single point. Similarly when I wanted to see Senator Joseph Biden and knew that an appointment would be a long wait or that I might end up speaking with a staffer and not necessarily the chief of staff I arranged through the lobbyist to attend a fund raising reception. There I had a brief chat with Biden because it was unusual for an ambassador to attend such an event. The ambassador on such an occasion must be careful not to make a donation lest this be interpreted as taking a position in favor of one political party or of getting involved in the politics of the host country. Such an indiscretion could be fatal to the perception of the political neutrality of the ambassador and indeed the government represented.

Strengthening the Staff of the Embassy

In order to improve the capacity to accomplish special objectives it is advisable that the staff of the country's embassy in Washington, D.C., be strengthened and in some cases increased as some governments have to when facing crisis or special challenges. As a small developing country with fiscal difficulties Jamaica could not afford to increase the staff complement provided by the Ministry of Foreign Affairs but it did allow me to upgrade the staff of the Embassy of Jamaica by allowing me to select and recruit the personnel I recognized as necessary for the successful execution of the work of the mission. This was done by organizing the staff along functional lines, e.g., economic, political, trade, and legal and placing the appropriate specialist in each post. The upgrading of the staff of the Embassy of Jamaica is shown in table 8.1. Two posts were added: that of a legal attaché and that of a security attaché staffed by an officer from the Jamaica Constabulary Force (police). For a year the embassy benefitted from the services of an investment officer provided and funded by the Jamaica Investment Promotion.

Support of Lobbyists

U.S. foreign policy is the end-product of a complex inter-agency process within which is the mix of departments, branches, and personalities. The combination of these elements differs depending on the issue and over time the mix differs on the same issue. A foreign government wishing to influence U.S. policy must monitor and adjust to these changes. In this aspect a seasoned and well connected lobbyist can be particularly

Table 8.1.   Staff of the Embassy of Jamaica 1990–1995

POSTS	QUALIFICATIONS 1990	QUALIFICATIONS 1994/95
Ambassador	Tertiary	PhD, Economics
Deputy Chief of Mission	PhD, Political Science	PhD, Social Science
Economics Attaché	BA General	PhD, International Relations
Trade Attaché	BA General	B.Sc. International Relations and J.D., Law
Legal Attaché	Post did not exist	BA, J.D. Law
Consular Officer	BA Arts	BA, MPA
Information Attaché	BA General	PhD Mass Communications
Security Attaché	Post did not exist	Senior Police Officer

Source: Embassy files.

useful in keeping their client full and quickly briefed on changes. Indeed, the lobbyist can sometimes alert the foreign government before the changes in personnel actually take place. The retention of the services of lobbyists is important because, first, Americans tell Americans information that they will not tell foreigners; second, the staff of the lobbyists have been in Washington "circles" in many instances far longer than any ambassador's tenure; and third, they have a wide network of contacts that will take an ambassador and/or embassy staff many years to develop and cultivate. The government of Jamaica's efforts to influence U.S. policy benefit from the utilization of the services of lobbyists in securing aid, debt relief, trade legislation, and certification for cooperation on counter narcotics. Regardless of how small and impecunious a country may be it is essential for the government to retain the services of a firm of lobbyists. The cost depends on which firm is hired and how much service is required. The government should arrange for what it can afford and choose the appropriate firm.

Carefully Designed and Implemented Strategy

To gain success in influencing U.S. foreign policy countries must have a strategy that is carefully designed, continuously redacted, and consistently implemented and that embodies the following elements:

1. A clearly defined objective that can be ambitious but must be feasible,

2. The strategy must be proactive and definitely on a stance of reacting to events but of envisioning and shaping outcomes,
3. The strategy must be capable of mobilizing U.S. government and domestic constituencies because they have been convinced that it is in their interest and the interest of the United States,
4. The appropriate personnel and necessary institutional capacity must be identified and marshalled or created or acquired,
5. The strategy must be multi-dimensional encompassing all the institutions and actors that affect the desired outcome,
6. The implementation must be followed consistently at all levels,
7. The strategy will have to be redacted on a continuous basis to take account of changing circumstances and entry and exit of players.

Effective Modes of Engagement

A small country in addition to the usual array of techniques of engagement has to be creative in its efforts to engage the "behemoth" that is the U.S. government. For example, invitations to Congressmen to attend receptions on the country's national day usually get passed to "staffers" who while not to be ignored are not the Congressman. However, an enjoyable after working hours event that the Congressional representative can spend a short time at is often more effective in attendance. For example, I arranged for Sandals to purchase all the seats for the 8 PM performance of Jamaican jazz pianist Monty Alexander at Blues Alley and this brought in several very important people. Similarly, an event at the Caribbean club/restaurant Zanzibar at which free Jamaican cigars (five brands), coffee, and rum was dispensed pulled in a couple Senators. While they could not accept a gift of Jamaican cigars there is no rule against accepting some samples. Targeting is most efficacious when the individual is studied (their curriculum vitae, their interest, their recent achievements, their recent television appearance, their family holiday in Jamaica, etc.) to find the right "angle" of approach. This type of personal information can be the way to establish a personal rapport before introducing any official business. For example, I recall referring to a point made in a book authored by a senior State Department official that was particularly flattering, a chance encounter at a Mozart concert at the Kennedy Center was a bond with a key World Bank official, and a discussion of a brass rubbing of a 16th-century English tombstone with a top Treasury technocrat.

Professor Braveboy-Wagner writing in April 1991 described the modalities of Caribbean diplomats in Washington, D.C., as: "Luncheons, parties, dinners, functions, and occasional small gifts are the favored ways in which Caribbean diplomats seek to influence the U.S. bureaucracy and congress."[166] This mode of engagement was at variance with the political culture in Washington, D.C., in the 1990s because time was of the essence. Congressional representatives are beholden to the voters of their district and foreign policy issues are of limited importance to staying in office (with exceptions) and a representative being re-elected can be jeopardized by supporting foreign policy issues that appear to send U.S. business and jobs abroad or divert funds from U.S. projects into foreign aid. They do not have time for long engagements such as dinners, preferring to appear for 20–30 minutes at a reception, make brief remarks if necessary, and move on to the next engagement. When calling on a Congressman in his office the Ambassador must get to the point quickly. A typical meeting would be brief salutations, introduction of all present, and appreciation for acceding to the request for the meeting given the very busy schedule of the Congress. Photos are taken if requested by either party. Immediately the Congressman will say: "What can I do for you, Mr. Ambassador?" The Ambassador will explain what he wants, something like, "Congressman, I would like your support for the draft bill." Three to five points are presented as to why he should support the bill, e.g., creates jobs in the member's district, increases U.S. exports, etc. and why it is important for the ambassador's country, which is a friend and partner of the American people. A brief exchange occurs and then the Ambassador or his aide presents a two page memo to the Congressman's staffer. Thank you and departure follow. The meeting should be followed by a letter from the Ambassador to the Congressman the next day reiterating the points made and formally acknowledging any verbal commitments. A skillful diplomat will add to this barebones engagement points that build or consolidate relations with the Congressman, e.g., laudatory reference to some recent speech, television interview, or deed or an expression of appreciation for the member's support for the issue at hand. Beyond this the skilled diplomat might say something like "we both support the same team in the NBA, hope they make the play-offs this year."

An example of being business-like. I had waited three weeks for an appointment to see Congressman Sam Gibbons, Democrat from Florida, and Chair of the Trade Sub-Committee of the Ways and Means Committee of the House of Representatives. The moment after the salutations the light and bell in his office indicated that it was time to make a vote in the House, which was in another building 15 minutes away. Rather than miss my opportunity I asked if I could walk with him and he readily agreed. I traveled with him on the underground rail reserved for members and in the members-only elevator and by the time we arrived at the voting venue I had unloaded my agenda. This established me as a business-like person and thereafter I had no problem in seeing him at any time. Meetings can be even briefer, for example, I and the staffer from the lobbyist would stand outside a room in which a Congressional committee was meeting and the staffer would take a note or send a verbal message that the Ambassador of Jamaica would like to speak to the member for a few minutes if he could step out. I do not recall a refusal and these two-minute encounters were very productive, apart from facilitating a quick coffee for the member.

Building American Support

The key to getting U.S. foreign policy to support objectives of a foreign country is to have the various elements in the U.S. process of policy decision making to see the objective as being in the interest of the United States. While not entirely dismissing support for foreign policy objectives for altruistic and enlightened reasons it is wise to be cynically wise and realistic. The extent to which a small developing country or for that matter any country is able to mobilize support for its positions and goals depends largely on identifying and gaining the support of a constituency in the U.S. political process. The onus is on the foreign country to point out why supporting their position is good for the United States. Indeed, the process is often one of educating Congressional representatives who are astonishingly ignorant about the world beyond the borders of the United States. One effective way to educate members of Congress is to enlighten the staff who in turn will brief the member. For example, in lobbying for the United States-Caribbean Trade Partnership Act (CBTPA) legislation it was often the case that members had to be told the value of exports from their state to the Caribbean and to explain why jobs in the United States would not be lost but would benefit from support of joint or shared production in which the international division of labor would distribute economic gains between the United States and the Caribbean. A coping strategy had to be developed to neutralize domestic opponents, for example, in pushing for trade legislation Jamaica and the Caribbean were supported by the apparel producers and advocates of free trade while the opposition came from the textile producers and the trade unions.

It is American interests and voters that matter most to members of Congress and to Federal government officials. A problem that often arises when U.S. interests diverge and even where interests do not clash with local interests are frequently in the position of competing for the same pool of resources as foreign governments. For example, when a certain congressman for a district in New York with a large number of Caribbean voters would not commit to supporting trade legislation beneficial to the Caribbean I arranged through a friendly journalist to have an article about his lack of support published in the local newspaper. Within days he signed on as a co-sponsor for the bill.

A very important aspect of building support and influence is to engage prominent and influential Americans born in Jamaica or born in the United States of Jamaican parents. Harry Belafonte[167] is an example of the first and General Colin Powell[168] is an outstanding example of the latter. The networking encompassed Jamaican-Americans in all fields of endeavor and was extended to people who had a special relationship with Jamaica and to people of Caribbean origin or affiliation. For example, in the business sector is Walt Braithwaite, a Vice President of Boeing Corporation in Seattle who was born in Jamaica and William "Bill" Rhodes[169] Vice President of Citibank, an American whose early career with the bank was in Kingston, Jamaica.

Strategic Alliances

Jamaica has had many years of building strategic alliances with CARICOM countries, other small countries, and developing countries in a wide variety of fora and a broad range of economic, political, and security issues. In Washington, D.C., Jamaica operated on several issues with other CARICOM states, in particular the issue of trade legislation for the Caribbean. Beyond CARICOM its next strategic alliance was with the Central American countries that were beneficiaries of the CBERA Act. The Revised Treaty of Chaguaramas in Article 6 (g) and (h) establishes as objectives "the achievement of a greater measure of economic leverage and effectiveness" in external relations and "enhanced coordination of Member States' foreign and (foreign) economic policies."[170] It obligates member states of CARICOM to coordinate their trade policies and pursue the negotiation of external trade agreements on a joint basis. The establishment of the Caribbean Regional Negotiating Machinery[171] has facilitated a common approach to external trade negotiations at a time when the region was simultaneously involved in an unprecedented number of external negotiations, notably the WTO, the FTAA, and the EU-ACP arrangements.

An indispensable part of influencing U.S. foreign policy for a small country is strategic alliances with other parties who have common interests. These strategic alliance may be with other like-minded governments or with U.S. corporate interests. These alliances may vary from one issue to another. For example, the English-speaking Caribbean countries and the Central American countries were in very close coordination lobbying for preferential access to the U.S. market provided by the CBERA but the Central Americans vigorously opposed preferential treatment for small economies in the Free Trade of the Americas negotiation even before it was decided whether they would be classified as one of the small economies. Collaboration among CARICOM in Washington, D.C., was made easier by the tradition of coordination that dated back to the 1960s. The coordination extended to having common positions in the Organization of American States and during the Summit of the Americas process. The common positions involved the group taking and advocating positions on issues that did not directly affect individual countries. For example, Barbados, Guyana, and Trinidad and Tobago consistently supported the common positions of CARICOM in the banana dispute with the United States although these countries did not export bananas. There were exceptions such as not being able to agree to support one candidate in the election of a new Secretary-General of the OAS and there have been difficulties with joint representation. [172]

The tradition of coordination and common positions goes back to the colonial era when the then West Indies colonies jointly negotiated with the British colonial authorities over the marketing arrangements for sugar and bananas. During the brief West Indies Federation the governments at a single diplomatic mission in the United Kingdom and subsequently joint diplomatic representative has been an ideal position to aspire to. The Federation broke up in 1961 but the goal of foreign policy was retained and in 1973 it was formally mandated as one of the goals of the newly established Caribbean Community [173] and later in the OECS charter. The CARICOM negotiators acted as a single unit in negotiations for the Lome Conventions with the European Union as well as in other international engagements at the United Nations and the World Trade Organization and international fora such as the Non-Aligned Movement. The practice was observed in dealing with the United States; for example, CARICOM operated as a joint team in the negotiations with the United States of the Barbados Accord signed in Bridgetown by President Bill Clinton and the heads of governments of CARICOM. The negotiations consisted of two parallel processes: the economic component was led by Richard Bernal of Jamaica and the security component was led by David Simmons, Attorney General of Barbados, both superintended by P. J. Patterson, Prime Minister of Jamaica.

Entering Policy Formation Through Think Tanks

The strategy must start with where the policy ideas start or are intellectually legitimized, which is in the think tanks. The think tanks and research institutes consist of former government officials with contacts and some of whom are on sabbatical waiting to resume a post in government when their political party returns to power. These institutions are also incubators for those aspiring to posts in the U.S. government and are establishing their policy advice and technical expertise. Others include a core of long-term commentators available for TV commentaries and opinion editorials. These "research fellows" include a mix of future and former actors. They include especially those who were in academia, or are comfortably retired from institutions such as the IMF or World Bank and who are finally free to speak their minds or those regarded as too old for federal government posts.

Think tanks have the special role of reviewing and initiating policy that the various departments of the U.S. government adapt and incorporate as U.S. foreign policy. Michael Manley understood this very well and wherever and whenever he engaged these institutions he was able to influence their discussions. As a former university academic he was comfortable in the milieu of the think tank community and very active. Indeed, on many occaisions I was the only ambassador present and almost at every event was the only developing country diplomat. Some of the contacts reinforced or made in the think tanks later became members of the U.S. government, for example, Richard Feinberg, formerly of the Overseas Development Council was later in charge of Latin America and the Caribbean in the National Security Council. Several persons on the staff of think tanks were former U.S. government officials and gave valuable insights into the workings of the U.S. government system. They usually retained contacts and influence in their former departments and could be very helpful. I was able to establish a presence, and even became a "regular" in the think tank community on economic issues, in particular international trade and Caribbean issues in general. In this regard my testimonies to Congress were ideal calling cards. In spite of being an ambassador (a post viewed with patronizing condescension by "policy wonks") I was frequently cited in print media and had papers published by the Center for Strategic and International Studies, the North-South Center, the National Planning Association, Trans-Africa as well as scholarly law journals published by Georgetown University, American University, Columbia University, and in a book published by the World Bank. I also had the rare distinction of being the lead speaker on NAFTA on a panel at the annual American Bar Association conference in New Orleans. The most effective way to reach a wide cross-section of American public opinion is an opinion editorial in one of the leading nationally read newspapers in particular the *Wall Street Journal*, the *Washington Post*, and the *New York Times*. This is an extremely difficult venture to accomplish because these newspapers are bombarded with far more submissions than they can possibly publish. They are especially skeptical of diplomats who they view correctly as seek to "use" their paper. To succeed the editorial has to be topical so the timing of submission is critical and as they say in the press jargon, there has to be a "hook," i.e., current event. Regardless of how important the issue is to the writer's country or government it has to be of current interest to the American public. Opinion editorials more likely to succeed if the author is known and well regarded and has the best chance of succeeding if piloted by somebody with sufficient contracts to get it to the top of the pile of the editor in charge of opinion editorials. The editorial has to be short conforming to the number of words of the particular newspaper and must be written in the appropriate style. Specifically it must engage the reader in the first two sentences and must have a punch line at the end. The actual title is the prerogative of the editor. It must be free of jargon as far as possible and sentences must be short and each paragraph convey a single thought. In my case fortune favour the brave and I had to two opinion editorials on two of the most important topics for Jamaica and they appeared at the most politically propitious moment in the *Wall Street Journal* and the *Washington Post*.

PART III: THE LESSONS

The preceding explanation of why Jamaica was successful in influencing U.S. foreign policy yields lessons that can be useful to all countries, in particular small states and small developing countries. The key lessons are enumerated below.

1. A critically important factor for Jamaica was the belief that it could accomplish its goals and that derived from a national tradition and national character. A government must first believe that it is possible and that it can succeed in influencing U.S. foreign policy. It can draw some confidence based on the Jamaican experience set out and explained in this book.

2. The government of a country wishing to influence the United States must carefully devise a strategy to get on the foreign policy agenda of the United States hopefully not as a crisis or problem but as a country of interest or concern. It must formulate a strategy that is practical given its human and financial resources.

3. The quality of the political leadership in the country wishing to influence U.S. policy is critical. The leaders must elicit the attention and respect of the U.S. government and should ideally have the personality, intellect, and political astuteness to build relationships with key members of government in particular with the President and the Secretary of State but additionally with any member of the Cabinet. There is no guarantee that the leadership with the right attitude, vision, and appropriate skills will emerge but should keep in mind the dictum of Norman Manley, architect of Jamaica's movement to political independence from Britain: "Great causes are not won by doubtful men and women." [174]

4. The efforts of a foreign government in the United States can benefit considerably from the services of a firm of lobbyists. There are lobbyists and lobbyists and care must be taken to select the one that is most appropriate for the agenda that is to be advanced. Large lobbying firms have a range of skills and connections with both Democrats and Republicans but are not necessarily the most appropriate and may be much more expensive than a smaller firm with a smaller client list.

5. The foreign government must deploy an ambassador whose skills are appropriate to the objectives; for example, if the agenda is largely economic then the ambassador should have a strong economic background. The ambassador must be supported by the best personnel the country can provide to staff the embassy. Recruitment must be guided by identifying the most qualified by their training and professional experi-

ence and skills, including bringing in skills from outside the career cadre of the ministry of foreign affairs. The "brightest and the best" is what is need.

The contemporary relevance of the lessons derived from the experience of Jamaica and the United States is two-fold: first, to embolden small states to have the belief and confidence in their capacity to influence even a superpower such as the United States. The case studies of the Jamaican experience document the possibility to succeed in such a daunting endeavor. Second, the lessons point to the type of actions and requirements for such actions that a small state must undertake to influence a superpower, or at least a more powerful state. Both impacts are particularly relevant because by any definition the majority of countries are small and indeed, in interacting with the United States nearly all countries will be in a situation of asymmetrical power.

The United States has been a superpower since World War II and for long periods its dominance in global affairs has been unchallenged. What the United States does affects all countries in one way or another. In this context all countries are interested in influencing U.S. foreign policy in general and in particular how it impacts their country, and hence most if not all countries are actively engaged in attempting to influence U.S. foreign policy. It is understood that large, developed, and powerful countries will exert some influence on U.S. foreign policy and accepted that small, developing, and poor countries will not be able to affect U.S. foreign policy. Jamaica, a small, developing country of no strategic importance to the United States, did influence U.S. foreign policy. This experience challenges the conventional wisdom expressed by Rose as a situation in which countries in the Caribbean inclusive of Jamaica "are not only dependent because of their small size and limited resources. Rather, dependency has destroyed their national capacity to act as autonomous units."[175] This poses the possibility that if even a small country can influence the United States, then a large number of countries could do the same. This raises the question of whether the United States should worry.

NOTES

1. "U.S. Issues Warnings for Trips to Jamaica, Mexico," Chicago Tribune, 8 September 1991. articles.chicagotribune.com/1991 . . . /travel/9103070805_. Accessed 27 September, 2014.

2. Travel Advisories. State Needs Better Practices for Informing Americans of Dangers Overseas (Washington, D.C.: United States General Accounting Office, August 1991).

3. Mike Shoup, "State Department changes its way of warning travelers," Baltimore Sun, November 22, 1992.

4. David Winner, Brilliant Orange. The Neurotic Genius of Dutch Football (London: Bloomsbury Publishing, 2000).

5. Amelia Hadfield-Amkhan, British Foreign Policy, National Identity and Neo-classical Realism (Lanham: Rowman & Littlefield Publishers, 2010) page 1.

6. Henry Kissinger, On China (New York: Penguin Press, 2011) pages 92–106.

7. Henry Kissinger, On China (New York: Penguin Press, 2011) pages 202–93 and Margaret Macmillan, Nixon and Mao. The Week That Changed the World (New York: Random House, 2007).

8. W. Travis Hanes III and Frank Sanello, The Opium Wars. The Addiction of One Empire and the Corruption of Another (New York: Barnes & Noble, 2002) pages 13–35.

9. It has been argued that there are two contending aspects of American character, see Arthur Schlesinger, Jr., "Foreign Policy and the American Character," Foreign Affairs, Vol. 62, No. 1 (Fall, 1983) pages 1–16.

10. The literature on the concept of "national character" is discussed in Alex Inkeles, National Character. A Psycho-Social Perspective (New Brunswick: Transaction Publishers, 1997) pages 3–124.

11. It may even be defined by the absence of particular traits found in many other countries/states. Seymour Martin Lipset, American Exceptionalism. A Double-Edged Sword (New York: W. W. Norton and Company, 1996).

12. There are those who dispute the basis for this such as Godfrey Hodgson, The Myth of American Exceptionalism (New Haven: Yale University Press, 2009).

13. Seymour Martin Lipset, American Exceptionalism. A Double-Edged Sword (New York: W. W. Norton and Company, 1996).

14. The Most Hon. Prof. Kenneth Hall, "Jamaica in the International Arena: Leader or Follower. Historical Perspectives on Jamaica's Contribution to the International Community" in Kenneth Hall and Myrtle Chuck-A-Sang (eds.), Paradigm Shifts & Structural Changes - in Pursuit of Progress in the Caribbean Community (Bloomington: Trafford Publishing, 2013) pages 104–14. See 104.

15. Randolph B. Persaud, Counter-Hegemony and Foreign Policy. The Dialectics of Marginalized and Global Forces in Jamaica (Albany: State University of New York Press, 2001) page 121.

16. Laurie Gunst, Born Fi' Dead: A Journey Through the Jamaican Posse Underworld (New York: Henry Holt and Company, 1995).

17. Cited in Ashante Infantry, "No One Has Swagger Like Jamaicans," Toronto Star, June 16, 2014.

18. Doreen Miller, An Introduction to Jamaican Culture for Rehabilitation Services Providers, Center for International Rehabilitation Research Information and Exchange, 2002. http://cirrie.buffalo.edu/culture/monographs/jamaica . Accessed 12 August 2014.

19. Geert Hofstede, Culture's Consequences: Comparing Values, Behaviors, Institutions and Organizations Across Nations (Thousand Oaks, CA: SAGE Publications, 2nd ed. 2001).

20. Jamaica - Geert Hofstede, http://geert-hofstede.com/jamaica.html. Accessed 24 February 2015.

21. Victor Stafford Reid, The Horses of the Morning. About the Right Excellent N. W. Manley, Q.C, M.M. National Hero of Jamaica (Kingston: Caribbean Authors Publishing, 1985) page 321.

22. Victor Stafford Reid, The Horses of the Morning. About the Right Excellent N. W. Manley, Q.C, M. M. National Hero of Jamaica (Kingston: Caribbean Authors Publishing, 1985) page 323.

23. Gerald Horne, Cold War in a Hot Zone: The United States confronts Labor and Independence Struggles in the British West Indies.(Philadelphia: Temple University Press, 20007).

24. Trevor Munroe, The Cold War and the Jamaican Left 1950–55 (Kingston: Kingston Publishers, 1992).

25. Peter Abrahams, Jamaica. An Island Mosaic (London: Her Majesty's Stationery Office, 1957) page 196.

26. Trevor Munroe, The Cold War and the Jamaican Left 1950–55 (Kingston: Kingston Publishers, 1992) page 72.

27. Anthony Bogues, "Michael Manley, Trade Unionism, and the Politics of Equality" in Perry Mars and Alma H. Young (eds.), Caribbean Labor and Politics: Legacies of Cheddi Jagan and Michael Manley (Wayne State University Press, 2004) pages 41–42.

28. Memorandum for the President. Secretary of State. Visit of Premier of Jamaica. 3 April, 1961, page 1. Courtesy of the John F. Kennedy Library.

29. Memorandum from Secretary of State Dean Rusk to President John F. Kennedy re Call by Norman Manley, Premier of Jamaica, 19 April, 1961, page 1. Courtesy of the John F. Kennedy Library.

30. Jamaica was concerned that non-quota purchases would be at world market price, which would be below the cost of production in Jamaica.

31. "Jamaica's problems: JFK understanding," The Daily Gleaner, April 20, 1961, page 1.

32. Memorandum for the President. Secretary of State. Visit of Premier of Jamaica. 3 April, 1961, page 1. Courtesy of the John F. Kennedy Library.

33. Philip Sherlock, "Prospects in the Caribbean," Foreign Affairs, Vol. 41, No. 4 (July, 1963) pages 744–50. See page 750.

34. Memorandum to McGeorge Bundy, White House from William H. Brubeck, State Department, Visit of Sir Alexander Bustamante, Premier of Jamaica, 26 June, 1962, page 2. Courtesy of the John F. Kennedy Library.

35. Interview with Dorell Callender on 3 March, 2014.

36. Edward Seaga, Edward Seaga. My Life and Leadership, Vol. 1: Clash of Ideologies 1930–1980 (Oxford: Macmillan, 2009) page 237.

37. Government of Jamaica, Ministry Paper No. 60, A Proposal that Jamaica should become a member of the Organization of American States, June, 1969, page 24.

38. Randolph B. Persaud, Counter-Hegemony and Foreign Policy. The Dialectics of Marginalized and Global Forces in Jamaica (Albany: State University of New York Press, 2001) page 123.

39. Principles and Objectives of page 52.

40. These historic events are recounted in Patrick H. O. Rousseau, Negotiating Change. Pat Rousseau and the Bauxite Negotiations 1974–77 (Kingston: Heinemann Educational Books Caribbean Ltd, 1987) and Carlton E. Davis, Jamaica in the World Aluminium Industry, Vol. II. 1974–1988. Bauxite Levy Negotiations (Kingston: Jamaica Bauxite Institute, 1995).

41. Carlton E. Davis, Jamaica in the World Aluminium Industry, Vol. II. 1974–1988. Bauxite Levy Negotiations (Kingston: Jamaica Bauxite Institute, 1995) pages 181–96.

42. Patrick H. O. Rousseau, Negotiating Change. Pat Rousseau and the Bauxite Negotiations 1974–7 (Kingston: Heinemann Educational Books Caribbean Ltd, 1987) page 110.

43. Michael Manley, The Politics of Change. A Jamaican Testament (Washington, D.C.: Howard University Press, 1975) page 262.

44. Kenneth N. Rogers, Political Officer, U.S. Embassy, Kingston (1968–1972). Jamaica Country Readers, adst.org/wp-content/uploads/2012/09/. Accessed 28 August 2014.

45. Article 9 of the Vienna Convention on Diplomatic Relations allows a receiving State "at any time and without having to explain its decision" to declare any member of a diplomatic staff persona non grata. A person so declared is considered unacceptable and is usually recalled to his or her home nation. If not recalled, the receiving State "may refuse to recognize the person concerned as a member of the mission."

46. Kenneth N. Rogers, Political Officer, U.S. Embassy, Kingston (1968–1972). Jamaica Country Readers, adst.org/wp-content/uploads/2012/09/. Accessed 28 August 2014.

47. George Crile, Jr., "Our Man in Jamaica," Harper's Magazine, October, 1974, pages 87–96. See page 87.

48. "JAMAICA: Our Man in Kingston," Time magazine, August 6, 1973.

49. Darrel E. Levi, Michael Manley. The Making of a Leader (Kingston: Heinemann Publishers (Caribbean), 1989) page 139.

50. Darrel E. Levi, Michael Manley. The Making of a Leader (Kingston: Heinemann Publishers (Caribbean), 1989) page 139.

51. Darrel E. Levi, Michael Manley. The Making of a Leader (Kingston: Heinemann Publishers (Caribbean), 1989) page 139.

52. Darrel E. Levi, Michael Manley. The Making of a Leader (Kingston: Heinemann Publishers (Caribbean), 1989) page 139.

53. Darrel E. Levi, Michael Manley. The Making of a Leader (Kingston: Heinemann Publishers (Caribbean), 1989) page 139.

54. Carlton Davis, "Michael Manley's Foreign Policy of Non-alignment," Jamaica Journal, Vol. 34, Nos. 1–2 (August, 2012) pages 38–47. See page 40.

55. R. B. Manderson-Jones, Jamaica Foreign Policy in the Caribbean 1962–1968 (Kingston: CARICOM Publishers, 1990) page 127.

56. Rex Nettleford (ed.), Manley and the New Jamaica. Selected speeches and writings 1938–1968 (Kingston: Longman Caribbean, 1971) page 381.

57. Anna Kasafi Perkins, Justice as Equality. Michael Manley's Caribbean Vision of Justice (New York: Peter Lang Publishing, 2010).

58. Anthony Bogues, "Michael Manley, Trade Unionism, and the Politics of Equality" in Perry Mars and Alma H. Young (eds.), Caribbean Labor and Politics: Legacies of Cheddi Jagan and Michael Manley (Wayne State University Press, 2004) page 43.

59. Rex Nettleford, "Preface: Michael Manley and Caribbean Development. The Culture of Resistance," Caribbean Quarterly, Vol. 48, No. 1 (March, 2002) pages 1–4. See page 1.

60. Carlton Davis, "Some Visions That Still Remain Relevant" in Delano Franklyn (ed.), Michael Manley. Putting People First (Kingston: Winston Franklyn Barnes Publishers, 2013) page 200.

61. Michael Manley, Jamaica. Struggle in the Periphery (London: Third World Media/Writers and Readers Publishing Cooperative Society, 1982) pages 66–67.

62. Michael Manley, "Overcoming Insularity in Jamaica," Foreign Affairs, Vol. 49, No. 1(October, 1970) page 106.

63. Michael Manley, Jamaica. Struggle in the Periphery (London: Third World Media/Writers and Readers Publishing Cooperative Society, 1982) pages 66–67.

64. Michael Manley, Jamaica. Struggle in the Periphery (London: Third World Media/Writers and Readers Publishing Cooperative Society, 1982) page 67.

65. Delano Franklyn (ed.), Michael Manley. The Politics of Equality (Kingston: Wilson Franklyn Barnes, 2009) page 29.

66. Delano Franklyn (ed.), Michael Manley. The Politics of Equality (Kingston: Wilson Franklyn Barnes, 2009) page 28.

67. Delano Franklyn (ed.), Michael Manley. The Politics of Equality (Kingston: Wilson Franklyn Barnes, 2009) page 29.

68. Michael Manley, "Overcoming Insularity in Jamaica," Foreign Affairs, Vol. 49, No. 1 (October, 1970) page 101.

69. Michael Manley, "Overcoming Insularity in Jamaica," Foreign Affairs, Vol. 49, No. 1 (October, 1970) page 109.

70. Michael Manley, Jamaica. Struggle in the Periphery (London: Third World Media/Writers and Readers Publishing Cooperative Society, 1982) page 123.

71. Denis Benn, Multilateral Diplomacy and the Economics of Change. The Third World and the New International Economic Order (Kingston/Miami: Ian Randle Publishers, 2003).

72. Michael Manley, "Overcoming Insularity in Jamaica," Foreign Affairs, Vol. 49, No. 1 (October, 1970) page 109.

73. Michael Manley, "Overcoming Insularity in Jamaica," Foreign Affairs, Vol. 49, No. 1 (October, 1970) page 108.

74. Michael Manley, "Overcoming Insularity in Jamaica," Foreign Affairs, Vol. 49, No. 1 (October, 1970) page 108.

75. Vijay Prashad, The Darker Nations: A People's History of the Third World (New York: New Press, 2008) page 210.

76. Anthony Bogues, "Michael Manley and the Politics of Decolonization" in Delano Franklyn (ed.), Michael Manley. Putting People First (Kingston: Winston Franklyn Barnes Publishers, 2013) pages 212–35.

77. Anthony Bogues, "Michael Manley and the Politics of Decolonization" in Delano Franklyn (ed.), Michael Manley. Putting People First (Kingston: Winston Franklyn Barnes Publishers, 2013) page 229.

78. Peter Phillips, "Preserving the Michael Manley Legacy: Towards a Progressive Political Agenda for the Current Period" in Delano Franklyn (ed.), Michael Manley. Putting People First (Kingston: Winston Franklyn Barnes Publishers, 2013) pages 103–15. See page 105.

79. Michael Manley, A Voice at the Workplace (London: Andre Deutsch, 1975) page 223.

80. Michael Manley, The Poverty of Nations. Reflections on Underdevelopment and the World Economy (London: Pluto Press, 1991) pages 88–109.

81. Dudley Thompson, former RAF pilot and Rhodes Scholar was a lawyer for Komo Kenyatta during the Mau-Mau trials. See Dudley Thompson, From Kingston to Kenya. The Making of a Pan-African Lawyer (Dover: The Majority Press, 1993).

82. Marc Goodman, "Interview with Dudley Thompson," Jamaica Journal, Vol. 34, Nos. 1–2 (August, 2012) pages 23–31. See page 26.

83. John Hearne (ed.), The Search for Solutions. The Speeches and Writings of Michael Manley (Oshawa: Maple House Publishing Co., 1976) page 189.

84. Michael Manley, The Politics of Change (London: Andre Deutsch,1974) page 138.

85. Richard L. Bernal, "Restructuring Jamaica's Economic Relations with Socialist Countries, 1974–1980" Development and Change, Vol. 17, No. 4 (October, 1986) pages 607–34.

86. Global Challenge. From Crisis to Co-Operation: Breaking the North-South Stalemate (London: Pan Books, 1985).

87. Michael Manley and Willy Brandt, "Introduction," Global Challenge. From Crisis to Co-Operation: Breaking the North-South Stalemate (London: Pan Books, 1985) pages 13–21.

88. Michael Manley, The Poverty of Nations (London: Pluto Press, 1991) pages 88–109.

89. The Challenge to the South: The Report of the South Commission (New York: Oxford University Press, 1990).

90. George L. Beckford, Persistent Poverty. Underdevelopment in Plantation Economies of the Third World (New York: Oxford University Press, 1972).

91. Norman Girvan, "Multinational Corporations and Dependent Underdevelopment in Mineral-Export Economies," Social and Economic Studies, Vol. 19, No. 4 (December, 1970) pages 490–526 and Corporate Imperialism. Conflict and Expropriation (White Plains, N.Y.: M.E. Sharpe, 1976).

92. Norman Girvan, The Caribbean Bauxite Industry: The Scope for Rationalization and Regional Collaboration. Mona: Institute of Social and Economic Research, (I.S.E.R.), University of the West Indies, 1967.

93. Fred Bergsten, "A New OPEC in Bauxite," Challenge, July-August, 1976, pages 12–20.

94. Michael Manley, Jamaica. Struggle in the Periphery (London: Third World Media/ Writers and Readers Publishing Cooperative Society, 1982) pages 115–16.

95. Roger D. Hansen, "Introduction" in Albert Fishlow, Carlos F. Diaz-Alejandro, Richard R. Fagen, and Roger D. Hansen, Rich and Poor Nations in the World Economy. (New York: McGraw-Hill, 1978) pages 12–13.

96. Mark Mazower, Governing the World. The History of an Idea (New York: Penguin Books, 2012) page 345.

97. Carlos F. Diaz-Alejandro, "Delinking North and South: Unshackling or Unhinging?" in Albert Fishlow, Carlos F. Diaz-Alejandro, Richard R. Fagen, and Roger D. Hansen, Rich and Poor Nations in the World Economy (New York: McGraw-Hill, 1978) paged 87–164. See page 127.

98. Ernest Mandel, Late Capitalism (London: Verso, 1977).

99. Clive Y. Thomas, Dependence and Transformation. The Economics of the Transition to Socialism (New York: Monthly Review Press, 1974).

100. Raul Prebisch, The Economic Development of Latin America and Its Principal Problems (New York: United Nations Economic Commission for Latin America, 1950) and "Commercial Policy in the Underdeveloped Countries." American Economic Review, Vol. 49, No. 2 (May 1959) pages 251–73.

101. H. W. Singer, "The Distribution of Gains Between Investing and Borrowing Countries." American Economic Review, Vol. 40, No. 2 (May, 1950) pages 473–85.

102. Michael Manley, Down the Up Escalator and Jamaica. Struggle in the Periphery (London: Third World Media/ Writers and Readers Publishing Cooperative Society, 1982).

103. Eric Williams, Capitalism and Slavery (London: Andre Deutsch, 1964).

104. Lloyd Best, " An Outline Model of Pure Plantation Economy," Social and Economic Studies, Vol. 17, No. 3 (1968) pages 283–326 and Lloyd Best and Kari Levitt, "Revised and Expanded Model of Pure Plantation Economy" in Lloyd Best and Kari Polanyi Levitt (eds.), The Theory of Plantation Economy. A Historical and Institutional Approach to Caribbean Economic Development (Kingston: University of the West Indies Press, 2009) pages 41–119.

105. Andre Gunder Frank, Latin America: Underdevelopment or Revolution: Essays on the Development of Underdevelopment (New York: Monthly Review Press, 1969).

106. Fernando Henrique Cardoso and Enzo Faletto, Dependency and Development in Latin America (Berkeley: University of California Press, 1979).

107. Samuel L. Parmar, "Self-Reliant Development in an Interdependent World"in Guy F. Erb and Valeriana Kallab (eds.), Beyond Dependency. The Developing World Speaks Out (Washington, D.C.: Overseas Development Council, 1975) pages 3–27.

108. For a detailed account of the negotiations see Carlton E. Davis, Jamaica in the World Aluminium Industry, Vol. II 1974–1988. Bauxite Levy Negotiations (Kingston: Jamaica Bauxite Institute, 1995) pages 1–196.

109. Norman Girvan, "Why We Need to Nationalize Bauxite, and How," New World Pamphlet No. 6, 1971 in Norman Girvan and Owen Jefferson (eds.), Readings in the Political Economy of the Caribbean (Kingston: New World Group, 1971) pages 217–40.

110. "After Oil, Bauxite" Washington Post, June 3, 1974 cited in Carlton E. Davis, Jamaica in the World Aluminium Industry, Vol. II 1974–1988. Bauxite Levy Negotiations (Kingston: Jamaica Bauxite Institute, 1995) page 207.

111. Michael Manley, Jamaica. Struggle in the Periphery (London: Third World Media/ Writers and Readers Publishing Cooperative Society, 1982) page 117.

112. James Reston, "Cuban Expansion," New York Times, March, 1977.

113. Michael Manley, "The Caribbean Basin: Its Political Dynamic and Possible Directions" in Third World Affairs 1985 (London: Third World Foundation for Social and Economic Studies, 1985) pages 243–50. See page 247.

114. Alexander Kruger, Jamaica after the Election: Opportunity for Recovery, the Heritage Foundation, January 26, 1981.

115. Michael Manley, "The Caribbean Basin: Its Political Dynamic and Possible Directions" in Third World Affairs 1985 (London: Third World Foundation for Social and Economic Studies, 1985) pages 243–50. See page 248.

116. Michael Kaufman, Jamaica Under Manley. Dilemmas of Socialism and Democracy (London: Zed Books, 1985).

117. Evelyne Huber Stephens and John D. Stephens, Democratic Socialism in Jamaica. The Political Movement and Social Transformation in Dependent Capitalism (Princeton: Princeton University Press, 1986).

118. Randolph B. Persaud, Counter-Hegemony and Foreign Policy. The Dialectics of Marginalized and Global Forces in Jamaica (Albany: State University of New York Press, 2001).

119. Holger Henke, Self-Determination and Dependency. Jamaica's Foreign Policy 1972–1989 (Kingston: University of the West Indies Press, 2000).

120. Jamaica Scope Paper, 22 June 1962, page 1. Archives of the Kennedy Presidential Library.

121. Richard L. Bernal, "Foreign Investment and Development in Jamaica," Inter-American Economic Affairs, Vol. 38, No. 2 (Autumn, 1984) page 9.

122. Remarks of the Newly Appointed Ambassador of Jamaica to the United States Neville Noel Ashenheim upon the Occasion of the Presentation of his Letter of Credence.

123. Anthony P. Maingot, The United States and the Caribbean (London: Macmillan Press, 1994) pages 114–39.

124. Evelyne Huber Stephens and John D. Stephens, Democratic Socialism in Jamaica. The Political Movement and Social Transformation in Dependent Capitalism (Princeton: Princeton University Press, 1986) page 251.

125. Edward Seaga, My Life and Leadership Vol. I: Clash of Ideologies 1930–1980 (Oxford: Macmillan, 2009) page 238.

126. Patrick E. Bryan, Edward Seaga, and the Challenge of Modern Jamaica (Kingston: University of the West Indies Press, 2009) page 165.

127. George Schultz, Kiron K. Skinner, Annelise Anderson, and Martin Anderson (eds.), Reagan, In His Own Hand: The Writings of Ronald Reagan That Reveal His Revolutionary Vision for America (New York: Free Press, 2001) 196–97.

128. "Ronald Reagan's Showcase," Newsweek, October 26, 1981, page 48.

129. Ronald Reagan, The Reagan Diaries, edited by Douglas Brinkley (New York: Harper Perennial, 2007) page 1.

130. Ronald Reagan, The Reagan Diaries, edited by Douglas Brinkley (New York: Harper Perennial, 2007) pages 133 and 654.

131. Remarks Following a Meeting with Barbadian Prime Minister J.M.G. Adams in Barbados, April 8, 1982. http://www.reagan.utexas.edu/archives/speeches/1982/40882b.htm . Accessed 23 March, 2014.

132. The Most Hon. Prof. Kenneth Hall, "Jamaica in the International Arena: Leader or Follower. Historical Perspectives on Jamaica's Contribution to the International Community" in Kenneth Hall and Myrtle Chuck-A-Sang (eds.), Paradigm Shifts & Structural Changes - In Pursuit of Progress in the Caribbean Community (Bloomington: Trafford Publishing, 2013) pages 104–14, see 109.

133. Ronald Reagan, An American Life (New York: Pocket, 1999) 549–59.

134. For an overview of the U.S. invasion of Grenada see Anthony Payne, Paul Sutton, and Tony Thorndike, Grenada: Revolution and Invasion (London: Croom Helm, 1984).

135. Ronald Reagan, The Reagan Diaries, edited by Douglas Brinkley (New York: Harper Perennial, 2007) page 189.

136. Ronald Reagan, The Reagan Diaries, edited by Douglas Brinkley (New York: Harper Perennial, 2007) page 192.

137. Ronald Reagan, The Reagan Diaries, edited by Douglas Brinkley (New York: Harper Perennial, 2007) page 191.

138. Ronald Reagan, Speaking My Mind: Selected Speeches (New York: Simon & Schuster, 2004) pages 184–95.

139. The Michael Manley-Kari Levitt Exchange reprinted in Kari Levitt, Reclaiming Development: Independent Thought and Caribbean Community (Kingston: Ian Randle Publishers, 2005) pages 267–310.

140. Robert Pear, "Jamaican Criticizes Panama Invasion," New York Times, January 30, 1990.

141. Robert Borosage and Saul Landau, "Lonely Manley," Mother Jones, March/April 1991, pages 26–29. See page 26.

142. Delano Franklyn (ed.), The Challenges of Change. P. J. Patterson Budget Presentations 1992–2002 (Kingston: Ian Randle Publishers, 2004) page 33.

143. The Most Hon. P. J. Patterson, "CARICOM Beyond Thirty. Charting New Directions, Chairman's Perspectives" in Kenneth Hall and Myrtle Chuck-A-Sang (eds.), CARICOM Single Market and Economy. Genesis and Prognosis (Kingston: Ian Randle Publishers, 2007) page 469.

144. The Most Hon. P. J. Patterson, "CARICOM Beyond Thirty. Charting New Directions, Chairman's Perspectives" in Kenneth Hall and Myrtle Chuck-A-Sang (eds.), CARICOM Single Market and Economy. Genesis and Prognosis (Kingston: Ian Randle Publishers, 2007) page 481.

145. The Most Hon. P. J. Patterson, "CARICOM Beyond Thirty. Charting New Directions, Chairman's Perspectives" in Kenneth Hall and Myrtle Chuck-A-Sang (eds.), CARICOM Single Market and Economy. Genesis and Prognosis (Kingston: Ian Randle Publishers, 2007) page 481.

146. Jacqueline Anne Braveboy-Wagner, The Caribbean in World Affairs. The Foreign Policies of the English-Speaking States (Boulder: Westview Press, 1989) page 131.

147. Delano Franklyn (ed.), A Jamaican Voice in Caribbean and World Politics. P. J. Patterson. Selected Speeches 1992–2000 (Kingston: Ian Randle Publishers, 2002) page 130.

148. Delano Franklyn (ed.), The Challenges of Change. P. J. Patterson Budget Presentations 1992–2002 (Kingston and Miami: Ian Randle Publishers, 2004) pages 31–32.

149. Delano Franklyn (ed.), A Jamaican Voice in Caribbean and World Politics. P. J. Patterson. Selected Speeches 1992–2000 (Kingston: Ian Randle Publishers, 2002) page 157.

150. Delano Franklyn (ed.), A Jamaican Voice in Caribbean and World Politics. P. J. Patterson. Selected Speeches 1992–2000 (Kingston: Ian Randle Publishers, 2002) page 102.

151. Delano Franklyn (ed.), A Jamaican Voice in Caribbean and World Politics. P. J. Patterson. Selected Speeches 1992–2000 (Kingston: Ian Randle Publishers, 2002) page 105.

152. Delano Franklyn (ed.), A Jamaican Voice in Caribbean and World Politics. P. J. Patterson. Selected Speeches 1992–2000 (Kingston: Ian Randle Publishers, 2002) page 105.

153. Delano Franklyn (ed.), A Jamaican Voice in Caribbean and World Politics. P. J. Patterson. Selected Speeches 1992–2000 (Kingston: Ian Randle Publishers, 2002) page 105.

154. Delano Franklyn (ed.), A Jamaican Voice in Caribbean and World Politics. P. J. Patterson. Selected Speeches 1992–2000 (Kingston: Ian Randle Publishers, 2002) page 107.

155. "What the PM said," Jamaica Observer, July 3, 2000, page 9.

156. Delano Franklyn (ed.), A Jamaican Voice in Caribbean and World Politics. P. J. Patterson. Selected Speeches 1992–2000 (Kingston: Ian Randle Publishers, 2002) page 131.

157. Delano Franklyn (ed.), A Jamaican Voice in Caribbean and World Politics. P. J. Patterson. Selected Speeches 1992–2000 (Kingston: Ian Randle Publishers, 2002) page 133.

158. Delano Franklyn (ed.), A Jamaican Voice in Caribbean and World Politics. P. J. Patterson. Selected Speeches 1992–2000 (Kingston: Ian Randle Publishers, 2002) page 135.

159. Jessica Byron, "Strategic Repositioning: Foreign Policy Shifts in Barbados and Trinidad and Tobago 1992–2000," Social and Economic Studies, Vol. 56, Nos. 1&2 (March/June, 2007) pages 209–39.

160. Sir Shridath Ramphal, Caribbean Challenges. Sir Shridath Ramphal's Collected Counsel (London: Hansib Publishers, 2012) page 121.

161. Aristide says U.S. deposed him in a "coup d'etat." White House calls allegation "nonsense." http://edition.cnn.com/2004/WORLD/americas/03/01/aristide.claim/ . Retrieved 27 July 2014.

162. Gail Scott, Diplomatic Dance. The New Embassy Life in America (Golden, Colorado: Fulcrum Publishing, 1999) page xviii.

163. Anthony J. Payne, Politics in Jamaica (Kingston: Ian Randle Publishers, rev. ed., 1994) page 203.

164. David Brock, "The New Ambassadors," the American Enterprise, July/August, 1991, pages 70–75. See page 71.

165. Keb Adelman, "Fields of Influence. Canadian Ambassador Allan Gotlieb on How to Get Through to Decision Makers," The Washingtonian, December, 1988, pages 121–124. See page 124.

166. Jacqueline Anne Braveboy-Wagner, The United States and the Caribbean: The Washington Bureaucracy (Washington, D.C.: Center for Strategic and International Studies, April, 1991).

167. Harry Belafonte and Michael Shnayerson, My Song: A Memoir (New York: Knopf, 2011).

168. Colin L. Powell with Joseph E. Persico, My American Journey (New York: Random House, 1996).

169. William Rhodes, Banker to the World: Leadership Lessons from the Front Lines of Global Finance (New York: McGraw-Hill, 2011).

170. Revised Treaty Establishing the Caribbean Community including the Caricom Single Market and Economy, Article 6, page 8.

171. Richard L. Bernal, Globalization, Trade and Economic Development: A Study of the CARIFORUM-EU Economic Partnership Agreement (New York: Palgrave MacMillan, 2013).

172. Patsy Lewis, Surviving Small Size. Regional Integration in Caribbean Ministates (Mona: University of the West Indies, 2012) pages 63–65.

173. Anthony J. Payne, The Political History of CARICOM (Kingston: Ian Randle Publishers, 2008) pages 175–88.

174. Kenneth Hall and Myrtle Chuck-A-Sang (eds.), The Caribbean Single Market and Economy. Towards a Single Economic Space (Bloomington: Trafford, 2013) page 35.

175. Euclid A. Rose, Dependency and Socialism in the Modern Caribbean: Superpower Intervention in Guyana, Jamaica, and Grenada, 1970–1985 (Lanham: Lexington Books, 2002) page 9.

Appendix A

The English-Speaking Caribbean

In this study many of the issues on which Jamaica sought to influence U.S. foreign policy were issues common to many or all of the states of the ESC as they shared objectives and coordinated their policy actions in furtherance of these goals. Given the focus of this study, the limitations of space, and the well-documented historical, social, economic, and political similarities between the countries of the ESC[1] it is not necessary to provide a detailed discussion of the ESC. This section therefore presents information on selected issues and aspects, to complement the overview of Jamaica and its foreign policy towards the United States.

The ESC consists of: Antigua and Barbuda, Bahamas, Barbados, Belize, Dominica, Grenada, Guyana, Jamaica, Montserrat, St. Kitts and Nevis, St. Lucia, St. Vincent, and Trinidad and Tobago. Basic economic data for the ESC are shown in table 9.1.

First, the ESC can be studied as a group because of (1) the commonality of their historical experience, social characteristics, economic problems, political systems, and culture.[2] (2) The states of the region while not having identical interests as is to be expected among any group of countries have a substantial similarity of policy objectives. (3) The governments of the ESC and Suriname are committed to the coordination of their foreign policies as part of their membership in the Caribbean Common Market and Community. (4) The United States treats these countries as a homogeneous entity for foreign policy and administrative simplicity and makes a distinction between the ESC and Cuba, Haiti, and the Dominican Republic.

Second, U.S. foreign policy towards the Caribbean has been a subset of a wider Latin American policy within an overall foreign policy framework dominated by Cold War perspectives. As a superpower, the United States has pursued a foreign policy of global reach and engagement within which the Caribbean has not always been the subject of a clear, distinctive, and sustained policy. In fact, the United States has pursued separate policies for Central America, Cuba, Haiti, the Dominican Republic, and the CARICOM, albeit within the leitmotif of free trade, anti-communism, and democracy. A distinctive U.S. policy towards the ESC emerged after the 1960s when these countries attained their political independence from Great Britain beginning with Jamaica in 1962.

Table A.1. Land Area, Population, GDP, and GDP per Capita for the CARICOM Countries and the United States (1999)

COUNTRY	LAND AREA (sq km)	POPULATION	GDP US$ Million	GDP Per Capita US$
Antigua & Barbuda	440	66,860	639	9,432
Bahamas	13,880	290,400	4,560	14,998
Barbados	430	265,630	2,469	9,789
Belize	2,960	238,550	705	2,949
Dominica	750	73,000	273	3,690
Grenada	340	96,200	360	3,758
Guyana	214,970	849,180	782	998
Jamaica	10,990	2,576,000	7,445	2,893
St. Kitts & Nevis	360	40,820	305	7,193
St. Lucia	620,390	152,000	639	3,677
St. Vincent & the Grenadines	163,270	113,220	320	2,874
Suriname	5,130	412,070	1,104	2,474
Trinidad & Tobago	9,363,520	1,285,140	6,380	4,666
United States	440	270,299,008	9,256,150	33,933

Source: IMF, World Economic Outlook Database (http://www.imf.org)

Third, much of Jamaica's foreign policy towards the United States, and that of the other ESC countries was taken up with responding to foreign policy initiatives of the United States, such as the Enterprise for the Americas Initiative and the NAFTA. The reactions to U.S. policies have varied from cooperation, e.g., combating drug smuggling, to seeking to influence, e.g., sugar, to resistance, e.g., bananas. At times the countries of the ESC have operated as a very cohesive group, e.g., lobbying for the CBI, and on occasions they have differed, e.g., the U.S. invasion of Grenada. In some instances the issue may not be of vital interest, e.g., debt relief was important only to Guyana and Jamaica, but it was normal that all CARICOM countries would support the interests of even one state, e.g., for Trinidad and Tobago against anti-dumping action by the United States. Jamaica and to a lesser extent the ESC acting in unison have influenced thinking in U.S. foreign policy circles. The most notable examples were Seaga's input to the design of the CBI and Manley's impact on the EAI.

Fourth, the prominent feature of Jamaica and the ESC countries is their vulnerability, which has both economic and security dimensions.

This vulnerability is particularly evident in relations between the small states of the region and the United States where the enormous disparities in size, power, and development have led to acute dependence rather than interdependence to which the ESC rightfully aspired.

The ESC economies are small and highly open, i.e., external transactions are large in relation to total economic activity, as indicated by the high ratio of trade to GDP. The United States has a trade/GDP ratio of 15 percent. By contrast, ESC economies have trade/GDP ratios between 40 and 204 percent. The limited range of economic activity in these small economies is reflected in the concentration on one to three exports, accompanied in the majority of cases, by a relatively high reliance on primary commodities. In extreme instances, one primary product export accounts for nearly all of exports. For example, in 1991, bananas accounted for 92 percent of total exports in Dominica and 87 percent in St. Lucia. Export concentration is compounded by the dependence on one or two export markets, e.g., Britain absorbs 80 percent of Dominica's bananas and 90 percent of St. Lucia's exports. Economic vulnerability can be a feature of an economy of any size and level of development, but it is compounded by the CARICOM countries' small size, susceptibility to natural disasters, remoteness, and insularity. Studies of developing countries have demonstrated that there is a direct relationship between vulnerability and size, with the smallest developing countries being the most vulnerable. A World Bank/Commonwealth Secretariat study shows that of 111 developing countries, 26 of the 28 most vulnerable were small countries and the 28 least vulnerable were all large states. Canada, Brazil, Argentina, and the United States have vulnerability indexes of 0.2 or less, while Caribbean and Central American economies exceed 0.4. The smallest economies have vulnerability indexes ranging from 0.595 for Barbados to 0.843 for Antigua.[3]

Volatility in national income is a pronounced characteristic of small, developing countries, which export a few primary products, particularly minerals and agricultural commodities and experience erratic fluctuations in capital flows. This is particularly the case in small developing countries because of the severely constrained adjustment capacity that limits their ability to react. Volatility is costly because of the adverse impact on investment, resource allocation, productivity, inflation, exchange rates, and economic growth. Small economies experience higher income volatility than larger economies, estimated by the World Bank/Commonwealth Secretariat, as 25 percent higher. A recent study of foreign direct investment flows in the last 20 years reveals that small developing countries are at a disadvantage in attaining FDI relative to larger developing countries, because even when they have sound economic policies, small, developing countries are rated 28 percent more risky.[4]

Fifth, the states of the ESC have sought to overcome the disadvantage of the enormous disparities in power, wealth, and size between themselves and the sole superpower, the United States, by cooperation and coordination in foreign policy through CARICOM. A. N. R. Robinson, Prime Minister of Trinidad and Tobago explained that in the region "we are convinced that national self-determination can often be most effectively pursued within the framework of regional groupings. We are firmly of the view that it is through such associations that small nations are afforded the best opportunity to contribute to the solution of the world's problems and their own."[5] In 1967 the countries of the ESC established the Caribbean Free Trade Association and in 1973 they created CARICOM as a vehicle of regional economic integration for promoting economic development.[6] The Treaty establishing the Caribbean Community (1973) speaks of "a common front in relation to the external world"[7] and Article 34.1 states as an objective "the coordination of the foreign policies of Member States."[8] The 1981 report, "The Caribbean Community in the 1980's" admonished the governments of the region to "intensify their efforts to achieve coordination of their external trade relations." The report of the West Indian Commission, "Time For Action" called on member states to "adopt a collective approach to current and potential changes in the international community, including international political and financial institutions, and reflect this approach in common arrangements for international economic negotiations and diplomatic representation."[9]

There have been problems in the execution of collective or joint representation. The unresolved dilemma, which Bryan points out, is the willingness of these states and their leaders "to concede a little national sovereignty for the greater supranationality of the region."[10] A virulent strain of nationalism has made operations more difficult than they have to be but cooperation has been bolstered by the policy of developed countries of dealing only with small states in groups, especially when they are in the same physical region or in an integration process. Costa Rica approached the United States for a free trade agreement only to be rebuffed and much to their chagrin told that the United States would only countenance an approach by Central America. This is the same approach taken to relations with the CARICOM by the United States and Britain. This should not cause CARICOM any discomfort given its collaboration in external affairs for almost a half a century. Yet the Ambassador of Grenada to the United States as recently as 2007 was prompted to bemoan group "therapy" stating that: "One is not taken seriously when all the small countries are grouped in one bloc. To the extent that frontline countries like to talk to Caricom, a country such as Grenada does not get much attention."[11] Certainly to be heard as part of a group with a common position must be better than not being seen or heard.

NOTES

1. The commonalities of the ESC are discussed and documented in Franklin W. Knight, The Caribbean. The Genesis of a Fragmented Nationalism (New York: Oxford University Press, 1990), Sedro Sanitarian, Trade and Development. A Study of the Small Caribbean Countries and Large Multinational Corporations (Georgetown: University of Guyana, 1976), Clive Y. Thomas, The Poor and the Powerless. Economic Policy and Change in the Caribbean (London: Latin American Bureau, 1988), Anthony T. Bryan (ed.), The Caribbean. New Dynamics in Trade and Political Economy (Miami: North-South Center, University of Miami, 1995), Stanley Lalta and Marie Freckleton (eds.), Caribbean Economic Development. The First Generation (Kingston: Ian Randle Publishers, 1995), and Winston C. Dookeran (ed.), Choices and Change. Reflections on the Caribbean (Washington, D.C.: Inter-American Development Bank, 1996).

2. The Meaning of the Caribbean differs depending on whether it is defined culturally, geographically, or geo-politically and definitions based on culture and geo-politics have changed over time. See Norman Girvan, "Creating and Recreating the Caribbean" in Kenneth Hall and Denis Benn (eds.), Contending with Destiny. The Caribbean in the 21st Century (Kingston: Ian Randle Publishers, 2000) pages 31–36.

3. Richard L. Bernal, The Integration of Small Economies in the Free Trade Area of the Americas, CSIS, Policy Paper on the Americas, Vol. IX, Study No. 1 (Washington, D.C.: Center for Strategic and International Studies, 1998).

4. Richard Bernal, "Globalization and Small Developing Economies. The Challenges and Opportunities," in David Peretz, Rumman Faruqi, and Eliawony J. Kisanga (eds.), Small States in the Global Economy (London: Commonwealth Secretariat, 2001) pages 39–51.

5. A. N. R. Robinson, Caribbean Man. Selected Speeches from a Political Career 1960–1986 (Port of Spain: Inprint Publication, 1986) page 98.

6. The rationale for economic integration in promoting economic development in the small economies of the ESC is explained in Havelock Brewster and Clive Y. Thomas, The Dynamics of West Indian Economic Integration (Mona, Jamaica: Institute of Social and Economic Research, University of the West Indies, 1967) and William Demas, Essays on Caribbean Integration and Development (Mona, Jamaica: Institute of Social and Economic Research, University of the West Indies, 1976). For an assessment of the rationales for regional integration see Ian Boxill, Ideology and Caribbean Integration (Mona, Jamaica: Consortium Graduate School of Social Sciences, University of the West Indies, 1993).

7. Treaty establishing the Caribbean Community, Chaguaramas, 4th July 1973 (Georgetown: Caribbean Community Secretariat, June, 1987) page 2.

8. Treaty establishing the Caribbean Community, Chaguaramas, 4th July 1973 (Georgetown: Caribbean Community Secretariat, June, 1987) page 38.

9. Time For Action. The report of The West Indian Commission (Black Rock, Barbados: The West Indian Commission, 1992) page 457.

10. Anthony T. Bryan "The International Dynamics of the Commonwealth Caribbean: Challenges and Opportunities in the 1990's," Journal of Interamerican Studies and World Affairs, Vol. 31, No. 3 (Fall, 1989) pages 1–7. See page 7.

11. Franklin W. Knight, "Caribbean Diplomacy in Washington," The Jamaica Observer, January 24, 2007.

Appendix B

Members of the government advocacy team who worked for the government of Jamaica included:

George Dalley, Senior Consultant and Partner at the Law Office of Holland & Knight worked for Jamaica since 1988. During that time, he worked on a wide range of issues relating to Jamaica's agenda in Washington, including trade, aid, debt, counter narcotics, and tourism promotion. Mr. Dalley, whose parents were Jamaicans, had extensive contacts in the bureaucracy and in Congress and was instrumental in helping Jamaica establish a presence on the "Hill." In the mid-1970s, Dalley helped Prime Minister Michael Manley and the government of Jamaica establish a relationship with the Congressional Black Caucus. As a Deputy Assistant Secretary of State for International Organization Affairs in the Carter Administration, he contributed to shaping U.S. policy in international economic issues and galvanized support for the international anti-apartheid movement. Appointed to the U.S. Civil Aeronautics Board by President Carter, Dalley specialized in the liberalization of international aviation regimes. As Chief of Staff to Congressman Charles B. Rangel of New York, Dalley was a chief architect of the Caribbean Basin Initiative (CBI) and the Section 936 tax incentive program for U.S. investment in the Caribbean.

Denis M. Neill, Senior Consultant, began working for Jamaica in 1988. Before working for Jamaica he spent the past 14 years working for a broad range of foreign governments and trade associations in Washington, helping them design and implement legislative strategies relating to foreign aid, trade, and defense issues. He assisted Jamaica in undertaking its government relations efforts in Washington, working on a variety of trade, aid, and security issues. Previously, he served as assistant administrator of the Agency for International Development (AID), where he oversaw the Agency's Congressional relations. Mr. Neill was a well-known foreign policy advocate in Congress and the Executive Branch. He also maintained close links with key officials in the Democratic National Party through his active work with, and memberships in numerous policy groups, including the Center for National Policy, the National Democratic Institute, and the Democratic Leadership Council.

Ann Wrobleski, President of Jefferson, Waterman International assisted several government clients obtain Congressional earmarks for foreign aid and worked with American-based corporations to secure U.S.

export financing. Before joining Jefferson, Waterman International, she served as Assistant Secretary of State for International Narcotics Matters during the Reagan Administration. In this position, she oversaw the multi-million dollar counter narcotics budget and was responsible for designing and implementing the U.S. worldwide response to stem the flow of narcotics and oppose narcotics related activities, such as money laundering. As assistant secretary she testified repeatedly before a variety of House and Senate Committees. She previously worked as Special Projects Director for First Lady Nancy Reagan, where she organized the "Just Say No" campaign. Before joining the Reagan Administration, Mrs. Wrobleski served a number of years as a key staff aide to several Republican and Democrat Senators and Congressmen from Florida.

Stephen E. Lamar, vice president at Jefferson, Waterman International, has led several legislative and lobbying campaigns to expand trade and tax preferences for Caribbean clients. He has worked daily with Congress and the Administration on the Caribbean Basin Initiative (CBI), the Interim Trade Program and Caribbean parity, the Section 936 Caribbean Investment Fund, and the Enterprise for the Americas Initiative (EAI). As a result, he has become closely identified with Caribbean issues in Congress. In undertaking his responsibilities on behalf of Africa, Caribbean, and Asian clients, Mr. Lamar has developed extensive links with members of staff in the House Ways and Means Committee, the Senate Finance Committee, and the House and Senate Foreign Relations Committees. Mr. Lamar previously worked at the U.S. Department of Commerce, where he designed U.S. trade and export promotion policies for developing countries. He has spoken at numerous conferences and has written frequently on export promotion and the development of trade policy.

Walter Jones pounded the long corridors of the Congressional buildings with Ambassador Bernal on innumerable visits to members of Congress. Mr. Jones served as a Legislative Assistant on the personal staff of United States Senator Paul Sarbanes (D-MD) handling foreign relations and banking matters. He is a graduate of the Woodrow Wilson School of Public Affairs of Princeton University, Harvard Law School, and the George Washington University School of Business and Management.

Appendix C

Ross-Robinson & Associates was a Washington-based firm of foreign policy consultants headed by Hazel Ross-Robinson, a former senior-level Congressional staffer who had served as foreign policy advisor in the office of William H. Gray III (D-PA) during his tenure as U.S. House Budget Committee Chairman, U.S. House Democratic Caucus Chairman, and U. S. House Majority Whip. Ross-Robinson had also served as associate staff on the House Appropriations Committee Subcommittee on Foreign Operations, and was a member of the Chairman's Group of Policy Advisers, U.S. House Armed Services Committee. As the Washington representative of Caribbean banana exporting nations during their battle with Chiquita, RR&A worked closely with Caribbean embassies, the U.S. executive and legislative branches, Caribbean nationals in the United States, U.S. interest groups, and the American media in order to raise public awareness of and action on the issue. This resulted in a high profile delegation of Congresspersons, labor leaders, and policy specialists meeting with the U.S. Trade Representative to strongly urge a change in U.S. policy; an Eminent Persons Group comprised of members of Congress, U.S. labor leaders, environmentalists, university professors, and others traveled to the Caribbean's banana-producing nations so as to familiarize themselves with the concerns of governments and the farmers themselves, in order to serve as informed opponents of U.S. policy upon their return. RR&A also arranged for then-former Prime Minister of Dominica Eugenia Charles, U.S. General John Sheehan, Congresswoman Maxine Waters (D-PA), and others to hold a widely carried press conference in Washington, D.C., warning of the destabilizing immediate and long-term effects of U.S. policy on banana-exporting Caribbean nations. Demonstrations at the White House, U.S. executive and legislative branch meetings by Caribbean government officials, editorial board meetings with Caribbean officials, Congressional letter-writing campaigns, and legislative branch policy fora were also among the actions organized by RR&A, resulting in broad-based print and electronic coverage of the concerns of Caribbean governments and peoples regarding U.S. policy on this matter, and the negative immediate and long-term impact of this U.S. policy on the Caribbean.

Appendix C

Appendix D

Dear Sir:

Larry Rohter's otherwise excellent article on U.S./Caribbean Basin relations (10/24/96, p. A13) incorrectly suggests that Caribbean countries engage in counter-narcotics efforts as a way to earn aid and trade benefits from the United States. To the contrary, Caribbean countries are battling drug lords and money launderers because it is in their own self-interest. Although some forms of U.S. assistance play an important role in supporting our counter-narcotics efforts, we accept such help to supplement our resources, not as a *quid pro quo* for our basic commitment in this struggle.

Located between the major drug-producing regions of the Andes and drug users in the United States, Caribbean Basin countries are on the front line in the war against drugs. While many drugs are headed for the U.S. market, their damaging impact has taken a deadly toll across the Caribbean. In Jamaica, for example, the drug trade has stimulated an increase in gun smuggling from the United States. We can no more ignore this war on drugs than we can ignore other security threats.

Of course, our ability to prosecute this war can only be effective if Caribbean economies remain strong. Rohter correctly catalogued Caribbean concerns over signs of a "scaling back of Washington's economic commitment" in the Caribbean, particularly in the area of trade. He failed to note, however, that U.S. disengagement in this region undermines U.S. national security interests. Without access to markets and capital, Caribbean economies can easily become susceptible to the destabilizing influences of narcotics. And without effective partners in the Caribbean, U.S. efforts at narcotics interdiction will be eviscerated.

Sincerely
Dr. Richard L. Bernal
Ambassador

APPENDIX

Appendix E

Dear Mr. President,

We are writing to express our concern in response to an article that appeared in The New York Times on Sunday, February 6, which suggests that Jamaica is in danger of being "de-certified" at the end of this month.

Our most immediate concern arises from the article's implication that the failure to conclude a maritime cooperation agreement should serve as some sort of litmus test for full cooperation with the United States. The intent of the certification process is to gauge the entirety of the counternarcotics relationship with the United States, and then assess if the foreign country's intent and actions reveal a pattern of cooperation and partnership. On this basis, it would appear that Jamaica has met, as it has every year since the process was initiated, the test for full certification.

In the past year, Jamaica has enacted money-laundering legislation even though there is no evidence of significant money laundering activities on the island. Passage of this landmark legislation, which was long sought by the United States, was accomplished despite vocal domestic opposition from some parties. Jamaica is also moving to strengthen the way in which it discourages and responds to drug-related activities. It recently toughened penalties for a series of drug-related crimes and is now moving ahead on its first asset forfeiture cases. We understand that the legislature is preparing to take up precursor chemical legislation during the coming year.

In other areas, cooperation appears to be on par with previous years. Jamaica continues a potent marijuana eradication campaign with the assistance of U.S. supplied helicopters. We would note that eradication figures would likely have been even higher but for the fact that the U.S. personnel grounded the helicopters for part of the year for servicing. Jamaica remains an active partner in joint legal efforts, and our two countries are now availing themselves of the provisions in the recently implemented Mutual Legal Assistance Treaty (MLAT). In September, Prime Minister Patterson opened a U.S.-funded UN regional training center to strengthen Caribbean –wide anti-drug efforts.

While we agree that a U.S./Jamaican maritime cooperation agreement is in the best interests of both the United States and Jamaica, and would urge the rapid conclusion of such an agreement, we understand that the Jamaican authorities already cooperate fully with U.S. requests to conduct counter-narcotics efforts in and near Jamaican waters. We also understand that U.S. and Jamaican negotiating teams have met on several occasions in the past six months and have made some progress toward a final agreement. Indeed, in early December, Jamaica withdrew an exemption it had taken to the 1988 UN Convention, clearing one of the remaining obstacles to the successful conclusion of this agreement. Such a step certainly demonstrates that Jamaica is operating in full faith, and under the auspices of a fully cooperative relationship with United States.

We are concerned that the rhetoric that has been exchanged—as reported in the article—significantly damages what should be an even more productive atmosphere. Jamaica and the other countries of the Caribbean Basin are the front line in our defense against drug trafficking from South America. Our efforts should be aimed at fortifying the resolve and supporting the commitment of the Caribbean leaders to take the most aggressive stance possible against this terrible scourge. We can best accomplish this through dialogue and reinforcement rather than through casual threats of decertification. Where decertification is merited, we should move unequivocably to pursue that course. But when it is not, as appears to be the case with Jamaica, we should resolve our differences amicably and speedily and work to confront the common enemy—the narco-traffickers.

On a related point, we would like to commend you for your decision to visit two Caribbean Basin countries—Barbados and Costa Rica—during your upcoming visit to Latin America. We are particularly pleased to note that you will be using those two visits to meet with regional leaders. We would urge you to take the opportunity of these meetings to reaffirm American leadership—including your own personal commitment—to strengthen regional anti-narcotics cooperation.

Thank you for your consideration and prompt attention to this matter.

Sincerely
Dr. Richard L. Bernal
Ambassador

Appendix F

March 3, 1997

Dear:

I am writing to thank you for your efforts in urging full certification of Jamaica during the annual certification process last week.

As you know, Jamaica greatly values its relationship with the United States, both in the fight against narcotics as well as in many other issues. Our cooperation with the United States has been fully certified every year since the process began. I am pleased to note that, with your support, Jamaica was again fully certified last week.

We have made the fight against drugs an important priority and have consistently dedicated ourselves to this struggle – at every level and with a firm expression that this is in our own national self-interest.

Jamaica participates on many levels with U.S. Government agencies and organizations to help stem the flow of narcotics through the Caribbean and to help eradicate drug use and production in our country. This week, for example, a team of Jamaican negotiators is meeting with U.S. officials to conclude a maritime cooperation agreement with the United States. In the coming months, we hope to achieve other notable accomplishments as we jointly undertake steps to eradicate this menace.

Thank you again for your personal leadership and support for the U.S./Jamaican counter-narcotics partnership. I look forward to working with you in the coming year as we work to further strengthen this relationship.

In the meantime, please accept my best wishes and the assurances of my highest consideration.

Sincerely
Richard Bernal, Ambassador

Appendix G

Chronology of Activities by Jamaica in Support of Caribbean Basin Trade Enhancement

September 18–19, 1987	Testimony by Richard Bernal on the Caribbean Basin Initiative to the Hearings before the Sub-Committee on 1987 International Economic Policy and Trade on Western Hemispheric Affairs of the Committee on Foreign Affairs.
July 31, 1990	Testimony by Richard Bernal before the joint hearing of the Sub-Committee on Western Hemisphere Affairs and the Sub-Committee on International Economic Policy and Trade of the U.S. House of Representatives on HR 5196, The Caribbean Debt Act for Development Act of 1990.
January 22, 1992	Testimony by Richard Bernal before the U.S. International Trade Commission Hearings on U.S. Market Access in Latin America, Recent Liberalization Measures, and Remaining Barriers.
July 1, 1992	House Subcommittees on International Economic Policy and Trade and Western Hemisphere Affairs hold a joint hearing on the effect of NAFTA on the Caribbean.
February 4, 1993	Opinion Editorial by Ambassador Bernal in the *Miami Herald*.
March 18, 1993	Congressman Sam Gibbons introduces HR 1403 — The Caribbean Basin Free Trade Agreements Act. Other sponsors include: Pickle, Crane, Rangel, McKinney, Mfume, Torres, Towns, de la Garza, Deutsch, Serrano, and Hutchinson, T.
April 1, 1993	Testimony by Richard Bernal before the U.S. House Ways and Means Committee on the Role of 936 Funds in Economic Development of Caribbean Countries.
May 1993	A review of the statements received during the initial public comment period reveals

	overwhelming support for Caribbean parity with NAFTA among business groups, officials from southern U.S. states, and Caribbean representatives.
June 7, 1993	House Ways and Means Trade Subcommittee publishes written comments on Caribbean parity (HR 1403).
June 24, 1993	Senator Bob Graham introduces Senate version of HR 1403—S. 1155. Other sponsors include: Senators Durenberger and Mack. Ambassador Bernal and other witnesses testify in support of Caribbean parity. Labor groups—who broadly oppose NAFTA—testify in opposition to parity. The Congressional Black Caucus identifies the adverse effects on the Caribbean as one of its main concerns of NAFTA.
June 24, 1993	House Ways and Means Trade Subcommittee holds a hearing on Caribbean parity.
June 24, 1993	Testimony by Richard Bernal before the U.S. House Ways and Means Subcommittee on Trade.
July 1993	A pre-recess drive nets an additional roster of co-sponsors to HR 1403, including the Chairmen of the Black and Hispanic Caucus, and the Chairman of the House Agriculture Committee.
August 1993	President Clinton instructs Ambassador Kantor to study the effects of NAFTA on CBI countries and to recommend steps to enhance U.S./Caribbean trade in response to visit by the Caribbean heads of government, incl. PM Patterson.
September 1993	The Florida Congressional delegation sends a letter to the President asking for parity in the NAFTA implementing legislation.
September–November 1993	Members of Congress and Senators make repeated statements to the President, urging the inclusion of Caribbean parity in the NAFTA bill. The statement by Congressman Ed Towns prompted the visit of Dr. Paul Robertson, Foreign Minister of Jamaica.
October 1, 1993	Opinion Editorial by Ambassador Bernal in the *Washington Times*.
November 1993	Congress considers and adopts NAFTA implementing bill without parity provisions.

Senator Graham announces his intention to submit new legislation on Caribbean parity during the next session. The President publicly reconfirms his intention before Central American heads of government to take short-term steps to protect the CBI countries from the effects of NAFTA.

December 8, 1993   President Clinton signs NAFTA Implementation Act into law.

January 1, 1994   NAFTA takes effect.

January 18, 1995   Congressman Phil Crane (R-IL) introduces The Caribbean Basin Trade Security Act (HR 553). Sponsors include: Shaw, Gibbons, Rangel, Towns, Deutsch, Owens, Torres, Menendez, Hastings, A., McKinney, Mfume, Wynn, Meek, Jackson-Lee, Tucker, Wilson, Johnson, E., Fattah, and Kolbe.

February 10, 1995   House Ways and Means Trade Subcommittee holds a hearing on Caribbean parity. CBI interests and Ambassadors meet at the U.S. Chamber of Commerce.

March 10, 1995   Senator Bob Graham (D-FL) introduces The Caribbean Basin Trade Security Act (S. 529). Sponsors include: Mack, Lott, Bradley Moseley-Braun, Hatch, Grassley, McCain, Pryor, Lugar, Dodd, and Gregg.

March 29, 1995   The House Ways and Means Trade Subcommittee marks up and adopts HR 553 by a vote of 12 to 3. At the mark-up, Deputy U.S.TR Charlene Barshefsky announces that parity is "enthusiastically supported" by the Administration.

April 1995   Congressman L. F. Payne (D-VA) and 72 House members write House Ways and Means Committee Chairman Bill Archer (R-TX) asking that NAFTA parity provisions on tariff preference levels (TPLs) be modified.

April 1995   At the request of the Embassy and Jamaica's advocacy team, eight House members sign on as additional co-sponsors of NAFTA parity.

May 3–5, 1995   Jamaica's Minister of Foreign Affairs and Foreign Trade meets with NSC (Feinberg), Department of

State (Talbot), U.S.TR (Barshefsky), and Congress (Brown, Hastings, Payne, Wynn, Jackson-Lee).

May 15, 1995	Senate Finance Trade Subcommittee holds a hearing on pending Caribbean parity legislation. Ambassadors of the CBI region hold strategy meeting.
May 15, 1995	Anthony Hylton, Parliamentary Secretary in the Ministry of Foreign Affairs and Foreign Trade in Jamaica gives testimony to Senate Committee.
June–September 1995	Gained additional co-sponsors, which brought the total co-sponsorship to eight House members and ten Senators.
September 12, 1995	President Clinton meets with Prime Minister Patterson at the White House. As a follow-up, the White House issues a statement reiterating the President's support for NAFTA parity, providing the highest level Administration endorsement for the bill.
September 12, 1995	The House Ways and Means Committee defers consideration of NAFTA parity in an Omnibus Budget Reconciliation Bill, which subsequently stalled in Congressional/Executive Branch negotiations.
September 12, 1995	Congressman L. F. Payne and 60 House members write Chairman Archer urging that parity be dropped from the budget bill.
October 3, 1995	A broad coalition of textile and apparel associations expressed support for parity in a letter to Senate Finance Committee Chairman Bill Roth (R-DE).
October 20, 1995	Senator Graham unveils a modified parity proposal, which he promises to introduce as an amendment on the first trade-related bill that is considered by the Senate.
November 1995	Chairman Phil Crane makes a number of speeches and statements where he identifies NAFTA parity as one of the three or four pending trade items he will include in an omnibus trade bill that will be considered in early 1996.
December 1995	Congressman L. F. Payne and 70 other labor Democrats in the House ask the President to

exclude NAFTA parity from any budget agreement.

January 5, 1996	U.S.TR Ambassador Kantor announces the Administration is still committed to seeking enactment of parity, and announces a new Administration effort to draft and propose a parity bill within 60 days.
March 19, 1996	President Clinton submits FY 1997 budget funding a Caribbean Basin parity trade package.
March 22, 1996	Opinion Editorial by Ambassador Bernal in the *Wall Street Journal*.
October 1, 1996	USTR releases Second Annual Report on Operation of the CBERA, noting the Administration's intention to seek enactment of Caribbean trade enhancement legislation.
February 6, 1997	President Clinton submits FY 1998 budget funding Caribbean Basin Trade Enhancement package.
May 8, 1997	President Clinton pledges to Central American leaders to seek enactment of Caribbean Trade Enhancement provisions at San Jose, Costa Rica.
May 10, 1997	President Clinton repeats the pledge to Caribbean leaders at Bridgetown, Barbados.
June 17, 1997	USTR Charlene Barshesfky transmits copy of draft Caribbean Basin Trade Enhancement Act (CBTEA) to Congress.
June 22, 1997	Testimony by Richard Bernal before the Subcommittee on Trade of the Committee on Ways and Means, House of Representatives.
June 26, 1997	Senator Bob Graham (D-FL) introduces CBTEA (S 984) on behalf of the Administration.
June 26, 1997	Congressman Charles B. Rangel (D-NY) introduces CBTEA (HR 2096) on behalf of the Administration.
June 26, 1997	House approves Taxpayer Relief Act of 1997 (HR 2014). Subtitle H of Title IX contains a one-year parity bill.
July 31, 1997	Conferees on Taxpayer Relief Act of 1997 (HR 2014) file joint conference report without CBI parity provisions.

September 11, 1997   Testimony by Richard Bernal before the
                    Subcommittee on Trade of the Committee on Ways
                    and Means, House of Representatives.

September 17, 1997   Senate Finance Committee holds a hearing and
                    requests comments on fast track, Caribbean parity,
                    and Africa trade legislation.

October 1, 1997   Senate Finance Committee approves by voice vote
                    a three-year Caribbean Trade Enhancement bill (S.
                    1278).

October 9, 1997   House Ways and Means Committee approves by
                    voice vote a 14-month Caribbean Basin Trade
                    Partnership bill (H 2264).

November 4, 1997   House defeats HR 2264 by a vote of 182 to 234.

January 25, 1998   Senate Majority Leader Trent Lott (R-MS) issues
                    the first of several public calls for passage of S.
                    1278.

February 2, 1998   President Clinton includes funding for CBI Trade
                    Enhancement in the FY 1999 budget.

April 6, 1998   Secretary of State Albright tells Caribbean heads of
                    state that the Administration is committed to
                    pressing for passage of CBI trade enhancement in
                    1998.

June 24, 1998   At a hearing on an Africa trade bill, Finance
                    Committee members and Administration witnesses
                    repeatedly discuss the need to "move" CBI trade
                    enhancement legislation as soon as possible.

July 21, 1998   Senate Finance Committee approves Caribbean
                    trade enhancement legislation on a vote of 18–2 as
                    part of an omnibus trade package.

July 23, 1998   Following Finance Committee action, President
                    Clinton makes first of several calls to urge
                    enactment of CBI trade legislation before end of
                    105th Congress.

October 24, 1998   President Clinton expresses disappointment that
                    CBI trade legislation was not enacted during 105th
                    Congress and restates his support for enactment
                    during 106th Congress.

November 9, 1998   Central American Presidents issue a plea for
                    passage of Caribbean Basin Trade Enhancement to
                    aid in reconstruction of Hurricane Mitch.

December 11, 1998	After meeting with Central American leaders in Washington, President Clinton declares, "We will continue to support Caribbean Basin enhancement legislation to make trade more free and more fair, and to help Central American nations restore their economies. I hope very much that it will pass in this coming Congress."
January 19, 1999	President Clinton calls for measures to aid in reconstructing Central America and foster trade with Latin America in his State of the Union.
January 25, 1999	Senate Majority Leader Trent Lott (R-MS) issues the first of several statements calling for passage of CBI trade enhancement legislation.
February 2, 1999	President Clinton includes funding for CBI trade enhancement in his FY 2000 budget.
February 3, 1999	Senator Bob Graham (D-FL), joined by a bipartisan mix of nine other Senators, introduces CBI trade enhancement legislation as part of a package of relief measures for hurricane reconstruction.
February 3, 1999	Led by the Chamber of Commerce, a broad coalition of several dozen business organizations and trade associations—representing, among other things, every element of the garment supply chain from cotton to consumer—call for enactment of CBI trade enhancement legislation as part of a package of relief measures for hurricane reconstruction.
March 4, 1999	Reps. Phil Crane (R-IL), Jim Kolbe (R-AZ), Charlie Rangel (D-NY), and Bob Matsui (D-CA) introduce CBI trade enhancement legislation as part of a package of relief measures for hurricane reconstruction.
March 4, 1999	The Administration transmits a CBI trade enhancement bill to the Congress.
March 9, 1999	President Clinton pledges support for CBI trade enhancement during a two-day visit to the Central America region.
March 23, 1999	House Ways and Means Trade Subcommittee holds hearing on CBI trade enhancement legislation (HR 984).

May 18, 1999	House Ways and Means Trade Subcommittee approves CBI trade enhancement legislation (HR 984).
June 10, 1999	House Ways and Means Committee approves CBI trade enhancement legislation (HR 984).
November 3, 1999	Senate Caribbean Basin Trade Enhancement legislation as Title II of the Trade and Development Act of 1999 (HR 434) by a vote of 76 to 19.
January 27, 2000	In his final State of the Union Address, President Clinton asked Congress to "finalize" the CBI trade enhancement legislation.
January 29, 2000	At a World Trade Forum in Davos, Switzerland, President Clinton again cites his strong support for CBI trade enhancement.
February 7, 2000	FY 2001 budget includes funds for Caribbean Basin Trade Enhancement.
April 13, 2000	Breaking a months-long logjam, Congressional leaders reach "agreement in principle" on CBI and Africa trade enhancement. Staff spends next two weeks working out details.
May 4, 2000	Conference agreement on HR 434 approved by the House on a vote of 309 to 110.
May 11, 2000	Conference agreement on HR 434 approved by Senate on a vote of 77 to 19.
May 17, 2000	Testimony by Richard Bernal on the Caribbean/ U.S. Relations to the Hearings before the Subcommittee on the Western Hemisphere of the House Committee on International Relations.
May 18, 2000	In South Lawn ceremony before more than 300 guests, President Clinton signs HR 434 into law (PL 106-200).

Appendix H

Side by Side Comparison of Caribbean Basin Trade Enhancement Bills—1999

Provision	House	Senate	Administration
Name	Title I of HR 984. United States—Caribbean Trade Partnership Act.	Title I of S. 371. United States—Caribbean Basin Trade Enhancement Act.	United States—Caribbean Basin Trade Enhancement Act.
Date of introduction	Introduced on 3/4/99 by Rep. Phil Crane and three other co-sponsors.	Introduced on 2/4/99 by Senator Bob Graham (D-FL) and nine other co-sponsors.	Submitted by Administration on 3/4/99
Coverage of originating textile and apparel items.	Benefits described below occur upon enactment. 1. Tariff treatment similar to Mexico under NAFTA. No quotas. 2. Duty and quota free treatment for 807A with U.S. yarn 3. Duty and quota free treatment for 809 with U.S. yarn 4. Duty and quota free treatment for knit to shape in region with U.S. yarn 5. Duty and quota free treatment for knit in region with U.S. yarn, or	Benefits described below occur upon enactment. 1. Duty and quota free treatment for 807A with U.S. yarn 2. Duty and quota free treatment for 809 with U.S. yarn with U.S. sewing thread. 3. Duty and quota free treatment for knit to shape in region with U.S. yarn 4. Duty and quota free treatment for handloomed, etc. 5. Duty and quota free treatment for textile luggage if	Tariff benefits described below occur subject to Presidential discretion and proclamation. Quota benefits occur upon enactment. 1. Duty and quota free treatment for 807A with U.S. yarn 2. Duty and quota free treatment for 809 with U.S. yarn with U.S. sewing thread. 3. Duty and quota free treatment for handloomed, etc.

	6. Duty and quota free treatment for handloomed, etc.	assembled according to (1) or (2) above. 6. De minimis rule for findings and trimmings not exceeding 25 percent of the cost of assembled components of product. Based on existing CBI de minimis rule.	
Ratchet down of existing quotas.	No provision.	No provision	President may reduce quotas on existing quotas on non-originating goods to counter increased benefits.
Coverage of non-originating textile and apparel items.	Presidential authority to proclaim tariff preference levels subject to absolute and allocation limitations.	No provisions.	No provisions.
Bilateral emergency actions for T/A products.	Permits bilateral tariff emergency actions similar to those contained in NAFTA for originating T/A goods. Permits bilateral quota emergency actions similar to those contained in NAFTA for non-originating T/A goods. No compensation.	Permits bilateral tariff emergency actions similar to those contained in NAFTA for originating T/A goods. No compensation.	Permits bilateral tariff and quota emergency actions similar to those contained in NAFTA for originating T/A goods. No compensation.
Coverage of products other than T/A products.	Identical to NAFTA tariff treatment for all CBERA excluded goods. Exceptions for goods described in US Note 2(b) and	No provisions.	President may proclaim tariff treatment identical to NAFTA for all CBERA excluded goods. Exceptions for goods described

	subsection (h), which already have duty free treatment or treatment lower than NAFTA.		in US Note 2(b) and subsection (h), which already have duty free treatment or treatment lower than NAFTA.
Customs procedures.	Similar to NAFTA	Similar to NAFTA	Similar to NAFTA.
Transshipment safeguards.	President to deny benefits to exporters for two years if they transship. USTR/Customs study analyzing how partnership countries cooperate on transshipment issues.	President to deny benefits to exporters for two years if they transship. Countries that do not take steps to halt transshipment to be triple charged on quota.	Countries that do not take steps to halt transshipment to be charged on quota (in amount to be determined by President).
Duration.	Five years or date of accession to NAFTA or similar free trade area.	Six years. From 10/1/1999 to 9/30/2005.	21 months. From 10/1/1999 to 6/30/2001.
Rule of origin.	Similar to NAFTA, except only refers to U.S. and partnership, or combination of partnership, countries.	No explicit provision.	Similar to NAFTA, except only refers to U.S. and partnership, or combination of partnership, countries.
Eligibility and retention of designation.	Partnership countries must be CBERA designated beneficiary countries. Presidential authority to withdraw, suspend, or limit preference based on regular reviews.	Enhancement countries must be CBERA designated beneficiary countries.	Enhancement countries must be CBERA designated beneficiary countries and must be undertaking obligations under WTO and participating in FTAA negotiations. President may also consider CBERA criteria as well as 11 other requirements relating to economic and non-economic factors.

			Presidential authority to withdraw, suspend, or limit preference based on review of eligibility criteria. Links GSP status to CBERA status. If GSP is withdrawn, CBERA shall also be withdrawn.
Changes to existing eligibility requirements.	No provisions.	Establishes new discretionary criteria to permit President to determine that a country denies adequate and effective IPR even if in compliance with TRIPs.	Changes existing discretionary criteria for CBERA to mandatory criteria. Establishes new criteria to permit President to determine that a country denies adequate and effective IPR even if in compliance with TRIPs.
Reporting requirements.	USTR/Customs transshipment report. Due 10/1/1999. Presidential review on operation of USCTPA, including discussion of continued eligibility of partnership countries using CBERA criteria. Due one year after enactment of USCTPA and every three years thereafter. USTR report on economic development and market oriented reforms in Caribbean Basin and ability of	Changes annual ITC report to biannual report. First report due on September 30 following enactment of USCBTEA. Similar change made to report due under Andean Trade Preference Act.	Presidential review on operation of CBTEA, including discussion of continued eligibility of partnership countries using existing CBERA and new CBTEA criteria. Due on December 1, 2000, and every three years thereafter. Changes annual ITC report to triennial report. First report due on September 1, 2000. Reaffirms existing requirement for U.S. Dept. of Labor (DOL) study on CBERA to clarify inclusion of CBTEA.

	CBERA countries to accede to NAFTA. Due two years after enactment of USCTPA. USTR to provide review discussing impact on CBERA countries if new countries reach free trade agreement with United States.		Modifies USTR, ITC, and DOL ATPA report due dates.
Follow-up meetings.	President shall take steps to convene meeting with trade ministers to discuss timetable for initiation of trade negotiations with United States.	No provision.	No provision.
Sugar.	President to monitor effect of NAFTA on CBI sugar access. If adverse, President will take actions or recommend action to ameliorate adverse effect.	No provision.	No provision.
Rum.	Contains provisions to facilitate NAFTA preferential treatment for Canadian products using Virgin Island or CBI rum.	Contains provisions to facilitate NAFTA preferential treatment for Canadian or Mexican products using Virgin Island or CBI rum.	No provision.

Appendix I

Table 8.2. Side by Side Comparison of Caribbean Basin Trade Enhancement Bills—2000

Provision	House	Senate (Graham)	Senate (Roth)	Administration
Name.	Title I of HR 984. United States—Caribbean Trade Partnership Act.	Title I of S. 371. United States—Caribbean Basin Trade Enhancement Act.	S. 1389. United States Caribbean Basin Trade Enhancement Act. Incorporated as Title II of Senate passed version of HR 434.	United States—Caribbean Basin Trade Enhancement Act.
Coverage of originating textile and apparel items.	Benefits described below occur upon enactment. 1. Tariff treatment similar to Mexico under NAFTA. No quotas. 2. Duty and quota free treatment for 807A or apparel entered under Chapters 61, 62, and 63 (but for incidental processes) with U.S. yarn 3. Duty and quota free treatment for 809 with U.S. yarn 4. Duty and quota free treatment for knit to shape in region with U.S. yarn 5. Duty and quota free treatment for knit in region with U.S. yarn 6. Duty and quota free treatment for hand	Benefits described below occur upon enactment. 1. Duty and quota free treatment for 807A or apparel entered under Chapters 61 and 62 (but for incidental processes) with U.S. yarn 2. Duty and quota free treatment for 809 with U.S. yarn with U.S. formed sewing thread. 3. Duty and quota free treatment for knit to shape in region with U.S. yarn 4. Duty and quota free treatment for hand loomed, etc. Determined by President. 5. Duty and quota free treatment for textile	Benefits described below occur upon enactment, subject to eligibility determination. 1. Duty and quota free treatment for 807A or apparel entered under Chapters 61 and 62 (but for incidental processes) with U.S. yarn 2. Duty and quota free treatment for 809 with U.S. yarn with U.S. formed sewing thread. 3. Duty and quota free treatment for handloomed, etc. Determined by President. 4. Duty and quota free treatment for textile luggage if assembled according to (1) or	Tariff benefits described below subject to eligibility determination and Presidential proclamation. Quota benefits occur upon enactment, subject to eligibility determination. 1. Duty and quota free treatment for 807A or apparel entered under Chapters 61, 62, and 63 (but for incidental processes) with U.S. yarn 2. Duty and quota free treatment for 809 with U.S. yarn with U.S. formed sewing thread. 3. Duty and quota free treatment for hand loomed, etc. Determined by President.

loomed, etc. Determined by USTR.	luggage if assembled according to (1) or (2) above. 6. De minimis rule for findings and trimmings not exceeding 25 percent of the cost of assembled components of product. Based on existing CBI de minimis rule.	(2) above.	
Ratchet down of existing quotas.	No provision.	No provision.	President may reduce existing quotas on non-originating goods to counter increased benefits.
Coverage of non-originating textile and apparel items.	Presidential authority to proclaim tariff preference levels subject to absolute and allocation limitations.	No provisions.	No provisions.
Bilateral emergency actions for T/A products.	Permits bilateral tariff emergency actions similar to those contained in NAFTA for originating T/A goods. Permits bilateral quota emergency actions similar to those contained in NAFTA for non-originating T/A goods. No compensation.	Permits bilateral tariff emergency actions similar to those contained in NAFTA for originating T/A goods. No compensation.	Permits bilateral tariff and quota emergency actions similar to those contained in NAFTA for originating T/A goods. No compensation.

Coverage of products other than T/A products.	Identical to NAFTA tariff treatment for all CBERA excluded goods. Exceptions for goods described in U.S. Note 2(b) and subsection (h), which already have duty free treatment or treatment lower than NAFTA.	No provisions.	Identical to NAFTA tariff treatment for all CBERA excluded goods. Exceptions for goods described in U.S. Note 2(b) and subsection (h), which already have duty free treatment or treatment lower than NAFTA.	President may proclaim tariff treatment identical to NAFTA for all CBERA excluded goods. Exceptions for goods described in U.S. Note 2(b) and subsection (h), which already have duty free treatment or treatment lower than NAFTA.
Customs procedures.	Similar to NAFTA.	Similar to NAFTA.	Similar to NAFTA.	Similar to NAFTA.
Transshipment safeguards.	President to deny benefits to exporters for two years if they transship. USTR/Customs study analyzing how partnership countries cooperate on transshipment issues.	President to deny benefits to exporters for two years if they transship. Countries that do not take steps to halt transshipment to be triple charged on quota.	President to deny benefits to exporters for two years if they transship. Countries that do not take steps to halt transshipment to be triple charged on quota.	Countries that do not take steps to halt transshipment to be charged on quota (in amount to be determined by President).
Duration.	25 months. From 7/1/2000 to 8/1/2002 or date of accession to NAFTA or similar free trade agreement. Originally introduced to last for five years or date of accession.	Six years. From 10/1/1999 to 9/30/2005	Four years, three months. From 10/1/00 to 12/31/04 or date of entry into force of FTAA with CBTEA country.	21 months. From 10/1/1999 to 6/30/2001.
Rule of origin.	Similar to NAFTA, except only refers to U.S. and partnership, or combination of partnership, countries.	No explicit provision.	Similar to NAFTA, except only refers to U.S. and enhancement, or combination of enhancement, countries.	Similar to NAFTA, except only refers to U.S. and enhancement, or combination of enhancement, countries.
Eligibility and retention of designation.	Partnership countries must be CBERA	Enhancement countries must be CBERA	Enhancement countries must be CBERA	Enhancement countries must be CBERA

designated beneficiary countries. Presidential authority to withdraw, suspend, or limit preference based on regular reviews that include following criteria:

a. continues to meets existing CBERA criteria
b. follows international trade rules
c. protects IPR
d. protects investment
e. provides non-discriminatory treatment for CBERA products
f. provides workers rights
g. cooperates in administering CBERA provisions.

designated beneficiary countries.

designated beneficiary countries and must have designated commitment to undertake obligations under WTO and participate in FTAA negotiations. President shall also consider CBERA criteria as well as ten other requirements relating to economic and non-economic factors. Those criteria, include:

a. follows international trade rules
b. protects IPR
c. protects investment
d. provides non-discriminatory market access for CBERA products
e. provides workers rights
f. meets drug certification
g. takes steps to observe Anti-Corruption treaty
h. supports USG government procurement objectives

designated beneficiary countries and must have designated commitment to undertake obligations under WTO and participate in FTAA negotiations. President may also consider CBERA criteria as well as 11 other requirements relating to economic and non-economic factors. Those criteria, include:

a. follows international trade rules
b. protects IPR
c. protects investment
d. provides non-discriminatory market access for CBERA products
e. provides workers rights
f. provides environmental protection
g. meets drug certification
h. takes steps to observe Anti-Corruption treaty
i. supports USG

			i. follows WTO customs valuation j. affords U.S. products non-discriminatory treatment Presidential authority to withdraw, suspend, or limit preference based on review of eligibility criteria. No benefits under Act to countries that do not meet and adequately enforce provisions regarding child labor in ILO Convention 182.	government procurement objectives i. follows WTO customs valuation k. affords U.S. products non-discriminatory treatment Presidential authority to withdraw, suspend, or limit preference based on review of eligibility criteria. Links GSP status to CBERA status. If GSP is withdrawn, CBERA shall also be withdrawn.
Changes to existing eligibility requirements.	No provisions.	Establishes new discretionary criteria to permit President to determine that a country denies adequate and effective IPR even if in compliance with TRIPs.	Establishes new criteria to permit President to determine that a country denies adequate and effective IPR even if in compliance with TRIPs. Effectively changes existing discretionary criteria for CBERA to mandatory criteria.	Establishes new criteria to permit President to determine that a country denies adequate and effective IPR even if in compliance with TRIPs. Effectively changes existing discretionary criteria for CBERA to mandatory criteria.
Labor provisions.	Partnership country eligibility depends on extent to which it meets the internationally recognized workers rights criteria specified in existing CBERA.	Enhancement countries must meet existing CBERA labor conditionality.	Enhancement country eligibility depends on extent to which it provides internationally recognized workers rights, including right of association, right to bargain collectively,	Enhancement country eligibility depends on extent to which it provides internationally recognized workers rights, including right of association, right to bargain collectively,

	prohibition on forced labor, minimum age, and acceptable conditions with respect to minimum compensation and health and safety. Benefits linked to child labor treaty implementation.		prohibition on forced labor, minimum age, and acceptable conditions with respect to minimum compensation and health and safety.	prohibition on forced labor, minimum age, and acceptable conditions with respect to minimum compensation and health and safety.
Reporting requirements.	USTR/Customs transshipment report. Due 10/1/1999. Presidential review on operation of USCTPA, including discussion of continued eligibility of partnership countries using CBERA criteria. Due one year after enactment of USCTPA and every three years thereafter. USTR report on economic development and market-oriented reforms in Caribbean Basin and ability of CBERA countries to accede to NAFTA. Due two years after enactment of USCTPA. USTR to provide review, discussing impact on CBERA countries if new countries reach free trade agreement with U.S.	Changes annual ITC report to biannual report. First report due on September 30 following enactment of USCBTEA. Similar change made to report due under Andean Trade Preference Act.	USTR biennial review on operation of CBTEA, including discussion of continued eligibility of enhancement countries using existing CBERA and new CBTEA criteria. Due on December 31, 2001 and every two years thereafter. Changes annual ITC report to biennial report. First report due on September 30, 2001. Modifies ITC and USTR report due dates for ATPA.	Presidential review on operation of CBTEA, including discussion of continued eligibility of partnership countries using existing CBERA and new CBTEA criteria. Due on December 1, 2000, and every three years thereafter. Changes annual ITC report to triennial report. First report due on September 1, 2000. Reaffirms existing requirement for U.S. Dept. of Labor (DOL) study on CBERA to clarify inclusion of CBTEA. Modifies USTR, ITC, and DOL ATPA report due dates.

Follow-up meetings.	President shall take steps to convene meeting with trade ministers to discuss timetable for initiation of trade negotiations with the United States.	No provision.	No provision.	No provision.
Sugar.	President to monitor effect of NAFTA on CBI sugar access. If adverse, President will take actions or recommend action to ameliorate adverse effect.	No provision.	No provision.	No provision.
Rum.	Contains provisions to facilitate NAFTA preferential treatment for Canadian products using Virgin Island or CBI rum.	Contains provisions to facilitate NAFTA preferential treatment for Canadian or Mexican products using Virgin Island or CBI rum.	No provision.	No provision.

References

BOOKS

Aaronson, Susan Ariel. *Trade and the American Dream. A Social History of Postwar Trade Policy.* Lexington: The University Press of Kentucky, 1996.

Abrahams, Peter. *The Coyaba Chronicles. Reflections of the Black Experience in the 20th Century.* Kingston: Ian Randle, 2000.

————. *Jamaica. An Island Mosaic.* London: Her Majesty's Stationery Office, 1957.

Adams, Gordon. *The Politics of Defense Contracting: The Iron Triangle.* New Brunswick: Transaction Books, 1982.

Adelman, Irma, and Joan Taft Morris. *Economic Growth and Social Equity in Developing Countries.* Stanford: Stanford University Press, 1973.

Agee, Philip. *Inside the Company. A C. I. A. Diary.* New York: Stonehill, 1975.

Aguilar, Alonso. *Pan-Americanism: From Monroe to the Present.* New York: Monthly Review Press, 1965, page 53, 70.

Alba, Victor. *Alliance without Allies. The Mythology of Progress in Latin America.* New York: Praeger, 1964.

Alberbach, Joel D. *Keeping a Watchful Eye. The Politics of Congressional Oversight.* Washington, D.C.: Brookings Institution, 1990.

Alleyne, Mervyn. *Roots of Jamaican Culture.* London: Pluto Press, 1988.

Allison, Graham T. *The Essence of Decision. Explaining the Cuban Missile Crisis.* Boston: Little, Brown and Company, 1971.

Almadhagi, Ahmed Norman. *Yemen and the USA: A Super-Power and a Small-State Relationship 1962–1994.* London: I. B. Tauris, 1996.

Ambrose, Stephen E., and Douglas G. Brinkley. *Rise to Globalism. America Foreign Policy since 1938.* Harmondsworth: Penguin, 8th Revised Edition, 1997, page 77.

Ambrose, Stephen E., Douglas G. Brinkley, and H. W. Brands. *The Devil We Knew. Americans and the Cold War.* Oxford: Oxford University Press, 1993.

Amersfoort, Herman, and Wim. Klinkert (eds.). *Small Powers in a World of Total War, 1900–1940.* Leiden: BRILL, 2011.

Amin, Samir. *Accumulation on a World Scale.* New York: Monthly Review Press, 1974.

————. *Capitalism in the Age of Globalization.* London: Zed Books, 1997.

————. *Imperialism and Unequal Development.* New York: Monthly Review Press, 1977.

————. *Unequal Development.* New York: Monthly Review Press, 1976.

Amin, Samir, Giovanni Arrighi, Andre Gunder Frank, and Immanuel Wallerstein, *Dynamics of Global Crisis.* New York: Monthly Review Press, 1982.

Amos Jr., William Taylor, and Lawrence Kort, *American National Security: Policy and Process.* Baltimore: Johns Hopkins Press, 4th ed, 1993.

Anderson, Perry. *Considerations of Western Marxism.* London: New Left Books, 1976.

———— (ed.). *Western Marxism. A Critical Reader.* London: Verso, 1978.

Andre, Irving W., and Gabriel J. Christian. *In Search of Eden. The Travails of a Caribbean Mini State.* Upper Marlboro: Pond Case Press, 1992.

Ashby, Timothy. *Missed Opportunities: The Rise and Fall of Jamaica's Edward Seaga.* Indianapolis: Hudson Institute, 1989.

Ayub, Mahmood Ali. *Made in Jamaica. The Development of the Manufacturing Sector, World Bank, Staff Occasional Paper, No. 31.* Washington, D.C.: World Bank, 1981.

Badaraco, Joseph L. Jr. *The Knowledge Link. How Firms Compete through Strategic Alliances.* Boston: Harvard Business School Press, 1991.

Bakan, Abigail B., David Cox, and Colin Leys (eds.). *Imperial Power and Regional Trade. The Caribbean Basin Initiative.* Waterloo: Wilfred Laurier University Press, 1993.

Baker, James. *The Politics of Diplomacy: Revolution, War and Peace 1989–1992.* New York: Putnam Publishers, 1995.

Baldwin, Robert E., and Christopher S. Magee. *Congressional Trade Votes: From NAFTA Approval to Fast-Track Defeat.* (Washington, D.C.: Institute for International Economics, 2000) page 9.

Bandow, Doug (ed.). *US Aid to the Developing World: A Free Market Agenda.* Washington, D.C.: Heritage Foundation, 1985.

Bansa, Stephen. *The American Mediterranean.* New York: Maffatt, Yard & Co., 1913.

Baptiste, Fitzroy. *War, Cooperation and Conflict: The European Possessions in the Caribbean, 1939–1945.* New York: Greenwood Press, 1988.

Baran, Paul, and Paul Sweezy. *Monopoly Capital.* New York: Monthly Review Press, 1968.

Barbour, Haley. *Agenda for America. A Republican Direction for the Future.* Washington, D.C.: Regency Publishing, 1996.

Baritz, Loren. *City on a Hill: A History of Ideas and Myths in America.* New York: John Wiley and Sons, 1964.

Barnett, Richard J. *Intervention and Revolution. The United States in the Third World.* London: Paladin, 1972.

Barnett, Richard J., and John Cavanagh. *Global Dreams. Imperial Corporations and the New World Order.* New York: Simon & Schuster, 1994) pages 346–47.

Barrett, Leonard. *The Rastafarians. Sounds of Cultural Dissonance.* Boston: Beacon Press, 1977.

Barry, Tom, and Deb Preusch. *Soft War.* New York: Grove Press, 1988.

Basedeo, Sahadeo, and Graeme Mount. *The Foreign Relations of Trinidad and Tobago, 1962–2000. The Case of a Small State in the Global Arena.* Port of Spain: Lexicon Trinidad, 2001.

Bauer, Raymond A. Ithaiel de Sola Pool and Lewis Anthony Dexter. *American Business and Public Policy. The Politics of Foreign Trade.* New York: Atherton, 1963.

Baum, Daniel Jay. *The Banks of Canada in the Commonwealth Caribbean.* New York: Praeger, 1974.

Beck, Roy. *The Case Against Immigration. The Moral, Economic, Social and Environmental Reasons for Reducing US Immigration Back to Traditional Levels.* New York: WW Norton, 1996.

Beckford, George L. *Persistent Poverty. Underdevelopment in Plantation Economies of the Third World.* New York: Oxford University Press, 1972.

Beckles, Hilary, and Verene Shepherd (eds.). *Caribbean Slave Society and Economy: A Student Reader.* New York: New Press, 1993.

Belafonte, Harry, and Michael Shnayerson. *My Song: A Memoir.* New York: Knopf, 2011.

Bell, Wendell. *Jamaican Leaders. Political Attitudes in a New Nation.* Berkeley: University of California Press, 1964.

Bello, Walden. *People and Power in the Pacific. The Struggle for the Post-Cold War Order.* London: Pluto Press, 1992, pages 37–49.

Benn, Denis. *Multilateral Diplomacy and the Economics of Change. The Third World and the New International Economic Order.* Kingston/Miami: Ian Randle Publishers, 2003.

Bennett, W. Lance, and David L. Paletz (eds.). *Taken by Storm: The Media, Public Opinion and US Foreign Policy in the Gulf War.* Chicago: University of Chicago, 1994.

Bent, R. M., and Enid L. Bent-Golding. *A Complete Geography of Jamaica.* London: Collins, 1966.

Bentley, Arthur. *The Process of Government.* Chicago: University of Chicago Press, 1908.

Berbusse, Edward J. *The United States in Puerto Rico, 1898–1900.* Chapel Hill: University of North Carolina Press, 1966.

Bergsten, C. Fred. *America in the World Economy. A Strategy for the 1990s.* Washington, D.C.: Institute for International Economics, 1988.

Berry, Tom, Beth Wood, and Deb Preusch. *The Other Side of Paradise. Foreign Control in the Caribbean.* New York: Grove Press, 1984.

Best, Lloyd, and Kari Polanyi Levitt (eds.). *The Theory of Plantation Economy. A Historical and Institutional Approach to Caribbean Economic Development.* Kingston: University of the West Indies Press, 2009.

Bhagwati, Jagdish. *The World Trading System at Risk.* Princeton: Princeton University Press, 1991.

Birnbaum, Jeffrey H. *The Lobbyists. How Influence Peddlers Work Their Way in Washington.* New York: Times Books, 1992.

Bishop, Maurice. *Forward Ever! Three Years of the Grenadian Revolution.* Sidney: Pathfinder Press, 1982.

———. *Whose Freedom?* London: Latin America Bureau, 1984.

Black, Clinton V. *History of Jamaica.* London; Collins, 1958.

Blackburn, Robin. *The Making of New World Slavery. From the Baroque to the Modern 1492–1800.* London: Verso, 1997.

———. *The Overthrow of Colonial Slavery 1776–1848.* London: Verso, 1988.

Blanchard, James J. *Behind the Embassy Door. Canada, Clinton, and Quebec.* Chelsea: Sleeping Bear Press, 1998.

Blasier, Cole. *The Hovering Giant. US Responses to Revolutionary Change in Latin America.* Pittsburgh: University of Pittsburgh Press, 1976.

Block, Fred L. *The Origins of International Economic Disorder.* Berkeley: University of California, 1977.

Bogues, Anthony. *Caliban's Freedom. The Early Political Thought of C. L. R. James.* London: Pluto Press, 1997.

Bolland, O. Nigel. *On the March. Labour Rebellion in the British Caribbean, 1934–1939.* Kingston: Ian Randle Publishers, 1995.

Booker, Cedella, and Anthony Winkler. *Bob Marley. An Intimate Portrait by His Mother.* London: Viking, 1996.

Bovard, James. *The Fair Trade Fraud.* New York: St. Martin's Press, 1991.

Boyd, Derick. *Economic Management, Income Distribution, and Poverty in Jamaica.* Westport: Praeger Publishers, 1988.

Boyes, Roger. *Meltdown Iceland: Lessons on the World Financial Crisis from a Small Bankrupt Island.* New York: Bloomsbury, 2009.

Boxill, Ian. *Ideology and Caribbean Integration.* Mona, Jamaica: Consortium Graduate School of Social Sciences, University of the West Indies, 1993.

Brands, H. W. *The Devil We Knew. Americans and the Cold War.* Oxford: Oxford University Press, 1993.

———. *What America Owes the World. The Struggle for the Soul of Foreign Policy.* Cambridge: Cambridge University Press, 1998.

Brathwaithe, Edward. *The Development of Creole Society in Jamaica, 1770–1820.* Oxford: Clarendon Press, 1971.

Braudel, Fernand. *Civilization and Capitalism. 15th-18th Century.* New York: Harper & Row, 1981–1984, Vols. 1–3.

Braveboy-Wagner, Jacqueline A. *Caribbean Diplomacy. Focus on Washington, Cuba and the Past Cold War Era.* New York: Caribbean Diaspora Press, 1995.

———. *The Caribbean in World Affairs. The Foreign Policies of the English-Speaking Caribbean States.* Boulder: Westview Press, 1989.

———. *Small States in Global Affairs. The Foreign Policies of the Caribbean Community (CARICOM).* New York: Palgrave Macmillan, 2008.

———. *The Venezuelan-Guyana Border Dispute. Britain's Colonial Legacy in Latin America.* Boulder: Westview Press, 1984.

Bray, Charles. *The Media and Foreign Policy in the Post-Cold War World.* New York: Freedom Forum Media Studies Center, Columbia University, 1993.

Brewer, Anthony. *Marxist Theories of Imperialism*. London: Routledge & Kegan Paul, 1980.

Brewster, Havelock, and Clive Y. Thomas. *The Dynamics of West Indian Economic Integration*. Mona, Jamaica: Institute of Social and Economic Research, University of the West Indies, 1967.

Brezinski, Zbigniew. *Out of Control. Global Turmoil on the Eve of the 21st Century*. New York: Charles Scribner & Sons, 1993.

Briggs, Philip J. *Making American Foreign Policy. President-Congress Relations from the Second World War to the Post Cold War Era*. Lanham: Rowman & Littlefield, 2nd ed., 1994.

Brimelow, Peter. *Alien Nation, Common Sense about America's Immigration Disaster*. New York: Random House, 1995.

Brodber, Erna. *The Second Generation of Freemen in Jamaica, 1907–1944*. Gainesville: University Press of Florida, 2004.

Brown, Michael Barrett. *Economics of Imperialism*. Harmondsworth: Penguin, 1974.

Bryan, Anthony T. (ed.). *The Caribbean. New Dynamics in Trade and Political Economy*. Miami: North-South Center, University of Miami, 1995.

Bryan, Anthony T., Edward Greene, and Timothy Shaw (eds.), *Peace, Development and Security in the Caribbean. Perspectives to the Year 2000*. London: Macmillan, 1990.

Bryan, Patrick. *The Jamaican People: 1880–1902: Race, Class and Social Control*. Kingston: University of the West Indies Press, 2002.

Buddan, Robert. *The Foundations of Caribbean Politics*. Kingston: Arawak Publications, 2001.

Bull, Headley. *The Anarchical Society. A Study of Order in World Politics*. London: Macmillan, 1977.

Burrowes, S. I., and J. A. Carnegie. *George Headley*. London: Thomas Nelson and Sons, 1971.

Burtless, Gary, Robert Z. Lawrence, Robert E. Litan, and Robert J. Shapiro. *Globaphobia. Confronting Fears About Open Trade*. Washington, D.C., Brookings Institution, Progressive Policy Institute and Twentieth Century Fund, 1998.

Burton, John, Frank Dukes, and George Mason. *Conflict. Resolution and Prevention*. London: Macmillan, 1990.

Burton, John (ed.). *Conflict. Human Needs Theory*. London: Macmillan, 1990.

———. *International Relations. A General Theory*. Cambridge: Cambridge University Press, 1965.

———. *World Society*. Cambridge: Cambridge University Press, 1972.

Bush, George, and Brent Scowcroft. *A World Transformed*. New York: Alfred A. Knopf, 1998.

Bustamante, Lady. *The Memoirs of Lady Bustamante*. Kingston: Kingston Publishers Ltd., 1997.

Calleo, David P. *Beyond American Hegemony. The Future of the Western Alliance*. New York: Twentieth Century Fund, 1987.

Calleo, David P., and Benjamin M. Rowland. *America and the World Political Economy: Atlantic Dreams and National Realities*. Bloomington: Indiana University Press, 1973.

Campbell, Charles S. Jr., *Social Business Interests and the Open Door Policy*. New Haven: Connecticut College and University Press, 1951.

Campbell, Horace. *Rasta and Resistance: From Marcus Garvey to Walter Rodney*. Africa World Press, 1987.

Campbell, Mavis C. *The Maroons of Jamaica 1655–1796. A History of Resistance, Collaboration and Betrayal*. Trenton, NJ: Africa World Press, 1990.

Cardoso, Fernando Henrique, and Enzo Faletto. *Dependency and Development in Latin America*. Berkeley: University of California Press, 1979.

Carey, Beverley. *The Maroon Story. The Authentic and Original History of the Maroons in the History of Jamaica*. Gorton Town, Jamaica: Agouti Press, 1997.

CARICOM Secretariat. *CARICOM. Our Caribbean Community*. Kingston: Ian Randle Publishers, 2005.

Carley, Mary Manning. *Jamaica. The Old and the New*. London: George Allen & Unwin, 1963.

Carmichael, Stokely, and Charles V. Hamilton. *Black Power. The Politics of Liberation*. New York: Vintage Books, 1967.

Carnegie, James. *Great Jamaican Olympians*. Kingston: Kingston Publishers, 1996.

———. *Some Aspects of Jamaica's Politics 1918–1938*. Kingston: Institute of Jamaica, 1973.

Carothers, Thomas. *In the Name of Democracy, US Policy Toward Latin America in the Reagan Years*. Berkeley: University of California Press, 1991.

Carr, E. H. *The Twenty Years Crisis, 1919–1939. An Introduction to the Study of International Relations*. London: Macmillan, 1939: Harper & Row, 1964.

———. *What is History?*. London: Macmillan, 1961.

Carrington, Selwyn. *The West Indies during the American Revolution. A Study in Colonial Economy and Politics*. Leiden: Koninklijk Instituut Voor Taal Landen Volkenkunde, 1987.

Carter, Jimmy. *Keeping Faith: Memory of a President*. New York: Bantam Books, 1982.

Carter, Ralph G. *Essentials of U.S. Foreign Policy Making*. New York: Pearson, 2014.

Cassen, Robert, and Associates. *Does Aid Work?*. Oxford: Clarendon Press, 1986.

Castaneda, Jorge G. *The Mexican Shock. Its Meaning for the U.S.* New York: Free Press, 1995.

Chamberlain, M. E. *Decolonization. The Fall of the European Empires*. Oxford: Blackwell Publishers, 1985.

Chase-Dunn, Christopher. *Global Formation. Structures of the World Economy*. Cambridge: Basil Blackwell, 1989.

Chenery, Hollis B., and M. Syrquin. *Patterns of Development, 1950–1970* (London: Oxford University Press, 1975).

Chevannes, Barrington A. *Rastafari. Roots and Ideology*. Syracuse: Syracuse University Press, 1995.

Choate, Pat. *Agents of Influence. How Japan's Lobbyists in the United States Manipulate America's Political and Economic System*. New York: Alfred Knopf, 1990.

Chomsky, Aviva. *West Indian Workers and the United Fruit Company in Costa Rica, 1870–1940*. Baton Rouge: Louisiana State University Press, 1996.

Christopher, Warren. *Chances of a Lifetime*. New York: Simon & Schuster, 2001.

———. *In the Stream of History*. Stanford: Stanford University Press, 1998.

Clarke, Colin, and Tony Payne (eds.). *Politics, Security and Development in Small States* London: Allen & Unwin, 1987.

Clarke, Edith. *My Mother Who Fathered Me. A Study of the Family in Three Selected Communities in Jamaica*. London: Allen & Unwin, 1957.

Cline, Howard F. *The United States and Mexico*. Cambridge: Howard University Press, 1967.

Cline, William R. *International Debt: Systematic Risk and Policy Response*. Washington, D.C.: Institute of International Economics, 1984.

Clinton, Bill, and Al Gore. *Putting People First: How We Can All Change America*. New York: Times Books, 1992.

Cockburn, Alexander, and Ken Silverstein. *Washington Babylon*. London: Verso, 1996.

Cohen, Bernard C. *The Press and Foreign Policy*. Princeton: Princeton University Press, 1963.

Cohen, Stephen, Joel R. Paul, and Robert A Blecker. *Fundamentals of US Foreign Trade Policy*. Boulder: Westview Press, 1996.

Coll, Steve. *Private Empire: ExxonMobil and American Power*. New York: Penguin Press, 2012.

Connell, John. *Sovereignty and Survival: Island Microstates in the Third World*. Sydney: University of Sydney, 1988.

Conrad, Peter. *Islands. A Trip Through Time and Space*. London: Thames and Hudson, 2009.

Conti, Delia B. *Reconciling Free Trade, Fair Trade, and Interdependence. The Rhetoric of Presidential Economic Leadership*. Westport: Praeger Publishers, 1998.

Cooper, Carolyn (ed.). *Global Reggae*. Mona: University of the West Indies Press, 2012.

Cooper, Wayne (ed.). *The Passion of Claude McKay. Selected Prose and Poetry 1912–1948*. New York: Schlocken Books, 1973.

Corwin, Edward S. *The President: Office and Powers, 1787–1957*. New York: New York University Press, 4th ed., 1957.

Cowhey, Peter F., and Jonathan Aronson. *Managing the World Economy. The Consequences of Corporate Alliances*. New York: Council on Foreign Relations, 1993.

Cox, Robert W. *Production, Power, and World Order. Social Forces in the Making of History*. New York: Columbia University Press, 1987.

Cox, Michael. *US Foreign Policy after the Cold War: Superpower Without a Mission?*. London: The Royal Institute of International Affairs, 1995.

Cox, Robert W. *Approaches to World Order*. Cambridge: Cambridge University Press, 1996.

Crabb, Cecil V. *Policymakers and Critics. Conflicting Theories of American Foreign Policy*. New York: Praeger Publishers, 1976.

Crabb Jr., Cecil V., Glenn J. Antizzo, and Leila E. Sarieddine. *Congress and the Foreign Policy Process. Modes of Legislative Behavior*. Baton Rouge: Louisiana State University Press, 2000.

Crahan, Margaret E., and Franklin W. Knight (eds.) *Africa and the Caribbean. The Legacies of a Link*. Baltimore: Johns Hopkins University Press, 1979.

Crane, Philip M. *Surrender in Panama: The Case Against the Treaty*. New York: Dale Books, 1978.

Cronon, Edmund David. *Black Moses. The Story of Marcus Garvey and the Universal Negro Improvement Association*. Madison: University of Wisconsin Press, 1968.

Cundall, Frank. *Historic Jamaica*. Kingston: Institute of Jamaica, 1915.

Curtin, Philip D. *Two Jamaicas. The Role of Ideas in a Tropical Colony 1830–1865*. Cambridge, MA: Harvard University Press, 1955.

Curtin, Philip D. *The Atlantic Slave Trade*. Madison: University of Wisconsin Press, 1969.

Dahl, Robert A. *A Preface to Democratic Theory*. Chicago: University of Chicago Press, 1963.

———. *Who Governs?*. New Haven: Yale University Press, 1961.

Davidson, Roger H., and Walter J. Oleszek. *Congress and Its Members*. Washington, D.C.: Congressional Quarterly Press, 7th ed. 2000.

Davies, Peter N. *Fyffes and the Banana: Musa Sapientum. A Centenary History 1888–1988*. London Athlone Press, 1990.

Davis, Carlton E. *Jamaica in the World Aluminium Industry 1938–1973*. Kingston: Jamaica Bauxite Institute, 1989.

———. *Jamaica in the World Aluminium Industry, Vol. II 1974–1988. Bauxite Levy Negotiations*. Kingston: Jamaica Bauxite Institute, 1995.

Davis, Ralph. *The Rise of the Atlantic Economies*. London: Weidenfeld and Nicolson, 1973.

Davis, Stephen. *Bob Marley*. London: Arthur Barker, 1983.

Davison, R. B. *Black British. Immigrants to England*. London: Oxford University Press, 1966.

DeConde, Alexander. *Ethnicity, Race and American Foreign Policy: A History*. Boston: Northeastern University Press, 1992.

Demas, William G. *The Economics of Development in Small Countries with Special Reference to the Caribbean*. Montreal: McGill University Press, 1965.

———. *Essays on Caribbean Integration and Development* (Mona, Jamaica: Institute of Social and Economic Research, University of the West Indies, 1976).

Destler, I. M. *American Trade Politics*. Washington, D.C.: Institute for International Economics, 3rd ed., 1995.

————. *Making Foreign Economic Policy.* Washington, D.C.: The Brookings Institution, 1980.

————. *Presidents, Bureaucratics, and Foreign Policy.* Princeton: Princeton University Press, 1972.

Destler, I. M., Leslie I. Gelb, and Anthony Lake. *Our Own Worst Enemy. The Unmaking of American Foreign Policy.* New York: Simon and Schuster, 1984.

Destler I. M., and Peter J. Balint. *The Politics of American Trade: Trade, Labour and Environment.* Washington, D.C.: Institute for International Economics, 1999.

Deutsch, Karl W. *The Analysis of International Relations* (Englewood Cliffs: Prentice Hall, 2nd ed., 1978).

Dickerson, Kitty G. *Textiles and Apparel in the Global Economy.* Englewoods Cliffs, New Jersey: Prentice Hall, 2nd edition, 1995.

Diskin, Martin (ed.). *Trouble in our Backyard. Central America and the United States in the Eighties.* New York: Pantheon Books, 1983.

Dobrynin, Anatoly. *In Confidence: Moscow's Ambassador to America's Six Cold War Presidents 1962–1986.* New York: Times Books, 1995.

Dolman, A. J. *Islands in the Shade: The Performance and Prospects of Small Island Developing Countries.* The Hague: Institute of Social Studies Advisory Service, 1984.

Domhoff, G. William. *The Higher Circles. The Governing Class in America.* New York: Vintage Books, 1971.

————. *Who Rules America?.* Englewoods Cliffs: Prentice-Hall, 1967.

————. *Who Rules America Now?* New York: Simon & Schuster, 1983.

Dookeran, Winston C. (ed.), *Choices and Change. Reflections on the Caribbean.* Washington, D.C.: Inter-American Development Bank, 1996.

Doran, Charles. *Canada and Congress: Lobbying in Washington.* Halifax: Centre for Foreign Policy Studies, Dalhousie University, 1985.

Doran, Charles F., and Sokolsky, Joel J. *Canada and Congress: Lobbying in Washington.* Halifax: Centre for Foreign Policy Studies, 1986.

Dorman, William A., and Mansour Farhang. *The US Press and Iran: Foreign Policy and the Journalism of Deference.* Berkeley: University of California Press, 1987.

Dougherty, James E., and Robert L. Pfaltzgraff, Jr. *Contending Theories of International Relations. A Comprehensive Survey.* New York: Harper Collins Publishers, 3rd ed., 1990.

Drew, Elizabeth. *Politics and Money. The New Road to Corruption.* New York: Macmillan, 1983.

————. *Showdown. The Struggle Between the Gingrich Congress and the Clinton White House.* New York: Simon & Schuster, 1996.

Dryden, Steve. *USTR and the American Crusade for Free Trade.* New York: Oxford University Press, 1995.

Dumbrell, John. *The Making of US Foreign Policy.* Manchester: Manchester University Press, 2nd ed., 1997.

Dunn, Richard S. *Sugar and Slaves. The Rise of the Planter Class in the English West Indies, 1624- 1713.* New York: W. W. Norton, 1972.

Dutt, R. Palme. *Britain's Crisis of Empire.* London: Lawrence and Wishart, 1949.

Eaton, George. *Alexander Bustamante and Modern Jamaica.* Kingston: Kingston Publishers, 1975.

Edwards, David. *An Economic Study of Small Farming in Jamaica.* Mona: Institute of Social and Economic Studies, University College of the West Indies, 1961.

Eisenhower, Milton S. *The Wine is Bitter. The United States and Latin America.* New York: Doubleday, 1963, page 302.

Eisner, Gisela. *Jamaica 1830–1930. A Study in Economic Growth.* Manchester: Manchester University Press, 1961.

Emmanuel, Arghiri. *Unequal Exchange. A Study of the Imperialism of Trade.* New York: Monthly Review Press, 1972.

Enders, Thomas O., and Richard P. Mattione. *Latin America: The Crisis of Debt and Growth.* Washington, D.C.: Brookings Institution, 1984.

Erb, Guy F., and Valeriana Kallab (eds.). *Beyond Dependency. The Developing World Speaks Out*. Washington, D.C.: Overseas Development Council, 1975.

Fallows, James M. *Media Rules. How the American Press Undermines American Diplomacy*. New York: Pantheon, 1996.

Fanon, Frantz. *The Wretched of the Earth*. New York: Grove Press, 1963.

Farer, Tom (ed.). *Transnational Crime in the Americas*. New York and London: Routledge, 1999.

Faulkner, M. V. *American Economic History*. New York: Harper & Row, 8th edition, 1959.

Fauriol, George A. *Foreign Policy Behavior of Caribbean States. Guyana, Haiti and Jamaica*. Lanham: University Press of America, 1984.

Feinberg, Richard E. *The Intemperate Zone, The Third World Challenge to US Foreign Policy*. New York, W. W. Norton & Company, 1945.

———. *Summitry in the Americas. A Progress Report*. Washington, D.C.: Institute of International Economics, 1997.

Feinberg, Richard E., and Robin L. Rosenberg (eds.). *Civil Society and the Summit of the Americas: The 1998 Santiago Summit*. Miami: North-South Center Press at the University of Miami, 1999.

Fenno, Richard F. *The Power of the Purse*. Boston: Little, Brown, 1966.

Fenno, Richard F. Jr. *Congressmen in Committees*. Boston: Little Brown, 1973.

Ferguson, William S. *Greek Imperialism*. New York: Biblo and Tanner, 1941.

Fieldhouse, D. K. (ed.). *The Theory of Capitalist Imperialism*. London: Longmans, 1967.

Fisher, William. *Experiment in Development: The US Business Committee on Jamaica*. New York: US Business Committee on Jamaica, Inc, 1985.

Fishlow, Albert, Carlos F. Diaz-Alejandro, Richard R. Fagen, and Roger D. Hansen. *Rich and Poor Nations in the World Economy*. New York: McGraw-Hill, 1978.

Fishlow, Albert, and James Jones (eds.). *The United States and the Americas. A Twenty-first Century View*. New York: W. W. Norton, 1999.

Fix, Michael, and Jeffrey S. Passel. *Immigration and Immigrants, Setting the Record Straight*. Washington, D.C.: Urban Institute, 1994.

Foner, Nancy. *Jamaica Farewell: Jamaican Migrants*. London: Routledge & Kegan Paul, 1979.

Fordham, Freida. *An Introduction to Jung's Psychology*. Harmondsworth, England: Penguin 1953.

Fox, Annett Baker. *The Power of Small States*. Chicago: University of Chicago Press, 1959.

Francis, Vivienne. *With Hope in Their Eyes*. London: Nia, 1998.

Frank, Andre Gunder. *Capitalism and Underdevelopment in Latin America. Historical Studies of Chile and Brazil*. New York: Monthly Review Press, 1967.

———. *Lumpenbourgeoisie. Lumpendevelopment, Dependence, Class and Politics in Latin America*. New York: Monthly Review Press, 1973.

Franklyn, Delano (ed.). *The Jamaican Diaspora. Building an Operational Framework*. Kingston: Wilson Franklyn Barnes, 2010.

———. *A Jamaican Voice in Caribbean and World Politics. P. J. Patterson. Selected Speeches 1992–2000*. Kingston: Ian Randle Publishers, 2002.

———. *Michael Manley. The Politics of Equality*. Kingston: Wilson Franklyn Barnes, 2009.

———. *Michael Manley. Putting People First*. Kingston: Winston Franklyn Barnes, 2013.

Friedman, Thomas L. *The Lexus and the Olive Tree. Understanding Globalization*. New York: Farrer Straus, Giroux, 1999.

Fuchs, Lawrence H. *The American Kaleidoscope: Race, Ethnicity and the Civic Culture*. Hanover, N. H.: University Press of New England, 1990.

Furtado, Celso. *Development and Underdevelopment. A Structuralist View of the Problems of Developed and Underdeveloped Countries*. Berkeley: University of California Press, 1964.

Galbraith, John Kenneth. *American Capitalism*. Harmondsworth: Penguin, 1952.

Gardener, Lloyd C. *Economic Aspects of New Deal Diplomacy*. Boston: Beacon Press, 1964.

Gardner, Richard N. *Sterling-Dollar Diplomacy in Current Perspective*. New York: Columbia University Press, 1980, Part 1.

Garten, Jeffrey E. *The Big Ten. The Big Emerging Markets and How They Will Change Our Lives*. New York: Basic Books, 1977.

Gates, Jeff. *Democracy at Risk. Rescuing Main Street from Wall Street*. Cambridge: Perseus Publishing, 2000.

Garvey, A. Jacques. *Garvey and Garveyism*. Kingston: A. Jacques Garvey, 1963.

Garwood, Darrel. *Undercover, 35 Years of CIA Deception*. New York: Grove, 1985.

Gerassi, John. *The Great Fear in Latin America*. New York: Macmillan, 1971.

——— (ed.). *Vinceramos: The Speeches and Writings of Che Guevera*. London: Panther Books, 1969.

Gerson, Alan. *The Kirkpatrick Mission. Diplomacy Without Apology. America at the United Nations 1981–1985*. New York: Free Press, 1991.

Gerson, Louis L. *The Hyphenated and Recent American Politics and Diplomacy*. Lawrence: University of Kansas Press, 1964.

Gilbert-Roberts, Terri-Ann. *The Politics of Integration. Caribbean Sovereignty Revisited*. Kingston and Miami: Ian Randle Publishers, 2013.

Gill, Stephen (ed.). *Gramsci, Historical Materialism and International Relations*. Cambridge: Cambridge University Press, 1993.

Gilpin, Robert. *War and Change in World Politics*. New York: Cambridge University Press, 1981.

Girvan, Norman. *Corporate Imperialism: Conflict and Expropriation*. New York: Monthly Review Press, 1978.

———. *Foreign Capital and Economic Underdevelopment in Jamaica*. Mona, Jamaica: Institute of Social and Economic Research, University of the West Indies, 1971.

Goldberg, David H. *Foreign Policy and Ethnic Interest Groups: American and Canadian Jews Lobby for Israel*. Westport: Greenwood Press, 1990.

Goldstein, Judith. *Ideas, Interests and American Trade Policy*. Ithaca: Cornell University Press, 1993.

Goldstein, Judith, and Robert O. Keohane (eds.). *Ideas and Foreign Policy*. Ithaca: Cornell University Press, 1993.

Gomes-Casseres, Benjamin. *The Alliance Revolution. The New Shape of Business Rivalry* Cambridge: Harvard University Press, 1996.

Goodwin, Jacob. *Brotherhood of Arms. General Dynamics and the Business of Defending America*. New York: New York Times Books, 1985.

Gordon, David M. *Fat and Mean. The Corporate Squeeze of Working Americans and the Myth of Managerial Downsizing*. New York: Free Press, 1996.

Gordon, Shirley C. *God Almighty Make Me Free. Christianity in Preemancipation Jamaica*. (Bloomington: Indiana University Press, 1996).

———. *Our Cause for His Glory. Christianity and Emancipation in Jamaica*. Mona, Jamaica: The Press University of the West Indies, 1998.

Gotlieb, Allan. *I'll Be with You in a Minute, Mr. Ambassador. The Education of a Canadian Diplomat in Washington*. Toronto: University of Toronto Press, 1991.

Gray, Obika. *Radicalism and Social Change in Jamaica, 1960–1972*. Knoxville: University of Tennessee Press, 1991.

Grayson, George W. *The North American Free Trade Agreement, Regional Community and the New World Order*. Lanham: University Press of America, 1995.

Green, William A. *British Slave Emancipation. The Sugar Colonies and the Great Experiment 1830–1865*. Oxford: Oxford University Press, 1976.

Greene, John Robert. *The Limits of Power. The Nixon and Ford Administrations* Bloomington: Indiana University Press, 1992.

Greenfield, Meg. *Washington*. New York: Public Affairs, 2001.

Greenspan, Allan. *The Age of Turbulence*. New York: Penguin Press, 2007.

Greider, William. *Who Will Tell the People? The Betrayal of American Democracy.* New York: Simon & Schuster, 1992.

Grey, Rodney De C. *Concepts in Trade Diplomacy and Trade in Services.* London: Harvester Wheatsheaf, 1990.

Griffin, Keith. *Underdevelopment in Spanish America.* London: George Allen and Unwin, 1967.

Griffith, Ivelaw L. *Caribbean Security on the Eve of the 21st Century, McNair Paper 54.* Washington, D.C.: Institute for National Strategic Studies, National Defense University, 1996.

———. *Drugs and Security in the Caribbean. Sovereignty under Siege.* University Park: Pennsylvania State University Press, 1997.

Gross, Peter. *Continuing the Inquiry. The Council of Foreign Relations from 1971 to 1996.* New York: Council on Foreign Relations, 1996.

Grugel, Jean. *Politics and Development in the Caribbean Basin. Central America and the Caribbean in the New World Order.* Bloomington: Indiana University Press, 1995.

Gunst, Laurie. *Born Fi' Dead. A Journey Through the Jamaican Posse Underworld.* New York: Henry Holt and Company, 1995.

Gwertzman, Bernard. *The Lobby: Jewish Political Power and American Foreign Policy.* New York: Simon and Schuster, 1988.

Haas, Ernst B. *Beyond the Nation State.* Stanford: Stanford University Press, 1964.

Haass, Richard N. *The Reluctant Sheriff. The United States after the Cold War.* New York: Council of Foreign Relations, 1997.

———. *The Use of American Military Force in the Post-Cold War World.* Washington, D.C.: Carnegie Endowment for International Peace, 1994.

Hadfeld-Amkhan, Amelia. *British Foreign Policy, National Identity and Neoclassical Realism.* Lanham: Rowman & Littlefield Publishers, 2010.

Haig, Alexander M. Jr., with Charles McCarry, *Inner Circles. How America Changed the World. A Memoir.* New York: Time Warner, 1992.

Halberstam, David. *The Fifties.* New York: Villard Books 1993.

Hall, Douglas. *Free Jamaica 1838–1865. An Economic History.* Kingston: Caribbean Universities Press, 1969.

Hall, Kenneth O. (ed.). *Integrate or Perish. Perspectives of Leaders of the Integration Movement 1963–1999.* Mona: University of the West Indies Press, 2000.

Hall, Kenneth, and Myrtle Chuck-A-Sang (eds.). *The Caribbean Single Market and Economy. Towards a Single Economic Space.* Bloomington: Trafford, 2013.

———. *CARICOM Single Market and Economy. Genesis and Prognosis.* Kingston: Ian Randle Publishers, 2007.

———. *Paradigm Shifts & Structural Changes - in Pursuit of Progress in the Caribbean Community.* Bloomington: Trafford Publishing, 2013.

Halley, Laurence. *Ancient Affections, Ethnic Groups and Foreign Policy.* New York: Praeger, 1979.

Halliday, Fred. *Rethinking International Relations.* London: Macmillan, 1994.

Hallin, Daniel. *The Uncensored War.* Oxford: Oxford University Press, 1986.

Halperin, Morton H. *Bureaucratic Politics and Foreign Policy.* Washington, D.C.: Brookings Institution, 1974.

Handel, Michael. *Weak States in the International System.* London: Frank Cass & Co, 1990.

Hanes, W. Travis III, and Frank Sanello. *The Opium Wars. The Addiction of One Empire and the Corruption of Another.* New York: Barnes & Noble, 2002.

Hanson, Simon G. *Dollar Diplomacy Modern Style. Chapters in the Failure of the Alliance for Progress.* Washington, D.C.: Inter-American Affairs Press, 1970.

Harden, Sheila. *Small Is Dangerous. Micro States in a Macro World.* London: Palgrave Macmillan, 1985.

Harding, Earl. *The Untold Story of Panama.* New York: Athen Press, 1959.

Haring, C. H. *The Spanish Empire in America.* New York: Harcourt, Brace & World, 1947.

Harpelle, Ronald N. *The West Indians of Costa Rica. Race, Class and the Integration of an Ethnic Minority*. Kingston: Ian Randle, 2001.

Harriott, Anthony. *Police and Crime Control in Jamaica. Problems of Reforming Ex-Colonial Constabularies*. Kingston: University of the West Indies Press, 2000.

Hart, Michael, with Bill Dymond and Colin Robertson. *Decision at Midnight. Inside the Canada-US Free Trade Negotiations*. Vancouver: University of British Columbia Press, 1994.

Hart, Richard. *The End of Empire. Transition to Independence in Jamaica and Other Caribbean Region Colonies*. Kingston; Arawak Publications, 2006.

———. *Rise and Organize. The Birth of the Workers and National Movements in Jamaica 1936–1939*. London: Karia Press, 1989.

———. *The Slaves Who Abolished Slavery*. Mona: University of the West Indies Press, 1985.

———. *Towards Decolonization. Political, Labour and Economic Development in Jamaica, 1938–1945*. Kingston: Canoe Press University of the West Indies, 1999.

Haughton, Suzette A. *Drugged Out. Globalisation and Jamaica's Resilience to Drug Trafficking*. Lanham: University of the Americas Press, 2011.

Hayes, Margaret Daly. *Building the Hemisphere Community: Lessons from the Summit of the Americas Process*. Washington, D.C.: Inter-American Dialogue, July, 1996.

———. *Latin America and the US National Interest. A Basis for US Foreign Policy*. Boulder: Westview Press, 1984.

Headley, Bernard. *The Jamaican Crime Scene. A Perspective*. Mandeville: Eureka Press, 1994.

Heeney, Arnold. *The Things That Are Caeser's. Memoirs of a Canadian Public Servant*. Toronto: University of Toronto Press, 1972.

Henke, Holger. *Between Self-Determination and Dependency: Jamaica's Foreign Relations, 1972–1989*. Mona: University of the West Indies Press, 2000.

Henriques, Fernando. *Family and Colour in Jamaica*. London: Eyre & Spottiswoode, 1953.

Hertz, Noreena. *The Silent Takeover. Global Capitalism and the Death of Democracy*. New York: The Free Press, 2001.

Hey, Jeanne A. K. *Theories of Dependent Foreign Policy and the Cast of Ecuador in the 1980s*. Athens: Ohio University Center for International Studies, 1995.

Higman, Barry W. *Writing West Indian Histories*. London: Macmillan 1999.

Hill, Howard C. *Roosevelt and the Caribbean*. Chicago: University of Chicago Press, 1927.

Hilsman, Roger. *The Politics of Policy-Making in Defense and Foreign Affairs. Conceptual Models and Bureaucratic Politics*. New York: Prentice -Hall, 3rd ed., 1993.

Hilsman, Roger, Laura Gaughran, and Patricia A. Weitsman. *The Politics of Policy Making in Defense and Foreign Affairs. Conceptual Models and Bureaucratic Politics*. Englewood Cliffs, NJ: Prentice-Hall, 3rd ed., 1993.

Hinckley, Barbara. *Less than Meets the Eye. Congress, the President and Foreign Policy*. Chicago: University of Chicago, 1994.

Hirschman, Albert O. *The Strategy of Economic Development*. New Haven: Yale University Press, 1958.

Ho, Christine. *Salt-Water Trinnies*. New York: AMS Press, 1991.

Hobson, J. A. *Imperialism*. Ann Arbor: University of Michigan Press, 1965, originally published in 1902.

Hodgson, Godfrey. *The Myth of American Exceptionalism*. New Haven: Yale University Press, 2009.

Hofstede, Geert. *Culture's Consequences: Comparing Values, Behaviors, Institutions and Organizations Across Nations*. Thousand Oaks, CA: SAGE Publications, 2nd ed., 2001.

Hofstadter, Richard. *Social Darwinism in American Thought*. Boston: Beacon Press, 1955.

Holbrand, Carsten. *Danish Neutrality: A Study in the Foreign Policy of a Small State*. Oxford: Oxford University Press, 1991.

Holmes, Kim R., and James G. Moore. *Restoring American Leadership: A U.S. Foreign and Defense Policy Blueprint*. Washington, D.C.: Heritage Foundation, 1996.

Holsti, K. J. *The Dividing Discipline. Hegemony and Diversity in International Theory*. Boston: Allen & Unwin, 1985.

Holt, Thomas C. *The Problem of Freedom: Race, Labor, and Politics in Jamaica and Britain, 1832–1938*. Baltimore: Johns Hopkins Press 1991.

Hopkins, Terrace K., and Immanuel Wallerstein (eds.). *Processes of the World System*. Beverly Hills: Sage, 1981.

―――. *World-System Analysis. Theory and Methodology*. Beverly Hills: Sage Publications, 1982.

Horne, Gerald. *Cold War in a Hot Zone: The United States Confronts Labor and Independence Struggles in the British West Indies*. Philadelphia, PA: Temple University Press, 2007.

Horowitz, David. *Corporations and the Cold War*. New York: Monthly Review Press, 1969.

Hufbauer, Gary Clyde, and Jeffrey J. Schott. *NAFTA. An Assessment*. Washington, D.C.: Institute for International Economics, 1993.

―――. *NAFTA Revisited: Achievements and Challenges*. Washington, D.C.: Institute for International Economics, 2005.

―――. *Western Hemisphere Economic Integration*. Washington, D.C.: Institute for International Economics, 1994.

Huffington, Arianna. *How to Overthrow the Government*. New York: Regan Books, 2000.

Hunt, Michael H. *Ideology and US Foreign Policy*. New Haven: Yale University Press, 1987.

Hunter, Robert E. *Presidential Control of Foreign Policy. Management or Mishap? Center for Strategic and International Studies, Washington Papers No. 91*. New York: Praeger, 1982.

Huzar, Elias. *The Purse and the Sword*. Ithaca: Cornell University Press, 1950.

Hyland, William G. *Clinton's World: Remaking American Foreign Policy*. Westport, CT: Praeger Publishers, 1999.

―――. *The Cold War is Over*. New York: Random House Inc., 1990.

Ingebritsen, Christine, Iver Neuman, Sieglinde Gstohl, and Jessica Beyer (eds.). *Small States in International Relations*. Seattle: University of Washington Press/Reykjavik: University of Iceland Press, 2006.

Ikenberry, G. John, David A. Lake, and Michael Mastanduno (eds.). *The State and American Foreign Economic Policy*. New York: Cornell University Press, 1988.

Ince, Basil (ed.). *Contemporary International Relations in the Caribbean*. St. Augustine: Institute of International Relations, University of the West Indies, 1979.

Ince, Basil, Anthony Bryan, Herb Addo, and Ramesh Ramsaran (eds.). *Issues in Caribbean International Relations*. Lanham: University Press of America, 1983.

Inkeles, Alex. *National Character. A Psycho-Social Perspective*. New Brunswick: Transaction Publishers, 1997.

Irwin, Douglas A. *Free Trade Under Fire*. Princeton: Princeton University Press, 2002.

Isbister, John. *The Immigration Debate. Remaking America*. West Hartford: Kumarian Press, 1996.

Jacobs, W. Richard, and Ian Jacobs. *Grenada. The Route to Revolution*. Habano: Casa de las Americas, 1980.

Jagan, Cheddi. *The West on Trial. The Fight for Guyana's Freedom*. Berlin: Seven Seas Publishers, rev. ed., 1972.

Jainarain, Iserdeo. *Trade and Development. A Study of the Small Caribbean Countries and Large Multinational Corporations*. Georgetown: University of Guyana, 1976.

Jalee, Pierre. *The Pillage of the Third World*. New York: Monthly Review Press, 1967.

James, C. L. R. *Beyond a Boundary*. London: Hutchinson & Co., 1963.

―――. *The Black Jacobins. Toussaint L'Ouverture and the San Domingo Revolution*. New York: Random House, 1963.

James, Winston. *Holding Aloft the Banner of Ethiopia. Caribbean Radicalism in Early Twentieth-Century America*. London: Verso Press, 1998.

Janda, Kenneth, Jeffrey M. Berry, and Jerry Goldman. *The Challenge of Democracy. Government in America*. Boston: Houghton, Mifflin, 2nd ed., 1989.

Jazbec, Milan. *The Diplomacies of Small States: The Case of Slovenia with Some Comparisons from the Baltics*. London; Ashcraft Publishing, 2001.

Jefferson, Owen. *The Post-War Economic Development of Jamaica*. Mona: Institute of Social and Economic Studies, University of the West Indies, 1972.

Jervis, Robert. *Perception and Misperception in International Politics*. Princeton: Princeton University Press, 1976.

Johnson, Haynes. *Sleepwalking Through History. America in the Reagan Years*. New York: W. W. Norton and Company, 1991.

Johnson, Paul E., Gary J. Miller, John H. Aldich, David W. Rohde, and Charles W. Ostrom. *American Government, People, Institutions and Policies*. Boston: Houghton Mifflin Co., 3rd. ed., 1994.

Jones, Gordon S., and John Marini (eds.). *The Imperial Congress. Crisis in the Separation of Powers*. New York: Pharos Publishers, 1988.

Jones, Ronald E. "Cuba and the English-speaking Caribbean" in Cole Blasier and Carmelo Mesa-Lago (eds.). *Cuba in the World*. Pittsburgh: University of Pittsburgh Press, 1979 pages 131–33.

Jonsson, Asgeir. *Why Iceland? How One of the World's Smallest Countries Became the Meltdown's Biggest Casualty*. New York: McGraw-Hill, 2009.

Josephson, Matthew. *The Robber Barons. The Great American Capitalists, 1861–1901*. New York: Harcourt Brace and Company, 1934.

Judas, John B. *The Paradox of American Democracy. Elites, Special Interests and the Betrayal of Public Trust*. New York: Pantheon Books, 2000.

Kasinitz, Philip. *Caribbean New York. Black Immigrants and the Politics of Race*. Ithaca: Cornell University Press, 1992.

Katzenstein, Peter J. *Small States in World Markets: Industrial Policy in Europe*. Ithaca: Cornell University Press, 1985.

Kaufman, Burton I. *Trade and Aid: Eisenhower's Foreign Economic Policy*. Baltimore: Johns Hopkins University Press, 1982.

Kaufman, Michael. *Jamaica Under Manley. Dilemmas of Socialism and Democracy*. London: Zed Books, 1985.

Kay, Cristobal. *Latin American Theories of Development and Underdevelopment*. London: Routledge, 1989.

Kennan, George F. *American Diplomacy*. Chicago: University of Chicago Press, 1951.

Kennedy, Paul. *The Rise and Fall of the Great Powers*. New York: Vintage Books, 1987.

Keohane, Robert O., and Joseph S. Nye (eds.). *Transnational Relations and World Politics*. Cambridge, Mass.: Harvard University Press, 1972.

Keohane, Robert O., and Joseph S. Nye. *Power and Interdependence. World Politics in Transition*. Boston: Little, Brown, 1977.

Keohane, Robert O. *After Hegemony. Cooperation and Discord in the World Political Economy*. Princeton: Princeton University Press, 1984.

Kerr, Madeline. *Personality and Conflict in Jamaica*. London: Collins, 1963.

Kindleberger, Charles P. *Power and Money*. New York: McMillan, 1970.

———. *The World in Depression, 1929–1939*. Berkeley: University of California Press, 1973.

Kingdom, John W. *Congressman's Voting Decisions*. Ann Arbor: University of Michigan Press, 1989.

Kinzer, Stephen. *Bitter Fruit: The Untold Story of the American Coup in Guatemala*. New York: Doubleday, 1981.

Kirkpatrick, Jeane J. *Dictatorships and Double Standards. Rationalism and Reason in Politics*. New York: Touchstone Books, 1982.

Kissinger, Henry. *Does America Need a Foreign Policy? Toward a Diplomacy for the 21st Century*. New York: Simon & Schuster, 2001.

———. *On China*. New York: Penguin Press, 2011.

———. *The White House Years*. Boston: Little, Brown, 1979.

———. *A World Restored. The Politics of Conservationism in a Revolutionary Age*. New York: Grosset and Dunlap, 1964.

———. *Years of Renewal*. New York: Simon & Schuster, 1978.

———. *Years of Upheaval*. Boston: Little, Brown 1982.

Klingberg, Frank L. *Cyclical Trends in American Foreign Policy Moods: The Unfolding of America's World Role*. Lanham: University Press of America, 1983.

Knight, Franklin W. *The Caribbean, The Genesis of a Fragmented Nationalism*. New York: Oxford University Press, 2nd, ed., 1990.

Knight, Franklin W., and Colin A. Palmer (eds.). *The Modern Caribbean*. Chapel Hill: University of North Carolina, 1989.

Knorr, Klaus. *Power and Wealth*. New York: Basic Books, 1973.

Koning, Hans. *Columbus. His Enterprise*. New York: Monthly Review Press, 1976.

Korten, David C. *When Corporations Rule the World*. West Hartford: Kumarian Press, 1995.

Kotchikan, Asbed. *The Dialectics of Small States: Foreign Policy Making in Armenia and Georgia*. VDM Verlag, 2008.

Kounalakis, Eleni. *Madam Ambassador: Three Years in Budapest*. New York: New Press, 2015.

Krasner, Stephen. *Defending the National Interest. Raw Material Investments and U.S. Foreign Policy*. Princeton: Princeton University Press, 1978.

———. *Structural Conflict. The Third World Against Global Liberalism*. Berkeley: University of California Press, 1985.

Krause, Walter. *Economic Development*. Wadsworth, 1961.

Krueger, Anne O. *Economic Policies at Cross Purposes. The United States and Developing Countries*. Washington, D.C.: The Brookings Institution, 1993.

Kupchan, Charles A. *The End of the American Era. U.S. Policy and the Geopolitics of the Twenty-First Century*. New York: Alfred A. Knopf, 2002.

Kurlansky, Mark. *Cod: A Biography of the Fish That Changed the World*. London: Penguin, 1998.

Lacey, Terry. *Violence and Politics in Jamaica, 1960–1970*. London: Manchester University Press, 1972.

Lafeber, Walter. *The American Age. United States Foreign Policy at Home and Abroad Since 1750*. New York: W. W. Norton and Company, 1989.

Lake, Anthony. *Samoza Falling. The Nicaraguan Dilemma: A Portrait of Washington at Work*. Boston: Houghton Mifflin, 1989.

Lalta, Stanley and Marie Freckleton (eds.). *Caribbean Economic Development. The First Generation*. Kingston: Ian Randle Publishers, 1995.

Landau, David. *Kissinger. The Uses of Power*. Boston: Houghton Mifflin, 1972.

Langley, Lester D. *The United States and the Caribbean in the Twentieth Century*. Athens: University of Georgia Press, 1989.

———. *The United States and the Caribbean 1900–1970*. Athens, GA: University of Georgia Press, 1980.

Larsen, Henrik. *Analysing the Foreign Policy of Small States in the EU: The Case of Denmark*. London: Palgrave Macmillan, 2005.

Lasswell, Harold D. *Politics. Who Gets What, When, How*. New York: McGraw-Hill, 1936.

Lefever, Ernest W. *America's Imperial Burden: Is the Past Prologue?*. Colorado: Westview Press, 1999.

Leibenstein, Harvey. *Economic Backwardness and Economic Growth*. New York: John Wiley, 1957.

Lenin, V. I. *Imperialism. The Highest Stage of Capitalism*. New York: International Publishers, 1939, originally published in 1917.

Leslie, Winsome J. *Zaire. Continuity and Political Change in an Oppressive State*. Boulder: Westview Press, 1993.

Levi, Darrell E. *Michael Manley. The Making of a Leader.* Kingston: Heinemann Publishers Caribbean, 1989.

Levinson, Jerome and J. De Onis. *The Alliance That Lost Its Way.* Chicago: Quadrangle Books, 1970.

Levitt, Kari Polanyi. *The Origins and Consequences of Jamaica's Debt Crisis 1970–1990.* (Mona: Consortium School of Graduate Studies, Social Science, University of the West Indies, 1991).

———. *Reclaiming Development: Independent Thought and Caribbean Community.* Kingston: Ian Randle Publishers, 2005.

Lewis, Arthur. *Labour in the West Indies. The Birth of a Workers Movement.* London: Victor Gollancz, 1939, reprinted London: New Beacon Books, 1977.

Lewis, Bernard. *What Went Wrong? Western Impact and Middle Eastern Response.* Oxford: Oxford University Press, 2002.

Lewis, Charles. *The Buying of the Congress.* New York: Avon Books, 1998.

Lewis, Gordon K. *The Growth of the Modern West Indies.* New York: Monthly Review Press, 1968.

Lewis, John P. and Valeriana Kallab (eds.) *US Foreign Policy and the Third World, Agenda 1983.* New York: Praeger Publishers, 1983.

Lewis, Patsy. *Surviving Small Size. Regional Integration in Caribbean Ministates.* Kingston: Ian Randle Publishers, 2002.

Lewis, Rupert, and Maureen Warner-Lewis (eds.). *Garvey. Africa, Europe, the Americas.* Kingston: Institute of Social and Economic Research, 1986.

Lewis, Rupert, and Patrick Bryan (eds.). *Garvey. His Work and Impact.* Kingston: University of the West Indies, 1988.

Lewis, Vaughan A. (ed.). *Size, Self-determination and International Relations: The Caribbean* (Mona: Institute of Social and Economic Research, University of the West Indies, 1976).

Lieuwen, Edward. *U.S. Policy in Latin America: A Short History.* New York: Praeger, 1965.

Lieuwen, Edwin. *Arms and Politics in Latin America.* New York: Praeger, 1961.

Lindsay, James M. *Congress and the Politics of the US Foreign Policy.* Baltimore: John Hopkins University Press, 1994.

Lipset, Martin Seymour. *American Exceptionalism. A Double-Edged Sword.* New York: W. W. Norton, 1996.

Little, Richard, and Michael Smith (eds.). *Perspectives on World Politics.* London: Routledge, 2nd ed., 1991.

Look Lai, Walton. *Indentured Labor, Caribbean Sugar: Chinese and Indian Migrants to the British West Indies, 1838–1918.* Baltimore: Johns Hopkins University Press, 2004.

Louis, Roger William. *Imperialism at Bay: The United States and the Decolonization of the British Empire 1941–1945.* New York: Oxford University Press, 1978.

Lowenthal, Abraham F. *Partners in Conflict. The United States and Latin America in the 1990s.* Baltimore: Johns Hopkins University Press, 1987.

———. *Partners in Conflict. The United States and Latin America in the 1990s.* Baltimore: Johns Hopkins University Press, rev. ed., 1990.

Lowenthal, Abraham F., and Gregory F. Treverton (eds.). *Latin America in a New World.* Boulder: Westview Press, 1994.

Lowenthal, David. *The West Indies Federation. Perspectives on a New Nation.* New York: Columbia University Press, 1961.

Lowi, Theodore J. *The End of Liberalism. The Second Republic of the United States.* New York: W. W. Norton, 2nd ed., 1979.

———. *The Personal President.* Ithaca: Cornell University Press, 1985.

Lukacs, Georg. *History and Class Consciousness: Studies in Marxist Dialectics.* Cambridge: MIT Press, 1972.

Lundberg, Ferdinand. *The Rich and Super-Rich. A Study in the Power of Money Today.* New York: Bantam Books, 1969.

Lustig, Nora, Barry Bosworth, and Robert Z. Lawrence (eds.). *North American Free Trade. Assessing the Impact*. Washington, D.C.: The Brookings Institution, 1992.

Lutchman, Harold Alexander. *From Colonialism to Co-operative Republic. Aspects of Political Development in Guyana*. Rio Piedras: Institute of Caribbean Studies, 1974.

McArthur, John R. *The Selling of Free Trade, NAFTA, Washington and the Subversion of American Democracy*. New York: Hill and Wang, 2000.

MacDonald, Scott B. and Andrew R. Novo. *When Small Countries Crash*. New Brunswick: Transaction Publishers, 2011.

Mack, Charles S. *Lobbying and Government Relations*. Westport, CT: Quorum Books, 1989.

Magdoff, Harry. *The Age of Imperialism. The Economics of U.S. Foreign Policy*. New York: Monthly Review Press, 1969, pages 45–54.

Mahler, Vincent A. *Dependency Approaches to International Political Economy. A Cross-National Study*. New York: Columbia University Press, 1980.

Maingot, Anthony. *The United States and the Caribbean*. London: Macmillan, 1994.

Mair, Lucille. *Rebel Women*. Kingston: Institute of Jamaica, 1995.

Maizels, Alfred. *Exports and Economic Growth in Developing Countries*. Cambridge: Cambridge University Press, 1968.

Makinson, Larry. *Open Secrets. The Dollar Power of PACs in Congress*. Washington, D.C.: Congressional Quarterly Press, 1990.

Maldonado-Denis, Manuel. *Puerto Rico: A Socio-Historic Interpretation*. New York: Vintage Books, 1972.

Mandel, Ernest. *Late Capitalism*. London: New Left Books, 1975.

Mandelbaum, Michael. *The Frugal Superpower. America's Global Leadership in a Cash-Strapped Era*. New York: Public Affairs, 2010.

Manderson-Jones, R. B. *Jamaican Foreign Policy in the Caribbean, 1962–1988*. Kingston: CARICOM Publishers, 1990.

Manheim, Jarol B. *Strategic Public Diplomacy and American Foreign Policy. The Evolution of Influence*. New York: Oxford University Press, 1994.

Manley Michael. *Global Challenge. From Crisis to Co-operation: Breaking the North-South Stalemate*. London: Pan Books, 1985.

———. *A History of West Indies Cricket*. London: Andre Deutsch, 1988.

———. *Jamaica. Struggle in the Periphery*. London: Third World Media/Writers & Readers Publishing Cooperative Society, 1982.

———. *The Politics of Change*. London: Andre Deutsch, 1974.

———. *The Politics of Change. A Jamaican Testament*. Washington, D.C.: Howard University Press, 1975.

———. *The Poverty of Nations. Reflections on Underdevelopment and the World Economy*. London: Pluto Press, 1991.

———. *Up the Down Escalator. Development and the International Economy. A Jamaican Case Study*. London: Andre Deutsch, 1987.

———. *A Voice at the Workplace*. London: Andre Deutsch, 1975.

Manley, Rachel (ed.). *Edna Manley. The Diaries*. Kingston: Heinemann, 1989.

———. *Slipstream: A Daughter Remembers* (Kingston: Ian Randle Publishers, 2000).

Mann, Thomas (ed.). *The Question of Balance: The President, the Congress, and Foreign Policy*. Washington, D.C.: Brookings, 1990.

Mars, Perry, and Alma H. Young (eds.) *Caribbean Labor and Politics: Legacies of Cheddi Jagan and Michael Manley*. Wayne State University Press, 2004.

Marshall, Don D. *Caribbean Political Economy at the Crossroads, NAFTA and Regional Development*. London: Macmillan, 1998.

Martin, John Bartlow. *US Policy in the Caribbean*. Boulder: Westview Press, 1978.

Martin, Tony. *Race First. The Ideological and Organizational Struggles of Marcus Garvey and the Universal Negro Improvement Association*. Westport: Greenwood Press, 1976.

Martz, John D. (ed.). *United States Policy in Latin America. A Quarter Century of Crisis and Challenge, 1961–1986*. Lincoln: University of Nebraska, 1988.

Marx, Robert F. *Pirate Port. The Story of the Sunken City of Port Royal.* London: Pelham Books, 1968.

Mayhew, David R. *Congress: The Electoral Connection.* New Haven: Yale University Press, 1974.

Macmillan, Margaret. *Nixon and Mao. The Week That Changed the World.* New York: Random House, 2007.

McAfee, Kathy. *Storm Signals, Structural Adjustment and Development Alternatives in the Caribbean.* London: Zed Books, 1991.

McCormick, James M. (ed.). *Essentials of U.S. Foreign Policy Making.* Lanham: Rowman & Littlefield Publishers, 6th ed., 2012.

McDonald, Scott B. *Dancing on a Volcano: The Latin American Drug Trade.* New York: Praeger, 1992.

McDougall, Walter A. *Promised Land, Crusader State. The American Encounter with the World Since 1776.* New York: Houghton Mifflin, 1997.

McGehee, Ralph. *Deadly Deceits. My 25 years with CIA.* New York: Sheridan Square Publications, 1983.

McGibben, Bill. *The End of Nature.* New York: Random House, 1987.

Mead, Walter Russell. *Special Providence. American Foreign Policy and How It Has Changed the World.* New York: Alfred A. Knopf, 2001.

Mearsheimer, John J. and Stephen M. Walt. *The Israel Lobby and U.S. Foreign Policy.* New York: Farrar, Straus and Giroux, 2008.

Mecham, J. L. *The U.S. and Inter-American Security, 1889–1960.* Austin: University of Texas Press, 1961, page 352.

Medvetz, Thomas. *Think Tanks in America.* Chicago: University of Chicago Press, 2012.

Meeks, Brian. *Radical Caribbean. From Black Power to Abu Bakar.* Kingston: University of the West Indies Press, 1996.

Meier, Gerald M. and Robert E. Balwin. *Economic Development, Theory, History and Policy.* New York: John Wiley, 1966.

Melanson, Richard A. *American Foreign Policy since the Vietnam War.* New York: M. E. Sharpe, 2nd ed., 1996.

Melville, Thomas and Marjorie. *Guatemala – Another Vietnam?.* Harmondsworth: Penguin, 1971.

Merk, Frederick. *Manifest Destiny and Mission in American History.* New York: Vintage Books, 1966.

―――. *Manifest Destiny and Mission in American History: A Reinterpretation.* Cambridge, MA: Harvard University Press, 1995.

Meyer, Christopher. *DC Confidential. The Controversial Memoirs of Britain's Ambassador at the Time of 9/11 and the Iraq War.* London: Weidenfeld & Nicolson, 2006.

Mfume, Kweisi, with Ron Stodghill II. *No Free Ride. From the Mean Streets to the Mainstream.* New York: Ballantine Books, 1996.

Mikesell, Raymond F. *The Economics of Foreign Aid.* London: Weidenfeld and Nicolson, 1968.

Millet, Richard, and W. Marvin Will (eds.). *The Restless Caribbean. Changing Patterns of International Relations.* New York: Praeger Publishers, 1979.

Mills, Don. *Journeys and Missions at Home and Abroad.* Kingston: Arawak Publishers, 2009.

―――. *The New Europe, the New Order and the Caribbean.* Kingston: Grace, Kennedy Foundation, 1991.

Mills, C. Wright. *The Power Elite.* New York: Oxford University Press, 1956.

Mintz, Sidney W. *From Plantation to Peasantries in the Caribbean.* Washington, D.C.: Woodrow Wilson International Center for Scholars, 1984.

Mitchell, Christopher (ed.). *Western Hemisphere Immigration and the United States Foreign Policy.* University Park: Pennsylvania State University Press, 1992.

Mitchell, James F. *Guiding Change in the Islands.* Waitsfield, Vermont: Concepts Publishing, 1996.

Molineu, Harold. *US Policy Toward Latin America. From Regionalism to Globalism*. Boulder: Westview Press, 1990.

Monbiot, George. *Captive State. The Corporate Takeover of Britain*. London: Macmillan, 2000.

Moon, P. T. *Imperialism and World Politics*. London: Macmillan, 1926.

Moore, Robert J. *Third World Diplomats in Dialogue with the First World*. London: Macmillan, 1985.

Morgenthau, Hans J. *Politics Among Nations: The Struggle for Power and Peace*. New York: Alfred A. Knopf, originally published in1948, 5th ed., 1978.

Mosk, Sandford A. *Industrial Revolution in Mexico*. Berkeley and Los Angeles: University of California Press, 1950.

Mullerleile, Christoph. *CARICOM Integration. Progress and Hurdles. A European View*. Kingston: Kingston Publishers, 1996.

Munroe, Trevor. *The Cold War and the Jamaican Left 1950–55*. Kingston: Kingston Publishers, 1992.

———. *For a New Beginning. Selected Speeches. 1990–1993*. Kingston: Caricom Publishers, 1994.

———. *The Politics of Constitution Decolonization. Jamaica, 1944–1962*. Mona: Institute of Social and Economic Research, University of the West Indies, 1972.

Myint, H. *The Economic of Developing Countries*. Hutchinson University Press, 1964.

Nacos, Brigitte Lebens. *The Press, President and Crises*. New York: Columbia University Press, 1990.

Nader, Ralph, et al. *The Case Against Free Trade. GATT, NAFTA and the Globalization of Corporate Power*. San Francisco: Earth Island Books, and Berkeley: North Atlantic Books, 1993.

National Association of Manufacturers. *Proceedings of the Twenty-first Annual Convention*. New York: National Association of Manufacturers, 1916.

Nau, Henry R. *The Myth of America's Decline*. Oxford: Oxford University Press, 1990.

Naughtie, James. *The Accidental American: Tony Blair and the Presidency*. New York: Public Affairs, 2004.

Neibuhr, Reinhold. *Moral Man and Immoral Society*. New York: Charles Scribner's Sons, 1932.

Neita, Hartley. *Hugh Shearer. A Voice for the People*. Kingston: Ian Randle Publishers, 2005.

Nettleford, Rex. *Caribbean Cultural Identity. The Case of Jamaica. An Essay in Cultural Dynamics*. Kingston: Institute of Jamaica, 1978.

——— (ed.). *Manley and the New Jamaica. Selected Speeches and Writings 1938–1968*. London: Longmans Caribbean, 1970.

———. *Mirror Mirror. Identity, Race and Protest in Jamaica*. London and Kingston: William Collins & Sangsters Jamaica, 1970.

———. *Political Leadership in the Commonwealth Caribbean. Responsibilities Options and Challenges at End of Century*. Mona: School of Continuing Studies, University of the West Indies, 1994.

Neustadt, Richard E. *Presidential Power and the Modern Presidents*. New York: The Free Press, 1990.

———. *Presidential Power: The Politics of Leadership*. New York: John Wiley, 1960.

Newfarmer, Richard. (ed.). *From Gunboats to Diplomacy. New US Policies for Latin America*. Baltimore: Johns Hopkins University Press, 1984.

Newsom, David D. *Diplomacy and the American Democracy*. Bloomington: Indiana University Press, 1988.

Nicholls, David. *From Dessalines to Duvalier*. Cambridge: Cambridge University Press, 1979.

Niebuhr, Reinhold. *Moral Man and Immoral Society*. New York: Charles Scribner's Sons, 1932.

Nixon, Richard. *The Memoirs of Richard Nixon*. New York: Grosset & Dunlop, 1978.

————. *Seize the Moment. America's Challenge in a One-Superpower World*. New York: Simon and Schuster, 1992.

Nordlinger, Eric A. *Isolationism Reconfigured. American Foreign Policy for a New Century*. Princeton: Princeton University Press, 1995.

Nurkse, Ragnar. *Problem of Capital Formation in Underdeveloped Countries and Pattern of Trade and Development*. Oxford of Ghana, 1969.

Nye, Joseph S. *Bound to Lead*. New York: Basic Books, 1990.

————. *The Future of Power*. New York: Public Affairs, 2011.

————. *The Paradox of American Power. Why the World's Only Superpower Can't Go It Alone*. Oxford: Oxford University Press, 2002.

O'Heffernan, Patrick. *Mass Media and American Foreign Policy: Insider Perspectives on Global Journalism and the Foreign Policy Process*. Norwood, NJ: Ablex Publishing Co., 1991.

O'Shaughnessy, Hugh. *Grenada. Revolution, Invasion and Aftermath*. London: Sphere Books, 1984.

Olson, Moncur. *The Logic of Collective Action*. Cambridge: Harvard University Press, 1965.

Ortiz, Frank V. *Ambassador Ortiz: Lessons from a Life of Service*. Albuquerque: University of New Mexico Press, 2005.

Ostry, Sylvia. *Governments and Corporations in a Shrinking World*. New York: Council on Foreign Relations Press, 1990.

Owen, Roger, and Bob Sutcliffe (eds.). *Studies in the Theory of Imperialism*. London: Longman Group, 1972.

Owens, Joseph. *Dread. The Rastafarians of Jamaica*. Kingston: Sangsters Bookstores, 1976.

Palmer, Colin A. *Eric Williams & the Making of the Modern Caribbean*. Kingston; Ian Randle Publishers, 2006.

————. *Freedom's Children. The 1938 Labor Rebellion and the Birth of Modern Jamaica*. Chapel Hill: University of North Carolina Press, 2014.

Panton, David. *Jamaica's Michael Manley: The Great Transformation 1972–92*. Kingston: Kingston Publishers, 1993.

Parenti, Michael. *Against Empire*. San Francisco: City Lights Books, 1995.

————. *Democracy for the Few*. New York: Saint Martin's Press, 5th ed., 1988.

Parry, J. H. *The Spanish Seaborne Empire*. London: Hutchinson & Co., 1966.

Parascandola, Louis J. (ed.) *"Look for Me All Around You": Anglophone Caribbean Immigrants in the Harlem Renaissance*. Cleveland: Wayne State University Press, 2005.

Pastor, Robert A. *Congress and the Politics of U.S. Foreign Economic Policy 1929–1976*. Berkeley: University of California Press, 1980.

————. *Exiting the Whirlpool. U.S. Foreign Policy Towards Latin America and the Caribbean*. Boulder: Westview Press, 2001.

————. *Whirlpool. U.S. Foreign Policy Towards Latin America and the Caribbean*. Princeton University Press, 1992.

Pastor, Robert A. and Rafael Fernandez de Castro (eds.) *The Controversial Pivot. The US Congress and North America*. Washington, D.C.: The Brookings Institution, 1998.

Patterson, Orlando. *Slavery and Social Death. A Comparative Study*. Cambridge, Mass.: Harvard University Press, 1982.

————. *The Sociology of Slavery. An Analysis of the Origins, Development and Structure of Negro Slave Society in Jamaica*. London: Granada Publishing, 1967.

Payne, Anthony J. *The Political History of CARICOM*. Kingston: Ian Randle Publishers, 2008.

————. *Politics in Jamaica*. Kingston: Ian Randle Publishers, rev. ed., 1994.

Payne, Anthony J., and Paul Sutton. *Charting Caribbean Development*. London: Macmillan, 2001.

Payne, Anthony J., Paul Sutton, and Tony Thorndike. *Grenada: Revolution and Invasion*. New York: St. Martin's Press, 1984.

Payne, Douglas W., Mark Falcoff, and Susan Kaufman Purcell. *Latin America: US Policy After the Cold War*. New York: America's Society, 1991.

Payne, Richard J. *The Clash with Distant Cultures. Values, Interests, and Force in American Foreign Policy*. Albany: State University of New York Press, 1995.

Paxman, Jeremy. *The English. A Portrait of a People*. London: Michael Joseph, 1998.

Peachman, Joseph A. (ed.). *Setting National Priorities, Agenda for the 1980s*. Washington, D.C.: The Brookings Institution, 1980.

Pearce, Jenny. *Under the Eagle: U.S. Intervention in Central America and the Caribbean*. London: Latin American Bureau, 1982.

Peckenham, Robert A. *Liberal America and the Third World. Political Development Ideas in Foreign Aid and Social Science*. Princeton: Princeton University Press, 1973.

Pendle, George. *A History of Latin America*. Harmondsworth: Penguin, 1971.

Perkins, Anna Kasafi. *Justice as Equality. Michael Manley's Caribbean Vision of Justice*. New York: Peter Lang Publishing, 2010.

Perkins, Whitney. *Constraint of Empire. The United States and Caribbean Interventions*. Westport: Greenwood Press, 1981.

Perlo, Victor. *The Empire of High Finance*. New York: International Publishers, 1957.

Perot, Ross, and Pat Choate. *Save Your Job, Save Your Country: Why NAFTA Must be Stopped-Now*. New York: Hyperion, 1993.

Persaud, Randolph B. *Counter-Hegemony and Foreign Policy. The Dialectics of Marginalized and Global Forces in Jamaica*. Albany: State University of New York Press, 2001.

Peterson, Paul E. (ed.) *The President, Congress and the Making of Foreign Policy*. Oklahoma University Press, 1994.

Peterson, Peter G. *Gray Dawn. How the Coming Age Wave Will Transform America and the World*. New York: Random House, 1999.

Petras, James, and Morris Morley. *The United States and Chile: Imperialism and the Overthrow of the Allende Government*. New York: Monthly Review Press, 1975.

Philips, Fred. *Caribbean Life and Culture. A Citizen Reflects*. Kingston: Heinemann, 1991.

Phillips, Kevin. *Arrogant Capital. Washington, Wall Street and the Frustration of American Politics*. New York: Little, Brown and Company, 1995.

Pifer, Drury. *Hanging the Moon. The Rollins Rise to Riches*. Newark: University of Delaware Press, 2001.

Plischke, Elmer. *Microstates in World Affairs. Policy Problems and Options*. Washington, D.C.: American Enterprise Institute for Public Policy Research, 1977.

Poole, Bernard L. *The Caribbean Commission: Background of Cooperation in the West Indies*. Columbia: University of South Carolina Press, 1951.

Post, Ken. *Arise Ye Starvelings. The Jamaican Labour Rebellion of 1938 and Its Aftermath*. The Hague: Martinus Nijhoff, 1978.

———. *Strike the Iron. A Colony at War: Jamaica 1939–1945*. Atlantic Highlands, N. J.: Humanities Press, 1981.

Poulantzas, Nicos. *Classes in Contemporary Capitalism*. London: New Left Books, 1975.

———. *Political Power and Social Classes*. London: Verso, 1978.

Powell, Colin L. with Joseph E. Persico, *My American Journey*. New York: Random House, 1996.

Prashad, Vijay. *The Darker Nations: A People's History of the Third World* (New York: New Press, 2008).

Pratt, Julius W. *A History of U.S. Foreign Policy*. Englewood Cliffs, NJ: Prentice-Hall, rev. ed., 1965.

Preeg, Ernest. *The Haitian Dilemma. A Case Study in Demographics, Development and US Foreign Policy*. Washington, D.C.: Center for Strategic and International Studies, 1996.

Prestowitz Jr., Clyde V. *Trading Places. How We Allowed Japan to Take the Lead*. New York: Basic Books, 1988.

Price, Richard (ed.). *Maroon Societies. Rebel Slave Communities in the Americas*. Baltimore: Johns Hopkins University Press, 1979.

Rabe, Stephen G. *Eisenhower and Latin America. The Foreign Policy of Anticommunism.* Chapel Hill: University of North Carolina Press, 1988.

————. *The Most Dangerous Area in the World: John F. Kennedy Confronts Communist Revolution in Latin America.* London: The University of North Carolina Press, 1999.

Rabie, Mohammed. *The Politics of Foreign Aid: US Foreign Assistance and Aid to Israel.* New York: Praeger, 1988.

Ragatz, L. F. *The Fall of the Planter Class in the British Caribbean, 1763- 1833. A Study in Social and Economic History.* New York: American Historical Association, 1928.

Ramirez-Faria, C. *The Origins of Inequality between Nations.* London: Unwin Hyman, 1991.

Ramsaran, Ramesh F. *U.S. Investment in Latin America and the Caribbean.* London: Hodder and Sroughton, 1985.

Rauch, Jonathan. *Demosclerosis. The Silent Killer of American Government.* New York: Times Books, 1994.

Raven-Hansen, Peter. *National Security Law and the Power of the Purse.* New York: Oxford University Press, 1994.

Reagan, Ronald. *The Reagan Diaries, edited by Douglas Brinkley.* New York: Harper Perennial, 2007.

Reich, Bernard. *The United States and Israel: Influence in the Special Relationship.* New York: Praeger Publishers, 1994.

Reid, George L. *The Impact of Very Small Size on the International Behavior of Microstates.* Beverly Hills: Sage Publications, 1974.

Reid, Victor Stafford. *The Horses of the Morning. About The Rt. Excellent N. W. Manley, Q. C., M. M. National Hero of Jamaica. An Understanding.* Kingston: Caribbean Authors Publishing, 1985.

Reston, James. *The Artillery of the Press: Its Influence on American Foreign Policy.* New York: Harper and Row, 1966.

Reviere, Bill. *State Systems in the Caribbean.* Mona: Institute of Social and Economic Studies, University of the West Indies.

Rhodes, William. *Banker to the World: Leadership Lessons From the Front Lines of Global Finance.* New York: McGraw-Hill, 2011.

Ricci, David. *The Transformation of American Politics. The New Washington and the Rise of Think Tanks.* New Haven: York University Press, 1993.

Rippy, J. Fred. *The Caribbean Danger Zone.* New York: G. P. Putnam's Sons, 1940.

Robinson, Carey. *The Fighting Maroons of Jamaica.* Kingston: Collins & Sangsters Jamaica, 1969.

————. *The Iron Torn: The Defeat of the British by the Jamaican Maroons.* Kingston: LMH Publishing Company, 2007.

Robinson, Jane. *Mary Seacole: The Most Famous Black Woman of the Victorian Age.* New York: Basic Books, 2004.

Robinson, Patrick. *Jamaican Athletics: A Model for 2012 and the World.* Arcadia Books, 2009.

Robinson, Randall. *Defending the Spirit. A Black Life in America.* New York: Dutton, 1998.

Rock, David (ed.) *Latin America in the 1940s. War and Postwar Transitions.* Berkeley: University of California, 1994, pages 5–40.

Rockefeller, Nelson. *The Rockefeller Report on the Americas: The Official Report of a United States Presidential Mission for the Western Hemisphere.* Chicago: Quadrangle Books, 1969.

Rogowsky, Robert A., Linda A. Linkins, and Karl S. Tsuji. *Trade Liberalization. Fears and Facts, Center for Strategic and International Studies, Washington Papers, No. 179.* Westport: Praeger, 1997.

Rose, Euclid A. *Dependency and Socialism in the Modern Caribbean: Superpower Intervention in Guyana, Jamaica, and Grenada, 1970–1985.* Lanham: Lexington Books, 2002.

Rosner, Jeremy D. *The New Tug-of-War. Congress, the Executive Branch and National Security.* Washington, D.C.: Carnegie Endowment for International Peace, 1995.

Rostow, W. W. *The Stages of Economic Growth: A Non-Communist Manifesto.* Cambridge: Cambridge University Press, 1965.

Rostow, W. W., and Harvey Leibenstein. *Economic Backwardness and Economic Growth.* New York: John Wiley, 1957.

Rostow, W. W., and Max Millikan. *A Proposal: Key to an Effective Foreign Policy.* New York: Greenwood Press, 1967.

Rothstein, Robert L. *Alliances and Small Powers.* New York: Columbia University Press, 1968.

————. *The Weak in the World of the Strong. The Third World in the International System.* New York: Columbia University Press, 1980.

Rourke, Francis. *Bureaucracy and Foreign Policy.* Baltimore: Johns Hopkins University Press, 1972.

Rouse, Irving. *The Tainos. The Rise and Decline of the People Who Greeted Columbus.* New Haven: Yale University Press, 1992.

Rousseau, Patrick H. O. *Negotiating Change. Pat Rousseau and the Bauxite Negotiations 1974- 1977.* Kingston: Heinemann Educational Books Caribbean Ltd., 1987.

Rubinstein, Alvin Z. (ed.). *Anti-Americanism in the Third World: Implications for U.S. Foreign Policy.* New York: Praeger, 1985.

Rusk, Dean. *As I Saw It.* Harmondsworth: Penguin, 1991.

Ruttan, Vernon W. *United States Development Assistance Policy. The Domestic Politics of Foreign Economic Aid.* Baltimore: Johns Hopkins University Press, 1996.

Ryan, Selwyn D. *Race and Nationalism in Trinidad & Tobago.* Mona, Jamaica: Institute of Social and Economic Research, University of the West Indies, 1972.

Sabato, Larry J. *PAC Power: Inside the World of Political Action Committees.* New York: W. W. Norton, 1985.

Sabic, Zlatko and Charles Bukowski. *Small States in the Post-Cold War World: Slovenia and NATO Enlargement.* New York: Praeger Publishers, 2002.

Sale, Kirkpatrick. *The Conquest of Paradise.* New York: Alfred A. Knopf, 1990.

Sampson, Anthony. *The Sovereign State of ITT.* New York: Stein and Day, 1973.

Sanders, Sir Ronald. *Crumbled Small. The Commonwealth Caribbean in World Politics.* London: Hansib, 2005.

Sanitarian, Sedro. *Trade and Development. A Study of the Small Caribbean Countries and Large Multinational Corporations.* Georgetown: University of Guyana, 1976.

Schattschneider, E. E. *The Semi-sovereign People: A Realist's View of Democracy in America.* New York: Rinehart & Winston, 1960.

Scheman, Ronald L. (ed.). *The Alliance for Progress. A Retrospective.* New York: Praeger, 1988.

Schott, Jeffrey. *The Uruguay Round. An Assessment.* Washington, D.C.: Institute for International Economics, 1994.

Schlesinger, Arthur M. Jr. *The Cycles of American History.* Boston: Houghton Mifflin Company, 1986.

————. *The Imperial Presidency.* New York: Houghton Miflin, 1973.

————. *A Thousand Days: John F. Kennedy in the White House.* Boston: Houghton Mifflin, 1965.

Schlesinger, Stephen, and Stephen Kinzer. *Bitter Fruit: The Untold Story of the American Coup in Guatemala.* New York: Doubleday, 1981.

Schultz, George P. *Turmoil and Triumph. Diplomacy, Power, and the Victory of the American Ideal.* New York: Charles Scribner & Sons, 1993.

Schulzinger, Robert D. *The Wise Men of Foreign Affairs. The History of the Council of Foreign Relations.* Oxford: Oxford University Press, 1984.

Seacole, Mary. *Wonderful Adventures of Mrs Seacole in Many Lands.* London: Penguin, 2005.

Searle, Chris. *Grenada. The Struggle Against Destabilization.* London: Writers and Readers Publishing Cooperative, 1983.

Serfaty, Simon (ed.). *The Media and Foreign Policy*. New York: St. Martin's Press, 1990.

Shabecoff, Philip. *A Fierce Green Fire. The American Environmental Movement*. New York: Hill and Wang, 1993.

Shain, Yossi. *Marketing the American Creed Abroad: Diasporas in the U.S. and Their Homelands*. New York: Cambridge University Press, 1999.

Shaw, John. *The Ambassador: Inside the Life of a Working Diplomat*. Capital Books, 2006

Shepherd, Verene. *Transients to Settlers: East Indians in Jamaica in the Late 19th and Early 20th Century*. London: Peepal Tree Press, 1991.

Sherlock, Phillip and Hazel Bennett. *The Story of the Jamaican People*. Kingston: Ian Randle, 1998.

Shoch, James. *Trading Blows. Party Competition and U.S. Trade Policy in a Globalizing Era*. Chapel Hill: University of North Carolina Press, 2001.

Shoup, Laurence H. and William Minter. *Imperial Brain Trust*. New York: Monthly Review Press, 1977.

Slotkin, Richard. *Gunfighter Nation. The Myth of the Frontier in the Twentieth Century America*. New York: Atheneum, 1992.

Smith, Gaddis. *The Last Years of the Monroe Doctrine. 1945–1993*. New York: Hill and Wang, 1994, page 97.

———. *Morality, Reason and Power. American Diplomacy in the Carter Years*. New York: Hill and Wang, 1986.

Smith, Hendrick. *The Power Game. How Washington Works*. New York: Ballantine Books, 1989.

Smith, James A. *The Idea Brokers. Think Tanks and the Rise of the New Policy Elite*. New York: Free Press, 1991.

Smith, M. G. *Plural Society in the West Indies*. Berkeley: University of California Press, 1965.

Smith, Mark A. *American Business and Political Power. Public Opinion, Elections and Democracy*. Chicago: University of Chicago, 2000.

Smith, Robert F. *The United States and Cuba: Business and Diplomacy, 1917–1960*. New Haven: College and University Press, 1960.

Smith, Stanley A. De. *Microstates and Micronesia: Problems of America's Pacific Islands and Other Minute Territories*. New York: New York University Press, 1970.

Smith, Steven S. *Committees in Congress*. Washington, D.C.: Congressional Quarterly Press, 1990.

Smith, Tony. *America's Mission. The United States and the Worldwide Struggle for Democracy in the Twentieth Century*. Princeton: Princeton University Press, 1994.

———. *Foreign Attachments. The Power of Ethnic Groups in the Making of American Foreign Policy*. Cambridge: Harvard University Press, 2000.

Smyrl, Marc E. *Conflict or Codetermination? Congress, the President, and the Power to Make War*. Cambridge, Mass.: Ballinger, 1988.

Snyder, Richard C., H. W. Bruck, and Burton Sapin. *Foreign Policy Decision Making. An Approach to the Study of International Politics*. New York: Free Press, 1962.

Sobel, Richard. *The Impact of Public Opinion on Foreign Policy Since Vietnam*. New York: Oxford University Press, 2001.

——— (ed.). *Public Opinion in U.S. Foreign Policy. The Controversy over Contra Aid*. Lanham, Maryland: Rowman & Littlefield, 1993.

Solnick, Bruce. *The West Indies and Central America to 1898*. New York: Alfred A. Knopf, 1970.

Sorenson, Theodore. *Kennedy*. New York: Harper & Row, 1965.

Spiegel, Steven L. *Dominance and Diversity. The International Hierarchy*. Boston: Little Brown, 1972.

Springer, Hugh W. *Reflections on the Failure of the West Indies Federation*. Cambridge, Mass.: Center for International Affairs, Harvard University Press, July, 1962.

Starr, Martin K. *Global Corporate Alliances and the Competitive Edge*. New York: Quarium Books, 1991.

Steel, Ronald. *Temptations of a Superpower. America's Foreign Policy After the Cold War.* Cambridge: Howard University Press, 1995.

Steil, Benn. *The Battle of Bretton Woods. John Maynard Keynes, Harry Dexter White and the Making of the New World Order.* Princeton: Princeton University Press, 2013.

Stephanson, Anders. *Manifest Destiny. American Expansionism and the Empire of Right.* New York: Hill and Wang, 1995.

Stephens, Evelyne Huber, and John D. Stephens. *Democratic Socialism in Jamaica. The Political Movement and Social Transformation in Dependent Capitalism.* Princeton: Princeton University Press, 1986.

Stern, Gary M., and Morton H. Halperin (eds.). *The U.S. Constitution and the Power to Go to War.* Westport: Greenwood Press, 1993.

Stern, Philip M. *The Best Congress Money Can Buy.* New York: Pantheon Books, 1988.

Stone, Carl. *Class, Race and Political Behavior in Urban Jamaica.* Mona: Institute of Social and Economic Research, University of the West Indies, 1973.

———. *The Political Opinions of the Jamaican People 1976–1981.* Kingston: Blackett Publishers, 1982.

Strobel, Warren P. *Late-Breaking Foreign Policy. The News Media's Influence on Peace Operations.* Washington, D.C.: United States Institute of Peace Press, 1997.

Subversion in Chile: A Case Study in US Corporate Intrigue in the Third World. London: Spokesman Books, 1972.

Sussman, Barry. *What Americans Really Think and Why Our Politicians Pay No Attention.* New York: Pantheon, 1988.

Sutton, Paul K. (ed.) *Forged from the Love of Liberty. Speeches of Dr. Eric Williams.* Port of Spain: Longman Caribbean, 1981.

Sweezy, Paul M. *The Theory of Capitalist Development.* New York: Monthly Review Press, 1942.

Sylvan, D. and S. Chan (eds.). *Foreign Policy Decision-making: Perception, Cognitive and Artificial Intelligence.* New York: Praeger Publishers 1984.

Tafari, I. Jabulani. *A Rastafari View of Marcus Mosiah Garvey. Patriarch, Prophet, Philosopher.* Kingston: Great Company Jamaica. Ltd. 1996.

Taylor, Frank Fonda. *To Hell with Paradise. A History of the Jamaican Tourist Industry.* Pittsburgh: University of Pittsburgh Press, 1993.

Teitelbaum, Michael S. *Latin Migration North: The Problem for US Foreign Policy.* New York: Council on Foreign Relations, 1985.

The Economic Development of Latin America and its Principal Problems. Santiago: United Nations Economic Commission for Latin America, 1950.

Thomas, Clive Y. *Dependence and Transformation. The Economics of the Transition to Socialism.* New York: Monthly Review Press, 1974.

———. *The Poor and the Powerless. Economic Policy and Change in the Caribbean.* London: Latin American Bureau, 1988.

Thompson, Dudley. *From Kingston to Kenya. The Making of a Pan-African Lawyer.* Dover: The Majority Press, 1993.

Thurow, Lester. *Head to Head. The Coming Economic Battle Among Japan, Europe and America.* New York: William Morrow & Co., 1992.

Time For Action. *The Report of The West Indian Commission.* Black Rock, Barbados: The West Indian Commission, 1992.

Tivnan, Edward. *The Lobby. Jewish Political Power and US Foreign Policy.* New York: Simon and Schuster, 1987.

Truman, David. *The Governmental Process. Political Interests and Public Opinion.* New York: Knopf, 1951.

Tucker, Robert W. *The Radical Left and American Policy.* Baltimore: Johns Hopkins Press, 1971.

Tucker, Robert W. and David C. Hendrickson. *The Imperial Temptation. The New World Order and American Purpose.* New York: Council on Foreign Relations Press, 1992.

Tulchin, Joseph S. *Aftermath of War. World War I and US Policy Toward Latin America.* New York: New York University, 1971, pages 118–54.

Turner, Joyce Moore. *Caribbean Crusaders and the Harlem Renaissance*. Chicago: University of Illinois Press, 2005.

Turner, Mary. *Slaves and Missionaries. The Disintegration of Jamaican Slave Society, 1787–1834*. Urbana: University of Illinois Press, 1982.

Tyson, Laura D'Andrea. *Who's Bashing Whom? Trade Conflict in High Technology Industries*. Washington, D.C.: Institute for International Economics, 1992.

Van Alstyne, Richard W. *The Rising American Empire*. Chicago: Quadrangle Books, 1965.

Vance, Cyrus. *Hard Choices, Critical Years in America's Foreign Policy*. New York: Simon & Schuster, 1983.

Vega, Bernardo. *Diario de una Mision en Washington*. Santo Domingo: Fundacion Cultural Dominicana, 2002.

Vincent, Theodore G. *Black Power and the Garvey Movement*. New York: Ramparts Press, 1970.

Viner, Jacob. *International Trade and Economic Development*. Oxford: Oxford University Press, 1953.

Vital, David. *The Inequality of States. A Study of the Small Powers in International Relations*. Oxford: Clarendon Press, 1967.

———. *Fluctuating Fortunes. The Political Power of Business in America*. New York: Basic Books, 1989.

Von Bertrab, Hermann. *Negotiating NAFTA. A Mexican Envoy's Account*. New York: Praeger Publishers, 1997.

Wagner, R. Harrison. *United States Policy Toward Latin America. A Study in Domestic and International Politics*. Stanford: Stanford University Press, 1970.

Wallerstein, Immanuel. *The Modern World System I. Agriculture and the Origins of the European World-Economy in the Sixteenth Century*. New York: Academic Press, 1974.

———. *The Modern World System II. Mercantilism and the Consolidation of the European World Economy, 1600–1750*. New York: Academic Press, 1980.

Waltz, Kenneth. *Man, the State and War*. New York: Columbia University Press, 1959.

———. *Theory of International Politics*. New York: Random House, 1979.

Warren, Bill. *Imperialism. Pioneer of Capitalism*. London: Verso, 1981.

Weinberg, Albert K. *Manifest Destiny: A Study of Nationalist Expansionism in American History*. Gloucester, Mass.: 1958.

White, Timothy. *Catch a Fire. The Life of Bob Marley*. Holt, Reinert and Winston, 1983.

Wiarda, Howard J. *American Foreign Policy: Actors and Processes*. New York: HarperCollins College Publishers, 1996.

Wilkinson, Alec. *Big Sugar. Seasons in the Cane Fields of Florida*. New York: Alfred A. Knopf, 1989.

Williams, Eric. *Capitalism and Slavery*. London: Andre Deutsch, 1964.

———. *From Columbus to Castro. The History of the Caribbean 1492–1968*. London: Andre Deutsch, 1970.

Williams, Gwyneth. *Third World Political Organizations*. London: Macmillan, 1981.

Williams, William Appleman. *The Tragedy of American Diplomacy*. New York: W. W. Norton, rev. ed., 1972.

Wills, Garry, *John Wayne's America. The Politics of Celebrity*. New York: Simon & Shuster, 1997.

Wilson, Joan Hoff. *American Business and Foreign Policy 1920–1933*. Boston: Beacon Press, 1964.

Winner, David. *Brilliant Orange. The Neurotic Genius of Dutch Football*. London: Bloomsbury,2000.

Winslow, E. M. *The Pattern of Imperialism*. New York: Columbia University Press, 1948.

Wise, David, and Thomas B. Ross. *The Invisible Government*. New York: Random House, 1964.

Wittkopf, Eugene R. *Faces of Internationalism: Public Opinion and American Foreign Policy*. Durham: Duke University Press, 1990.

Wolfers, Arnold. *Discord and Collaboration*. Baltimore: Johns Hopkins University Press, 1962.

Wolpe, Bruce C. *Lobbying Congress. How the System Works*. Washington, D.C.: Congressional Quarterly Press, 2nd ed., 1996.

Wolpe, Bruce C., and Bertram J. Levine. *Lobbying Congress. How the System Works*. Washington, D.C.: Congressional Quarterly, 2nd ed., 1996.

Wood, Bryce. *The Making of the Good Neighbor Policy*. New York: W. W. Norton and Co., 1967.

Woods, Patricia D. *The Dynamics of Congress. The Guide to the People and the Process of Law-making*. Washington, D.C.: Woods Institute, 1999.

Woodward, Bob. *Inside the Clinton White House*. New York: Simon & Schuster, 1994.

———. *The Maestro: Greenspan's Fed and the American Boom*. New York: Simon & Schuster, 2000.

———. *Veil. The Secret Wars of the CIA, 1981–1987*. New York: Simon and Schuster, 1987.

Woods, Patricia D. *The Dynamics of Congress. The Guide to the People and the Process of Lawmaking*. Washington, D.C.: The Woods Institute, 1999.

Woolf, Leonard. *Economic Imperialism*. London: Swarthmore Press, 1920.

Wright, Ashton G. *No Trophies Raise*. Kingston: Ashton G. Wright.

Wright, Robin, and Doyle McManus, *Flashpoints. Promise and Peril in a New World*. New York: Alfred A. Knopf, 1991.

Yankelovich, Daniel, and I. M. Destler (eds.). *Beyond the Beltway. Engaging the Public in U.S. Foreign Policy*. New York: W. W. Norton, 1994.

ARTICLES IN JOURNALS

Abrams, Elliot. "The Shiprider Solution Policing the Caribbean," *The National Interest*, No. 43 (Spring, 1996) pages 86–92.

Ahiram, E. "Income Distribution in Jamaica, 1958," *Social and Economic Studies*, UWI, Vol. 13, No. 3 (September 1964), pages 36–69.

Ambrose, Stephen E. "The Presidency and Foreign Policy," *Foreign Affairs*, Vol. 70, No. 5 (Winter, 1991/92) pages 120–37.

Amin, Samir. "Accumulation and Development: A Theoretical Model," *Review of African Political Economy*, No. 1 (August–November, 1974) pages 9–26.

Arthur, Owen S. "The Promise and the Peril: A Caribbean Perspective on the FTAA," *Social and Economic Studies*, Vol. 51, No. 3 (September, 2002) pages 183–94.

Baldacchino, Godfrey. "Bursting the Bubble: The Pseudo-Development Strategies of Microstates," *Development and Change*, Vol. 24 (1993) pages 29–51.

Baptiste, Fitzroy. "The Federal Process in the West Indies as Seen by the United States, 1947–1962," *Social and Economic Studies*, Vol. 48, No. 4 (December, 1999) pages 185–210.

Bell, Philip W. "Colonialism as a Problem in American Foreign Policy," *World Politics*, Vol. 5, No. 1 (1952) pages 86–109.

Bell, Wendell, and J. William Gibson Jr. "Independent Jamaican Faces the Outside World," *International Studies Quarterly*, Vol. 22, No. 1 (March, 1978) pages 5–48.

Berger, Samuel R. "A Foreign Policy for the Global Age," *Foreign Affairs*, Vol. 79, No. 6 (November-December, 2000) pages 22–39.

Bernal, Richard L. "Caribbean Debt Relief," *Caribbean Affairs*, Vol. 4, No. 2 (June 1991) pages 45–58.

———. "China and Small Island Developing States," *Africa-East Asian Affairs, The China Monitor*, Issue 1 (August, 2012) pages 3–30.

———. "Debt, Drugs and Development in the Caribbean," *Transafrica Forum*, Vol. 9, No. 2 (Summer, 1992) pages 83–92.

———. "Emmanuel's Unequal Exchange as a Theory of Underdevelopment," *Social and Economic Studies*, Vol. 29, No. 4 (December, 1980) pages 152–74.

———. "Foreign Investment and Development in Jamaica," *Inter-American Economic Affairs*, Vol. 38, No. 2 (Autumn, 1984) pages 3–21.

———. "From NAFTA to Hemispheric Free Trade," *Columbia Journal of World Business*, Vol. 29, No. 3 (Fall, 1994) pages 22–31.

———. "The Great Depression, Colonial Policy and Industrialization in Jamaica," *Social and Economic Studies*, Vol. 37, Nos. 1 & 2 (March-June, 1988) pages 33–64.

———. "The Integration of Small Economies into the Free Trade Area of the Americas," *Policy Papers on the Americas*, Vol. IX, No. 1 (Washington, D.C.: Center for Strategic and International Studies, February, 1998) pages 23–24.

———. "IMF and Class Struggle in Jamaica, 1977–1980," *Latin American Perspectives*, Vol. 11, No. 3 (Summer, 1984) pages 53–82.

———. "Resolving the Global Debt Crisis," *Economia Internazionale*, Vol. XL, Nos. 2–3, (Maggio-Agosto, 1987) pages 1–19.

———. "Restructuring Jamaica's Economic Relations with Socialist Countries, 1974–1980," *Development and Change*, Vol. 17, No. 4 (October, 1986) pages 607–34.

———. "The Significance of Garvey," *New World Quarterly*, Vol. 5, No. 4 (1972) pages 69–72.

———. "Transnational Banks, the International Monetary Fund, and External Debt of Developing Countries," *Social and Economic Studies*, Vol. 31, No. 4 (December, 1982) pages 71–101.

———. "The Unimportance of the English Speaking Caribbean in US Foreign Policy as told by Presidents and Secretaries of State," *Caribbean Journal of International Relations & Diplomacy*, Vol. 1, No. 1 (February, 2013) pages 132–50.

Bernal, Richard L., and Vilma McNeish, "The Caribbean in the OAS." *Jamaica Journal*, Vol. 26, No. 3 (December, 1998) pages 33–36.

Best, Lloyd. "A Model of Pure Plantation Economy," *Social and Economic Studies*, Vol. 17, No. 3 (September, 1969) pages 283–326.

Bishop, Matthew Louis. "The Political Economy of Small States: The Enduring Vulnerability?," *Review of International Political Economy*, Vol. 19, No. 5 (December, 2012) pages 942–60.

Bores, John. "Money Business and the State: Material Interests, Fortune 500 Corporations and the Size of the Political Action Committee," *American Sociological Review*, Vol. 54, No. (October, 1989) pages 821–33.

Braithwaite, Lloyd. "Progress Toward Federation, 1938–1956," *Social and Economic Studies*, Vol. 6, No. 2 (June 1957) pages 133–84.

———. "Social Stratification and Cultural Pluralism," *Annals of the New York Academy of Sciences*, Vol. 83, No. 5 (January, 1960) pages 816–36.

Braveboy–Wagner, Jacqueline Anne. "Caribbean Foreign Policy," *Caribbean Studies*, Vol. 1, No. 3 (Third Quarter, 1988) pages 77–89.

———. "Opportunities and Limitations of the Exercise of Foreign Policy Power by a Very Small State: The Case of Trinidad and Tobago," *Cambridge Review of International Affairs*, Vol. 23, No. 3 (2010) pages 407–27.

Bray, Charles W. "The Media and Foreign Policy," *Foreign Policy*, No. 16 (Fall, 1974) pages 109–25.

Brenner, Robert. "The Origins of Capitalist Development: A Critique of Neo-Smithian Marxism," *New Left Review*, No. 104 (July-August, 1977) pages 25–92.

Brotherson, Festus, Jr. "The Foreign Policy of Guyana, 1970–1985: Forbes Burnham's Search for Legitimacy," *Journal of Interamerican Studies and World Studies*, Vol. 31, No. 3 (Fall, 1989) pages 9–36.

Bryan, Anthony T. "The International Dynamics of the Commonwealth Caribbean: Challenges and Opportunities in the 1990's," *Journal of Interamerican Studies and World Affairs*, Vol. 31, No. 3 (Fall, 1989) pages 1–7.

Brzezinski, Zbigniew, "Selective Global Commitment," *Foreign Affairs*, Vol. 70, No. 4, (Fall 1991) pages 1–20.

Buchanan, Patrick. "America First and Second, and Third," *National Interest*, No. 19 (Spring, 1990) pages 77–82.

Byron, Jessica. "Strategic Repositioning: Foreign Policy Shifts in Barbados and Trinidad and Tobago 1990–2000," *Social and Economic Studies*, Vol. 56, Nos. 1 & 2 (March/June, 2007) pages 209–39.

Cardoso, Fernando Henrique. "Dependency and Development in Latin America," *New Left Review*, No. 74 (July-August, 1972) pages 83–95.

Carrington, Selwyn. "The United States and Canada: The Struggle for the British West Indian Trade," *Social and Economic Studies*, Vol. 37, Nos. 1 & 2 (March-June, 1988) pages 69–106.

Chase-Dunn, Christopher and Richard Rubinson, "Toward a Structural Perspective on the World System," *Politics and Society*, Vol. 7, No. 4 (1977) pages 453–76.

Chenery H. B., and L. Taylor. "Development Patterns: Among Countries Over Time," *Review of Economics and Statistics*, Vol. 50, No. 4 (1968) pages 391–416.

Chenery, Holis, and Alan Strout, "Foreign Assistance and Economic Development," *American Economic Review*, Vol. 56, No. 4 (September, 1966) pages 679–733.

Chilcote, Ronald H. "Issues in the Theory of Dependency and Marxism." *Latin American Perspectives*. Vol. VIII, Nos. 3 and 4 (Summer and Fall, 1981) pages 3–16.

Choate, Pat. "Can a Keiretsu Work," *Harvard Business Review*, Vol. 68, No. 5 (September-October, 1990) pages 187–97.

Christopher, Warren. "America's Leadership, America's Opportunity," *Foreign Policy*, No. 98 (Spring, 1995) pages 6–27.

Clarke, Jonathan G. "A Foreign Policy Report Card on the Clinton-Gore Administration," *Policy Analysis No. 382* (Washington, D.C., Cato Institute, October 3, 2000) pages 10–11.

Coll, Alberto R. "America as the Grand Facilitator," *Foreign Policy*, No. 87 (Summer, 1992) pages 47–65.

Coore, David. "The Role of the Internal Dynamics of Jamaican Politics in the Collapse of the Federation," *Social and Economic Studies*, Vol. 48, No. 4 (December, 1999) pages 65–82.

Cox, Robert. "Social Forces, States and World Orders: Beyond International Relations Theory," *Millennium: Journal of International Studies*, Vol. 10, No. 2 (1981) pages 126–55.

Crowards, Tom. "Defining the Category of Small States." *Journal of International Development*, Vol. 14, No. 2 (March 2002) pages 143–79.

Daniel, S., A. A. Francis, D. Nelson, B. Nembhard, and D. H. Ramjeesingh, "A Structural Analysis of the Jamaican Economy, 1974. An Application of the Input-Output Technique," *Social and Economic Studies*, Vol. 34, No. 3 (September, 1985) pages 1–69.

Davis, Carlton. "Michael Manley's Foreign Policy of Non-alignment," *Jamaica Journal*, Vol. 34, Nos. 1–2 (August, 2012) pages 38–47.

Destler, I. M. "Foreign Policy and the Public: Will Leaders Catch the Full Message," *The Brown Journal of World Affairs*, Vol. III, Issue 1 (Winter/Spring, 1996) pages 265–70.

———. "Trade Policy at a Crossroad. An Approach for 1999 and Beyond," *Brookings Review*, Vol. 17, No. 1 (Winter, 1999) pages 27–30.

Devlin, Robert. "Economic Restructuring in Latin America in the Face of the Foreign Debt and the External Transfer Problem," *CEPAL Review*, No. 32 (August, 1987) pages 75–101.

Dickey, Christopher. "Central America: From Quagmire to Cauldron?" *Foreign Affairs*, Vol. 62, No. 3 (1983) pages 659–94.

Diebel, Terry L. "Reagan's Mixed Legacy," *Foreign Policy*, No. 75 (Summer, 1989) pages 34–55.

Dos Santos, Theotonio. "The Structure of Dependence," *American Economic Review*, Vol. LX, No. 2, (May 1970) pages 231–36.

Downes, Andrew S. "On the Statistical Measurement of Smallness. A Principal Component Measure of Country Size," *Social and Economic Studies*, Vol. 37, No. 3 (September, 1988) pages 75–96.

Enders, Thomas O. "A Comprehensive Strategy for the Caribbean Basin," *Caribbean Review*, Vol. 11, No. 2 (Spring, 1982) pages 10–13.

Erisman, H. Michael. "The Caricom States and US Foreign Policy: The Danger of Central Americanization," *Journal of Interamerican Studies and World Affairs*, Vol. 31, No. 3 (Fall 1989) pages 141–89.

Falco, Mathea. "America's Drug Problem and Its Policy of Denial," *Current History*, Vol. 97, No. 618 (April, 1998) pages 145–49.

———. "U.S. Drug Policy: Addicted to Failure," *Foreign Policy*, No. 102 (Spring, 1996) pages 120–33.

Fouts, Joshua. "Social Media, Virtual Worlds and Public Diplomacy," *World Politics Review*, October 13, 2009. http://www.worldpoliticsreview.com/articles/4440/social-media-virtual-worlds-and-public-diplomacy. Accessed October 9, 2014.

Friedman, Milton. "Foreign Economic Aid: Means and Objectives," *The Yale Review*, Vol. 47, No. 4 (Summer, 1958) pages 500–16.

Friedman, Will, and John Immerwahr. "Discussing Foreign Policy with the Post-Cold War Public," *The Brown Journal of World Affairs*, Vol. III, Issue 1 (Winter/Spring, 1996) pages 259–70.

Galtung, Johan. "A Structural Theory of Imperialism." *Journal of Peace Research*, Vol. 13, No. 2 (1971) pages 81–98.

Galbis, Vincent. "Ministate Economies," *Finance and Development* (June, 1984) pages 36–38.

Girvan, Norman. "The Development of Dependency Economics in the Caribbean and Latin America: Review and Comparison," *Social and Economic Studies*, Vol. 22, No. 1 (March, 1973) pages 1–33.

Girvan, Norman, and Richard L. Bernal. "The IMF and the Foreclosure of Development Options: The Case of Jamaica," *Monthly Review*, Vol. 38, No. 9 (February, 1982) pages 48–68.

Girvan, Norman, Richard L. Bernal, and Wesley Hughes. "The IMF and the Third World: The Case of Jamaica, 1974–1980," *Development Dialogue*, No. 2 (1980) pages 113–15.

Gonzales, Anthony P. "Recent Trends in International Economic Relations of the CARICOM States," *Journal of Interamerican Studies and World Affairs*, Vol. 31, No. 3 (Fall, 1989) pages 63–95.

Goodman, Marc. "Interview with Dudley Thompson," *Jamaica Journal*, Vol. 34, Nos. 1–2 (August, 2012) pages 23–31.

Grossman, Lawrence S. "British Aid and Windwards Bananas, The Case of St. Vincent and the Grenadines," *Social and Economic Studies*, Vol. 43, No. 1 (March, 1994) pages 151–79.

Hamilton, Lee H., and Van H. Dunson. "Making the Separation of Powers Work," *Foreign Affairs*, Vol. 57, No. (Fall, 1978) pages 21–33.

Handa, Sudhanshu, and Damian King. "Structural Adjustment Policies, Income Distribution and Poverty: A Review of the Jamaican Experience" *World Development*, Vol. 25, No. 6 (1997) pages 915–30.

Harris, Donald J. "Jamaica's Export Economy. Towards a Strategy of Export-led Growth," *Critical Issues in Caribbean Development* No. 5 (Kingston: Ian Randle Publishers, 1977).

Harris, William S. "Microstates in the United Nations. A Broader Purpose," *Columbia Journal of Transnational Law*, No. 9 (Spring, 1970) pages 23–53.

Harrison, Faye V. "Drug Trafficking in World Capitalism: A Perspective on Jamaican Posses in the U.S.," *Social Justice*. Vol. 16, No. 4 (1989) pages 115–31.

Helms, Jesse. "American Sovereignty and the UN" *National Interest*, No. 62 (Winter, 2000–1) pages 31–34.

Henke, Holger. "Jamaica's International Relations. Between the West…and the Rest," *Jamaica Journal*, Vol. 34, nos. 1–2 (August, 2012) pages 32–37.

Holsti, Ole. "Cognitive Process Approach to Decision-making," *American Behavioral Scientists*, Vol. 20, No. 1 (September-October, 1976) pages 11–32.

Huntington, Samuel P. "The Erosion of American National Interests," *Foreign Affairs*, Vol. 76, No. 5 (September-October, 1977) pages 28–49.

"Jamaica, Free to Go Where?," *The Economist*, August 11, 1962, page 519.

Kennan, George. "The Sources of Soviet Conduct," *Foreign Affairs*, Vol. 25, No. 4 (July, 1947) pages 566–82.

King, Damien. "The Evolution of Structural Adjustment and Stabilization Policy in Jamaica," *Social and Economic Studies*, Vol. 50, No. 1 (March 2001) pages 1–53.

Kirkpatrick, Jeane. "Dictatorship and Double Standards," *Commentary* (November, 1979) pages 34–35.

Klare, Michael. "The New Geography of Conflict," *Foreign Affairs*, Vol. 80, No. 3 (May/June, 2001) pages 49–61.

Krasner, Stephen D. "Are Bureaucracies Important? (Or Allison Wonderland)" *Foreign Policy*, No. 7 (Summer, 1972) pages 159–79.

Krauthammer, Charles. "The Unipolar Moment" *Foreign Affairs*, Vol. 17, No. 1 (1990/91) pages 23–33.

Legarda, Benito. "Small Island Economies." *Finance and Development*, Vol. 21 (June, 1984) pages 42–43.

Leogrande, William M. "Enemies Evermore: US Policy Towards Cuba After Helms-Burton," *Journal of Latin American Studies*, Vol. 29 (1997) pages 211–21.

Levy, Deborah M. "Advice for Sale," *Foreign Policy*, No. 67 (Summer, 1987) pages 64–86.

Lewis, Vaughan A. "The Small State Alone. Jamaican Foreign Policy, 1977–1980," *Journal of Inter-American Studies and World Affairs*, Vol. 25, No. 2 (May, 1983) pages 139–70.

Liou, F. M., and C. G. Ding. "Subgrouping of Small States Based on Socioeconomic Characteristics," *World Development*, Vol. 30, No. 7 (July, 2002) pages 1289–306.

"Lori's War": *The FP Interview, Foreign Policy*, No. 118 (Spring, 2000) pages 29–55.

Lowenthal, Abraham F. "Rediscovering Latin America," *Foreign Affairs*, Vol. 69, No. 4 (Fall, 1990) pages 27–41.

Mandelbaum, Michael. "The Bush Foreign Policy," *Foreign Affairs* Vol. 70, No. 1 (1991) pages 14–16.

"The Manley/Levitt Exchange," *Small Axe*, No. 1 (1997) page 81–115.

Manley, Michael. "The Integration Movement, the CBI and the Crisis of the Mini-State," *Caribbean Affairs*, Vol. 1, No. 1 (January-March, 1998) pages 6–15.

———. "Overcoming Insularity in Jamaica" *Foreign Affairs*, Vol. 49, No. 1 (October, 1970) pages 100–110.

———. "Southern Needs," *Foreign Policy*, No. 80 (Fall, 1970) pages 40–51.

Manning, Bayless. "The Congress, the Executive and Intermestic Affairs: Three Proposals," *Foreign Affairs*, Vol. 55, No. 2 (January, 1977) pages 306–24.

Mason, Edward S. "American Security and Access to Raw Materials," *World Politics*, Vol. 1, No. 2 (January 1949) pages 147–60.

Massing, Michael. "Grenada Before and After," *The Atlantic Monthly* (February 1984) pages 75–87.

McMathias Jr., Charles. "Ethnic Groups and Foreign Policy," *Foreign Affairs*, Vol. 59, No. 4 (1981) pages 978–79.

Miller, Linda B. "American Foreign Policy: Beyond Containment?" *International Affairs*, Vol. 66, No. 2 (April, 1990) pages 313–24.

Muniz, Humberto Garcia and Borges, Jose Lee. "US Consular Activism in the Caribbean, 1783–1903. With Special Reference to St. Kitts-Nevis' Sugar Depression, Labor Turmoil and Its Proposed Acquisition by the United States," *Revista Mexicana del Caribe*, Ano. III, No. 5 (1998) pages 32–79.

Nelson, Richard R. "A Theory of the Low Level Equilibrium Trap," *American Economic Review*, Vol. XLV No. 5 (December, 1956) pages 894–905.

Nettleford, Rex. "Manley and the Politics of Jamaica," *Social and Economic Studies*, Vol. 20, No. 3 (September, 1971) Supplement.

————. "Preface: Michael Manley and Caribbean Development. The Culture of Resistance," *Caribbean Development*, Vol. 48, No. 1 (March, 2002) pages 1–4.

Newman, Peter K. "Canada's Role in West Indian Trade Before 1912," *Inter-American Economic Affairs*, Vol. XIV, No. 1 (March, 1960) pages 25–49.

Nitze, Paul. "America: the Honest Broker," *Foreign Affairs*, Vol. 69, No. 4 (Fall, 1990) pages 1–14.

Obey, David R., and Carol Lancaster, "Funding Foreign Aid," *Foreign Policy*, No. 71 (Summer, 1988) pages 141–55. See page 141.

O'Flaherty, J. Daniel. "Finding Jamaica's Way," *Foreign Policy*, No. 31 (Summer, 1978) pages 137–58.

Padmore, Overand R. "Federation: The Demise of an Idea," *Social and Economic Studies*, Vol. 48, No. 4 (December, 1999) pages 21–65.

Pastor, Robert A. "Sinking in the Caribbean Basin," *Foreign Affairs*, Vol. 60, No. 3, (Summer, 1982) pages 1038–58.

Pastor, Robert, and Richard Fletcher, "The Caribbean in the 21st Century," *Foreign Affairs*, Vol. 70, No. 3 (Summer, 1991) pages 98–114.

Pinto, Anibal, and Jan Knakal, "The Center-Periphery System Twenty Years Later," *Social and Economic Studies*, Vol. 22, No. 1 (March, 1973) pages 34–89.

Prebisch, Raul. "Commercial Policy in the Underdeveloped Countries," *American Economic Review*, Vol. 49, No. 2 (May, 1959) pages 251–73.

Robbins, Carla Anne. "Dateline Washington: Cuban-American Clout," *Foreign Policy*, Issue 88 (Fall, 1992) pages 162–82.

Rosenstein-Rodan, Paul N. "Problem of Industrialization of Eastern and South-Eastern Europe," *Economic Journal*, Vol. 52, No. 210–211 (June-September, 1943) pages 202–11.

Ross, K. "The Commonwealth A Leader for the World's Small States," Round Table, Vol. 86, No. 343 (1997) 411–19.

Schlesinger, Arthur Jr. "Foreign Policy and the American Character," *Foreign Affairs*, Vol. 62, No. 1 (Fall, 1983) pages 1–16.

Selwin, Percy. "Smallness and Islandness," *World Development*, Vol. 8, No. 12 (1980) pages 945–51.

Sherlock, Philip. "Prospects in the Caribbean" *Foreign Affairs* Vol. 41, No. 4 (July, 1963) pages 744–50.

Singer, J. David. "International Conflict. Three Levels of Analysis," *World Politics*, Vol. 12 No. 3 (April, 1960) pages 453–61.

"Small but Perfectly Formed," *The Economist*, January 3, 1998, page 65.

Smith, Wayne. "Waving the Big Stick. The Helms-Burton Affair," *NACLA Report on the Americas*, Vol. XXXI, No. 2 (September-October, 1997) pages 27–28.

Sorensen, Theodore C. "The President and the Secretary of State," *Foreign Affairs*, Vol. 66 No. 2 (Winter, 1987/88) pages 231–48.

Srebrnik, Henry. "Small Island Nations and Democratic Values," *World Development* Vol. 32, No. 2 (2004) pages 329–41.

Srinivasan, T. N. "The Costs and Benefits of Being, a Small, Remote, Island, Landlocked or Ministate Economy," *World Bank Research Observer*, Vol. 1, No. 2 (1986) pages 205–18.

Streeten, Paul. "The Special Problems of Small Countries," *World Development*, Vol. 21, No. 2 (February, 1993) pages 197–202.

Sunkel, Osvaldo. "Transnational Capitalism and National Disintegration in Latin America," *Social and Economic Studies*, Vol. 22, No. 1 (March, 1973) pages 132–76.

Sutton, Paul "The Concept of Small States in the International Political Economy," *The Round Table: The Commonwealth Journal of International Affairs*, Vol. 100, No. 413 (2011) pages 141–53.

Swandby, Robert. "Economics and Politics of Oil in the Caribbean." *Maryland Journal of International Law*, Vol. 4, Issue 1 (Winter, 1978) pages 65–68.

Tarnoff, Peter. "An End to Foreign Policy. The Need to Reconcile Foreign and Domestic Strategies," *Harvard International Review*, Vol. XIV, No. 4 (Summer, 1992) pages 4–6.

Thorup, Cathryn. "The Politics of Free Trade and the Dynamics of Cross-Border Coalitions in US-Mexican Relations." *Columbia Journal of World Business* Vol. 26, No. 2 (1991) pages 12–26.

Tidrick, Gene. "Some Aspects of Jamaican Migration to the United Kingdom 1953–1962," *Social and Economic Studies*, Vol. 15, No. 1 (March, 1966) pages 22–39.

Tollefson, Scott D. "Jamaica. The Limits of a Showcase Policy," *SAIS Review*, Vol. 5, No. 2 (Summer - Fall, 1985) pages 189–204.

Tower, John. "Congress versus the President: The Formulation and Implementation of American Foreign Policy," *Foreign Affairs*, Vol. 60, No. 4 (Winter, 1981/82) pages 229–46.

Tucker, Robert W. "The Future of a Contradiction," *National Interest*, No. 43 (Spring, 1996) pages 20–27.

———. "The Purposes of American Power," *Foreign Affairs*, Vol. 59, No. 2 (Winter, 1980/81) page 265.

Tulchin, Joseph S. "The United States and Latin America in the 1960s" *Journal of Inter-American Studies*, Vol. 30, No. 1 (Spring, 1988) pages 1–36.

Vasciannie, Stephen. "Political and Policy Aspects of The Jamaica/United States Shiprider Negotiations" Vol. 43, No. 3 (September, 1997) pages 34–53.

Vellut, Jean-Luc. "Smaller States and the Problem of War and Peace: Some Consequences of the Emergence of Smaller States in Africa," *Journal of Peace Research*, Vol. 4, No. 3 (1967) pages 252–69.

Walker, H. S. "Jamaica and the United Nations 1962–1995," *Jamaica Journal*, Vol. 25, No. 3 (1995) pages 2–9.

Warren, Bill. "Imperialism and Capitalist Industrialization," *New Left Review*, No. 81 (September-October 1973) pages 3–44.

Welch, Barbara. "Banana Dependency: Albatross or Life Raft for the Windwards," *Social and Economic Studies*, Vol. 43, No. 1 (March, 1994) pages 123–49.

Wright, Theodore P., Jr. "United States Electoral Intervention in Cuba," *Inter-American Economic Affairs*, Vol. 13, No. 3 (Winter, 1959) pages 50–71.

ARTICLES IN BOOKS

Ambursley, Fitzroy. "Jamaica from Michael Manley to Edward Seaga," in *Crisis in the Caribbean*, ed. Fitzroy Ambursley and Robin Cohen. (London: Heinemann, 1983) pages 72–104.

Armstrong, H., and R. Reid. "Determinants of Economic Growth and Resilience in Small States" in *Building the Economic Resilience of Small States*, ed. Lino Briguglio, Gordon Cordina, and E. Kisanga. (London and Malta: Commonwealth Secretariat and University of Malta, 2006).

Ashley, Paul. "Jamaican Foreign Policy in Transition: From Manley to Seaga" in *The Caribbean and World Politics: Cross Currents and Cleavages*, ed. Jorge Heine and Leslie F. Manigat, (New York: Holmes & Meier, 1988) pages 144–62.

Bartson, R. P. "The External Relations of Small States" in *Small States in International Relations*, ed. August Schou and Arne Olav Bruntland. (New York: John Wiley & Sons, 1971).

Basch, Linda G. "The Politics of Caribbeanization: Vincentians and Grenadians in New York" in *Caribbean Life in New York: Socio-cultural Dimensions*, ed. Constance R. Sutton and Elsa M. Chaney. (New York: Center for Migration Studies of New York, 1987) pages 160–81.

Bauer, P. T. "Foreign Aid: Issues and Implications" in *Reality and Rhetoric: Studies in the Economics Development*, ed. P. T. Bauer. (Cambridge: Harvard University Press, 1984) pages 38–62.

Beckford, George L. "Issues in the Windwards – Jamaica Banana War" in *Readings in the Political Economy of the Caribbean*, ed. Norman Girvan and Owen Jefferson, (Kingston: New World, 1974).

Berg, Elliott. "Recent Trends and Issues in Development Strategies and Development Assistance" in Richard E. Feinberg and Ratchick M. Avakov (eds.), *U.S. and Soviet Aid to Developing Countries. From Confrontation to Cooperation* (New Brunswick: Transaction Publishers, 1991) pages 67–89.

Bernal, Richard L. "The Caribbean in the International System: Outlook for the First 20 years of the 21st Century" in *Contending with Destiny. The Caribbean in the 21st Century*, Kenneth Hall and Denis Benn (Kingston: Ian Randle, 2000) pages 295–325.

————. "Economic Growth and External Debt in Jamaica," in *External Debt and Economic Growth in Latin America*, ed. Antonio Jorge, Rene F. Higonnet, and Jorge Salazar –Carillo (New York, Pergamon Publishers, 1982) pages 89–108.

————. "Globalization and Small Developing Countries: Challenges and Opportunities" in *Small States in the Global Economy*, ed. David Peretz, Rumman Faruqi, and Eliawony J. Kisanga (London: Commonwealth Secretariat, 2001) pages 39–51.

————. "Globalization and Small Developing Countries: The Imperative for Repositioning," in *Globalization: A Calculus of Inequality*, ed. Denis Benn and Kenneth Hall (Kingston: Ian Randle Publishers, 2000) pages 88–128.

————. "Jamaica: Democratic Socialism Meets the IMF" in *Banking on Poverty: The Global Impact of the IMF and World Bank*, ed. Jill Torrie (Toronto: Between the Lines, 1983) pages 217–40.

————. "Special and Differential Treatment for Small Developing Economies" in *WTO at the Margins. Small States and the Multilateral Trading System*, ed. Roman Grynberg (Cambridge: Cambridge University Press, 2006) pages 309–55

————. "The Vicious Circle of Foreign Indebtedness: The Case of Jamaica," in *External Debt and Development Strategy in Latin America*, ed. Antonio Jorge, Jorge Salazar-Carrillo, and Frank Diaz-Pou (New York: Pergamon, 1985) pages 111–28.

Bernal, Richard L., Winsome J. Leslie, and Stephen E. Lamar, "Debt, Drugs and Structural Adjustment in the Caribbean," in *The Political Economy of Drugs in the Caribbean*, ed. Ivelaw L. Griffith (London: Macmillan, 2000) pages 58–80.

Bogues, Anthony. "Michael Manley, Trade Unionism, and the Politics of Equality" in *Caribbean Labor and Politics: Legacies of Cheddi Jagan and Michael Manley*, ed. Perry Mars and Alma H. Young (Wayne State University Press, 2004) pages 40–53.

Bolton, John R. "Unilateralism Is Not Isolationism" in *Understanding Unilateralism in American Foreign Relations*, ed. Gwyn Prins (London: Royal Institute of International Relations, 2000) pages 50–82.

Boohoo, Ken I. "US-Caribbean Relations in the Post-Cold War Era: Implications for Globalization and Development" in *Caribbean Survival and the Global Challenge*, ed. Ramesh Ramsaran (Kingston: Ian Randle Publishers, 2002) pages 149–62.

Brana-Shute, Gary. "Narco-criminality and Political Economy in the Caribbean," in *The Political Economy of Drugs in the Caribbean*, ed. Ivelaw L. Griffith (London: Macmillan, 2000) pages 97–112.

Brodber, Erna. "Raggae as Black Space" in *Global Raggae*, ed. Carolyn Cooper (Mona: University of the West Indies, 2012) pages 21–36.

————. "Socio-cultural Change in Jamaica" in *Jamaica in Independence. Essays on the Early Years*, ed. Rex Nettleford (Kingston: Heinemann,1989) pages 55–74.

Burchill, Scott. "Liberal Internationalism" in *Theories of International Relations*, ed. Scott Burchill and Andrew Linklater (London: Macmillan Press, 1996) pages 28–66.

Buzan, Barry. "Peoples, States and Fear" in *National Security in the Third World: The Management of Internal and External Conflicts*, ed. Edward E. Azar and Chung-In Moon (Cheltenham: Edward Elgar, 1988).

Byron, Jessica. "The Impact of Globalisation on the Caribbean" in *Globalisation, a Calculus of Inequality. Perspectives from the South*, ed. Denis Benn and Kenneth Hall (Kingston: Ian Randle Publishers, 2000) pages 135–42.

———. "Migration, National Identity, and Regionalism in the Caribbean: A Leeward Islands Case Study" in *Contending with Destiny. The Caribbean in the 21st Century*, ed. Kenneth Hall and Denis Benn (Kingston: Ian Randle, 2000) pages 80–90.

Cardoso, Fernando Henrique. "Associated-dependent Development: Theoretical and Practical Implications" in *Authoritarian Brasil: Origins, Policies and Future*, ed. Alfred Stephan (New Haven: Yale University Press, 1973) pages 142–78.

Chase-Dunn, Christopher. "Core-Periphery Relations: The Effects of Core Competition," in *Social Change in the Capitalist World-Economy*, Barbara Hockey Kaplan (Beverly Hills: Sage Publications, 1978) pages 159–77.

———. "Interstate System and Capitalist World-Economy: One Logic or Two?" in *World-System Structure. Continuity and Change*, ed. W. Ladd Hollist and James N. Rosenau (Beverly Hills: Sage Publications, 1981) pages 30–53.

Cigler, Allan J. "Interest Groups and Financing of the 2000 Elections" in *Financing the 2000 Election*, ed. David B. Maglegy (Washington, D.C.: Brookings Institution Press, 2002) pages 163–87.

Cigler, Allan J., and Burdett A. Loomis. "From Big Bird to Bill Gates: Organized Interests and the Emergence of Hyperpolitics" in *Interest Group Politics*, ed. Allan J. Cigler and Burdett A. Loomis (Washington, D.C.: Congressional Quarterly Press, 5th edition), pages 389–403.

Cohen, Bernard C. "Foreign Policy Makers and the Press" in *International Politics and Foreign Policy* ed. James N. Rosenau (New York: Free Press, 1961) pages 220–28.

Conway, M. Margaret and Joanne Connor Green, "Political Action Committees and Campaign Finance, in *Interest Group Politics*, ed. Allan J. Cigler and Burdett A. Loomis (Washington, D.C.: Congressional Quarterly Press, 5th edition, 2002) pages 193–216.

Cooper, Carolyn. "Jamaican Popular Music A Yard and Abroad" in *Global Reggae*, Carolyn Cooper (Mona: University of the West Indies, 2012) pages 1–19.

Dean, Heather. "Scarce Resources: The Dynamics of American Imperialism" in *Readings in U.S. Imperialism*, ed. K. T. Fann and Donald C. Hodges (Boston: Porter Sargent Publisher, 1971) pages 139–54.

Destler, I. M. "Delegating Trade Policy" in *The President, Congress and the Making of Foreign Policy*, ed. Paul E. Peterson (Norman: University of Oklahoma Press, 1994) pages 228–45.

———. "Foreign Policymaking with the Economy at Center State" in *Beyond the Beltway. Engaging the Public in US Foreign Policy*, ed. Daniel Yankelovich and I. M. Destler (New York: W. W. Norton, 1994) pages 26–42.

Devetak, Richard. "Critical Theory" in *Theories of International Relations*, ed. Scott Burchill and Andrew Linklater (London: Macmillan, 1996) pages 179–209.

Domhoff, G. William. "Who Made American Foreign Policy, 1945–1963?" in *Corporations and the Cold War*, ed. David Horowitz (New York: Monthly Review Press, 1969) pages 25–70.

Dominguez, Jorge I. "The Future of Inter-American Relations: States, Challenges and Likely Responses" in *The Future of Inter-American Relations*, ed. Jorge I. Dominguez (New York: Routledge, 2000) pages 3–34.

Dosi, Giovanni, "Trade, Technologies and Development" in *Politics and Productivity. The Real Story Why Japan Works*, ed. Laura D'Andrea Tyson, John Zysman, and Chalmers Johnson (New York: Harper Collins, 1989).

Dos Santos, Theotonio. "The Crisis of Development Theory and the Problem of Dependence in Latin America" in *Underdevelopment and Development. The Third World Today*, H. Bernstein (Harmondsworth: Penguin, 1973) pages 57–80.

Dulles, John Foster "International Communism in Guatemala," in *The United States and Latin America*, ed. Earl T. Glauert and Lester D Langley (Reading: Addison-Wesley, 1971) pages 141–45.

Duncan, Neville C. "Domestic Policy and International Relations" in *Barbados. Thirty Years of Independence*, ed. Trevor A. Carmichael (Kingston: Ian Randle Publishers, 1996) page 52–66.

Duvall, Raymond, et al. "A Formal Model of Dependencia Theory. Structure and Measurement" in *From National Development to Global Community*, ed. Richard Merritt and Bruce Russett (London: George Allen & Unwin, 1981).

Edmondson, Locksley, and Peter Phillips, "The Commonwealth Caribbean and Africa: Aspects of Third World Racial Interactions, Linkages and Challenges," in *Contemporary International Relations in the Caribbean*, ed. Basin A. Ince (St. Augustine: Institute for International Relations, University of the West Indies, 1979) pages 33–55.

Einaudi, Luigi. "Latin America's Development and the United States" in *Beyond Cuba: Latin America Takes Charge of Its Future*, ed. Luigi R. Einaudi (New York: Crane, Russak and Co., 1974) pages 209–28.

———. "U.S. Latin American Policy in the 1970's: New Forms of Control?" in *Latin America and the United States. The Changing Political Realities*, ed. Julio Cotler and Richard R. Fagen (Stanford: Stanford University Press, 1974) pages 238–55.

Eisenhower, Dwight D. "The Military-Industrial Complex" in *Defense and Disarmament. The Economics of Transition*, ed. Rodger E. Bolton (Englewood Cliffs: Prentice Hall, 1966) pages 173–75.

Ellis, H. S. and H. Wallich (eds.) "Notes on the Theory of the Big Push" in *Economic Development for Latin America* (London: Macmillan, 1961) pages 57–66.

Francis, Michael J. "United States Policy toward Latin America during the Kissinger Years" in *United States Policy in Latin America. A Quarter Century of Crisis and Challenge 1961–1986*, ed. John D. Martz (Lincoln: University of Nebraska, 1990) pages 28–60.

Frank, Andre Gunder. "The Development of Underdevelopment in Latin America" in *Latin America. Underdevelopment or Revolution*, ed. Andre Gunder Frank (New York: Monthly Review Press, 1969).

Gardener, Lloyd C. "The New Deal, New Frontiers and the Cold War: A Re-examination of the American Expansion, 1933–1945" in *Corporations and the Cold War*, ed. David Horowitz (New York: Monthly Review Press, 1970) pages 105–42.

Gill, Stephen. "Gramsci and Global Politics: Towards a Post-Hegemonic Research Agenda" in *Gramsci, Historical Materialism and International Relations*, ed. Stephen Gill (Cambridge: Cambridge University Press, 1993) pages 1–18.

Girvan, Norman. "Creating and Recreating the Caribbean" in *Contending with Destiny. The Caribbean in the 21st Century*, ed. Kenneth Hall and Dennis Benn (Kingston: Ian Randle Publishers, 2000) pages 31–36.

Gonzales, Anthony P. "World Restructuring and Caribbean Economic Diplomacy" in *Diplomacy for Survival: CARICOM States in a World of Change*, ed. Lloyd Searwar (Kingston: Frederick Ebert Stiftung, 1991) pages 1–18.

Grant, Cedric. "The Association of Caribbean States and US-Caribbean Relations" in *The Repositioning of US-Caribbean Relations in the New World Order*, ed. Ransford W. Palmer (Westport: Praeger Publishers, 1997) page 27–50.

Grayson, George W. "Lobbying by Mexico and Canada" in *The Controversial Pivot. The US Congress and North America*, ed. Robert A. Pastor and Rafael Fernandez de Castro (Washington, D.C.: Brookings Institution Press, 1998) pages 70–94.

Greene, J. Edward. "External Influences and Stability in the Caribbean" in *Peace, Development and Security in the Caribbean. Perspectives to the Year 2000*, ed. Anthony T. Bryan, J. Edward Greene, and Timothy M. Shaw (London: Macmillan, 1990) pages 205–23.

Griffith, Ivelaw. "Transnational Crime in the Americas: A Reality Check" in *The Future of Inter-American Relations*, ed. Jorge I. Dominguez (New York: Routledge, 2000) pages 63–86.

Hall, Douglas, "The Early Banana Trade from Jamaica, 1868–1905. A Descriptive Account" in *Ideas and Illustrations in Economic History*, Douglas Hall (New York: Holt, Rinehart and Winston, 1964) pages 56–79.

Hall, Kenneth. "Jamaica in the International Arena: Leader or Follower. Historical Perspectives on Jamaica's Contribution to the International Community" in *Paradigm Shifts & Structural Changes - in Pursuit of Progress in the Caribbean Community,* ed. Kenneth Hall and Myrtle Chuck-A-Sang (Bloomington: Trafford Publishing, 2013) pages 104–14.

Heclo, Hugh. "Issue Networks and the Executive Establishment" in *The New American Political System*, Anthony King (Washington, D.C.: American Enterprise Institute, 1978) pages 87–124.

Hein, P. "The Study of Microstates" in *States, Microstates and Islands*, Edward Dommen and Phillipe Hein (London: Croom Helm, 1985).

Jones, Ronald E. "Cuba and the English-speaking Caribbean" in *Cuba in the World*, ed. Cole Blasier and Carmelo Mesa-Lago (Pittsburgh: University of Pittsburgh Press, 1979) pages 131–33.

Keohane, Robert O. "The Theory of Hegemonic Stability and Changes in International Economic Regimes 1967–1977" in *Changes in International System*, Ole R. Holsti, Randolph M. Silverson, and Alexander L. George (Boulder: Westview Press, 1980) pages 132–62.

Kirkpatrick, Jeane. "U.S. Security and Latin America" in *Rift and Revolution. The Central American Imbroglio*, Howard Wiarda (Washington D.C.: American Enterprise Institute for Public Policy Research, 1984) pages 329–59.

Kotschwar, Barbara. "Small Countries and the Free Trade Area of the Americas" in *Trade Rules in the Making. Challenges in Regional and Multilateral Negotiations*, Miguel Rodriguez Mendoza, Patrick Low, and Barbara Kotschwar (Washington, D.C.: Brookings Institution Press/ Organization of American States, 1999) pages 134–58.

Kurbalija, Jovan. "The Impact of the Internet and ICT on Contemporary Diplomacy" in *Diplomacy in a Globalizing World*, ed. Pauline Kerr and Geoffrey Wiseman (Oxford University Press, 2012) pages 141–59.

Kuznets, Simon. "Economic Growth of Small Nations" in *Economic Consequences of the Size of Nations*, ed. E. A. G. Robinson (London: Macmillan, 1960) pages 14–32.

Lamming, George. "Concepts of the Caribbean" in *Frontiers in Caribbean Literature in English*, Frank Birlbalsingh (London: Macmillan, 1996) pages 1–14.

Lande, Steve, and Nellis Crigler. "CBI and NAFTA Provisions Compared" in *U.S.-Caribbean Relations into the 21st Century*, ed. Georges A. Fauriol and G. Philip Hughes (Washington, D.C.: Center for Strategic and International Studies, 1995) pages 29–42.

Lewis, John P. "Can We Escape the Path of Mutual Injury?" in John P. Lewis and Valeria Kallab (eds.), *US Foreign Policy and the Third World Agenda 1983* (New York: Praeger, 1983) pages 7–48.

Lewis, Vaughan A. "The Commonwealth Caribbean Policy of Non-Alignment" in *Contemporary International Relations of the Caribbean*, ed. Basil A. Ince (Port of Spain: Institute of International Relations, 1979) pages 1–11.

———. "Issues and Trends in Jamaican Foreign Policy 1972–1977" in *Perspectives on Jamaica in the Seventies*, ed. Carl Stone and Aggrey Brown (Kingston: Publishing House, 1981).

Lovett, William A. "Balancing U.S. Trade" in *U.S. Trade Policy. History, Theory and the WTO*, ed. William A. Lovett, Alfred E. Eckes Jr., and Richard L. Brinkman (Armonk, New York: M. E. Sharpe, 1999) pages 136–82. See page 148.

Lowenthal, Abraham F. "Latin America and the Caribbean: Toward a New US Policy" in *US Foreign Policy and the Third World*, ed. John P. Lewis and Valleriana Kallab (New York: Praeger 1983) pages 51–65.

———. "Ronald Reagan and Latin America: Coping with Hegemony in Decline," in *Eagle Defiant: US Foreign Policy in the 1980s*, ed. Kenneth Oye, Robert Lieber, and Donald Rothchild (Boston: Little Brown and Co. 1983) pages 311–35.

———. "United States–Latin American Relations at the Century's Turn: Managing the Intermemestic Agenda" in *The United Nations and the Americas*, ed. Albert Fishlow and James Jones (New York: W. W. Norton, 1999) pages 109–36.

Maingot, Anthony. "The Decentralization Imperative and Caribbean Criminal Enterprises" in *Transnational Crime in the Americas*, ed. Tim Farer (New York: Routledge, 1999) pages 42–170.

———. "The Internationalization of Corruption and Violence: Threat to the Caribbean in the Post-Cold War World" in Jorge I. Dominguez, Robert Pastor, and DeLisle Worrell (eds.) *Democracy in the Caribbean: Political, Economic and Social Perspective* (Baltimore: Johns Hopkins University Press, 1993) pages 42–56.

Malone, David D. "The Modern Diplomatic Mission" in *The Oxford Handbook of Modern Diplomacy*, ed. Andrew F. Cooper, Jorge Heine, and Ramesh Thakur (Oxford: Oxford University Press, 2013) pages 124–41. See page 138.

Manley, Michael. "The Caribbean Basin: Its Political Dynamic and Possible Directions" in *Third World Affairs 1985* (London: Third World Foundation for Social and Economic Studies, 1985) pages 243–50.

Marsh, Bennett. "CBI in the Shadow of NAFTA" in *Recommendations for a North American Free Trade Agreement and for Future Hemispheric Trade, Miami Report III* (Miami: North-South Centre, 1992) pages 43–52.

Mazrui, Ali A. "Uncle Sam's Hearing Aid," in *Estrangement. America and the World*, ed. Sanford J. Unger (Oxford: Oxford University Press, 1985) pages 179–92.

Miller, Errol. "Educational Development in Independent Jamaica" in *Jamaica in Independence. Essays on the Early Years*, ed. Rex Nettlefor (Kingston: Heinemann Caribbean, 1989) pages 205–28.

Millett, Richard. "Imperialism, Intervention and Exploitation: The Historical Context of International Relations in the Caribbean," in The *Restless Caribbean, Changing Patterns of International Relations*, ed. Richard Millett and Marvin Will (New York: Praeger, 1979).

Mills, Don. "Jamaica's International Relations in Independence" in *Jamaica in Independence: Essays on the Early Years*, ed. Rex Nettleford (Kingston: Heinemann Publishers (Caribbean), 1989) page 131–71.

Munroe, Trevor. "Cooperation and Conflict in the US-Caribbean Drug Connection," in *The Political Economy of Drugs in the Caribbean*, ed. Ivelaw Griffith, (London: Macmillan, 2000) pages 183–200.

O'Brien, Philip J. "Dependency Revisited" in *Latin America,Economic Imperialism and the State. The Political Economy of the External Connection from Independence to the Present*, ed. C. Abel and C. M. Lewis (London: Athlone Press, 1985) pages 40–69.

Pastor, Robert. "The Cry-and-Sigh Syndrome: Congress and Trade Policy" in *Making Economic Policy in Congress*, Allen Schick (Washington, D.C.: American Enterprise Institute for Public Research, 1983) pages 158–95.

———. "Introduction: The Policy Challenge" in *Migration and Development in the Caribbean. The Unexplored Connection* (Boulder: Westview Press, 1985) pages 1–2.

———. "The United States: Divided by a Revolutionary Vision" in *A Century Journey. How the Great Powers Shape the World*, ed. Robert A. Pastor (New York: Basic Books, 1999) pages 191–238.

Pastor, Robert A., and Richard D. Fletcher. "Twenty-first Century Challenges for the Caribbean and the United States: Toward a New Horizon" in *Democracy in the Caribbean. Political, Economic and Social Perspectives*, ed. Jorge I. Dominguez, Robert A. Pastor and R. DeLisle Worrell (Baltimore: Johns Hopkins University Press, 1993) pages 255–76.

Payne, Anthony. "The Foreign Policy of the People's Revolutionary Government," in *A Revolution Aborted. The Lessons of Grenada*, ed. Jorge Heine (Pittsburgh; University of Pittsburgh Press, 1990) pages 123–51.

Pratt, Julius W. "The Ideology of American Expansion," in *American Expansion in the Late Nineteenth Century*, ed. J. Rogers Hollingsworth (New York: Holt Rinehart, Winston, 1968).

Preeg, Ernest H. "An Anatomy of the US Foreign Assistance Program" in Richard E. Feinberg and Ratchick M. Avakov (eds.), *U.S. and Soviet Aid to Developing Countries. From Confrontation to Cooperation* (New Brunswick: Transaction Publishers, 1991) pages 123–44.

References

Pryor, Frederic L. "Socialism via Foreign Aid: The PRG's Economic Policies with the Soviet Bloc," in *A Revolution Aborted. The Lessons of Grenada*, ed. Jorge Heine (Pittsburgh Press, 1990) pages 153–80.

Reid, Stanley. "An Introductory Approach to the Concentration of Power in the Jamaican Corporate Economy and Notes on its Origins," in *Essays in Power and Change in Jamaica*, ed. Carl Stone and Aggrey Brown (Kingston: Jamaica Publishing House, 1977) pages 15–45.

Rosenau, James. "Pre-Theories and Theories of International Politics" in *Approaches to Comparative and International Politics*, ed. R. Barry Farrell (Evanston: Northwestern University Press, 1966) pages 27–92.

Rosenstein-Rodan, Paul N. "Notes on the Theory of the Big Push," in *Economic Development for Latin America*, ed. H. S. Ellis and H. Wallich (London: Macmillan, 1961) pages 57–66.

Rowland, Benjamin M. "Preparing the American Ascendency: The Transfer of Economic Power from Britain to the United States," 1933–1944" in *Balance of Power or Hegemony: The Interwar Monetary System*, Benjamin M. Rowland (New York: New York University Press, 1976) pages 195–228.

Sanders, Ron. "The Drug Problem: Policy Options for the Caribbean Countries" in *Democracy in the Caribbean: Political, Economic and Social Perspective*, Jorge I. Dominquez, Robert Pastor, and DeLisle Worrell (Baltimore: Johns Hopkins University Press, 1993) pages 229–37.

Serrano, Monica. "Transnational in the Western Hemisphere" in *The Future of Inter-American Relations*, Jorge I. Domiquez (New York and London: Routledge, 2000), pages 87–110.

Smith, Robert F. "American Foreign Relations, 1920–1942" in *Towards a New Past: Dissenting Essays in American History*, ed. Barton J. Berstein (New York: Vintage Books, 1969), pages 232–62.

———. "Republican Policy and Pax Americana 1921–1932" in *From Colony to Empire: Essays in the History of American Foreign Relations*, ed. William Appleman Williams (New York: John Wiley & Sons, 1972) pages 253–92.

Smith, R. T. "Social Stratification, Cultural Pluralism and Integration in West Indian Societies" in *Caribbean Integration*, ed. S. Lewis and T. G. Mathews (Rio Praedas: University of Puerto Rico, 1967) pages 226–58.

Sutton, Paul. "The Caribbean as a Focus for Strategic and Resource Rivalry" in *The Central American Security System: North-South or East-West?*, ed. Peter Calvert (New York: Cambridge University Press 1988) pages 18–44.

Sylvan, David, and Associates. "The Peripheral Economies. Penetration and Distortion" in *Contending Approaches to World System Analysis*, William R. Thompson (Beverly Hills: Sage Publications, 1983).

Taylor, Charles L. "Statistical Typology of Microstates and Territories: Towards a Definition of a Micro-State" in J. Rapaport, E. Muteba, and J. Therattil, *Small States and Territories: Status and Problems, United Nations Institute for Training and Research Study* (New York: Arno Press, 1971) pages 183–202.

Thompson, Kenneth W. "The President, the Congress and Foreign Policy: The Policy Paper," in *The President, the Congress and Foreign Policy*, ed. Edmund S. Muskie, Kenneth Rush, and Kenneth W. Thompson (New York: University Press of America, 1986) pages 3–34.

Walcott, Derek. "The Muse of History" in *What the Twilight Says. Essays*, ed. Derek Walcott (New York: Farrar, Strauss and Giroux, 1998) pages 36–64.

Waltz, Kenneth N. "Realist Thought and Neorealist Theory," in *Controversies in International Relations Theory: Realism and the Neoliberal Challenge*, ed. Charles W. Kegley (New York: St. Martin's Press, 1995) pages 67–83.

Warf, Phillip S., and Steven Kull. "Tepid Traders: U.S. Public Attitudes on NAFTA and Free Trade Expansion" in *NAFTA in the New Millennium*, Edward J. Chambers and Peter H. Smith (La Jolla: University of California and Edmonton: University of Alberta Press, 2002) pages 213–38. See page 230.

Watson, Hilbourne A. "Global Restructuring and the Prospects for Caribbean Competitiveness: With a Case Study of Jamaica," in *The Caribbean in the Global Political Economy*, ed. Hilbourne A. Watson (Boulder: Lynne Rienner / Kingston: Ian Randle, 1994) pages 67–90.

Webb Hammond, Susan. "Congress in Foreign Policy" in *President, the Congress and Foreign Policy*, ed. Edmund Muskie, Kenneth Rush, and Kenneth W. Thompson (Lanham: University Press of America, 1986) pages 67–91.

Williams, William Appleman. "The Large Corporation and American Foreign Policy" in *Corporations and the Cold War*, David Horowitz (New York: Monthly Review Press, 1970) pages 71–104.

Wiltshire-Brodber, Rosina. "Trinidad and Tobago Foreign Policy 1962–1987: An Evaluation," in *Trinidad and Tobago. The Independence Experience 1962–1987*, ed. Selwyn Ryan (St. Augustine: Institute of Social and Economic Studies, University of the West Indies, 1988) pages 281–302.

MONOGRAPHS

Ashby, Timothy. *Missed Opportunities: The Rise and Fall of Jamaica's Seaga* (Indianapolis: Hudson Institute, 1989).

Bernal, Richard L. *The Integration of Small Economies in the Free Trade Area of the Americas, CSIS, Policy Paper on the Americas, Vol. IX, Study No. 1* (Washington, D.C.: Center for Strategic and International Studies, February 2, 1998).

———. "Resolving the International Debt Crisis," in *The Debt Problem in Jamaica: Situations and Solutions, Monograph No. 1, Department of Economics, University of the West Indies, Mona*, ed. Omar Davies (September 1986) pages 82–114.

———. *Strategic Global Restructuring and the Future Economic Development of Jamaica, North South Agenda Paper No. 18* (Miami: North-South Center, University of Miami, May, 1999).

———. "U.S. Caribbean Relations at the Dawn of the Twenty-First Century" in *The United States and Caribbean Strategies. Three Assessments, Policy Papers on the Americas, Vol. XII, Study 4*, ed. Richard L. Bernal, Anthony T. Bryan, and Georges A. Fauriol (Washington, D.C.: Center for Strategic and International Studies, 2002) pages 3–25.

Bernal, Richard L., and Steve Lamar. *Caribbean Basin Economic Development and the Section 936 Tax Credit, North-South Agenda Paper. No. 22* (Miami: North-South Center, University of Miami, December 1996).

Bositis, David. *Blacks and the 1992 Democratic National Convention* (Washington, D.C.: Joint Center for Political and Economic Studies, 1992).

Braveboy-Wagner, Jacqueline Anne. *The United States and the Caribbean: The Washington Bureaucracy* (Washington, D.C.: Center for Strategic and International Studies, April, 1991).

Bryan, Anthony T. "Caribbean Trends and a U.S. Policy Agenda" in *The United States and Caribbean Strategies. Three Assessments, Policy Papers on the Americas, Vol. XII, Study 4*, ed. Richard L. Bernal, Anthony T. Bryan, and Georges A. Fauriol, (Washington, D.C.: Center for the Strategic and International Studies, 2001) pages 26–38.

———. *Transnational Organized Crime: The Caribbean Context, Working Paper Series, Working Paper No. 1* (Miami: Dante B. Fascell North-South Center, University of Miami, October, 2000).

Castro, Max J. *Immigration and Integration in the Americas* (Miami: North South Centre, University of Miami, Agenda Paper No. 46, May, 2001).

De Varona, Adolfo Leyva. *Propaganda and Reality: A Look at the US Embargo Against Castro's Cuba* (Miami: Cuban American National Foundation, July 1994).

Harris, Donald J. *Jamaica's Export Economy. Towards a Strategy of Export-led Growth, Critical Issues in Caribbean Development No. 5* (Kingston: Ian Randle Publishers, 1977).

Hendrickson, Alan K. *Diplomacy and Small States in Today's World, The Dr. Eric Williams Memorial Lecture*, Twelfth Lecture, 22 May, 1998.

Hughes, G. Philip. "A US Policy Outlook on the Caribbean" in *U.S.-Caribbean Relations into the 21st Century, Policy Papers on the Americas Vol. VI, Study 4*, ed. Georges A. Fauriol and G. Philip Hughes (Washington, D.C.: Center for Strategic and International Studies, 1995).

Kim, Namsuk. *The Impact of Remittances on Labor Supply: The Case of Jamaica*, World Bank Policy Research Working Paper 4120 (Washington, D.C.: World Bank, February, 2007).

Levitt, Kari Polyani. *The Origins and Consequences of Jamaica's Debt Crisis 1970–1990* (Mona Consortium School of Graduate Studies and Social Science, University of the West Indies, 1991).

Mills, Don. *The New Europe, the New Order and the Caribbean* (Kingston: Grace Kennedy Foundation, 1991).

Mintz, Sidney W. *From Plantation to Peasantries in the Caribbean* (Washington, D.C.: Woodrow Wilson International Center for Scholars, 1984).

Payne, Douglas W. *Emerging Voices: The West Indian, Dominican and Haitian Diasporas in the United States, CSIS Americas Program Policy Papers on the Americas, Vol. IX, Study 11* (Washington, D.C.: Centre for Strategic and International Studies, October 22, 1998).

Rothstein, Jesse, and Robert E. Scott, *NAFTA's Casualties Employment Effects on Men, Women and Minorities* (Washington, D.C.: Economic Policy Institute, 1997).

Sutton, Paul K. "The Caribbean as a Subordinate State System, 1945–1976," *Hull Papers in Politics No. 16*, (Dept. of Politics, University of Hull, 1980).

Taylor, Margaret H., and T. Alexander Aleinikoff. *Deportation of Criminal Aliens: A Geopolitical Perspective* (Washington, D.C. Inter-American Dialogue, June 1998).

The Trading Game: Inside Lobbying for the North American Free Trade Agreement (Washington, D.C.: The Centre for Public Integrity, N. D.).

Thorburn, Diana, and Dana Marie Morris. *Jamaica's Foreign Policy. Making the Economic Development Link* (Kingston: Caribbean Policy Research Institute, June, 2007).

Tulchin, Joseph S., and Ralph H. Espach, *Addressing the Challenges of Cooperative Security in the Caribbean, Peace and Security in the Americas, Woodrow Wilson Center/Facultad Latinamericana de Ciencias Sociales*, (September, 1997, page 2).

TESTIMONIES TO CONGRESS

Bernal, Richard L. "The Caribbean Basin Free Trade Agreement Act" (H. R. 1403) in Hearing before the Subcommittee on Trade and the Subcommittee on Oversight of the Committee on Ways and Means, House of Representatives, One Hundred Third Congress, First Session, June 24, 1993, (Washington, D.C.: U.S. Government Printing Office, 1993) pages 68–75.

———. "The Caribbean Basin Initiative," in Hearings before the Subcommittee on International Economic Policy and Trade on Western Hemisphere Affairs of the Committee on Foreign Affairs, House of Representatives, One Hundredth Congress, First Session, September 18 and 19, 1987 (Washington, D.C., U.S. Government Printing Office, 1987) pages 48–56.

———. "Caribbean/US Relations" Testimony before the Subcommittee on the Western Hemisphere House Committee on International Relations, May 17, 2000.

———. "Debt Relief for Caribbean Countries" in Hearings before the Subcommittees on Human Rights and International Organizations, Western Hemisphere Affairs and International Economic Policy and Trade of the Committee on Foreign Affairs, House of Representatives, One Hundredth First Congress, Second Session, June 28th, July 11, 18, 31 and September, 1990 (Washington, D.C.: U.S. Government Printing Office, 1991) pages 225–38.

————. "Enterprise for the Americas Initiative Act 1991," (H. R. 4059) in hearing before the Committee on Agriculture, House of Representatives, One Hundred Second Congress, Second Session, June 17, 1992 (Washington, D.C.: U.S. Government Printing Office, 1992) pages 73–82.

————. "Foreign Aid to Jamaica," in Senate Hearings before the Committee on Appropriations. Foreign Operations, Export Financing, and Related Programs Appropriations. Foreign Operations Appropriations, 1995 (H. R. 4426). (Washington, D.C.: U.S. Government Printing Office, 1994) pages 768–76.

————. "NAFTA at Three: The Case for NAFTA Parity," Statement submitted to the House on Ways and Means Trade Subcommittee, House of Representatives, One Hundred Fifth Congress, First Session, September 11, 1997 (Washington, D.C.: Government Printing Office, 1998) pages 261–63.

————. "936 Funds: Contributing to Jamaica's Development," (H. R. 5270) in hearing before the United States House of Representatives Committee on Ways and Means, One Hundred and Second Congress, Second Session, July 21–22, 1992. (Washington, D.C.: U.S. Government Printing Office, 1992) pages 1075–78.

————. "The Role of 936 Funds in Economic Development of Caribbean Countries," in Hearings before the Committee on Ways and Means, House of Representatives, One Hundred and Third Congress, First Session, March 23, 31 and April 1, 1993. (Washington, D.C.: U.S. Government Printing Office, 1993) pages 1305–10.

————. *Testimony on the Caribbean Basin Initiative to the Hearings before the Sub-Committee on 1987 International Economic Policy and Trade and on Western Hemispheric Affairs of the Committee on Foreign Affairs*, House of Representatives, One hundredth Congress, First Session (Washington, D.C.: Government Printing Office, 1988) pages 45–56.

————. "U.S. Foreign Assistance and Economic Reform," in Hearings before a Subcommittee of the Committee on Appropriations, House of Representatives, One Hundred Third Congress, Second Session, April, 1994 (Washington, D.C.: U.S. Government Printing Office, 1994) pages 768–76.

————. "U.S. Foreign Assistance and Sustainable Growth in Jamaica" in Hearings before the Committee on Appropriations, Subcommittee on Foreign Operations, Export Financing, and Related Agencies, United States House of Representatives, One Hundred Fourth Congress, Second Session, April 25, 1996. (Washington, D.C.: U.S. Government Printing Office, 1996) pages 369–78.

————. "U.S. Foreign Assistance and Sustainable Growth in Jamaica" in Hearings before a Subcommittee of the Committee on Appropriations, U.S. Senate, One Hundred Fifth Congress, First Session, May 22, 1997 (Washington, D.C.: U.S. Government Printing Office, 1998), pages 351–56.

————. "U.S. Foreign Assistance and Sustainable Growth in Jamaica" in Hearings before the House Committee on Appropriations Subcommittee on Foreign Operations, Export Financing, and Related Agencies. April 24, 1997. (Washington, D.C.: U.S. Government Printing Office, 1997), pages 682–93.

Bryan, Anthony T. *Hearing before the Subcommittee on Trade of the Committee on Ways and Means*, House of Representatives, One Hundred Fourth Congress, First Session, February 10, 1995 (Washington, D.C.: Government Printing Office, 1995) pages 170–72.

Christopher, Warren in "Review of United States Foreign Policy," Hearing before the Committee on International Relations, House of Representatives, One Hundred Fourth Congress, Second session, July 31, 1996 (Washington, D.C.: Government Printing Office, 1997) pages 2–8 and 41–53.

de Roulet, Vincent. *Testimony of Vincent de Roulet*, U.S. Ambassador to Jamaica, United States Senate, Subcommittee on Multinational Corporations of the Committee on Foreign Relations, July 19, 1973, pages 109–44.

Hearings before the Subcommittee on Trade of the Committee of Ways and Means Ninety-Seventh Congress, *Second Session of the Administration's Proposed Trade and*

Tax Measures affecting the Caribbean Basin, March 17, 23, 24, and 25, 1982 (Washington, D.C.: U.S. Government Printing Office, 1982).

Hearings before the United States Senate, *Subcommittee on Multinational Corporations of the Committee on Foreign Relations*, (Washington, DC: Government Printing Office, 1973) pages 109–34.

Johnson, Peter B. Statement published in H. R. 533, *The Caribbean Basin Trade Security Act. Hearing before the Subcommittee on Trade of the Committee on Ways and Means House of Representatives*, One Hundred and Fourth Congress, First Session, February 10, 1995. (Washington, D.C.: U.S. Government Printing Office, 1995) pages 156–62.

Kantor, Michael. *The Administration's Case for NAFTA. Testimony of Ambassador Michael Kantor*, U.S. Trade Representative before the Senate Committee on Agriculture, Nutrition and Forestry, 21 September 1993.

Martin, Larry. Testimony - *American Apparel Manufacturers Association, in Hearings before the Subcommittee on Trade of the Committee on Ways and Means, House of Representatives*, One Hundred Fourth Congress, First Session, February 10, 1995 (Washington, D.C.: U.S. Government Printing Office, 1995) pages 93–96.

Pregelj, Vladimir N. "*US Foreign Trade and Investment Policy in the Caribbean Basin Region*," in The Caribbean Basin Economic and Security Issues. Joint Economic Committee Print (S. Print. 102–10) (Washington, D.C.: Government Printing Office, 1993).

Statement of Hon. Charlene Barshefsky, *Deputy United States Representative, Hearing before the Subcommittee on Ways and Means, House of Representatives*, One Hundred Fourth Congress, February 10, 1995 (Washington, D.C.: U.S. Government Printing Office, 1995).

Statement of Peter Johnson, *Caribbean/Latin American Action in Hearings before the Subcommittee on Trade of the Committee on Ways and Means, House of Representatives*, One Hundred Fourth Congress, First Session, February 10, 1995 (Washington, D.C.: US Government Printing Office, 1995) pages 154–62.

Statement of Senator Bob Graham of Florida in *Hearing before the Subcommittee on Trade of the Committee on Ways and Means*, House of Representatives, One Hundred Fourth Congress, First Session, February 10, 1995. (Washington, D.C.: Government Printing Office, 1995).

Statement of the Hon. Bob Graham, Senator from the State of Florida, *Hearing before the Subcommittee on Trade and the Subcommittee Oversight of the Committee on Ways and Means, House of Representatives*. One Hundred Third Congress, June 24, 1993 (Washington, D.C.: Government Printing Office, 1995).

REPORTS

A Future for Small States: Overcoming Vulnerability (London: Commonwealth Secretariat, 1997).

A New Inter-American Policy for the Eighties (Washington, D.C.: Council for Inter-American Security, 1980).

A National Security Strategy for a New Century (Washington, D.C.: The White House, May 1997).

A Regional Integration Fund of the Free Trade Area of the Americas, ECLAC, LC/R 1738, 10 July, 1997.

Annual Report for 1991 (Washington, D.C.: Neill & Company).

Bovey, Freda. *Economic Impact of the Caribbean Basin Free Trade Area* (Washington, D.C.: International Trade Administration, U.S. Department of Commerce, March 1982).

Caribbean Banana Exporters Association U.S.-EU Dispute Targets Fragile Economies of the Caribbean (Washington, D.C.: The Caribbean Coalition, June 1, 1995).

Caribbean/Latin American Action, Annual Report 1999–2000 (Washington, D.C.: Caribbean/Latin American Action, 2000).

Carifta and the New Caribbean (Georgetown: Commonwealth Caribbean Regional Secretariat, 1971).

Census of Agriculture 1968–1969. Jamaica Final Report, Vol. 3, Part A (Kingston: Department of Statistics, 1974).

Central America in Crisis. A Programme for Action. (Washington, D.C.: Washington Institute for Values in Public Policy, 1983).

Communist Interference in El Salvador (Washington, D.C.: U.S. Department of State, Special Report No. 80, February 23, 1981).

Council on International Economic Policy, Special Report: Critical Imported Materials (Washington, D.C.: Government Printing Office, December 1977).

Diplomacy and Development: A Review of the Foreign Policy of Barbados (Bridgetown, Barbados: Ministry of Foreign Affairs, 1987).

Drug Certification and US Policy in Latin America (Washington, D.C.: The Woodrow Wilson International Center, The Latin American Program, April 1988).

Economic and Social Progress in Latin America. External Debt: Crisis and Adjustment (Washington, D.C.: Inter- American Development Bank, 1985).

Economic and Social Survey. Jamaica (Kingston: Planning Institute of Jamaica, various years).

Embassy of Jamaica Annual Report 1974 (Washington, D.C.: Embassy of Jamaica, 1974) page 1.

Feinberg, Richard. *Summitry in the Americas. A Progress Report* (Washington, D.C.: Institute of International Economies, 1997).

Fenton, Allison A., Trevor A. Jackson, and Dennis A. Minott. *Natural Resources, Assessment and Development: A Regional Study in CARICOM Territories.* (CARICOM Secretariat, July, 1984) pages 1–46.

Foreign Policy in the 21st Century. The U.S. Leadership Challenge (Washington, D.C.: Center for Strategic and International Studies, September, 1996).

Gill, Henry S., and Anthony P. Gonzales. *Economic Consequences of a Banana Collapse in the Caribbean.* Report prepared for the CARICOM Secretariat, May, 1995.

Global Challenge. *From Crisis to Cooperation: Breaking the North-South Stalemate* (London: Pan Books, 1985) pages 95–99.

Hallam, David, and Steve McCorriston. *"Fair Trade in Bananas?"* Agricultural Economics Unit, University of Exeter, December, 1992.

International Narcotics Control Strategy Report, April 1993 (Washington, D.C., United States Department of State, Bureau of International Narcotics Matters, April 1, 1993).

International Narcotics Control Strategy Report, April 1994 (Washington, D.C., United States Department of State, Bureau of International Narcotics Matters, April 1 1994).

International Narcotics Control Strategy Report, March 1995 (Washington, D.C., United States Department of State, Bureau of International Narcotics Matters, March 1995).

International Narcotics Control Strategy Report, March 1997 (Washington, D.C.: United States Department of State, Bureau of International Narcotics Matters, August 1997).

International Narcotics Control Strategy Report, Mid-Year Update, August 1989 (Washington, D.C., United States Department of State, Bureau of International Narcotics Matters, August, 1989).

International Narcotics Control Strategy Report, Mid-Year Update, March 1996 (Washington, D.C., United States Department of State, Bureau of International Narcotics Matters, March 1996).

Jamaica Socio-Economic Report, (Washington, D.C.: Inter-American Bank, July 1979), Vol. 1, page 49.

Latin American Market Report, 1982. *Master Plan for Sustainable Tourism Development Jamaica* (London: Commonwealth Secretariat, 2002).

National Coalition on Caribbean Affairs, *Creating New Strategies to Meet New Challenges* (Washington, D.C.: National Coalition on Caribbean Affairs , 1997).

1997 Caribbean Basin Profile, (Washington, D.C.: Caribbean Latin American Action/ Caribbean Publishing Co., 1996).

Open Markets Matter. The Benefits of Trade Liberalization (Paris: Organization for Economic Cooperation and Development, 1998).

Partnership for Prosperity and Security in the Caribbean, Bridgetown, Barbados, May 10, 1997.

Production Sharing: Use of U.S. Components and Materials in Foreign Assembly Operations, 1991–95 (Washington, D.C.: United States International Trade Commission, USITC Publication No. 2966, May 1996) pages 5-1 to 5-3.

Report of the CARICOM Secretariat, Caribbean/United States Summit, REP. 97/1/61 CAR/ US, Bridgetown, Barbados, November 4, 1997.

Report Submitted to the Committee on International Relations. Committee on Ways and Means of the U.S. House of Representatives and the Committee on Foreign Relations, Committee on Finance of the U.S. Senate by the Department of State, February 1995 (Washington, D.C.: Government Printing Office, 1995).

A Regional Integration Fund of the Free Trade Area of the Americas, ECLAC, LC/R 1738, 10 July, 1997.

Restructuring and the Loss of Preferences. Labour Challenges for the Caribbean Banana Industry (Geneva: International Labour Organization, January, 1999).

Rethinking International Drug Control: New Directions for US Policy, A Task Force Report by the Council on Foreign Relations (New York, NY: Council on Foreign Relations, February, 1997).

Rockefeller, Nelson. *The Rockefeller Report on the Americas: The Official Report of a United States Presidential Mission for the Western Hemisphere* (Chicago, 1969).

Roofed, David. *Geopolitics, Security and US Strategy in the Caribbean Basin*. A Project Air Force Report prepared for the United States Air Force (California: The Rand Corporation, 1983).

Second Report to Congress on the Operation of The Caribbean Basin Recovery Act (Washington, D.C.: United States Trade Representative, October 16, 1996) page 16–18.

Small States. Meeting the Challenges of the Global Economy (London and Washington, D.C.: Commonwealth Secretariat/ World Bank, 2000).

Structural Adjustment of the Jamaican Economy, 1982–1987 (Kingston: National Planning Agency, 1982).

Taylor, Timothy G., and Patrick A Antoine. *Banana Diversification. Major Issues and Constraints*, Report prepared for the Food and Agriculture Organization of the United Nations, 1996).

The Americas in a New World (Washington, D.C.: Inter-American Dialogue/Aspen Institute, 1990).

The Caribbean Community in the 1980s, Report by a Group of Experts (Georgetown: CARICOM Secretariat, 1981).

The Economic and Social Contribution of the Banana Industry in the OECS, Research and Information Department, Eastern Caribbean Central Bank, September, 1997.

The Economic Development of Latin America and Its Principal Problems (Santiago: United Nations Economic Commission of Latin America, 1950).

The Five Year Independence Plan, 1963–1968 (Kingston: Government Printer, 1965).

Towards Global Tax Co-operation. Report of the 2000 Ministerial Council Meeting and Recommendations by the Committee on Fiscal Affairs. (Paris: Organization for Economic Co-operation and Development, 2000).

Treaty Establishing the Caribbean Community, Chaguaramas, 4th July 1973 (Georgetown: Caribbean Community Secretariat, June 1987).

The US International Trade Commission Annual Report on the Impact of the Caribbean Basin Economic Recovery Act on US Industries and Consumers No. 2225 (Washington, D.C.: U.S. International Trade Commission, 1992).

Vulnerability: Small States in the Global Society (London: Commonwealth Secretariat, 1985).

World Bank, *Annual Report 1991* (Washington, D.C.: World Bank, 1992).

World Development Report 2000/2001 (Washington, D.C.: World Bank, 2001).

MAGAZINES

"AAMA Letter on NAFTA Parity for CBI," *Inside Nafta*, Vol. 3, No. 9, May 1, 1996.
"A Tidal Wave of Drugs," *Economist*, June 24, 2000.
Bartlett, Donald L., and James P. Steele. "How to Become a Top Banana," *Time*, February 7, 2000, page 49.
"Benefits for Poor People Face Deepest Budget Cuts," *New York Times*, February 14, 1981, page 30.
Bergsten, C. Fred. "A New OPEC in Bauxite," *Challenge* (July-August, 1976), pages 12–20.
Bernal, Richard L. "NAFTA Parity," *Latin Trade*, May, 1993.
———. "Next Stop, Caribbean Debt Relief," *International Economy*, Vol. 5, No. 4 (July/August 1991) pages 71–74.
Boothe, Cathy, and Tammerlin Drummond. "Caribbean Blizzard," *Time Magazine*, February 26, 1996.
Borosage, Robert. "Lonely Manely," *Mother Jones*, March-April, 1991, pages 26–29.
Calonius, Erik. "A Comeback in Jamaica," *Newsweek*, Vol. 113, Issue 8, 20 February, 1989, page 29.
"Caribbean Nations Warn US on Drug Cooperation after Banana Retaliation," *Inside US Trade*, Vol. 17, No. 11, March 12, 1999.
"Caribbean Vision and Nightmare," *New York Times*, Editorial, February 25, 1982.
Clarke, Jonathan. "The Conceptual Poverty of US Foreign Policy," *Atlantic Monthly*, September, 1993), pages 54–66.
Cohodas, Nadine. "Black House Members Striving for Influence," *Congressional Quarterly*, April 13, 1985, pages 675–81.
Cunningham, Kitty. "Black Caucus Flexes Muscle on Budget – and More," *Congressional Quarterly*, July 3, 1993, pages 1711–15.
De Borchgrave, Arnaud. "Cuba's Role in Jamaica," *Newsweek*, February 1977, pages 37–38.
Evans, Judith. "Big Mack Attack," *LatinFinance*, September 1997, pages 59–62.
Farnsworth, Clyde H. "Congressional Battles Seem Likely Over Aid Plan," *New York Times*, February 25, 1982.
Fox, John, and Nancy Fuior. "Bananasplit," *Mother Jones*, November/December, 1988, page 62.
Godsell, James Nelson. "U.S. Offers Marshall Plan to Caribbean to Check Soviets" *Christian Science Monitor*, June 5, 1981.
Greenfield, Karl Taro. "Banana Wars," *Time Magazine*, February 8, 1999.
Hughes, Ann H. "The Caribbean Basin Economic Renewal," *U.S. Department of Commerce, Business America*, Vol. 5, No. 5, 8 March 1996, page 20.
"In a Fiercely Hawkish Mood," *Time*, February 11, 1980, pages 16–17.
Isikoff, Michael, and Brook Larmer. "And Now, Bananagate?," *Newsweek*, April 28, 1997, pages 13–14.
Jacobs, Brenda A. "U.S. Moves to Control 807 Trade." *Bobbin*. June, 1995, pages 12–17.
"Jamaica, Free to Go Where?" *Economist*, August 11, 1962, page 519.
Kaplan, Arthur. Galaxy of Graphics, "Goodbye, Art," *Time*, February 7, 2000, page 56.
Krauthammer, Charles. "The Lonely Superpower" *The New Republic*, 29 July 1991, pages 23–27.
Larmer, Brook. "The Banana Wars," *Newsweek*, April 28, 1997.
Lewis, Charles, and Margaret Ebrahim. "Can Mexico and Big Business USA Buy NAFTA," *The Nation*, June 14, 1993, pages 826–39.
Massing, Michael. "Grenada Before and After," *The Atlantic Monthly*, February 1984, pages 75–87.

Mendora, Rick, and Sarah Acosta. "The D. C. Cash Flow," *Hispanic Business*, October 1993, pages 20–26.

Nichols, John Spicer. "The Power of the Anti-Fidel Lobby," *The Nation*, October 24, 1988, pages 389–91.

Ray, Ellen. "CIA and Local Gunmen Plan Jamaican Coup," *Counterspy*, Vol. 3, No. 2 (December, 1976).

Roberts, Steven V. "Aid Plan Generally Praised by Leaders of Both Parties," *New York Times*, February 25, 1982, page 6.

———. "Poll shows a Majority Want U.S. to Stay out of Salvador," *New York Times*, February 21, 1982, page 1.

"Ronald Reagan's Showcase," *Newsweek*, October 26, 1981, page 48.

Ruble, Nicolas S. "Think Tanks: Who's Hot and Who's Not," *The International Economy*, Vol. xiv, No. 5 (September/October, 2000) pages 10–16.

Samuels, Michael A. "Time for an Activist Export Policy," *Business America*, Vol. 5, No. 3 (8 February, 1982).

Shapiro, Harvey D. "America's Conservatives Close in on the World Bank," *Institutional Investor*, September 1981, pages 111–20.

"Small but Perfectly Formed," *Economist*, January 3, 1998.

Stanfield, Rochelle L. "Lobbyists for the Lowly," *National Journal*, April 8, 1990, pages 1882–86.

Stein, Jeff. "The Caribbean Connection," *GQ Magazine*, August, 1999, pages 164–71 and 209–11.

Stone, Peter H. "Cuban Clout," *National Journal*, February 20, 1993, pages 449–53.

Tarnoff, Peter. "An End to Foreign Policy. The Need to Reconcile Foreign and Domestic Strategies," *Harvard International Review*, Vol. XIV, No. 4 (Summer, 1992).

"The Carousels of Power," *The Economist*, May 25, 1991, pages 23–26.

Tondson, Alan. "What Is the National Interest?" *The Atlantic Monthly*, July 1991, pages 35–81.

Wallerstein, Immanuel. "The Incredible Shrinking Eagle, The End of Pax Americana," *Foreign Policy*, July-August 2002, pages 60–68.

Weisman, Stephen R. "The Mugs That Weren't There," *Newsweek*, November 19, 1994, pages 8–11.

———. "The Struggle for Backing on Strategy in Salvador," *New York Times*, March 14, 1982, Section 4, page 1.

"What the PM said," *Jamaica Observer*, July 3, 2000, page 9.

Whichard, Obie G. "US Direct Investment abroad in 1976," *Survey of Current Business*, US Department of State, Vol. 57, No. 8 (August 1977) pages 32–55.

Wills, Garry. "Late Bloomer," *Time Magazine*, April 23, 1990, pages 28–34.

NEWSPAPERS

Adams, James, and Jaimie Seaton. "Washington goes bananas over Britain's colonial fruit run," *London Sunday Times*, April 9, 1995.

Alden, Edward. "US and EU still split on beef and bananas," *Financial Times*, December 19, 2000.

———. "US carousel sanctions are ready to spin," *Financial Times*, July 13, 2000.

Alden, Edward, and Christopher Bowe. "Chiquita sues Brussels over losses caused by banana import curbs," *Financial Times*, January 26, 2001.

Archibald, George. "Banana baron peeled off half a mil. White House paid back in WTO fight," *Washington Times*, August 25, 1997.

———. "Did Democrats trade WTO help for 500k skins from banana king?" *The Washington Times*, August 25, 1997.

Ashante Infantry, "No one has swagger like Jamaicans," *Toronto Star*, June 16, 2014.

Baker, Gerard. "The future of America: Liberty's triumph." *Financial Times*, December 23, 1999.

References 413

"Banana Republic," *Washington Post*, October 26, 2000.
"Banana split," Editorial, *Financial Times*, December 18, 1998.
"Banana trade vital to Caribbean," *The Journal of Commerce*, February 3, 1999.
Beard, David. "In Jamaica, they'll have no bananas," *Sun Sentinel*, March 29, 1998.
"Benefits for poor people face deepest budget cuts," *New York Times*, February 14, 1981.
Bernal, Richard L. "Caribbean nations need NAFTA, too," *Washington Times*, October 1, 1993.
———. "Fighting a banana battle now will mean US will lose lots of trade later," *Washington Times*, August 24, 1995.
———. "A Jamaican's case for trade parity with NAFTA," *Wall Street Journal*, March 22, 1996, page A13.
———. "Jobs for the US, jobs for the Caribbean," *International Business Chronicle*, March 29-April 11, 1993, page 23.
———. "Parity for the Caribbean," *Journal of Commerce*, July 2, 1997. September 18 & 19, 1987.
———. "A US-Caribbean tax lifeline." *Journal of Commerce*, April 16, 1993.
———. "A way out of the Caribbean debt trap," *Washington Post*, November 5, 1991
———. "Why Caribbean nations need parity with NAFTA," *The Miami Herald*, February 4, 1993.
———. "WTO Banana case, friendly fire hits Caribbean," *Journal of Commerce*, April 24, 1997.
Best, Tony. "The Caribbean, bananas and the OAS," *New York, Carib News*, week ending June 24, 1997.
———. "CARICOM and Black Caucus set course for close relationship," *CaribNews*, November 21, 2000.
———. "U.S. Congress rejects NAFTA parity," *Carib News*, November 18, 1997.
Bohning, Don. "U.S. relations with Caribbean under strain," *Miami Herald*, October 27, 1998.
Broder, David S. "Gephardt warns against trade pact with Chile." *Washington Post*, March 14, 1995.
Buchanan, Patrick J. "Now that red is dead, come home America," *Washington Post*, 8 September 1991.
Bumiller, Elizabeth. "The caucus & the cause," *Washington Post*, September 20, 1982.
Callejas, Rafael Leonardo. "Prosperity for the americas," *Journal of Commerce*, February 3, 1991.
"Caribbean disturbance," Editorial, *The Miami Herald*, August 10, 1998.
"Caribbean growers' lobby goes bananas," *The Washington Times*, April 16, 1997.
"Caribbean Vision and Nightmare," *New York Times*, Editorial, February 25, 1982.
"Chiquita shares on debt woe," *Financial Times*, January 17, 2001.
"Clinton lied," *The Daily Gleaner*, March 19, 1999.
Constantine, Gus. "Caribbean nations hurt by banana dispute threaten to retaliate," *Washington Times*, March 9, 1999.
Cooper, Helene. "Dole fails to find much appeal in accord to end to Banana War." *Wall Street Journal*, April 13, 2001.
Dalley, George A. "C'bean leaders contribute to the passage of CBI," *Carib News*, May 23, 2000.
———. "NAFTA parity: Caribbean must hold Congress responsible, *Carib News* week ending November 18, 1997, page 5.
de Jonquieres, Guy and Nancy Dunne. "A partnership in peril," *Financial Times*, March 8, 1999.
De Palma, Anthony. "Citing European banana quotas, Chiquita says bankruptcy looms," *New York Times*, January 17, 2001.
———. "U.S. and Europeans agree on deal to end banana trade war," *New York Times*, April 12, 2001.

Dove, Timothy. Action Battery, "Hit by a $200,000 bill from the blue," *Time*, February, February 7, 2000.

Emling, Shelley. "Hills to hear Central Americans; Trade pact fears," *Journal of Commerce*, August 1991.

"End the Cold War against Cuba," *Journal of Commerce*, February 9, 1993.

"The EU and US go bananas," Editorial, *Financial Times*, November 11, 1998.

Evans, Roy. "WTO approves US sanctions," *Journal of Commerce*, April 20, 1999.

Farah, Douglas. "Caribbean key to US drug trade," *Washington Post*, 23 September 1996.

———. "Double identity." *Washington Post*. February 17, 1998.

———. "Drug corruption over the top," *Washington Post*, February 17, 1998.

———. "Russian mob, drug cartels joining forces," *Washington Post*, September 29, 1997.

Farnsworth, Clyde H. "Congressional battles seem likely over aid plan," *New York Times*, February 25, 1982.

Faul, Michelle. "Albright advises islands to hit drugs," *Washington Times*, April 7, 1998.

Fineman, Mark. "Lone superpower's shadow darkens the frustration of caribbean nations" *Los Angeles Times*, 8th July 1998.

"Florida business leaders still wary with new manley," *Miami Times*, May 11, 1989.

Frantz, Douglas. "Chiquita still under a cloud after newspaper's retreat," *New York Times*, July 17, 1998.

Gallagher, Mike, and Cameron McWhirther. "Chiquita: An empire built on controversy," *Cincinnati Enquirer*, May 3, 1998.

Godsell, James Nelson. "U.S. offers marshall plan to Caribbean to check Soviets" *Christian Science Monitor*, June 5, 1981.

Greenhouse, Steven. "New calls to lift embargo on Cuba," *New York Times*, February 20, 1993.

———. "Third wrld's rapid growth gives a lift to U.S. economy," *New York Times*, 19 August, 1993.

Guzowski, Samuel. "Aid plus trade equals relief," *Journal of Commerce*, April 2, 1999.

Hakim, Peter. "US drug certification process is in serious need of reform," *Christian Science Monitor*, March 27, 1997.

Hakim, Peter, and Moses Naim. "The case for trading with cuba," *Journal of Commerce*, December 30, 1994.

Heath, Edward. "Seizing the moment in the Caribbean," *Times* (London), December 10, 1980.

Herbert, Bob. "Banana bully," *New York Times*, May 13, 1996.

"How to become a top banana," *Time*, February 7, 2000.

Ignatius, David. "Rooting out dirty money," *Washington Post*, May 31, 2000.

"Importers go bananas over sanctions on EU trade," *Journal of Commerce*, March 5, 1999.

Isikoff, Michael. "Jamaican urges anti-drug force," *Washington Post*, June 11, 1989.

James, Canute. "Caribbean leaders ask Canada for assistance in banana dispute," *Journal of Commerce*, March 11, 1996.

———. "Caribbean lose patience with US over banana row," *Financial Times*, July 13, 1995.

———. "Caribbean, US blame each other in banana split," *Journal of Commerce*, December 15, 1997.

———. "Clinton backs preferences for Caribbean bananas," *Journal of Commerce*, June 20, 1995.

———. "Drugs tide rises around the Caribbean," *Financial Times*, October 25, 1996.

———. "US banana move shocks Caribbean," *Financial Times*, April 30, 1996.

James, Canute, and George Parker. "U.S. faces Caribbean threat to quit drugs treaty" *Financial Times*, March 8, 1999.

Juday, Dave. "Lift the embargo," Editorial, *Wall Street Journal*, August 26, 1994.

Kirkpatrick, Jeane. "Caribbean, Central America - U.S. 'fourth border,'" *Daily Gleaner*, March 3, 1982.

Knight, Franklin W. "Caribbean diplomacy in Washington," *Jamaica Observer*, January 24, 2007.

Koppel, Naomi. "Banana dispute deadlocks US, EU," *Washington Times*, January 26, 1999.

Kovaleski, Serge F., and Douglas Farah. "Organized crime exercises clout in island nations," *Washington Post*, February 17, 1998.

Lamb, Christina. "US action on bananas a nightmare for islands," *Washington Times*, March 16, 1999.

Lande, Stephen, and Ambler Moss. "Give Central America a trade break," *Journal of Commerce*, February 24, 1999.

Lawrence, Richard. "Plan to extend NAFTA-like benefits to Caribbean backed in Congress," *The Journal of Commerce*, February 13, 1995, page 3.

Lee, Gary. "Crime in the Caribbean: A reality check," *Washington Post*, April 8, 2001.

Liu, Betty. "Presidential rivals feel the power of Hispanic voters," *Financial Times*, October 4, 2000.

Machalaba, Daniel. "Even legitimate ships are falling victim to drug smugglers," *Wall Street Journal*, May 24, 1989.

Maggs, John. "In banana dispute, discretion gives way to politics," *Journal of Commerce*, May 2, 1995.

Marquis, Christopher. "Bananas or drugs, Caribbean tells US," *Miami Herald*, June 13, 1996.

Martin, Larry. "A humanitarian trade bill," *Journal of Commerce*, May 2, 1999.

McLarty, Mack, and Jim Kolbe. "Central America needs help, not handouts," *Journal of Commerce*, March 16, 1999.

McLarty, Thomas F. III. "Trade means good jobs for Americans," *Washington Post*, September 15, 1997.

McWhirther, Cameron, and Mike Gallagher. "Influence: 'This is just money politics,'" *Cincinnati Enquirer*, May 3, 1998.

Morgan, Dan. "Think tanks: Corporations' quiet weapon," *Washington Post*, January 29, 2000.

Morgan, Jeremy. "Give Castro a carrot," *New York Times*, February 17, 1994.

"NAFTA vote exposes false friends," editorial, *Carib News*, November 18, 1997, page 4.

Navarro, Mireya. "Outpost in bananas and marijuana wars," *New York Times*, March 4, 1999.

"New opportunity for Investment: Jamaica 1982," Jamaica Government Advertisement, *Wall Street Journal*, February 19, 1982.

"The "new" Jamaica," Editorial, *Washington Times*, May 23, 1989.

Ogletree, Charles, and Randall Robinson. "The banana war's missing link – campaign funding," *Christian Science Monitor*, March 31, 1999.

O'Leary, Jeremiah. "Bush, Black Caucus meet, open way for cooperation," *Washington Times*, May 24, 1989.

Olson, Elizabeth. "Banana talks with Europe turn nasty," *The New York Times*, January 26, 1999.

Oppenheimer, Andres. "US target: Banks holding dirty money," *Miami Herald*, March 26, 2000.

Peale, Cliff. "Report blasts Chiquita's Honduran links" *Washington Post*, November 21, 1996.

Pear, Robert. "Jamaican criticizes Panama invasion," *New York Times*, January 30, 1990.

Rangel, Charles. "Will dispute squash banana growers?" *Washington Times*, February 16, 1999.

Reich, Robert B. "Trading insecurities," *Financial Times*, May 20, 1999.

Reston, James. "Cuban expansion," *New York Times*, March, 1977.

Roberts, Michael D. "Caribbean-American lobbying group meets with Clinton's special envoy at White House" *Carib News*, July 6, 1999.

———. "Lobbying Washington on Caribbean issues: Historic first" *Carib News*, July 6, 1999.

Roberts, Steven V. "Aid plan generally praised by leaders of both parties," *New York Times*, February 25, 1982.

———. "Poll shows a majority want U.S. to stay out of Salvador," *New York Times*, February 21, 1982.

Roberts, William. "Bipartisan group of Senators press for Caribbean economic package," *Journal of Commerce*, February 4, 1999.

Rodriguez, Angel Miguel, "After Hurricane Mitch," *Washington Post*, November 24, 1998.

Rogers, David. "House approves $21.5 billion bill on energy and water," *Wall Street Journal*, May 30, 1991.

"Ronald Reagan's showcase," *Newsweek*, October 26, 1981, page 48.

Safire, William. "Bananagate," *New York Times*, March 26, 1997.

Scully, Sean. "Minorities gain ground on whites in 2000 census, Hispanics pass blacks in population," *The Washington Times*, March 13, 2001.

Shoup, Mike. "State Department changes its way of warning travelers," *Baltimore Sun*, November 22, 1992.

Sinclair, Glenroy. "Drug busts on the ports," *Daily Gleaner*, December 4, 1997.

Smith, Wayne. "Don't isolate Cuba – Open It to New Ideas," *Christian Science Monitor*, August 25, 1994.

Stone, Carl. "Buying power," *Weekly Gleaner*, April 28, 1987.

Taylor Martin, Susan. "Banana war squeezes tiny Dominica," *The Washington Times*, April 15, 1997.

Thurow, Lester C. "When trade partners go bananas, don't ease up; get tough," *USA Today*, March 31, 1999.

"The U.S. and EU go bananas," *Financial Times*, November 11, 1998.

"U.S. issues warnings for trips to Jamaica, Mexico," *Chicago Tribune*, 8 September 1991. articles.chicagotribune.com/1991. . . /travel/9103070805_. Accessed 27 September, 2014.

Walker, Ian. "Caribbean finds itself in US trade deal slow lane," *Financial Times*, February 11, 1992.

Weisman, Steven R. "The struggle for backing on strategy in Salvador," *New York Times*, 1.

Wemple, Erik. "Washington Times columnist: Originality deficit?," *Washington Post*. 2012. Retrieved July 21, 2014. March 14, 1982, Section 4, page 1.

"What in the world? A debate over America's responsibilities as the lone superpower" *US News & World Report*, April 24, 2000.

Whitefield, Mimi. "Basin plan cuts worry White House," *Daily Gleaner*, May 14, 1982, page 1.

Wickham, DeWayne. "Banana wars: Give Caribbean a break," *USA Today*, May 15, 1995.

Williams, Frances. "Island growers spike US sanctions move," *Financial Times*, January 26, 1999.

Winestock, Geoff. "U.S. starts a fight with Dole Food Co. in the banana war," *Wall Street Journal*, Monday, October 9, 2000.

Yeutter, Clayton. "The Banana battlements," *Washington Times*, August 7, 1995.

Zaldivar, R. A. "Jamaican leader urges global anti-drug squad," *Miami Herald*, June 10, 1989.

Zimbalist, Andrew. "The great US-Cuba embargo debate (cont'd). Ease tensions," *Miami Herald*, March 23, 1994.

LETTERS

"Dear Colleague" Letter, "A Trade War? Over Bananas?" from Representatives Maxine Waters, David Bonior, Marcy Kaptur, Carrie Meek, Carolyn Maloney, and Peter Defazio, March 18, 1999.

Letter from Ambassador Richard Bernal to Hon. Edolphus Towns, U.S. House of Representatives, July 20, 1992.

Letter from Ambassador Richard Bernal to Hon. Robert Graham, U.S. Senate, July 9, 1992.

Letter from Manuel Esquivel, Prime Minister of Belize and Chairman of CARICOM to Mickey Kantor, U.S. Trade Representative, March 21, 1995.

Letter from Nicholas Brady and James Baker III to Thomas Foley, Speaker, U.S. House of Representatives, July 1992.

Letter from President William Clinton to Congresswoman Maxine Waters, December 12, 1997.

Letter from President William Clinton to Congressman Peter A. DeFazio, December 12, 1997.

Letter from Prime Minister P. J. Patterson to President William J. Clinton, June 2, 1997.

Letter from the Congressional Black Caucus to President Clinton, October 22, 1997.

Letter to Ambassador Charlene Barshefsky from Senator Paul D. Coverdell and Representative Saxby Chambliss, September 9, 1998.

Letter to Ambassador Dr. Richard L. Bernal from Representative Carrie Meek, Member of Congress, September 27, 1994.

Letter to Ambassador Richard Bernal from Carl T. C. Gutierrez, Governor of Guam, March 11, 1999.

Letter to Ambassador Richard Bernal from Peter Allgeier, Associate U.S. Trade Representative for the Western Hemisphere, February 7, 1996.

Letter to Ambassador Richard L. Bernal from Congressman Bill Archer, October 17, 1995.

Letter to Ambassador Richard L. Bernal from Lloyd Bentsen. Secretary of the Treasury, October 5, 1994.

Letter to Charlene Barshefsky, USTR from Congresswoman Maxine Waters, March 5, 1999.

Letter to Congressman Ben Gilman from Gary K. Smith, President of the American Uniform Company, February 2, 1999.

Letter to Congressman Charles Rangel from Charlene Barshefsky, USTR, June 23, 1997.

Letter to Hazel Ross-Robinson by Amy Musher, *Time* Magazine, February 18, 1999.

Letter to Janice Oliver, Acting Deputy Director for Systems and Support, U.S. Food and Drug Administration from Richard Bernal, Ambassador of Jamaica to the United States, August 13, 1993.

Letter to Mr. Aaron T. Manaigo, Chairman, National Council of Black Republicans, March 11, 1999.

Letter to Mr. Don Logan, Chairman, CEO Time Magazine by Hazel Ross-Robinson, February 10, 1999.

Letter to Ms. Rose Lanam, President, Jamaica Awareness Association in Los Angeles from Ambassador Richard Bernal, March 15, 1990.

Letter to President Clinton, from 40 Members of Congress - See appendix 3, July 31, 1997.

Letter to President Clinton, November 6, 1996, from Bill Cosby, Earl Graves, Bob Johnson, Ed Lewis, Jesse Jackson, Joseph Lowery, Susan Taylor and Danny Glover.

Letter to President William Clinton by Maxine Waters, Ronald Dellums, Marcy Kaptur, Duncan Hunter, Roscoe Bartlett, June 9, 1997.

Letter to President William Clinton from Donald G. Morgan, President of the Jamaica Volunteers Association, November 13, 1998.

Letter to President William Clinton from 40 Members of Congress including Maxine Waters, Charles Rangel, Marcy Kaptur, J. C. Watts, Sheila Jackson Lee, David Bonior, Ed Towns, John Lewis, and Joseph P. Kennedy II.

Letter to President William Clinton from Newt Gingrich and Trent Lott, October 9, 1998, *Inside U.S. Trade*, Vol. 16, No. 40, October 9, 1998.

Letter to the Editor by Richard Bernal, "Bananas and Drugs," *Washington Post*, October 23, 1999.

Letter to the Editor of the *Washington Post* from Donald G. Morgan, President of the Jamaica Volunteers Association, December 3, 1998.

Letter to the Governors of all states from Ambassador Richard L. Bernal, February 22, 1999.

Letter to Hon. Michael Kantor, Secretary of Commerce from the Ambassadors of the ESC Banana Exporting Countries, April 16, 1996.

DISSERTATIONS

Bernal, Richard L. "The Political Economy of IMF Programs in Jamaica 1977–1984." (Doctoral Dissertation, New School for Social Research, May 1988).

Palmer, Annette Catherine. "The United States and the Commonwealth Caribbean: 1940–45" (Unpublished Ph. D. thesis, Fordham University, 1979) page 29.

EMBASSY OF JAMAICA FILES

Ackee File, Part I, July 1972-November 1974, Embassy of Jamaica.

Ackee File, Part II. April 1999, Embassy of Jamaica.

Background on Jamaican Counter-narcotics Efforts, Embassy of Jamaica and Jefferson Waterman International February 3, 1997.

Briefing Book, Visit of the Hon. Prime Minister of Jamaica to Washington, D.C., August 26–31, 1993, (Embassy of Jamaica, Washington, D.C., August 25, 1993).

CBI files. Embassy of Jamaica.

Congressional/Administration Action Matrix (Washington, D.C.: Neill and Company, April 1, 1991).

Embassy of Jamaica Annual Report 1974 (Washington, D.C.: Embassy of Jamaica, 1974).

Embassy of Jamaica files, Jamaica's Debt Reduction Under the EAI, August 1991.

Embassy of Jamaica files, Memorandum from George Dalley to Hugh Small, Minister of Finance, June 24, 1992.

Embassy of Jamaica Files, Third World Debt, May 1988.

Embassy of Jamaica Telegram No. 141, August 9, 1972.

Embassy of Jamaica, Report of the Western Hemisphere Banana Meeting, Coral Gables, Miami, April 9, 1996.

Files from Jefferson Waterman, Inc.

Files of the Embassy of Jamaica, Washington, D.C.

Neill & Company, Jamaica's Annual Report 1991 (Washington, D.C.: 1992).

Summary of Accomplishments of Neill and Company on behalf of Jamaica, 1st Session, 103rd Congress, 1994.

The Official Working Visit to Washington, D.C. of the Right Honorable Michael Manley, Prime Minister of Jamaica, May 2 to May 4, 1990. Files of Neill and Company.

Work Plan for 1993, Neill and Company.

INTERVIEWS

Interview with Dorrell Callender, September 2014.
Interview with Andrew Young, August 3, 2002.
Interview with Anne Sabo, October 12, 2000.
Interview with Denis Neill, August 12, 2001.
Interview with Denis Neill, August 12, 2001.
Interview with Senator Dudley Thompson, October 18, 2000.
Interview with Robert A. Pastor at the Carter Center, Atlanta, August 5, 1994.

OTHER

Agreement Establishing the Multilateral Investment Fund/Agreement for the Administration of the Multilateral Investment Fund (Washington, D.C.: Inter-American Development Bank, February 1992).

All of these organizations submitted statements to Congressional Hearings, see *Hearing before the Subcommittee on Trade of the Committee on Ways and Means*, House of Representatives, One Hundred Fourth Congress, First Session, February 10, 1995 (Washington, D.C.: Government Printing Office, 1995) page 203.

All of these organizations submitted statements to Congressional Hearings, see *Hearing before the Subcommittee on Trade of the Committee on Ways and Means*, House of Representatives, One Hundred Fourth Congress, First Session, February 10, 1995 (Washington, D.C.: Government Printing Office, 1995).

A New Inter-American Policy for the Eighties (Washington, D.C.: Council for Inter-American Security, 1980) page 46.

Annual Report for 1991 (Washington, D.C.: Neill and Company, 1992).

Appointments Diary of Ambassador Dr. Richard L. Bernal, 1997.

The Banana Agreement: Opportunity and Challenge for the Caribbean, Press Release, Congressman Charles Rangel, U.S. House of Representatives, Washington, D.C., April 13, 2001.

Bandow, Doug. "Rethinking U.S. Foreign Aid," *Heritage Foundation Backgrounder No. 653* (Washington, D.C.: the Heritage Foundation, June 1, 1998).

Basedeo, Sahadeo, and Graeme Mount. *The Foreign Relations of Trinidad and Tobago, 1962–2000. The Case of a Small State in the Global Arena* (Port of Spain: Lexicon Trinidad, 2001).

Bernal, Richard L. Impact of NAFTA on the Apparel Industry in the Caribbean. Address to the Miami Conference, December 2, 1992.

Bernal, Richard L., and Pamela Coke Hamilton. "Region seeks to redress apparel issue," Hemisfile, Vol. 8, No. 2 (March/April, 1997) pages 3–4.

Borrell, Brent, and Yang Maw-Cheng. *"EC Bananarama 1992: The Sequel,"* Washington, D.C., World Bank, Working Paper, No. 958, 1992.

———. "EC Bananarama 1992," Washington, D.C., World Bank, Working Paper No. 523, 1990.

Borrell, Brent. *"EU Bananarama III,"* Washington, D.C., World Bank, Policy Research Working Paper, No. 1388, 1994.

Bovey, Freda. *Economic Impact of the Caribbean Basin Free Trade Area* (Washington, D.C.: International Trade Administration, U.S. Department of Commerce, March 1982).

Brown, Lester. *"The Global Politics of Resource Scarcity."* Testimony to Sub-Committee on Foreign Economic Policy, House Committee on Foreign Affairs, 93rd Congress, 1974, page 247.

Bryan, Anthony. *Transnational Crime* (Miami: North-South Centre, University of Miami, 2000).

———. "U.S.-Caribbean Relations Strained Over U.S.-European Banana Dispute," North South Center Update, October 3, 1999.

Burning Spear. 100th Anniversary (Island Records, 1976), Social Living (Island Records, 1980), and Hail H. I. M. (Heartbeat, 1994).

Caribbean Banana Exporters Association, U.S.-E.U. Dispute Targets Fragile Economies of the Caribbean, The Caribbean Coalition.

Caribbean Development Strategy and Private Enterprise. Speech by Rt. Hon. Edward Seaga, Prime Minister of Jamaica (Kingston: Jamaica Information Service, April 1982), pages 11 and 3.

Caribbean Division, International Trade Administration, U.S. Department of Commerce, reported in Ann H. Hughes, "The Caribbean Basin Economic Renewal: New Opportunities for American Business," *Business America*, Vol. 5, No. 5, March 8, 1982, page 19.

"Caribbean Nations Ask U.S. to Abandon Harmful Trade Proceeding," *The Caribbean Coalition*, Washington, D.C., March 22, 1995.

Carifta and the New Caribbean (Georgetown: Commonwealth Caribbean Regional Secretariat, 1971).

"Chiquita's Brand of Doing Business in Honduras," *COHA Occasional Paper*, Vol. 1, No. 3, November 1996.

Christopher, Warren. Statement of Secretary of State before the Senate Finance Committee, 15 September 1993.

Comments made to Ambassador Bernal by several State Department officials on many occasions.

Committee Approves Debt-for-Environment Swaps. News Release. Committee on Agriculture. U.S. House of Representatives, July 1, 1992.

Communique, Miami Conference on the Caribbean (Washington, D.C.: Caribbean Latin American Action, 1993).

Confidential Memorandum, Update on Narcotics from Ann Wrobleski, George Dallet, and Steve Lamar to Ambassador Richard L. Bernal, February 21, 1997.

Confidential notes of Ambassador Richard Bernal.

Congressional/Administration Action Matrix (Washington, D.C.: Neill & Company, April 1, 1991).

Dominguez, Jorge I. The Caribbean in a New International Context: Are Freedom and Peace a Threat to Its Prosperity? Presented at the North South Center, Miami, September, 1993.

Economic and Social Survey. Jamaica (Kingston: Planning Institute of Jamaica, various years).

Enterprise for the Americas Initiative, *A Vision for Economic Growth in the Western Hemisphere*, February 1992.

European Institute, Washington, D.C., April, 2001.

Fact Sheet: *Caribbean Basin Policy* (U.S. Department of State, February 1982).

Feinberg, Richard E. "Substantive Symmetry in Hemisphere Relations," *U.S. Department of State Dispatch*, Vol. 5, No. 11 (March 14, 1994).

Fenton, Allison A., Trevor A. Jackson, and Dennis A. Minott. Natural Resources, Assessment and Development: A Regional Study in CARICOM Territories. Report prepared for the CARICOM Secretariat (July, 1984) pages 1–46.

Files from Jefferson Waterman Inc.

Files of Neill & Company and various reports to the government of Jamaica from Neill and Company.

FinCEN Advisory, *United States Department of the Treasury Financial Crimes Enforcement Network*, Issue No. 13. July 2000.

The Governor of Guam assured the Ambassador that "in my interaction at the National Governors' Association, I will be sensitized to the unique needs of the Caribbean." Letter to Ambassador Richard Bernal from Carl T. C. Guitierrez, Governor of Guam, March 11, 1999.

Graham, Tracey E. *Jamaican Migration to Cuba, 1912–1940*, Doctoral Dissertation, Department of History, University of Chicago, March 2013.

Grimmett, Richard F. *War Powers Resolution: Presidential Compliance, Congress Research Service,* Issue Brief No. 81050 (Washington, D.C.: Congressional Research Service, April 19, 1999).

Haig, Alexander. *Official Text of Address by Secretary of State to the Organization of American States,* Castries, Saint Lucia, 4 December 1981.

Harker, Trevor. *Caribbean Integration in the Changing Global Context, Economic Commission for Latin American and the Caribbean,* (WP/19/3, 31 October 1991).

Henderson Tyson, Carole and Daniel J. Seyler. "US Foreign Aid to the Caribbean in the 1980's" in Mark Sullivan (ed.), *The Caribbean Basin: Economic and Security Issues, Study Papers submitted to the Joint Economic Committee, Congress of the United States,* (Washington, D.C.: U.S. Government Printing Office, January 1993) pages 42–64.

Hughes, Ann H. The Caribbean Basin Economic Renewal. *U.S. Department of Commerce, Business America, Vol. 5, No. 5,* (8 March 1982) page 20.

Jamaica Scope Paper. 22 June 1962, page 1. Archives of the Kennedy Presidential Library.

Jamaica-Geert Hofstede. http://geert-hofstede.com/jamaica.html. Accessed February 24, 2015.

Jamaican Prime Minister Proposing International Anti-Drug Strike Force. Media Advisory for August 18, 1989, Fenton Communications, Washington, D.C.

The JLP government of Seaga has a foreign policy that was outlined by the late JLP leader and Prime Minister Alexander Bustamante in 1962. He stated: "I am for the West. I am against communism." See Jamaica Hansard, November 7, 1962, page 87.

Kantor, Michael. "Trade Central to America's Future in the World" *U.S. Department of State Dispatch,* Vol. 4, No. 20 (May 17, 1993).

Kantor, Mickey. U.S. Trade Policy and the Post-Cold War World, *Department of State Dispatch,* Vol. 4, No. 11 (15 March 1993).

"Latin American and Caribbean Lobbying for International Trade in Washington, D.C." *United Nations Commission on Latin America and the Caribbean* (ECLAC) LC/G. 1632. LC/WAS/L. 9, June 29, 1990.

"Latins to Seek WTO Panel on EU Banana Regime This Month," *Inside U.S. Trade,* April 12, 1996.

Maingot, Anthony "The Decentralization Imperative and Caribbean Criminal Enterprises" in Tom Farer (eds.), *Transnational Crime in the Americas:* (New York: Routledge, 1999) pages 42–170.

"The Manley/Levitt Exchange," Small Axe, No. 1 (1997) page 2.

Manley, Michael. *"Address to Parliament,"* May 1974.

———. *Jamaica's New Economic Direction* (Kingston: Jamaica Information Services, September 16, 1990).

———. *Not For Sale, Address by Hon. Michael Manley, Prime Minister of Jamaica, at the 38th Annual Conference of the People's National Party, September 19, 1976* (San Francisco: Editoral Consultants, 1976).

———. *Our Movement Is Irreversible Because Our Cause Is Just, Speech at the Sixth Summit of the Non-Aligned in Havana, Cuba, September 4, 1979* (Kingston Agency for Public Information, 1979).

Members Guide 1997 (Kingston: The American Chamber of Commerce of Jamaica, 1997).

Memorandum from Secretary of State Dean Rusk to President John F. Kennedy re Call by Norman Manley, Premier of Jamaica, 19 April, 1961, page 1. Courtesy of the John F. Kennedy Library.

Memorandum for the President. Secretary of State. Visit of Premier of Jamaica. 3 April, 1961, page 1. Courtesy of the John F. Kennedy Library.

Memorandum to McGeorge Bundy, White House from William H. Brubeck, State Department, Visit of Sir Alexander Bustamante, Premier of Jamaica, 26 June, 1962, page 2. Courtesy of the John F. Kennedy Library.

Miller, Doreen. An Introduction to Jamaican Culture for Rehabilitation Services Providers, Center for International Rehabilitation Research Information and Exchange,

2002. http://cirrie. buffalo.edu/culture/monographs/jamaica/. Accessed 12 August 2014.

Mulford, David C. *A Blueprint for Economic Expansion from Alaska to Antarctica, Heritage Lectures, No. 375* (Washington, D.C.: Heritage Foundation, 1992).

1994 CLAA Retreat. *List of Participants* (Washington, D.C.: Caribbean Latin American Action, 1994).

Nixon, Richard M. "Action for Progress for the Americas," *Department of State Bulletin, Vol. 61, No. 1586*, (November 17, 1969) pages 409–14.

Notes of Ambassador Bernal, January 1997.

Office of Press Secretary. *Remarks by the President in an Address to the Council of Americas Dinner*, Washington, D.C., White House, 23 April, 1992.

Patterson, Percival James. "None But Ourselves," *Budget Presentation 1991/92*, May 9, 1991, page 8.

"The possibility of an exception to the systemically related polar opposites of development and underdevelopment was espoused" by Bill Warren, *Imperialism. Pioneer of Capitalism* (London: Verso, 1981).

Press Statement of Prime Ministers of the Windward Islands, Panama and Belize, November 11, 1998.

Principles and Objectives. *People's National Party* (Kingston: People's National Party, 1970).

Public Papers of the Presidents of the United States, Harry S. Truman, 1947 (Washington, D.C.: Government Printing Office, 1960).

Quick, Stephen A. "The International Economy and the Caribbean: The 1990s and Beyond," *The Caribbean Basin: Economic and Security Issues Joint Economic Committee Print* (S. Print 102–10), (Washington, D.C.: Government Printing Office, January 1993).

Reagan, Ronald. *Official text of an Address by the President to the Organization of American States*, Washington, D.C., February 24, 1982, (United States International Communication Agency, 1982).

Remarks by president-elect, Bill Clinton, to the Annual Conference on Trade, Investment and Development in the Caribbean Basin, Miami, Florida, December 2, 1992.

Remarks by the President to the Wall Street Project Conference, The White House, Office of the Press Secretary, January 15, 1998.

"Report on the Impact of the United States Challenge to the European Union Banana Regime on Political, Economic and Social Order in the Caribbean, and the Consequences for U.S. National Interests," *Eminent Persons Group*, Mission to Jamaica, Dominica and St. Lucia, January 1997.

Rogers, Kenneth N. Political Officer, U.S. Embassy, Kingston (1968–1972). The Association for Diplomatic Studies and Training Foreign Affairs Oral History Project. Jamaica Country Readers, adst. org/wp-content/uploads/2012/09/. Accessed 28 August 2014.

Scott, Robert E. *NAFTA's Hidden Costs. Trade Agreement results in job losses, growing inequality and wage suppression for the United States* (Washington, D.C.: Economic Policy Institute, 2001).

———. *North American Trade after NAFTA. Rising Deficits, Disappearing Jobs* (Washington, D.C.: Economic Policy Institute, 1996).

———. *Rebuilding the Caribbean. A Better Foundation for Sustainable Growth* (Washington, D.C.: Economic Policy Institute, 2000).

Seaga, Edward. *Speech to the Annual Meeting of the Council of the Americas.* New York, December 5, 1980.

Second Report to Congress on the Operation of the Caribbean Basin Economic Recovery Act of 1990 (Washington, D.C.: United States Trade Representative, October 10, 1996).

Speaking Notes. Ambassador Richard Bernal at Media Luncheon, the National Press Club, June 12, 1992 at 12:30 P. M.

Speech by Ambassador Fletcher at Business Luncheon in New York, October 25, 1972.

Speech by Honorable Michael Manley Prime Minister of Jamaica at Howard University, 10th August 1972, page 22.

Sutton, Eric. *Forged From the Love of Liberty – Selected Speeches of Dr. Eric Williams.* Compiled by Dr. Paul K. Sutton (Longman Caribbean, 1981).

Sweeney, John P. "The High Cost of Clinton's Trade War with the European Union," *Executive Memorandum, No. 584*, Washington, D.C., The Heritage Foundation, March 26, 1999.

Text of a letter from the President to the Chairman and Ranking Members of the House Committee on Appropriations and International Relations and the Senate Committees on Appropriations and Foreign Relations (Washington, D.C.: The White House, Office of the Press Secretary, 3 December 1996).

Text of the Remarks of the President on the Enterprise for Americas Address, June 27, 1990.

Third Annual Survey of Public Opinion on International Trade (Washington, D.C.: The Association of Women in International Trade, 1999).

"Travel Advisories. State Needs Better Practices for Informing Americans of Dangers Overseas" (Washington, D.C.: United States General Accounting Office, August 1991).

Treaty Establishing the Caribbean Community, Chaguaramas, 4th July 1973 (Georgetown: Caribbean Community Secretariat, June, 1987), page 4.

Truman, Harry S. Public Papers of the Presidents of the United States (Washington, DC: Government Printing Office, 1960) pages 178–79.

U.S. Department of Commerce, U.S. General Imports - Schedule a commodity by Country, FT 135 (Washington, D.C.: Government Printing Office, December 1977).

U.S. Department of Commerce, "North American Free Trade Agreement. Generating Jobs for Americans," (Washington, D.C., May 1991).

U.S. Department of Commerce/International Trade Administration and U.S. Agency for International Development, "U.S. Exports to Latin American and the Caribbean: A State-by-State Overview 1987–1990," (Washington, D.C., March 1992) page 7.

U.S. Department of Justice, Criminal Division. The Foreign Agents Registration Act of 1938 as Amended and the Rules and Regulations Prescribed by the Attorney General (Washington, D.C.: Department of Justice, n. d.).

The US/EU Banana Dispute, *European Union News*, No. 96/98, November 10, 1998.

Watson, Alexander F. "U.S. -Latin America Relations in the 1990s: Toward a Mature Partnership," *U.S. State Department Dispatch*, Vol. 5, No. 11 (March 14, 1994).

Wright, Lacy A. Jr. Deputy Chief of Mission, U.S. Embassy, Jamaica, 1991–1995. The Association for Diplomatic Studies and Training Foreign Affairs Oral History Project, pages 1–113. www.adst.org/wp-content/uploads/2012/09/Caribbean-Islands.pdf.

Index

bureaucracy: ambassadors and,
146–147; on CBI, 265–267; in counter
narcotics, 220–224; debt relief and,
186; U.S. Embassy and, 146–147;
U.S. foreign policy and, 145–149
Burnham, Forbes, 99
Burton, John, 29–30
Bush, George: Manley, M., and, 185; *A
World Transformed*, 79
Bush, George W., 71–72, 83
business sector: CBI relating to,
251–252, 267–270, 275–276; CLAA
and, 145, 269–270; corporate
disparity in, 18; of ESC, 275–276;
foreign aid relating to, 209–210;
private sector, 200, 305; U.S. foreign
policy relating to, 144–145
Bustamante, Alexander, 62, 90, 291, 292

CACTAC. *See* Caribbean Textiles and
Apparel Council
CAIO. *See* Caribbean American Inter-
cultural Organization
CAL. *See* Caribbean Action Lobby
Capitol Hill, 137
Caribbean: elected U.S. officials from,
159–160, 162; history, 114n13;
literature on, 3–4; media in, 165;
U.S. jobs dependent on, 251. *See also*
English-speaking Caribbean; *specific
countries; specific topics*
Caribbean Action Lobby (CAL), 158
Caribbean American Inter-cultural
Organization (CAIO), 158
Caribbean Basin Economic Recovery
Act (CBERA), 9, 249; Jamaica-
United States relations and, 103–105
Caribbean Basin Economic Recovery
Expansion Act (CBEREA), 9, 103,
250
Caribbean Basin Initiative (CBI), 7;
attempts to influence, 259;
bureaucracy on, 265–267; business
sector relating to, 251–252, 267–270,
275–276; campaign for, 252–253;
CBTPA and, 103, 250, 315; CLAA
relating to, 269–270; Clinton
administration on, 262–266;
conclusion on, 278–279; Congress

relating to, 252–253, 259–262;
economic reform relating to,
254–255; ESC on, 253–255; executive
branch and, 262–265; H.R. 1403 bill
on, 254, 257–259; Jamaica-United
States relations and, 201; lobbying
for, 270–271, 275–276; media and,
273–275; motivation for, 77; NAFTA
effects on, 255–257, 276–278;
overview of, 249–252; principal
obstacles to, 260; process, 276–278;
public opinion on, 261; taxes
relating to, 251–252; think tanks,
271–272; U.S./CBI trade, 1985–1999,
250; U.S. ESC community and, 276;
USTR relating to, 262, 265, 266–267
Caribbean Basin Trade Enhancement
Bills: side-by-side comparison of,
1999, 353
Caribbean Common Market and
Community, 89
Caribbean Community (CARICOM),
92–93; ESC and, 332; Grenada
relating to, 98–99; Jamaica in, 61;
lobbying by, 160–161; Patterson
and, 306–307, 308–309; strategic
alliances with, 316–317; United
States-CARICOM Summit, 102; in
U.S., 158–161
Caribbean Free Trade Association
(CARIFTA), 89–90
Caribbean/Latin American Action
(CLAA): business sector and, 145,
269–270; CBI relating to, 269–270;
lobbying by, 145
Caribbean Textiles and Apparel
Council (CACTAC), 275
CARICOM. *See* Caribbean Community
CARIFTA. *See* Caribbean Free Trade
Association
Carr, E. H., 21
Carter, James "Jimmy", 78; Manley, M.,
and, 185; on U.S. foreign policy,
78–79
Carter administration, 93–94
CBC. *See* Congressional Black Caucus
CBERA. *See* Caribbean Basin Economic
Recovery Act

non-governmental organizations
(NGOs), 182
Non-IMF Path, 96
nontraditional merchandise exports, 71
North American Free Trade
Agreement (NAFTA): aggravated
trade deficit and, 257; Bernal on,
261–262; CBI effected by, 255–257,
276–278; economic growth relating
to, 256; investment diversion
relating to, 256; job losses relating
to, 257, 272; lobbying for, 261–262;
media on, 140, 274; Mexico and,
103–104, 138–139, 140, 153, 163–164,
255; relocation of production
capacity and, 256; think tanks, 272;
trade diversion and, 256
NSC. *See* National Security Council
Nye, Joseph S., 24

OAS. *See* Organization of American
States
OECS. *See* Organization of Eastern
Caribbean States
Office of Management and Budget
(OMB), 191, 192
Olympics, 72, 74, 82
OMB. *See* Office of Management and
Budget
Organization of American States
(OAS), 292–293
Organization of Eastern Caribbean
States (OECS), 98
organization overview, 5–10
Ortiz, Frank, 4, 87
ownership, 297; in Jamaica, 65–66, 96

paternalism, 87
patriotism, 144
Patterson, P. J., 75, 81, 236, 244,
263–264; as astute political leader,
309–310; CARICOM and, 306–307,
308–309; Jamaica's foreign policy
under, 306–309; on United States'
foreign policy, 308
Payne, Anthony, 310
People's National Party (PNP), 61–62,
91; on counter narcotics, 230; debt
relief relating to, 178–179; Manley,

M., and, 100–101, 197–198; Manley,
N., and, 291; socialism and, 96,
197–198
perception, 40
plantation economy, 68–69
plantations, 59
pluralist models, 40–41
PNP. *See* People's National Party
political culture, U.S., 286–287
political leadership, 309–310, 319
political philosophy, 295–296
political vulnerability, 38
politics: domestic, 42, 44; foreign aid
relating to, 194–197; of interest
groups, 40–41; in Jamaica, 60–62;
Westerns and, 71–72
"Politics Among Nations"
(Morgenthau), 21–22
population: of ESC, 330; of Jamaica,
17–18, 62–63; of small economies,
36; of small states, 35; of U.S., 17–18
power, 15; in atomistic asymmetries,
20; in interest group model, 41–42;
Morgenthau on, 21–22;
vulnerability and relative
powerlessness, 37–40
presidents, 42. *See also* executive
branch; *specific presidents*
private sector, 200, 305
Prize for Human Rights, 120n131
production capacity, 256
public opinion: on CBI, 261; on foreign
aid, 196–197; media and, 139–140
public relations firms, 153–154

Quayle, Dan, 184, 207, 311

racism, 87
Rangel, Charles B., 148, 234
Rastafarianism, 64, 73
Rattray, Alfred, 81, 147
raw materials, 88
Reagan, Ronald, 78–79; foreign aid
and, 194–196; on Grenada, 305; on
Seaga administration, 304–305
realism: Allison on, 23; atomistic
asymmetries relating to, 21–24;
behaviorists on, 22–23; cognitive
thinking and, 23; critique of, 22–23,

About the Author

Ambassador Dr. Richard L. Bernal, diplomat and economist with over 40 years of experience, was Jamaica's Ambassador to the United States of America and Permanent Representative to the Organisation of American States (OAS) for the period May 6, 1991, to August 31, 2001. His ten-and-a-half-year period in office spanned the administrations of three presidents (George Bush, Bill Clinton, and George W. Bush) and five Secretaries of State (Baker, Eagleburger, Christopher, Albright, and Powell). When he demitted office he was the fourth most senior Ambassador in Washington, D.C., and Dean of the Caribbean Diplomatic Corps. During his tenure he gave testimonies to several Committees of Congress (House and Senate) and the U.S. International Trade Commission on issues of concern to the Caribbean such as aid, NAFTA, and the Caribbean Basin Initiative. He was involved in numerous negotiations on behalf of Jamaica and CARICOM with various agencies and departments of the U.S. government, including agreements on investment, intellectual property rights, textiles and apparel, trade, debt, and loans from multilateral financial institutions (IMF, World Bank, and IADB). His opinion editorials appeared in the *Washington Post*, *Wall Street Journal*, *Miami Herald*, and the *Washington Times* and he has been interviewed by CNN, PBS, and the BBC.

He is the author of *Globalization, Trade, and Economic Development: A Study of the CARIFORM-EU Economic Partnership Agreement* (New York: Palgrave Macmillan, 2013) and *Dragon in the Caribbean: China's Global Re-Positioning—Challenges and Opportunities for the Caribbean* (Kingston: Ian Randle Publishers, April, 2014).

He was educated at the University of the West Indies, University of Pennsylvania, New School for Social Research, and the School for Advanced International Studies of Johns Hopkins University. He holds the degrees of BSc, MA, PhD (Economics), and MIPP (International Public Policy).

9789766406660